# MOTHER-OF-PEARL

## Antiques and Collectibles

**PLATE 1**

A masterpiece of carving, this vignette of a medieval strolling minstrel playing his lute was carved in France, c. 1850, size 21.5 x 18 cm (8.5″ x 7.1″).

# MOTHER-OF-PEARL

## Antiques and Collectibles

Michael Meyer, Dawn Meyer and Patricia Martin

Photos by Stacey & Michael Meyer

Schiffer Publishing Ltd
4880 Lower Valley Road • Atglen, PA 19310

Library of Congress Control Number: 2013956370



Type set in University Roman Bd BT/Zurich BT

ISBN: 978-0-7643-4528-9
Printed in China

Published by Schiffer Publishing, Ltd.
4880 Lower Valley Road
Atglen, PA 19310
Phone: (610) 593-1777; Fax: (610) 593-2002
E-mail: Info@schifferbooks.com

For our complete selection of fine books on this and related subjects, please visit our website at www.schifferbooks.com. You may also write for a free catalog.

This book may be purchased from the publisher. Please try your bookstore first.

We are always looking for people to write books on new and related subjects. If you have an idea for a book, please contact us at proposals@schifferbooks.com

Schiffer Publishing's titles are available at special discounts for bulk purchases for sales promotions or premiums. Special editions, including personalized covers, corporate imprints, and excerpts can be created in large quantities for special needs. For more information, contact the publisher.

# Contents

# Acknowledgments

We owe a deep debt of gratitude to our coauthor, Patricia Martin, and her husband Bob, who have given us extensive advice and mentoring throughout our collecting days. Their knowledge of past collectibles is amazing. We urge collectors to support their antiques business of Home Farm Antiques: see http://www.homefarmantiques.com.

We acknowledge with thanks the help of the experts listed here. It was the task of the three authors of this book to research, verify, and draw educated conclusions, and we ask that if an error is found, it be considered our error and not the error of those who were kind enough to help us.

Religious Carvings: Dino Basilissi (Italy)<br>
Sewing: Carolyn Meacham (USA)<br>
Gaming counters: Bill Neal (UK)<br>
http://www.chezbill.com/<br>
Perfumes: Helen Farnsworth (USA)<br>
UK Antiques: Jean and Paul Mason (Discovery Antiques UK)<br>
Restorations: Peter Meyer (Australia)<br>
History of Palestine Pearl: Enrique Yidi (Colombia)

Thanks also go to the many unnamed collectors and dealers who have given us tidbits of information. Every bit of information has helped our understanding of this subject.

# Introduction

In researching this book, we found little definitive, published information on items created with mother-of-pearl. This made documentation difficult. We have therefore worked closely for over a decade with a worldwide group of cultural and social historians, collectors, artisans and antique dealers, professionals and experts. This work is an amalgamation of our findings. The purpose of this volume is to give readers a good idea of what can be found within the antiques, decorative arts, and collectibles markets in regard to mother-of-pearl works of art, their age, and their function.

It is important to remember that the majority of the early mother-of-pearl creations have been made by hand. This has given the carver the opportunity to experiment with a wide range of different designs and subjects. We've chosen to show as many examples as possible in each category, in order to further the reader's and researcher's understanding of the importance of the variety in carving made for the same item. By looking at a large number of similar productions, it is possible to isolate common denominators that are an aid to pinpointing the origin of carving. But it also shows that each carver has his own interpretation of the subject, and a different level of carving skills in the way he portrays a subject. The study of carving details helps us with both the historical and the regional tracing of the piece, and it also helps us with the sociology of the pieces, of the various markets for which pieces were created, and also with the evolution of artistic and technical practices of the science and art of carving.

The scope of this book is confined to material we have personally accumulated over the past ten years. It does not encompass museum collections or other private collections. This book is a snapshot in time to help future researchers recognize the availability of material during the last decade. Even with our extensive collection, we feel we've only scratched the surface of the use of mother-of-pearl in most fields. There is material still to discover and record and there is information in foreign languages that needs to be translated, researched, and collated. Modern online language translators have been an asset in learning more, but it is difficult to access the original publications from each country of origin. It is our hope that this book will be an inspiration to collectors and researchers worldwide to delve into this interesting field.

An interesting, and at the same time unfortunate, conclusion to which we have come while compiling our research is that carved and decorated mother-of-pearl is universally underappreciated. Master carvers of the past have produced stunning carvings in mother-of-pearl, and yet they sell for a mere pittance. This may very well be attributed to the lack of literature and education on the subject. Carving of mother-of-pearl requires advanced artistic skills, a well-versed cognizance of the material and its origins, strengths and fragilities, an impeccable eye for the aesthetic, along with talents in composition and a firm but gentle carving hand. The skill required is comparable to that of master painters and sculptors. Despite this, the development of appreciation of art in mother-of-pearl has been disappointing. Hopefully, this book will help correct that.

We feel that we are rapidly approaching the end of the era in which society and the arts enjoyed prolific use of mother-of-pearl. This era lasted over 250 years, reaching the height of popularity in the High Victorian period. The volume of mother-of-pearl items and the number of artisans capable of producing fine work have both been steadily decreasing over the past century. Wild stock of pearl is diminishing and therefore getting prohibitively expensive. Farmed stock of shell from pearl farms is seldom left long enough to grow thick, and is used mainly in the jewelry trades. The few craftsmen worldwide who can work in this material cannot get suitable or sufficient raw stock, and so they turn to other materials.

New production is presently reduced to a mere trickle. Most of what is currently produced has nowhere near the artistic value of early pieces. Pressures of modern life and the need for quick turnover have resulted in modern production being, in the main, no more than souvenir items with little or no artistic merit. There is good news, though. There are still fine examples of early mother-of-pearl creations available in the antiques market. Astute collectors are already accumulating amazing treasures from the past before they disappear for good.

It is our intention in the relatively near future to dispose of a portion of our collection. This will enable us to specialize in a more select grouping of mother-of-pearl categories. Collectors with information on historical aspects on mother-of-pearl to aid future research can let us know by emailing Michael@motherofpearlmuseum.com.

**PLATE 2**

**1.** An exceptional wall decoration with three putti, China, c. 2000, size 19 x 14 cm (7.5″ x 5.5″).

CHAPTER 1

# Source of Mother-of-Pearl

The pearl shell is home to a living animal, class Bivalvia, phylum Mollusca. This animal is protected by two plate-like shells joined by a flexible ligament called the hinge. They are filter feeders, using gills to capture food particles from the water. Sexes are separate; they practice external fertilization. The shell itself is made of calcium carbonate produced by the animal. A pearl is formed when the animal finds an irritant in the shell and covers it with calcium carbonate.

Dr. Shohei Shirai, author of *Pearls and Pearl Oysters of the World*, recorded 275 different species of mollusks that produce pearls and have mother-of-pearl or nacreous interiors. Of these, twenty-four are marine and the rest freshwater. Only a small portion of these are available in commercial quantities.

Plates 3 and 4 show the different types of mother-of-pearl shell you'll recognise, most with external and internal view.

## PLATE 3 – ABALONE SHELL

Two of the more popular abalone shells used for arts:

1. **Abalone/Paua shell.** Scientific name Haliotis iris (Family Haliotidae) New Zealand.
2. **Abalone/Awabi.** Scientific name Haliotis gigantea (Family Haliotidae) Japan.

## PLATE 4 – MOTHER-OF-PEARL OYSTERS

**1a 1b 1c. Yellow/gold lip mother-of-pearl oyster.** Scientific name Pinctada maxima (Family Pteriidae) Philippine Islands, (Especially Sulu Sea) Thailand and Indonesia.

**2a 2b 2c. White/silver lip mother-of-pearl oyster.** Scientific name Pinctada maxima (Family Pteriidae) Australia, Myanmar, Indonesia, and the Arafura Sea. This is the largest and thickest pearl oyster in the world and is the best for carving.

**3a 3b. Black lip mother-of-pearl oyster.** Scientific name Pinctada margaritifera (Family Pteriidae) Micronesia, French Polynesia, Melanesia, and Indo-Pacific.

**4a 4b. Brown mother-of-pearl (winged) oyster.** Scientific name Pteria penguin (Family Pteriidae) Philippines and Indo-Pacific.

**5a 5b. Trocha/Top Shell.** Scientific name Trochus niloticus (Family Trochidae) Indo Pacific.

**6a 6b. Green Turbo/Turban Shell.** Scientific name Turbo marmoratus (Family Turbinidae) Indo-Pacific. This shell was widely used for veneers in Victorian times.

**7a 7b 7c. Freshwater Clams.** Many different types, (Family Unionidae) freshwater rivers.

1a
1b
1c
2a
2b
2c
3a
3b
4a
4b
5a
5b
6a
6b
7a
7b
7c

CHAPTER 2

# A Brief History of Mother-of-Pearl

## THE EARLIEST YEARS

Records show that mother-of-pearl was used as far back as 2500 B.C. in the Royal Grave of Ur, or Mesopotamia, now South Iraq. Some scholars believe mother-of-pearl may have been used as far back as 4200 B.C. in Egypt, but as there seems to be no authentic, well-documented reference that this did indeed mean mother-of-pearl, and not pearls. As this work concerns mother-of-pearl, it is important that we make that distinction.

Mother-of-pearl was used for decorative inlay and was both carved and engraved. Throughout the ages, mother-of-pearl has been mentioned sporadically, mostly connected to decorative items that have been discovered in graves or archeological digs. It was not until the eighteenth century that mother-of-pearl was used primarily for decoration. It reached its height of popularity in the nineteenth century.

During the early days, the main mother-of-pearl oyster beds were known to exist in only three regions, the Persian Gulf, the Red Sea, and the India-Sri Lanka coast. It was after the major European voyages of discovery that pearl oyster beds were found to be widely distributed throughout tropical waters.

Many early civilizations have valued the mother-of-pearl shells more than the pearls themselves. Mother-of-pearl was used prior to any use of those pearls, which most likely did not begin until the fifth century B.C. It is said that in pre-nineteenth century Japan, divers who found pearls often discarded them. One legend tells us of Polynesian children using pearls as marbles.

With limited reference works on the subject of carved mother-of-pearl, and with the absence of hallmarks or artist marks indicating the carver, the place, and the date of origin, there has been considerable confusion in this field. A mother-of-pearl item with silver parts may have a silver mark. However, this does not mean the pearl part of the item was created at the same time as the silver part. For instance, an unmarked pearl handle may have been carved in France in 1850, and it may have been used to make a serving fork with silver bands and tines hallmarked London, 1895. This misleads some into thinking the piece in its entirety was made in London in 1895.

In this book, through extensive research and work with shell, and through our own experience in handling antique carved mother-of-pearl pieces, we will identify origins of carved mother-of-pearl works, and at the same time clear up some of the confusion and misconceptions.

Mention should be made that much information is recorded in languages foreign to our own language (English). We have translated thousands of pages of foreign language text with online translators and have had input from language professors and professionals. Although we have made many important discoveries, we feel further discoveries are waiting to be made by researchers in the future. Hopefully, in the near future.

## THE GROWTH OF THE MOTHER-OF-PEARL INDUSTRY

As the popularity of the use of mother-of-pearl grew, major manufacturing centers emerged in France, in England, and in Palestine. These centers supplied their pearl products throughout Europe and the world. In tandem with this was the growth of smaller, local production that took place in countries the world over.

Both silversmiths and trained artisans worked in the pearl industry. Very few of the items they made and decorated were signed. Carving was often undertaken behind closed doors to avoid competitors knowing what practices, techniques, effects, and motifs were being used. No pattern records were kept. We can only make educated assumptions based upon styles and subjects of carvings, and record our current understanding. Taking all this into account, and also considering the gradual demise of the craft on its artistic level and the passing of time, one can understand how difficult it is to trace exact origins of pearl pieces.

## PEARLING IN AUSTRALIA

It is commonly thought that the wealth in pearling was gained chiefly from the pearls themselves. It is a fact, however, that it has been the shell that was most valuable, and any pearls that accompanied the shell were simply an added bonus.

Australian pearl oysters were first exported in 1862. The shell was large and ideal for pearl workers. This pearl oyster was so plentiful, it could be found even at low tide.

However, once the shore stock was depleted, hard hat divers were employed to search deeper waters.

By 1914, Broome, the center of the Australian pearling industry, supplied seventy-five percent of the world's raw mother-of-pearl. World War I temporarily stopped the trade.

In the 1930s, Broome's local pearl industry was affected, both negatively and positively, by three factors. One was the Great Depression, a negative factor for all. Also, oyster beds in Australia were being depleted from constant fishing over a long period of time. This over-fishing led to the Australian government limiting harvesting. The third factor was a cyclone in northwest Australia. In 1935, this cyclone destroyed twenty pearl luggers or large pearl-fishing boats, and damaged sixteen others. Over 142 lives were lost. The wreckage put the foreign luggers out of operation and Broome experienced this as a positive effect of the cyclone. The storm had eliminated foreign harvesting and left Broome with the majority of the pearl business, simply due to location. A relative "boom" hit Broome's mother-of-pearl industry and this boom continued until the mid-twentieth century.

Pearling continues in this region today, and farming the pearl oyster for cultured pearls, a practice begun in 1956, goes on. Mother-of-pearl is mostly exported from Australia, and only a small amount is used within Australia by private hobbyists for carving and for jewelry.

## THE PEARL INDUSTRY IN CHINA

The use of mother-of-pearl in China dates back to the tenth century B.C. It was first used for decorative inlay in wood. It was in the twelfth century A.D. that China refined its lacquered goods to include mother-of-pearl inlay. Since then, pearl-encrusted lacquerware was an important trade item and was used as gifts in high-powered diplomacy.

At the same time, mother-of-pearl inlays were set into furniture. By the seventeenth century, China was supplying lacquerware with mother-of-pearl decoration to the world. It was extremely well received; the demand for it continued well into the nineteenth century.

China benefited from this advantage: they were the country closest to the supply of raw, or uncleaned, pearl oysters in the Dutch East Indies. Any excess of raw shell imports was sold overseas. In 1834, China sent Britain 119 tons of excess raw mother-of-pearl shell.

China was the first country to capitalize on the need for a large number of gaming counters for the European market. This need accompanied the growth of popularity of "spa life," which included spa visitations and trips seaside summers with gaming parties among the European wealthier classes. China produced incredibly fine, scratch-carved examples in mother-of-pearl. This production started in the early eighteenth century and continued until the 1840s, when the demand dwindled due to the new fashion of playing games that did not require counters. China itself had no market for game counters, as this sort of game was not popular in the culture. Pearl carvers turned their energies into making other sorts of mother-of-pearl items for their export markets. Pincushions, thread winders, needle cases, and other sewing tools, notebooks, pencils, inkwells and general desk accessories, and even lancet cases and dental kits for the medical professions were produced.

China produces mother-of-pearl jewelry and decorative items to this day.

## JAPAN AND THE PEARL INDUSTRY

Early lacquer work inlaid with mother-of-pearl dated from 710 onwards. By the late tenth century, Japan was sending lacquerware with pearl shell decoration to the Chinese court as gifts. Mother-of-pearl was also used extensively in the Hall of Gold (Konjikido) at the Chusonji Temple in 1124.

The Ryukyu Islands (later Okinawa) relied on lacquerware with mother-of-pearl as a primary source of income. They conducted trade with China.

In addition to lacquerware, which continued to be important until the late nineteenth century, Japan produced solid mother-of-pearl carvings, including dressing accessories such as inro, netsuke, ojime, and hair combs. Very beautiful, meticulously crafted, majestic pieces have come out of Japan.

## PEARL IN THE PHILIPPINES

The Philippines were and still are a major world supplier of raw mother-of-pearl. From the sixteenth century, Philippine raw shell would travel in galleons from Cebu Island to Acapulco in Mexico. From there, they were transported by land across Mexico to the port of Vera Cruz on the Gulf of Mexico. Here they were loaded onto the Spanish treasure fleet, bound for Spain.

Although most of the present day harvest is exported, there are a number of local manufacturers still using mother-of-pearl to make pearl carvings, pearl jewelry, and pearl boxes for the tourist trade.

## PEARL IN TAHITI, FRENCH POLYNESIA, THE SOUTH SEAS

Early divers in Tahiti and the Tuamotu Archipelago searched for mother-of-pearl shell rather than for actual pearls. This region was home of the black lip pearl oyster. Once Tahiti was annexed to France in 1843, large quantities of raw, black lip mother-of-pearl were exported to France.

The growth of this South Sea region as a tourist destination enabled a small local industry to develop. Craftsmen created tourist souvenirs and jewelry from the black lip mother-of-pearl oyster. With the exception of French Polynesia, most islanders in the South Sea Islands used mother-of-pearl in a decorative inlay in their woodwork, but they did not actually carve the mother-of-pearl shells, as they had no access to steel chisels.

## NEW CALEDONIA

In 1864, the French established a penal colony in New Caledonia, within Melanesia in the South Pacific. In 1872, thousands of exiled Communards arrived from Paris. Due to the high cost of placing, equipping, and feeding the deportees, the authorities let the prisoners make a living from trades they had learned in their lives before exile. The French cameo carvers turned their skills to carving mother-of-pearl oysters, trocha shell, green turban shell, and nautilus shell. These were sold to tourists on visiting ships.

There was a general amnesty late in the nineteenth century. While there were Frenchmen who returned home to France, many thousands remained in New Caledonia and continued their trades.

## THE PERSIAN GULF

In ancient days, the pearl oyster beds of the Persian Gulf were known throughout the world for their pearls. These beds remained in the control of Arabian and Persian princes, except for a one hundred year period in the sixteenth century when the Portuguese took control. Most of the pearls harvested were traded in Bahrain and shipped to the pearl market of Bombay.

The demand for pearls waned until the twelfth and thirteenth centuries, when early Crusaders returned to Europe with stories of the fabulous wealth of Persian and Indian royalty. These stories revived European interest in pearl.

## THE RED SEA

Even before the birth of Jesus Christ, the Red Sea was known for its important pearl oyster beds. With the expansion of the Holy Roman Empire, the pearl oyster beds came under control of the Romans. The Romans hoarded the pearl over the 500 years of their empire. They valued the pearls so highly, they traded huge amounts of gold for any available pearls. No records have been found of what happened to the pearl oyster shells.

Dating back to the sixteenth century, one of the major consumers of Red Sea mother-of-pearl shell was Palestine.

## INDIA'S HISTORY WITH MOTHER-OF-PEARL

There is evidence that mother-of-pearl shells with carvings were used in religious ceremonies in the eleventh or twelfth centuries.

When Marco Polo visited the Gulf of Mannar located off the southernmost tip of India in 1294, he saw up to 500 ships harvesting pearl oyster beds. By 1560, during the Mughal Dynasty (1525–1707), mother-of-pearl was used with lacquer as decoration for articles of domestic function. Carved pearl articles were created here for export to Europe. Gujarat in western India played an important role in using mother-of-pearl in decorative woodware.

During the twentieth century, extensive use of freshwater mother-of-pearl was used to create day-to-day articles in great numbers, which were exported throughout the entire world. The quality of this pearl was not as good as the sea equivalent. It was used mainly for souvenirs and inexpensive gifts.

## MOTHER OF PEARL IN ENGLAND

England gained an excellent reputation for her mother-of-pearl industry. They were universally known for their pearl buttons and pearl-handled tableware. Birmingham was the center of production of mother-of-pearl buttons and jewelry, while Sheffield was the center of production of pearl handled cutlery.

The pearl button industry was instrumental in the development of English towns like Birmingham. From the 1740s through the 1770s, fashion for gentlemen dictated large buttons. By the 1780s, French and Italian influence had extended to the Birmingham button industry. British gentlemen's buttons became elaborate and decorative. In 1767, eight companies are recorded as being in operation making buttons. With the increase in popularity and decoration, this number increased to the hundreds, with companies growing well into the nineteenth century. Unfortunately for the pearl industries, the plastic industry of the early twentieth century took its toll. Today, only one pearl carver is left in Birmingham.

Sheffield, known for its work with silver and silver plate, was the center of cutlery production. Early tableware was made with thin strips of mother-of-pearl. Once the large Australian shells were discovered, with thickness suitable to produce solid handles, the use of thin strips of pearl diminished.

Aside from the major industries of buttons and tableware, mother-of-pearl was used in England from the eighteenth century in the manufacture of a wide range of both functional and decorative objects for the home, such as snuff boxes, sewing tools, cards cases, notebooks, and a significant array of other small and lovely items. Mother-of-pearl was also used in jewelry. Early directories and ledgers classified these manufacturers as Ornament Makers.

Mother-of-pearl fine inlay in papier-mâché enjoyed an enthusiastic following and was very popular for a very long time. It remains so today. In the early nineteenth century, Aaron Jennens and John Bettridge patented a process for making this pearl inlay. Their patent expired in 1839, opening up their inlay process to all. The process continued to be used for the next twenty-five years.

Raw shell was imported from the Indian and Pacific Oceans and from Polynesia, Melanesia, Hawaii, Australia, and South Japan, as well as from countries that had surplus stock, such as China. St. Katherine docks in London were opened in 1828. These docks were dedicated to handling only mother-of-pearl shell and precious cargo like ivory, sugar, and carpets. It operated well into the twentieth century. An entire warehouse floor stocked only mother-of-pearl. Six times a year, buyers would come to sales, paying up to 10.00 GBP per pound. Large volumes were handled. In 1853, 782 tons of raw mother-of-pearl was imported. By 1870, this had increased to 1500 tons.

## Pearl Manufacture in Europe

Mother-of-pearl shell from the Persian Gulf was distributed throughout Europe via Gdansk, Venice, and Antwerp. The mother-of-pearl reached all major European destinations. By the eighteenth century, it was being used by silversmiths for high-level market creations such as *objet d'art*, snuff boxes, fans, and other decorative and presentation items. Austria, the Netherlands, Spain, and Portugal all made items, but none in large volumes.

Of the European countries, France and Germany held outstanding positions in the manufacture of mother-of-pearl articles. Their artisans became master craftsmen at carving, piercing, and otherwise processing the pearl.

In France in 1741, the law permitted small manufacturers, known as "tabletterie," the right to work mother-of-pearl and other natural materials such as ivory and horn. By the nineteenth century, France was the market leader the world over. Meru, north of Paris, was the capital of pearl-making for 150 years. In 1789, twelve hundred workers were employed in the pearl industry, producing vast amounts of mostly utilitarian items. There were other production centers within a radius of twenty-five kilometers, including Andeville. (Andeville is where pearl buttons were first hand-engraved.)

The height of mother-of-pearl carving in the western world was achieved during the 1790–1820 time period, when the finest mother-of-pearl goods were sold in the shops of the Palais Royal in Paris. These pieces were then, and remain today, exemplary of the highest standard in pearl work. Sets of sewing tools, desk accessories, tableware, and other fine pieces are highly desirable and are in constant demand by collectors, exhibitors, and museums.

Raw mother-of-pearl shell was imported from the French colonies and also by trading. The French East India Company traded with the Far East from 1664, stopping at ports in Madagascar and India, areas rich for pearl oysters. The black lip pearl oyster was supplied by the French colonies of French Polynesia and New Caledonia. Later in the nineteenth century, Indochina supplied pearl shell. Exact quantities of imports are unknown, but one statistic has been recorded that in 1879, France imported 1500 tons of pearl shell. The French use of mother-of-pearl in everyday items continued well into the twentieth century.

The Renaissance in Germany, from the fourteenth through the seventeenth centuries, saw the rise of mother-of-pearl art. Most of Germany's mother-of-pearl carving was associated with religious items, with holy places, and with themes from the New Testament and the Saints. Historic records point to Berchtesgaden as the center of early pearl carving work. Raw shell was imported from the Red Sea. The height of popularity during the Renaissance existed from mid-fifteenth to mid-sixteenth centuries.

Experts are undecided if the birth of mother-of-pearl carving in Germany originated from inspiration of carved shells purchases on pilgrimages to the Holy Land, or if it stemmed from that period's interest in Chinese art. By the end of the seventeenth century, Germany lost its significant role in the mother-of-pearl industry. Pearl became less popular in this region and was downgraded for use in furniture and small boxes.

The biggest centers of mother-of-pearl carving in Italy were Torre del Greco in the province of Naples, and Trapani in Sicily. Italy hosted craftsmen who carved pearl as far back as the sixteenth century. There seemed to never have been a very large mother-of-pearl production, as examples are rare and mostly in museums.

Italian carvers from the last century specialized in cameo production, preferring shells that had different layers of colors to add dimension to their cameos, rather than mother-of-pearl.

Our research led us to the discovery that many of the religious mother-of-pearl carvings thought to have been produced in Italy actually originated in Palestine. The confusion came about as the carvings were sent from the Franciscan Friars in Bethlehem to the Franciscan Order in Italy, from where they were distributed to wealthy patrons and churches all over Italy (and Europe). More research is needed to isolate and document the wonderful creations in mother-of-pearl produced in Italy.

## PALESTINE

The Holy Land, cradle of a great diversity of cultures and religions, was home to one of the largest mother-of-pearl industries in the world. It was to continue this way for over four hundred years.

One school of study believes that the Crusaders were the first to bring mother-of-pearl carvings to the Holy Land in the twelfth century. Another school believes the Franciscan fathers were the first to introduce the carvings in the fifteenth century.

Due to excellent documentation on the Franciscan order's involvement in the mother-of-pearl trade, we know much of their history. Other religious orders, such as various Orthodox churches, were involved in the pearl industry, ordering carvings to their particular designs. However, few records can be found today of their exact involvement.

Palestine had little arable land. The Franciscan Order of Friars Minor ran a convent in Bethlehem, and they had to find a way to help their congregation, who mostly lacked employment. In the fifteenth century, the Franciscan fathers brought pearl artists from Florence, Italy. These artists impressed the inhabitants of Bethlehem so much, the locals embarked on learning the skill. This was the start of the souvenir trade in Palestine.

Pilgrims visiting the Holy Land in 1588 were the first to see models of the Holy Sepulcher, crosses and crucifixes decorated with mother-of-pearl. The work was rough and the articles created were of little artistic merit. However, the mere fact that they were from the Holy Land gave them great significance. In time, quality improved. Pilgrims went home from Palestine with good supplies of these souvenirs. The balance of the production was sold to the local Franciscan order. The support of the Church in buying this inventory enabled the local inhabitants to receive continuous income.

The Franciscan order sent the mother-of-pearl souvenirs to their superiors in Italy, and they in turn distributed the souvenirs to benefactors, patrons, and churches throughout Europe. This supply was to ensure wide spread distribution of these mother-of-pearl arts. The abundance of pearl religious souvenirs in the European countries resulted in the misconception that the articles were actually made in Europe, particularly in Italy.

It was common to inscribe shells in Italian, since many residents of Bethlehem spoke Italian. Also taken into account was the trade's logical practice to use the native language of the pilgrims and their Church on souvenir items. Languages recorded on the Palestine shells include Italian, French, Russian, Greek, Latin, English, Arabic, and others. This plethora of languages has caused confusion to early researchers who thought the language used on the piece dictated the item's country of origin.

The Franciscans in Palestine took orders from all over Europe for carvings of specific religious subjects. Early carved shell souvenirs were sanctified, or blessed, by the Church.

This rite held tremendous importance for the pilgrim. Similar shells carved in other countries were merely *objet d'art* and not the highly valued, blessed items from Bethlehem. These sanctified pieces were believed to protect holders against evil, a very important belief in those early and very hazardous days of travel.

Grand Tours of the Holy Land began after 1852, when peace had come to the region. Thomas Cook started to bring tour groups to the Holy Land in the 1860s and so the souvenir and tourist trades blossomed. By the end of the nineteenth century, Palestine was more accessible to pilgrims. The mother-of-pearl industry managed to operate independently from the Church, although churches remained the main customer.

The war in Palestine in the latter part of the twentieth century resulted in shrinking the number of Christian pearl workers there. The Holy Land was no longer safe for pilgrimages. The pearl trade in Palestine, after flourishing for four hundred years, declined rapidly. Although pearl carving is still being done for the tourist market, both the quality and the volume have been greatly reduced.

## THAILAND AND MYANMAR

Archeological records show that mother-of-pearl may have been used in Thailand as early as the ninth century. By the eighteenth century, mother-of-pearl was used as inlay in architectural pieces, such as doors, in thrones, and also for decorative items. By the twentieth century, mother-of-pearl was used extensively in the production of cutlery handles, jewelry, and souvenir items.

In Myanmar (southern Burma), the Myeik Archipelago has been well known for its pearl oyster beds since ancient times.

## RUSSIA AND THE BALKANS

Confusion reigns when studying mother-of-pearl in this area. Although early Russian silversmiths did indeed make a small quantity of mother-of-pearl decorative and religious pieces, by far the majority of the items attributed to Russia were in fact made in the Holy Land. Bethlehem was a popular destination for Russian pilgrims. The pilgrims brought home a wealth of Holy Land pearl souvenirs. These souvenirs were highly regarded in Russia. Many were donated to the royal family and displayed in churches. Russian silversmiths used these pieces as inlay in silver, which was of course hallmarked for Russia. This gave the impression that the entire item was made in Russia, when in truth the pearl was created in the Holy Land. True Russian pearl work is rare.

## UNITED STATES OF AMERICA

Early explorers along the American Atlantic coastline found natives wearing pearls. This led to the discovery of rich pearl shell beds in the Ohio, Mississippi, and Tennessee River basins. The explorers recognized the true value of these pearl pieces. The best examples were sent to Europe. In 1887, a German button maker named John Boepple settled in Muscatine on the Mississippi River and opened the first American button factory in 1891, utilizing the river pearl shell.

Iowa became the center of the US button trade. In 1905, Muscatine produced one and a half billion buttons, nearly forty percent of the world's production. This increased to six billion buttons in 1912. The industry by then employed 9500 factory works and 9700 shell fishermen. The industry thrived until the mid-twentieth century, when plastic buttons were found to be less expensive to produce and longer lasting than the more delicate pearl. Luckily, there was an alternative outlet for the shell. By 1950, Japan pearl farms were importing hundreds of tons of pearl shell from the United States, to be cut into nuclei for seeding their cultured pearl oysters. At its height in 1993, the US exported nearly seven thousand tons of shell.

Unfortunately, over-fishing and pollution took its toll. Of the three hundred species of North American freshwater pearl shells, thirty-five are extinct and another forty percent endangered.

Large volumes of fancy goods were produced in the nineteenth and twentieth centuries in the USA. Souvenir pieces were the highest production for seaside towns and major tourist destinations. These consisted of spoons, purses, inkwells, dip pens, and so on. Most all had the name of the tourist destination written on them.

Major US manufactures of lighters, compacts, and vanity goods produced a limited line in mother-of-pearl.

## CONCLUSION

Most countries not mentioned here have had some history of hosting mother-of-pearl manufacture, but they were not main producers.

By the third quarter of the twentieth century, raw mother-of-pearl shell was getting scarce in many regions. The jewelry trade had gobbled up vast quantities. Natural raw stock was supplemented with mother-of-pearl shell from cultured pearl farms. These farm pieces were not as large as the naturally grown pearl shell, nor as thick. This made intricate carving virtually impossible.

There will always be a supply of mother-of-pearl shell from the world's pearl farms. This will most likely remain to be used mainly in jewelry design. Carved and inlaid pieces that for a time in history showed such impressive artisanry and unique craftsmanship will become a thing of the past. Study in the area of mother-of-pearl must continue so that the history of the aesthetic and the appreciation for the superb talent that created these intricate, meticulously done works of art will continue and will thrive.

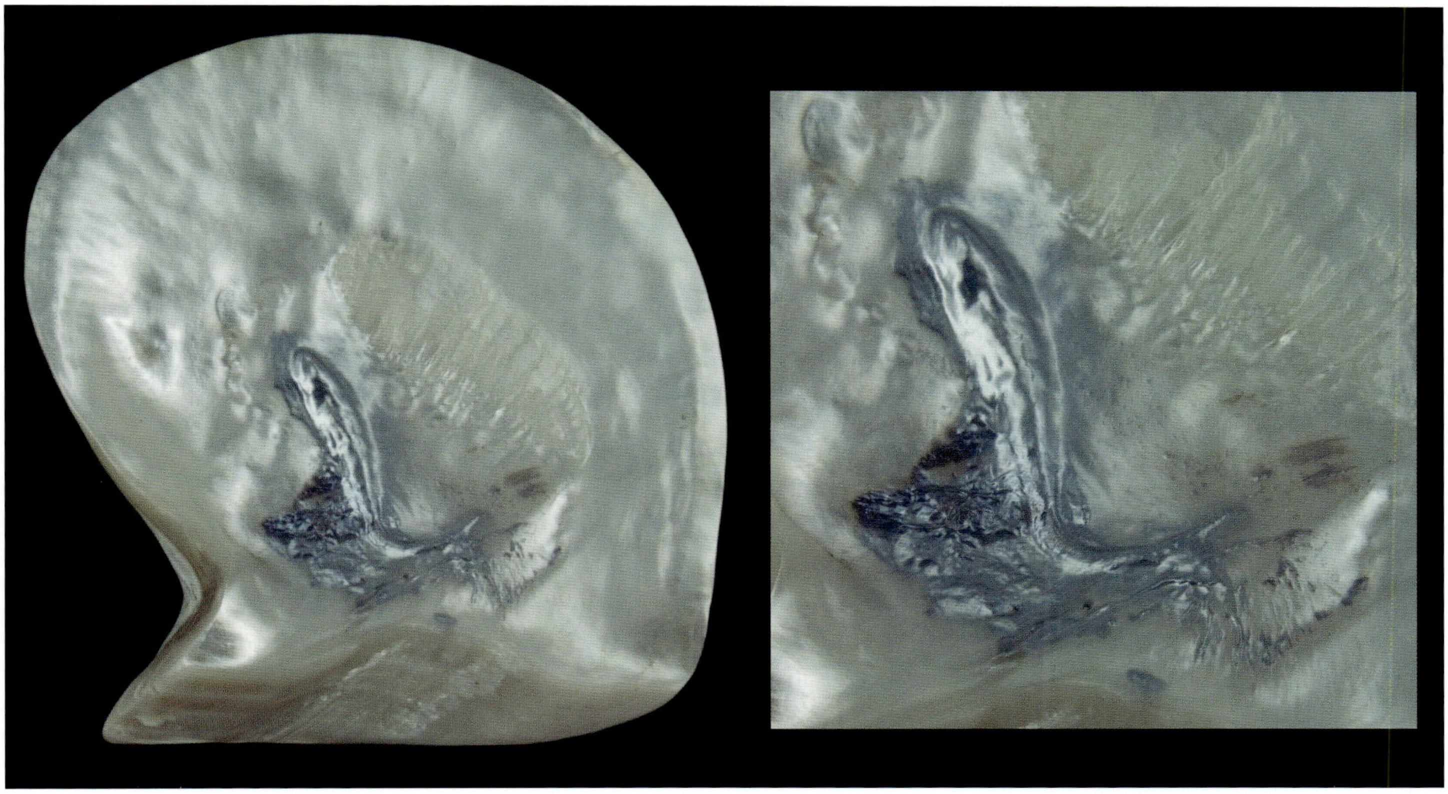

**PLATE 5**

An interesting pearl oyster from Myanmar/Burma that shows a fish was trapped in the living oyster and was completely covered in mother-of-pearl, 1995, size 21.5 x 20.5 cm (8.5″ x 8.1″)

CHAPTER 3

# Carvings

Due to the wonderful luster of mother-of-pearl and the softness of the shell when compared to stone, this material has enjoyed a long history of popularity for carving. Jewelry, buttons, and decorative objects are among the most numerous of items carved out of mother-of-pearl. The history of mother-of-pearl carving dates back to 2500 B.C. Although initially crude in design and detail, this art developed so that by the eighteenth and nineteenth century, master carvers who worked with mother-of-pearl achieved the highest level of carving known to mankind.

Unfortunately, by the twentieth century, this quality of artistry declined as the pressures of bulk production and the need for quick turnover left carvers insufficient time to produce pieces to high standards. By the early twenty-first century, the art of carving was virtually lost. Only a small number of artists worldwide continue to produce mother-of-pearl carvings.

After study of a large number of carvings, it gets easier to pinpoint the country of origin of the carving. The artists from different countries had different carving styles. The carving techniques were passed down from carver to apprentice, who carried on the style of his teacher. Also, the carvers were often restricted by the type of shell that was available for carving, so a careful study of the type of shell, the subject, and the style will give us the origin in most (but not all) carvings.

We have tried to illustrate a number of carvings from each locality so that readers can see the similar styles for themselves. Due to the large number of carvings on religious themes, these have been placed in a separate chapter entitled "Religion."

Carvings are important to us not only for their beauty and decorative value, but also from a historical point of view, as they give us glimpses of a way of life that has long since past.

**PLATE 6**

A Chinese pearl carver's image of Western culture's Bone-Shaker bicycle. This image dates to c. 1860–70.

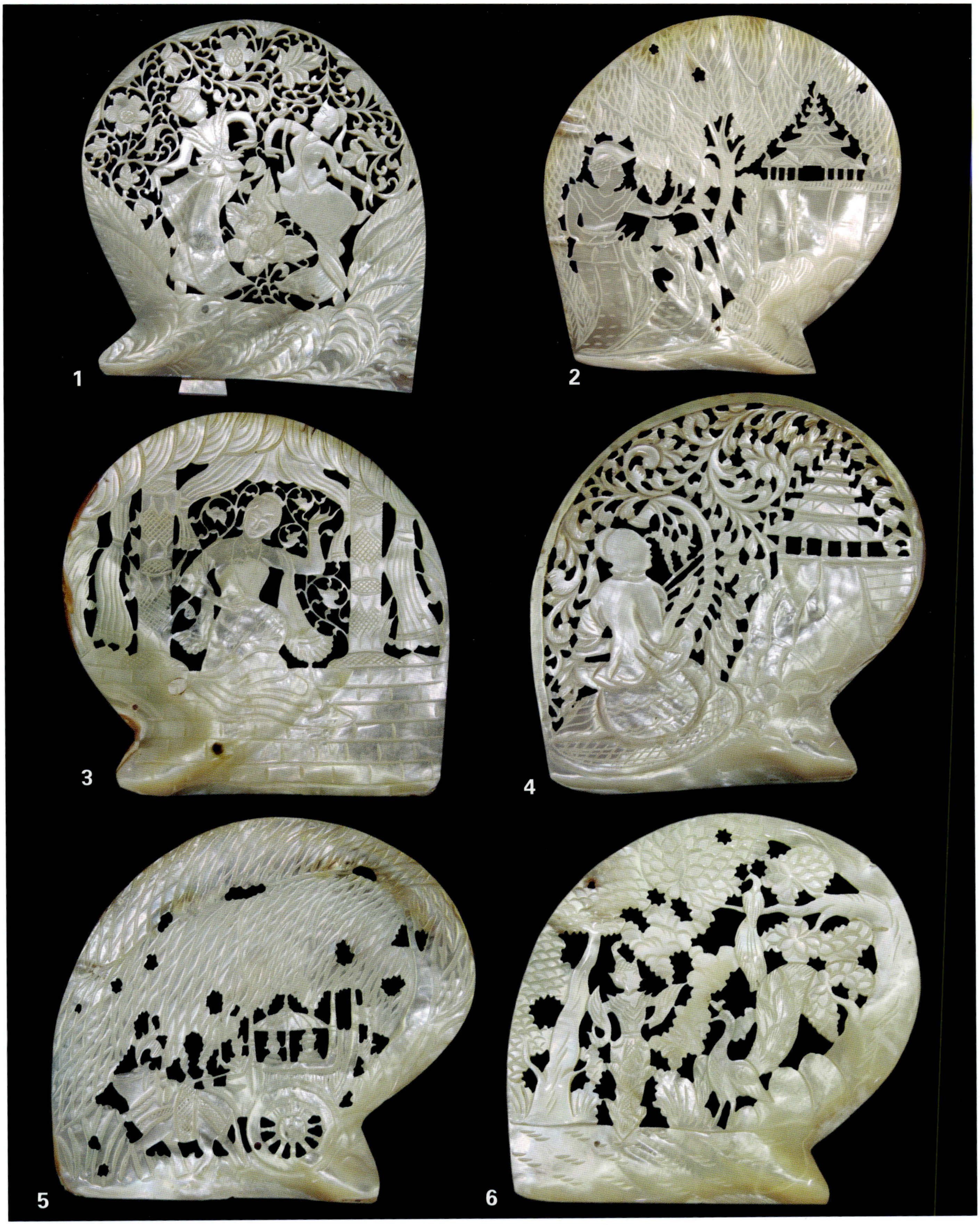


## PLATE 7 – CARVINGS FROM BURMA/MYANMAR 1

All carvings are from Burma/Myanmar. **1.** Two temple dancers, c. 1950–60, size 7.8″ x 7.2″ (19.9 x 18.2 cm). **2.** Dancing at the temple, c. 1960, size 8.3″ x 8.3″ (21 x 21 cm). **3.** Temple dancer, c. 1980, size 6.9″ x 6.9″ (17.5 x 17.5 cm). **4.** Temple musician playing a Saung Gauk, c. 1945, size 8.1″ x 7.9″ (20.5 x 20 cm). **5.** Riders in a Bullock cart, c. 1975, size 6.9″ x 6.5″ (17.5 x 16.5 cm). **6.** Temple dancer with a Burmese peacock, c. 1985, size 6.9″ x 6.8″ (17.5 x 17.3 cm).

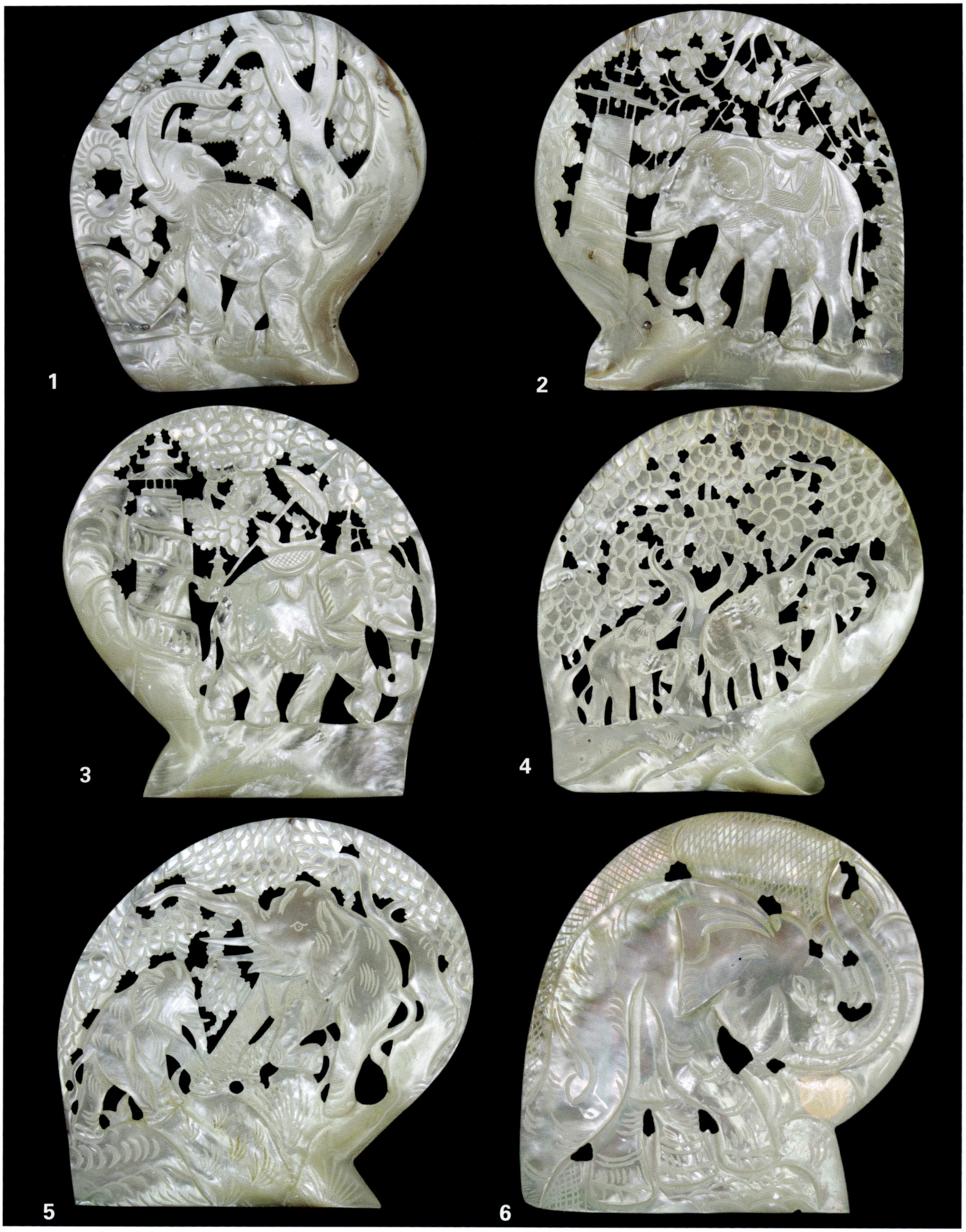


## PLATE 8 – CARVINGS FROM BURMA/MYANMAR 2

**1.** Elephant in a forest, c. 1999, size 7.3″ x 7.1″ (18.5 x 18 cm). **2.** Riders on an elephant, c. 1950, size 7.5″ x 7.3″ (19 x 18.5 cm). **3.** Men riding an elephant, c. 1985, size 6.9″ x 7.1″ (17.5 x 18 cm). **4.** Two elephants under large trees, c. 1996, size 6.3″ x 6.7″ (16 x 17 cm). **5.** Two elephants, c. 1996, size 8.3″ x 8.1″ (21 x 20.5 cm). **6.** Elephant, c. 1999, size 6.3″ x 6″ (16 x 15 cm).

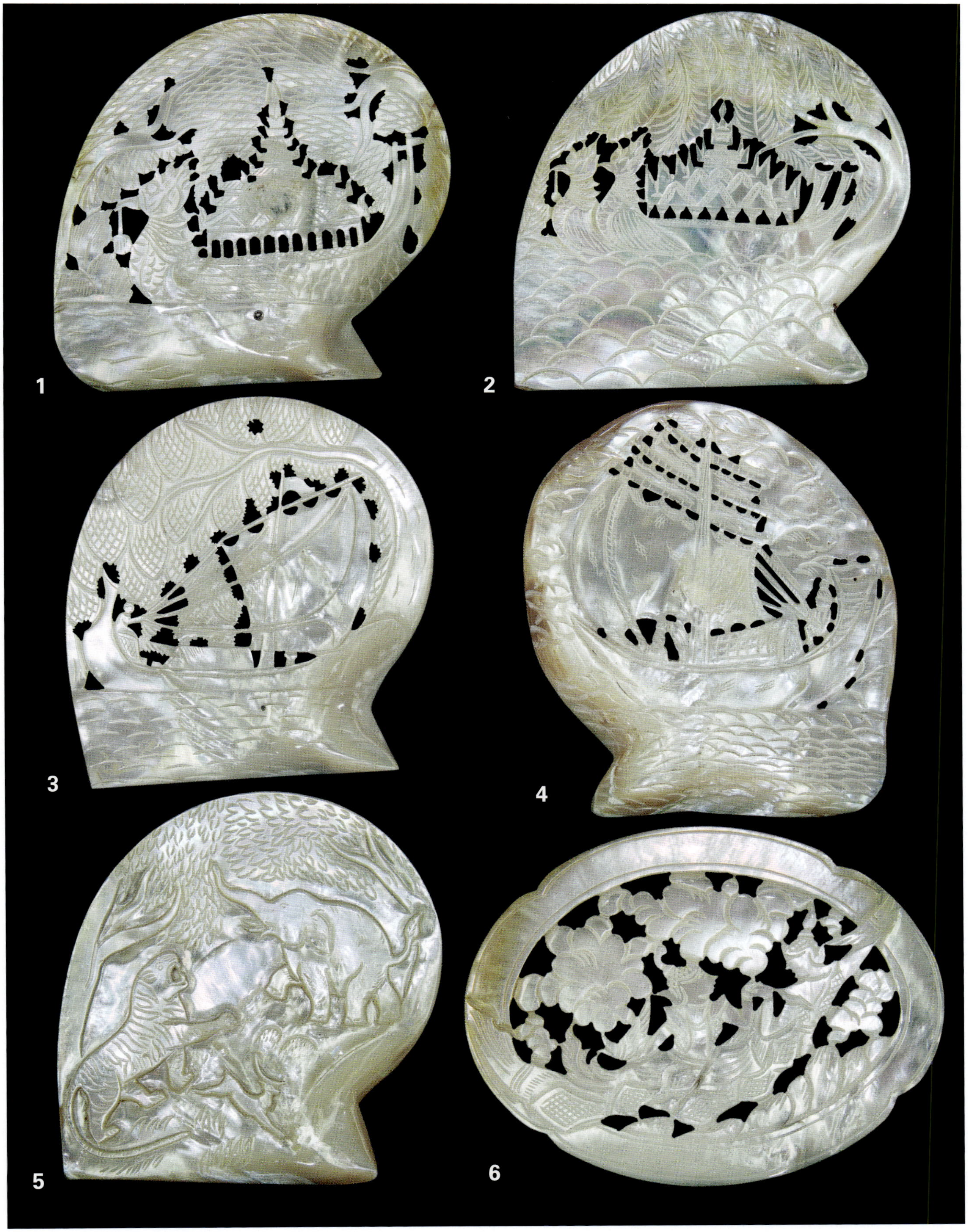


## PLATE 9 – CARVINGS FROM BURMA/MYANMAR 3

1. Dragon boat from Yangon, c. 1990, size 6.9″ x 6.7″ (17.5 x 17 cm). 2. Two-headed dragon boat from Yangon, c. 1970, size 7.1″ x 6.8″ (18 x 17.3 cm). 3. Sea trader arriving at Yangon, c. 1980, size 8.1″ x 7.9″ (20.5 x 20 cm). 4. Sea trader at Yangon, c. 1950, size 7.3″ x 6.9″ (18.5 x 17.5 cm). 5. Elephant and tiger with fleeing deer in background, c. 1966, size 7.2″ x 6.9″ (18.3 x 17.5 cm). 6. Two temple dancers, Yangon, c. 1999, size 5″ x 3.5″ (12 x 9 cm).

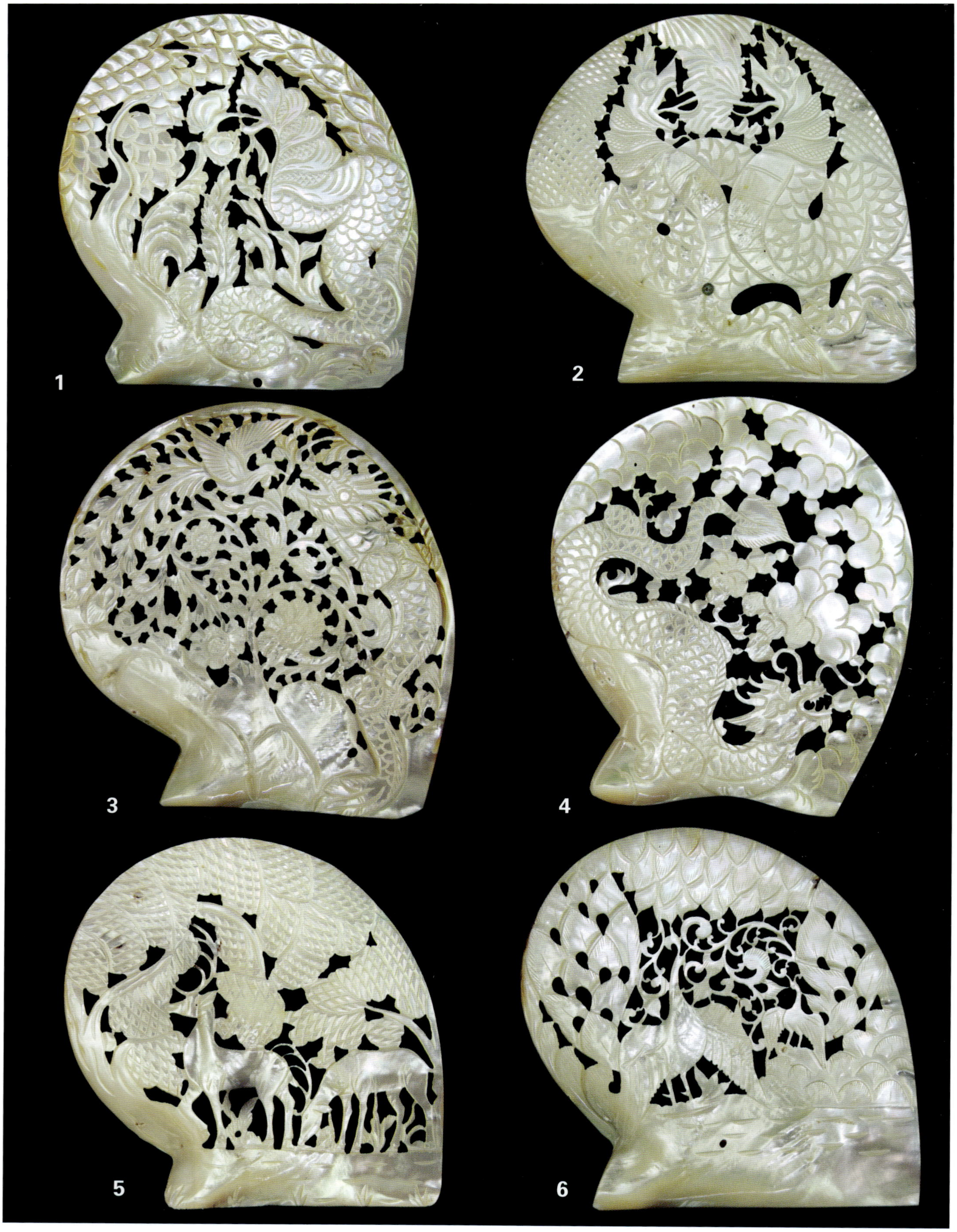


## PLATE 10 – CARVINGS FROM BURMA/MYANMAR 4

**1.** Dragon, c. 1999, size 7.5″ x 7.1″ (19 x 18 cm). **2.** Two dragons, c. 1970, size 7.3″ x 7.1″ (18.5 x 18 cm). **3.** Dragon and bird, c. 1988, size 8.1″ x 8.4″ (20.5 x 21.4 cm). **4.** Dragon, c. 1990, size 6.9″ x 6.3″ (17.5 x 16 cm). **5.** Two deer, c. 1950, size 8″ x 8″ (20.3 x 20.5 cm). **6.** Burmese peacock, c. 1990, size 7.7″ x 7.5″ (19.5 x 19 cm).

## PLATE 11 – CARVINGS FROM BURMA/MYANMAR 5

1. Fish, c. 1990, size 8.2″ x 7.1″ (20.8 x 18 cm). 2. Fish, c. 1996, size 7.5″ x 6.7″ (19 x 17 cm). 3. Carving of flowers, c. 1960, size 8.9″ x 6.5″ (22.5 x 16.5 cm). 4. Two sunflowers, c. 1998, size 5.7″ x 5.5″ (14.5 x 14 cm). 5. Scallop shell, c. 1996, size 5.4″ x 5″ (13.7 x 12.7 cm). 6. Leaf, c. 1995, size 7.3″ x 6.1″ (18.5 x 15.5 cm). 7. Tigers are common in Myanmar, c. 1999, size 5″ x 2.6″ (13 x 6.5 cm). 8. Elephants are tamed or bred in captivity for use as work animals, particularly in logging, c. 1999, size 4.7″ x 2.6″ (12 x 6.5 cm).

## PLATE 12 – CARVINGS FROM BURMA/MYANMAR 6

1. A water carrier balances two buckets, c. 1991, size 4.1″ x 3.9″ (10.5 x 9.8 cm). 2. A musician playing the Saung Guak, a Burmese arched harp with 16 strings, c. 1970, size 3.9″ x 3.5″ (10 x 9 cm). 3. A musician playing the Saung Guak, with a dancer, c. 1970, size 4.1″ x 4.1″ (10.5 x 10.3 cm). 4. Taj Mahal in India, c. 1999, size 4.3″ x 3.7″ (10.8 x 9.5 cm). 5. Elephants are tamed or bred in captivity for use as work animals particularly in logging, c. 1999, size 2.6″ x 2.6″ (6.5 x 6.5 cm). 6. Transport using a bullock cart, c. 1999, size 4.7″ x 3.9″ (12 x 10 cm). 7. Sampan in the Irrawaddy River, Yangon, c. 1999, size 6″ x 3.7″ (15.2 x 9.5 cm). 8. Dragon, as seen in Shinenandaw Kyaung Temple, Mandalay, c. 1999, size 4.7″ x 1.6″ (12 x 4 cm).

## PLATE 13 – CARVINGS FROM BURMA/MYANMAR 7

1. Fu lion (sometimes called Foo dog), a Chinese guardian figure that was believed to have mystic powers, c. 1999, size 1.7" x 1.2" (4.4 x 3 cm). 2. Two temple dancers, Yangon, c. 1999, size 4.4" x 3.3" (11.3 x 8.5 cm). 3. A musician playing the Saung Gauk, a Burmese arched harp with 16 strings, c. 1999, size 4.4" x 4.1" (11.3 x 10.5 cm). 4. A jester in Burma is known as a Nibhatkin, c. 1999, size 5" x 2.6" (13 x 6.5 cm). 5. Temple dancer, c. 1999, size 4.5" x 2.2" (11.5 x 5.6 cm). 6. Two temple dancers, Yangon, c. 1999, size 4.1" x 3" (10.5 x 7 cm). 7. A water carrier balances her load on her head in a rural area, c. 1999, size 4.9" x 1.2" (12.4 x 3 cm). 8. Sea trader arriving at Yangon, c. 1999, size 4.7" x 2.6" (12 x 6.5 cm) 9. Dragon boat as seen in Yangon, c. 1999, size 3.5" x 2.4" (9 x 6 cm) 10. Two-headed dragon boat as seen in Yangon, c. 1999, size 5.5" x 3.4" (14 x 8.5 cm)

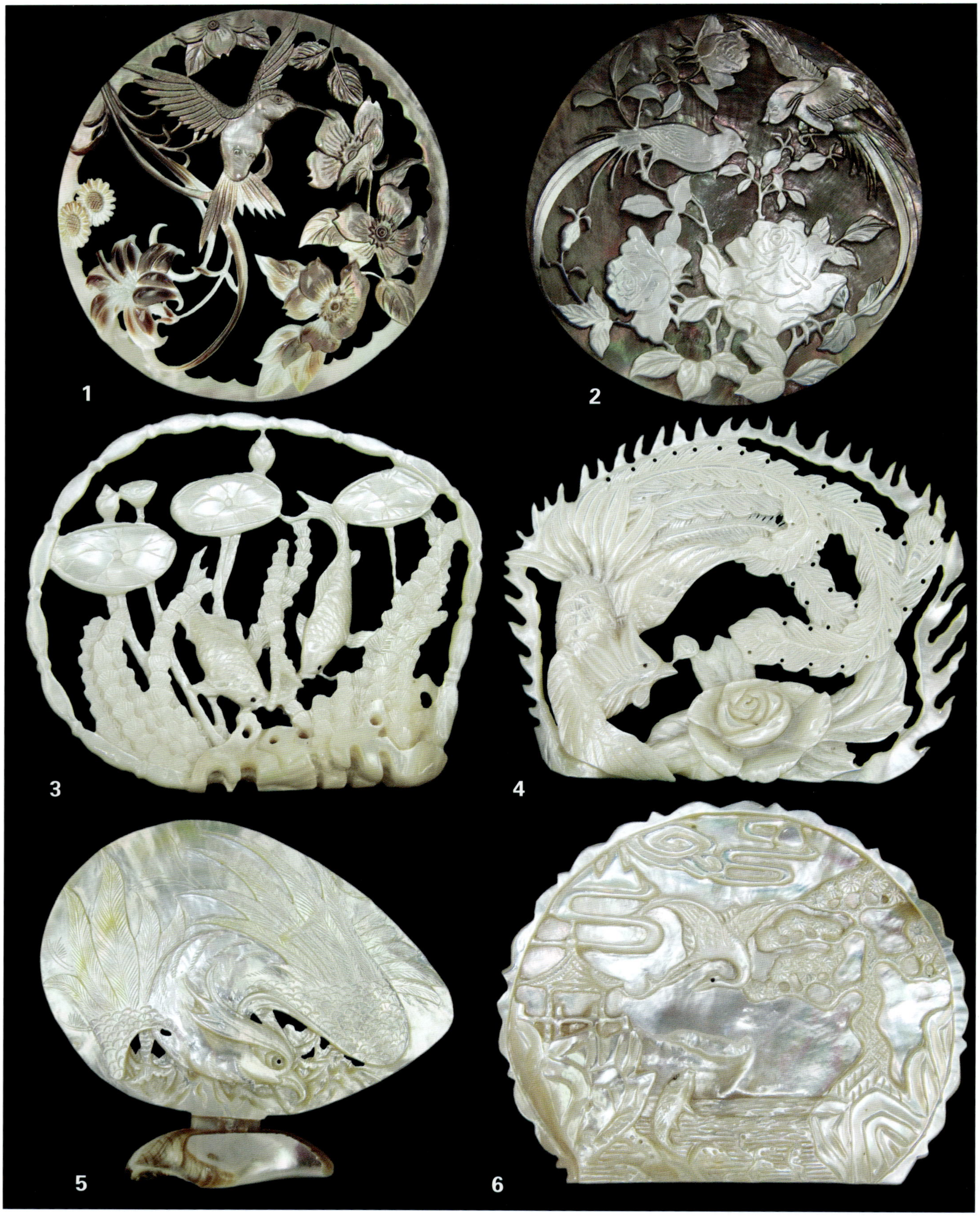


## PLATE 14 – CARVINGS FROM CHINA 1

Carvings from China, c. 1997–2000. 1. Honeyeater bird, also known as hummingbird, size 4.7" x 4.7" (12 x 12 cm). 2. Exotic birds, black lip pearl background, size 4.5" x 4.5" (11.5 x 11.5 cm). 3. Carp, size 6.5" x 5.4" (16.5 x 13.8 cm). 4. Rooster, believed to ward off evil spirits, size 5.9" x 4.7" (15 x 12 cm). 5. Rooster, size 7" x 5.3" (18 x 13.5 cm). 6. Crane, legendary in China for being the prince of all feathered creatures on earth and an ancient symbol for longevity, size 5.9" x 5" (15 x 12.5 cm).

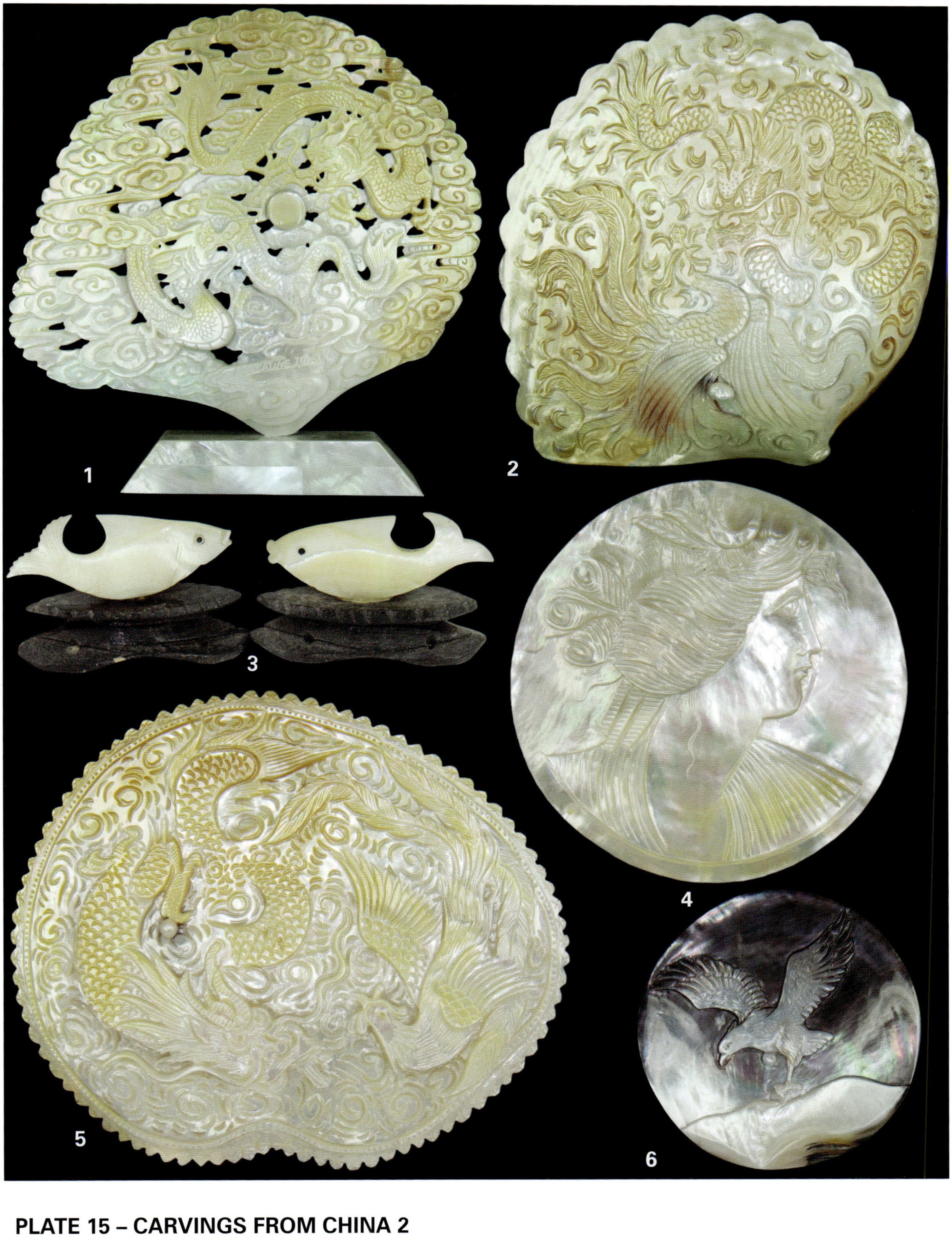


## PLATE 15 – CARVINGS FROM CHINA 2

1. Carved dragons with an attached mother-of-pearl stand, c. 1990, size 9″ x 7.6″ (23 x 19.5 cm). 2. Dragon and Phoenix. The phoenix is regarded as King of the winged kingdom, synonymous with good fortune, opportunity and luck. When combined with the dragon, the pair represent Yin energy, c. 1950, size 7.5″ x 7.3″ (19 x 18.5 cm). 3. A pair of small fish on stands, possible box lid decorations, c. 1910, size 2.6″ x 1.7″ (6.5 x 4.3 cm). 4. Profile of a lady in classical motif, c. 1990, size 4.7″ x 4.7″ (12 x 12 cm). 5. Dragon, c. 1960, size 7.1″ x 6.1″ (18 x 15.5 cm). 6. Eagle, c. 1980, size 3.7″ x 3.5″ (9.3 x 9 cm).

## PLATE 16 – CARVINGS FROM CHINA 3

These intricate carvings originally came in pairs, but many have been separated over the years. **1a, 1b.** Scene of warriors fighting, being watched by priests, matching pair, c. 1840, size 8.5″ x 7″ (21.2 x 17.6 cm). **2.** Miniature elephant on a stand, possible box lid decoration, c. 1890, size 1.7″ x 1.6″ (4.3 x 4 cm). **3.** Scene of people making tools, c. 1880-1900, size 7.1″ x 6.3″ (18 x 16 cm). **4.** Head and shoulders decoration, thought by many to be a gaming counter, but given that the carving is only on one side, it is more than likely a box decoration, c. 1800, size 1.6 x 1.7″ (4 x 4.4 cm). **5.** Village scene, c. 1850–1870, size 8.3″ x 8.3″ (21 x 21 cm). **6.** Western scene, note the bone shaker bicycle (only a central rod to hold onto) and multi-story buildings, c. 1860–70, size 9.4″ x 7.9″ (24 x 20 cm).

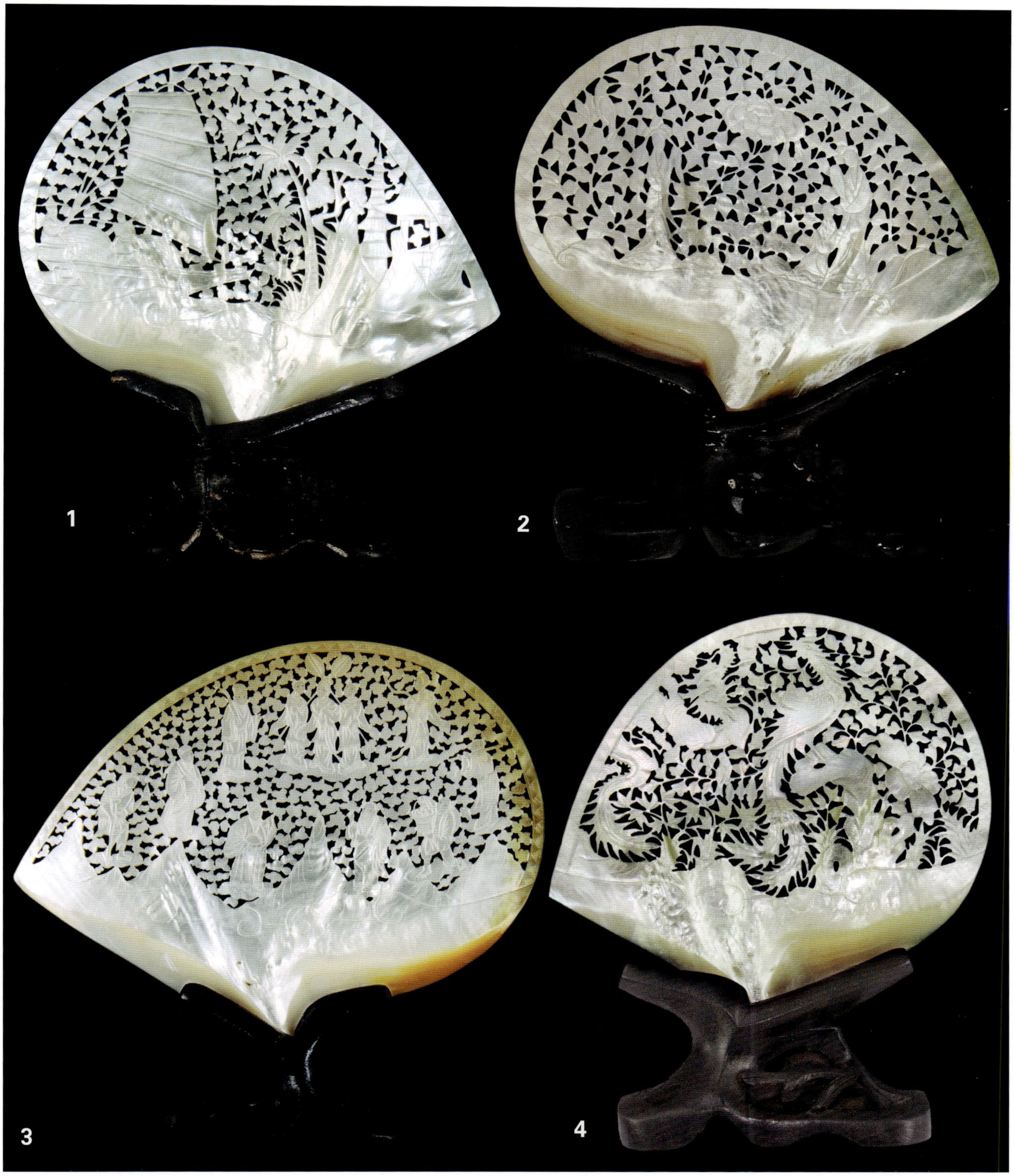


## PLATE 17 – CARVINGS FROM CHINA 4

These carvings were usually sold in identical pairs. **1.** Pierced carving of a Chinese sampan, a boat used in coastal waters and rivers, c. 1960–70, size 8.5″ x 8″ (21.5 x 20.4 cm). **2.** Pierced carving of two ladies, c. 1960–70, size 6.5″ x 6.3″ (16.5 x 16 cm). **3.** Eight immortals come to the Court of Heaven for celebration of the birthday of the Queen of the West, who is attended by two servants, China, c. 1950, size 10.2″ x 6.7″ (26 x 17 cm). **4.** Pierced carving of a dragon and phoenix. The phoenix is regarded as king of the winged kingdom, synonymous with good fortune, opportunity, and luck. When combined with the dragon, the pair represent Yin energy, c. 1960–70, size 6.7″ x 6.3″ (17 x 16 cm).

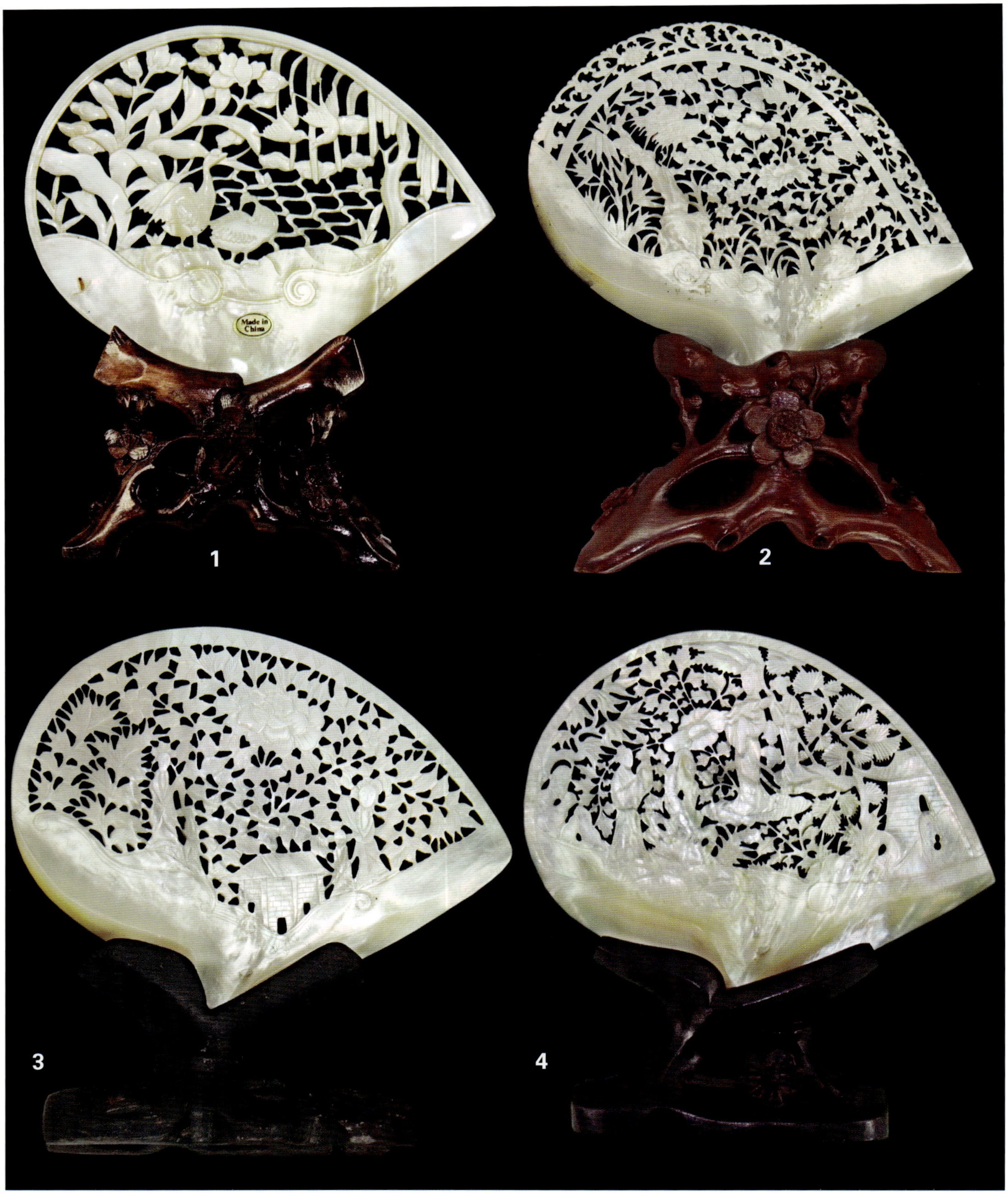


## PLATE 18 – CARVINGS FROM CHINA 5

These carvings are usually sold in identical pairs, but they often get separated with time. 1. Pierced carving of two geese, symbol of married bliss, c. 1960–70, size 5.3″ x 4.9″ (13.5 x 12.5 cm). 2. Pierced carving of two cranes, ancient symbol of longevity, c. 1960–70, size 6.7″ x 6.5″ (17 x 16.5 cm). 3. Pierced carvings of two ladies, with a house in the background, c. 1960–70, size 5.5″ x 5.5″ (14 x 14 cm). 4. The Queen of the West, who is attended by a servant, glancing down, symbolizing her constant vigilance over the world, c. 1960–70, size 7.1″ x 5.8″ (18 x 14.7 cm).

## PLATE 19 – CARVINGS FROM CHINA 6

These carvings were originally sold in identical pairs, but most have now been separated. **1.** Pierced carving of a bird in the trees, original box, c. 1960–70, size 6.1″ x 4.8″ (15.5 x 12.3 cm). **2.** Pierced carving of birds, original box, c. 1960–70, size 5.9″ x 4.3″ (15 x 11 cm). **3.** Pierced carving based on the Chinese classic masterpiece "Journey to the West" written by Wu Cheng-en. (1500–1582). The main characters are a monkey king, eight commandment pig, tang monk (with a crown), and Sha monk, c. 1945–50, size 7.6″ x 7.5″ (19.5 x 19 cm). **4.** Fish on a stand, possible box lid decoration, c. 1910, size 3 ¾″ x 1 ¾″ (9.7 x 4.5 cm). **5.** Fish on a stand, possible box lid decoration, c. 1910, size 3.7″ x 1.9″ (9.5 x 4.8 cm). **6.** Pierced carving of cranes, ancient symbol of longevity, c. 1950, size 6.7″ x 6.5″ (17 x 16.5 cm).

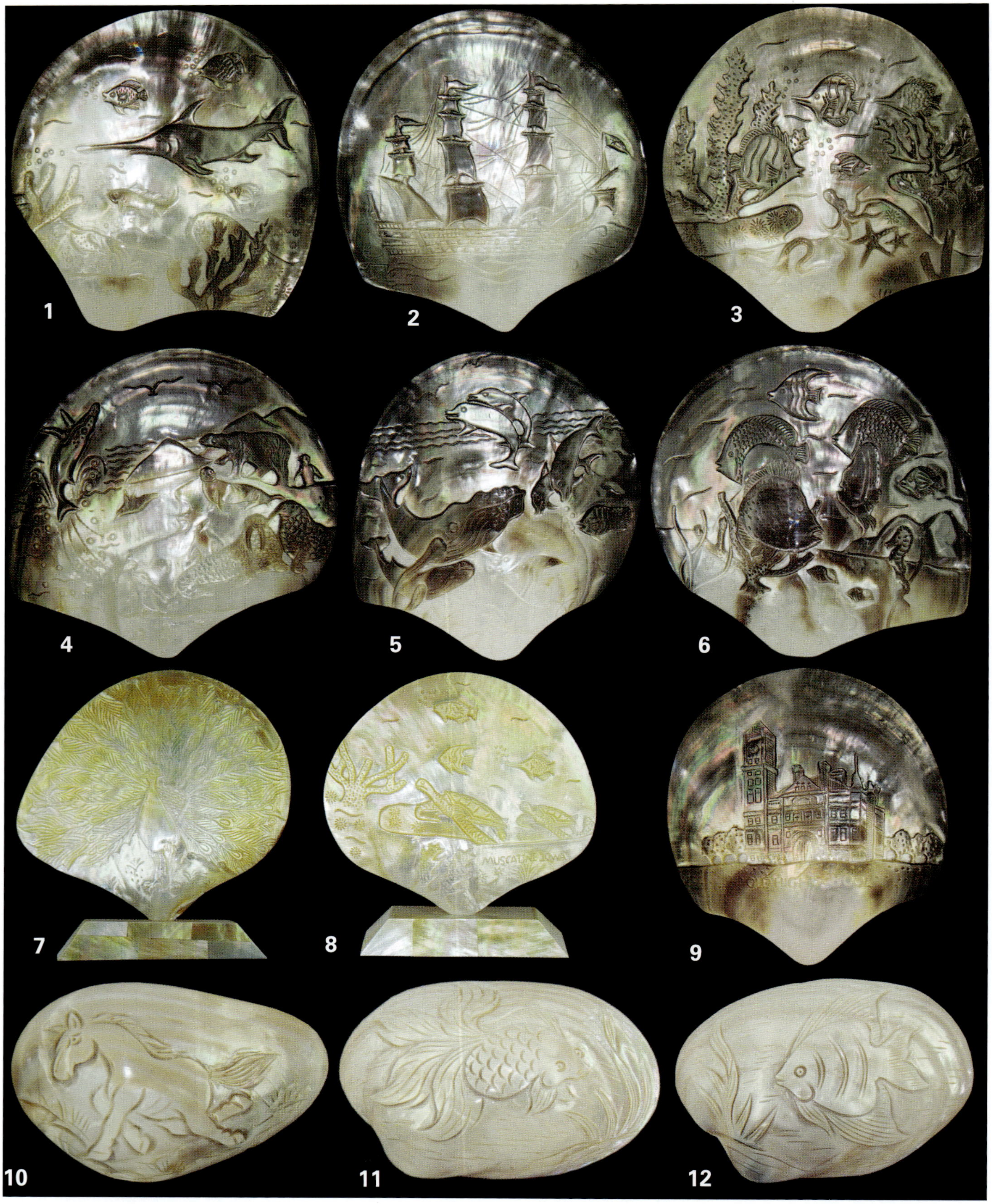


## PLATE 20 – CARVINGS FROM CHINA 7

These are carved in China, c. 1980–1990. **1.** Marlin, size 4.7″ x 5″ (12 x 12.5 cm). **2.** Galleon, size 5″ x 4.7″ (12.5 x 12 cm). **3.** Fish and marine life, size 4.7″ x 4.5″ (12 x 11.5 cm). **4.** Animals of the icy waters, size 4.6″ x 5.3″ (11.8 x 13.5 cm). **5.** Whales and dolphins, size 4.7″ x 4.3″ (12 x 11 cm). **6.** Fish, size 5.1″ x 4.7″ (13 x 12 cm). **7.** Peacock, size 5.3″ x 5.1″ (13.4 x 13 cm). **8.** Turtles, size 5.3″ x 4.7″ (13.5 x 12 cm). **9.** Old High School, Muscatine, Iowa, USA, size 5.3″ x 5.1″ (13.5 x 13 cm). **10.** Horse, carved in full shell, size 3.9″ x 2.4″ (10 x 6.2 cm). **11.** Gold fish, in full shell, size 3.5″ x 2.4″ (9 x 6 cm). **12.** Angel fish, in full shell, size 4.7″ x 3.3″ (12 x 8.5 cm).

## PLATE 21 – CARVINGS FROM CHINA 8

All these carvings are from China,1980–90. The use of white, yellow, black, and freshwater pearl oyster shows the different effect that can be achieved. 1. Tiger, size 3″ x 3″ (7.3 x 7.5 cm). 2. Donkey, size 2.3″ x 3.3″ (6 x 8.4 cm). 3. Cow, size 3.3″ x 2.5″ (8.3 x 6.4 cm). 4. Pegasus, winged horse-god sired by Poseidon, size 3.5″ x 3.1″ (9 x 8 cm). 5. Zebra, size 2.8″ x 2.8″ (7 x 7 cm). 6. Lion, size 2.6″ x 3″ (6.7 x 7 cm). 7. Leopard, size 3.7″ x 2″ (9.5 x 5 cm). 8. Elephant, size 3.7″ x 2.4″ (9.5 x 6 cm), made for and marked Muscatine, Iowa. 9. Dog, size 2.8″ x 3.3″ (7 x 8.5 cm). 10. Tortoise, size 3.7″ x 2″ (9.5 x 5 cm). 11. Bunny, size 2.8″ x 2.2″ (7 x 5.6 cm). 12. Mouse, size 3.1″ x 2.9″ (8 x 7.4 cm). 13. Rat, size 3″ x 2.8″ (7.6 x 7 cm). 14. Corn, size 3.5″ x 1.9″ (9 x 4.8 cm).

## PLATE 22 – CARVINGS FROM CHINA 9

All these carvings are from China, c. 1980–90. The use of white, yellow, black, and freshwater pearl oyster shows the different effect that can be achieved. 1. Angel fish, size 3.4" x 3" (8.6 x 7.4 cm). 2. Moorish idol, size 3.9" x 3.1" (10 x 8 cm). 3. Freshwater angel fish, size 3.5" x 3.3" (9 x 8.5 cm). 4. Moorish idol, size 3.3" x 3.1" (8.5 x 8 cm). 5. Long nose butterfly fish, size 3.5" x 2.8" (9 x 7 cm). 6. Long nose butterfly fish, size 3.9" x 2.8" (9.8 x 7 cm). 7. Butterfly fish, size 2.8" x 2.8" (7.2 x 7 cm) made for and marked Muscatine, Iowa. 8. Butterfly fish, size 3.5" x 2.8" (9 x 6.8 cm). 9. Long nose butterfly fish, size 3.8" x 2.4" (9.6 x 6.2 cm). 10. Sea horse, size 4.4" x 2.3" (11.2 x 5.8 cm). 11. Dolphin, size 3.5" x 2.1" (9 x 5.4 cm). 12. Whale, size 3.9" x 2.4" (10 x 6 cm).

## PLATE – 23 CARVINGS FROM CHINA 10

All these carvings are from China, c. 1980–90, using white, yellow, black, and freshwater pearl oyster. **1.** Bird, size 3.8″ x 2.8″ (9.7 x 7 cm). **2.** Bird of prey, size 3.1″ x 3.3″ (8 x 8.4 cm). **3.** Rooster, size 2.6″ x 3.3″ (6.5 x 8.4 cm). **4.** Eagle, size 3.9″ x 2.4″ (10 x 6 cm). **5.** Bird, size 4.2″ x 2.4″ (10.6 x 6 cm). **6.** Owl, size 3.4″ x 2″ (8.7 x 5 cm). **7.** Parrot, size 3.3″ x 2″ (8.5 x 5 cm). **8.** Turtle, size 2.4″ x 2.7″ (6.2 x 6.8 cm). **9.** Angel fish, size 3.5″ x 2.2″ (8.9 x 5.6 cm). **10.** Squirrel, size 2.4″ x 2.2″ (6 x 5.6 cm). **11.** Bee, size 3.1″ x 2.8″ (8 x 7 cm). **12.** Train, size 3″ x 1.8″ (7.5 x 4.5 cm). **13.** Starfish, size 2.8″ x 2.8″ (7 x 7 cm). **14.** Strawberries, size 3.5″ x 2.6″ (8.8 x 6.5 cm). **15.** Child, size 3.1″ x 1.4″ (8 x 3.5 cm).

## PLATE 24 – CARVINGS FROM CHINA 11

This selection has mostly been made with the freshwater pearl shell. 1. Goldfish, c. 1980, size 6.9″ x 4.3″ (17.5 x 11 cm). 2. Eagle, c. 1980, size 6.9″ x 3.9″ (17.5 x 9.8 cm). 3. Owl, c. 1980, size 4.1″ x 2.4″ (10.5 x 6 cm). 4. Goldfish, c. 1980, size 4.3″ x 2.4″ (11 x 6 cm). 5. Dolphin, c. 1980, size 7.1″ x 3.9″ (18 x 10 cm). 6. Swan, c. 1980, size 5.7″ x 3.9″ (14.6 x 9.8 cm). 7. Fan, c. 1985, size 5.7″ x 3″ (14.5 x 7.5 cm). 8. Goldfish, black lip pearl, c. 1975, size 4.1″ x 3″ (10.5 x 7.5 cm). 9. Flower, c. 1980, size 3.9″ x 2.2″ (10 x 5.6 cm). 10. Fan, c. 1985, size 5.7″ x 3″ (14.5 x 7.5 cm). 11. Elephant, c. 1980, size 5″ x 3.4″ (2.6 x 8.6 cm). 12. Peacock, c. 1970, size 5.5″ x 4.1″ (14 x 10.4 cm). 13. Native American in feathered headdress, made for USA market, c. 1970–80, size 4.5″ x 3.5″ (11.5 x 9 cm). 14. Owl, c. 1980, size 6.7″ x 4.9″ (17 x 12.5 cm)

## PLATE 25 – CARVINGS FROM CHINA 12

These carvings are all from China. 1. Carved lady's head, c. 1960, size 6.7" x 4.3" (17 x 11 cm). 2. Carved lady's head, c. 1960, size 6.5" x 4.1" (16.5 x 10.5 cm). 3. Birds, probably intended as a box top lid or decoration, c. 1880, size 3.9" x 3.1" (9.8 x 8 cm). 4. Dragon with 4 claws, pierced full shell carving, c. 1995, size 5.9" x 4.1" (15 x 10.5 cm). 5. Pagoda scene made with cut pearl pieces, c. 1960, size 7.1" x 4.3" (18 x 11 cm). 6. Lady, c. 1960, size 6.4" x 2" (16.2 x 5 cm). 7. Dragon with 4 toes, c. 1950, size 5.7" x 3.3" (14.5 x 8.5 cm). 8. Birds in a tree on a stand, c. 1993, size 5.5" x 3.5" (14 x 9 cm).

## PLATE 26 – CARVINGS FROM CHINA 13

These turban shells were carved in China, c. 1950–1980, mostly intended for lamp shades. **1.** Horses, size 5.7″ x 5.7″ (14.5 x 14.5 cm). **2.** Story book shell. Gold figures painted on the turban shell tell a story about a historic event, c. 1850, size 5.5″ x 5.5″ (14 x 14 cm). **3.** Sharks, size 5.9″ x 5.1″ (15 x 13 cm). **4.** Chinese fisherman, carved from a turban shell, size 3″ x 2.3″ (7.5 x 6 cm). **5.** Green dragon, size 7.9″ x 5.1″ (20 x 13 cm). **6.** Small dragon, size 7.9″ x 5″ (20 x 12.5 cm). **7.** Dragons, size 8.5″ x 6.2″ (21.5 x 15.7 cm). **8.** Elephants, size 7.1″ x 5.5″ (18 x 14 cm).

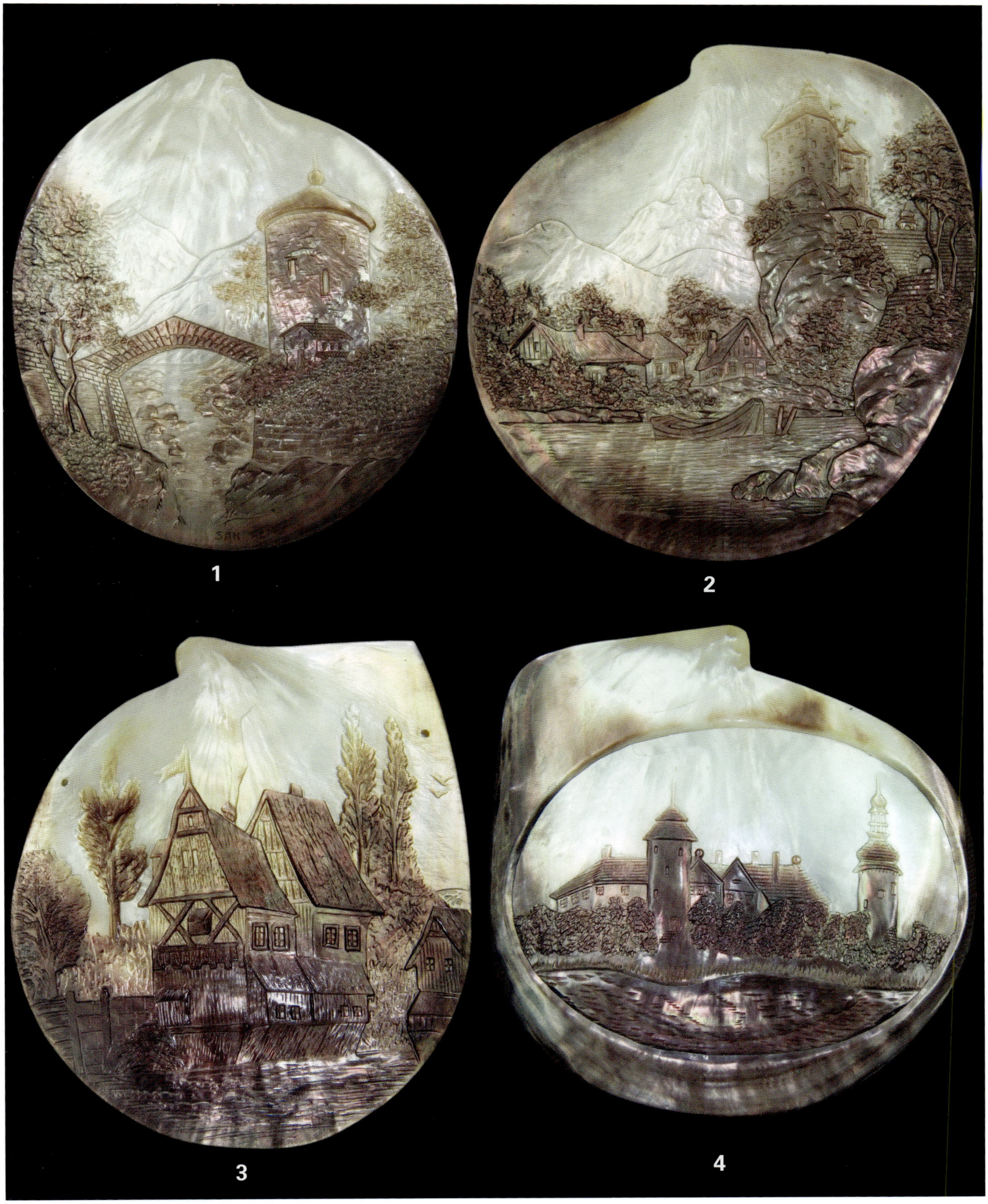


## PLATE 27 – CARVINGS FROM EUROPE

These carvings are typical of the work done in several European countries and further examples are needed to be able to pinpoint the exact origin. **1.** Scenic carving inscribed *Sanremo*, a town in Italy. Origin of carving could be Austria, Germany or Italy, c. 1875, size 6.1″ x 5.7″ (15.5 x 14.5 cm). **2.** Scenic carving inscribed *Maria-stein*, a town in Austria. Origin of carving could be Italy, Austria or Germany, c. 1875 size 6.1″ x 6.1″ (15.5 x 15.5 cm). **3.** Early house boat on a river, Germany, c. 1875, size 5.5″ x 4.9″ (14 x 12.5 cm). **4.** Chateau or lighthouse on the sea shore or river, Austria, Italy or Germany, c. 1880, size 5.5″ x 5.4″ (14 x 13.8 cm).

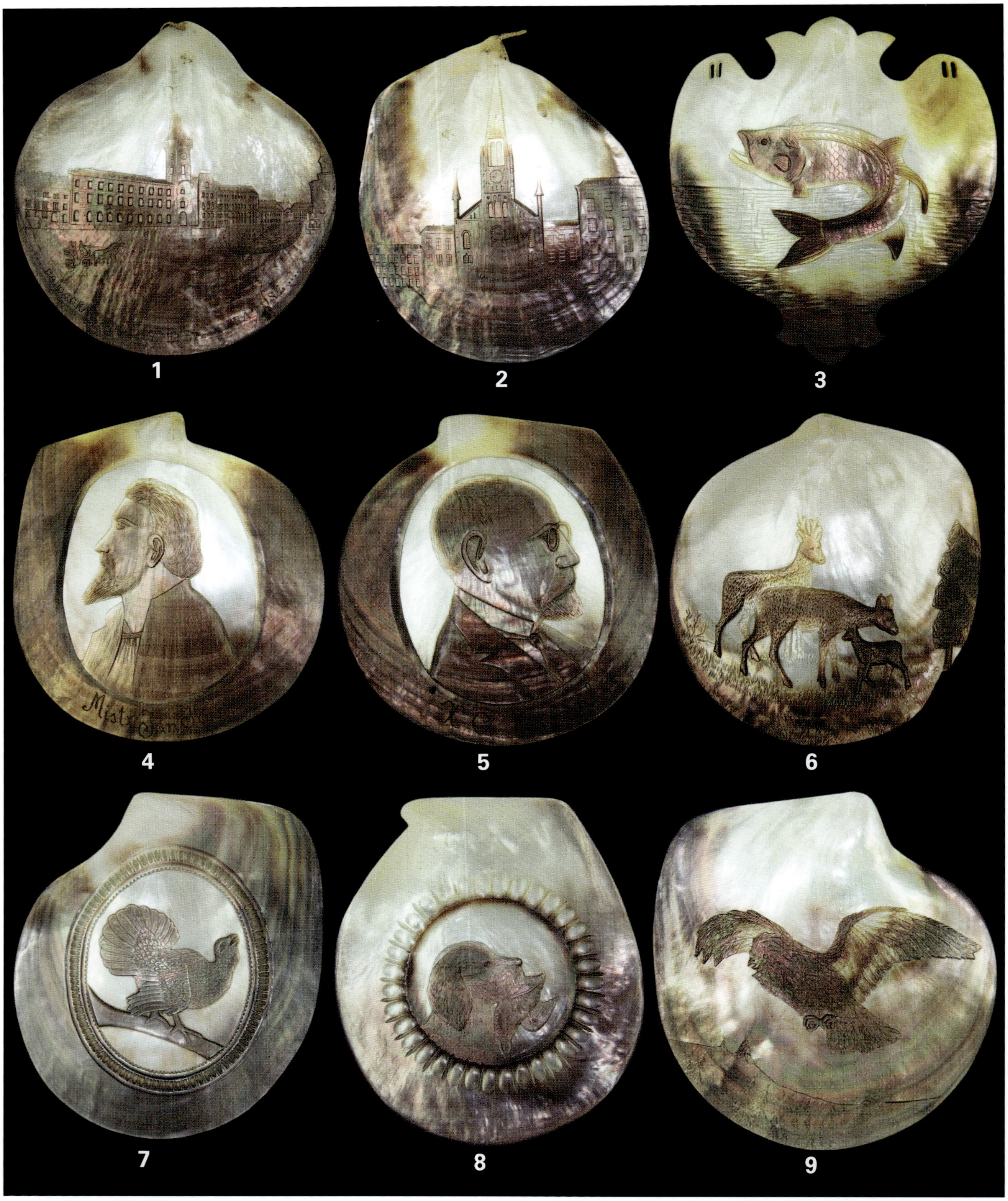


## PLATE 28 – CARVINGS FROM EUROPE

1. Royal Castle in Warsaw, Poland, c. 1880, size 6.9″ x 7.1″ (17.5 x 18 cm). 2. Evangelical Reformed Church in Warsaw, Poland, c. 1880, size 7.1″ x 6.3″ (18 x 16 cm). 3. Fish on badge shaped pearl, Austria, Italy, or Germany, c. 1880, size 5.5″ x 5.1″ (14 x 13 cm). 4. Jan Huys, (1369–1415), who pushed for reform, was burnt at the stake for his beliefs, Czechoslovakia, c. 1920, size 6.4″ x 6.1″ (16.2 x 15.5 cm). 5. T.G. Masaryk, (1850–1937) first President and chief founder of Czechoslovakia, c. 1920, size 6.1″ x 5.9″ (15.5 x 15 cm). 6. Grazing deer, Austria, Italy, or Germany, c. 1900, size 5.5″ x 5.1″ (14 x 13 cm). 7. Grouse, signed by the carver *K. Hava, Zirovnica*, Slovenia, c. 1980–90, size 7″ x 5.9″ (17.8 x 15 cm). 8. Hunting dog, Slovenia, c. 1980–90, size 6.9″ x 5.8″ (17.5 x 14.7 cm). 9. Falcon, possibly being used for hunting, Slovenia, c. 1980–90, size 6.1″ x 5.9″ (15.5 x 15 cm).

1

2

## PLATE 29 – CARVINGS FROM GERMANY

1–2. A set of two outstanding carvings of skittle or kegelen players, with a background of thatched homes and surrounding forests, Germany, c. 1750–1810, size 8.4" x 6.7" (21.3 x 17 cm).

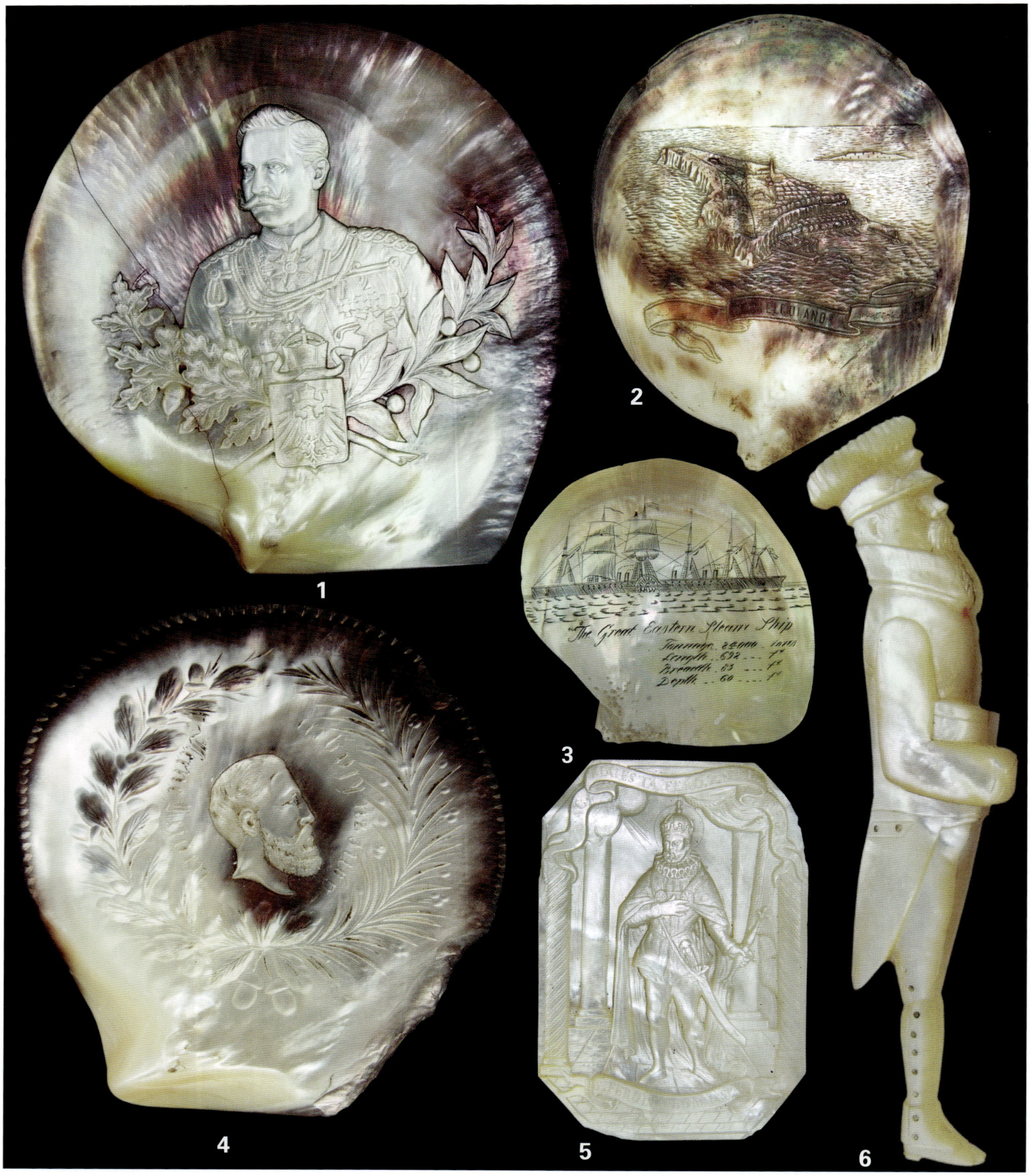


## PLATE 30 – CARVINGS FROM ENGLAND and EUROPE

1. Kaiser Wilhelm II, Emperor of Germany and Kingdom of Prussia, (1888–1918) Germany, c. 1890, size 7.2″ x 7.2″ (18.4 x 18.2 cm). 2. Heligoland, a small German archipelago in the North Sea, Germany, c. 1880, size 8.3″ x 7.2″ (21 x 18.4 cm). 3. Great Eastern Steamship, a commemorative item sold at the time of launching, England, c. 1858, size 3.1″ x 3.1″ (7.8 x 7.8 cm). 4. Kaiser Friedrich 111 (1831–1888) German Emperor and King of Prussia inscribed *Lerne leiden ohne zu klagen; Learn to suffer without complaining*, Germany, c. 1880, size 7″ x 6.3″ (17.8 x 16 cm). 5. King Ferdinand of Two Sicilies, from a box top, Italy, c. 1850, size 3.3″ x 2.3″ (8.5 x 6 cm). 6. Military gentleman or sea captain, although some believe this figure to be that of Jimmy the Rockman, famous for selling sweets at bull fights in Spain, England, c. 1870, size 6.3″ x 1.2″ (16 x 3.1 cm).

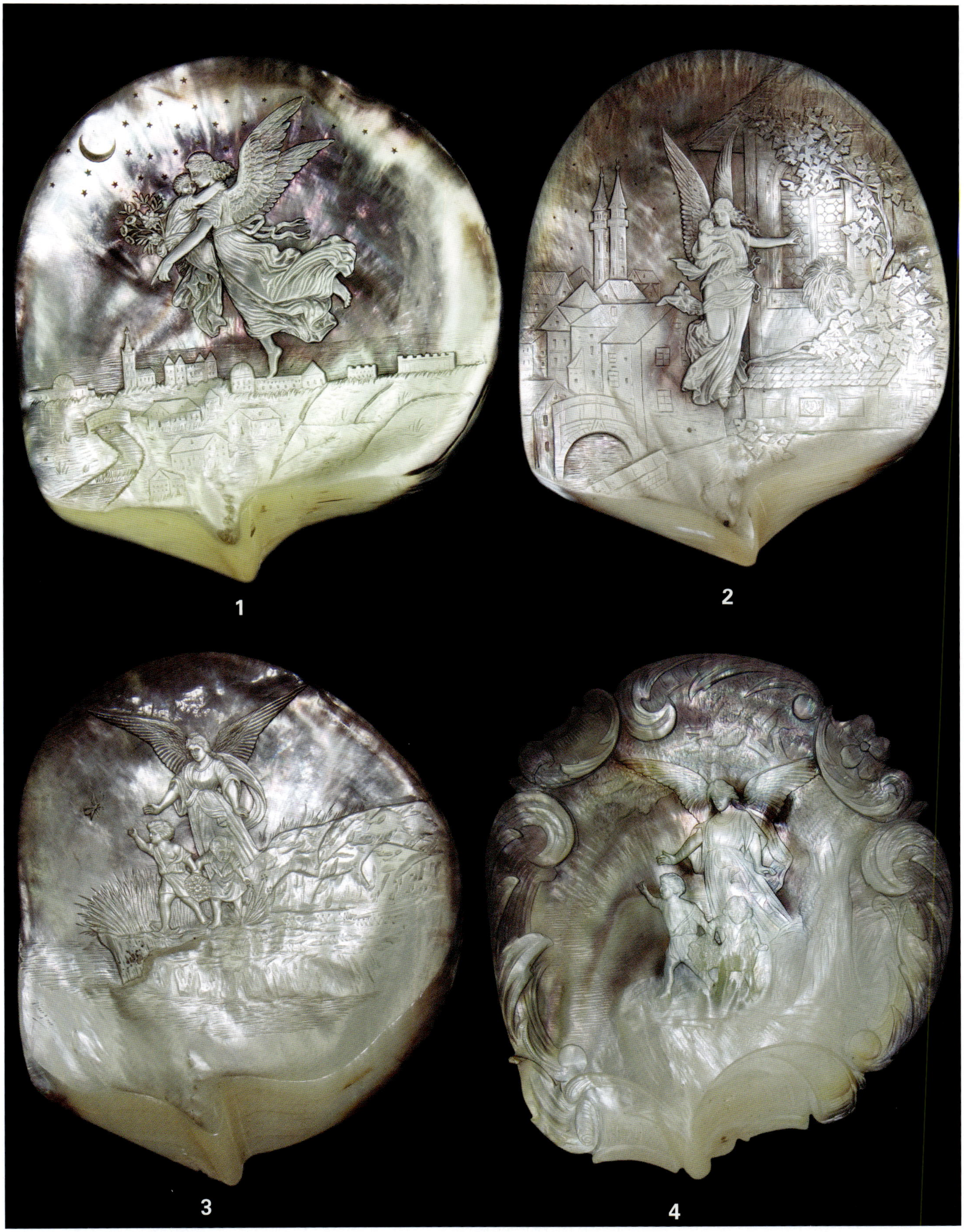


## PLATE 31 – CARVINGS FROM FRANCE 1

This interesting set is based on the painting, *The Guardian Angel,* 1656 by Pietro da Cortona. **1.** An angel holding a child, with a village in the background, c. 1830, size 7.9″ x 6.5″ (20 x 16.5 cm). **2.** An angel holding a child, c. 1830, size 7.9″ x 6.3″ (20 x 16 cm). **3.** An angel watching two children, c. 1860, size 8.7″ x 7.9″ (22 x 20 cm). **4.** An angel with two children, c. 1850, size 8.5″ x 7.3″ (21.5 x 18.5 cm).

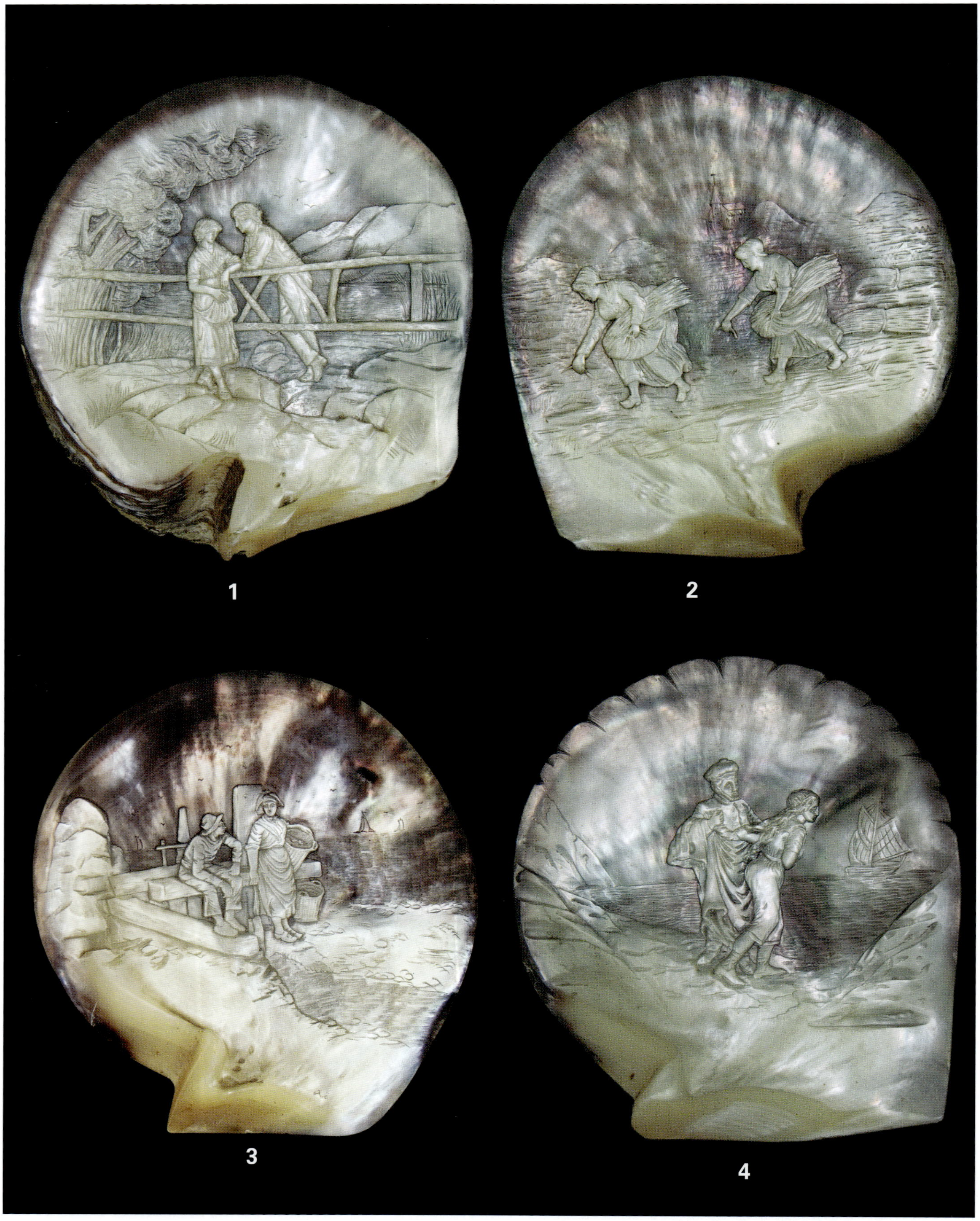


## PLATE 32 – CARVINGS FROM FRANCE 2

1. Woman and man in conversation at fence, c. 1830, size 9.1" x 8.6" (23 x 21.8 cm). 2. Two ladies harvesting corn, c. 1850-70, size 7.2" x 6.9" (18.5 x 17.5 cm). 3. Lady and man sitting on a wharf, c. 1870, size 8.3" x 7.9" (21 x 20 cm). 4. Lady going for a swim with a servant assisting, c. 1880, size 6.5" x 6.1" (16.5 x 15.4 cm).

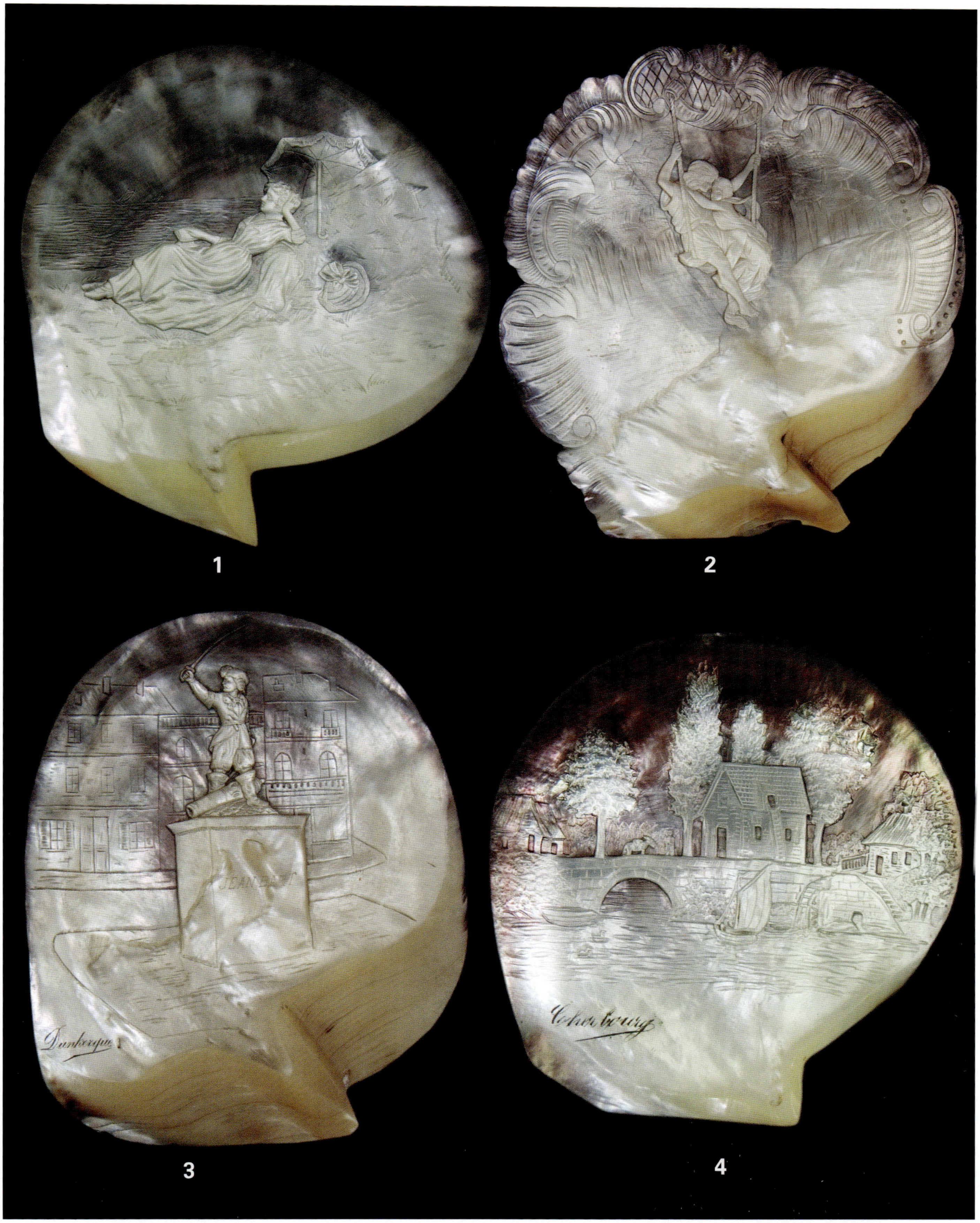


## PLATE 33 – CARVINGS FROM FRANCE 3

1. Reclining lady, c. 1860, size 7.5″ x 7.3″ (19 x 18.6 cm). 2. Two lovers on a swing, based on the painting, *Spring,* 1873, by Pierre Auguste Cot, c. 1875, size 9.6″ x 9″ (24.5 x 22.8 cm). 3. Statue of Jean Bart in the main square of Dunkirk. Bart captured 386 ships, becoming a hero of the Navy during the war of 1688–1697, c. 1870–90, size 7.9″ x 6.5″ (20 x 16.5 cm). 4. House beside a river, inscribed *Cherbourg*, c. 1880, size 4.4″ x 4.3″ (11.2 x 10.9 cm).

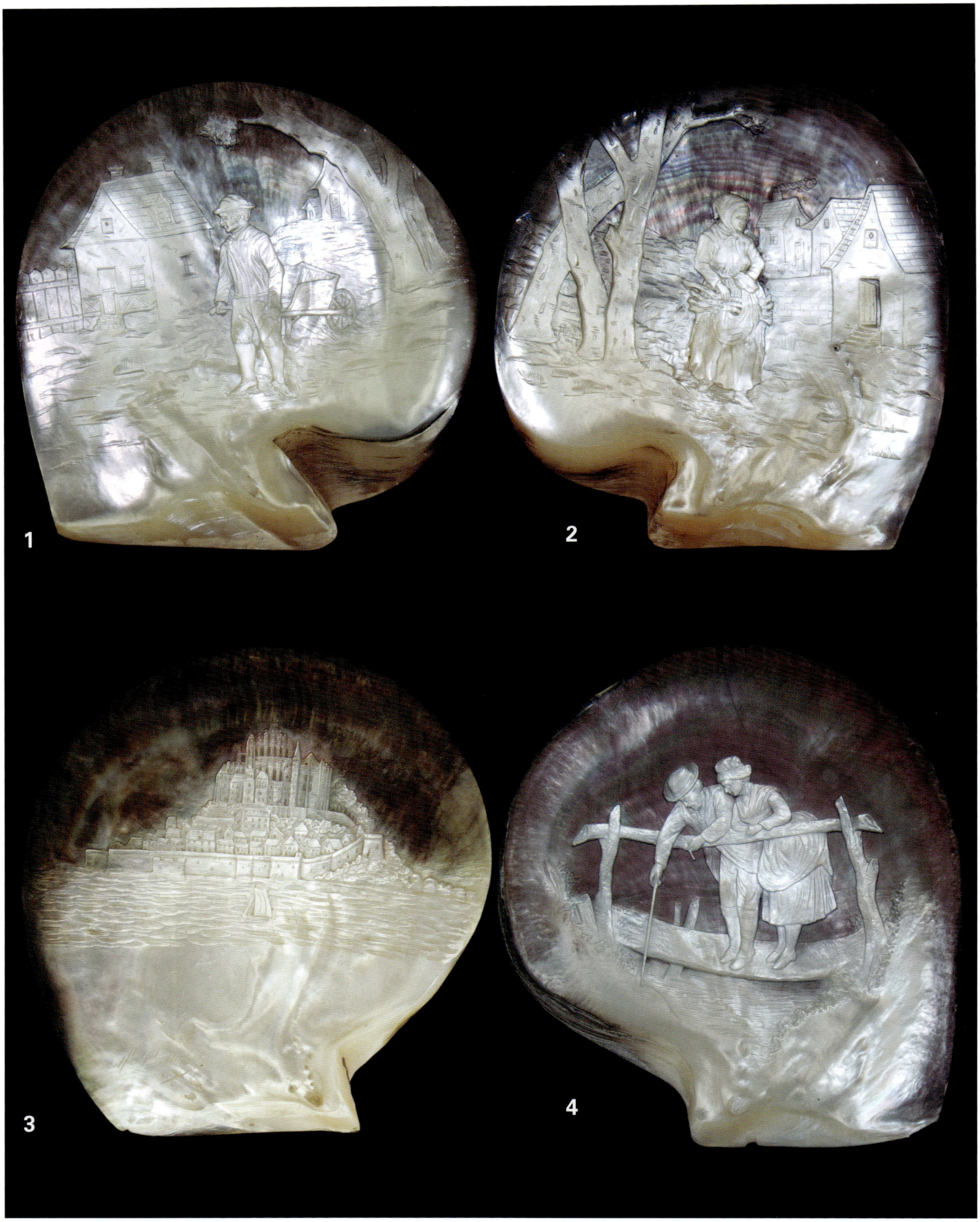

## PLATE 34 – CARVINGS FROM FRANCE 4

1. Man pulling a wheelbarrow, France, c. 1880, size 8.1″ x 7.7″ (20.5 x 19.5 cm). 2. Lady collecting firewood, France, c. 1880, size 8.2″ x 7.5″ (20.8 x 19 cm). 3. Mont Saint Michel, an island one kilometer off Normandy, France, c. 1890, size 7.1″ x 6.5″ (18 x 16.5 cm). 4. Lady and man on a bridge pointing at something on the river's edge, France, c. 1860–90, size 7″ x 6.3″ (17.8 x 16 cm).

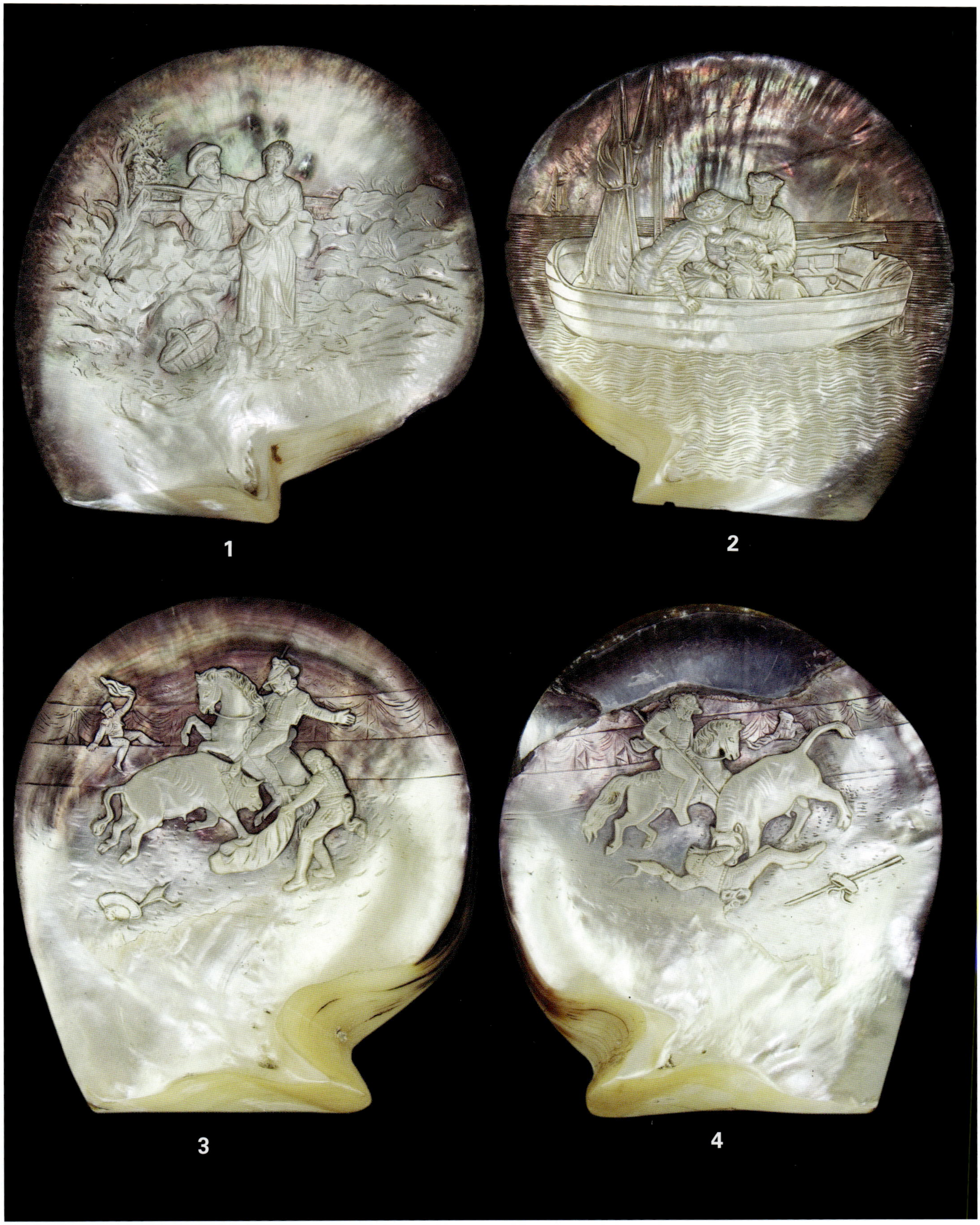

## PLATE 35 – CARVINGS FROM FRANCE 5

1. Lady with basket, talking to a man, c. 1850–75, size 7.5″ x 6.5″ (19 x 16.5 cm). 2. Lady fishing, accompanied by a boatman, c. 1850, size 7.2″ x 7″ (18.4 x 17.8 cm). 3. Bull fighting in Spain, possibly carved in Spain, more likely France, c. 1880, size 7.9″ x 7″ (20 x 17.8 cm). 4. Bull fighting in Spain, with an old repair, possibly carved in Spain, more likely France, c. 1880, size 8″ x 6.9″ (20.4 x 17.5 cm).

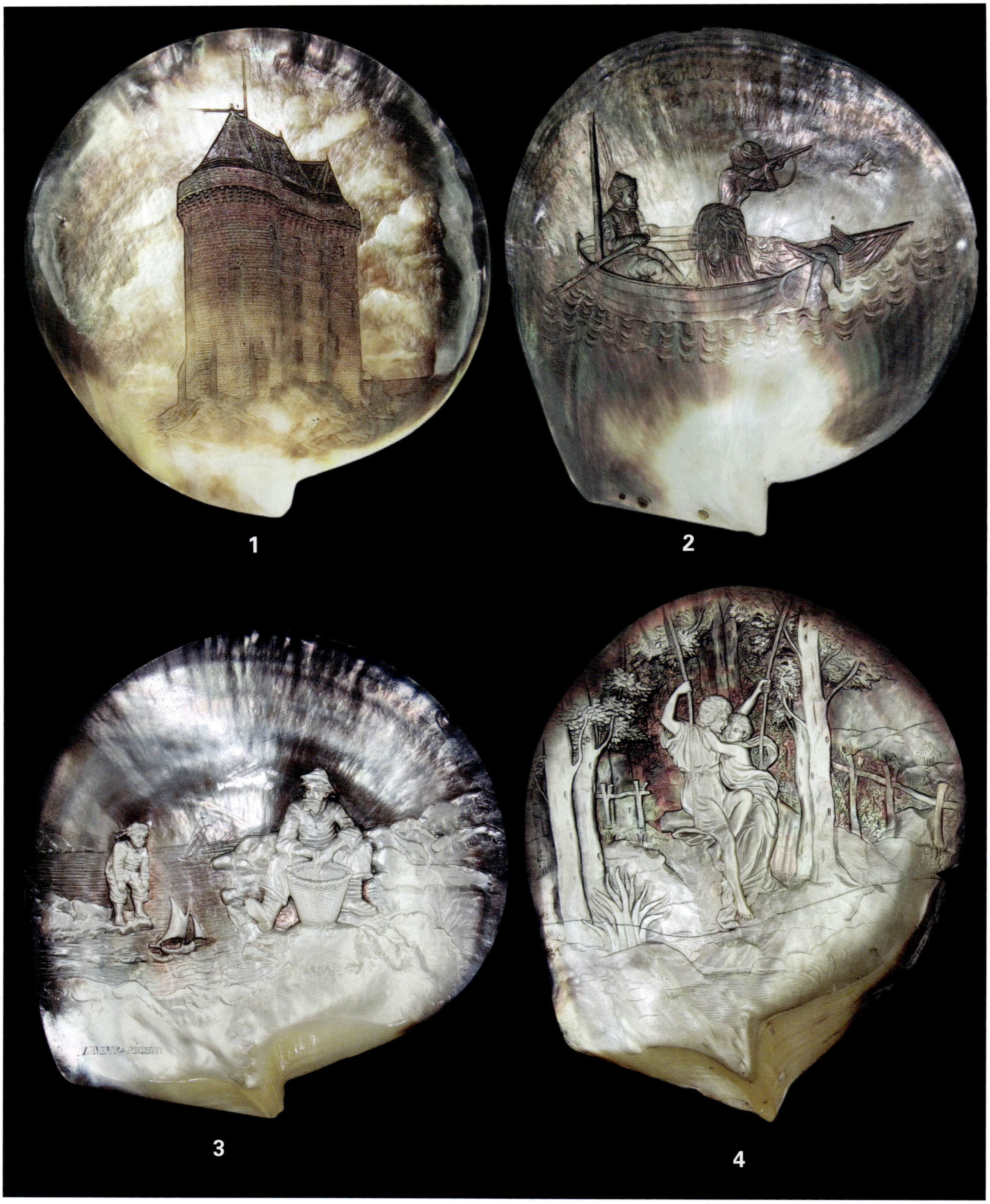


## PLATE 36 – CARVINGS FROM FRANCE 6

1. Solidor Tower of Saint-Servan (now falls under Saint-Marlo) on the coast of Brittany, built in the fourteenth century to control access to the river Rance, c. 1880, size 7.1″ x 6.9″ (18 x 17.4 cm). 2. Lady shooting ducks from a boat, accompanied by a boatman, c. 1870, size 8.3″ x 7.7″ (21 x 19.5 cm). 3. Man with child on seashore, entitled *L'avenir de pecheur, J. Ges Boyes*, c. 1850–70, size 7.7″ x 7.4″ (19.5 x 18.8 cm). 4. Two lovers on a swing, based on the painting *Spring,* 1873, by Pierre Auguste Cot, c. 1880, size 7.9″ x 6.9″ (20 x 17.5 cm).

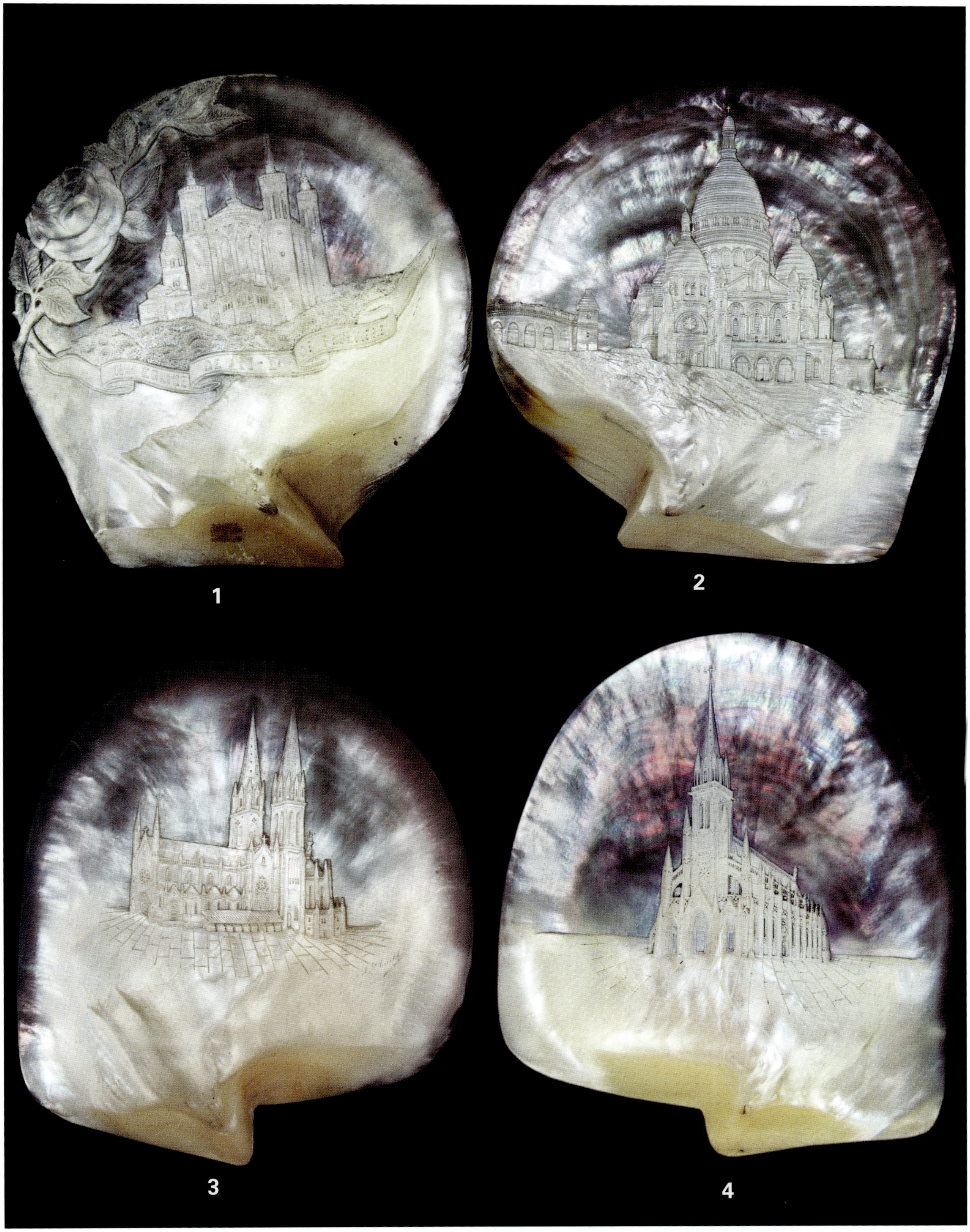

## PLATE 37 – CARVINGS FROM FRANCE 7

1. Basilica Notre Dame de Fourviere, Lyon, c. 1870–80, size 9.9″ x 9.3″ (25.2 x 23.5 cm). 2. Basilique de Sacre-Couer, (Basilica of Sacred Heart of Jesus,) Paris, c. 1840–50, size 8″ x 7.9″ (20.4 x 20 cm). 3. Basilica Notre Dame De La Delivrande, c. 1850–7, size 8″ x 7.1″ (20.3 x 18 cm). 4. Basilica Notre Dame de Bonsecours, Seine-Martime, c. 1875, size 8.3″ x 7.1″ (21 x 18 cm).

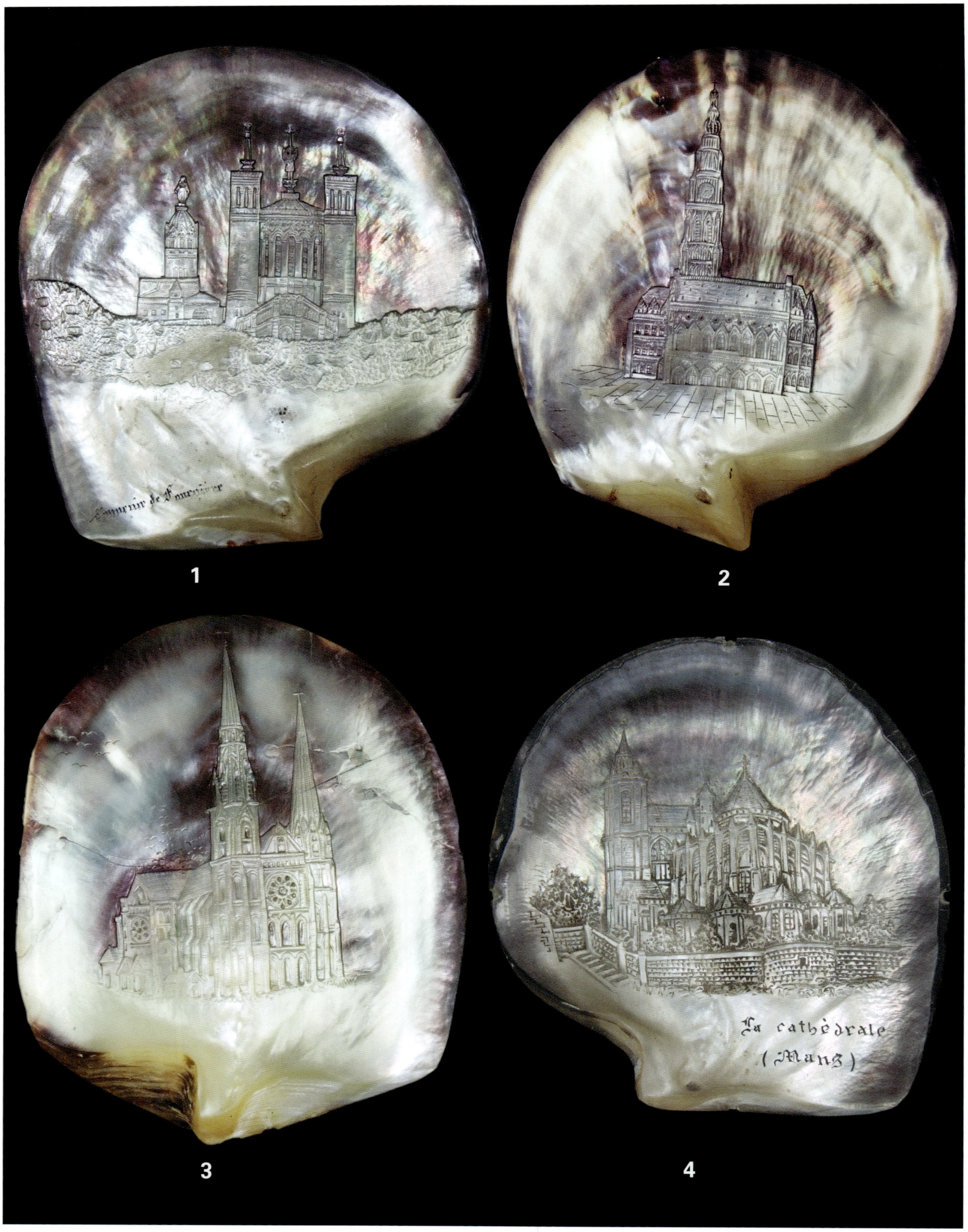


## PLATE 38 – CARVINGS FROM FRANCE 8

1. Basilica Notre Dame de Fourviere, Lyon, c. 1870–80, size 5.3″ x 5.5″ (13.5 x 14 cm). 2. Arras town hall with bell tower, Arras, c. 1875, size 6.5″ x 6.1″ (16.6 x 15.5 cm). 3. Cathedral Notre Dame de Chartres, c. 1875, size 7.1″ x 5.9″ (18 x 15 cm). 4. Le Mans Cathedral dedicated to Saint Julian of Le Mans, the city's first bishop, France, c. 1875, size 5.1″ x 4.9″ (13 x 12.5 cm).

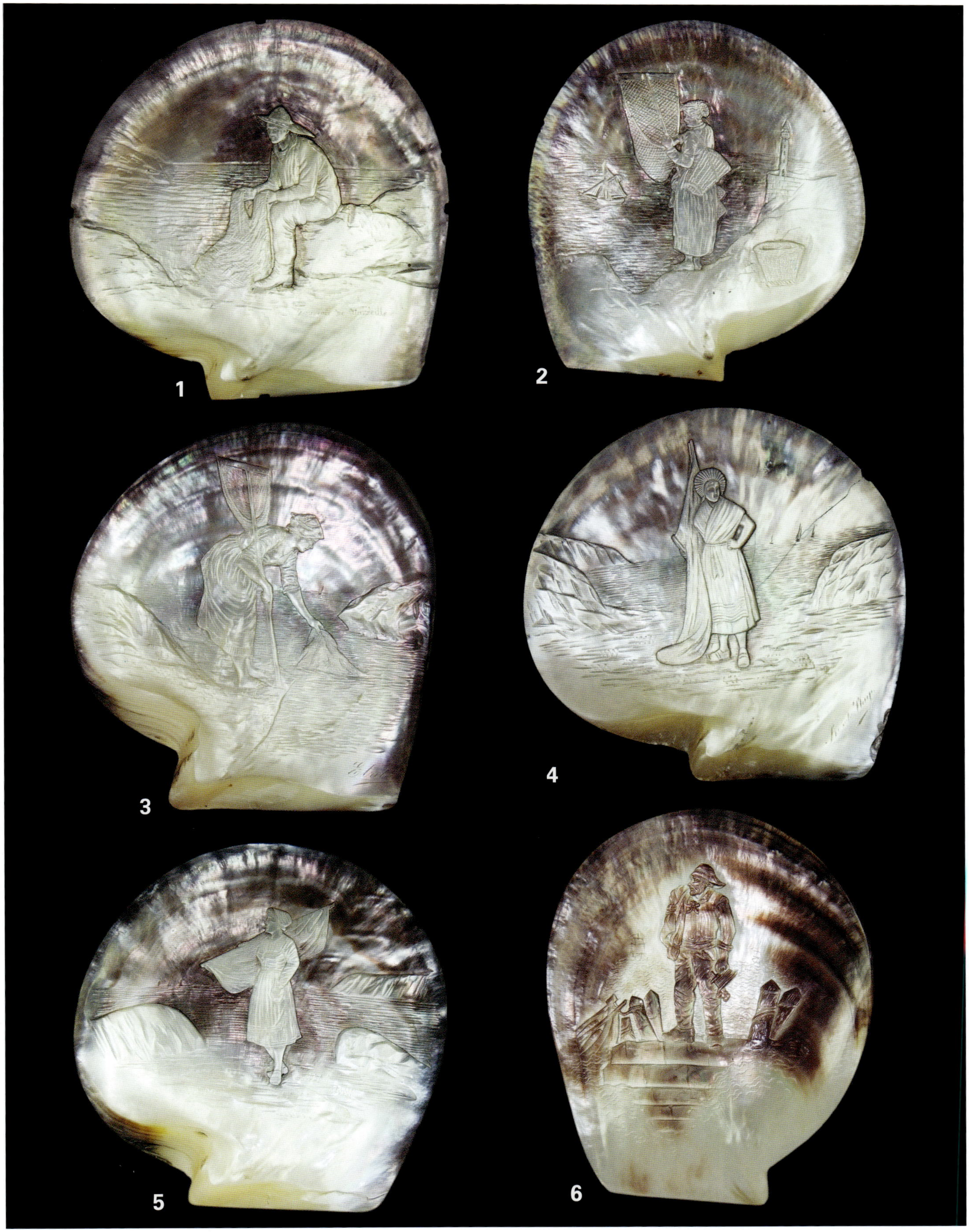


## PLATE 39 – CARVINGS FROM FRANCE 9

**1.** Fisherman sitting on rocks, inscribed *Marseille,* c. 1890, size 6.6″ x 6.5″ (16.8 x 16.6 cm). **2.** Fisherwoman with a large net, c. 1890, size 6.9″ x 6.3″ (17.5 x 16 cm). **3.** Fisherwoman with nets, inscribed *Etretat*, Northern France, c. 1890, size 7.6″ x 7.1″ (19.3 x 18 cm). **4.** Fisherwoman in period ethnic costume, holding a net, inscription worn, possibly *Sur La Plage* (on the beach,) c. 1890, size 7.1″ x 6.9″ (18 x 17.5 cm). **5.** Fisherwoman holding a net, c. 1890, size 6.6″ x 6.7″ (16.8 x 17 cm). **6.** Fisherman on a wharf, c. 1890, size 7.5″ x 7.2″ (19 x 18.4 cm).

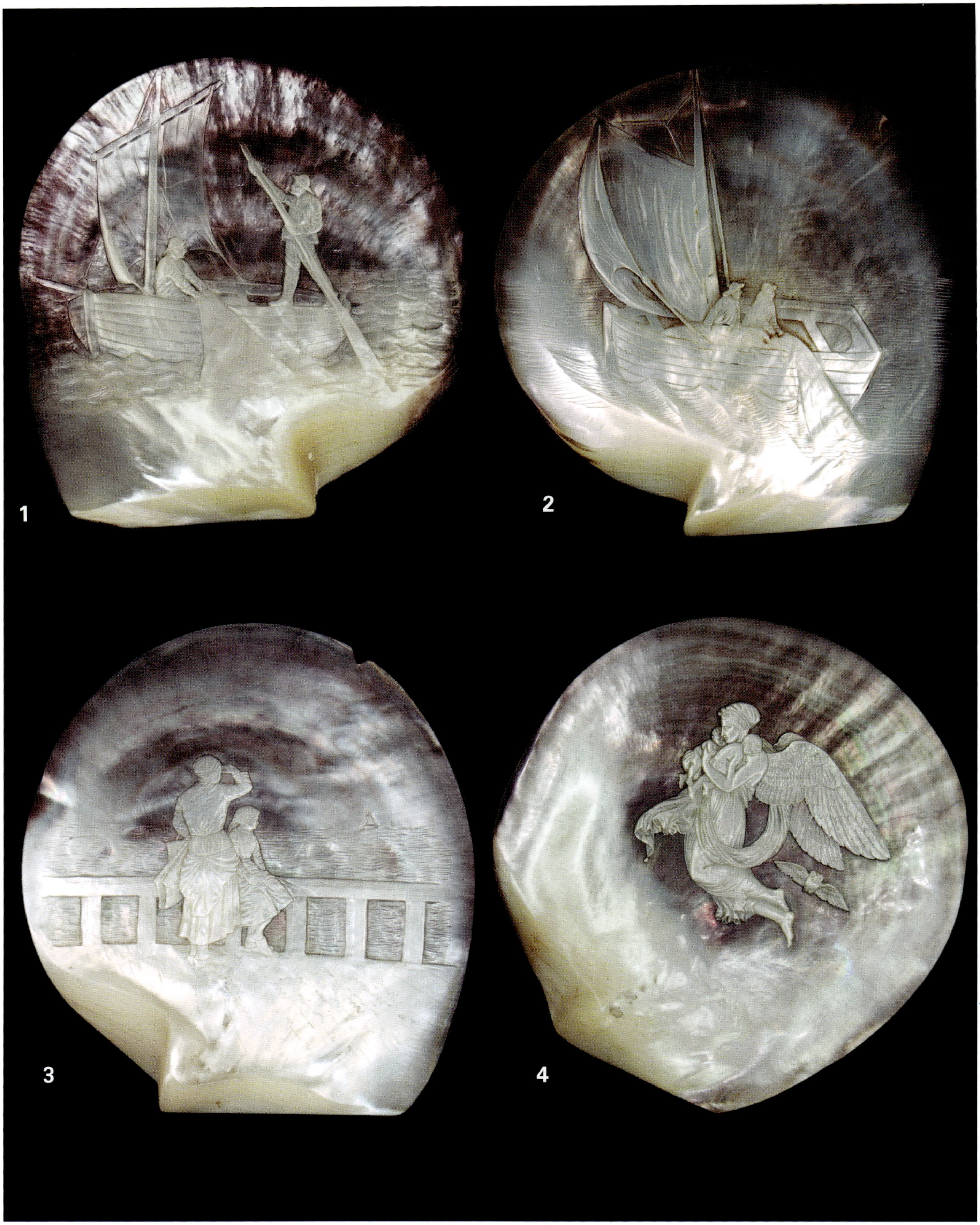

## PLATE 40 – CARVINGS FROM FRANCE 10

1. Two fisherman in a sailboat, c. 1890, size 6.7″ x 7.5″ (17 x 19 cm). 2. Pulling the fishing nets onto the boat, France, c. 1880, size 6.3″ x 5.7″ (16 x 14.5 cm). 3. A lady and child on a wharf waiting for the return of the fishing boats, France, c. 1880, size 7.5″ x 7.1″ (19 x 18 cm). 4. An angel with two children flying in the sky, based on the painting *The Guardian Angel,* 1656, by Pietro da Cortona, c. 1890, size 9.1″ x 8.5″ (23 x 21.5 cm).

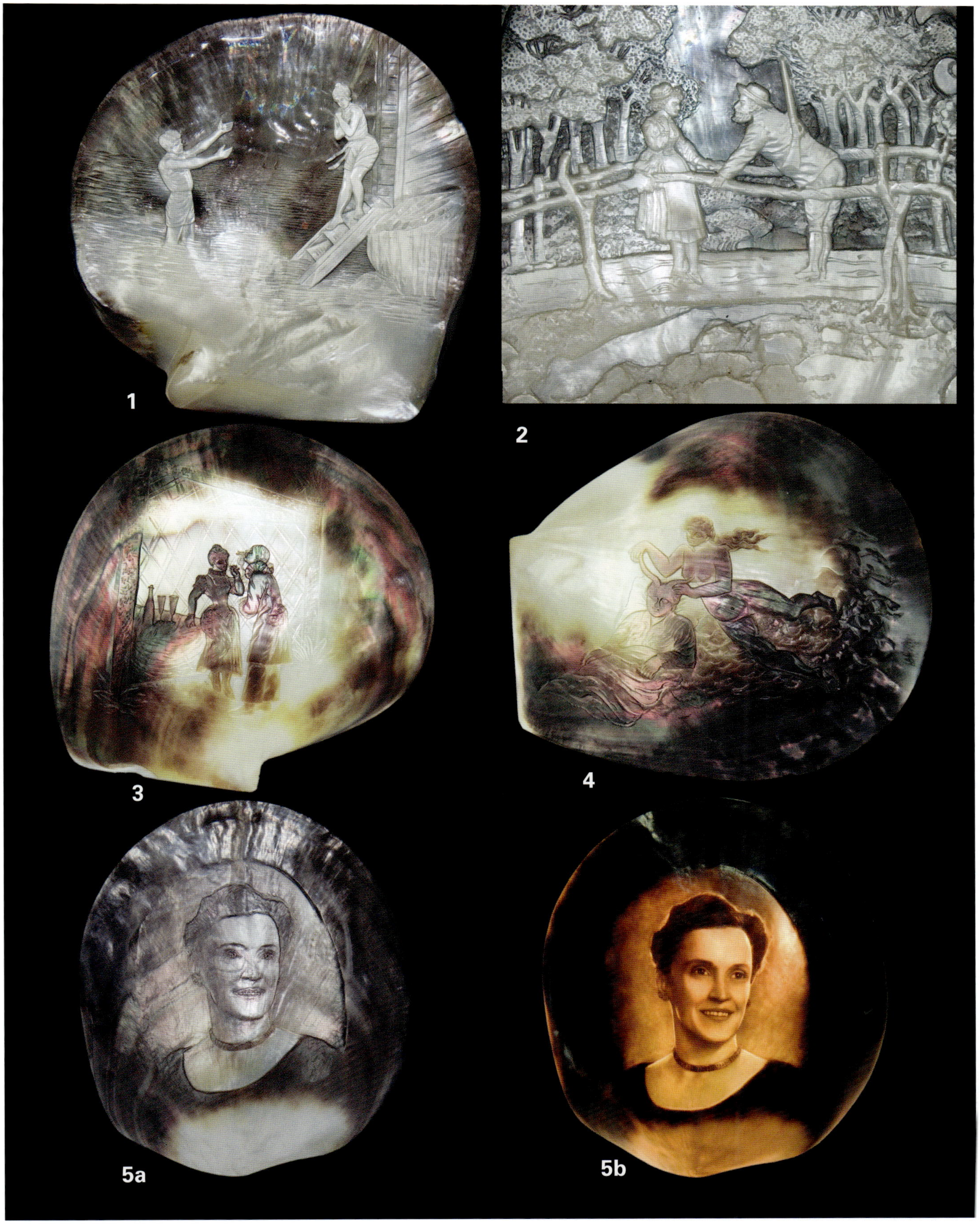


## PLATE 41 – CARVINGS FROM FRANCE 11

1. Swimmer descending from the steps of a bathing machine, c. 1918–1922, size 6.3″ x 6.3″ (16 x 16 cm).
2. Groundskeeper (or hunter) and a young woman in conversation on a bridge, France, c. 1850, size 8″ x 6.7″ (20.4 x 17 cm). 3. Two Pierrot acting on stage, holiday souvenir, c. 1890, size 6.7″ x 7.1″ (17 x 18 cm). 4. Scene from Greek myth of Europa, in which Europa grips the horns of Zeus who is in bull form, c. 1890, size 7.1″ x 6.2″ (18 x 15.5 cm).
5a, 5b. Lithophane of a lady's head. Under natural light, the carving looks rough (figure 5a), but with a light behind it, the figure comes to life (figure 5b), France or Germany, c. 1948–54, size 7.9″ x 7.1″ (20 x 18 cm).

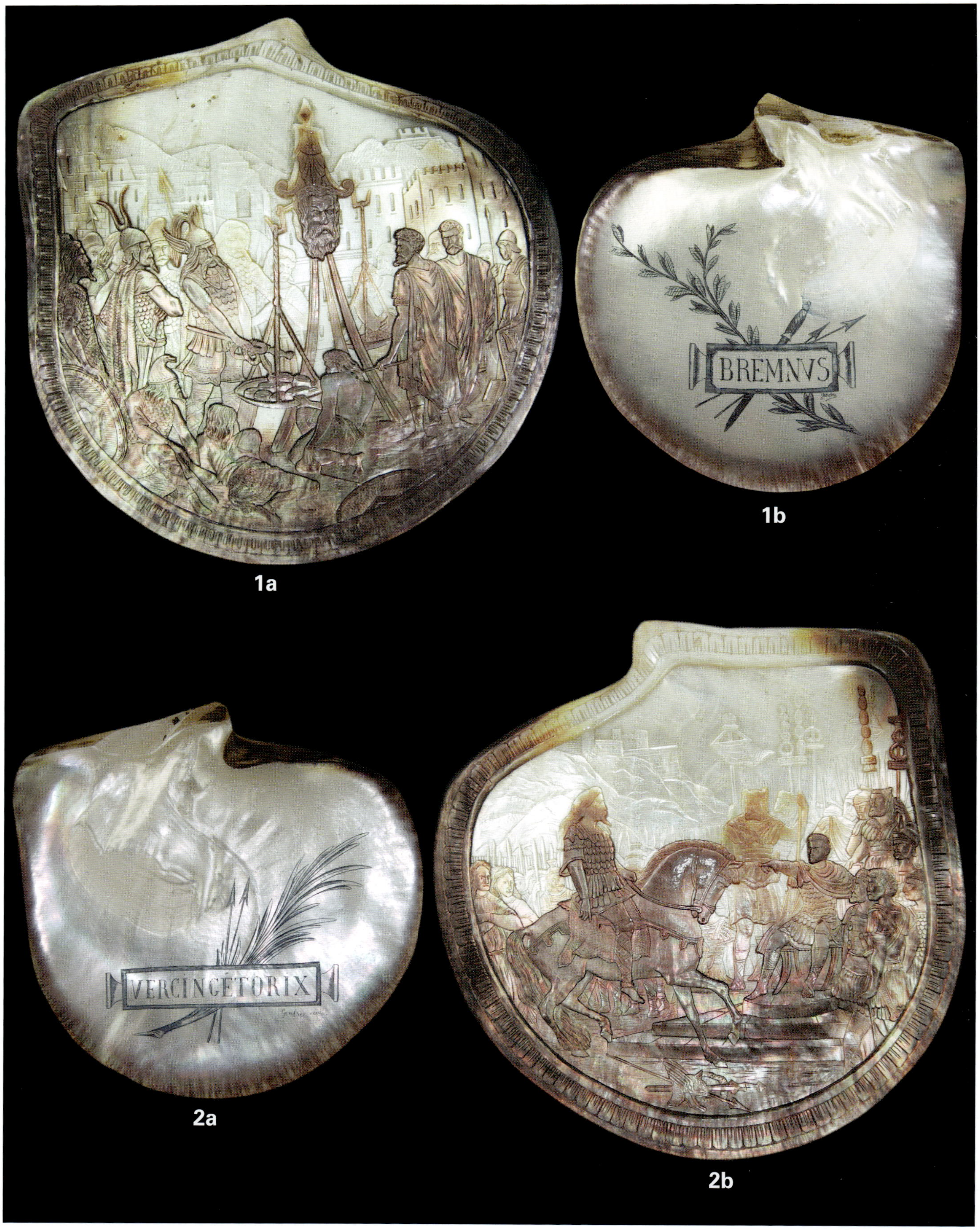


## PLATE 42 – CARVINGS FROM FRANCE 12

**1a, 1b.** Brennus at the Battle of Allia in 390 BC, when during a dispute over payment of gold by the Romans to stop his pillage of Rome, he uttered the famous words *"Vae victus"* (Woe to the vanquished), France, c. 1850–60, size 8.1″ x 8″ (20.5 x 20.3 cm). **2a, 2b.** Vercingetorix, King of the Gauls, surrenders to Julius Caesar in 52 BC, signed by the carver Gendre, France, c. 1850–60, size 8.1″ x 8″ (20.5 x 20.3 cm).

## PLATE 43 – CARVINGS FROM FRANCE 13

1. Commemorative box, showing Napoleon Bonaparte in front of the Pyramids of Giza, giving his soldiers his famous speech on 21st July 1798 before the Battle of the Pyramids; *"Songez que du haut des ces monumens quarante siecles vous contemplent"* (From the summit of these pyramids, forty centuries look down upon you), France, c. 1800, size 3" x 1.7" (7.5 x 4.5 cm). 2. Presentation box inscribed inside (roughly translated), "Dan Manuel, son of the king of France 1. Hassan HH Governor of Jerusalem 2. "Sheykh" Hasen general Visitator. 3. Sheykh Said Governor of Gaza. The other sirs to the right of the prince are from his court and the priest Mariano VII of Bethlehem, who had the honor of sitting with him on the table," France, c. 1750–1800, size 2 8" x 1.8" (7 x 4.5 cm). 3. Building *Les Invalides*, Paris, c. 1880, size 4.7" x 4.7" (12 x 12 cm). 4. Trinket box, Alexander the Great generously gives his most beautiful concubine Campaspe to the painter Apelles who fell in love with Campaspe when painting her portrait, Greece, c. 1780, size 3.4" x 2.6" (8.5 x 6.5 cm). 5. Classical woman with lyre, holding a child, possibly a box decoration, France, c. 1780, size 5.3" x 2.3" (13.5 x 5.9 cm). 6. Child sitting on a pier and fishing, France, c. 1880, size 5.7" x 5" (14.5 x 12.8 cm). 7. Lighthouse on the coast of Brittany, c. 1890–1900, size 6.3" x 6.3" (16 x 16 cm). 8. Trinket box with carved man and dog, France, c. 1850, size 1.8" x 1.4" (4.5 x 3.5 cm).

## PLATE 44 – CARVINGS FROM TAHITI, FRENCH POLYNESIA

**1.** Kihe Wahine from Polynesian mythology, c. 1970, size 8.1" x 7.3" (20.5 x 18.5 cm). **2.** Kihe Wahine, inscribed *Institute of Pacific Culture, Tokyo*, likely conference souvenir, c. 1985, size 6.1" x 5.4" (15.5 x 14 cm). **3.** Warrior's head, c. 1990, size 3.5" x 3.5" (9 x 9 cm). **4.** Decorative carving incorporating a Tiki, c. 1975, size 7.1" x 6.9" (18 x 17.5 cm). **5.** Fish, c. 1980, size 6.9" x 5.7" (17.5 x 14.5 cm). **6.** Flower lady, c. 1990, size 5" x 3.5" (12.8 x 9 cm). **7.** Hibiscus flower, engraved *Bora Bora*, c. 1995, size 4.7" x 4.7" (12 x 12 cm). **8.** Fish, tourist souvenir, engraved *Bora Bora*, c. 1995, size 5.1" x 4.9" (13 x 12.5 cm). **9.** Monk, c. 1970, size 2.8" x 2.8" (7.2 x 7 cm).

## PLATE 45 – CARVINGS FROM INDONESIA 1

This set has been carved in Indonesia and has inset rubies and gemstones, 2010–11. **1.** European dragon (differs from the Oriental versions by having wings), size 7.1″ x 7.1″ (18 x 18 cm). **2.** Two Chinese dragons, size 7.1″ x 6.9″ (18 x 17.5 cm). **3.** Roman chariot racing, size 7.4″ x 7.4″ (18.7 x 18.7 cm). **4.** European dragon, size 7″ x 6.9″ (17.8 x 17.6 cm).

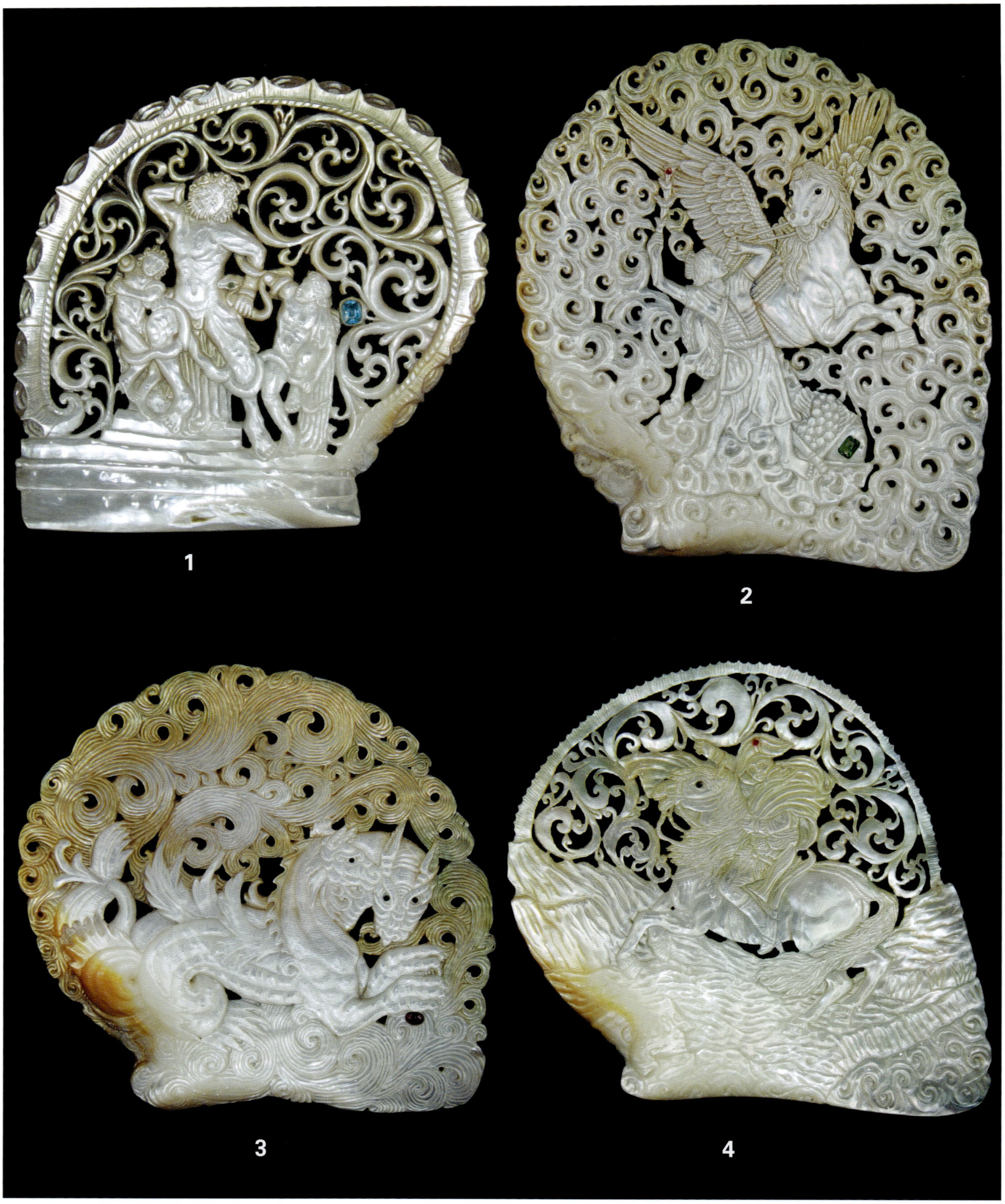

## PLATE 46 – CARVINGS FROM INDONESIA 2

1. Laocoon and his sons. The Trojan priest with his sons Antiphantes and Tymbraeus being strangled by sea serpents, based on the sculpture in the Vatican Museum, Rome, 2010, size 7.4″ x 7.5″ (18.7 x 19 cm). 2. Athena taming Pegasus, who was sired by Poseidon in Greek mythology, Indonesia, 2011, size 7.9″ x 7.3″ (20 x 18.5 cm). 3. Graceful flowing depiction of Hippocampus, mythological beasts who pulled Poseidon's chariot in Greek mythology, Indonesia, 2011, size 7.3″ x 7.3″ (18.5 x 18.5 cm). 4. Napoleon Bonaparte, political and military leader of France, crossing the Alps on horseback to Italy in 1800, Indonesia, 2011, size 6.9″ x 6.5″ (17.5 x 16.5 cm).

## PLATE 47 – CARVINGS FROM INDONESIA 3

1. Poseidon, God of the sea in Greek mythology and brother to Zeus and Hades (Romans called him Neptune), riding a magical horse, which foams the water as he rides over the sea (now known as a wind wave where the wind blows the top of the wave to form a crest known as white horses), Indonesia, 2011, size 7.7" x 8.3" (19.5 x 21 cm). 2. Poseidon in a shell chariot being pulled by sea horses also known as Hippocampus (from the ancient Greek hippos meaning horse and *kampos* meaning sea monster), Indonesia, 2011, size 7" x 6.9" (17.8 x 17.6 cm). 3. Poseidon calming the waters, while a triton leans backward to hand him a piece of coral. Based on the 1733 sculpture by Lambert-Sigisbert Adam in The Louvre, Paris, carved in Indonesia, 2011, size 7.7" x 7.7" (19.5 x 19.5 cm). 4a, 4b. Dragon carved into a nautilus shell, Indonesia, 2011, size 7.9" x 5.9" (20 x 15 cm).

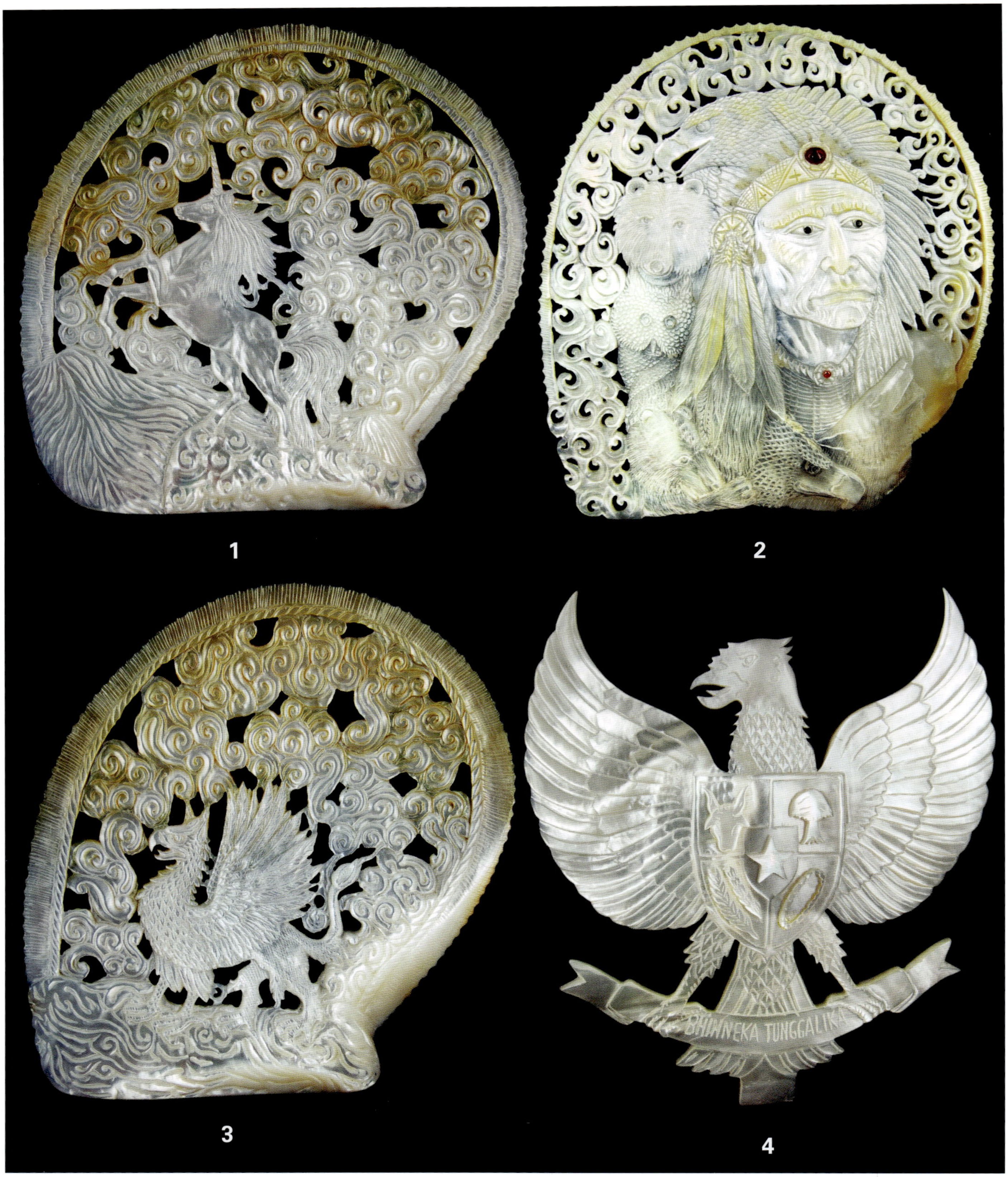


## PLATE 48 – CARVINGS FROM INDONESIA 4

**1.** Unicorn, a legendary animal from European folklore, 2011, size 6.6″ x 6.7″ (16.8 x 17 cm). **2.** Native American Chief with eagle, bear, owl, and wolf symbolizing the ancestral spirits of the Chief. The forceful carving fits well with the strength of the subject; Indonesia, 2011, size 7.3″ x 6.9″ (18.5 x 17.5 cm). **3.** Griffin, a legendary creature with the body of a lion and the wings of an eagle, Indonesia, 2011, size 6.3″ x 7″ (16 x 17.7 cm). **4.** Carving of the Indonesian national symbol, Garuda Pancasila with the national motto *Bhinneka Tunggal Ika* (Unity in Diversity), Indonesia, c. 1980, size 7.8″ x 7.7″ (19.8 x 19.5 cm).

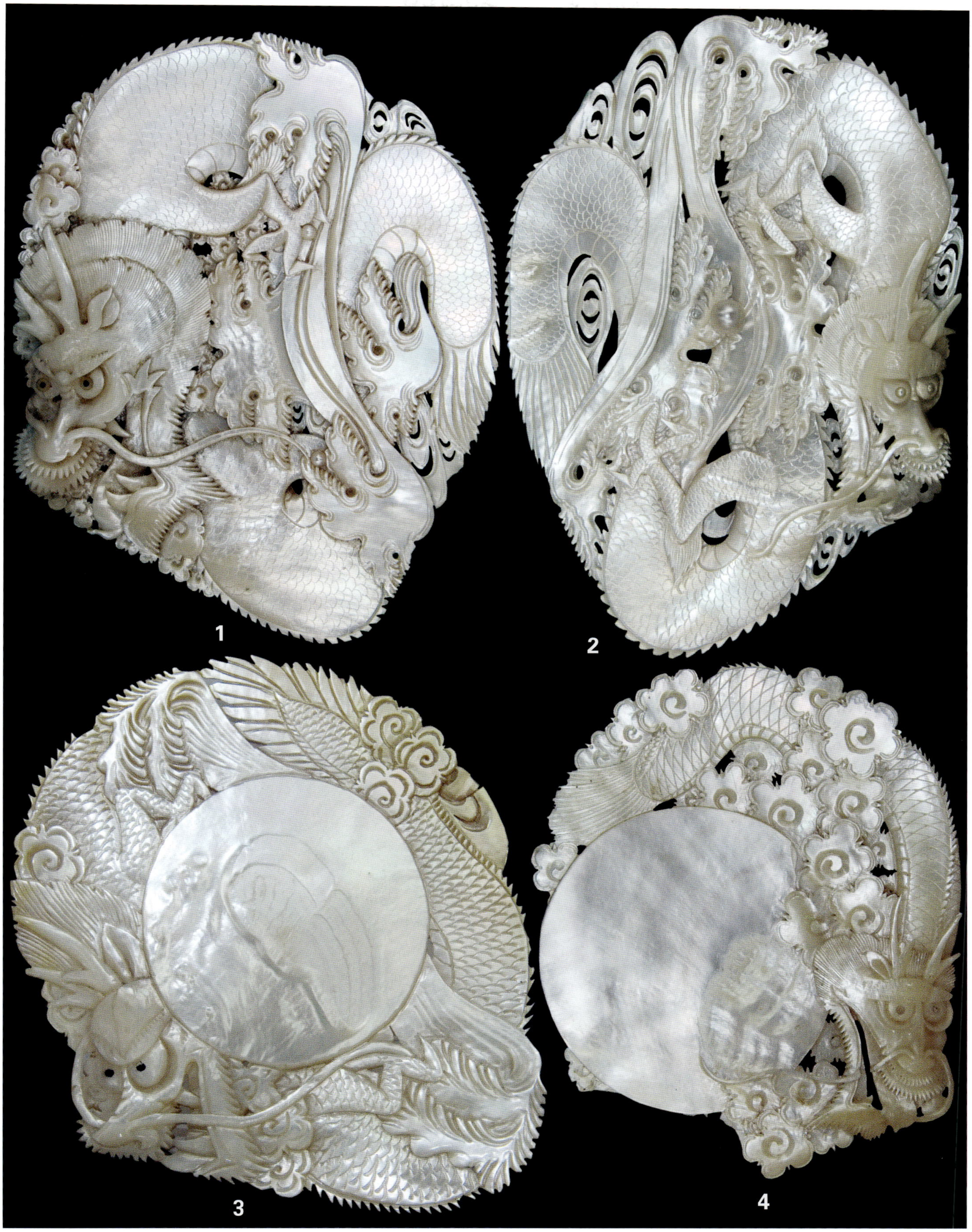

## PLATE 49 – CARVINGS FROM JAPAN 1

Dragons from Japan are easy to distinguish as they all have three toes (Chinese dragons have five toes). **1.** Dragon carving, c. 1890, size 8″ x 9.8″ (20.4 x 25 cm). **2.** Dragon carving, c. 1890, size 9.4″ x 6.9″ (24 x 17.5 cm). **3.** Dragon carving, c. 1870–90, size 7.1″ x 5.9″ (18 x 15 cm). **4.** Dragon carving, c. 1870–90, size 6.7″ x 5.9″ (17 x 15 cm).

## PLATE 50 – CARVINGS FROM JAPAN 2

**1.** Scene from Okinawa, house on stilts with palm trees and other trees, c. 1880–1900, size 9.6″ x 9.4″ (24.5 x 24 cm). **2.** Scene from Okinawa, house on stilts with trees and cattle, c. 1880–1900, size 8.9″ x 6.9″ (22.5 x 17.5 cm). **3.** Elephant souvenir or charm, c. 1860–1880, size 4.7″ (12 cm). **4.** Carved dish in floral motif, c. 1890–1900, size 6.3″ x 5.9″ (16 x 15 cm). **5.** Carved dish in floral motif, c. 1890–1900, size 6.3″ x 5.9″ (16 x 15 cm). **6.** Dragon carving, inscribed *Japan Pearls Export Co, Kobe & Tokyo*, c. 1920, size 7.5″ x 6.3″ (19 x 16 cm). **7.** Bird in flight, c. 1880–1900, size 7″ x 7″ (18 x 18 cm).

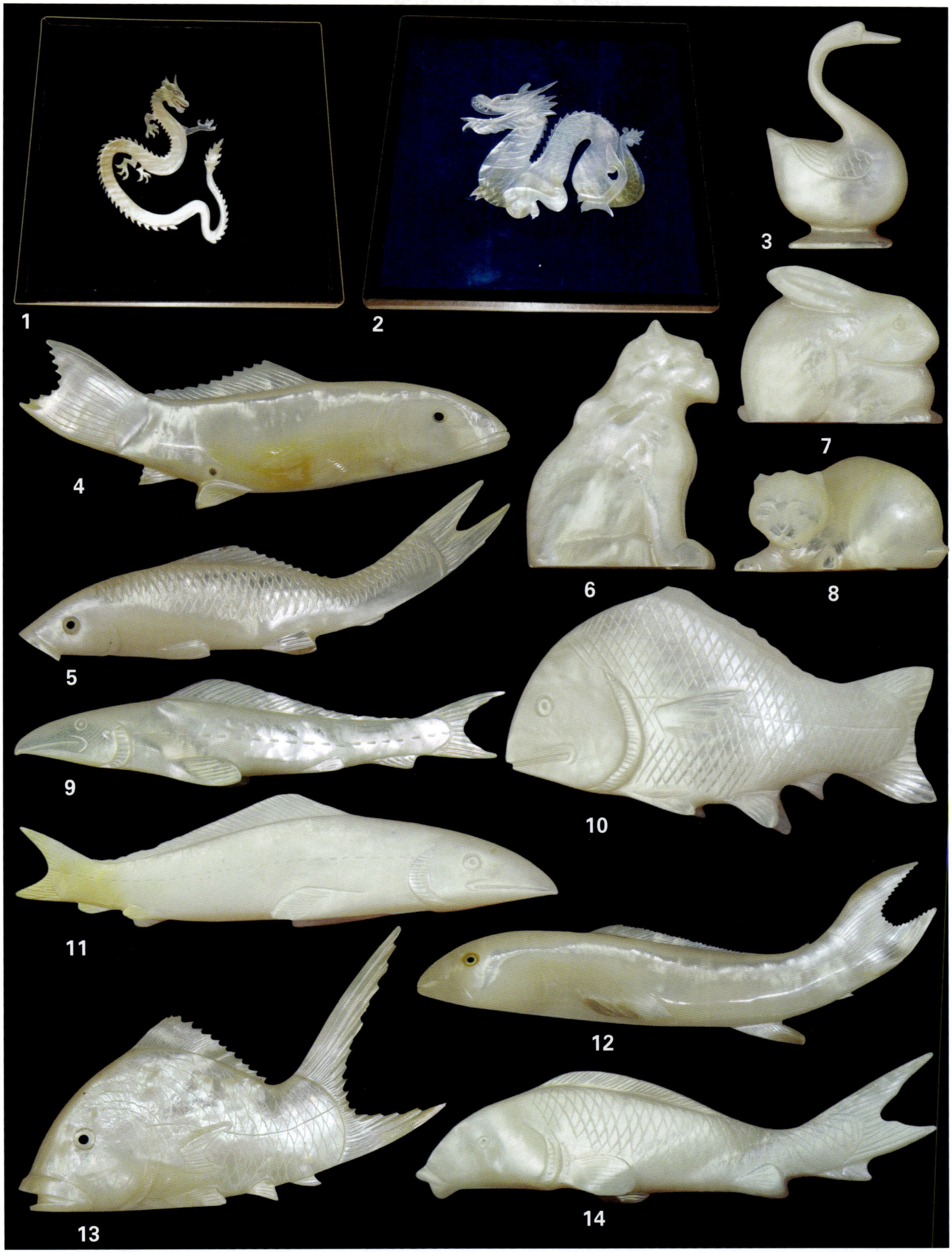

## PLATE 51 – CARVINGS FROM JAPAN 3

1. Framed dragon, c. 1970, size of carving 4.3" x 4.1" (11 x 10.5 cm). 2. Framed dragon, c. 1970, size of carving 3.1" x 4.7" (8 x 12 cm). 3–14. Souvenirs or charms, c. 1860–1880, size 4.7" to 6.9" (12 to 17.5 cm) includes different species of fish, rabbit, cat, swan, and dog.

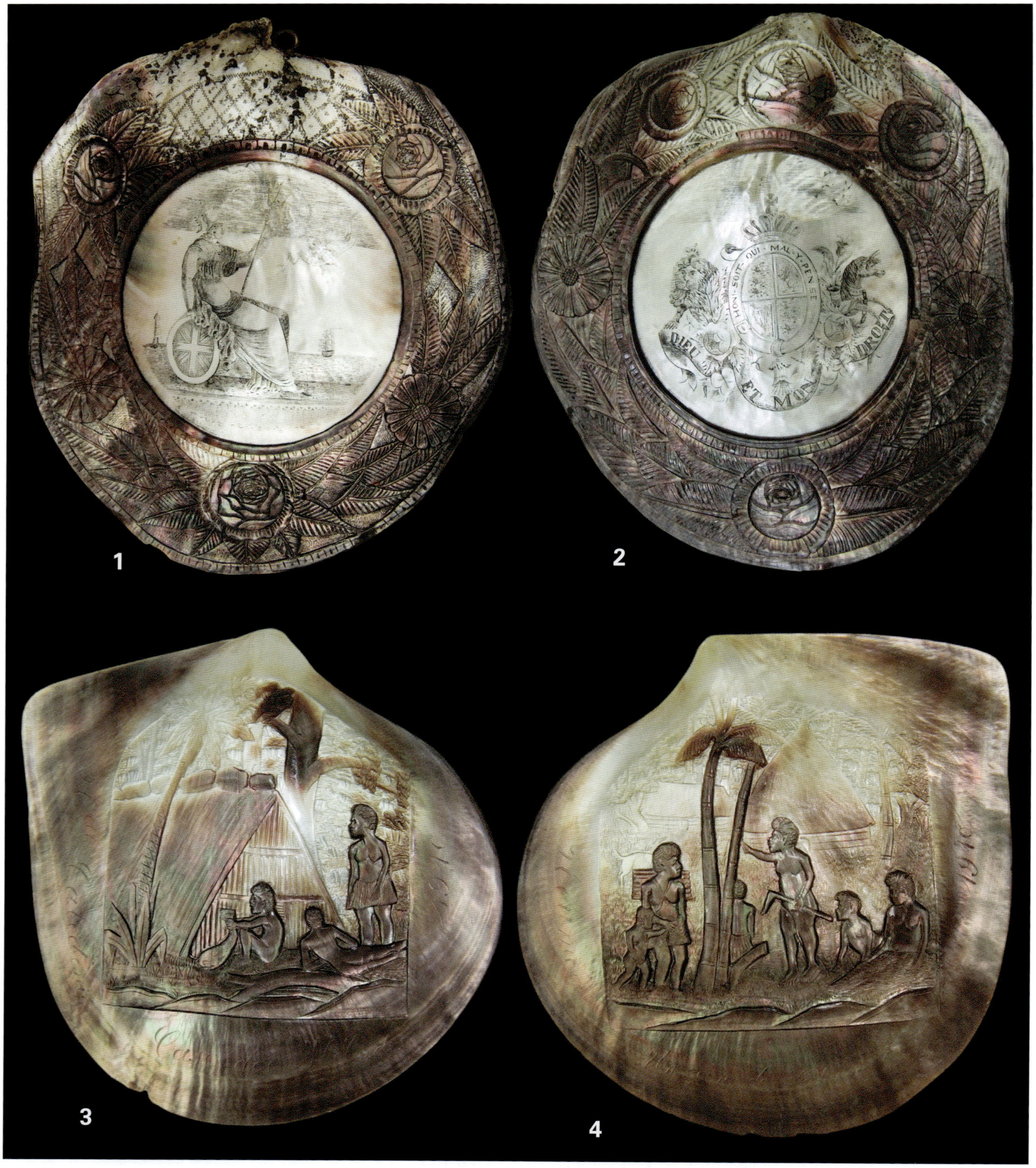

## PLATE 52 – CARVINGS FROM NEW CALEDONIA 1

This is a selection of carvings from the French penal colony established in Noumea in 1864. In 1872, over 4155 exiled Communards arrived from Paris and the authorities let prisoners make a living from their old trades. The French cameo cutters turned their skills to carving mother-of-pearl oysters, trocha shell, green turban shell, and nautilus shell. These were sold to tourists in visiting boats. Mostly carved in pairs, some have been separated over the years. **1.** Britannia (Personification of Britain), c. 1890, size 10.2″ x 8.7″ (26 x 22 cm). **2.** Royal Coat of Arms of England, c. 1890, size 10.2″ x 8.7″ (26 x 22 cm). **3.** Inscribed *Nelle Caledonie case de Hebrides 1910*, size 5.9″ x 5.7″ (15 x 14.5 cm). **4.** Inscribed *Noumea un coin de tribe O L'ouko 1910*, size 5.7″ x 5.5″ (14.5 x 14 cm).

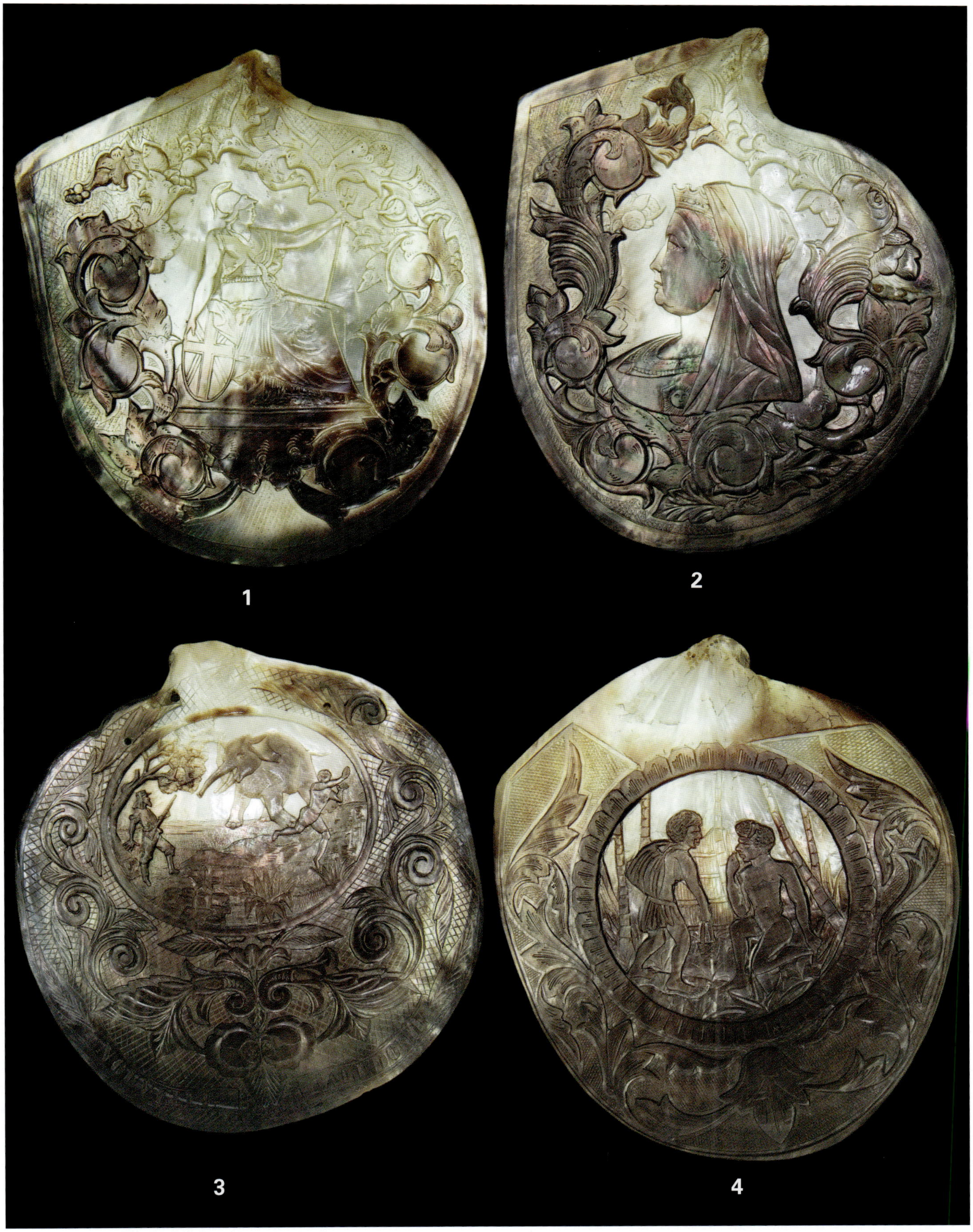


## PLATE 53 – CARVINGS FROM NEW CALEDONIA 2

1. Britannia (Personification of Britain), c. 1880, size 7.1" x 6.9" (18 x 17.5 cm). 2. Queen Victoria, c. 1880, size 7" x 6.3" (17.8 x 16 cm). 3. Hunting scene with elephant, inscribed *Nouvelle Caldonie 1886*, size 7.9" x 7.3" (20 x 18.5 cm). 4. View of Kanak life (indigenous inhabitants), c. 1875, size 6.9" x 6.1" (17.5 x 15.4 cm).

## PLATE 54 – CARVINGS FROM NEW CALEDONIA 3

**1–2.** Head of a Kanak, the name given to an indigenous inhabitant, matching pair, c. 1880, size 6.9″ x 6.7″ (17.6 x 16.9 cm) and 6.7″ x 6.4″ (17 x 16.2 cm). **3–4.** Marianne, national emblem of France representing liberty and reason, matching pair, c. 1875, size 8″ x 7.2″ (20.4 x 18.2 cm) and 8.6″ x 7.2″ (21.8 x 18.2 cm).

## PLATE 55 – CARVINGS FROM NEW CALEDONIA 4

**1.** Inscribed *Liberty*, Liberty being personified as a woman, c. 1890, size 4.1" x 3.7" (10.4 x 9.5 cm). **2.** Inscribed *Sperm Whale* c. 1890, size 4.1" x 3.9" (10.4 x 10 cm). **3.** Etched flowers, c. 1890, size 7.2" x 6.3" (18.3 x 16 cm). **4a, 4b.** Carved nautilus shell, includes an etching of Pan, god of shepherds, flocks and mountain wilds in Greek mythology, c. 1895, size 6.3" x 4.7" (16 x 12 cm). **5.** French deportee in the Penal colony, c. 1890, size 4.9" x 4.3" (12.5 x 11 cm). **6–7.** Native huts carved on trocha shells, c. 1895, size 4.3" x 3.3 (11 x 8.4 cm) and 4" x 3.7" (10.2 x 9.5 cm).

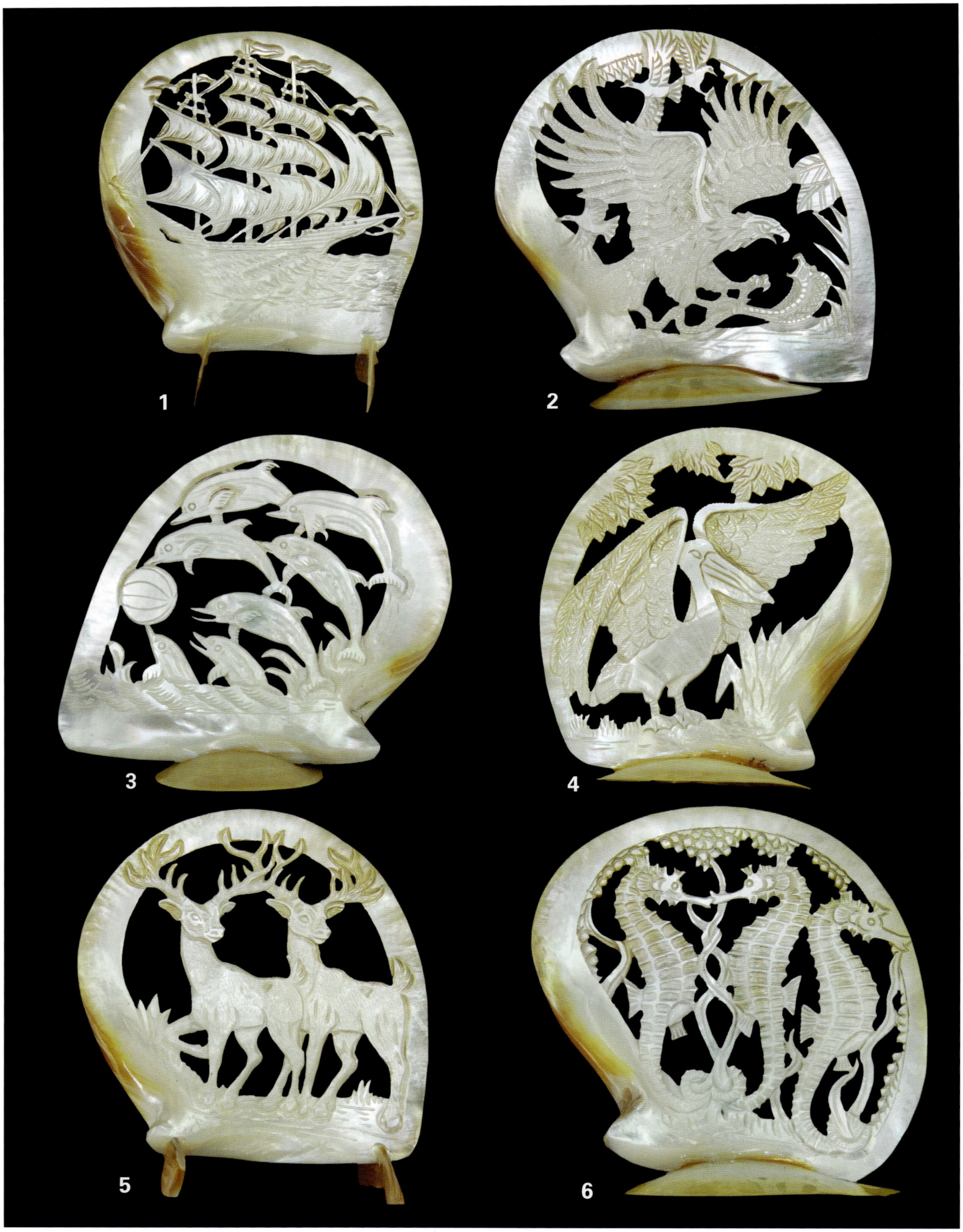


## PLATE 56 – CARVINGS FROM THE PHILIPPINE ISLANDS 1

1. Manila galleon, a Spanish trading ship that sailed between Manila and Acapulco (then New Spain, now Mexico) in the sixteenth to nineteenth century, Cebu, 2004, size 6.7″ x 6.9″ (17 x 17.5 cm). 2. Eagle attacking a snake, Cebu, 1998, size 7.1″ x 6.7″ (18 x 17 cm). 3. Dolphins playing with a ball, Cebu, 1998, size 7.3″ x 6.9″ (18.5 x 17.5 cm). 4. Pelican, Cebu, 2003, size 6.1″ x 6.1″ (15.5 x 15.5 cm). 5. Two deer, Cebu, 2004, size 6.9″ x 7.5″ (17.5 x 19 cm). 6. Three sea horses, Cebu, 1998, size 6.9″ x 6.3″ (17.5 x 16 cm).

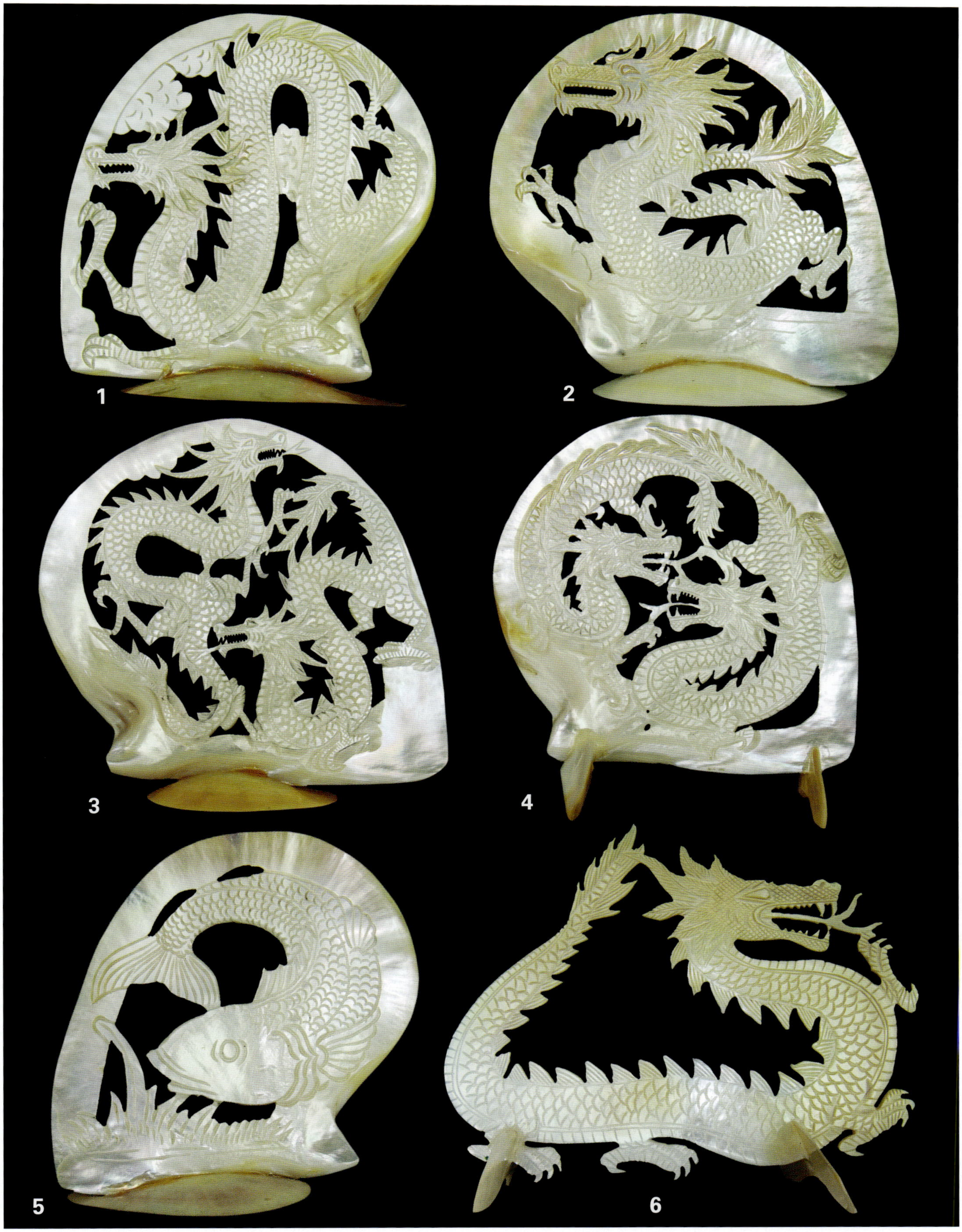

## PLATE 57 – CARVINGS FROM THE PHILIPPINE ISLANDS 2

1. Dragon, Cebu, 1996, size 7.1″ x 6.2″ (18 x 15.8 cm). 2. Dragon, Cebu, 1998, size 6.9″ x 6.3″ (17.5 x 16 cm). 3. Double dragon, as seen in Taoist temples, Cebu, 1998, size 7.4″ x 7.3″ (18.9 x 18.5 cm). 4. Two dragons, Cebu, 1998, size 6.3″ x 6.4″ (16 x 16.3 cm). 5. Fish, Cebu, 2003, size 5.9″ x 5.9″ (15 x 15 cm). 6. Standing dragon, Cebu, 2004, size 6.5″ x 4.7″ (16.5 x 12 cm).

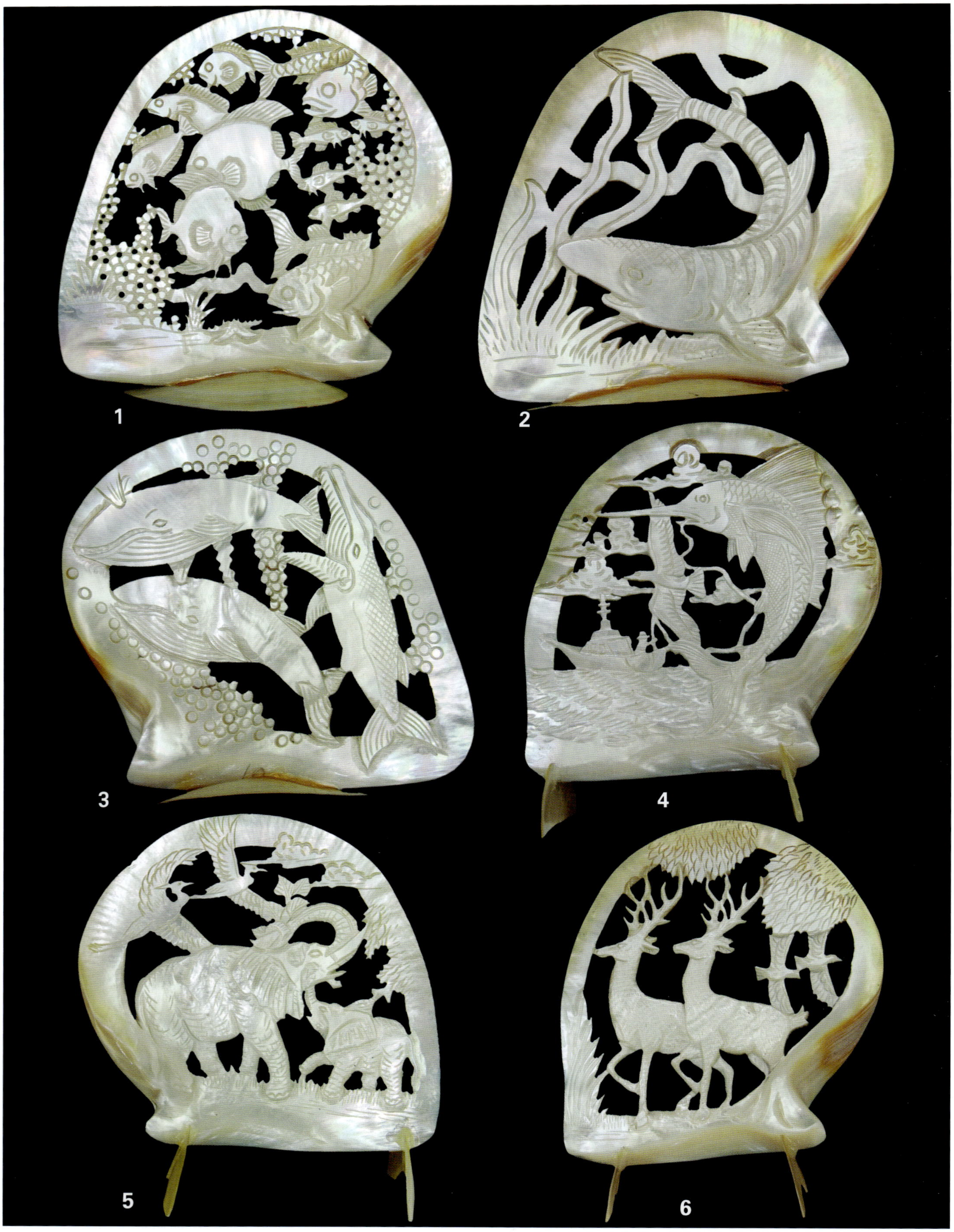

## PLATE 58 – CARVINGS FROM THE PHILIPPINE ISLANDS 3

**1.** A school of fish, Cebu, 2003, size 6.3" x 6.3" (16 x 16 cm). **2.** Shark, Cebu, 2003, size 6.1" x 6.1" (15.5 x 15.5 cm). **3.** Whales, Cebu, 2002, size 6.1" x 6.1" (15.5 x 15.5 cm). **4.** Marlin fishing, Cebu, 2004, size 6.3" x 6.7" (16 x 17 cm). **5.** Two elephants, Cebu, 2004, size 6.1" x 5.9" (15.6 x 15 cm). **6.** Two deer, Cebu, 2004, size 6.9" x 7.5" (17.5 x 19 cm).

## PLATE 59 – CARVINGS FROM THE PHILIPPINE ISLANDS 4

1–5. Scenes from Philippine country life. 1. Gilt edging Cebu, 1996, size 7.2″ x 7.2″ (18.4 x 18.3 cm). 2. Gilt edging, Cebu, 1996, size 6.3″ x 6.3″ (16 x 16 cm). 3. Gilt edged, 1996, size 6.3″ x 6.2″ (16 x 15.8 cm). 4. Manila, 1990, size 7.6″ x 7.6″ (19.2 x 19.2 cm). 5. Manila, 1990, size 7.7″ x 7.7″ (19.5 x 19.5 cm). 6. Manila galleon, a Spanish trading ship that sailed between Manila and Acapulco (then New Spain, now Mexico) in the sixteenth to nineteenth centuries, Cebu, 2004, size 6.2″ x 5.7″ (15.7 x 14.5 cm).

## PLATE 60 – CARVINGS FROM THAILAND 1

These carvings were all made by master carver Samai Sehua, Chanthaburi, Thailand, 2006. 1. Garuda, a mythological Eastern Indian bird usually depicted as part human, kills and eats poisonous snakes with no harmful consequences to himself, size 4.9″ x 4.9″ (12.5 x 12.5 cm). 2. Mythological bird-like creature Garuda holding a sea serpent in his legs, size 5.1″ x 3.7″ (13 x 9.5cm). 3. "Suprakorn" from Thai fairy tale of a giantess from the ocean. She tricked a man into believing she was a beautiful woman. They married, had a child, and then Suprakorn turned back to her true form, size 5.1″ x 3.7″ (13 x 9.5 cm). 4. Phoenix standing above a dragon, from Thai mythology, size 6.7″ x 4.9″ (17 x 12.5 cm). 5. Phoenix, a mythological bird, size 5.1″ x 7.1″ (13 x 18 cm).

## PLATE 61 – CARVINGS FROM THAILAND 2

**1.** General Taksin, on horseback and holding a sword, formed an army in 1767 to drive the Burmese out of Thailand and take control of Siam to form a new government. He became King of Siam in 1768. With mother-of-pearl calendar, c. 1925, size 8.5″ x 7.7″ (21.5 x 19.5 cm). **2.** General Taksin on horseback, talking to a lady, c. 1925, size 7.1″ x 6.9″ (18 x 17.5 cm). **3.** *Look Krok* amulet protects the owner from dangers, c. 1890, size 1.2″ x 0.6″ (3 x 1.5 cm). **4** General Taksin on horseback, c. 1950, size 6.3″ x 2.8″ (16 x 7 cm). **5.** *Kinari* from the Thai fairly tale of a lady with a bird body, by master carver Samai Sehua, Chanthaburi, Thailand, 2006, size 4.7″ x 3.7″ (12 x 9.5 cm). **6.** Dragon holding a pearl, from Thai mythology, by master carver Samai Sehua, Chanthaburi, 2006, size 4.3″ x 3.5″ (11 x 9 cm). **7.** Table lamp with a turban shell as a lamp shade, etched with a temple dancer, c. 1950, size 10.8″ x 5.1″ ( 27.5 x 13 cm). **8.** *Naga Eye* amulet which brings good luck to the owner, c. 1890, size 1.5″ x 0.8″ (3.8 x 2 cm). **9.** Carved turban shell for the tourist trade, Phuket, 1996, size 5.9″ x 5.9″ (15 x 15 cm). **10.** Carved turban shell for the tourist trade, Phuket, c. 1989, size 5.1″ x 5.1″ (13 x 13 cm).

## PLATE 62 – CARVINGS FROM AUSTRALIA and EGYPT

**1.** Aboriginal etching by L.J. Sampi, Kimberley region, Broome, Western Australia, c. 1948, size 7.1″ x 5.9″ (18 x 15 cm). **2.** Pearl Lugger inscribed *Broome, WA,* Australia, c. 1950, size 8.1″ x 7.9″ (20.5 x 20 cm). **3.** Colonel Arabi-Bey led the rebellion of the Egyptian army against dual control of the English and French in 1881–2, c. 1885, size 7.3″ x 5.8″ (18.5 x 14.7 cm), the coloring of this shell is typical of those from the Red Sea.

## PLATE 63 – CARVINGS FROM USA and RED SEA

**1. & 2.** Louisiana Creoles, c. 1950–60, size 3.9″ x 1.8″ (10 x 4.6 cm). **3.** Ronald Reagan, President of USA 1981–89, c. 1985, size 1.3″ x 1″ (3.2 x 2.6 cm). **4.** Mouse, Zuni fetish made by native American tribe living in the area of Zuni River, New Mexico, c. 1960, size 3.5″ x 0.7″ (9 x 1.8 cm). **5.** Anniversary memento of George Washington's axe and cherry tree story, c. 1899, size 2.4″ x 1.2″ (6 x 3 cm).

**RED SEA**

**6.** Geometric designs, Red Sea (Somalia to Egypt), c. 1930, size 5.9″ x 5.9″ (15 x 15 cm).

CHAPTER 4

# Decorative Arts

## PLATE 64 – FISH 1

These fish were made in Bali, Indonesia, c. 1990–95. Mother-of-pearl fish made in this region during this era represented, in the main, fish found around the coral reefs of Bali. They are all free standing and have pearl on both sides of the fish. Sizes: **1.** 9.3" x 7.1" (23.5 x 18 cm). **2.** 5.3" x 4.9" (13.5 x 12.5 cm). **3.** 8.3" x 6.2" (21 x 15.8 cm). **4.** 7.3" x 6.1" (18.5 x 15.4 cm). **5.** 15.7" x 5.5" (40 x 14 cm)

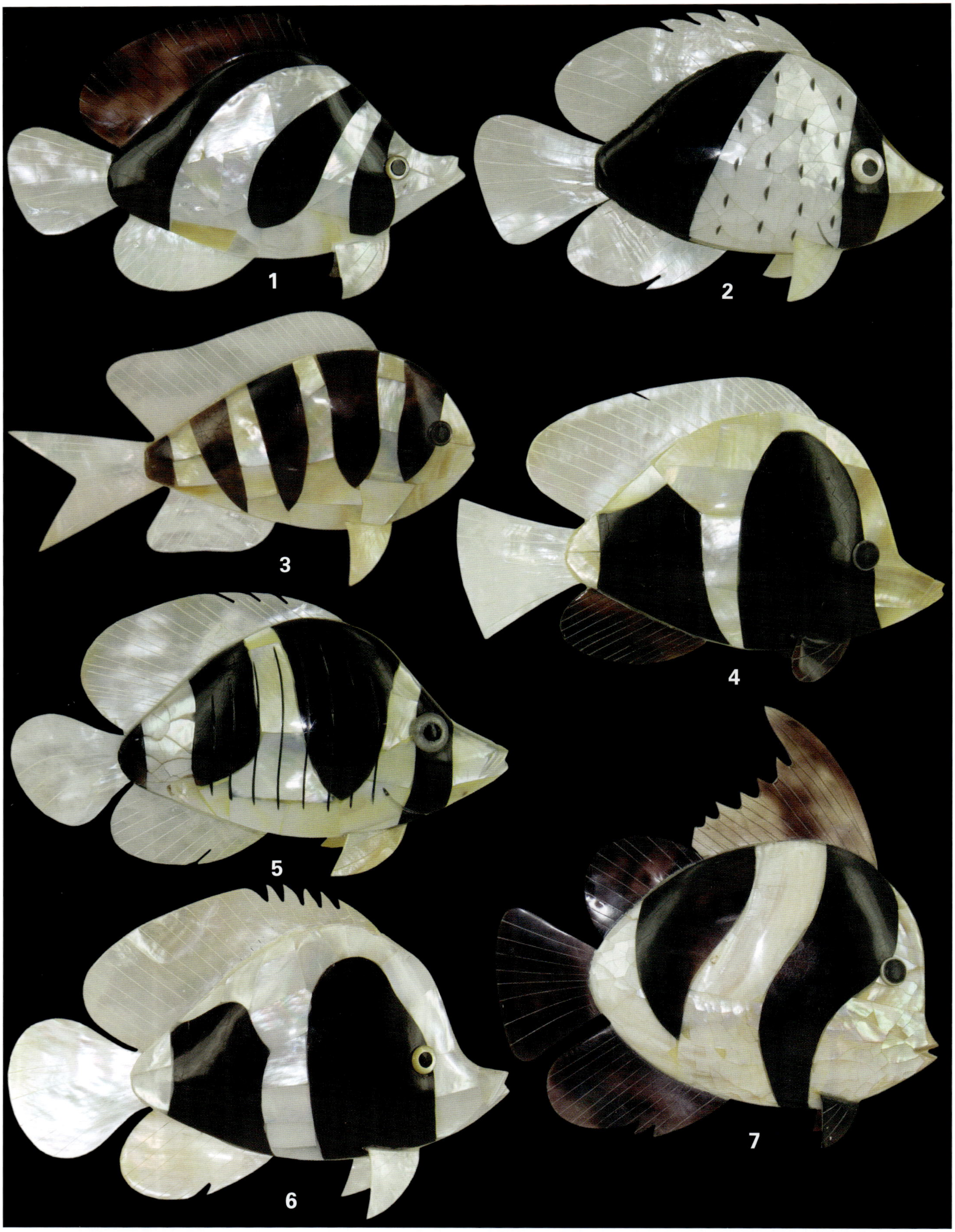

## PLATE 65 – FISH 2

These fish were made in Bali, Indonesia, c. 1990–95. Mother-of-pearl fish made in this region during this era represented, in the main, fish found around the coral reefs of Bali. They are all free standing and have pearl on both sides of the fish. Sizes: **1.** 7.1″ x 4.5″ (18 x 11.5 cm). **2.** 5.9″ x 3.1″ (15 x 8 cm). **3.** 7.9″ x 3.9″ (20 x 10 cm). **4.** 7.1″ x 4.3″ (18 x 11 cm). **5.** 5.5″ x 3″ (14 x 7.5 cm). **6.** 7.9″ x 5.5″ (20 x 14 cm). **7.** 7.1″ x 6.1″ (18 x 15.5 cm).

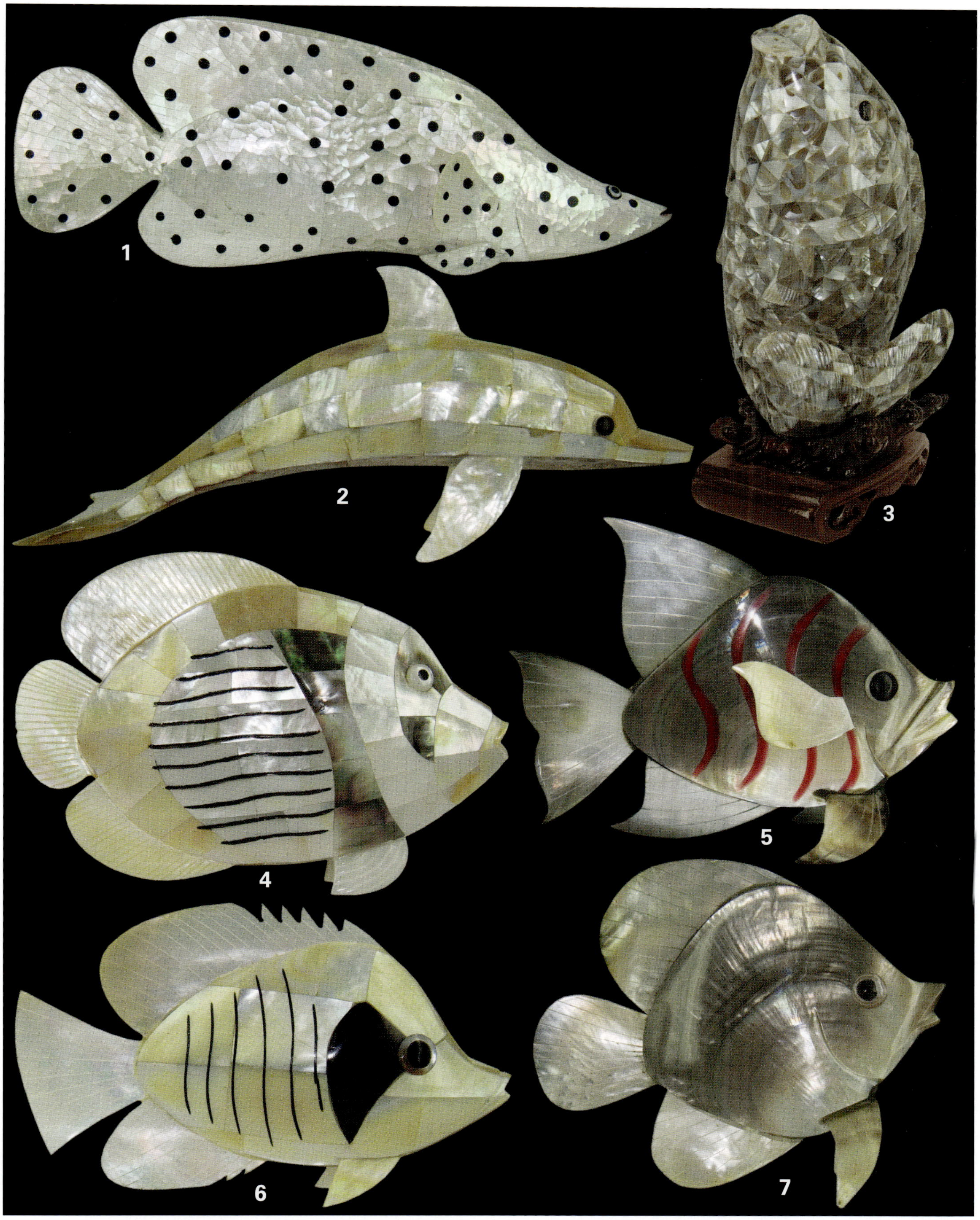


## PLATE 66 – FISH 3

All but two of these fish were made in Bali, Indonesia, c. 1990–95. They are all free standing and have pearl on both sides of the fish. Sizes: 1. 14.3" x 5.3" (36.5 x 13.5 cm). 2. Dolphin, size 12.2" x 5.7" (31 x 14.5 cm). 3. Royal Carp, China, c. 1990, size 6.9" x 5.9" (17.5 x 15 cm). 4. Angel fish, China, c. 1990, size 6.7" x 4.5" (17 x 11.4 cm). 5. 4.9" x 2.6" (12.5 x 6.6 cm). 6. 5.5" x 3.1" (14 x 8 cm). 7. 4.7" x 3.5" (12 x 9 cm).

## PLATE 67 – BIRDS 1

Made in China and sold by American Express USA as a special offer to their card holders, these birds were mostly sold as a boxed pair, c. 1970. **1a, 1b.** A pair of cranes, size 7″ x 2.8″ (17.8 x 7 cm). **2.** Peacock, size 5.1″ x 3.3″ (13 x 8.5 cm). **3a, 3b.** A pair of ducks, size 4.8″ x 2.2″ (12.2 x 5.5 cm). **4a, 4b.** A pair of small birds, maybe a Pipit, size 3.1″ x 2″ (8 x 5 cm). **5.** Black beaked bird, size 5.5″ x 4.1″ (14 x 10.5 cm). **6a, 6b.** A pair of parrots, size 3.9″ x 3.3″ (10 x 8.5 cm). **7.** Boxed set of parrots, size of each bird 3.9″ x 3.3″ (10 x 8.5 cm). **8.** Boxed set of cranes, size of each bird 7″ x 2.8″ (17.8 x 7 cm). **9.** Duck, size 2.8″ x 1.9″ (7 x 4.8 cm).

## PLATE 68 – BIRDS 2

1. Small bird, USA or Mexico, c. 1950, size 5.1" x 3.5" (13 x 9 cm). 2. Pewter duck, pearlized nautilus shell, India, c. 1960, size 10.4" x 6.7" (26.5 x 17 cm). 3. Pink bird, possible maker Los Castillo, Mexico, c. 1960, size 5.3" x 4.8" (13.5 x 12.2 cm). 4. Pewter crane, pearlized nautilus shell, India, c. 1980, size 8.7" x 4" (22 x 10.2 cm). 5. Owl, Thailand, 1996, size 1.8" x 0.9" (4.5 x 2.2 cm). 6. Pewter bird, turban shell, India, c. 1995, size 4.7" x 1.8" (12 x 4.5 cm). 7. Duck, China, c. 1990, size 6.7" x 3.5" (17 x 9 cm). 8. Peacock, turban shell, Thailand, 1996, size 3.9" x 3.1" (10 x 8 cm).

## PLATE 69 – TURTLES AND FROGS

It is interesting to compare items 1 to 3, to see the different effects that can be achieved with different types of mother-of-pearl. **1.** Turtle, white lip pearl, China, c. 1990, size 6.3″ x 5.5″ (16 x 14 cm). **2.** Turtle, yellow lip and white lip pearl, China, c. 1990, size 6.3″ x 5.5″ (16 x 14 cm). **3.** Turtle, black lip pearl, China, c. 1990, size 6.3″ x 5.5″ (16 x 14 cm). **4.** Pond turtle, freshwater pearl, China, c. 1990, size 4.7″ x 3.1″ (12 x 8 cm). **5.** Frog, yellow lip pearl, China, c. 1990, size 3.5″ x 2.8″ (9 x 7 cm). **6.** Frog, freshwater pearl, China, c. 1990, size 3.5″ x 2.8″ (9 x 7 cm).

## PLATE 70 – HORSES 1

**1.** Jumping horse, China, 2009, size 8.7″ x 8.1″ (22 x 20.5 cm). **2.** Horse's head, white lip pearl, China, 2009, size 7.1″ x 4.7″ (18 x 12 cm). **3.** Horse, winged pearl oyster, Thailand, 1995, size 8.5″ x 8.9″ (21.5 x 22.5). **4.** Horse's head, freshwater pearl. c. 1990, China, size 5.8″ x 5.5″ (14.8 x 14 cm).

## PLATE 71 – HORSES 2

**1.** Horse, extra large, white lip pearl, China, 2009, size 12.2″ x 9.4″ (31 x 24 cm). **2.** Horse, extra large, freshwater pearl shell, India, c. 1920, size 15.7″ x 15.7″ (40 x 40 cm).

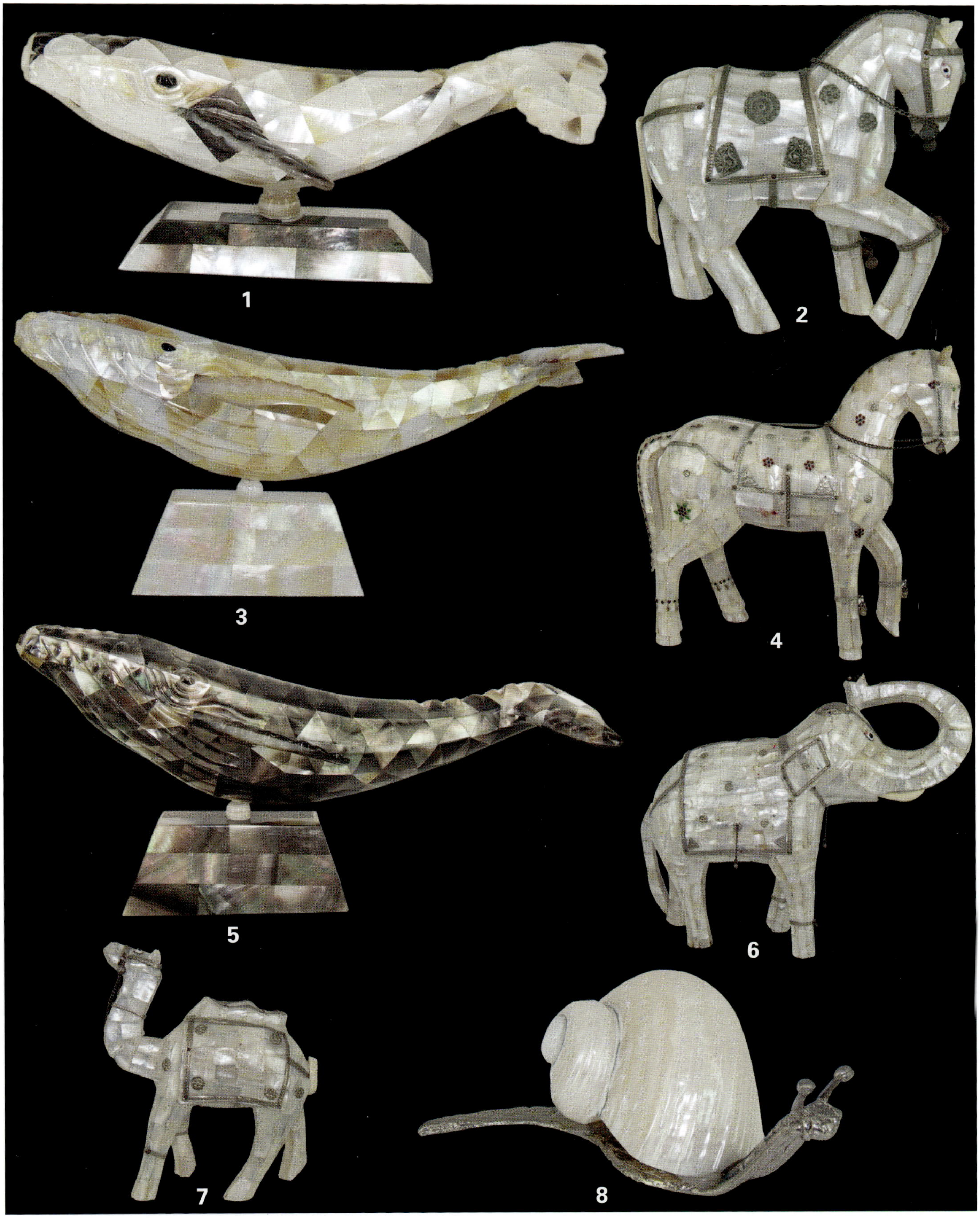


## PLATE 72 – WHALES and ANIMALS

1. Whale, white and black lip pearl, China, c. 1990, size 6.3″ x 4.1″ (16 x 10.5 cm). 2. Horse, symbolizing energy, is a popular wedding gift, India, c. 1970–80, size 5.1″ x 5.1″ (13 x 13 cm). 3. Whale, yellow and white lip pearl, China, c. 1990, size 10″ x 4.5″ (25.5 x 11.5 cm). 4. Horse, c. 1950–70, size 8.3″ x 7.5″ (21 x 19 cm). 5. Whale, black lip pearl, China, c. 1990, size 10″ x 4.5″ (25.5 x 11.5 cm). 6. Elephant, symbol of wisdom, a popular wedding gift in India, c. 1950–70, size 13.4″ x 11.4″ (34 x 29 cm). 7. Camel, India, c. 1950, size 4.9″ x 5.5″ (12.5 x 14 cm). 8. Snail, turban shell and silver plate, Thailand, 1995, size 4.5″ x 1.6″ (11.5 x 4 cm).

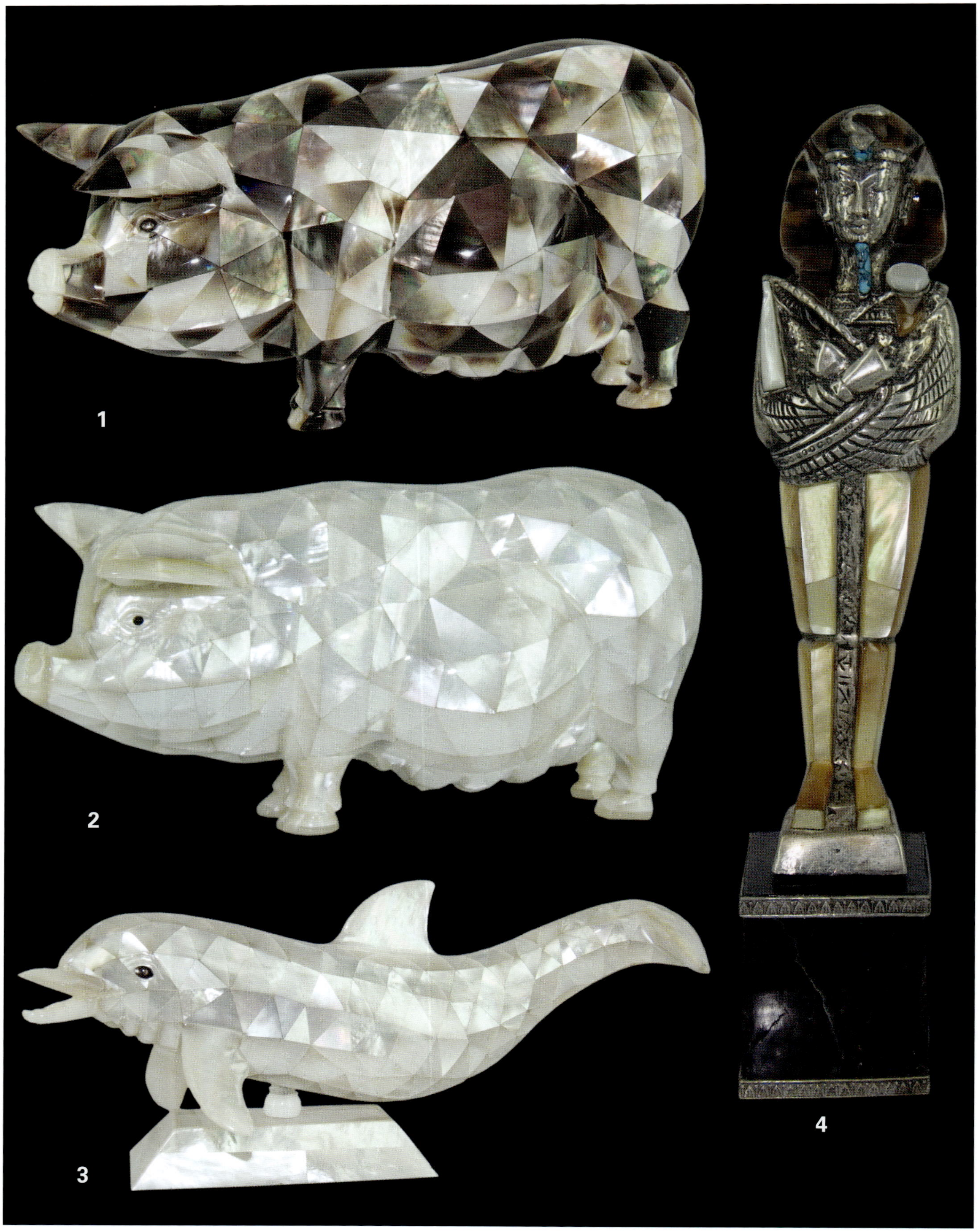

## PLATE 73 – PIGS, DOLPHIN, and STATUE

1. Pig, black and white lip pearl, China, c. 1990, size 6.7" x 3.7" (17 x 9.5 cm). 2. Pig, white lip pearl, China, c. 1990, size 6.7" x 3.7" (17 x 9.5 cm). 3. Dolphin, white lip pearl, China, c. 1990, size 8.7" x 3.7" (22 x 9.5 cm). 4. Tutankhamen, made during the wave of interest in Egyptology after the discovery of Tutankhamen's tomb in 1922, includes silver, onyx, turquoise, on a marble base, Europe, c. 1924–30, size 11.4" x 2" (29 x 5 cm).

## PLATE 74 – CHINESE JUNKS 1 and PEARL LUGGERS

These examples were all made in China, c. 1990. **1.** Pearl lugger, yellow lip pearl oyster, three sails, size 6.1" x 6.3" (15.5 x 16 cm). **2.** Pearl Lugger, black lip pearl oyster, three sails, size 6.1" x 6.3" (15.5 x 16 cm). **3.** Pearl lugger, yellow lip pearl oyster, two open sails, one folded sail, size 6.5" x 6.9" (16.5 x 17.5). **4.** Junk (a sailboat designed by the Chinese and dates back to ancient times), yellow lip pearl oyster, one sail, size 8.3" x 8.5" (21 x 21.5 cm).

## PLATE 75 – CHINESE JUNKS 2

The Junk is a sailboat designed by the Chinese and dates back to ancient times. These examples were all made in China, c. 1990. **1.** Yellow lip pearl oyster, three sails, size 8.1″ x 8.7″ (20.5 x 22 cm). **2.** Pink pearl shell (found in US rivers), three sails, size 9.8″ x 10.6″ (25 x 27 cm). **3.** Chinese swan junk, white lip pearl oyster, one sail, size 9.8″ x 8.9″ (25 x 22.5 cm). **4.** Freshwater pearl shell, two sails, size 8.5″ x 8.7″ (21.5 x 22 cm).

1

2

3

4

## PLATE 76 – CHINESE JUNKS 3 and LUGGER

The Junk is a sailboat designed by the Chinese and dates back to ancient times. The Lugger, a type of small sailing vessel with two or more sails, often used for pearling and fishing. These examples were all made in China, c. 1990. **1.** White lip pearl oyster, three sails, size 7.9" x 9.1" (20 x 23 cm). **2.** Yellow lip pearl oyster, three sails, size 9.8" x 10" (25 x 25.5 cm). **3.** Freshwater pearl shell, three sails, size 8.1" x 9.1" (20.5 x 23 cm). **4.** Lugger, freshwater pearl shell, size 9.8" x 9.1" (25 x 23 cm).

## PLATE 77 – CHINESE JUNKS 4

1. Dragon junk, China, 2009, size 13.8″ x 9.8″ (35 x 25 cm). 2. Rooster junk, China, c. 1920–30, size 9.3″ x 6.1″ (23.5 x 15.5 cm).

## PLATE 78 – CHINESE JUNKS 5 and SHIPS

1. Chinese junk, three decks, China, c. 1990, size 14.6″ x 9.8″ (37 x 25 cm). 2. Lugger, a small sailing vessel with sails on two or more masts used for pearling and fishing, white lip pearl oyster, China, 2009, size 9.4″ x 8.9″ (24 x 22.5 cm). 3. English Galleon, a multi-deck ship used for war and commerce, yellow lip pearl oyster, China, 2009, size 9.1″ x 9.6″ (23 x 24.5 cm).

## PLATE 79 – SHIPS

1. Model of H.M. *Bark Endeavour,* originally launched in 1768, Germany, c. 1900, size 14.6″ x 12.2″ (37 x 31 cm). 2. Sailing ship, Europe, c. 1970, size 10.6″ x 6.3″ (27 x 16 cm). 3. Sailing boat, dragon decoration, Vietnam, c. 1975, size 10.6″ x 11.8″ (27 x 30 cm). 4. Sailing ship, Cebu, Philippines, c. 1993, size 20.5″ x 13″ (52 x 33 cm). 5. Galleon, turban shell, France, c. 1880, size 11.8″ x 13.8″ (30 x 35 cm). 6. Extra large English galleon, inscribed July 1882, name of ship partly worn, France, 1882, size 31.5″ x 27.6″ (80 x 70 cm).

## PLATE 80 – DECORATIVE

1. *The Rose* etched on a pearl nautilus shell by Peter Meyer, Perth, Australia, 1993, size 13" x 6.7" (33 x 17 cm). 2. Egg, yellow lip pearl oyster, Cebu, Philippine Islands, 1995, size 2.6" x 1.7" (6.6 x 4.3 cm). 3. Pyramid, secret box, Philippine Islands, c. 1980, size 10.6" x 4.1" (27 x 10.5 cm). 4. Stand for a work of art, or a table for a high end doll house, France, c. 1880, size 3" x 3.1" (7.5 x 8 cm). 5. Aeroplane, yellow lip pearl oyster, China, c. 1990, size 4.7" x 5.7" (12 x 14.5 cm). 6. Pearl ball made from Australian abalone shell, Cebu, Philippine Islands, 2005, size 3.7" diameter (9.5 cm). 7. Small chest of drawers, Cebu, Philippine Islands, 2004, size 12.2" x 11.6" (31 x 29.5 cm). 8. Tennis racquet, made for a presentation box or plaque celebrating a tennis match, France, c. 1890, size 2.6" (6.5 cm). 9. Treasure chest, Cebu, Philippine Islands, 2001, size 30.3" x 14.1" x 18.1" (77 x 36 x 46 cm).

## PLATE 81 – DECORATIVE

1. Ceremonial sword made for the export market, China, c. 1980, size 35.8″ (91 cm). 2. Ceremonial sword, Cebu, Philippines, c. 2003, size 32.2″ (82 cm). 3. Miniature reproduction of an ancient Chinese sword, China, c. 1992, size 11.5″ (29.3 cm). 4. Miniature reproduction of an ancient Chinese sword, China, c. 1997, size 11.4″ (29 cm). 5. Pearl covered dagger, Thailand, c. 1996, size 8.1″ x 0.8″ (20.7 x 2 cm). 6. Baby piano covered in white pearl oyster, Australia, c. 1980–2000, size 11.4″ x 9.8″ (29 x 25 cm). 7. English galleon by artist Peter Meyer, Australia, c. 1990, size 5.1″ x 5.9″ (13 x 15 cm). 8. Large pewter jug, India, c. 1960, size 9″ x 4.7″ (23 x 12 cm). 9. Guitar, covered in white pearl oyster, Cebu, Philippine Islands, 2003, size 21.2″ x 6.5″ (54 x 16.5 cm).

## PLATE 82 – PAINTING ON MOTHER-OF-PEARL

**1a, 1b.** Pair painted scenes from Persia, Isfahan, Iran, c. 1960, size frame 10″ x 10″ (25.5 x 25.5 cm), shell 4.5″ x 4.8″ (11.5 x 12.3 cm). **2.** Wat Arun Temple, Bangkok, Thailand, c. 1950, size 8.7″ x 7.9″ (22 x 20 cm). **3a, 3b.** Pair painted scenes from Persia, Isfahan, Iran, c. 1960, size 4.5″ x 4.8″ (11.5 x 12.3 cm). **4.** Kuthodaw Pagoda, Mandalay, Myanmar, c. 1940–50, size 9.6″ x 7.7″ (24.5 x 19.5 cm). **5.** Framed English galleon, China, c. 1980, size 9.1″x 9.1″ (23 x 23 cm). **6.** English galleon made from pearl and set on porcelain, China, c. 1950, size 9.1″ (23 cm) diameter. **7.** Men spearing fish in shallow water, Cebu Island, Philippines, c. 1990, size 8.7″ x 8.7″ (22.2 x 22.2 cm).

## PLATE 83 – PICTURES and WALL PLAQUES 2

1. Dragon in colored mother-of-pearl, framed, Thailand, 1996, size 22.6″ x 13.8″ (57.5 x 35 cm). 2. Flower picture inscribed *Sulawesi Souvenir Shop, Ambon, Maluku,* Indonesia, c. 1960, size 10.6″ x 5.9″ (27 x 15 cm). 3-4. Painted lady and gentleman by Carol Meyer in a pearl frame, England, frame c. 1880, size 1.9″ x 1.9″ (4.7 x 4.7 cm). 5. Screen with ladies, China, c. 1950, size 47.2″ x 36.2″ (120 x 92 cm). 6. Bird sitting on a branch above two flowers, China, c. 1998, size 13″ x 9.8″ (33 x 25 cm). 7. Silver dragons mounted on a pair of hinged mother-of-pearl shells, China, c. 1870–90, size 13″ x 7.9″ (33 x 20 cm).

## PLATE 84 – CHINESE MINIATURE SCREENS

**1.** Screen with panels showing English galleons, China, c. 1970, size 26″ x 14.2″ (66 x 36 cm). **2.** Miniature screen of colored birds, China, c. 1993, size 18.2″ x 15″ (46.3 x 38 cm). **3.** Miniature screen of birds, China, c. 1995, size 14.4″ x 12″ (36.5 x 30.5 cm). **4.** Miniature screen of colorful birds, China, c. 1998, size 17.2″ x 12″ (43.8 x 30.5 cm). **5.** Miniature screen of Japanese Ladies, Vietnam, c. 1970, size 16.1″ x 11.5″ (41 x 29.3 cm).

## PLATE 85 – MASKS and DECOR

**1–2.** King Rama and Queen Sita, based on the classical Hindu stories *Ramayana* and *Mahabharata*, Madura Island, Java, Indonesia, c. 1980, size Rama 4.5″ x 3.3″ (11.5 x 8.5 cm), Sita 4.7″ x 3.6″ (12 x 9.2 cm). **3.** Teotihuacán style mask, Mexico, c. 2000, size 8.3″ x 6.9″ (21 x 17.5 cm). **4–5.** King Rama and Queen Sita, another style, Madura Island, Java, Indonesia, c. 1980, size 7.3″ x 5.7″ (18.5 x 14.5 cm). **6.** Teotihuacán style mask, Mexico, c. 1960, size 8.3″ x 6.9″ (21 x 17.5 cm). **7.** Fan-shaped wall décor, Vietnam, c. 1980, size 23.6″ x 13.4″ (60 x 34 cm). **8.** Teotihuacán style mask, Mexico, c. 1960, size 5.5″ x 4.7″ (14 x 12 cm).

CHAPTER 5

# Sewing Tools and Accessories

The use of mother-of-pearl in the making of sewing tools has been more extensive than in any other collectible. Most of these attractive tools were originally housed in a sewing kit, which was an essential in every household. The sets that we see at the antique markets today often have added and replaced tools from when the set is passed down from mother to daughter and is adapted to their preferences, which all adds to their charm.

In our opinion, the most stunning sewing sets of all were produced in France in the early nineteenth century, c. 1810–20. The finest of all were the Palais Royal pieces, having been made for sale at the Palais Royal, at one time the home of Cardinal Richelieu. The Palais Royal, Paris's social and political center for that period, had arcades that sold top quality items to the wealthy. The enameled pansy was the symbol the Palais Royal artisans put on the best quality items, many made and fit for royalty.

These early sewing boxes were often intricate feats of both art and science. Some had music boxes; some had secret drawers; some had several levels, all fit securely into one small box. The contents of the boxes often varied, as many boxes were made custom for clients who ordered the tools they desired to be fitted for the box. Some boxes were made by craftsman who bought sewing tools to fit from tool specialists.

The following pages take you through examples of these amazing sets and tools. It should be understood that after the passing of two hundred years, age may have taken its toll on some of the tools, requiring repair or replacement. Repairs, unless done by a talented professional, are visible upon inspection and the clue to spotting a replacement is that it seldom fits exactly into its designated nest in the kit.

Production of the early nineteenth century boxes with mother-of-pearl tools came to an end in the 1830s, when silver gilt and gold tools came into fashion. There was a revival period of the internal style of the Palais Royal sewing boxes around 1860–80, but these sets where in a flatter box (example on plate 92 number 2a–c). It is thought that these were made up with both old tools from 1810–30 and newly made tools, which do not show the crisp lines of the earlier carving.

**PLATE 86**

Two horses pulling a mother-of-pearl carriage, which contains a thimble, France, c. 1870–90, size 3.6" x 2.4" (9.2 x 6 cm).

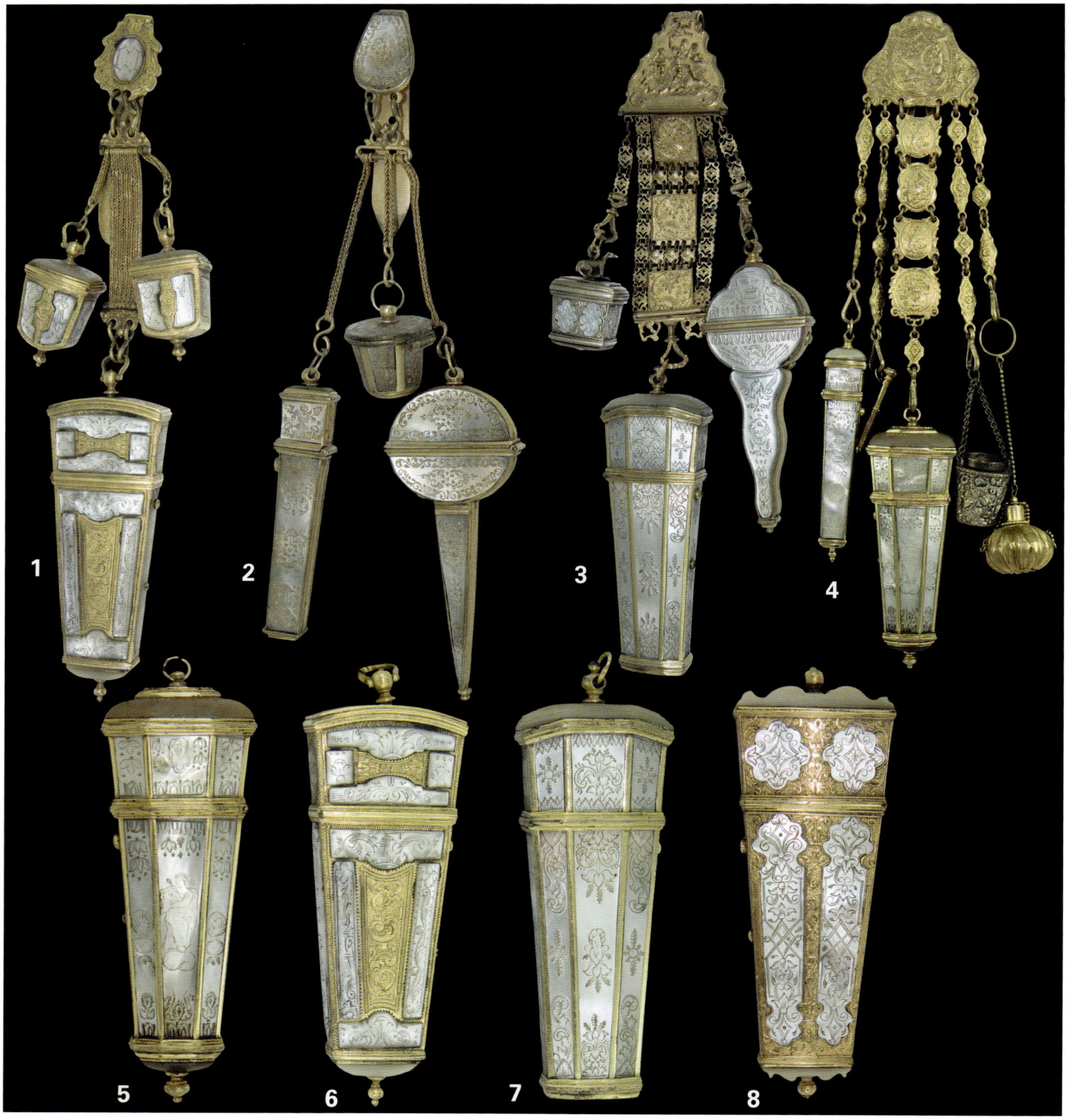


## PLATE 87 – CHATELAINES and ETUI

Worn on a belt around the waist, the sewing chatelaine was very popular in its day and allowed quick access to tools needed for sewing repairs or small tasks. The etui usually contained the essentials for sewing: a thimble, scissors, bodkin, stiletto, needle, or bodkin case, and at times other items like a pencil, ear spoon, and a knife. Most of the contents have been lost over the centuries, but the outer cases have survived. **1.** Sewing chatelaine with etui, thimble case, and pin cushion or reel case, France, c. 1730, overall size 8.3″ (21 cm). **2.** Sewing chatelaine with needle or bodkin case, scissor case, and thimble case, France, c. 1740–50, overall size 7.9″ (20 cm). **3.** Sewing chatelaine with etui, needle or bodkin case, and scissor case, France, c. 1730–40, overall size 8″ (20.3 cm). **4.** Sewing chatelaine, which reminds us that these items were treasured and were often handed down from mother to daughter, who would add her own favorite tools to replace missing or damaged items. This example has tools from 1730 to 1860 added by the different owners. Included is an etui, perfume flask, sliding pencil, needle, or bodkin case and thimble holder, France, c. 1730–1860, overall size 10.2″ (26 cm). **5–8.** Sewing etui that would have been attached to a chatelaine, France, c. 1730–40, average size 4.1″ x 1.5″ (10.5 x 3.8 cm).

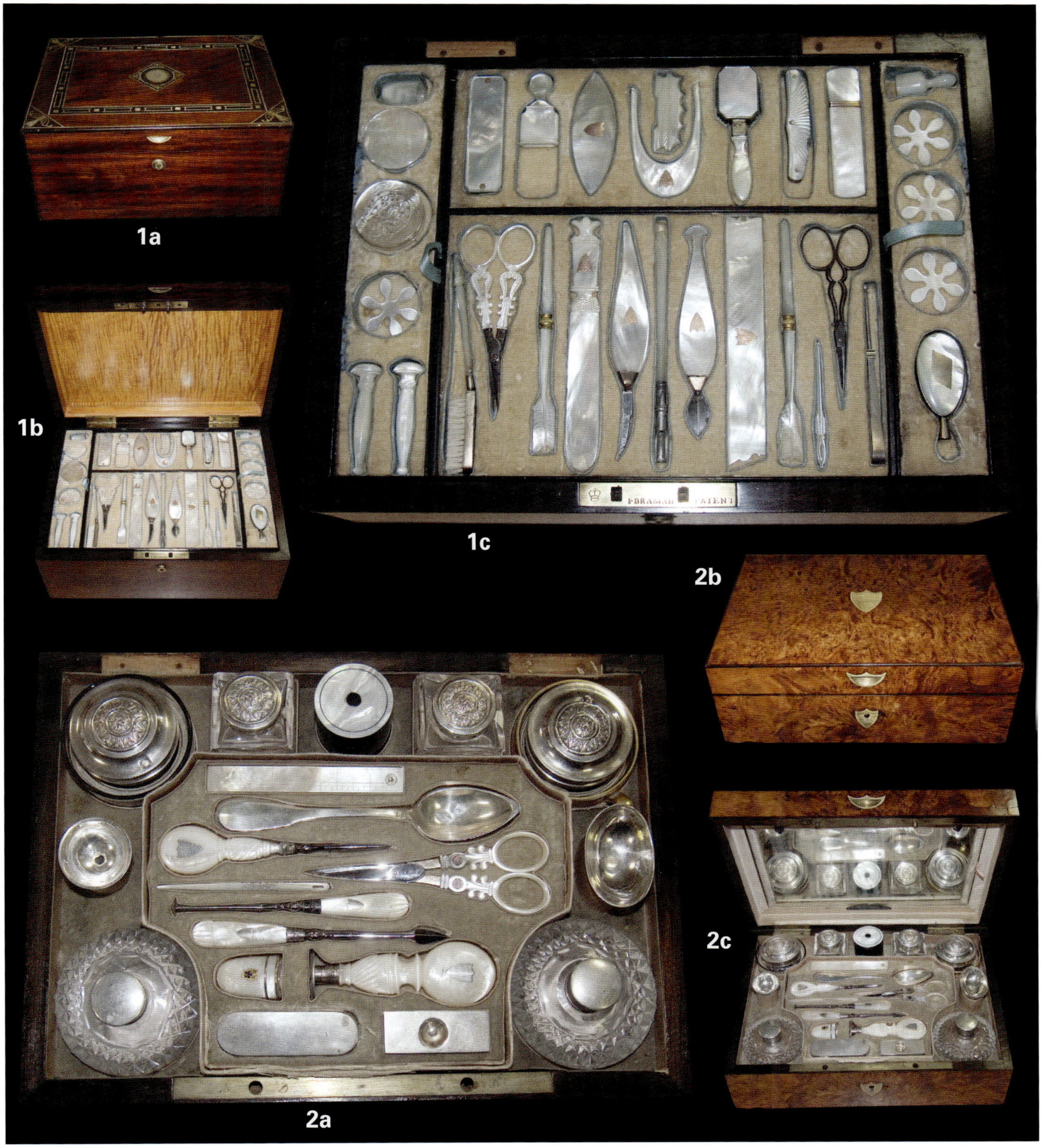


## PLATE 88 – *NECESSAIRE DE VOYAGE*

These were boxes filled with the basic essentials for a sea voyage, each set with custom ordered contents. **1a, 1b, 1c.** Includes two scissors, bodkin, lucet, thimble, two knitting guards, tatting shuttle, needle case, four thread winders, straight edge, dip pen, quill sharpener, ink eraser, letter opener, whist marker set in a round box, mustache brush, two brush handles, comb, toothbrush, ear spoon on the end of tweezers, round box, perfume container with lid missing, knife rest, pen knife, two quill-like objects that convert to a dip pen, lock made by Bramah England, assembled in Austria or France, c. 1820, size 14.2" x 10.2" (36 x 26 cm). **2a, 2b, 2c.** Includes ruler, stiletto, scissors, bodkin, thimble, seal, brush, silver patch box, spoon, two dental cleaning tools, two matching cut glass perfume bottles, two matching cut glass jars, silver funnel, silver eye bath, two silver topped ink wells, seal wax box, lead crystal drinking glass, Limoge gilt decorated cup and saucer, silver spoon, a secret compartment, France, c. 1820, size 10.6" x 7.5" (27 x 19 cm).

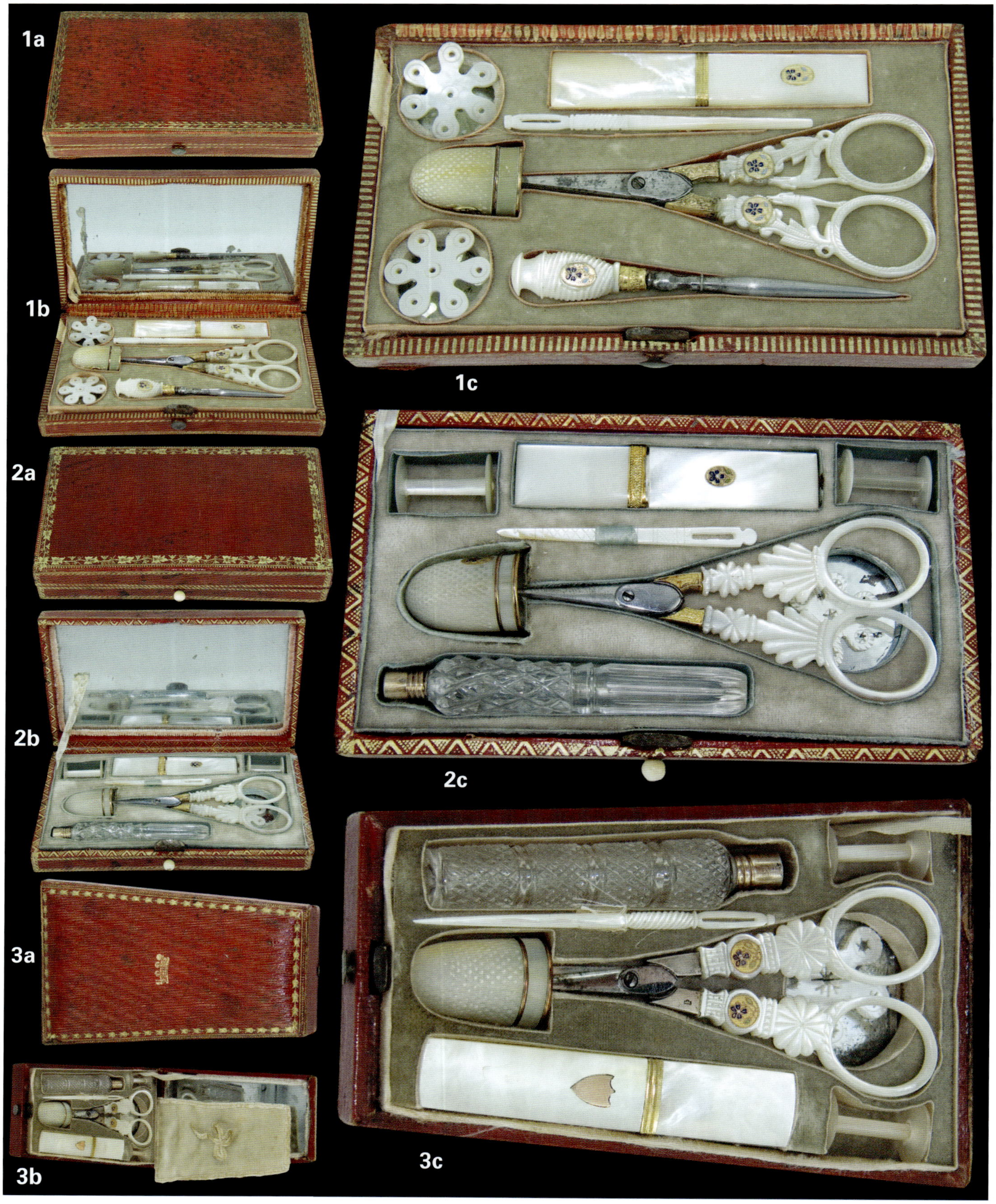


## PLATE 89 – BOXED FRENCH SEWING SETS 1

Red Morocco leather boxed sewing sets that would have been sold in the arcades of the Palais Royal, Paris, France, c. 1810–20, some with the enameled pansy symbol of higher quality. **1a, 1b, 1c.** Includes scissors, stiletto, bodkin, thimble, needle case, and two thread winders, size 5.2" x 3" (13.3 x 7.5 cm). **2a, 2b, 2c.** Includes, scissors, thread winder, two reels, needle case, bodkin, thimble, and perfume bottle, size 5.2" x 3" (13.3 x 7.5 cm). **3a, 3b, 3c.** Includes needle case, scissors, thread winder, two reels, thimble, bodkin, perfume bottle, and a tray cover, size 4.6" x 2.9" (11.7 x 7.3 cm).

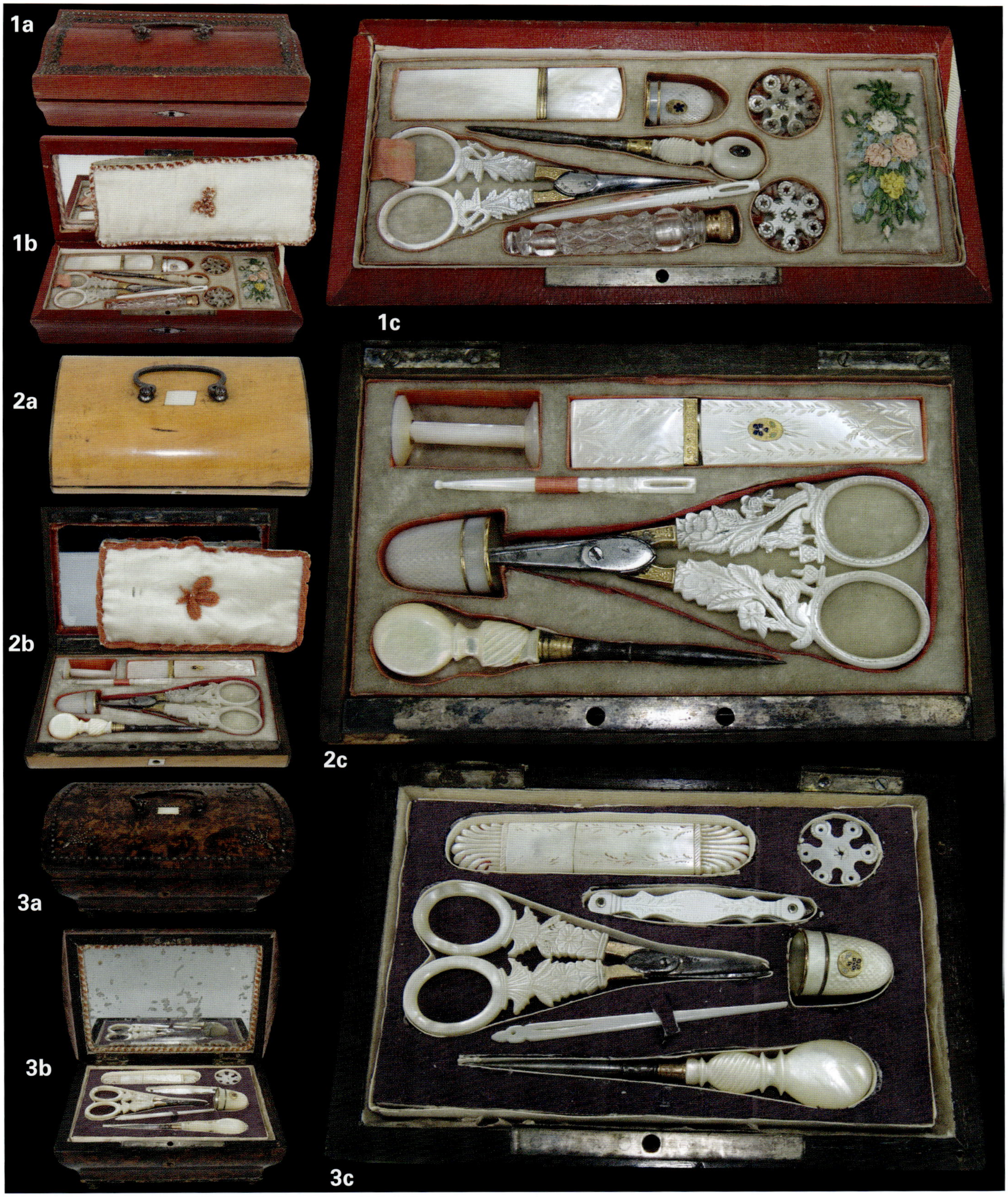


## PLATE 90 – BOXED FRENCH SEWING SETS 2

These larger boxed sewing sets would have been sold in the arcades of the Palais Royal, Paris, France, c. 1810–20, some with the enameled pansy symbol of higher quality. **1a, 1b, 1c.** Includes needle case thimble, two thread winders, stiletto, scissors, bodkin, perfume bottle, tray cover, an embroidered pincushion incorporated in the tray, size 7.5″ x 3.5″ (19 x 9 cm). **2a, 2b, 2c** Includes needle case, reel, bodkin, scissors, thimble, stiletto, and a tray cover, size 5.1″ x 3.2″ (13 x 8.2 cm). This set belonged to William Tallon, UK, butler to the Queen Mother. **3a, 3b, 3c.** Includes needle case, ear spoon, scissors, thimble, bodkin, thread winder, and stiletto, size 6″ x 4″ (15.3 x 10.2 cm).

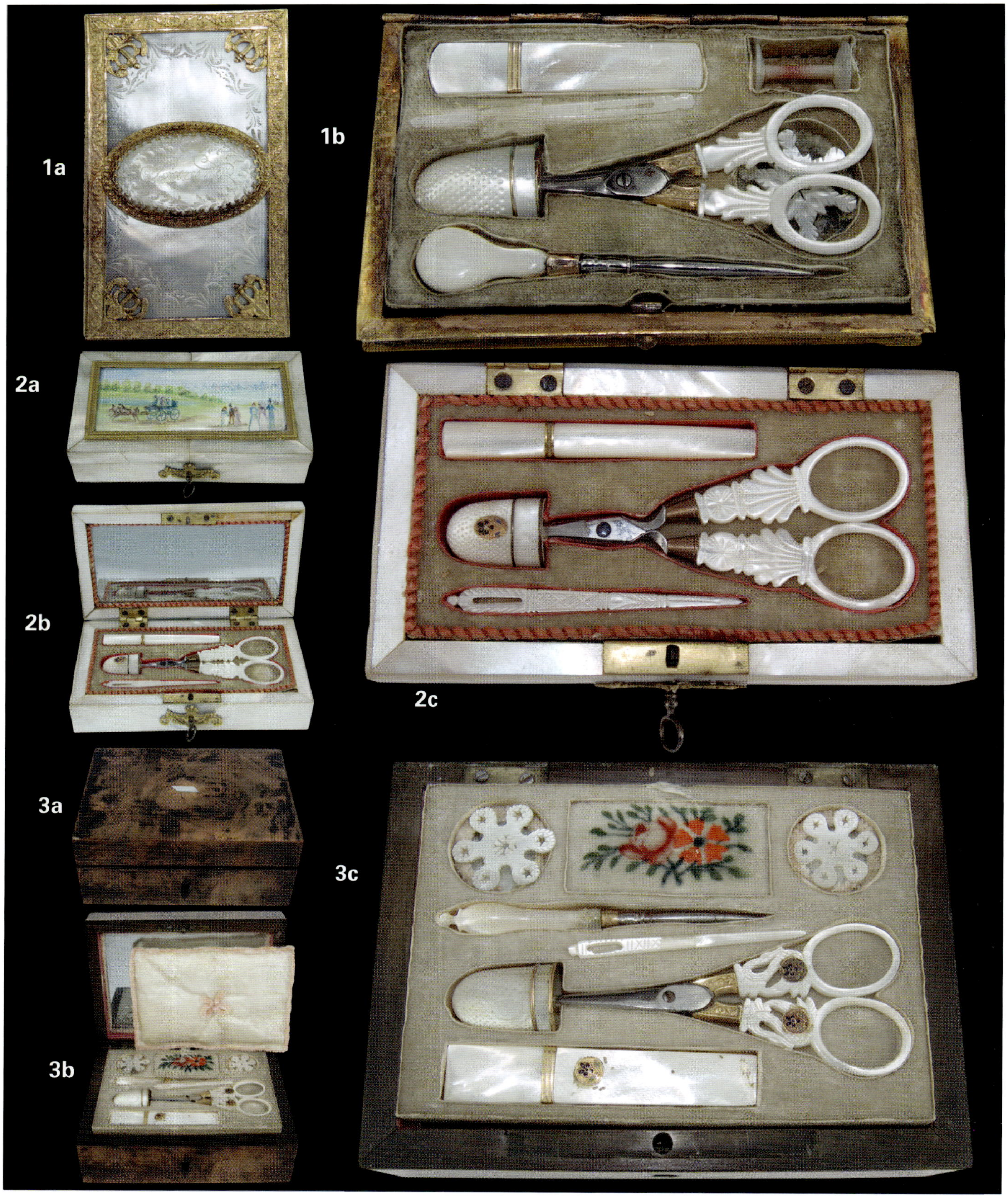


## PLATE 91 – BOXED FRENCH SEWING SETS 3

More boxed sewing sets that would have been sold in the arcades of the Palais Royal, Paris, France, c. 1810–20, some with the enameled pansy symbol of higher quality. **1a, 1b.** Unusual gilt metal and pearl box in the shape of two books, inscribed *Souvenir*, which includes needle case, reel, bodkin, thimble, scissors, thread winder, stiletto, size 4.1" x 2.6" (10.5 x 6.5 cm). **2a, 2b, 2c.** Pearl case, painting under glass, includes needle case, scissors, bodkin, and thimble, size 5" x 2.8" (12.8 x 7 cm). **3a, 3b, 3c.** Includes two thread winders, stiletto, bodkin, thimble, scissors, needle case, tray cover, and an embroidered pincushion incorporated in the tray, size 5.3" x 3.9" (13.4 x 9.8 cm).

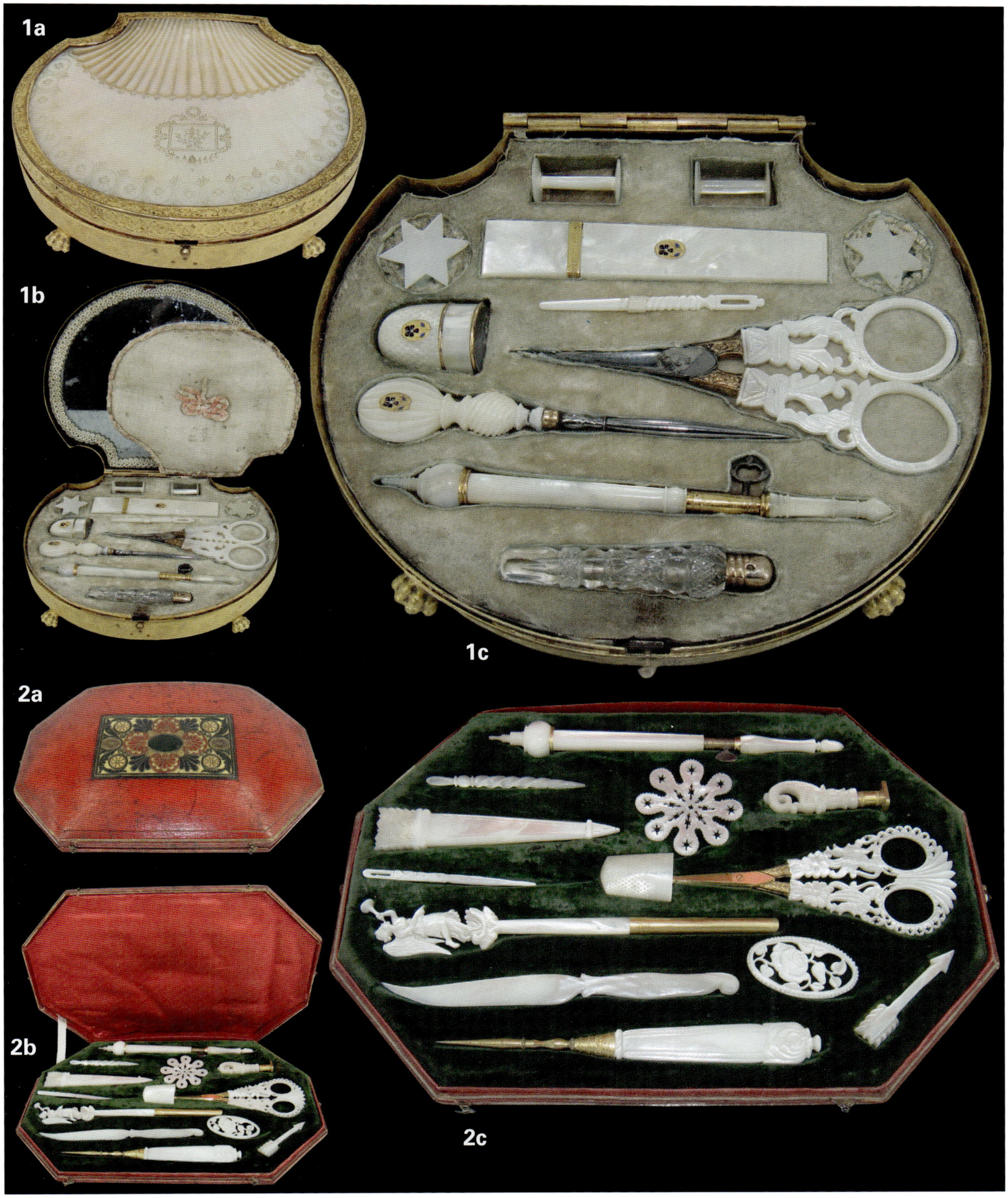


## PLATE 92 – BOXED FRENCH SEWING SETS 4

**1a, 1b, 1c.** Rare design boxed sewing set that would have been sold in the arcades of the Palais Royal: solid pearl top in the shape of a scallop, includes two reels, two thread winders, needle case, bodkin, scissors, thimble, stiletto, tambour, a perfume bottle, and tray cover, some with the enameled pansy symbol of higher quality, Paris, France, c. 1810, size 6.1" x 5.1" (15.4 x 13 cm). **2a, 2b, 2c.** Revival period sewing box, includes tambour, ear spoon, thread winder, seal, needle case, bodkin, thimble, scissors, dip pen, paper knife, stiletto, arrow, and rose carving ex brooches for decoration, made up of a mix of original 1810–30 and 1860–80 tools, France, c. 1860–80, size 9.3" x 6.1" (23.5 x 15.5 cm).

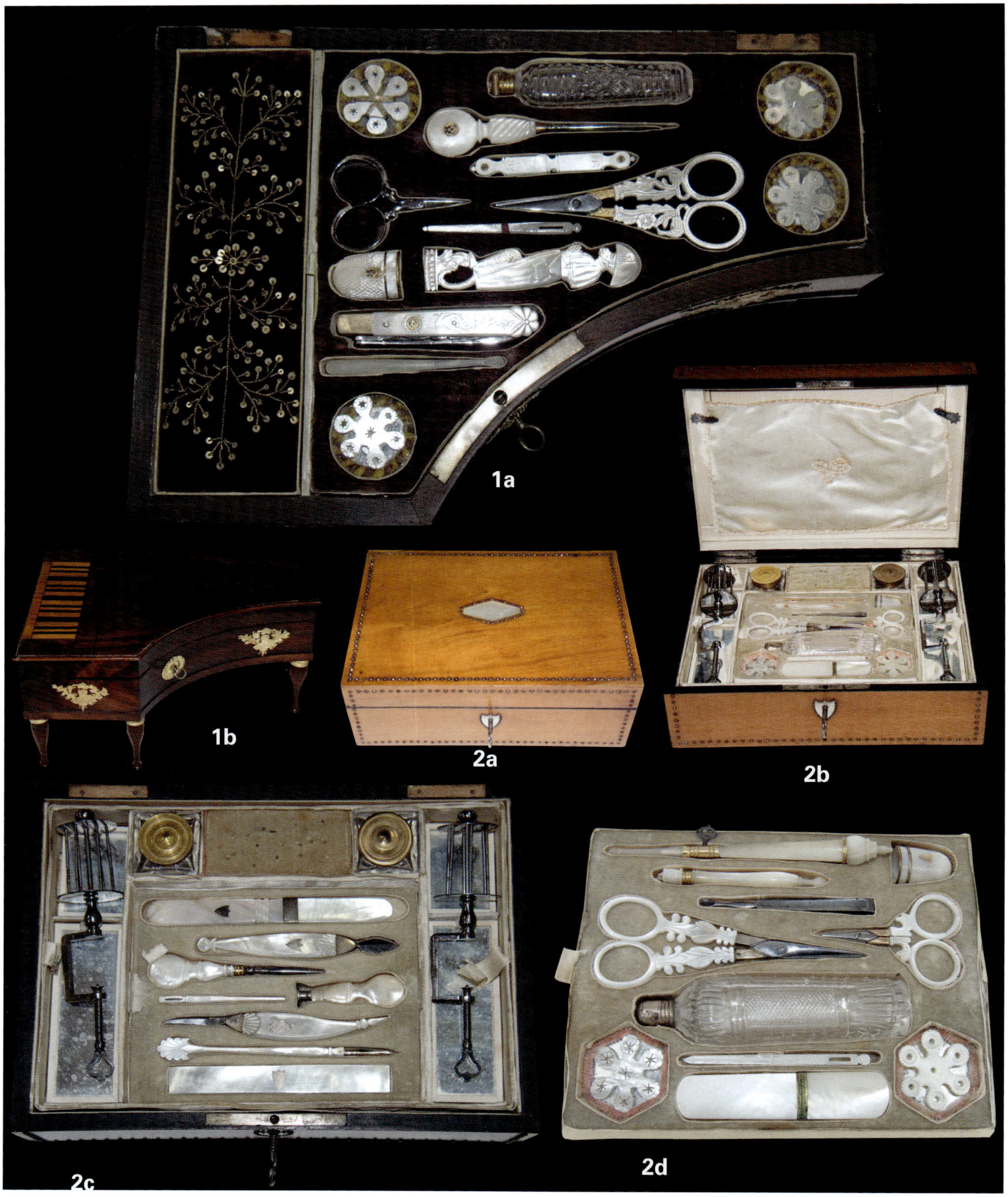


## PLATE 93 – BOXED FRENCH SEWING SETS 5

Boxed sewing sets that would have been sold in the arcades of the Palais Royal, Paris, France, c. 1810–20, some with the enameled pansy symbol of higher quality. **1a, 1b.** Case in the shape of a spinet, includes four thread winders, perfume bottle, stiletto, combined toothpick and ear spoon, two scissors, bodkin, needle case, thimble, knife, and tray cover, size 11.6″ x 8″ (29.5 x 20.2 cm). **2a, 2b, 2c, 2d.** Boxed set with two trays: top tray: tambour, thimble, lace picker, tweezers, two scissors, perfume bottle, bodkin, needle case, two thread winders; bottom tray: two sewing clamps, two ink wells, page turner, ink eraser, stiletto, seal, bodkin, quill sharpener, dip pen, ruler, size 10.6″ x 7.3″ (27 x 18.5 cm).

## PLATE 94 – BOXED FRENCH SEWING SETS 6

The finest sewing box that we have seen from the arcades of Palais Royal, Paris, France, c. 1810, with tools enhanced with inset gem stones. **1a, 1b, 1c.** Painting under glass on top, painted mirror on inside top, includes a stiletto with snake carving, dip pen, ear spoon, two tools for dental hygiene, bodkin, ink scraper, quill sharpener, two scissors, toothbrush, perfume bottle, two thread winders, thimble, needle case, thread spool, two inkwells, and two jars, size 10.6" x 7.9" (27 x 20 cm).

1a

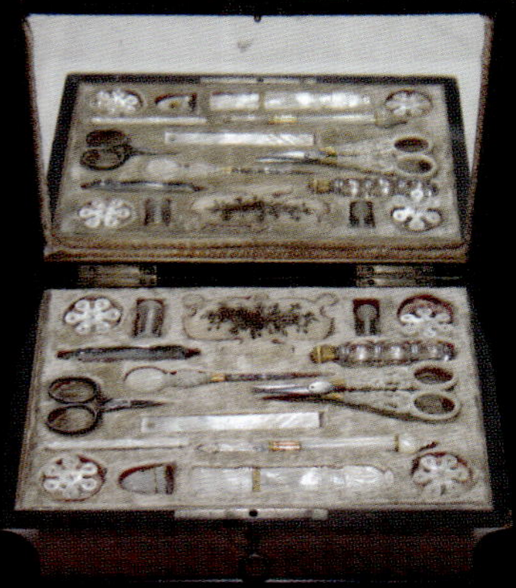

1b

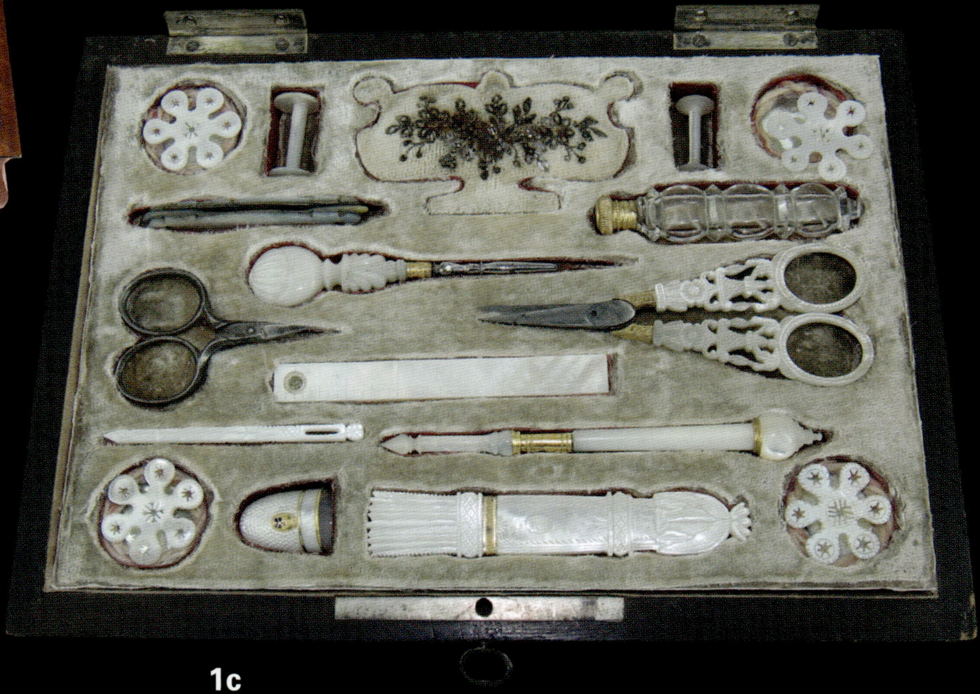

1c

2a

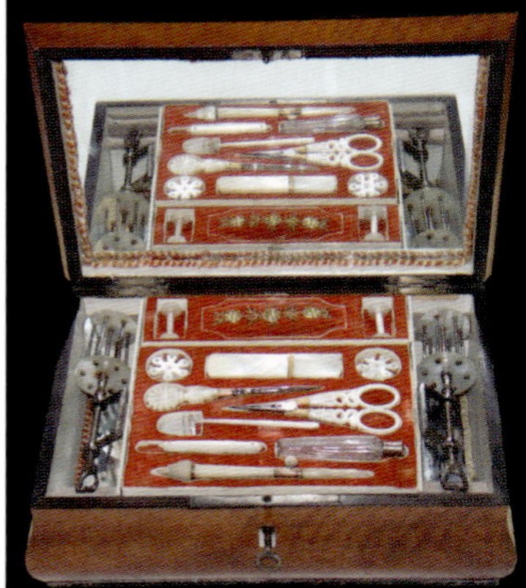

2b

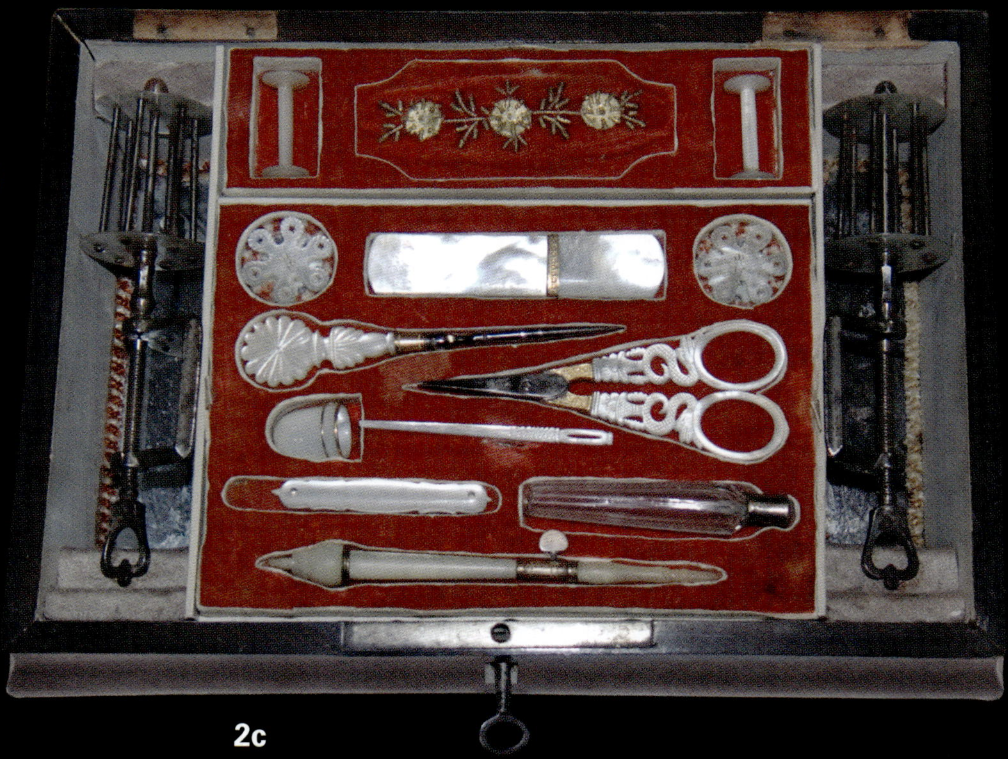

2c

## PLATE 95 – BOXED FRENCH SEWING SETS 7

Boxed sewing sets that would have been sold in the arcades of the Palais Royal, Paris, France, c. 1810–20. **1a, 1b, 1c.** Includes four thread winders, two reels, perfume bottle, ear spoon, stiletto, two scissors, folding ruler, bodkin, tambour, thimble, and needle case, size 9.3″ x 6.7″ (23.8 x 17 cm). **2a, 2b, 2c.** Includes two mother-of-pearl clamps, two reels, two thread winders, needle case, stiletto, scissors, thimble, bodkin, ear spoon, perfume bottle, and tambour, size 10.3″ x 7.1″ (26.2 x 18 cm).

## PLATE 96 – BOXED ENGLISH SEWING SETS 1

Mid-nineteenth century English fitted sewing boxes (c. 1840–80) were popular due to their attractive contents, some of which included articles like matched pearl-topped reel holders, emeries, tape measures, and waxers, among other tools. **1a, 1b.** Blue silk and velvet lining, contents: four cotton reel holders, tape measure, emery, waxer, corkscrew, stiletto, crochet hook, button hook, scissors, thimble, pins, and needle packs, c. 1880, size 11.8″ x 8.9″ (30 x 22.5 cm). **2a, 2b.** Coromandel wood box with purple silk lining, with contents, six cotton reel holders, thimble, penknife, stiletto, crochet hook, tweezers, and needle packs, c. 1880, size 11.6″ x 8.5″ (29.5 x 21.5 cm). **3a, 3b.** Red silk lining with gilt decoration, contents: six cotton reel holders, tape measure, emery, waxer, thimble, scissors, button hook, tweezers, crochet hook, stiletto, and corkscrew, c. 1840, size 9.8″ x 7.3″ (25 x 18.5 cm). **4a, 4b.** Interior blue silk, contents: six cotton reel holders, two thimbles, crochet hook, stiletto, button hook, ribbon threader, and needle pack, c. 1850, size 10.8″ x 8″ (27.5 x 20.4 cm).

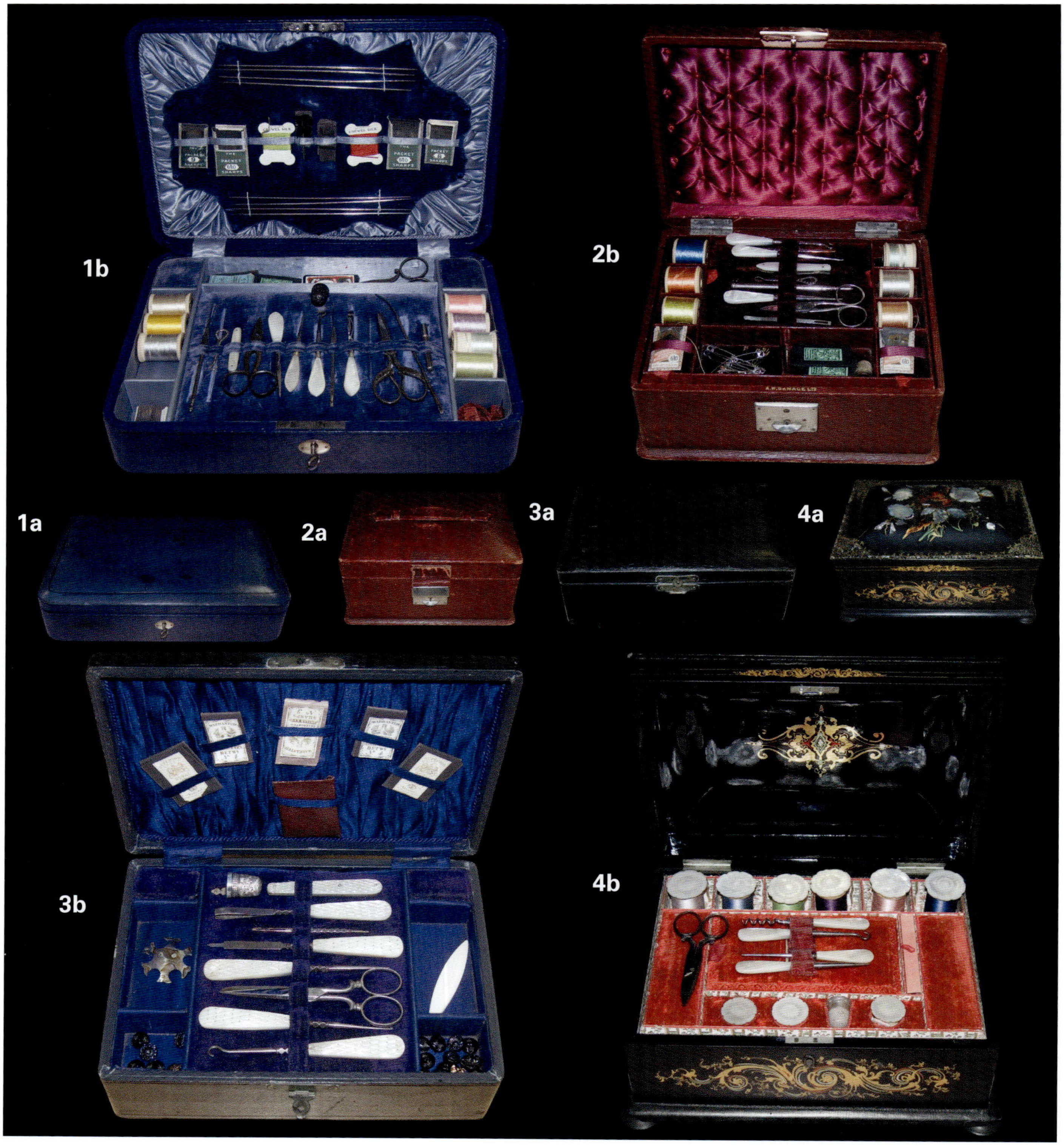


## PLATE 97 – BOXED ENGLISH SEWING SETS 2

The pearl handled tools are the main feature in these English sewing boxes. Many different designs were produced in the second half of the nineteenth century. **1a, 1b.** Blue leather box with blue silk and velvet interior, contents: needle packs, knitting needles, cotton on reels, scissors, tape measure, thimble, needle case, tweezers, stiletto, crochet hook, button hook, pen knife, pins, c. 1890, size 12.6" x 8.7" (32 x 22 cm). **2a, 2b.** Red leather box with red silk and velvet interior with contents: needle packs, cotton on reels, button hook, crochet hook, stiletto, scissors, pencil, bodkin, thimble, inscribed *A. W. Gamage,* c. 1900–14, size 9.8" x 7.5" (25 x 19 cm). **3a, 3b.** Black leather box with blue silk and velvet interior with contents: thimble, pen knife, tweezers, file, crochet hook, stiletto, button hook, scissors, tatting shuttle, thread winder, needle packs, pins, pincushion, pattern, c. 1890, size 9.5" x 6.3" (24 x 16 cm). **4a, 4b.** Black lacquer papier-mâché with pearl inlaid box, red velvet interior with contents: six cotton reel holders, scissors, waxer, emery, tape measure, thimble, corkscrew, button hook, stiletto, crochet hook, needle book, c. 1850, size 10.7" x 7.9" (27.3 x 20 cm).

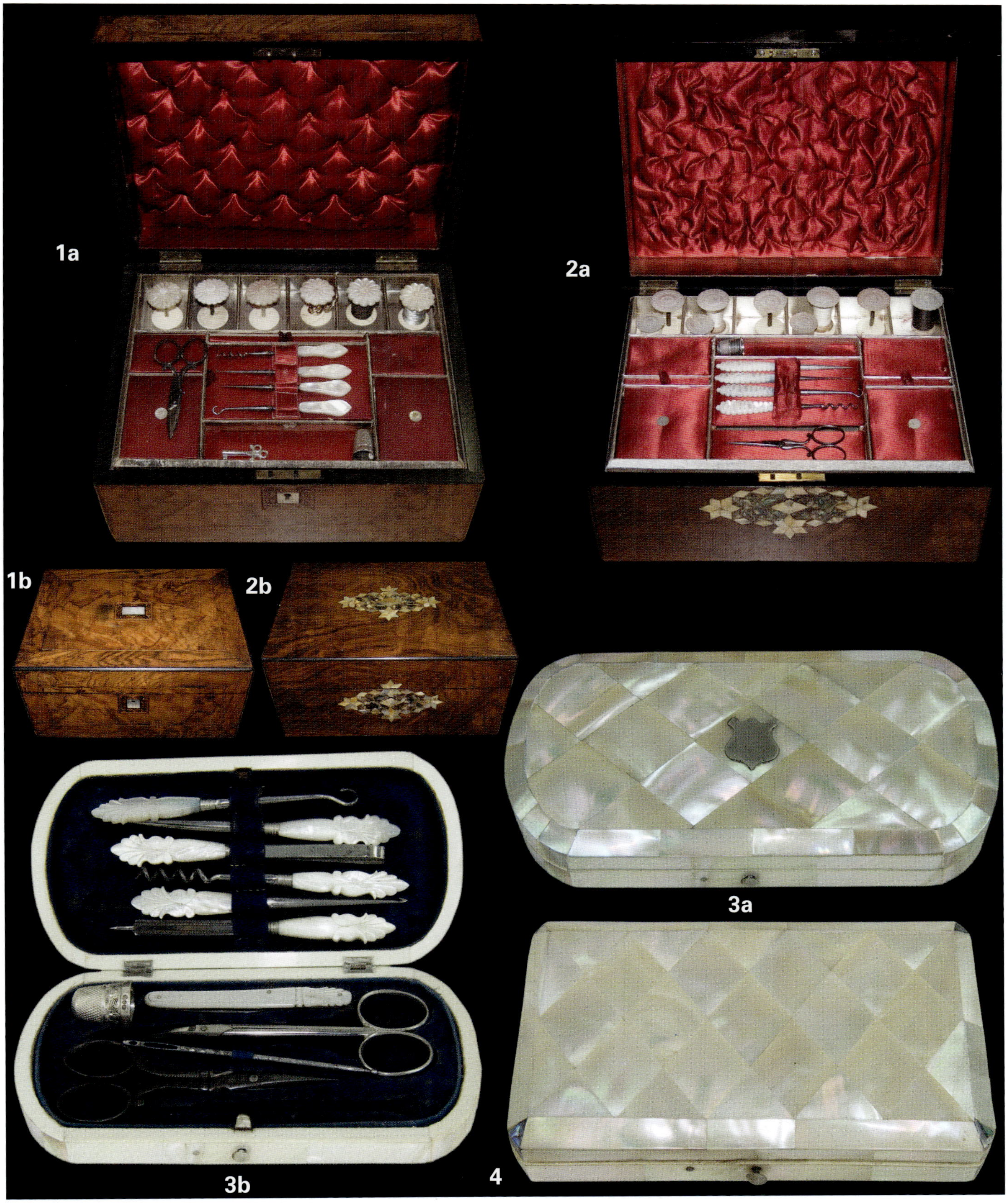


## PLATE 98 – BOXED ENGLISH SEWING SETS 3

Besides the wooden boxed sets, England also produced sewing sets in lustrous mother-of-pearl cases (item 3 and 4). **1a, 1b.** Padded red silk interior with contents of six cotton reel holders, scissors, thimble, corkscrew, stiletto, crochet hook, button hook, and needle book, c. 1850, size 11.8″ x 8.9″ (30 x 22.5 cm). **2a, 2b.** Red interior, contents: six cotton reel holders, waxer, emery, tape measure, thimble, stiletto, crochet hook, button hook, corkscrew, scissors, needle packs, c. 1870, size 11.6″ x 8.7″ (29.5 x 22 cm). **3a, 3b.** Mother-of-pearl case, contents two scissors, pen knife, thimble, needle, button hook, file, tweezers, stiletto, and crochet hook, c. 1875–90, size 6.1″ x 3″ (15.5 x 7.6 cm). **4.** Mother-of-pearl cased sewing set, c. 1875–90, size 6.1″ x 3.5″ (15.5 x 9 cm).

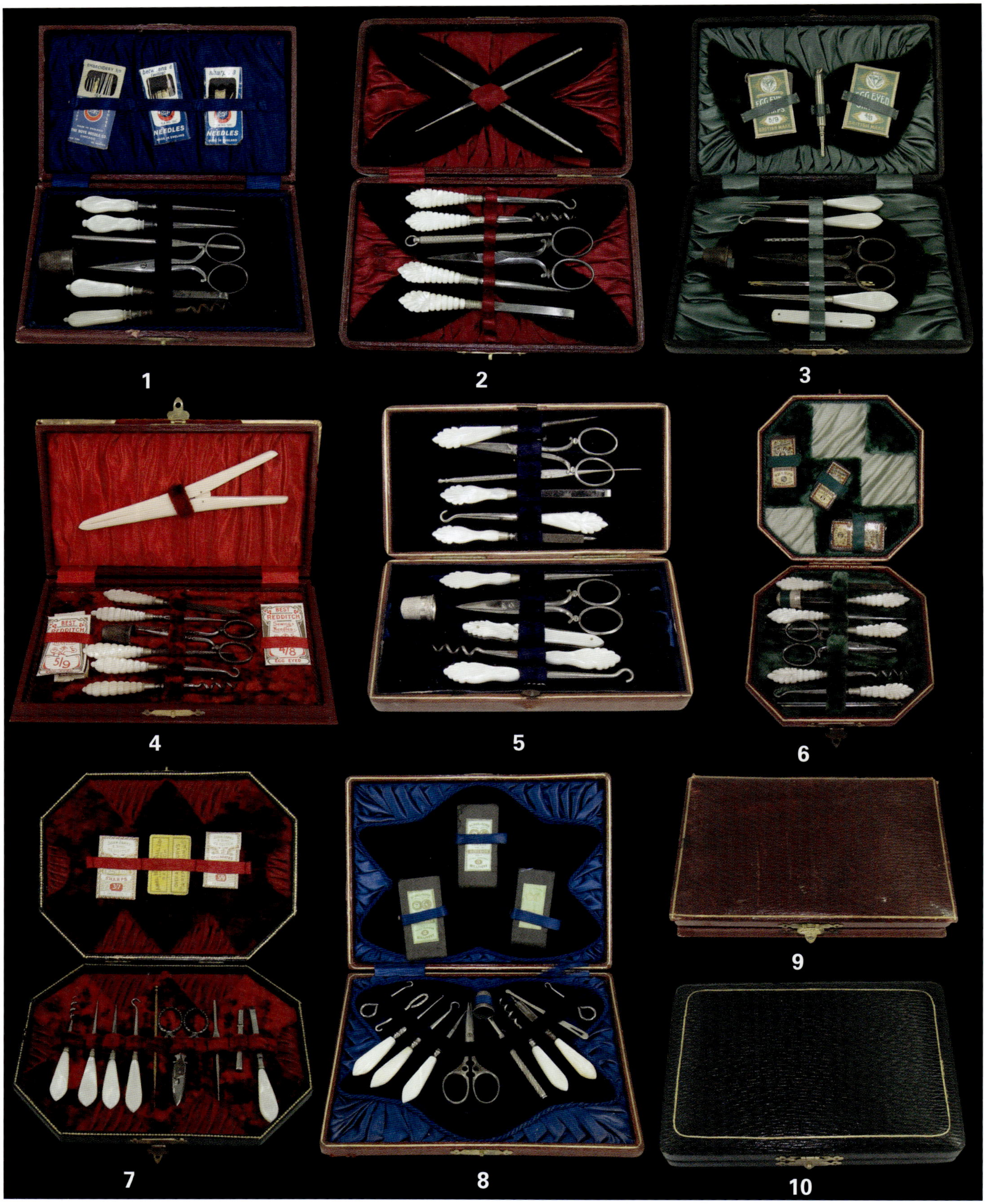


## PLATE 99 – ENGLISH SEWING SETS 1

Mother-of-pearl handled sewing tools were very popular in sewing sets made in England, which came in all shapes and sizes as this series shows. The sewing tools have a large variety of differently carved pearl handles. Production was from 1850 to 1920. A typical set would consist of stiletto, crochet hook, thimble, corkscrew, button hook, and packs of needles, but interestingly every set is different. **1.** Size 6.7″ x 4.1″ (17 x 10.5 cm). **2, 9.** Size 6.9″ x 4.1″ (17.5 x 10.5 cm). **3, 10.** Size 7.1″ x 4.9″ (18 x 12.5 cm). **4.** Size 7.9″ x 4.3″ (20 x 11 cm). **5.** Size 6.7″ x 3.6″ (17 x 9 cm). **6.** Size 5.3″ x 5.3″ (13.5 x 13.5 cm). **7.** Size 8.5″ x 6.1″ (21.5 x 15.5 cm). **8.** Size 7.1″ x 5.1″ (18 x 13 cm).

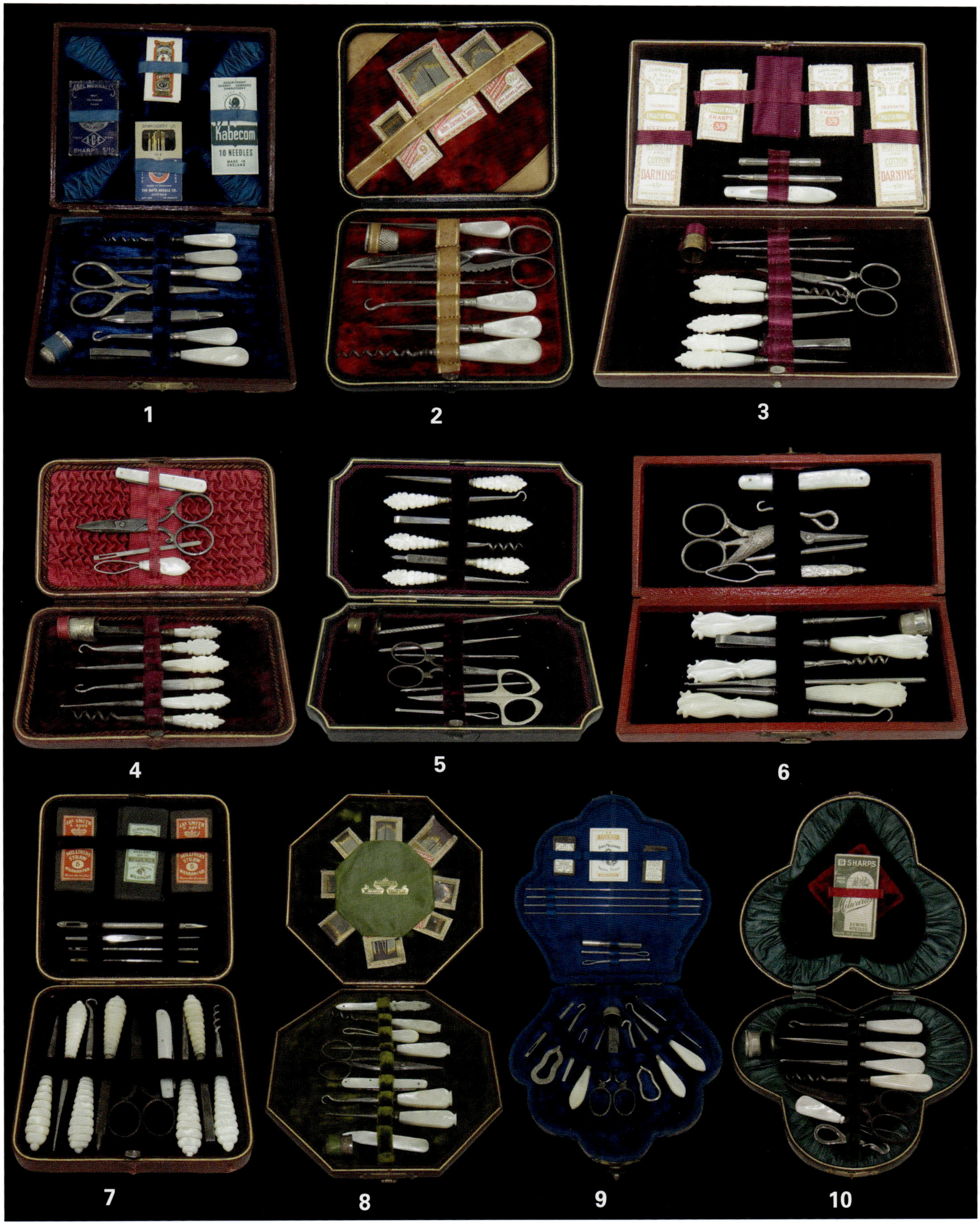


## PLATE 100 – ENGLISH SEWING SETS 2

Showing more variety in shape with different pearl handles, these sewing sets are all from England, c. 1850–1920. A typical set would consist of stiletto, crochet hook, thimble, corkscrew, button hook, and packs of needles. **1.** Size 6.2" x 5.3" (15.8 x 13.4 cm). **2.** Size 4.9" x 3.5" (12.5 x 9 cm). **3.** Size 7.9" x 4.5" (20 x 11.5 cm). **4.** Size 6.3" x 3.5" (16 x 9 cm). **5.** Size 7.3" x 4.1" (18.5 x 10.5 cm). **6.** Size 6.7" x 3.1" (17 x 7.8 cm). **7.** Size 5.1" x 5.1" (13 x 13 cm). **8.** Size 6.7" x 6.7" (17 x 17 cm). **9.** Size 7.5" x 7.1" (19 x 18 cm). **10.** Size 6.7" x 5.9" (17 x 15 cm).

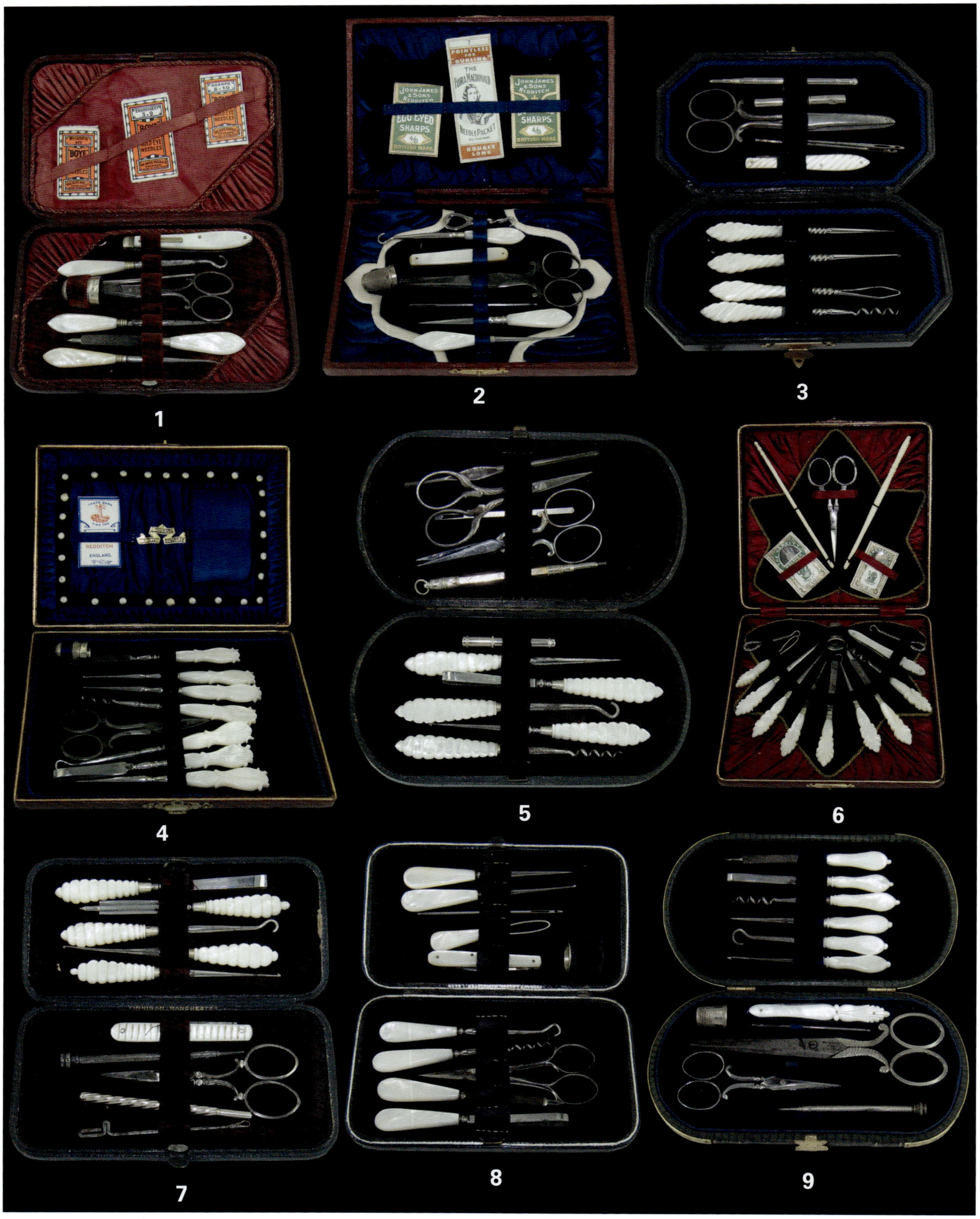


## PLATE 101 – ENGLISH SEWING SETS 3

The English sewing set, c. 1850–1920, was extremely popular in its day and the many varieties were produced to appeal to all tastes. A typical set would consist of stiletto, crochet hook, thimble, corkscrew, button hook, and packs of needles. **1.** Size 6.5″ x 3.5″ (16.5 x 9 cm). **2.** Size 7.1″ x 4.7″ (18 x 12 cm). **3.** Size 6.3″ x 3.5″ (16 x 9 cm). **4.** Size 8.1″ x 6.1″ (20.5 x 15.5 cm). **5.** Size 6.7″ x 7.5″ (17 x 19 cm). **6.** Size 6.5″ x 6.1″ (16.5 x 15.5 cm). **7.** Size 5.7″ x 3″ (14.5 x 7.5 cm). **8.** Size 5.7″ x 3.4″ (14.5 x 8.3 cm). **9.** Size 6.9″ x 3.5″ (17.5 x 9 cm).

## PLATE 102 – LADIES' COMPANIONS

**1a, 1b.** Contents thimble, scissors, stiletto, thread winder, and needle book, England, c. 1840, size 4.3" x 3.1" (10.9 x 7.8 cm). **2a, 2b.** Pearl oyster and abalone shell case, contents scissors, crochet hook, stiletto, corkscrew, thimble, needle packs, England, c. 1850–60, size 4.1" x 2.5" (10.5 x 6.3 cm). **3a, 3b.** Contents waxer, stiletto, knife, scissors, and notebook, England, c. 1840–50, size 4.1" x 2.2" (10.3 x 5.6 cm). **4a, 4b.** Contents scissors, perfume bottle, stiletto, mirror, bodkin, and thimble, England, c. 1840–50, size 4" x 2.6" (10.2 x 6.5 cm). **5a, 5b.** Brown leather case, contents: thimble, needles in packs, pearl knife, pencil, notebook, stiletto, crochet hook, scissors, needle book, and mirror, England, c. 1850–75, size 4.1" x 2.4" (10.3 x 6 cm). **6a, 6b.** Red leather case, contents: thimble, pearl sewing tools, England, c. 1850–75, size 3.7" x 2.2" (9.5 x 5.5 cm).

## PLATE 103 – ETUI, BOXED SETS

**1a, 1b.** Egg etui, center opening with contents: scissors, stiletto, needle case, bodkin, and thimble, France, c. 1880, size 6.5" x 2.4" (16.4 x 6 cm). **2a, 2b.** Egg etui, top opening, lined with material for holding sewing tools, France, c. 1880, size 6.6" x 2.4" (16.7 x 6 cm). **3a, 3b, 3c.** Egg etui with side opening and red silk lining with contents: scissors, stiletto, needle case, and bodkin, France, c. 1880, size 6.7" x 4.7" (17 x 12 cm). **4.** Sewing etui inscribed *Souvenir* and *D'amitie* (friendship), France, c. 1750–1800, size 3.3" x 1.7" (8.3 x 4.4 cm). **5.** Etui to carry daily essentials such as sewing tools and writing items, Canton, China, for the export market, c. 1830, size 4.4" x 1.8" (11.3 x 4.5 cm). **6.** Boxed crochet hook set with interchangeable hooks, France, c. 1850, box size 5.7" x 1.4" (14.4 x 3.5 cm).

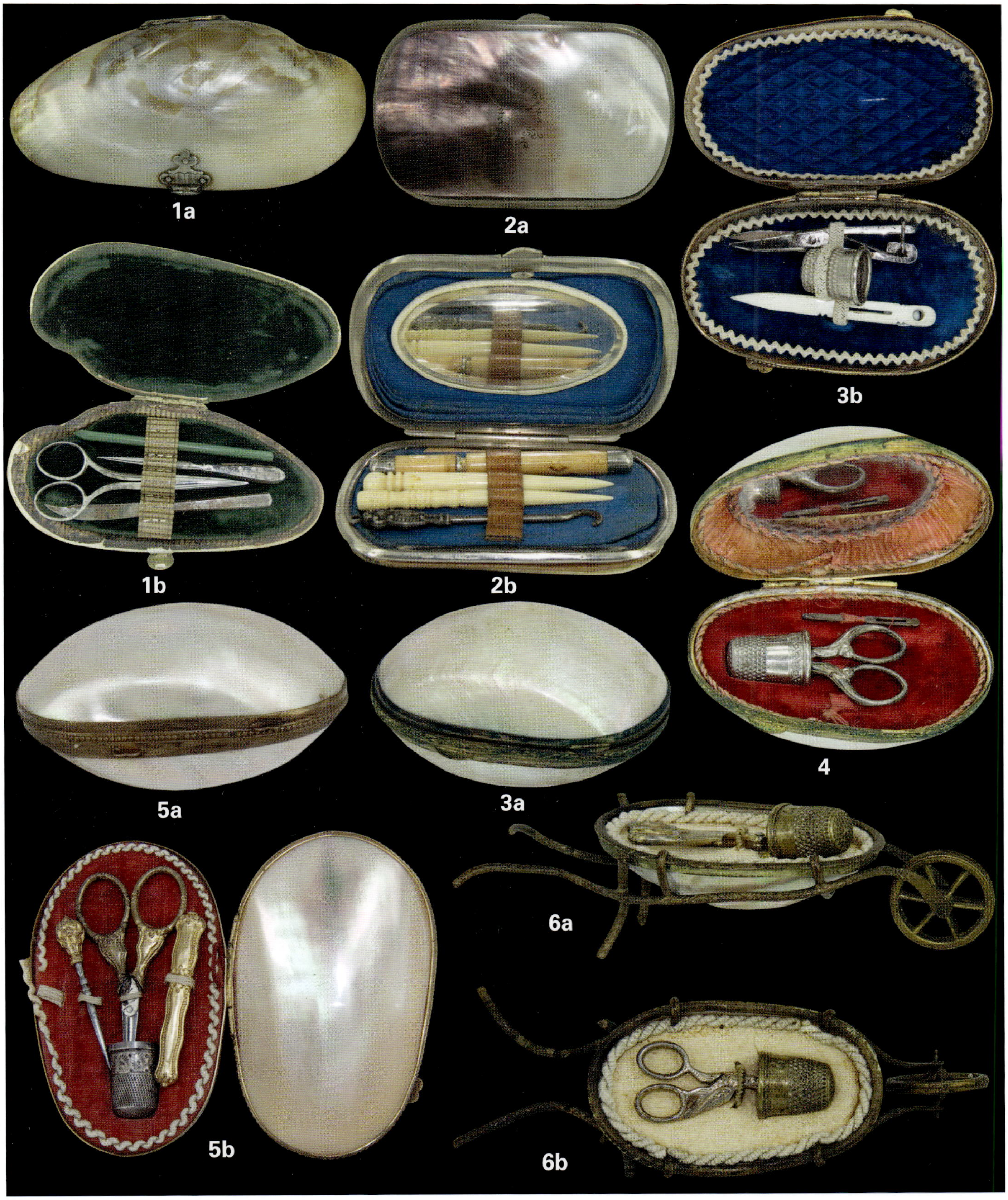


**PLATE 104 – ASSORTED SEWING SETS**

**1a, 1b.** Green velvet lined case made from a freshwater Unio pearl shell, USA, c. 1900, size 4.5″ x 2.2″ (11.5 x 5.6 cm). **2a, 2b.** Mother-of-pearl case containing a small sewing set inscribed *Souvenir Boatgate*, France, c. 1890, size 3.7″ x 2.3″ (9.3 x 5.8 cm). **3a, 3b.** Mother-of-pearl egg sewing set containing scissors, thimble, and stiletto, England, c. 1880, size 2.8″ x 1.6″ (7 x 4 cm). **4.** Mother-of-pearl egg sewing set containing thimble, scissors, and needle, France, c. 1880, size 2.8″ x 1.6″ (7 x 4 cm). **5a, 5b.** Mother-of-pearl egg sewing set containing scissors, needle case, stiletto, and thimble, France, c. 1880, size 3.7″ x 2.1″ (9.3 x 5.3 cm). **6a, 6b.** Wheelbarrow made from mother-of-pearl shell with scissors and thimble, France, c. 1880, size 4.7″ x 1.4″ (12 x 3.6 cm).

## PLATE 105 – FRENCH SCISSORS 1

Most of these scissors would have originally been from fitted sewing boxes sold in the arcades of the Palais Royal in Paris. 1. Griffin, c. 1800, size 4.2" (10.7 cm). 2. Griffin, c. 1860–80, size 4.3" (11 cm), this is a later example from the revival period with less pierced carving than earlier examples and with gold plated blades. 3. Rooster, c. 1800, size 4.4" (11.2 cm), this is the same example as illustrated by N. Taunton in her book *Antique Needlework Tools*. 4. Dog, c. 1810–20, size 4.1" (10.3 cm). 5. Pattern with the enameled pansy symbol of higher quality, c. 1810–20, size 3.7" (9.4 cm). 6. Spire in circle, c. 1810–20, size 3.7" (9.4 cm). 7. Urn shape, c. 1810–20, size 3.9" (10 cm). 8. Scallop shape, c. 1810–20, size 3.5" (9 cm), the blades are English, the carving French, so these are most likely replacement blades.

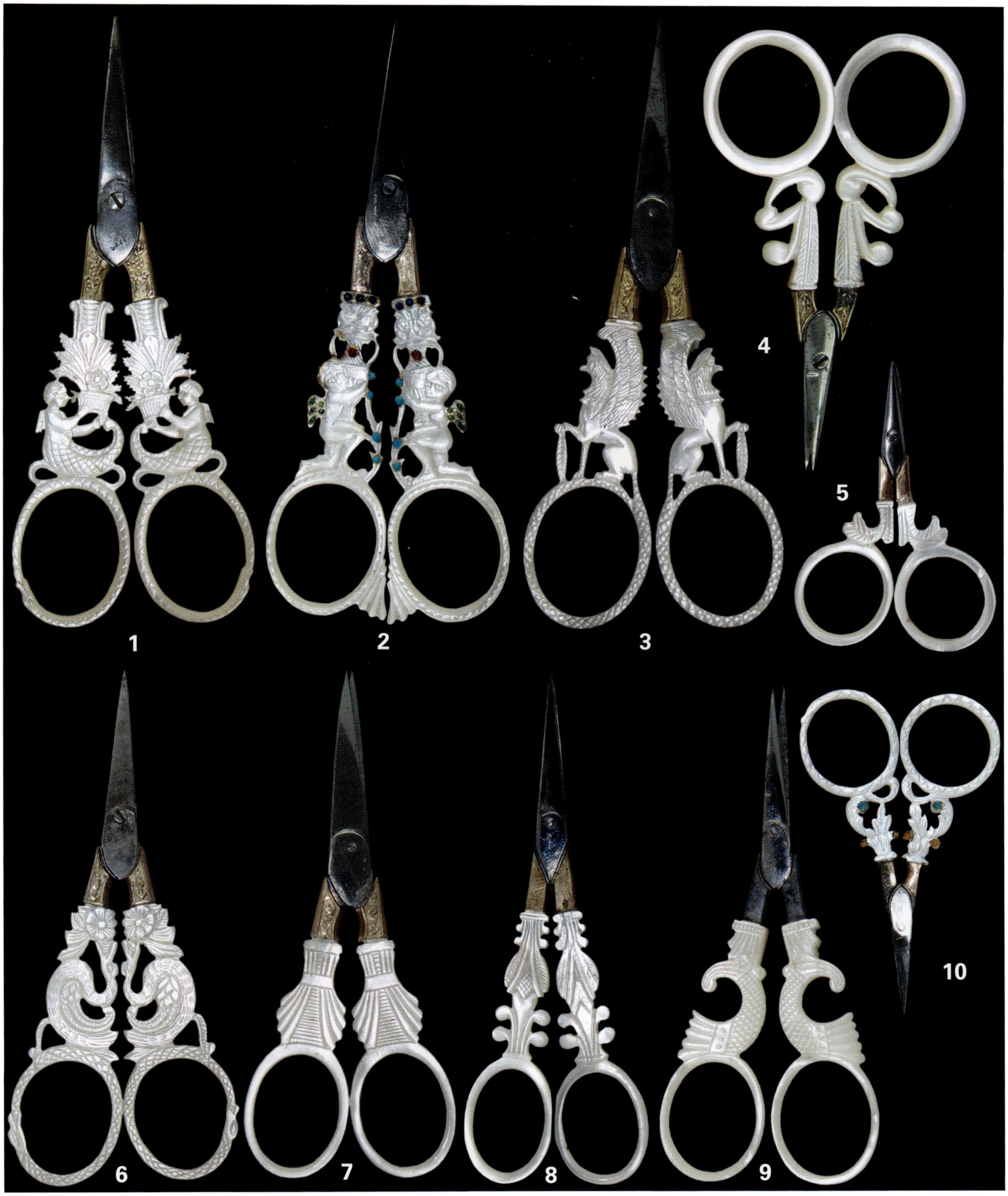


## PLATE 106 – FRENCH SCISSORS 2

Most of these scissors would have originally been from fitted sewing boxes sold in the arcades of the Palais Royal in Paris, c. 1810–20. The smaller sized scissors were usually a second pair seen in the larger sewing boxes. **1.** Mermaid, with a handle of a snake eating its tail also known as an ouroborus, an ancient symbol representing continuity and the cycle of life, size 3.8" (9.6 cm). **2.** Putti, with gemstone decoration, size 3.9" (10 cm). **3.** Griffin, size 3.8" (9.6 cm). **4.** Patterned, size 2.7" (6.9 cm). **5.** Miniature, size 2.3" (5.9 cm). **6.** Swan, with snake handle like number 1, size 3.9" (9.8 cm). **7.** Scallop pattern, size 3.5" (8.8 cm). **8.** Patterned, size 4.1" (10.3 cm). **9.** Patterned, size 3.3" (8.5 cm). **10.** Small-sized, with gemstone decoration, size 2.7" (6.8 cm).

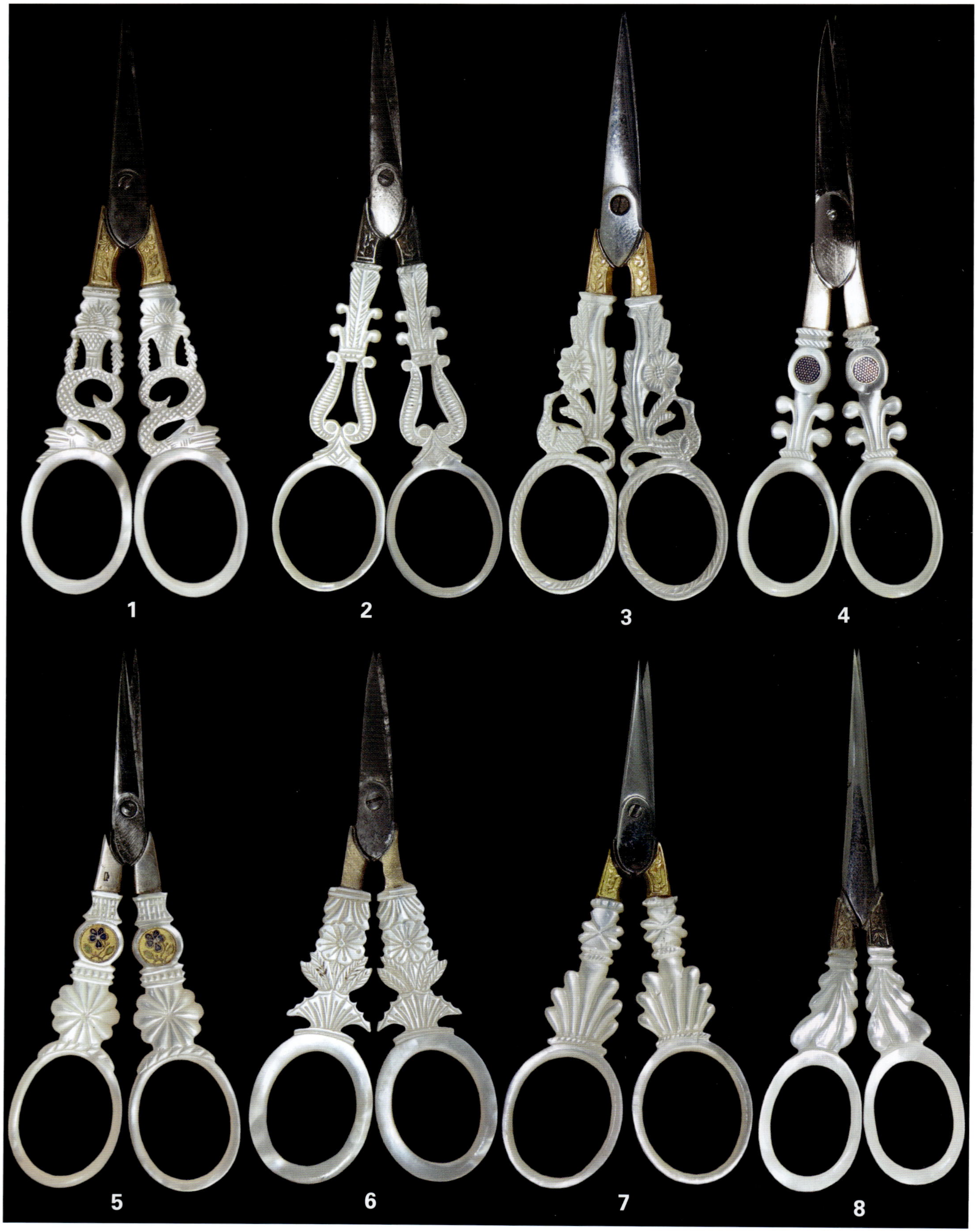


## PLATE 107 – FRENCH SCISSORS 3

Most of these scissors would have originally been from fitted sewing boxes sold in the arcades of the Palais Royal in Paris, c. 1810–20. **1.** Snake, size 3.9" (10 cm). **2.** Lyre, size 4.1" (10.3 cm). **3.** Birds, size 3.9" (9.8 cm). **4.** Pattern, size 3.9" (10 cm). **5.** Flower with enameled pansy symbol of higher quality, size 3.1" (8 cm). **6.** Patterned, size 3.5" (8.8 cm). **7.** Scallop shape, size 3.5" (9 cm). **8.** Patterned, size 3.9" (10 cm).

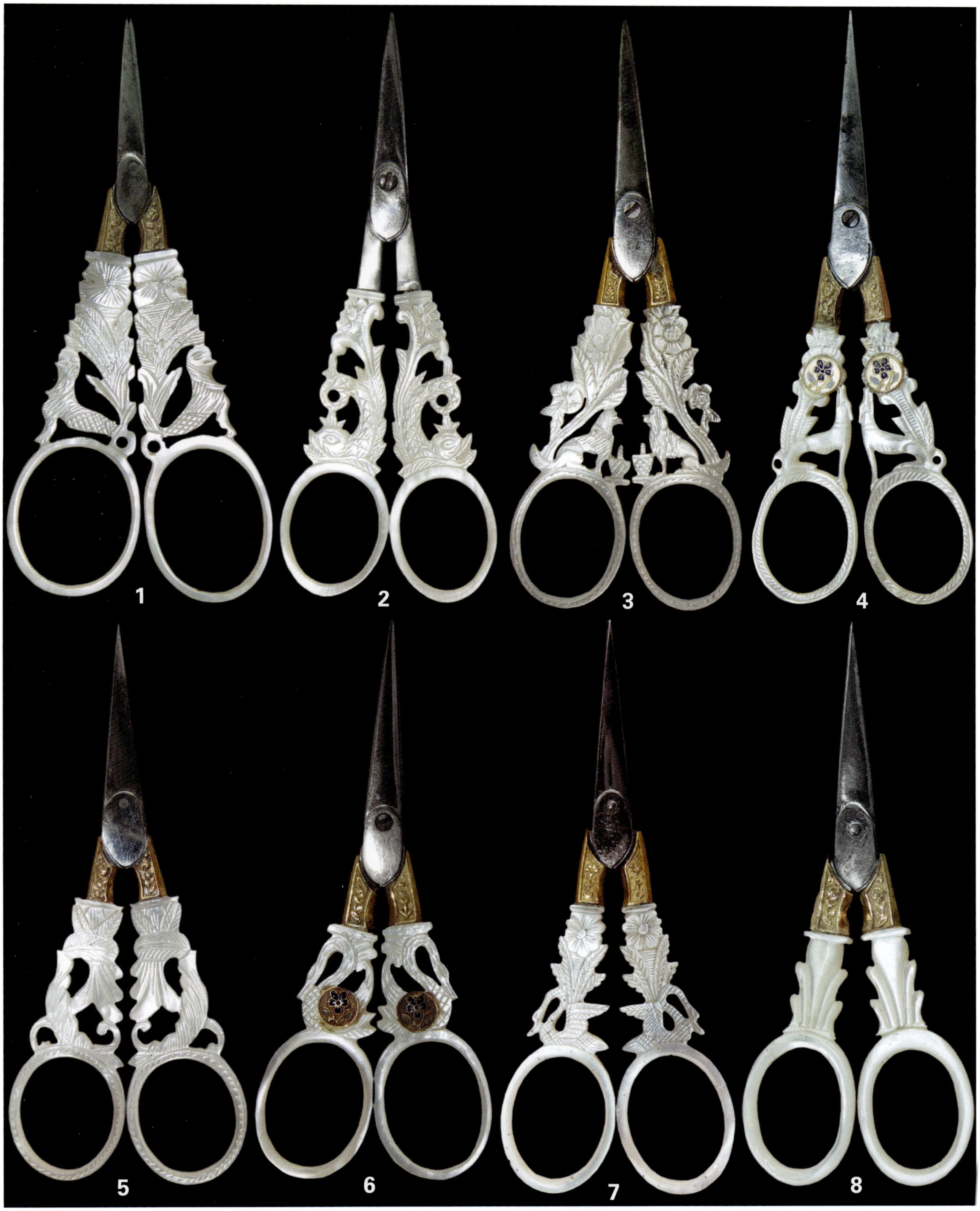


## PLATE 108 – FRENCH SCISSORS 4

Most of these scissors would have originally been from fitted sewing boxes sold in the arcades of the Palais Royal in Paris, c. 1810–20, some with the enameled pansy symbol of higher quality. 1. Seal, size 3.8″ (9.6 cm). 2. Dolphin, size 4.1″ (10.3 cm). 3. Dog, size 3.9″ (10 cm), the two handles do not match exactly, indicating two different carvers might have been involved in production, or one handle was a later replacement. 4. Greyhound, size 3.5″ (9 cm). 5. Floral pattern, size 3.9″ (10 cm). 6. Swan, size 3.1″ (8 cm). 7. Swan, size 3.9″ (10 cm). 8. Pattern, size 2.8″ (7 cm).

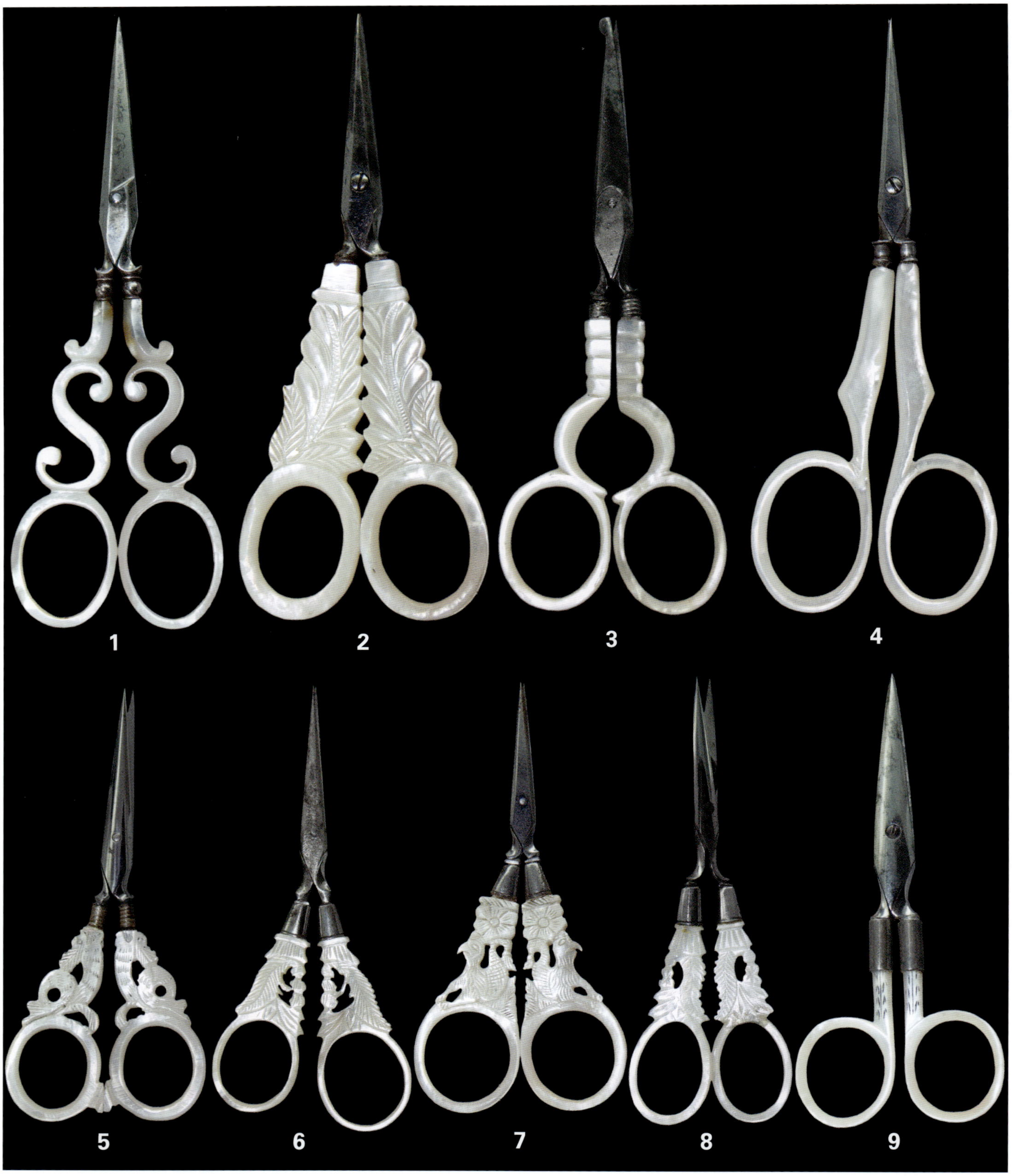

1 2 3 4 5 6 7 8 9

## PLATE 109 – ENGLISH, FRENCH, and GERMAN SCISSORS 1

The carved pearl-handled scissors (items 5–8) were originally thought to have been French, but are now considered English and were found in sets called ladies' companions or fitted sewing boxes. The carving is not as intricate as the French, and the blades are different to the French examples. **1.** Scroll carving, England, c. 1850, size 4.1" (10.5 cm). **2.** Floral decoration, England, c. 1840–50, size 3.8" (9.6 cm). **3.** Scissors used in Carrickmacross lace work, England, c. 1850, size 3.9" (9.8 cm). **4.** Sewing scissors, Germany, c. 1900, size 4.1" (10.3 cm). **5.** Floral, England, c. 1840–50, size 3.7" (9.3 cm). **6.** Floral, England, c. 1840–50, size 4.3" (11 cm). **7.** Bird-like, England, c. 1840–50, size 4.1" (10.5 cm). **8.** Floral, England, c. 1840–50, size 4.5" (11.5 cm). **9.** France, c. 1890, size 3.1" (8 cm).

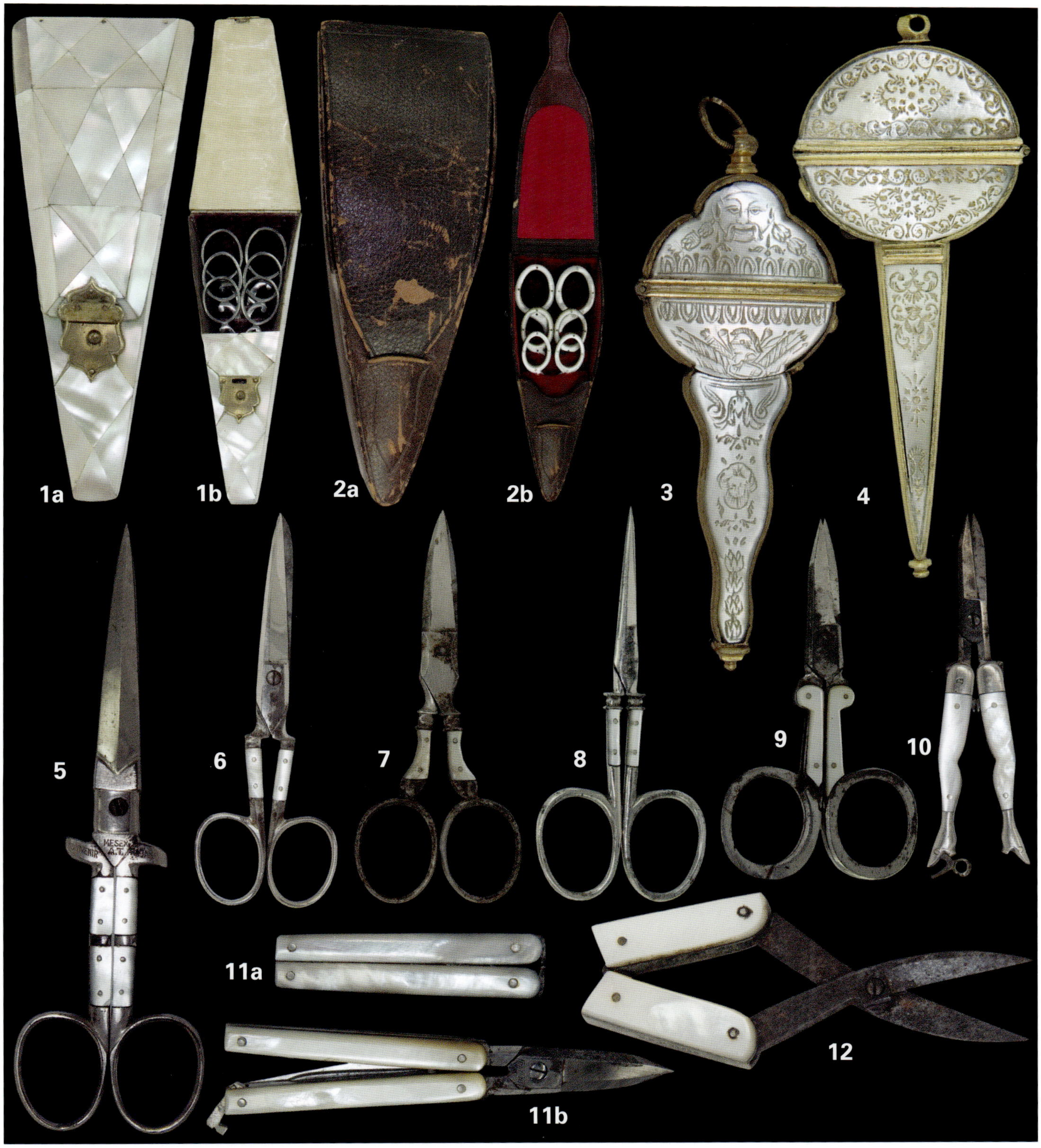


## PLATE 110 – ENGLISH, FRENCH, and GERMAN SCISSORS 2

**1a, 1b.** Scissor case with three scissors inscribed *Brookes Crookes*, England, c. 1870, size 6" x 2.4" (15.3 x 6 cm). **2a, 2b.** Leather scissor case with three pearl-handled scissors inscribed *Ed Husihof Solingen*, Germany, c. 1880–90, size 6" x 2.3" (15.3 x 5.8 cm). **3.** Pearl case for scissors from a chatelaine, France, c. 1730, size 3.9" x 1.4" (10 x 3.5 cm). **4.** Pearl case for scissors from a chatelaine, France, c. 1740, size 3.7" x 1.6" (9.5 x 4 cm). **5.** Dagger scissors, inscribed *Souvenir Habana Mesex At*, Germany for export market, c. 1910, size 6.3" (16 cm). **6.** Inscribed *Germany*, c. 1900, size 4.6" (11.6 cm). **7.** Inscribed *Germany*, c. 1880, size 4.3" (11 cm). **8.** Inscribed *NDH CO Germany*, c. 1890, size 3.5" (8.8 cm). **9.** Sewing machine scissors, Germany, c. 1890, size 4" (10.1 cm). **10.** Folding scissors, leg shape, Germany, c. 1890, size 2.3" (5.9 cm). **11a, 11b.** Treadle sewing machine scissors, Germany, c. 1875–90, size 2.3" closed, 4.1" open (5.9 cm–10.3 cm). **12.** Folding seamstress scissors, Germany, c. 1875–1900, size 3.5" (9 cm).

## PLATE 111 – BODKINS and BODKIN CASES

1–8. Bodkin cases, France, c. 1750–70, showing variety in size and design. 1. Size 5.5" x 0.9" (14 x 2.2 cm) diameter. 2. Size 4.5" x 0.8" (11.5 x 2 cm) diameter. 3. Size 4.4" x 0.6" (11.3 x 1.6 cm) diameter. 4. Size 4.1" x 0.6" (10.5 x 1.6 cm diameter). 5. Size 4.1" x 0.7" (10.5 x 1.8 cm) diameter. 6. Size 4" x 0.6" (10.2 x 1.5 cm) diameter. 7. Size 3.7" x 0.8" (9.3 x 2.1 cm) diameter. 8. Size 3.1" x 0.8" (7.8 x 2 cm) diameter. 9. Bodkin case, inscribed *M.E.Ball,* England, c. 1845–65, size 3.9" x 1.3" (10 x 3.3 cm). 10–25. Bodkins from fitted sewing sets that would have sold in the arcades of Palais Royal, France, c. 1800–20, size 2.1" to 2.9" (5.4 to 7.4 cm), showing variety in design (#11 in the shape of a fish or eel is exceptional). 26, 27. Bodkins, England, c. 1890, size 2" to 2.8" (5.2 to 7 cm). 28, 29. Bodkins, USA, c. 1900, size 3" to 3.1" (7.5 to 8 cm).

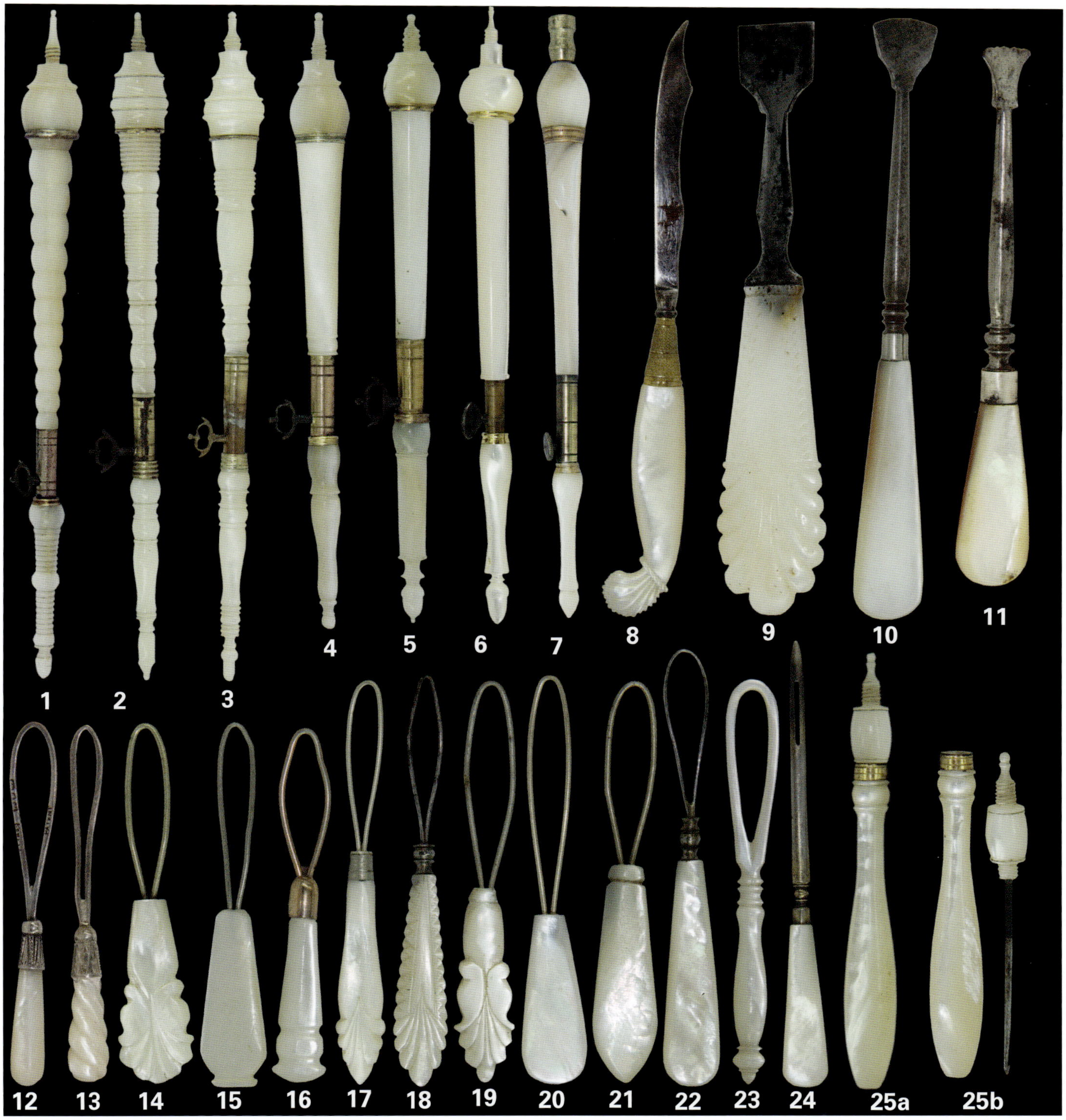


## PLATE 112 – SEWING TOOLS

The tambours (instruments designed to hold a variety of sizes of hooks for tambour embroidery) are all from fitted sewing sets that sold in the arcades of the Palais Royal in Paris. **1.** Tambour with fancy carving, France, c. 1800–1820, size 5.6″ (14.2 cm). **2.** Tambour with fancy carving, France, c. 1800–1820, size 5.6″ (14.2 cm). **3.** Tambour with fancy carving, France, c. 1800–1820, size 5.5″ (14 cm). **4.** Tambour, France, c. 1800–1820, size 4.9″ (12.5 cm). **5.** Tambour, France, c. 1800–1820, size 4.2″ (10.7 cm). **6.** Tambour with solid screw, France, c. 1800–1820, size 04.6″ (11.8 cm). **7.** Tambour with metal screw top that fits on top of the pearl spire lid, France, c. 1800–1820, size 5.1″ (13 cm). **8.** Seam cutter or ripper, France, c. 1820, size 5″ (12.7 cm). **9.** Buttonhole chisel, England, c. 1850, size 3.9″ (10 cm). **10.** Buttonhole chisel, England, c. 1850, size 3.9″ (10 cm). **11.** Buttonhole chisel, England, c. 1850, size 2.8″ (7 cm). **12, 13.** Ribbon threader, Adie & Lovekin, Birmingham, England, 1863, size 2.3″ (5.8 cm). **14–22.** Ribbon threader, England, c. 1860–1900, size 2.2″ to 3.9″ (5.5 to 9.8 cm). **23.** Solid pearl ribbon threader, France, c. 1810, size 2.4″ (6.1 cm). **24.** Ribbon threader, England, c. 1880, size 4.7″ (12 cm). **25a, 25b.** Lace picker ex Palais Royal sewing set, France, c. 1820, size 3.1″ (8 cm).

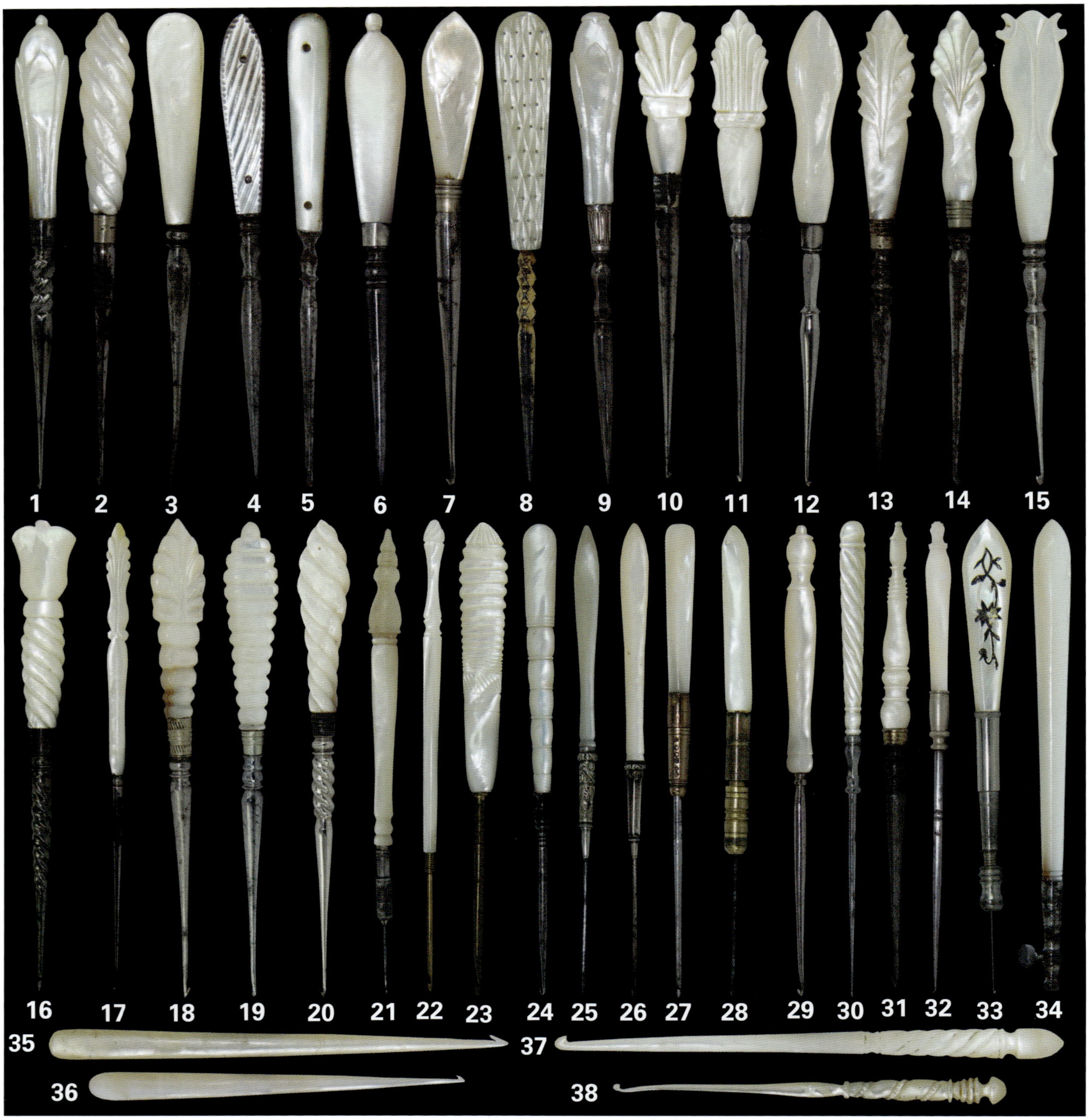


## PLATE 113 – CROCHET HOOKS

Crochet comes from the French word for little hook. There are two varieties: the solid form and one with an interchangeable hook. The latter examples were originally supplied with a range of hooks, but few of these have survived. **1–20.** Many different designed pearl handles for crochet hooks were produced during a seventy year period of peak popularity. Many were found in fitted sewing sets together with a matching set of sewing tools, England, c. 1850–1920, size from 3.6″ to 4.6″ (9.2 cm to 11.6 cm). **21.** Interchangeable hook, France, c. 1850, size 5.5″ (13.9 cm). **22, 23.** Reproduction, Bahamas, 2002, size 4.4″ to 4.8″ (11.3 to 12.2 cm). **24.** Crochet hook with interchangeable hook, England, c. 1860, size 5.7″ (14.5 cm). **25, 26.** With interchangeable hook, France, c. 1850, size 5.1″ (13 cm). **27, 28.** Front part interchangeable, inscribed *J Coney 6 Oct 46*, England, 1846, size 4.13″ to 4.4″ (10.5 to 11.3 cm). **29–32.** France, c. 1880, size 4.3″ to 4.7″ (11 to 12 cm). **33.** Front hook interchangeable, France, c. 1880, size 4.5″ (11.5 cm). **34.** Thumb screw for changing crochet hooks, England, c. 1830–40, size 4.1″ (10.3 cm). **35, 36.** Solid pearl crochet hook, England, c. 1860, size 3.6″ & 4.3″ (9.2 cm & 10.8 cm). **37, 38.** Solid pearl crochet hook, France, c. 1820–30, size 3.9″ & 4.9″ (10 cm & 12.5 cm).

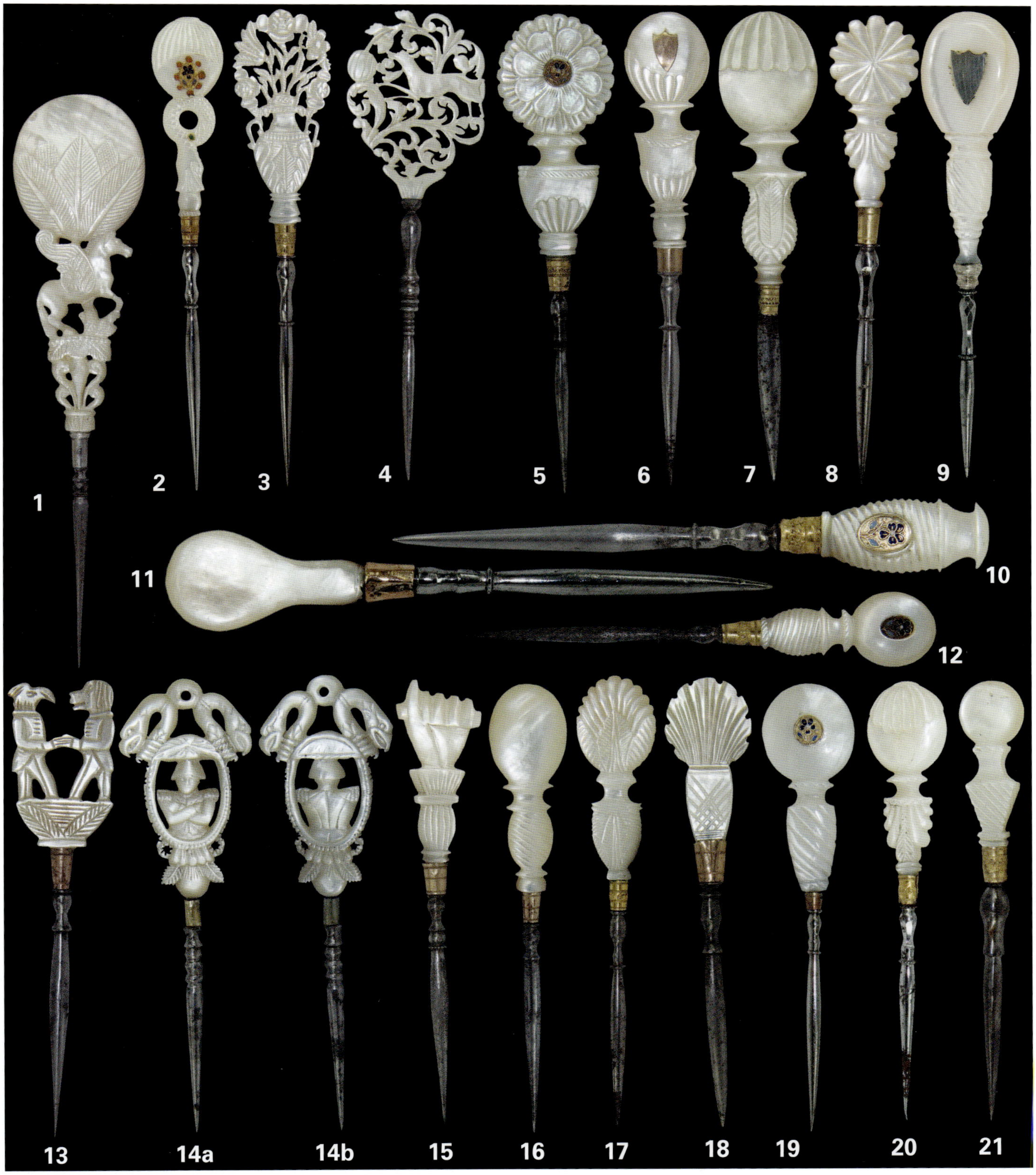


## PLATE 114 – FRENCH STILETTOS

Stilettos were used to make holes in material and had the advantage that they would not cut or tear the material. The selections on this page all came from France, and would have been found in fitted sewing boxes as were sold in the arcades of the Palais Royal, Paris, France, c. 1800–1820, some with the enameled pansy symbol of higher quality. **1.** Exceptionally large, with a carving of Pegasus in the stem, size 6.5″ (16.5 cm). **2.** A snake is carved into the stem with gemstone decoration, size 4.9″ (12.5 cm). **3.** Vase of flowers, size 4.1″ (10.5 cm). **4.** Dog in a floral design, size 4.9″ (12.5 cm). **5–12.** Assorted designs, size 3.1″ to 4.7″ (8 to 12 cm). **13.** Two military personnel characterized as a dog and eagle, perhaps referring to England-USA alliance, size 3.2″ (8.2 cm). **14a, 14b.** Napoleon with two eagles, the symbol of his new French empire, size 4.1″ (10.4 cm). **15–21.** Assorted designs, size 3.1″ to 4.7″ (8 to 12 cm).

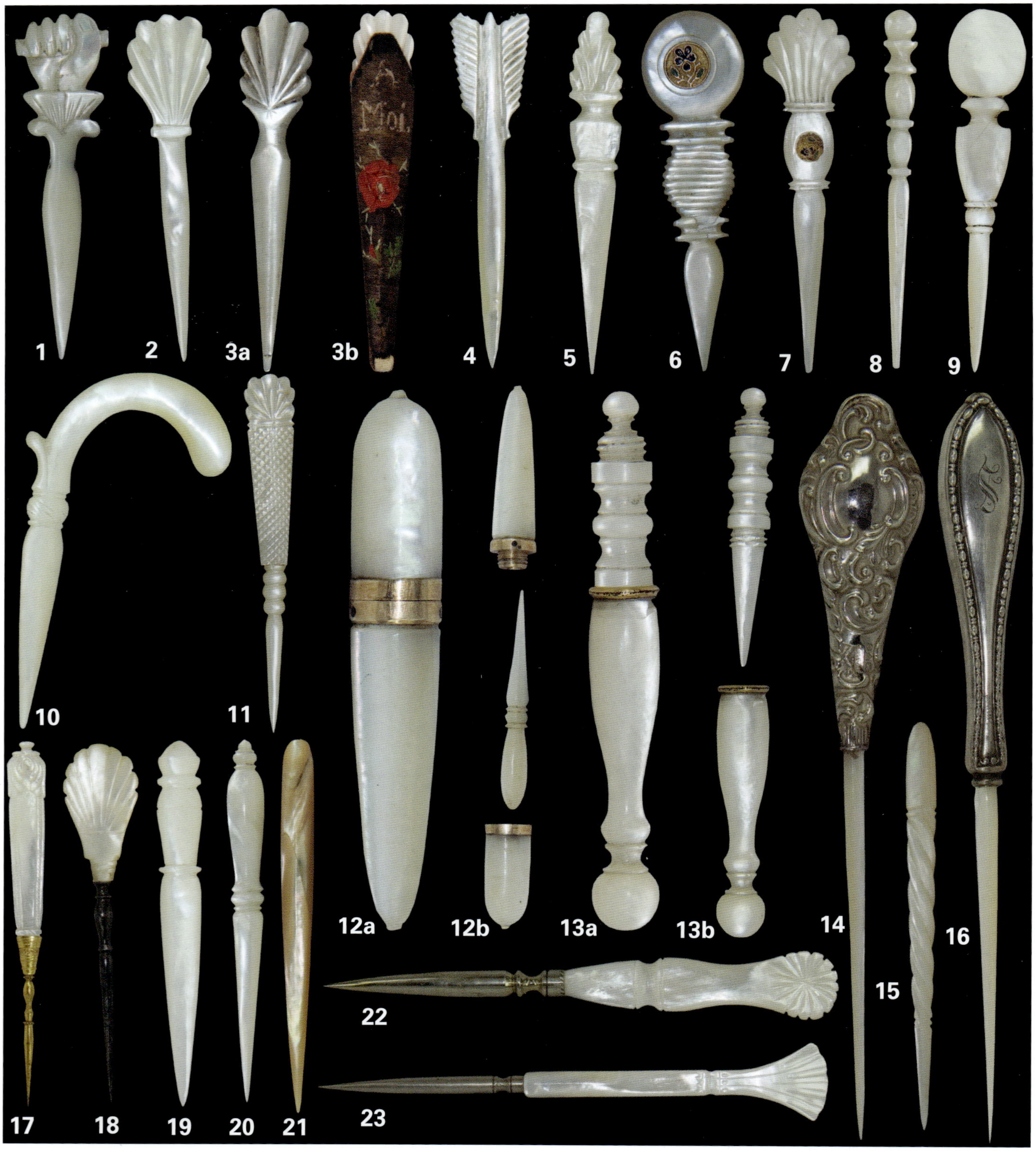


## PLATE 115 – FRENCH and WORLD STILETTOS

**1–9.** Solid mother-of-pearl stiletto, France, c. 1800–1820, some with the enameled pansy symbol of higher quality, size 1.9" to 3.1" (4.8 to 7.8 cm); item 3 has its own embroidered sheath. **10.** Rare design from a fitted sewing box, France, c. 1810, size 2.7" x 1.5" (6.8 x 3.8 cm). **11.** Carved in two pieces, France, c. 1850, size 3.3" (8.3 cm). **12a, 12b.** A small stiletto in its own mother-of-pearl case, France, c. 1810–20, size 1.9" (4.7 cm). **13a, 13b.** Stiletto which screws into a point protector, France, c. 1920, size 2.4" (6.1 cm). **14.** Large size, made by J & R Griffin, Chester, England, 1904, size 5.7" (14.5 cm). **15.** Solid pearl stiletto, France, c. 1870, size 3.3" (8.3 cm). **16.** Inscribed *sterling*, USA, c. 1890, size 6.8" (17.2 cm). **17.** Gilt steel, made during the Revival Period, France, c. 1860–80, size 5.1" (12.9 cm). **18.** Scallop shape, France, c. 1810, size 3.5" (9 cm). **19, 20.** Two solid pearl stilettos, France, c. 1810, size 2.4" (6.1 cm). **21.** Solid abalone shell, USA, c. 1880, size 2.7" (6.8 cm). **22, 23.** Modern reproduction, Bahamas, 1999, size 4.7" to 5.2" (12 to 13.2 cm).

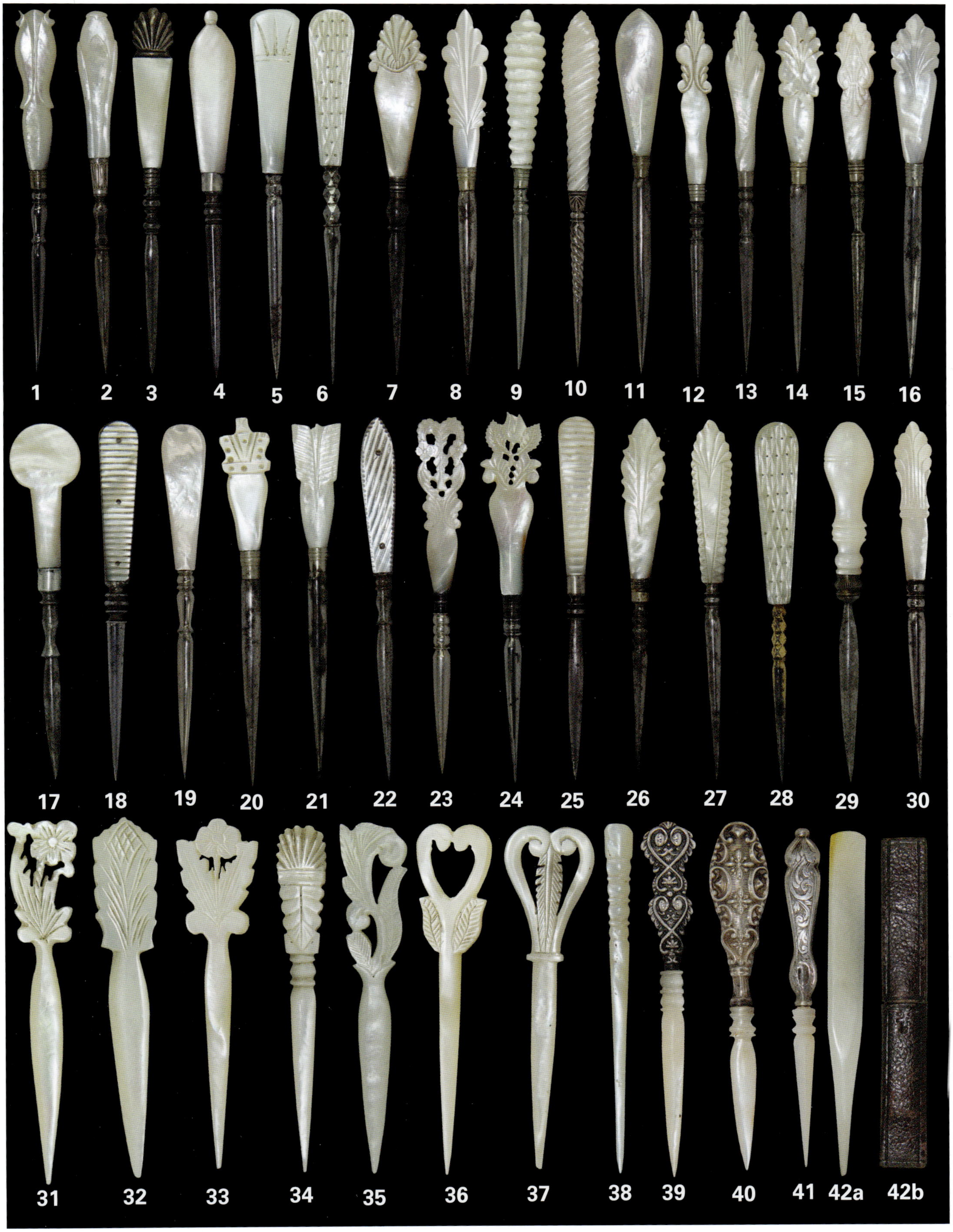

## PLATE 116 – ENGLISH STILETTOS

A large number of designs of mother-of-pearl stilettos were manufactured for over seventy years of peak popularity in England. Many were found in fitted sewing sets with a matching set of sewing tools. **1–30.** c. 1850–1920, size 3″ to 4.9″ (7.6 to 12.5 cm). **31–38.** Solid mother-of-pearl, c. 1850–70, size 2.2″ to 3.1″ (5.7 to 8 cm). **39–41.** Silver handles, c. 1840–50, size 2.6″ to 3.3″ (6.8 to 8.3 cm). **42a, 42b.** Solid mother-of-pearl stiletto in its own case, c. 1860, size 2.6″ (6.5 cm).

## PLATE 117 – NEEDLE BOOKS 1

Needle books have fabric pages used for storing needles. The fronts and backs of these needle books are made with mother-of-pearl and are often held together with ribbon ties. **1.** Bird amongst leaves, England, c. 1840–60, size 2.6″ x 1.8″ (6.5 x 4.5 cm). **2.** Flower pattern, England, c. 1840–60, size 1.8″ x 1.3″ (4.6 x 3.4 cm). **3.** Flower with dot decoration, England, c. 1840–60, size 1.7″ x 1.3″ (4.3 x 3.4 cm). **4.** Pierced flower like pattern, England, c. 1830–60, size 1.7″ x 1.4″ (4.4 x 3.5 cm). **5.** Chinese village life, might be converted from a note book, China, c. 1820–45, size 2.5″ x 2.1″ (6.4 x 5.3 cm). **6.** Chinese village life, China, c. 1820–45, size 2.4″ x 2.2″ (6.2 x 5.6 cm). **7.** Border pattern, England, c. 1840–60, size 2.1″ x 1.5″ (5.4 x 3.8 cm). **8.** Undecorated, England, c. 1860–80, size 1.7″ x 1.2″ (4.4 x 3 cm). **9.** An view of an open needle book.

## PLATE 118 – NEEDLE BOOKS 2

Needle books are fabric pages for storing needles. These fabric pages are protected within two covers of mother-of-pearl and often held together with ribbon ties. **1.** Pierced carving of flowers and leaves, England, c. 1830–60, size 2.6″ x 1.7″ (6.5 x 4.3 cm). **2.** Flower decoration, England, c. 1840–60, size 2″ x 1.5″ (5 x 3.8 cm). **3.** Pierced carving of a bird on a branch, England, c. 1830–60, size 2.2″ x 1.6″ (5.5 x 4 cm). **4.** Flower with dot decoration, England, c. 1840–60, size 1.7″ x 1.2″ (4.4 x 3 cm). **5.** Star with dot decoration, England, c. 1840–60, size 1.9″ x 1.5″ (4.8 x 3.8 cm). **6.** Heart pattern, England, c. 1830–60, size 2.5″ x 1.7″ (6.4 x 4.3 cm). **7.** Flowers in a vase, England, c. 1850–80, size 2.4″ x 1.6″ (6 x 4 cm). **8.** Leaves, England, c. 1850–80, size 2.2″ x 1.6″ (5.7 x 4 cm). **9.** Flower with leaves, England, c. 1850–80, size 2.2″ x 1.6″ (5.6 x 4 cm). **10.** Pagoda, England, c. 1850–80, size 2″ x 1.6″ (5 x 4 cm).

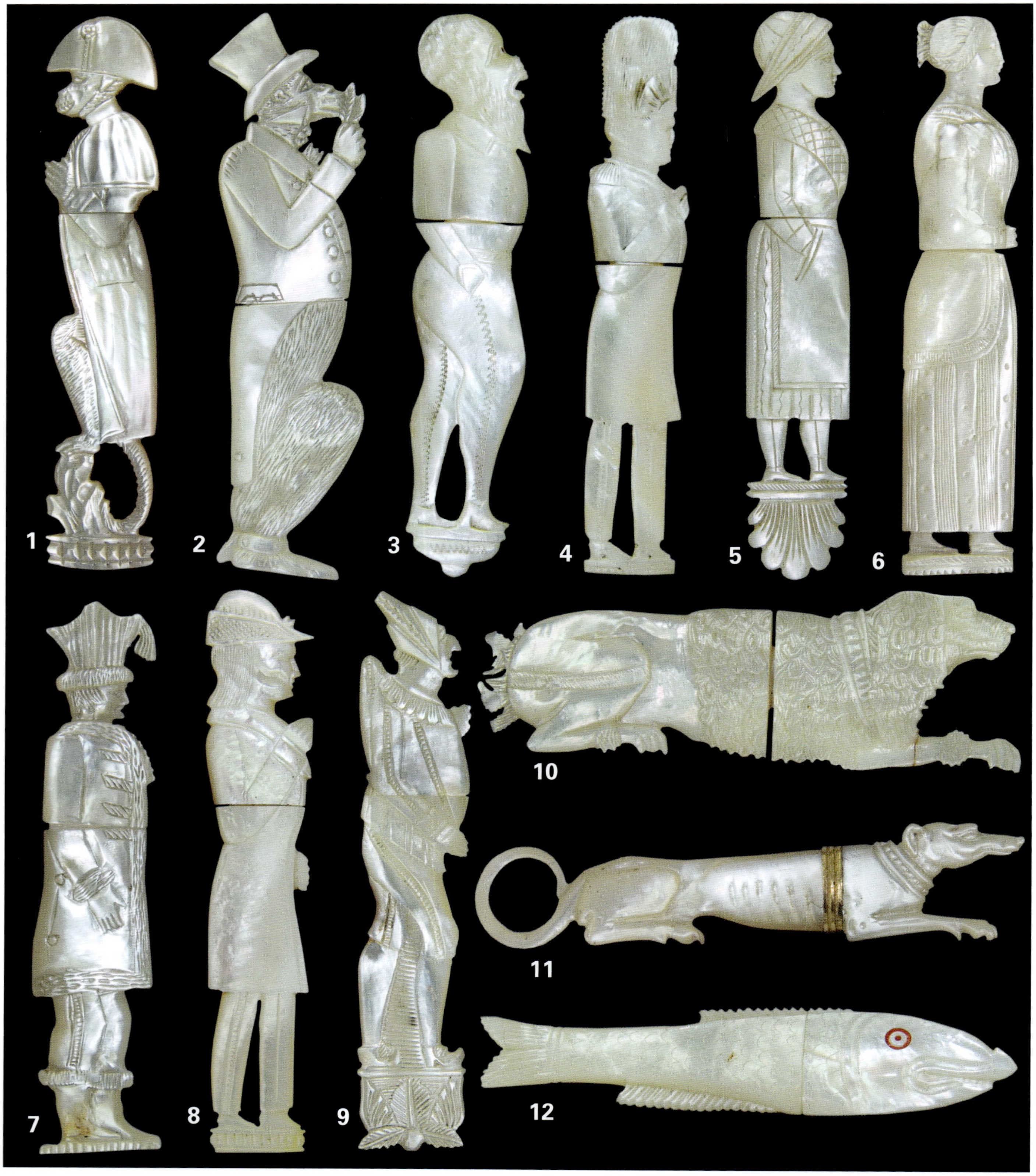


## PLATE 119 – FRENCH NEEDLE CASES 1

This selection of needle cases is from France, c. 1810–30. Many would have originally come out of fitted sewing boxes which sold in the arcades of the Palais Royal in Paris. 1. Napoleon in dress uniform, characterized as a monkey, size 3.7" x 0.7" (9.4 x 1.8 cm). 2. Napoleon drinking tea, characterized as a monkey, size 3.8" x 0.8" (9.6 x 2 cm). 3. Napoleon in uniform, characterized as a monkey, size 3.5" x 0.7" (9 x 1.7 cm). 4. Soldier with bearskin hat, size 4.3" x 0.8" (10.9 x 2 cm). 5. Lady, possibly a French Huguenot, size 4.4" x 0.8" (11.1 x 2.1 cm). 6. Columbine, a fictional character in the *Commedia dell'Arte*, size 3.7" x 0.8" (9.3 x 2 cm). 7. Soldier, size 3.1" x 0.6" (7.8 x 1.6 cm). 8. Huntsman, size 4.1" x 0.8" (10.5 x 2 cm). 9. Punchinello, a fictional character in the *Commedia dell'Arte*, size 3.8" x 0.7" (9.6 x 1.9 cm). 10. Poodle, size 3.6" x 1.1" (9.2 x 3 cm). 11. Greyhound, size 3.2" x 0.6" (8.2 x 1.5 cm). 12. Fish, inscribed *Trouville*, size 3.6" x 0.7" (9.2 x 1.9 cm).

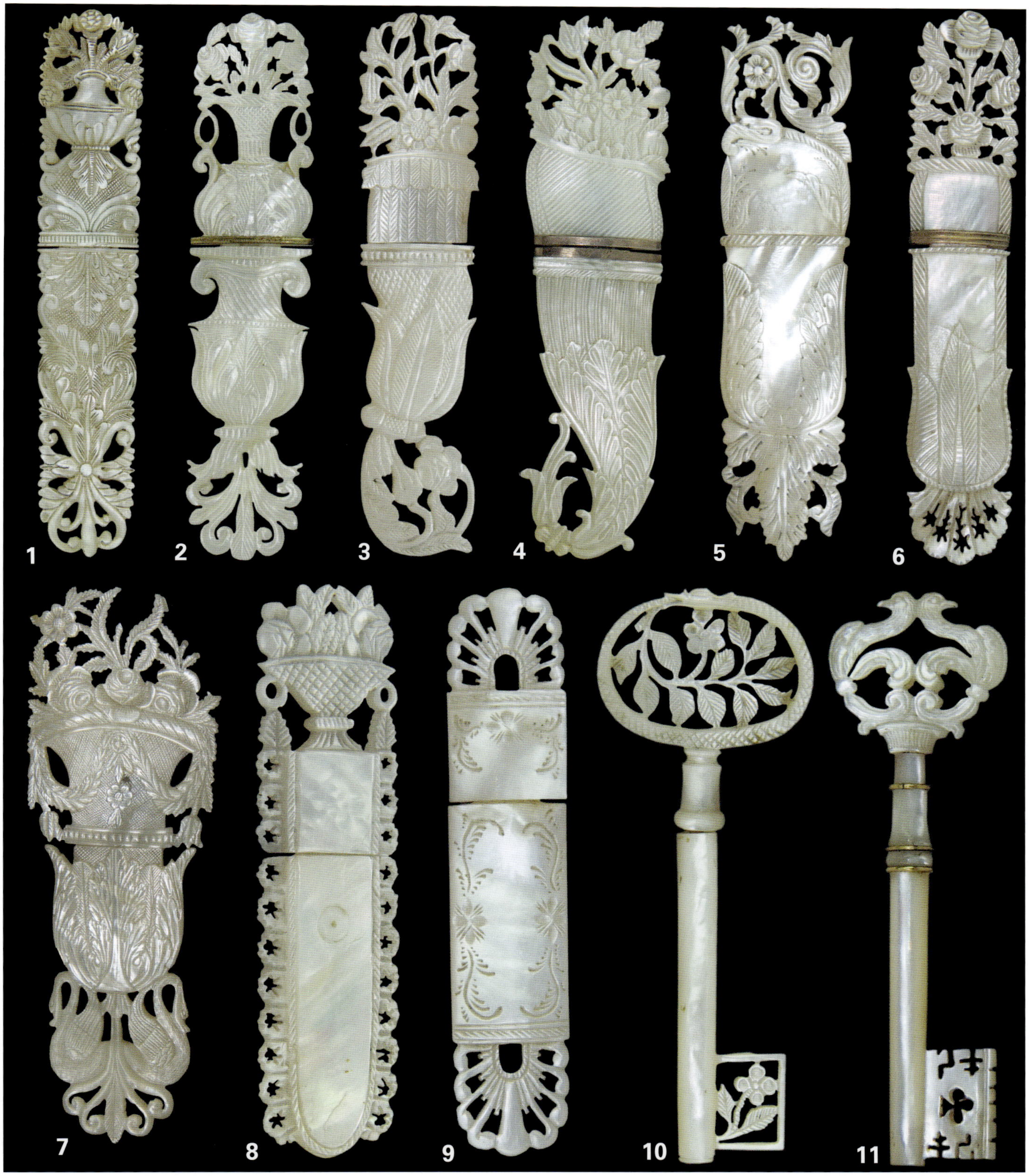


## PLATE 120 – FRENCH NEEDLE CASES 2

This selection of needle cases is from France, c. 1810–30. Many would have originally come out of fitted sewing boxes, which sold in the arcades of the Palais Royal in Paris. **1.** Urn with flowers, size 4.4" x 0.8" (11.3 x 2.1 cm). **2.** Bowl of flowers, size 4.1" x 0.9" (10.5 x 2.3 cm). **3.** Flower and floral decoration, size 4.1" x 0.9" (10.5 x 2.3 cm). **4.** Flower and floral decoration, size 4" x 1" (10.2 x 2.6 cm). **5.** Flowers, size 3.7" x 0.9" (9.5 x 2.2 cm). **6.** Flowers, size 4.2" x 0.8" (10.7 x 2 cm). **7.** Vase of flowers with imperfections , size 4.3" x 1.4" (11 x 3.6 cm). **8.** Vase of flowers, size 3.3" x 0.7" (8.4 x 1.8 cm). **9.** Decorated, size 3.3" x 0.7" (8.4 x 1.8 cm). **10.** Key shape decorated with flowers, with snake eating its tail handle also known as an ouroborus, an ancient symbol representing continuity and the cycle of life, size 4.4" x 1.6" (11.2 x 4.1 cm). **11.** Key shape with two swans, size 3" x 1" (7.7 x 2.5 cm).

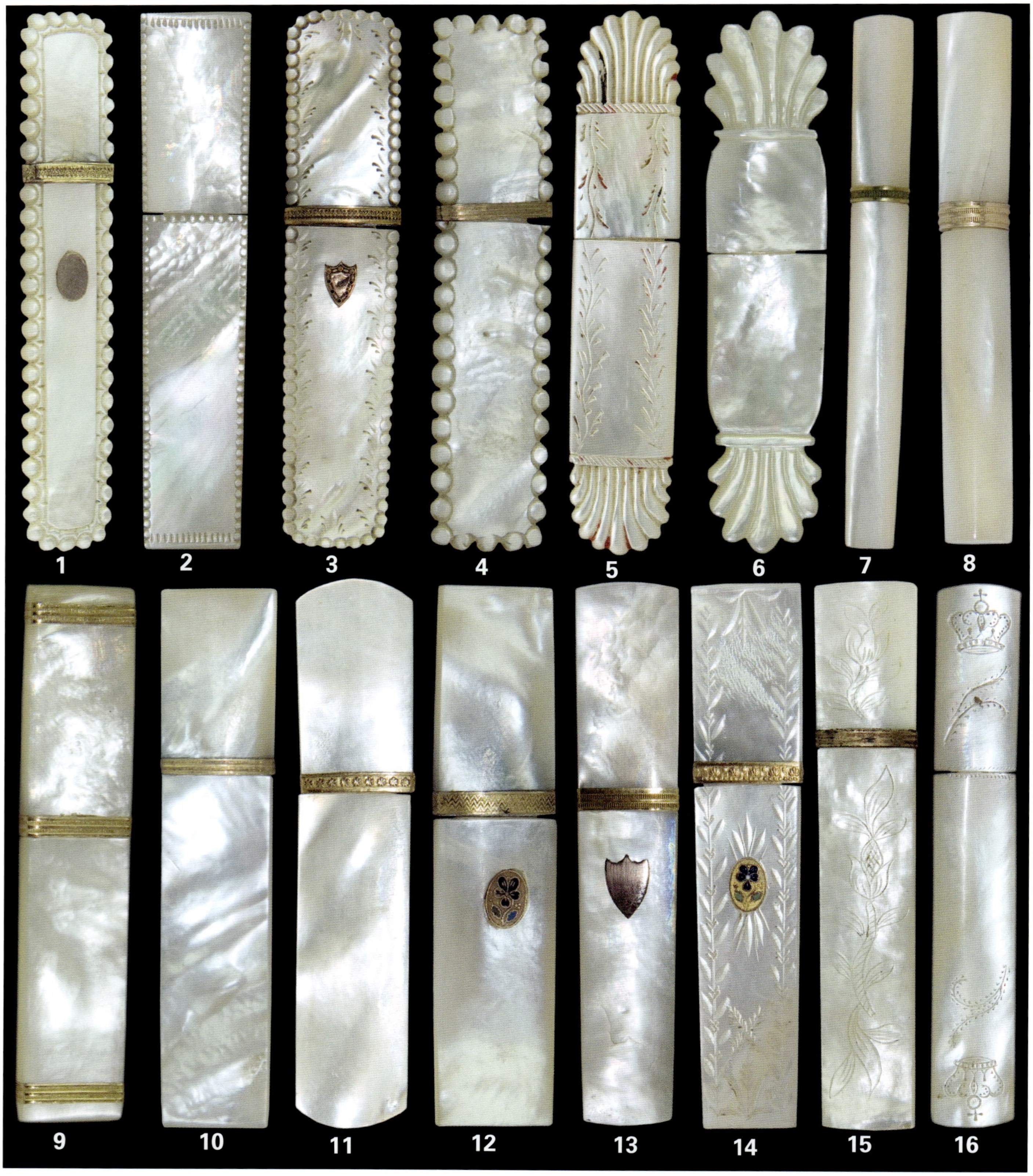


## PLATE 121 – FRENCH NEEDLE CASES 3

This selection of needle cases is from France, c. 1810–30. Many would have originally come out of fitted sewing boxes, which sold in the arcades of the Palais Royal in Paris. **1.** Gold oval, size 3.1" x 0.6" (8 x 1.5 cm). **2.** Size 3.4" x 0.7" (8.6 x 1.7 cm). **3.** Gold shield, size 3.6" x 0.7" (9.2 x 1.9 cm). **4.** Size 3" x 0.7" (7.6 x 1.7 cm). **5.** Size 3" x 0.7" (7.7 x 1.7 cm). **6.** Size 3.5" x 0.8" (9 x 2.1 cm). **7.** Tailored barrel shape, size 3" x 0.4" (7.6 x 0.9 cm). **8.** Tailored barrel shape, size 2.4" x 0.4" (6.1 x 0.9 cm). **9.** Size 3" x 0.6" (7.5 x 1.6 cm). **10.** Size 3.4" x 0.7" (8.6 x 1.8 cm). **11.** Size 3.8" x 0.7" (9.7 x 1.8 cm). **12.** With the enameled pansy symbol of higher quality, size 2.4" x 0.5" (6.2 x 1.3 cm). **13.** Gold shield, size 2.8" x 0.5" (7 x 1.3 cm). **14.** With the enameled pansy symbol of higher quality, size 2.9" x 0.6" (7.4 x 1.4 cm). **15.** Floral pattern, size 3.1" x 0.6" (7.9 x 1.5 cm). **16.** Crown representing the Infant of Prague, size 3" x 0.5" (7.5 x 1.2 cm).

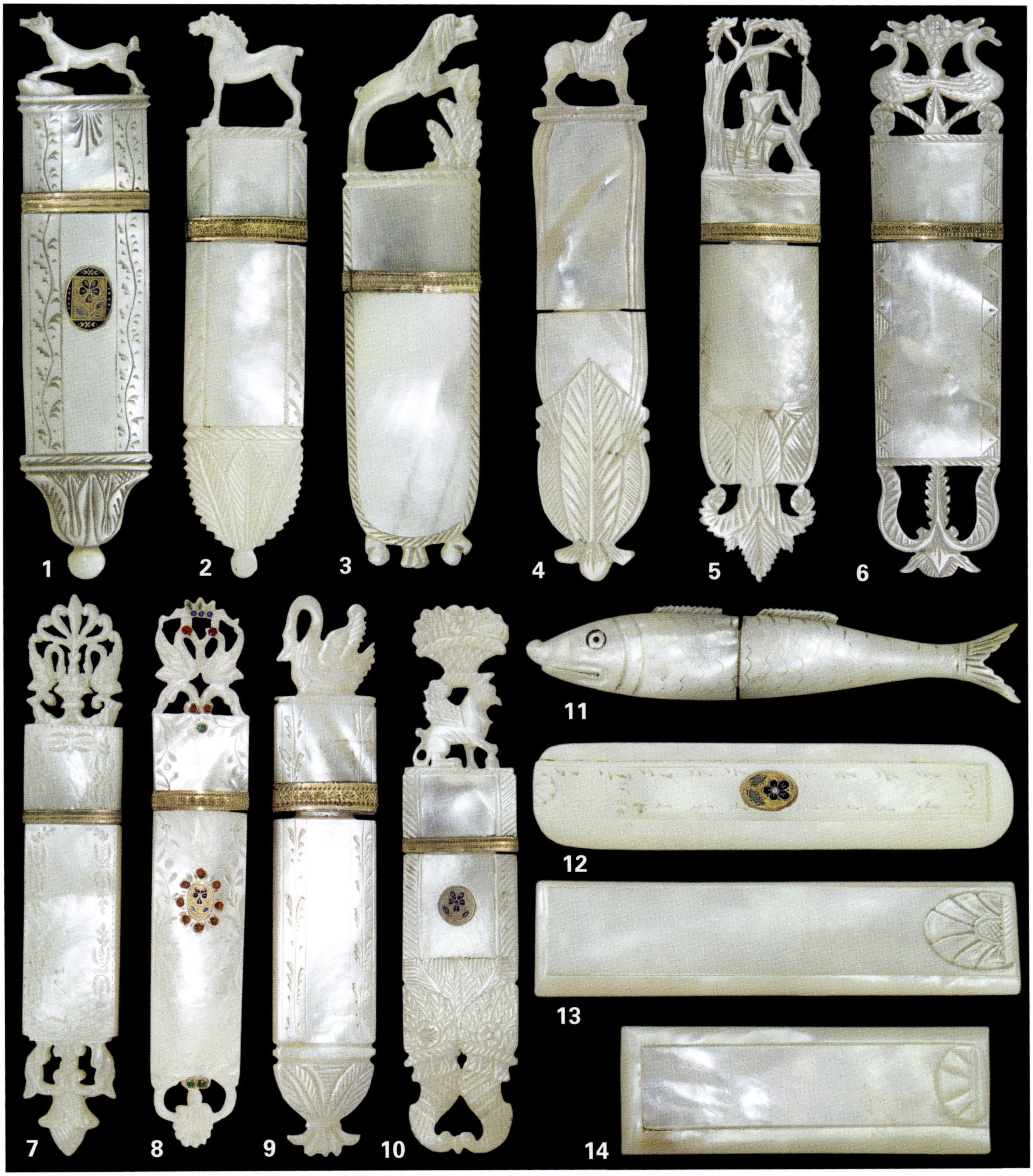


## PLATE 122 – FRENCH NEEDLE CASES 4

This selection of needle cases is from France, c. 1810–30. Many would have originally come out of fitted sewing boxes, which sold in the arcades of the Palais Royal in Paris, some with the enameled pansy symbol of higher quality. **1.** Dog, size 3.1″ x 0.7″ (7.8 x 1.8 cm). **2.** Horse, size 3.3″ x 0.7″ (8.5 x 1.8 cm). **3.** Poodle, size 3″ x 0.8″ (7.5 x 2 cm). **4.** Poodle, size 3.3″ x 0.6″ (8.3 x 1.6 cm). **5.** Soldier under a tree, size 3.6″ x 0.8″ (9.1 x 2 cm). **6.** Two swans, size 3.5″ x 0.8″ (9 x 2.1 cm). **7.** Two swans, size 4.3″ x 0.7″ (11 x 1.9 cm). **8.** Swans with gemstone decoration and pansy badge, size 4″ x 0.7″ (10.2 x 1.7 cm). **9.** A swan, size 2.9″ x 3.6″ (7.3 x 1.4 cm). **10.** Griffin, size 3.6″ x 0.8″ (9.2 x 2 cm). **11.** Fish, size 3.4″ x 0.7″ (8.7 x 1.7 cm). **12.** Box with sliding lid, size 2.4″ x 0.6″ (6.1 x 1.5 cm). **13.** Box with sliding lid, size 3.4″ x 0.8″ (8.5 x 2.1 cm). **14.** Box with sliding lid, size 1.8″ x 0.6″ (4.6 x 1.6 cm).

## PLATE 123 – FRENCH and CHINESE NEEDLE CASES 5

This selection of needle cases is mostly from France, and some would have originally come out of fitted sewing boxes. 1. Floral decoration, c. 1850, size 4.4″ x 1″ (11.1 x 2.4 cm). 2. Umbrella, c. 1840–50, size 3.5″ x 0.5″ (9 x 1.2 cm). 3. Umbrella with bird's head handle, c. 1840–50, size 3.7″ x 0.9″ (9.5 x 2.2 cm). 4. Peapod, c. 1810–20, size 3.4″ x 0.6″ (8.6 x 1.6 cm). 5. Quiver of arrows, c. 1860–80, size 3.5″ x 0.7″ (9 x 1.7 cm). 6. Edge carving, c. 1820, size 4.3″ x 0.7″ (11.1 x 1.7 cm). 7. A needle case's sliding lid with etched pattern and monogram M. The decorated sliding lids are often mistakenly identified as gauges; Canton, China, c. 1840, size 3″ x 0.5″ (7.8 x 1.3 cm). 8. China for export market, c. 1830–40, size 3″ x 0.5″ (7.7 x 1.3 cm). 9. Quiver of arrows, c. 1810–20, size 3.8″ x 0.7″ (9.6 x 1.7 cm). 10. Quiver of arrows with gold shield, c. 1810–20, size 3.7″ x 0.7″ (9.5 x 1.7 cm). 11. Quiver of arrows, c. 1810–20, size 3.3″ x 0.6″ (8.5 x 1.6 cm). 12. Quiver of arrows, c. 1810–20, size 3.6″ x 0.8″ (9.2 x 2 cm). 13. Decorated needle or bodkin case from a chatelaine, France, c. 1730, size 3.7″ x 0.7″ (9.5 x 1.7 cm). 14. Decorated needle or bodkin case from a chatelaine, France, c. 1740, size 3″ x 0.6″ (7.7 x 1.6 cm). 15. Box inscribed *Aiguilles* (Needles), c. 1840, size 2″ x 0.9″ (5.2 x 2.4 cm).

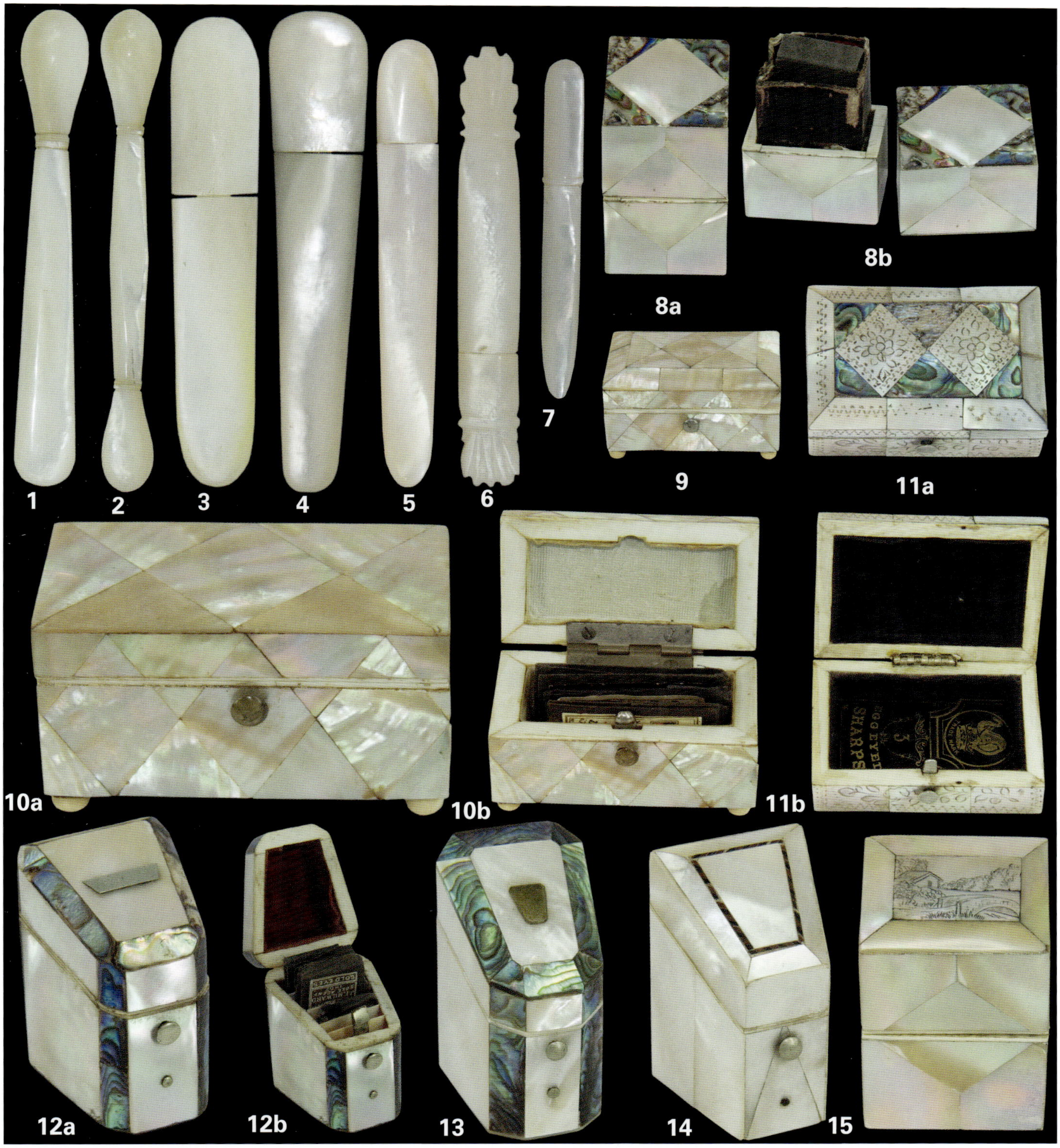


## PLATE 124 – ENGLISH NEEDLE CASES and NEEDLE BOXES

Needle cases number 1–6. Needle boxes 7-14. Needle boxes are different to needle cases in that they hold paper packs of needles as purchased in shops and not loose needles. **1.** Case, screws open, bulbous end for darning, c. 1850, size 3.4″ x 0.5″ (8.7 x 1.2 cm). **2.** Case, screws open, two bulbous ends for darning, c. 1850, size 3.8″ x 0.5″ (9.7 x 1.3). **3.** c. 1850–60, size 3″ x 0.6″ (7.6 x 1.5 cm). **4.** c. 1850–60, size 2.8 x 0.6″ (7.1 x 1.5 cm). **5.** c. 1850–60, size 3.1″ x 0.4″ (8 x 1.1 cm). **6.** c. 1850–60, size 2.2″ x 0.3″ (5.5 x 0.8 cm). **7.** Needle case with brass inner tube made for a sewing kit or a specialized type of needle, England, c. 1850, size 2″ (5 cm). **8a, 8b.** Needle pack box with removable lid, England, c. 1850–60, size 2.5″ x 0.6″ x 1″ (5.4 x 3.6 x 2.5 cm). **9.** Hinged lid, England, c. 1850–60, size 2.4″ x 1.3″ (6 x 3.3 cm). **10a, 10b.** Hinged lid, England, c. 1850–60, size 2.4″ x 1.2″ (6.2 x 3 cm). **11a, 11b.** Hinged lid, England, c. 1850–60, size 2.4″ x 1.6″ x 1″ (6 x 4 x 2.6 cm). **12a, 12b.** England, c. 1850–60, size 2″ x 1.5″ x 1.3″ (5 x 3.7 x 3.2 cm). **13.** England, c. 1850–60, size 2.2″ x 1.6″ x 1.3″ (5.5 x 4 x 3.2 cm). **14.** England, c. 1850–60, size 2.3″ x 1.4″ x 1.4″ (5.8 x 3.5 x 3.6 cm). **15.** Etched scene, England, c. 1850–60, size 2″ x 1.4″ x 1″ (5 x 3.5 x 2.7 cm).

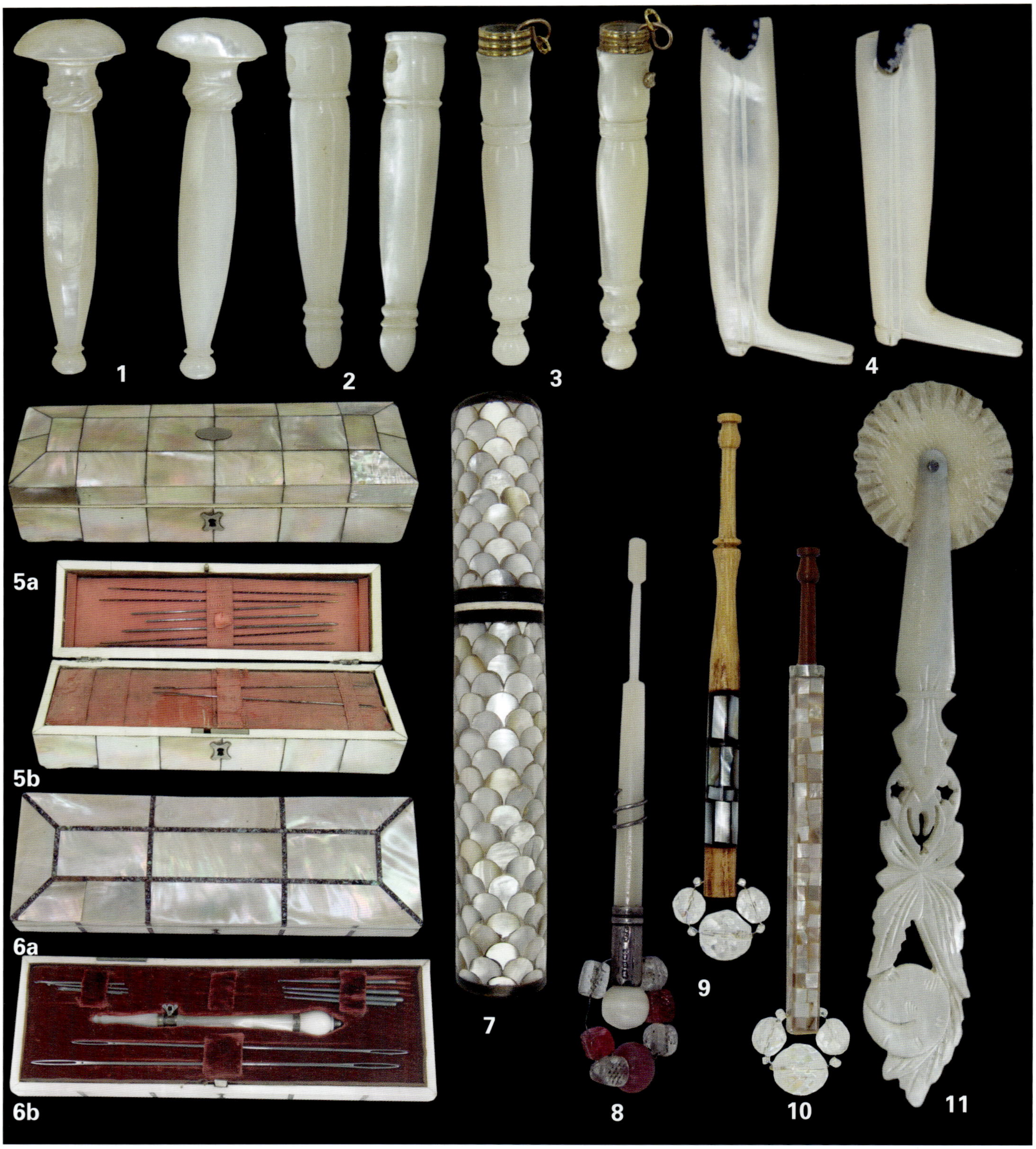


## PLATE 125 – NEEDLE GUARDS, DARNING, TRACING, BOBBINS

Needle guards (items 1–4) came in pairs and were usually attached with a ribbon or chain and were used to place on the end of knitting needles to protect the points and avoid accidental piercing of surrounding items when packed away. **1.** Needle guard, France, c. 1800–20, size 2.2″ (5.7 cm). **2.** Needle guard, France, c. 1800–20, size 2.4″ (6 cm). **3.** Needle guard, England, c. 1840–50, size 1.8″ (4.5 cm). **4.** Needle guard in the shape of boots, England, c. 1850, size 1.5″ (3.7 cm). **5a, 5b.** Needle box, France, c. 1850, size 9.6″ x 2.9″ (24.4 x 7.3 cm). **6a, 6b.** Boxed tambour set, France, c. 1800–20, size 7.9″ x 2.6″ (20 x 6.6 cm). **7.** Needle case for knitting or crocheting, England, c. 1900, size 10.4″ x 1.6″ (26.5 x 4 cm). **8.** Lace bobbin decorated with sterling silver hallmarked James Fenton, Birmingham, England, 1892, size 4.3″ (10.8 cm). **9.** Lace bobbin, wood and pearl, England, 2007, size 4.9″ (12.4 cm). **10.** Lace bobbin, wood and pearl, England, 2007, size 4.7″ (12 cm). **11.** Wheel for tracing patterns, France, c. 1870, size 4.5″ (11.5 cm).

## PLATE 126 – PIN CUSHIONS 1

Disk pin cushions, also known as pin wheels, were produced in a wide range of designs to meet the increasing demand. This selection is from England, c. 1840–60. Sizes are the diameter. **1.** Size 1.2″ (3 cm). **2.** Size 1.1″ (2.9 cm). **3.** Size 1.7″ (4.2 cm). **4.** Size 1.5″ (3.8 cm). **5.** Size 1.8″ (4.5 cm). **6.** Size 1.3″ (3.4 cm). **7.** Size 1.5″ (3.7 cm). **8.** Size 1.5″ (3.9 cm). **9.** Size 1.4″ (3.5 cm). **10.** Size 1.4″ (3.6 cm). **11.** Size 1.3″ (3.2 cm). **12.** Size 1.3″ (3.3 cm). **13.** Size 1.6″ (4.1 cm). **14.** Size 1.3″ (3.2 cm). **15.** Size 1.5″ (3.9 cm). **16.** Size 1.1″ (2.7 cm). **17.** Size 1″ (2.5 cm). **18.** Size 1.3″ (3.4 cm). **19.** Size 1.2″ (3 cm). **20.** Size 1.3″ (3.2 cm). **21.** Size 1.5″ (3.8 cm). **22.** Size 1.8″ (4.5 cm). **23.** Size 1.5″ (3.7 cm). **24.** Whimsy, a pin cushion created for a gift more than for use, England or France, c. 1840–59, size 2″ (5 cm).

## PLATE 127 – PIN CUSHIONS 2

Pin cushions were extremely popular and came in every shape imaginable. **1.** Lady outside a house, France, c. 1840, size 2″ (5 cm). **2.** Leaf shape, England, c. 1840–60, size 2.4″ x 1.4″ (6 x 3.5 cm). **3.** Octagonal with etched flower, England, c. 1850, size 1.6 x 1.6″ (4 x 4 cm). **4.** Etched pin cushion, England, c. 1850, size 2.4″ x 2.9″ (6.1 x 7.4 cm). **5.** Dimensional bird, England, c. 1820–30, size 1.7″ x 1.3″ (4.3 x 3.3 cm). **6.** Floral motif, England, c. 1830, size 1.9″ x 1.4″ (4.8 x 3.5 cm). **7.** Souvenir pin cushion inscribed *Souvenir de Dunkerque*, France, c. 1850, size 2″ x 1.2″ (5 x 3 cm). **8.** Figural pin cushion in the form of a harp, England, c. 1800–20, size 2″ x 1.4″ (5 x 3.6 cm). **9.** Carved carp, Japan, c. 1870, size 3.6″ x 3″ (9.1 x 7.5 cm). **10.** Shape of fireplace bellows, England, c. 1820–30, size 3.4″ x 1.2″ (8.7 x 3 cm). **11.** Fireplace bellows, inscription too worn to read, France, c. 1950, size 2.7″ x 1.1″ (6.8 x 2.8 cm).

## PLATE 128 – PIN CUSHIONS, PIN HOLDERS 3

China created a large range of pin cushions for the export market. Interestingly, pearl disks were sold individually, allowing the buyer the opportunity to create his or her own pin cushion. Item 9 is an example of how these loose disks were often packaged. Similar patterns were etched on both pieces, but the interior was blank. **1–10.** China, c. 1800–1830. **1.** Geometric form with floral motif, size 1.5″ x 1.5″ (3.7 x 3.7 cm). **2.** Figural butterfly, size 2.4″ x 1.2″ (6.1 x 3 cm). **3.** Fancy with Chinese scene, size 1.9″ x 1.9″ (4.9 x 4.9 cm). **4.** Fancy with Chinese scene, size 1.7″ x 1.2″ (4.2 x 3 cm). **5.** Round, size 1.6″ (4.1 cm). **6.** Etched pagoda, size 1.5″ x 1.5″ (3.7 x 3.7 cm). **7.** Abstract shaped, size 2″ x 1.3″ (5.2 x 3.3 cm). **8.** Figural heart shape, size 1.6″ x 1.5″ (4 x 3.9 cm). **9.** Packaged loose heart-shaped pieces, to be made into a pin cushion, size 1.6″ x 1.9″ (4 x 4.7 cm); the card is inscribed *Brought from China by first mate Gordon Conklin of "Old Lyme" who was lost at sea in 1870.*
**10.** Figural heart shape, size 1.7″ x 1.8″ (4.3 x 4.5 cm). **11.** Pin box with a goat carved on the top, France, c. 1875, size 2.4″ x 1.6″ (6 x 4 cm). **12.** Pin dish, France, c. 1895, size 2.5″ (6.4 cm).

## PLATE 129 – EMERIES

An emery contains polishing powder and is used to clean rust from needles and pins. The larger examples were from fitted sewing sets and matched the carved pattern in the cotton reel holders, waxer, and tape measure, c. 1840–80. Other examples that were much smaller were sold individually, c. 1840–70. All these examples are from England. **1–10.** Disk type, size 0.8″ (2.2 cm) diameter. **11–20.** Pearl topped, average size 1″ x 1″ (2.5 x 2.3 cm). **21.** Earlier type with pearl cylinder and emery hole in the base instead of in the barrel, c. 1840, size 1.1″ x 1.1″ (2.8 x 2.7 cm).

## PLATE 130 – WAXERS

These reels holding beeswax or white wax were used for strengthening of threads. All were from England. **1–17.** c. 1840–70, size 0.9" diameter x 0.4" (2.2 x 1 cm). **18.** c. 1850, size 1.3" diameter x 0.4" (3.2 x 1 cm). **19–30.** c. 1840–80, average size 1" diameter x 0.9" (2.5 cm x 2.3 cm).

## PLATE 131 – REEL HOLDERS 1

Reel holders were used to hold threads and flosses purchased in shops per pound, or in skeins. The threads were wound onto the spool at home. This plate of reel holders show just some of the wide variety of designs that were made in England, c. 1840–80. The average size is 1.2″ diameter x 1.4″ height (3 x 3.5 cm). This does not represent a full collection of designs and there are many hundreds of designs to collect.

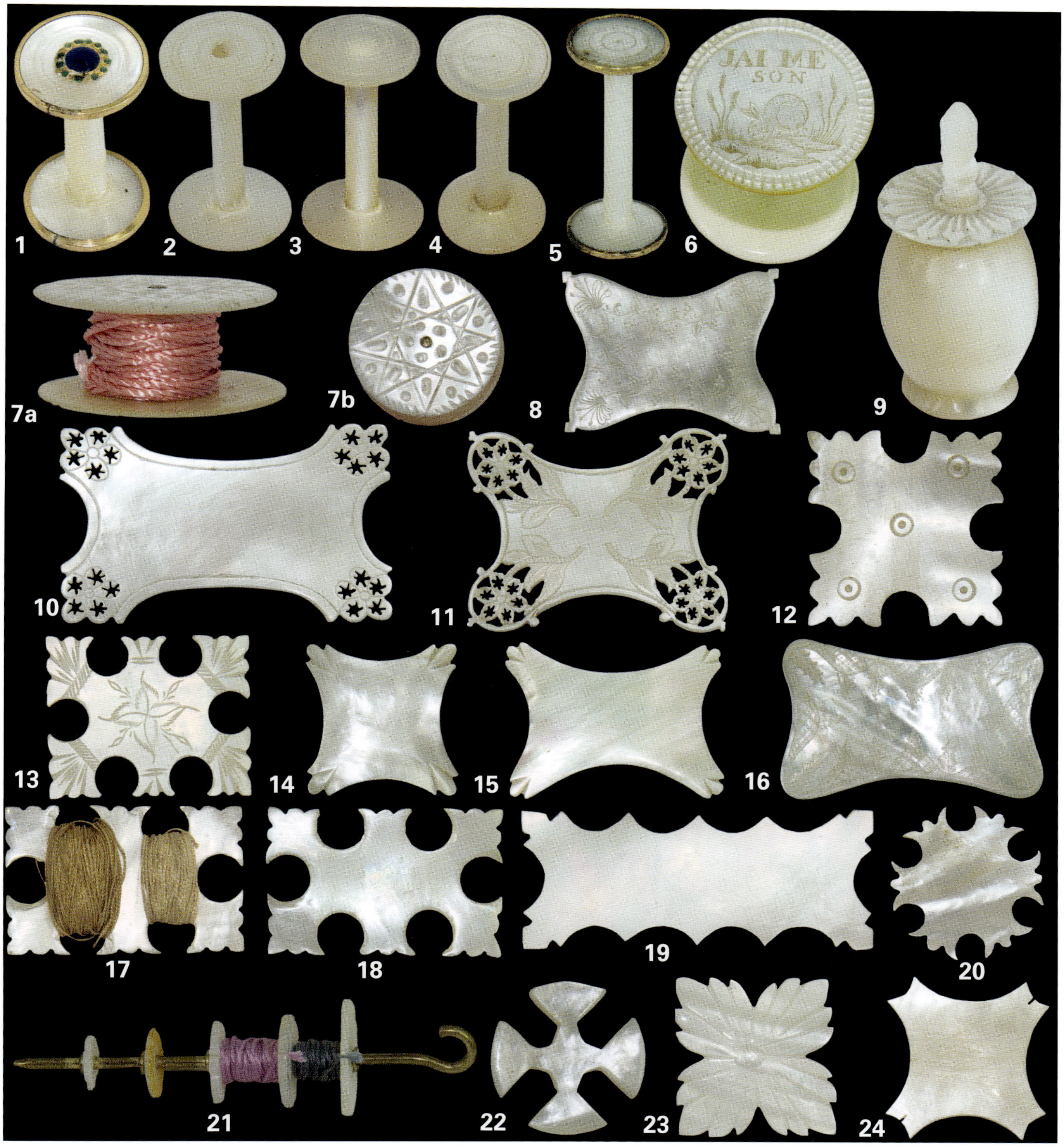


**PLATE 132 – REEL HOLDERS 4 and THREAD WINDERS 1**

Items 8 and 10–24 are thread winders from England, c. 1840–60. Some were found in fitted sewing kits. **1–5.** Thread reels from fitted sewing sets, France, c. 1810–20, size 0.8″ to 1.2″ (2 to 3 cm). **6.** Sold as a French reel holder, but in fact cleverly made up from a pearl button from c. 1850, size 1.4″ x 1.3″ (3.5 x 3.3 cm). France did not make large reels holders like the English. **7a, 7b.** Thread reel, England, c. 1860, size 1″ x 0.5″ (2.6 x 1.3 cm). **8.** Thread winder, size 2.1″ x 1.5″ (5.4 x 3.7 cm). **9.** Thread or cotton barrel, China, c. 1800–1840, size 1.6″ x 0.7″ (4 x 1.8 cm). **10.** Size 2.2″ x 1.3″ (5.8 x 3.4 cm). **11.** Size 2″ x 1.6″ (5 x 4 cm). **12.** Size 1.3″ x 1.3″ (3.2 x 3.2 cm). **13.** Size 1.9″ x 3.1″ (4.9 x 7.8 cm). **14.** Size 1.5″ x 1.5″ (3.7 x 3.7 cm). **15.** Size 2.1 x 1.5″ (5.2 x 3.8 cm). **16.** Size 2.2″ x 1.3″ (5.6 x 3.3 cm). **17, 18.** One example with original thread, size 1.7″ x 1″ (4.2 x 2.5 cm). **19.** Size 2″ x 0.8″ (5.2 x 2 cm). **20.** Size 1.3″ x 1.3″ (3.2 x 3.2 cm). **21.** Spool winder, size 3.5″ (9 cm). **22.** Reproduction, twentieth century, size 1″ x 1″ (2.6 x 2.6 cm). **23.** Reproduction, twentieth century, size 1.3″ x 1.3″ (3.4 x 3.4 cm). **24.** Size 1.5″ x 1.5″ (3.8 x 3.8 cm).

## PLATE 133 – THREAD WINDERS 2

A thread winder is used for the organized storing of threads and flosses, which were often purchased from shops per pound or skein and were wound onto the winder at home. This selection of thread winders is from France, c. 1800–1820. The pieces would have originally fit into sewing boxes that were sold in the arcades of the Palais Royal in Paris. Sometimes called snowflakes due to the variety in design, they show the incredible capabilities of early pearl carvers. **1.** Size 0.7″ (1.8 cm). **2.** Size 1.4″ (3.6 cm). **3.** Size 1.5″ (3.7 cm). **4.** Size 1″ (2.6 cm). **5.** Size 1.1″ (2.9 cm). **6.** Size 1.1″ (2.9 cm). **7.** Size 1.4″ (3.5 cm). **8.** Size 1.1″ (2.8 cm). **9.** Size 1.1″ (2.8 cm). **10.** Size 1″ (2.6 cm). **11.** Size 1.3″ (3.4 cm). **12.** Size 1.4″ (3.5 cm). **13.** Size 1.6″ (4.1 cm). **14.** Size 1.4″ (3.5 cm). **15.** Size 0.8″ (2.1 cm). **16.** Size 1.1″ (2.9 cm). **17.** Size 0.9″ (2.4 cm). **18.** Size 1.3″ (3.3 cm). **19.** Size 1.6″ (4.1 cm). **20.** Size 1.5″ (3.7 cm).

## PLATE 134 – THREAD WINDERS 3

This selection of thread winders is also from France, c. 1800–1820, and would have originally been from fitted sewing boxes that were sold in the arcades of the Palais Royal in Paris. Numbers 1 and 2 are interesting examples of a snake eating its tail, also known as an ouroborus. **1.** Size 1.3″ (3.3 cm). **2.** Size 1.4″ (3.5 cm). **3.** Exceptionally large, size 2.1″ (5.3 cm). **4.** Size 1″ (2.4 cm). **5.** Size 1.6″ (4.1 cm). **6.** Size 1.3″ (3.3 cm). **7.** Size 1.5″ (3.9 cm). **8.** Gemstone decoration, size 1.4″ (3.5 cm). **9.** Size 1.8″ (4.5 cm). **10.** Size 1.8″ (4.5 cm). **11.** Size 1.7″ (4.3 cm). **12.** Size 1″ (2.6 cm). **13.** Size 1.2″ (3 cm). **14.** Size 1.1″ (2.9 cm). **15.** Size 1.6″ (4.1 cm). **16.** Size 1.1″ (2.9 cm). **17.** Size 0.9″ (2.4 cm). **18.** Size 1.3″ (3.3 cm). **19.** Size 1.2″ (4 cm). **20.** Set of two thread winders in a fitted shagreen box, size box 1.4″ (3.5 cm), winders 1.1″ (2.7 cm).

## PLATE 135 – THREAD WINDERS 4

China created a range of thread winders for the export market (items 1–13). As Chinese-etched mother-of-pearl gaming counters were fast losing popularity in the early nineteenth century, manufacturers looked for new markets. They commenced making thread winders among other items, to enhance the declining business that had once been brought in by gaming counters. The winder often had a similar pattern to the gaming counter and has been mistaken for counters in the past. **1a, 1 b.** Inscribed *Bessie*, c. 1820, size 2.1″ (5.3 cm) diameter. **2.** c. 1820–40, size 2.2″ (5.7 cm) diameter. **3.** c. 1820–40, size 1.7″ (4.4 cm) diameter. **4.** c. 1820–40, size 1.8″ (4.5 cm) diameter. **5.** c. 1820–40, size 1.7″ (4.4 cm) diameter. **6.** c. 1820–40, size 1.8″ (4.5 cm) diameter. **7.** c. 1820–40, size 2″ (5 cm) diameter. **8.** c. 1820–40, size 1.6″ (4 cm) diameter. **9.** c. 1750–1800, size 1.7″ x 1.1″ (4.3 x 2.9 cm). **10.** c. 1750–1800, size 1.3″ x 0.9″ (3.3 x 2.4 cm). **11.** c. 1750–1800, size 1.5″ x 1″ (3.8 x 2.5 cm). **12.** c. 1750–1800, size 1.3″ x 0.9″ (3.4 x 2.2 cm). **13.** c. 1780–1820, size 2″ x 2″ (5 x 5 cm). **14.** Inscribed *Betlemme*, (Italian for Bethlehem,) Palestine, c. 1890, size 1.4″ (3.5 cm) diameter. **15.** Inscribed *Betelem*, (Bethlehem,) Palestine, c. 1890, size 1.7″ (4.2 cm) diameter.

## PLATE 136 – TAPE and SOLID MEASURES 1

This type of tape measure, which winds on internal barrels ( items **1–13**), was found in fitted sewing boxes, c. 1840–60. Tape measures are usually part of a matching set of cotton reel holders, emeries, and waxers. Tape measures with visible barrels (items **14–16**) were sold individually. These date to c. 1840. All items illustrated here are from England. **1–13.** Average size 0.9" x 0.9" (2.4 x 2.4 cm). Item 3 and 6 have mother-of-pearl barrels, which are only seen in the earliest examples. **14–16.** Reel type tape that winds from the top, average size 0.9" x 0.9" (2.3 x 2.4 cm). **17.** Tape measure carved in the shape of an acorn, c. 1850, size 1" (2.5 cm).

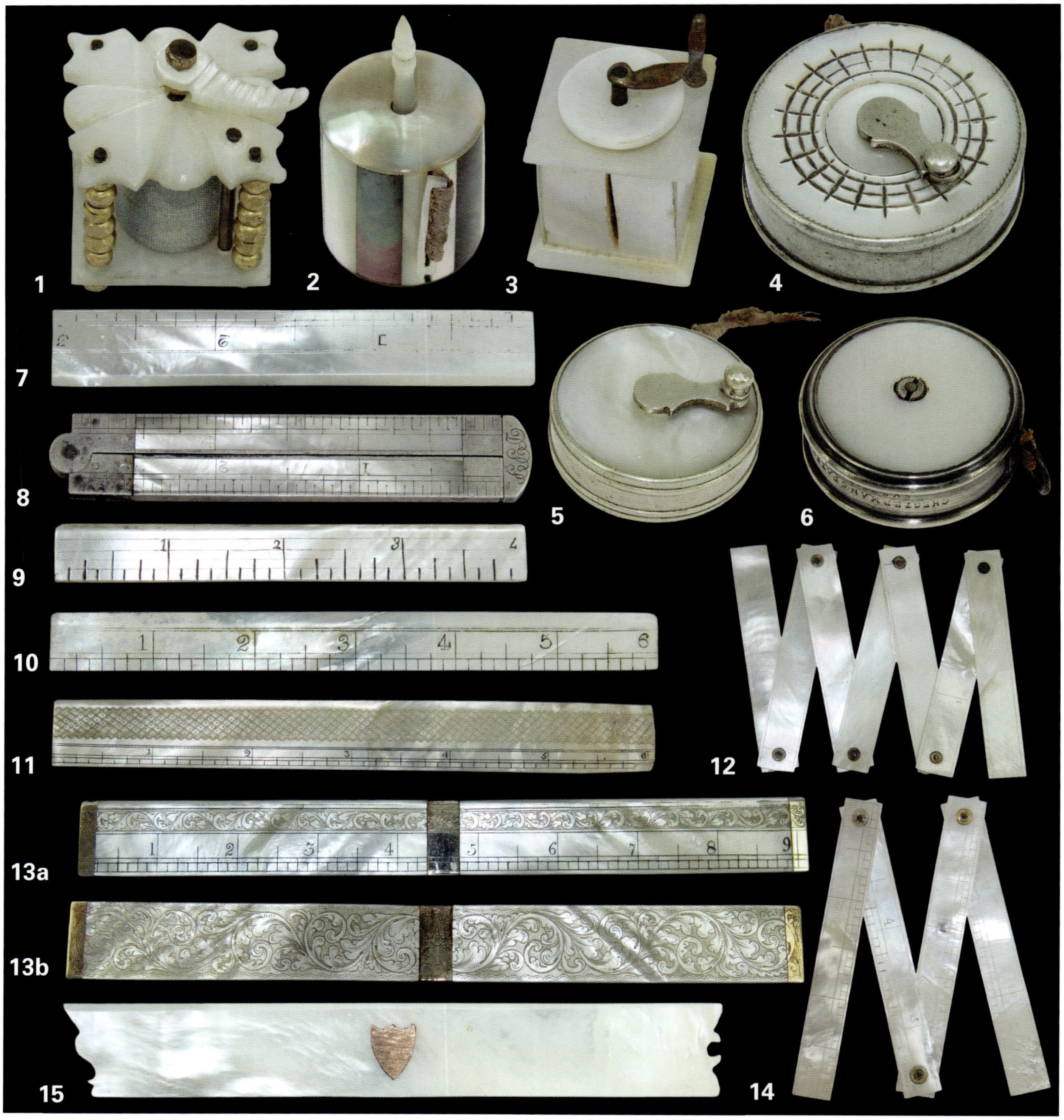


## PLATE 137 – TAPE and SOLID MEASURES 2

The rulers are mostly from fitted sewing sets. **1.** Tape measure, England, c. 1840–60, size 0.9" x 1" (2.4 x 2.5 cm). **2.** Barrel tape measure, France, c. 1850, size 0.6" x 1.1" (1.5 x 2.8 cm). **3.** Coffee grinder tape measure, England, c. 1840, size 0.9" x 1.7" (2.4 x 4.4 cm). **4.** Tape measure, England, c. 1840, size 1.3" (3.4 cm) diameter. **5.** Tape measure, England, c. 1840–50, size 1.1" (2.9 cm) diameter. **6.** Tape measure, hallmarked silver inscribed Chesterman's Patient, Sheffield, England, 1841, size 1.1" (2.9 cm) diameter. **7.** 3" Sewing ruler, England, c. 1840, size 3" (7.6 cm). **8.** 3 ½" Folding ruler inscribed *Theo B Starr Sterling*, USA, c. 1900–10, unfolds to 6" (15.3 cm). **9.** 4" sewing ruler, England, c. 1840, size 4" (10.1 cm). **10.** 6" Sewing ruler, England, c. 1860, size 6" (15.3 cm). **11.** 6" Sewing ruler with engraving, England, c. 1850, size 6" (15.3 cm). **12.** 21" Folding ruler, France, c. 1820, folds down to 3.3" (8.5 cm). **13a, 13b.** 9" Sewing ruler with exquisite etching, England, c. 1870, size 9" (23 cm). **14.** 11" Folding ruler, France, c. 1820, folds down to 3" (7.6 cm). **15.** Straight edge, used for drawing stencils and straight lines on fabrics. There are no measurements for it to be classed as a measure, France, c. 1820, size 5.1" (13 cm).

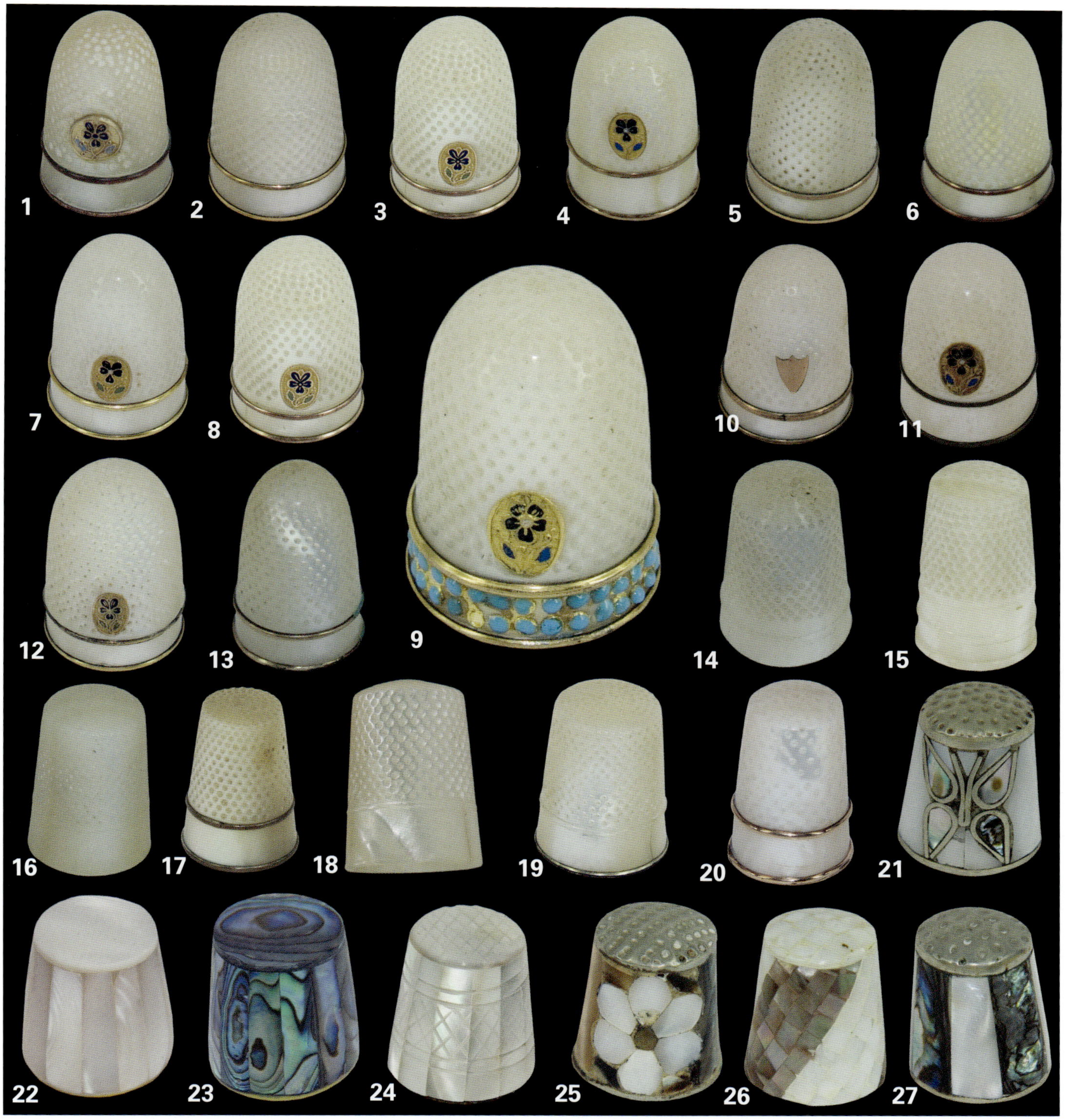


## PLATE 138 – THIMBLES

Solid mother-of-pearl thimbles are very rare as it took great skill to hand carve them out of the pearl shell. The very thick shell needed for this task was scarce. Interestingly, the study of existing examples show many different sizes were made, including for children. **1–13.** Thimbles carved out of solid mother-of-pearl from sewing sets that sold at the arcades of the Palais Royal, Paris, France, some with the enameled pansy symbol of higher quality, c. 1810–20, size 0.8″ to 1.1″ (2 to 2.7 cm) high; (item 9 has been enlarged to show the decoration of tiny turquoise stones.) **14–20.** These thimbles are different to round topped examples illustrated above due to their flat top and were made during the revival period when these pearl sewing sets again became popular, France, c. 1860–80, size 0.9″ to 1″ (2.3 to 2.5 cm) high. **21, 25, 27.** Thimbles with butterfly, flower, and abalone, Mexico, c. 1980, size 0.8″ x diameter 0.8″ (2 x 2 cm). **22, 23.** Thimble with pearl and abalone shell veneer, Philippines, 1996, size 0.8″ x diameter 0.8″ (2 x 2 cm). **24, 26.** Thimble, Thailand, c. 1985, size 0.8″ x diameter 0.8″ (2 cm x 2 cm).

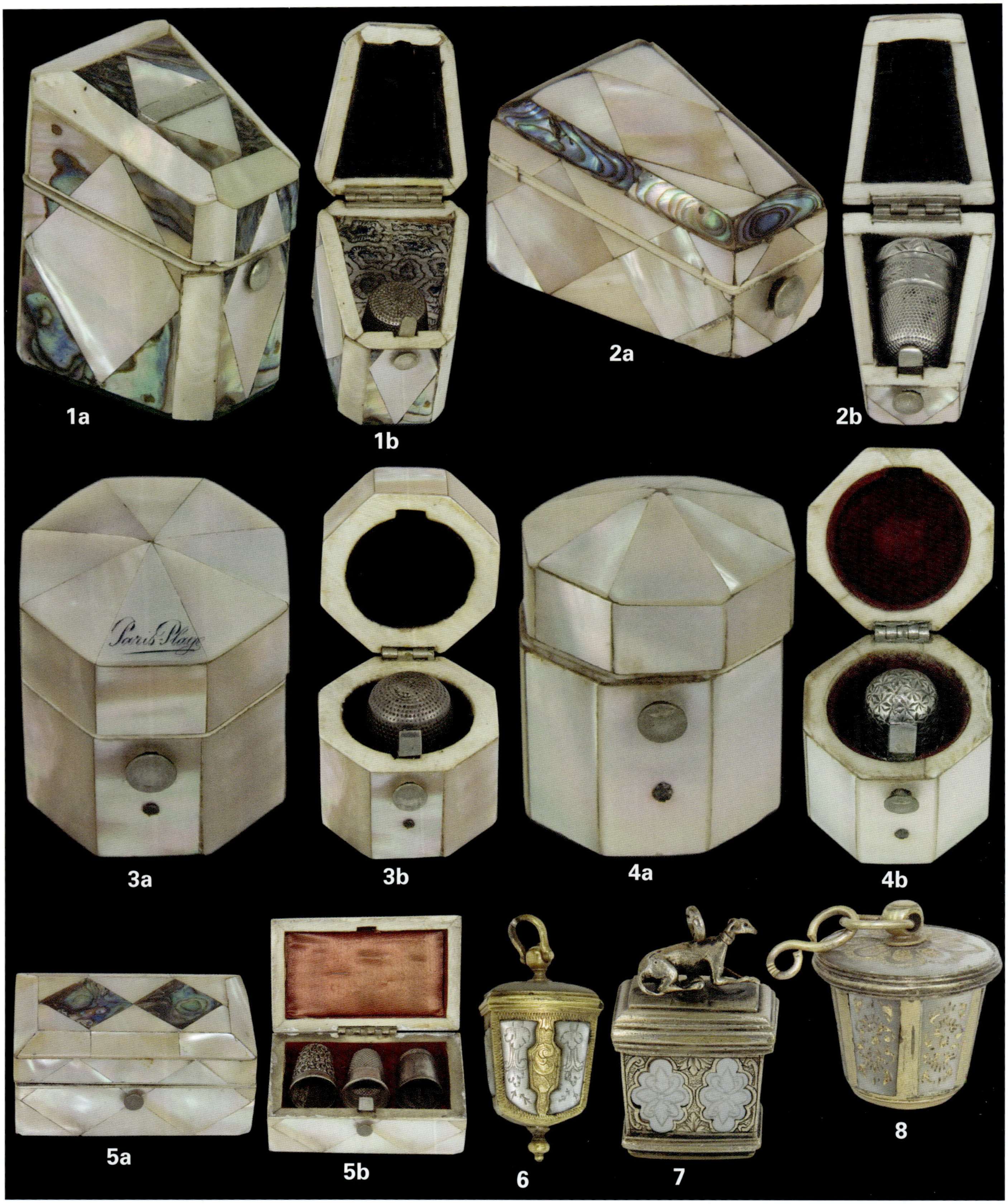


## PLATE 139 – THIMBLE HOLDERS 1

**1a, 1b.** Hinged thimble holder, England, c. 1850–60, size 2.1″ x 1.6″ x 0.8″ (5.3 x 4 x 2 cm). **2a, 2b.** Holder for a single thimble, England, c. 1860, size 1.4″ x 1.1″ x 1″ (3.6 x 2.9 x 2.5 cm). **3a, 3b.** Thimble holder inscribed *Paris Plage* (Paris beach), France, c. 1860, size 1.4″ x 1.3″ (3.6 x 3.2 cm). **4a, 4b.** Thimble holder, France, c. 1860, size 1.6″ x diameter 1.3″ (4 x 3.2 cm). **5a, 5b.** Holder for three thimbles, England, c. 1860, size 2.6″ x 1.6″ (6.5 x 4 cm). **6.** Thimble holder from a chatelaine, France, c. 1730, size 1.6″ x 0.9″ (4 x 2.4 cm). **7.** Thimble holder with dog on top from a chatelaine, France, c. 1730, size 1.3″ x 0.9″ (3.4 x 2.4 cm). **8.** Thimble holder from a chatelaine, France, c. 1740, size 0.9″ x 0.9″ (2.4 x 2.4 cm).

## PLATE 140 – THIMBLE HOLDERS 2

These delightful holders have a wide range of uses, including holding sewing items, knick knacks, salt, and table condiments. The owner can put them to any use. **1.** Two horses pulling a carriage that contains a thimble, France, c. 1870–90, size 3.6″ x 2.4″ (9.2 x 6 cm). **2.** Two horses pulling a carriage, France, c. 1870–90, size 3.5″ x 1.2″ (9 x 3 cm). **3.** Gcat pulling a cart, France, c. 1870–90, size 3.5″ x 1.3″ (9 x 3.4 cm). **4.** A goat pulling a carriage, France, c. 1870–90, size 3.1″ x 2″ (8 x 5 cm). **5.** Man pushing a wheelbarrow, France, c. 1870–90, size 4.9″ x 3.7″ (12.5 x 9.5 cm). **6.** Trolley, with egg thimble holder, France, c. 1870–90, size 2″ x 2″ (5 x 5 cm). **7.** Three wheeled carriage, France, c. 1870–90, size 5.8″ x 2.6″ (14.7 x 6.5 cm). **8.** Wheelbarrow thimble holder, with scissors and stiletto added by the previous owner, France, c. 1880–1900, size 6.1″ x 2.6″ (15.5 x 6.5 cm). **9.** Birds pulling an egg carriage, which contains a thimble, France, c. 1870–90, size 4.3″ x 2″ (11 x 5 cm). **10.** Sleigh thimble holder, France, c. 1870–90, size 7.2″ x 1.6″ (18.4 x 4 cm).

## PLATE 141 – THIMBLE HOLDERS 3

Ships were popular for thimble holders, and they were manufactured by many countries, making a determination of their origins difficult. **1.** Fancy ship thimble holder, France, c. 1870–90, size 6.3" x 6.3" (16 x 16 cm). **2.** Ship thimble holder, England, c. 1880, size 7.9" x 3.9" (20 x 10 cm). **3.** Ship thimble holder with Bisque sailor, England, c. 1870–90, size 3.9" x 3" (10 x 7.5 cm). **4.** Two sail ship, England, c. 1870–90, size 2.8" x 1.7" (7 x 4.3 cm). **5.** Ship thimble holder, USA, c. 1890, size 3" x 1.8" (7.6 x 4.5 cm). **6.** Ship thimble holder on wheels inscribed *Carrington & Co.*, England, c. 1900, size 4.9" x 3.7" (12.5 x 9.5 cm). **7.** One sail ship, England, c. 1870–90, size 2.8" x 1.7" (7 x 4.3 cm). **8.** Two sail ship, inscribed *Souvenir from Western Australia made in Germany,* c. 1880, size 3.1" x 3.3" (8 x 8.5 cm). **9.** One sail ship, England, c. 1870–90, size 2.9" x 1.3" (7.4 x 3.3 cm).

## PLATE 142 – THIMBLE HOLDERS 4

The pearl basket containers have a wide range of uses, including holding sewing items, knickknacks, salt and table condiments. The owner can put them to any use. **1.** Donkey standing behind an open thimble holder, France, c. 1870–90, size 4.1″ x 2.6″ (10.5 x 6.5 cm). **2.** Basket thimble holder, England c. 1870–90, size 2.2″ x 1.6″ (5.5 x 4 cm). **3a, 3b.** Fancy basket thimble holder, England, c. 1870–90, size 2.4″ x 1.4″ (6 x 3.5 cm). **4.** Thimble holder on a small stand, England, c. 1870–90, size 2.5″ x 1.6″ (6.4 x 4 cm), also could have been used for salt. **5.** Basket thimble holder, France, c. 1870–90, size 1.8″ x 1.1″ (4.5 x 3 cm). **6.** Fancy basket thimble holder, England, c. 1870–90, size 2.4″ x 1.6″ (6.1 x 4 cm). **7.** Thimble holder, basket shape, England, c. 1870–90, size 1.8″ x 1″ (4.5 x 2.5 cm). **8a, 8b.** Purse-like thimble holder, inscribed *Le Pouliglien*, France, c. 1880, size 1.7″ x 1″ (4.3 x 2.6 cm). **9a, 9b.** Egg-shaped thimble holder, Philippines, 1998, size 1.8″ x 1.2″ (4.5 x 3 cm). **10a, 10b.** Egg-shaped thimble holder with lined interior, England, c. 1880, size 2″ x 1.2″ (5 x 3 cm). **11.** Thimble holder, hallmarked W. Miller & Co., Scotland, 1870, size 2.4″ x 1.5″ (6 x 3.7 cm), also could have been used for salt.

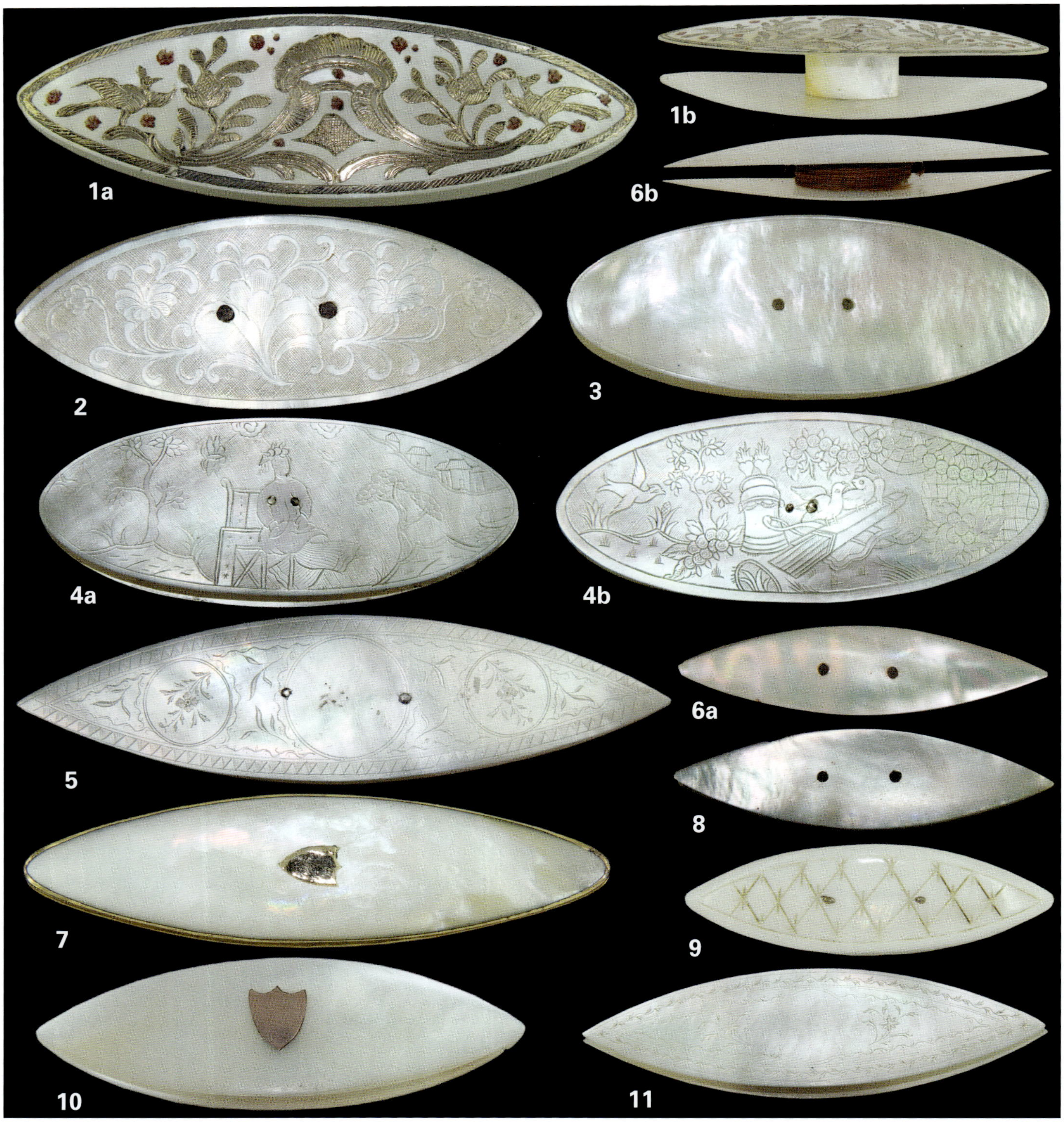


## PLATE 143 – KNOTTING and TATTING SHUTTLES

The knotting shuttle is flatter, with round ends, while the tatting shuttle has pointed ends nearly touching due to a convex top and bottom. They are used for different applications. The knotting shuttle uses a large thread to produce a cord for appliqué, whilst the tatting shuttle creates its own fabric. **1a, 1b.** Knotting shuttle with silver decoration, France, c. 1750, size 4.9″ x 1.6″ (12.7 x 4 cm). **2.** Knotting shuttle, China for the export market, c. 1800, size 3.1″ x 1.1″ (8 x 2.8 cm). **3.** Knotting shuttle, France, c. 1750–1810, size 4.3″ x 1.6″ (11 x 4 cm). **4a, 4b.** Knotting shuttle, China for the export market, c. 1800, size 3.4″ x 1.4″ (8.7 x 3.5 cm). **5.** Tatting shuttle, China for the export market, c. 1810–30, size 4.3″ x 1.1″ (11 x 2.8 cm). **6a, 6b.** Tatting shuttle, England, c. 1850–70, size 2.6″ x 0.6″ (6.6 x 1.4 cm). **7.** Tatting shuttle, France, c. 1810–20, size 3.3″ x 0.8″ (8.4 x 2 cm), likely out of a fitted sewing box. **8.** Tatting shuttle, England, c. 1850–70, size 3.3″ x 0.9″ (8.5 x 2.2 cm). **9.** Tatting shuttle, Bahamas, 2002, size 2.7″ x 0.8″ (6.8 x 2.1 cm). **10.** Tatting shuttle, France, c. 1810–20, size 2.9″ x 1″ (7.4 x 2.4 cm), from a Necessaire de Voyage. **11.** Tatting shuttle, China for the export market, c. 1810–30, size 3.5″ x 1.1″ (8.8 x 2.7 cm).

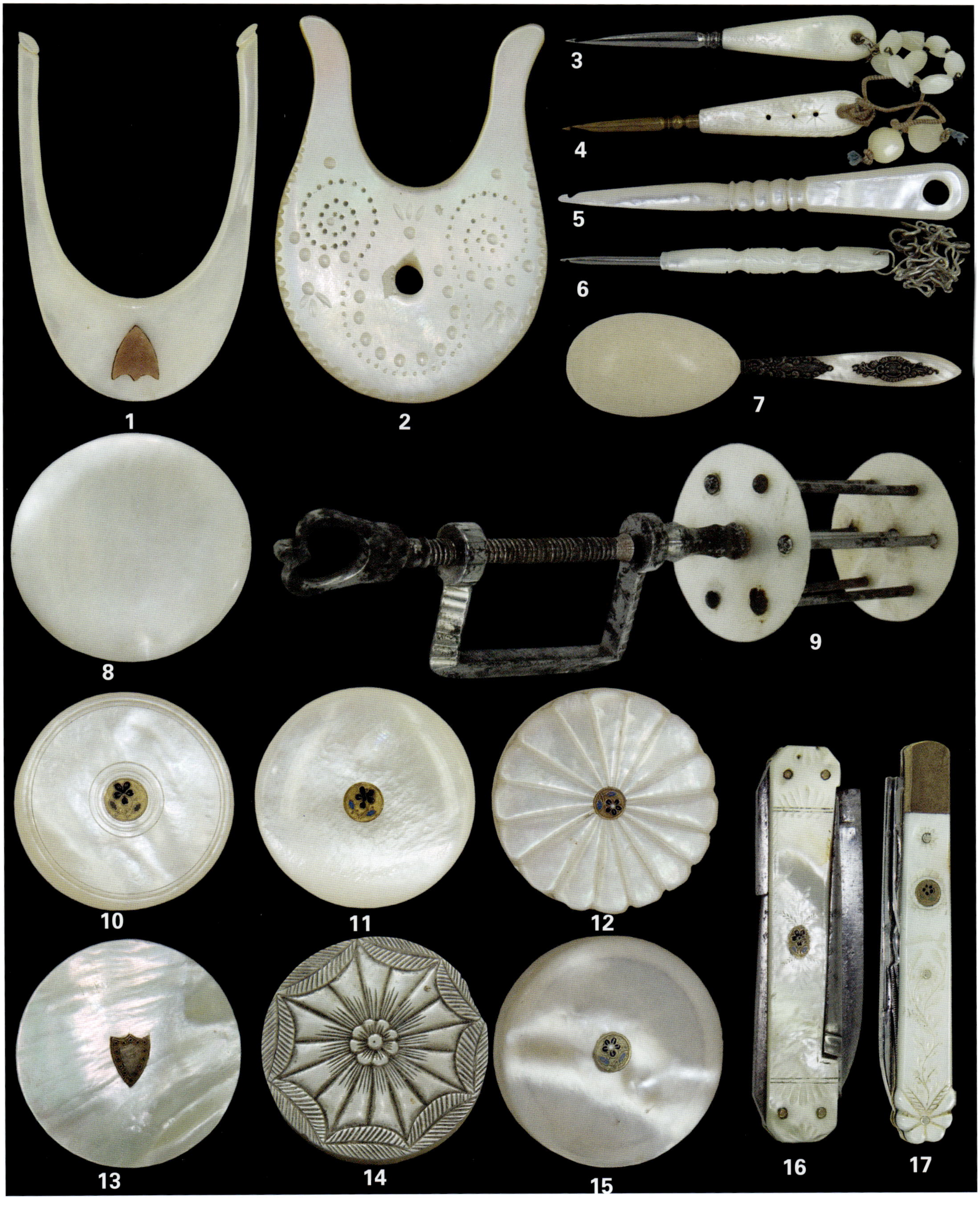


## PLATE 144 – SEWING TOOLS

1. Lucet from a *necessaire de voyage*, France, c. 1820, size 2.4″ x 1.5″ (6.2 x 3.7 cm). 2. Lucet, reproduction, Bahamas, 2006, size 2.4″ x 1.7″ (6 x 4.3 cm). 3–6. Picot hook, Bahamas, 2004, size #3 3.4″ (8.6 cm) #4 3″ (7.6 cm) #5 3″ (7.4 cm) #6 3.1″ (7.8 cm). 7. Darner with a pearl handle, inscribed *Sterling*, USA, c. 1850, size 6.3″ (16 cm). 9. Sewing clamp with mother-of-pearl, from a fitted sewing set, France, c. 1820, size 5.7″ (14.6 cm). 8, 10–15. Bead pots, some with the enameled pansy symbol of higher quality from fitted sewing sets, France, c. 1800–1820, size 1.2″ to 1.7″ (3 to 4.4 cm). 16–17. Sewing knife from sewing sets with the Palais Royal enameled pansy, France, c. 1820, size 3.1″ (8 cm).

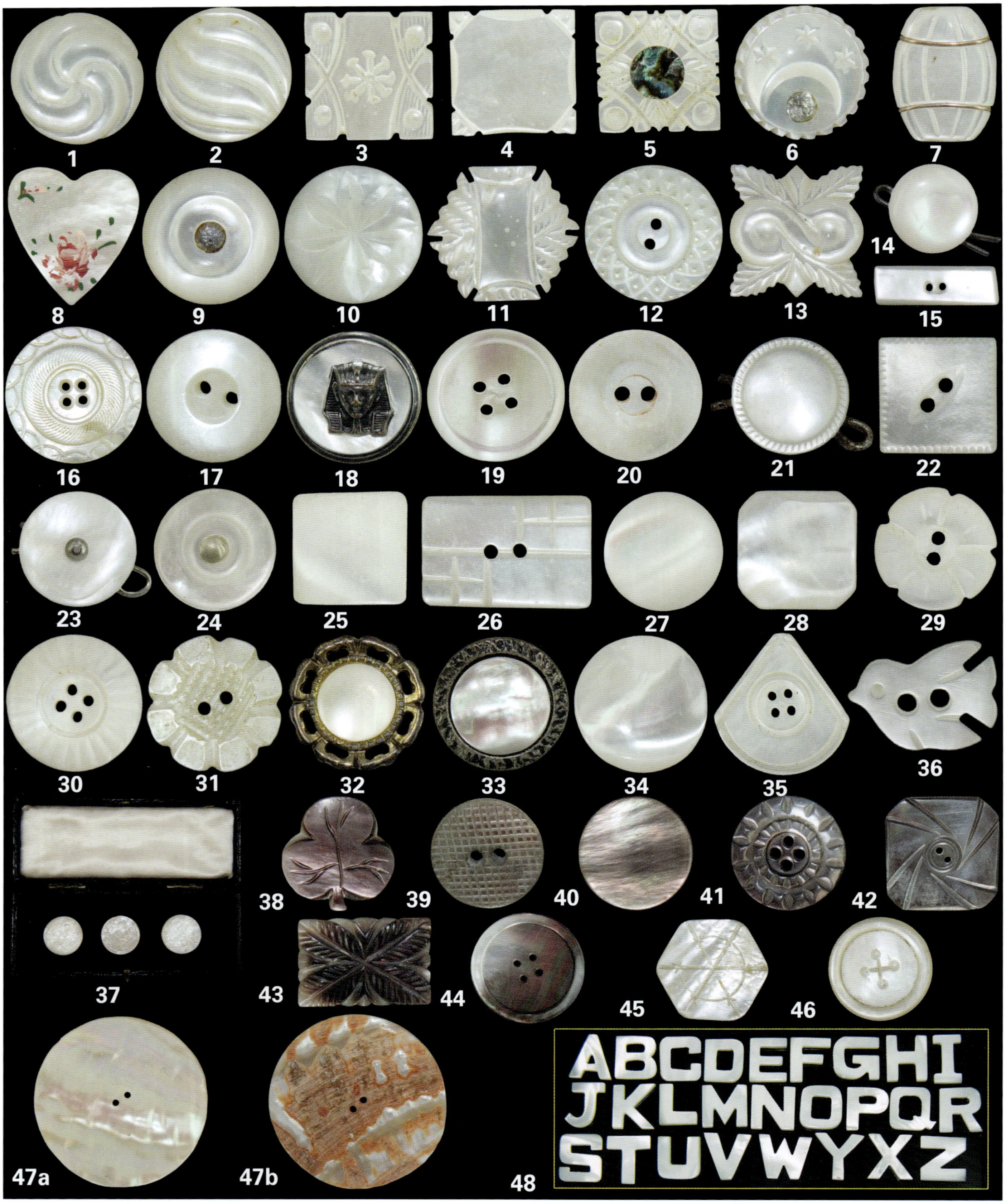


## PLATE 145 – BUTTONS and SEW-ONS

There are thousands of different styles of mother-of-pearl buttons that have been produced throughout the world, and this subject has been covered in many specialized books. This selection gives a very brief glimpse at a few of the more popular styles produced worldwide from 1850 to 1920, size 0.4″ to 2.4″ (1 to 6.2 cm). The variation is endless, especially when one realizes that in 1912 over six billion buttons were produced in the USA alone, employing 9500 factory workers and 9700 pearl fisherman. Item **37** is a carved and boxed set of buttons from China, c. 1840, size 0.8″ (2 cm) diameter. Item **48** is the alphabet carved out of mother-of-pearl and was used for sewing initials on garments, China, c. 1960, size per letter 0.5″ (1.3 cm).

CHAPTER 6
# Rattles

Mother-of-pearl was first used for handles on silver rattles in the eighteenth century. By the nineteenth century, these pearl-handled rattles were being hand crafted in large numbers in both England and France and sporadically in the rest of Europe. By 1870, this handcrafted work was replaced by bulk manufacture to keep up with the demand from the rising middle class.

English rattles were made from either sterling silver or silver plate. The sterling silver examples were hallmarked. Hallmarks were sometimes worn with age and use, making reading difficult but usually not impossible. French rattles were also hallmarked, but the marks were small and did not wear as well as English. The United States of America produced many rattles with pearl handles early in the twentieth century, which are all marked *sterling*.

New technologies in the twentieth century saw the introduction of synthetic materials, but there remained a limited demand for mother-of-pearl in rattle handles, especially as christening gifts or gifts to new parents. Even to this day, pearl-handled rattles are still being produced. These new rattles no longer have the thick handles seen in earlier days, but rather very thin, round pearl handles, which is a sign that the older, thicker pearl shells are no longer available to manufacturers. It is common to see rattles with damage, replacement handles or bells due to rough handling by babies.

This chapter also includes teethers, baby whistles, and dummies (pacifiers).

The phrase "all the bells and whistles...," meaning the item comes with everything, originated from the governess's rattles in this chapter.

**PLATE 146 – RATTLES FROM SPAIN, ENGLAND, and CHINA**

1. Two mermaids, J Mestre, Tarragona, 1895, size 5.9" (14.9 cm). 2. Baby's head, Spain, c. 1900, size 4.3" (11 cm). 3. Chinese export rattle, China, c. 1900, size 4.7" (12 cm). 4. Dog's head, Crisford & Norris, Birmingham, 1908, size 5.4" (13.6 cm).

## PLATE 147 – RATTLES FROM ENGLAND 1

1. Butterfly, Crisford & Norris, Birmingham, 1902, size 5.5″ (14 cm). 2. Rabbit, W H Collins, Birmingham, 1914, size 5.3″ (13.4 cm). 3. Bird, Crisford & Norris, Birmingham, 1926, size 5.7″ (14.5 cm). 4. Owl, London, 1898, size 4.9″ (12.5 cm). 5. Baby face, c. 1920, size 5.4″ (13.8 cm). 6. Dog, W H Collins, Birmingham, 1905, size 5.5″ (14 cm). 7. Teddy bear, Crisford & Norris, Birmingham, 1934, size 6″ (15.2 cm). 8. Teddy bear, W H Collins, Birmingham, 1942, size 6.1″ (15.5 cm). 9. Owl Head, William Adams, Birmingham, 1937, size 4.8″ (12.3 cm). 10. Cat, Birmingham, 1920, size 5.3″ (13.5 cm). 11. Boy Scout, Adie & Lovekin, Chester, 1916, size 3.5″ (9 cm).

## PLATE 148 – RATTLES FROM ENGLAND 2

1. Jester, Crisford & Norris, Birmingham, 1929, size 6″ (15.2 cm). 2. Jester with devil horns, William Aiken, Chester, 1913, size 6.7″ (17 cm). 3. Jester, Crisford & Norris, Birmingham, 1907, size 6.9″ (17.5 cm). 4. Jester, Crisford & Norris, Birmingham, 1929, size 7″ (17.7 cm). 5. Jester, Thomas Henry Vale, Birmingham, 1914, size 3.9″ (10 cm). 6. Peter Rabbit, Chester, 1915, size 7″ (17.8 cm). 7. Peter Pan, Crisford & Norris, Birmingham, 1913, size 7.2″ (18.2 cm). 8. Lady's Head, W H Collins, Birmingham, 1946, size 6.7″ (17 cm). 9. Boy's head, Crisford & Norris, Birmingham, 1905, size 5.9″ (15 cm). 10. Punch and Judy's dog, Toby, Crisford & Norris, Birmingham, 1931, size 4.1″ (10.5 cm). 11. Tom Kitten, a character from Beatrix Potter's book published in 1907, W H Collins, Birmingham, 1939–40, size 6.7″ (17 cm). 12. Cat, Crisford & Norris, Birmingham, 1914, size 5.8″ (14.8 cm).

## PLATE 149 – RATTLES FROM ENGLAND 3

1. Lord Kitchener, Crisford & Norris, Birmingham, 1914, size 8.3" (21 cm). 2. Peter Pan, EPNS, c. 1920, size 6" (15.4 cm). 3. Kate Greenway character, Crisford & Norris, Birmingham, 1927, size 4.8" (12.2 cm). 4. Glad Eye, possible William Aitken, Chester, 1906, size 4.8" (12.2 cm). 5. Girl, W H Collins, Chester, 1960, size 6.2" (16 cm). 6. Walrus, from Alice in Wonderland, EPNS, c. 1920, size 6.1" (15.4 cm). 7. Rattle inscribed *Baby*, EPNS, c. 1910, size 5.3" (13.5 cm). 8. Lady's head, William Vale & Sons, Birmingham, 1915, size 5.2" (13.2 cm). 9. Center square, Crisford & Norris, Birmingham, 1931, size 4.8" (12.2 cm). 10. Bird, Adie & Lovekin, Birmingham, 1922, size 5.1" (13 cm). 11. Personalized with etching *From Grandpa to AWP*, Crisford & Norris, Birmingham, 1898, size 4.8" (12.2 cm).

## PLATE 150 – RATTLES FROM ENGLAND 4

1. Jack and Jill, W H Collins, Birmingham, 1933, size 5.5″ (14 cm). 2. Bo Peep, Adie & Lovekin, Chester, 1924, size 4.7″ (12 cm). 3. Boy Blue, W H Collins, Birmingham, 1967, size 5.6″ (14.3 cm). 4. The cow jumps over the moon, W H Collins, Birmingham, 1922, size 5.1″ (13 cm). 5. Peter Pan, W H Collins, Glasgow, Scotland, 1930, size 5.1″ (12.9 cm). 6. Pied Piper, Crisford & Norris, Birmingham, 1902, size 6.1″ (15.5 cm). 7. Sun face, Richard Owen Williams, Birmingham, 1923, size 6.9″ (17.4 cm). 8. The pie man, Adie & Lovekin, Birmingham, 1921, size 5.1″ (13 cm). 9. Mother Hubbard, Adie & Lovekin, Birmingham, 1924, size 5.3″ (13.5 cm). 10. Little Jack Horner, Crisford & Norris, Birmingham, 1916, size 6.8″ (17.2 cm). 11. Dome, Crisford & Norris, Birmingham, 1926, size 6.9″ (17.5 cm). 12. Ribbon shape, marked "Baby Woodward," William Aiken, Chester, 1916, size 6.1″ (15.4 cm). 13. Whistle teether, Crisford & Norris, Birmingham, 1880, size 4.5″ (11.4 cm). 14. Baby, EPNS, c. 1910, size 5.7″ (14.4 cm).

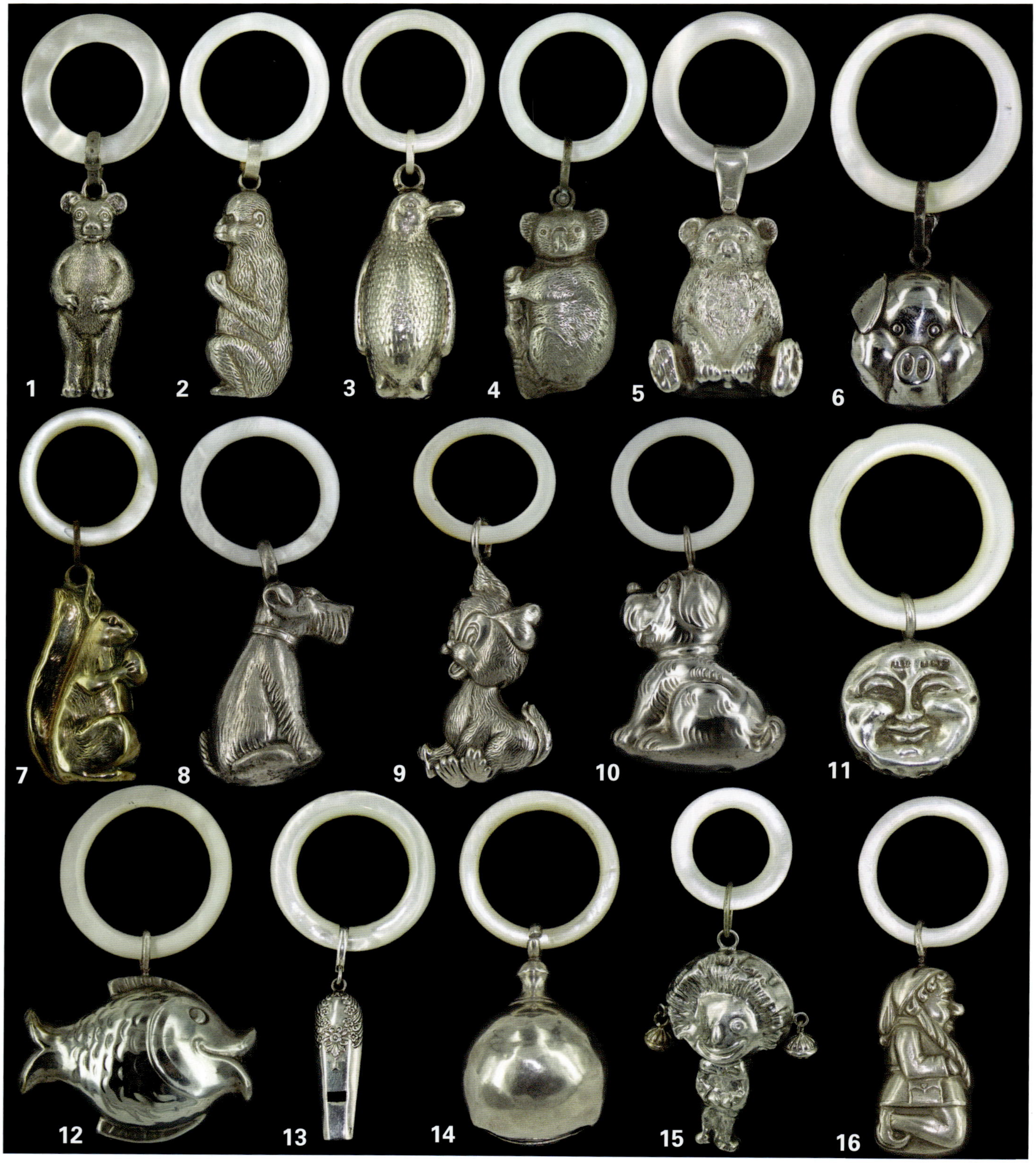

## PLATE 151 – RATTLES FROM ENGLAND 5

1. Teddy bear, c. 1925, size 4.2" (10.6 cm). 2. Monkey, *EPNS,* c. 1920, size 3.9" (10 cm). 3. Penguin, *EPNS*, c. 1930, size 4.1" (10.5 cm). 4. Koala, *EPNS*, c. 1920, size 3.9" (10 cm). 5. Teddy Bear, W Vale & Sons, Birmingham, 1909, size 3" (7.5 cm). 6. Pig's head, silver plate, c. 1920, size 3.3" (8.3 cm). 7. Squirrel, gilt metal, c. 1898, size 4.3" (11 cm). 8. Dog, silver plate, c. 1930, size 3.5" (9 cm). 9. Dog, silver plate, c. 1930–50, size 4.1" (10.5 cm). 10. Dog, silver plate, c. 1950, size 3.8" (9.7 cm). 11. Man in the moon, Adie & Lovekin, Birmingham, 1914, size 2.2" (5.5 cm). 12. Fish, silver plate, c. 1950, size 3.1" (8 cm). 13. Whistle teether, Charles Horner, Chester, 1921, size 3.5" (9 cm). 14 Bell, Crisford & Norris, Chester, 1918, size 3.9" (10 cm). 15. A Bernice Upton storybook character, William Aitken, Birmingham, 1936, size 3.3" (8.5 cm). 16. Dwarf, from *Snow White and the Seven Dwarfs*, *EPNS*, c. 1920, size 3.5" (9 cm).

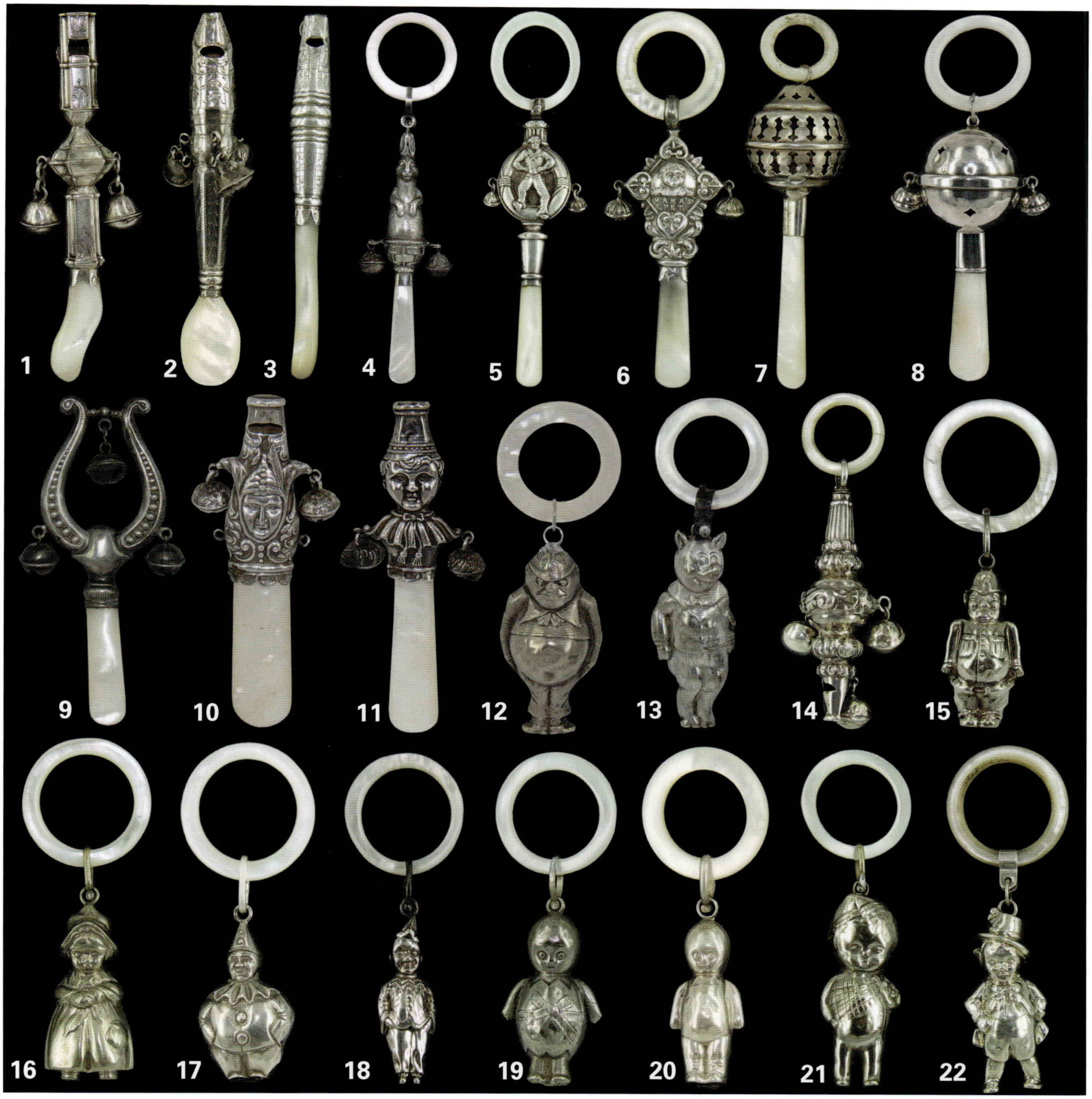


## PLATE 152 – RATTLES FROM ENGLAND 6

**1.** Reproduction of a 1720–50 rattle by James Edwards, London, c. 1850, size 4.7″ (12 cm). **2.** Whistle rattle, John Shekleton, London, c. 1806, size 5.1″ (13 cm). **3.** Whistle, John Lawrence, Birmingham, 1814, size 4.6″ (11.8 cm). **4.** Bunny on an egg, Birmingham, 1991, size 6.3″ (16 cm). **5.** Sailor, Crisford & Norris, Birmingham, 1920, size 5.7″ (14.5 cm). **6.** Inscribed *Mama's Pet,* Adie & Lovekin, Birmingham,1923, size 4.1″ (10.5 cm). **7** Pierced ball, Birmingham,1945, size 5.2″ (13.2 cm). **8.** Ball with stars, William Vale & Sons, Birmingham, 1942, size 5.5″ (14 cm). **9.** Lyre, Birmingham, 1857, size 4.1″ (10.5 cm). **10.** Jester, Hilliard and Thomason, Birmingham, 1901, size 3.9″ (9.8 cm). **11.** Boy's head, Hilliard and Thomason, Birmingham, 1901, size 3.7″ (9.5 cm). **12.** Tweedledum or Tweedledee, fictional characters in nursery rhymes, EPNS, c. 1920, size 4.1″ (10.5 cm). **13.** Podgy Pig, EPNS, c. 1920, size 4.3″ (11 cm). **14.** Whistle rattle, Sheffield, 1903, size 3.9″ (10 cm). **15.** Mr. Plodd the policeman (Noddy series), W H Collins, Birmingham, 1941, size 4.7″ (12 cm). **16.** Lady in a dress, *EPNS*, c. 1920, size 4.1″ (10.5 cm). **17.** Clown, silver plate, c. 1920, size 3.9″ (9.8 cm). **18.** Clown, W H Collins, Birmingham, 1937, size 3.9″ (10 cm). **19.** Kewpie, *EPNS*, c. 1920, size 4.1″ (10.5 cm). **20.** Kewpie, James Swann, Birmingham, 1925, size 3.3″ (8.5 cm). **21.** Scottish child, *EPNS*, Scotland, c. 1920, size 4.5″ (11.5 cm). **22.** Artful Dodger, a Charles Dickens character, silver plate, c. 1925, size 4″ (10.3 cm).

## PLATE 153 – RATTLES & OTHERS FROM ENGLAND 7

1. Inscribed *Our King*, King George V, with old repair to the handle, Hilliard & Thomason, Birmingham, 1900, size 3.5" (9 cm). 2. Whistle teether, Levi & Salaman, Birmingham, 1910, size 2.8" (7.2 cm). 3. Whistle teether, c. 1900, size 2.8" (7 cm). 4. Whistle teether, Hilliard & Thomason, Birmingham, 1949, size 3" (7.5 cm). 5. Monkey, silver plate, c. 1950, size 3.9" (10 cm). 6. Flowers, William Aiken, Chester, 1916, size 3.9" (10 cm). 7. Ball, Adie & Lovekin, Birmingham, 1911, size 3" (7.5 cm). 8. Jester, W H Collins, Chester, 1959, size 6.8" (17.2 cm). 9. Hey Diddle Diddle, Sydney & Co., Birmingham, 1907, size 3.7" (9.5 cm). 10. Hammer, F H Adams, Birmingham, 1920, size 3.1" (8 cm). 11. Punch and Judy's dog, Toby, Adie & Lovekin, Birmingham, 1920, size 3.9" (9.8 cm). 12. Flame shape, William Aiken, Chester, 1906, size 2.9" (7.4 cm). 13. Dummy (pacifier), Henry Williamson, Birmingham, 1914, size 2.8" (7 cm). 14. Dummy (pacifier), William Aiken, Chester, 1919, size 2" (5.2 cm). 15. Patterned, Crisford & Norris, Birmingham, 1912, size 5.5" (14 cm). 16. Toy Top, Chester, 1921, size 3.9" (10 cm). 17. King George V Guardsman, inscribed *Bom Priaur, EPNS*, 1920, size 4.2" (10.6 cm). 18. Bell, Crisford & Norris, Birmingham, 1923, size 4.4" (11.2 cm).

## PLATE 154 – RATTLES FROM FRANCE 1

1. Mary and Infant Jesus, c. 1850, size 6.3" (16 cm). 2. Figural doll, c. 1848, size 5.5" (14 cm). 3. Chinese Mandarin, c. 1850, size 6.3" (16 cm). 4. Punchinello, c. 1800, size 5.7" (14.5 cm). 5. Beehive style, c. 1870, size 6.6" (16.8 cm). 6. Gilt metal, c. 1850, size 6" (15.2 cm). 7. Scallop shell shape, c. 1850–70, size 5.8" (14.7 cm). 8. Flat scallop shell shape, c. 1850, size 5.7" (14.5 cm). 9. Wheel shape, c. 1860–70, size 5.2" (13.4 cm). 10. Flowers, c. 1850–70, size 5.1" (13 cm). 11. Diamond pattern, c. 1850–60, size 5.3" (13.4 cm).

## PLATE 155 – RATTLES FROM FRANCE 2

1. Six bells, c. 1840, size 6.5″ (16.5 cm). 2. Moveable center ball with acorn bells, c. 1840–50, size 5″ (12.7 cm). 3. Greek key decoration, c. 1850–60, size 5.6″ (14.2 cm). 4a, 4b. One side shows a weasel; the opposite side shows a lady in a garden, gilt highlights on silver, c. 1850–70, size 6.5″ (16.6 cm). 5. Gold ball, c. 1850–60, size 5.5″ (14 cm). 6. Two layers fancy design, c. 1860–1870, size 5.3″ (13.5 cm). 7. Star pattern with center flower, c. 1890, size 4.8″ (12.2 cm). 8. Multi-layered, c. 1850–70 size 5.3″ (13.5 cm). 9. Teether, c. 1840, size 4.9″ (12.5 cm). 10. Whistle teether often found in the homes of upper classes, including aristocrats,1803, size 6.2″ (15.7 cm).

## PLATE 156 – RATTLES FROM FRANCE 3

**1a, 1b.** Putto, inscribed *Bebe* on the back, c. 1880, size 4.5" (11.5 cm). **2.** Silver ball, c. 1850–70, size 5.1" (13 cm). **3.** Gold ball, c. 1850–70, size 4.8" (12.3 cm). **4.** Three balls, c. 1850–70, size 5.7" (14.5 cm). **5.** Dog's head whistle, probably also used on the hunt, c. 1850, size 2.1" (5.4 cm). **6.** Lyre, no whistle extension, c. 1870, size 3.9" (10 cm). **7.** Flowers, c. 1880, size 5.1" (13 cm). **8.** Scallop shell shape, c. 1860–70, size 4.8" (12.2 cm). **9.** Pattern with circle in the center, c. 1850–70, size 5.3" (13.5 cm). **10.** Baby face, c. 1850–70, size 5.1" (13 cm). **11.** Whistle rattle, inscribed *800 RSD*, c. 1820, size 6.1" (15.5 cm).

## PLATE 157 – RATTLES FROM USA 1

**1.** Humpty Dumpty, c. 1905, size 4.5″ (11.5 cm). **2.** Putto, kissing a lady, Unger Bros, c. 1900–10, size 4.6″ (11.6 cm). **3.** Putti, Unger Bros, c. 1900–10, size 4.5″ (11.5 cm). **4.** Bell, c. 1900, size 4.1″ (10.5 cm). **5.** Rabbit, McChesney Co., Newark, 1925, size 3.7″ (9.5 cm). **6a, 6b.** Inscribed *Little Bo Peep has lost her sheep*, Gorham, c. 1910, size 4.4″ (11.2 cm). **7a, & 7b.** Inscribed *This big pig went to market*, Gorham, c. 1910, size 4.5″ (11.5 cm). **8.** Inscribed *Mr. Bear*, c. 1910, size 3.3″ (8.4 cm). **9.** Roman head, on rear cat and a fiddle, c. 1920, size 3.8″ (9.6 cm). **10.** Man in the Moon teether, c. 1915–20, size 1.9″ (4.8 cm). **11.** Man in the Moon with two bells, c. 1915, size 2″ (5.2 cm). **12.** Teether with 2 bells, c. 1910, size 2.4″ (6 cm). **13.** Teether with 3 bells, c. 1910, size 2.6″ (6.5 cm).

## PLATE 158 – RATTLES FROM USA 2

1. Baby face with bonnet, c. 1905, size 5.1″ (13 cm). 2. Jester, c. 1890, size 4.6″ (11.8 cm). 3. Jester holding a small jester rattle, c. 1900, size 3.7″ (9.5 cm). 4. Winking man, Pryor, c. 1915, size 3.5″ (9 cm). 5. Head with hat, c. 1900, size 3.3″ (8.5 cm). 6. Smiling jester, c. 1910, size 3.3″ (8.5 cm). 7. Pirate, c. 1900, size 3.9″ (9.8 cm). 8. Elephant, Webster Co., Mass., c. 1910, size 3.9″ (10 cm). 9. Teether with two bells, c. 1915, size 3.8″ (9.6 cm). 10. Teether with two bells, c. 1900, size 5.1″ (13 cm).

## PLATE 159 – RATTLES FROM USA 3

**1.** Baby face, engraved *Thompson,* c. 1900, size 3.9" (9.8 cm). **2.** Whistle teether, c. 1890, size 3.5" (9 cm). **3.** Inscribed *Baby*, c. 1900–10, size 2.7" (6.8 cm). **4.** Teether, c. 1905, size 4.3" (11 cm). **5.** Raggedy Ann, Macmillan, c. 1950, size 4.7" (12 cm). **6.** Heart teether, c. 1915, size 2.8" (7 cm). **7.** Teether with one bell, c. 1880–1900, size 4.6" (11.8 cm). **8.** Teether with one bell, c. 1890, size 4.3" (10.8 cm). **9.** Griffin, Webster Co., Mass., c. 1900, size 3.8" (9.7 cm). **10.** Bunny bell, c. 1930, size 2.9" (7.4 cm). **11.** Ding Dong Bell, c. 1910, size 2.9" (7.4 cm).

# CHAPTER 7
# Dressing Accessories

The large variety of items used for both ladies' and men's dressing accessories in this chapter attests to the popularity of mother-of-pearl in the late nineteenth and early twentieth centuries. This is rather a new area in which to collect and prices are still low.

**A note about manicure sets:** some are sold under the name of American manufacturers, but the unfinished components were often imported and assembled by the US seller. For example, metal tool parts came from Germany and pearl buffers were imported from the Meru region of France.

## PLATE 160 – VINAIGRETTES, TUSSIE MUSSIES, and HEM LIFT

1–4. Vinaigrettes, containers having a single perforated inner layer under which is placed an aromatic sponge or a fabric bit soaked in oil or perfume, to combat unpleasant odors in cities before the time of effective sanitary practices, England, c. 1825, size 0.8" x 0.2" (2 cm x 0.5 cm) to 1" x 0.3" (2.5 cm x 0.7 cm). 5. Belt, carved cat, USA, c. 1960, size 5.1" x 3.1" (13 x 8 cm). 6. Hem lift: used by Victorian ladies to lift their hems while dancing, making for a graceful sweep across the ballroom floor, England, c. 1895–1908, size 5.1" (13 cm) opens to 6.7" (17 cm). 7–8. Tussie Mussies were held in the hand and contained a small bouquet or posey of flowers. As with the vinaigrette, the purpose was to mask unpleasant odors, #7: Europe, c. 1840–50, size 4.5" (11.5 cm), #8: England, c. 1850–70, size 4.5" (11.5 cm).

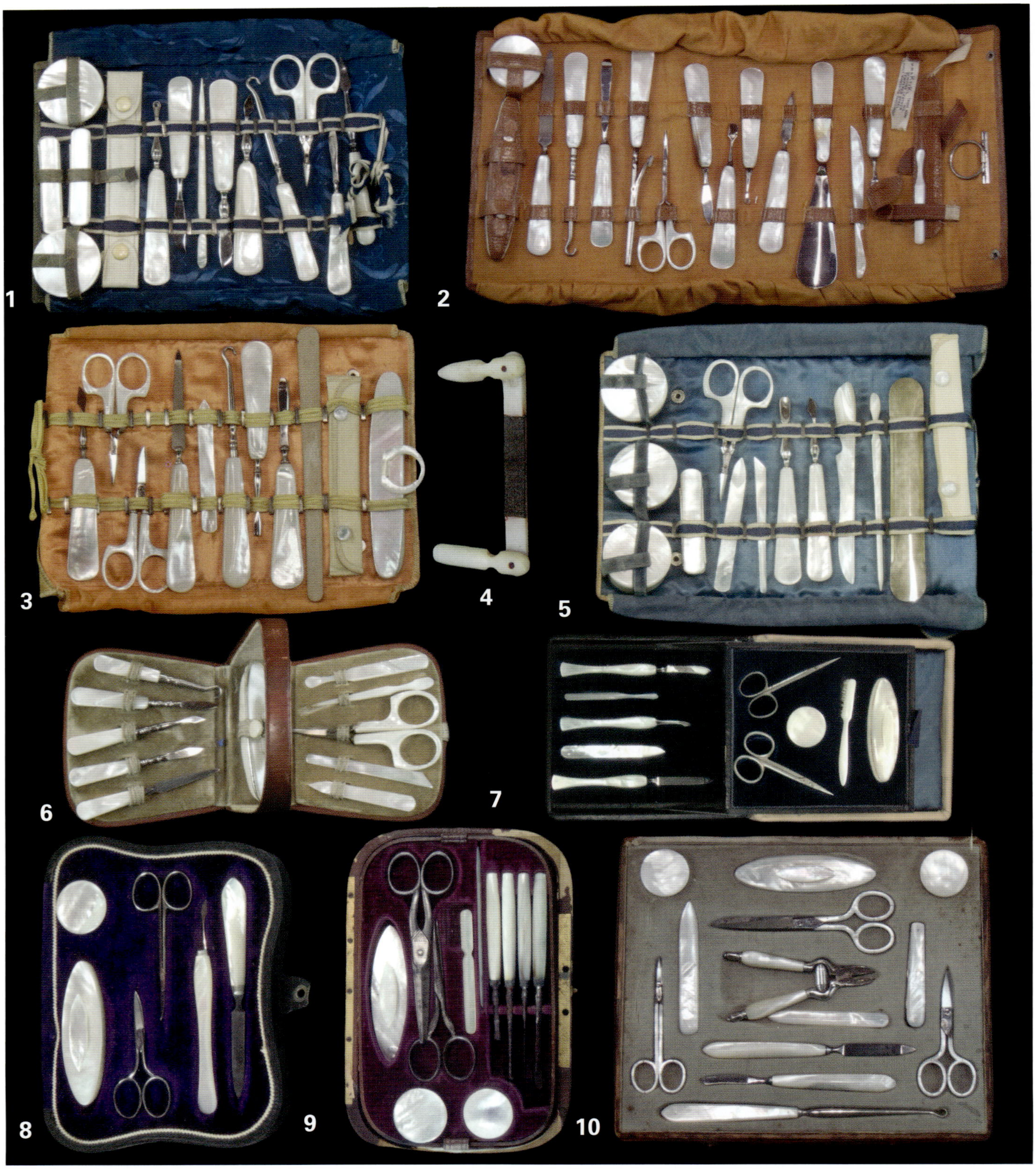


## PLATE 161 – MANICURE SETS

Although most of these manicure sets were assembled in the US, many of the metal tools came from Germany. Included are scissors, a range of manicure tools, nail buffer, file, button hook, and occasionally a shoe horn, powder box, and curling iron. **1.** USA, c. 1918–30, size 9.8″ x 7.1″ (25 x 18 cm). **2.** Praktikal, USA, c. 1918–30, size 16.5″ x 8.6″ (42 x 22 cm). **3.** USA, c. 1918–30, size 10.2″ x 8.7″ (26 x 22 cm). **4.** Traveler's folding manicure file, England, c. 1880, size 2.4″ (6.2 cm). **5.** USA, c. 1918–30, size 9.4″ x 7.1″ (24 x 18 cm). **6.** Krusius Bros, Germany, c. 1915, size 4.1″ x 3.7″ (10.5 x 9.5 cm). **7.** Set with fold out drawer, JA Henckels Twin Works, Germany, c. 1930, size 6.1″ x 7.1″ (15.5 x 18 cm), a toothbrush is an unusual inclusion. **8.** USA or UK, c. 1925–30, size 7.7″ x 6.1″ (19.5 x 15.5). **9.** Personal care set for teeth and manicure, Robert Collin, France, c. 1850–65, size 7.5″ x 5.3″ (19 x 13.5 cm), note tooth brush and tools for cleaning teeth. **10.** H. Boker, Germany, for markets in USA and Europe, c. 1880, size 11.4″ x 9.4″ (29 x 24 cm).

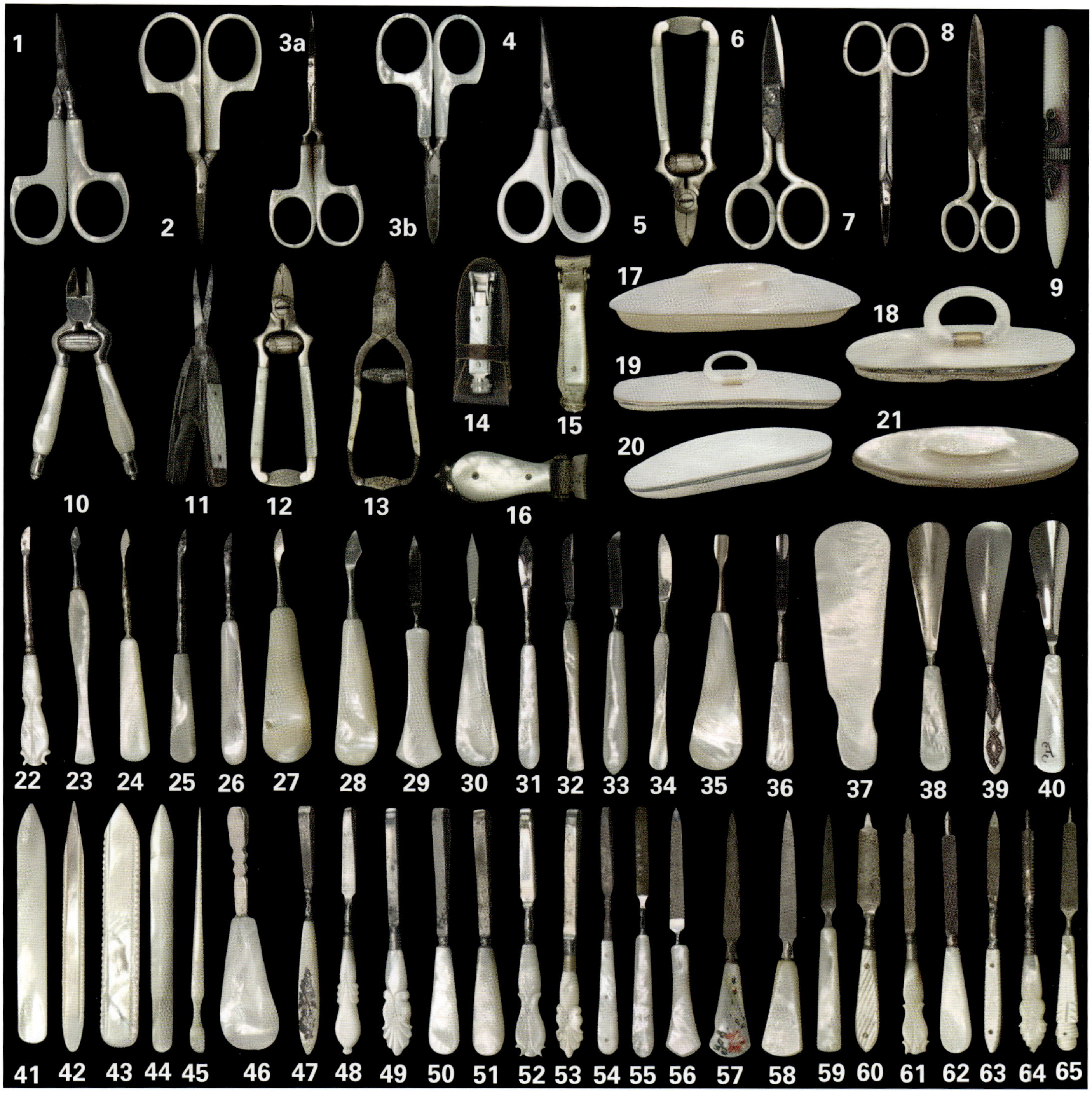


## PLATE 162 – MANICURE TOOLS

**1–5.** Manicure scissors, various designs, Germany for USA market, c. 1918–30, size 3.1″ to 4.5″ (8 to 11.5 cm). **6–8.** Manicure scissors, H. Boker, Germany, for the export market, c. 1880, size 3.9″ to 5.5″ (10 to 14 cm). **9.** Manicure tool for nail care, England, c. 1880, size 3.5″ (9 cm). **10.** Nail clippers, H. Boker, Germany, for the export market, c. 1880, size 4.7″ (12 cm). **11.** Nail clippers, Germany, for the export market, c. 1850, size 3.5″ (9 cm). **12.** Nail clippers inscribed *Gejtzl Geschutzt*, Germany, c. 1900–10, size 4.2″ x 1.3″ (10.7 x 3.3 cm). **13.** Nail clippers, Krusius Bros, Germany, c. 1910, size 4.1″ x 1.4″ (10.3 x 3.5 cm). **14.** Nail clippers, King Clip Co. NY, USA, c. 1905, size 2.3″ x 0.4″ (6 x 1 cm). **15.** Nail clippers, K.S. Koller, Germany, c. 1910–20, size 1.8″ x .4″ (4.5 x 0.9 cm). **16.** Nail clippers, possibly Ansonia, USA , c. 1910, size 1.5″ x 0.6″ (3.7 x 1.5 cm). **17–21.** Nail buffers, various designs, France for USA market, c. 1910–30, size 4.1″ x 5.1″ (10.5 to 13 cm) **22.** Manicure tool, England, c. 1890, size 4.3″ (11 cm) **23-36,41-45.** Manicure tools, USA, c. 1918-30, size 3.1″ to 6.3″ (8 to 16 cm). **37–40.** Shoe horn, various shapes, USA, c. 1910–30, size 4.3″ to 7.7″ (11 to19.5 cm). **46.** Tweezers, USA, c. 1910–30, size 3.5″ (9 cm). **47.** Tweezers, USA, c. 1880, sterling silver, size 5.5″ (14 cm). **48–54.** Tweezers, England, c. 1880–1910, size 3.5″ to 4.7″ (9 to 12 cm). **55–59.** Nail file, USA, c. 1910–30, size 3.5″ to 6.7″ (9 to 17 cm). **60–65.** Nail file, England, c1880–1910, size 3.7″ to 4.7″ (9.5 to 12 cm).

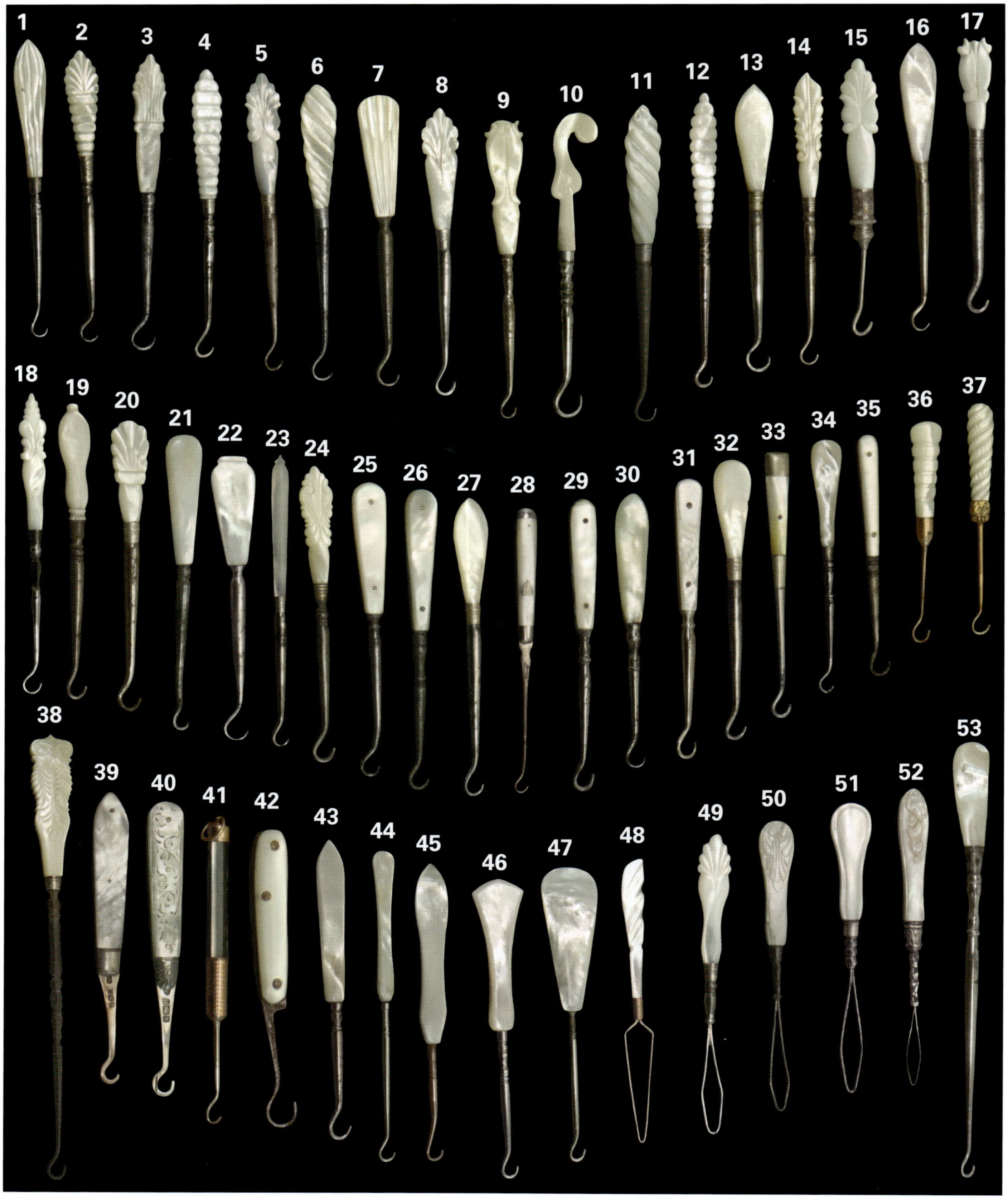


## PLATE 163 – BUTTON and SHOE HOOKS

**1–37.** Button hooks in various designs, England, c. 1850–1900, size 2.2″ to 4.7″ (5.5 to 12 cm). **38.** Shoe hook, France, c. 1880–1900, size 11.1″ (28.3 cm). **39–40.** Folding button hooks, hallmarked silver, Sheffield, England, 1901, size 2.2″ closed 3.3″ open (5.5 cm, 8.5 cm). **41.** Retractable button hook, USA, c. 1870, 2.2″ closed 3.1″ open (5.5 cm, 8 cm). **42.** Folding button hook, England, c. 1900, 1.2″ closed, 2.2″ open (3 cm, 5.5 cm). **43–47.** Button hooks, USA, c. 1900–1930, size 4.1″ to 5.9″ (10.5 to 15 cm). **48.** Looped buttoner, USA, c. 1910, size 4.3″ (11 cm). **49–52.** Looped buttoner, England, c. 1880–1900, size 3.1″ to 5.1″ (8 to 13.5 cm). **53.** Shoe hook, USA, c. 1920, size 8.5″ (21.5 cm).

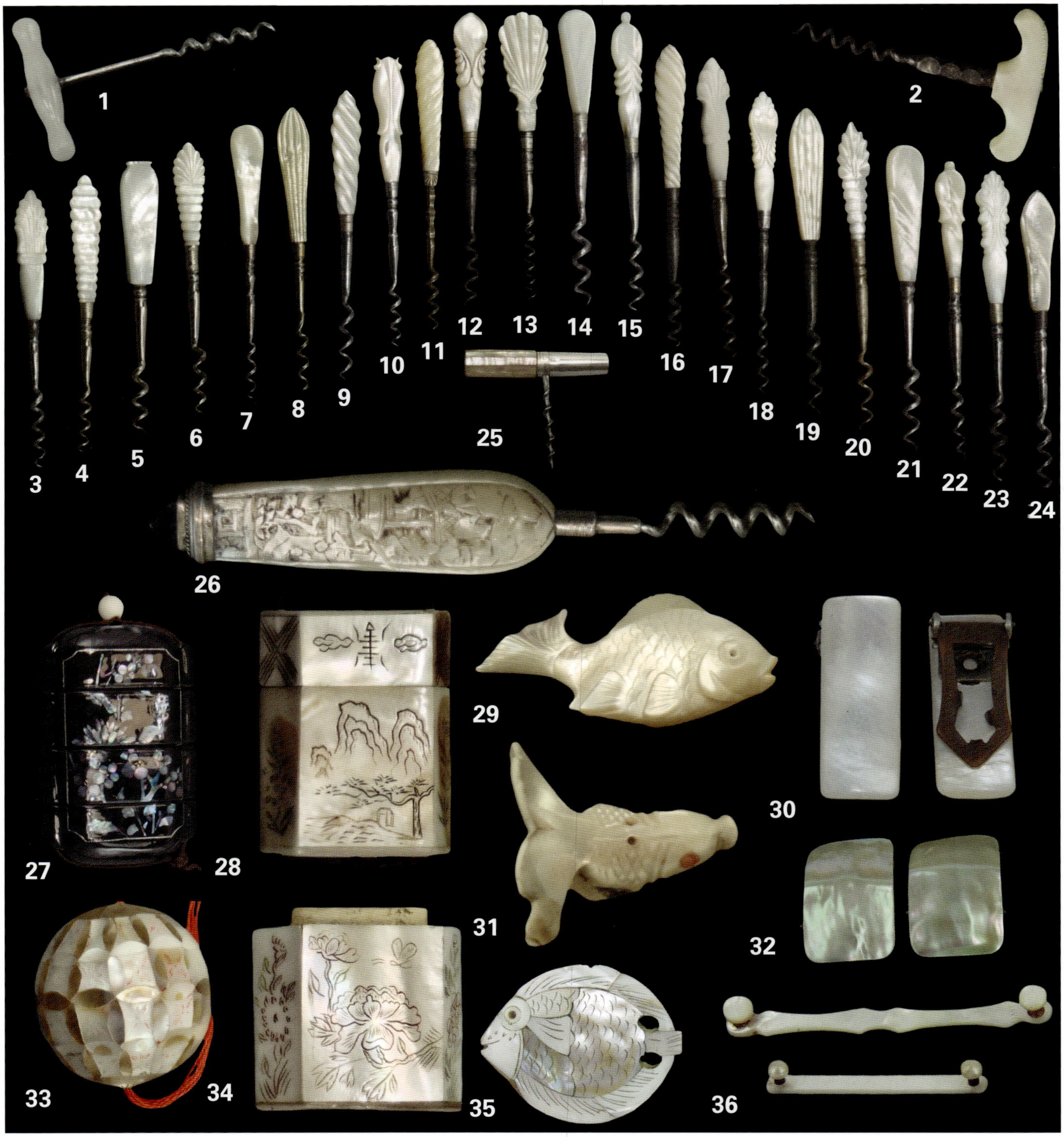


## PLATE 164 – PERFUME CORKSCREWS, ACCESSORIES

The smaller corkscrews are used for removing corks from early perfume bottles. **1.** Corkscrew, England, c. 1870–80, size 2″ x 1.2″ (5 x 3 cm). **2.** Corkscrew, England, c. 1850–80, size 2.4″ x 1.4″ (6 x 3.5 cm). **3–24.** Corkscrew, many designs were produced in over fifty years of production, England, c. 1850–1900, size 3.5″ to 4.5″ (9 to 11.5 cm). **25.** Corkscrew, France, c. 1900, marked Depose M, silver side unscrews to allow corkscrew to fit in the handle, size 3.5″ x 3″ (9 x 7.5 cm). **26.** Corkscrew, China, c. 1840, size 6.1″ x 0.8″ (15.5 x 2 cm). **27.** Lacquer inro, Japan, c. 1950, size 3.5″ x 2.4″ (9 x 6 cm). **28.** Inro, Japan, c. 1850, size 1.6″ x 1.4″ (4 x 3.5 cm). **29.** Netsuke in the shape of a fish, Japan, c. 1850, size 2.2″ (5.5 cm). **30.** Dress or lingerie clips, USA, c. 1920, size 1″ to 1.4″ (2.5 to 3.5 cm). **31.** Netsuke, goldfish, Japan, c. 1880, size 1.3″ (3.4 cm). **32.** Shoe buckles, England, c. 1920, size 2.4″ x 1.6″ (6 x 4 cm). **33.** Ojime bead to hold the inro closed, Japan, c. 1950, size 1″ (2.5 cm). **34.** Inro, missing its lid, Japan, c. 1850, size 1.2″ x 1.3″ (3 x 3.4 cm). **35.** Netsuke, fish, Japan, c. 1900, size 2″ x 1.5″ (5 x 3.8 cm). **36.** Cape clips, USA, c. 1890–1900, size 2″ to 3″ (5 to 7.5 cm).

## PLATE 165 – PERFUME CONTAINERS

Most of the smaller varieties of perfume containers in this section were designed to fit into a lady's purse or reticule. **1a–b.** Etui with four perfume bottles, France, c. 1870–90, size 10.6" x 5.5" (27 x 14 cm). **2.** Set of three perfume bottles in a mother-of-pearl stand, England, c. 1880–1900, size 5.7" x 2.9" (14.5 x 7.4 cm). **3.** Vanity set consisting of an atomizer, rouge pot, and powder compact. Made under name *La Clon*, manufactured by Marcel Franck, France, c. 1930, size of box 4.1" x 4.1" (10.5 x 10.5 cm). **4a–b.** Set of three cologne or perfume bottles in a mother-of-pearl box, England, c. 1860, size 6.2" x 3.9" (15.8 x 10 cm). **5a–b.** Perfume holder, France, c. 1870, size 4.3" x 4.5" (11 x 11.5 cm), with replacement Czech bottle, c. 1935. **6.** Box for holding a perfume bottle, France, c. 1820–35, size 3.1" x 2" (7.8 x 5 cm). **7.** Box with perfume bottle, France, c. 1820–35, size 2.9" x 1.3" (7.3 x 3.3). **8.** Perfume atomizer, Consul Amor, Germany, c. 1950, size 2.1" x 1.4" (5.3 x 3.6). **9.** Perfume atomizer, Narcon, Japan, c. 1950, size 2.1" x 1" (5.3 x 2.6 cm). **10.** Holder with three perfume bottles, USA, c. 1950–60, size 1.6" x 1.9" (4 x 4.8 cm). **11–12.** Perfume bottle, Wiesner of Miami, USA, c. 1950, size 1.8" x 1.2" (4.5 x 3 cm).

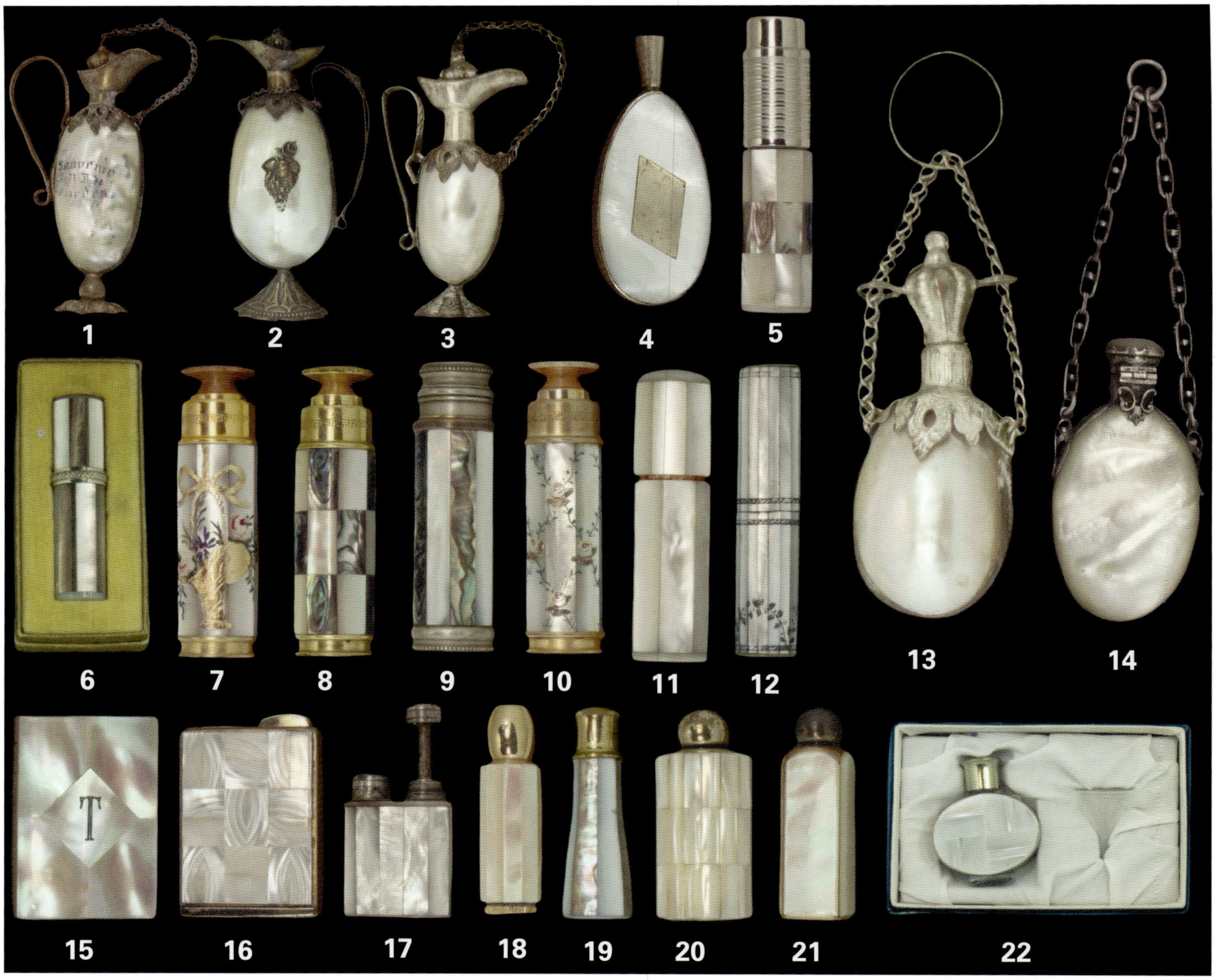


## PLATE 166 – PERFUME CONTAINERS

1. Ewer style table top Holy Water/Perfume bottle inscribed *Souvenir Lourdes*, France, c. 1870–1910, size 3.1" x 1.9" (8 x 4.7 cm). 2. Ewer style perfume bottle sold at world fairs and major tourist outlets, France, c. 1870–1910, size 4.7" x 2.8" (12 x 7 cm). 3. Ewer style table top perfume bottle sold at world fairs and major tourist outlets, France, c. 1870–1910, size 2.8" x 1.6" (7 x 4 cm). 4. Perfume bottle, France or Austria, c. 1810–20, from a *Necessaire de Voyage,* size 2" (5 cm). 5. Perfume atomizer, USA, c. 1950, size 3" x 0.7" (7.6 x 1.9 cm). 6. Perfume atomizer made under the name *Le Kismy,* manufactured by Marcel Franck, France, c. 1920, size 2.6" x 0.7" (6.6 x 1.7 cm), in original box. 7–10. Perfume atomizer, made under the name *Le Kid,* manufactured by Marcel Franck, France, c. 1920, size 2.6" x 0.7" (6.6 x 1.7 cm). 11. Perfume bottle holder, England, c. 1920–30, size 2.4" x 0.7" (6.2 x 1.8 cm). 12. Perfume bottle, France, c. 1909–1914, in a style echoing the Directoire period of 100 years prior to its manufacture, size 2.4" x 0.6" (6 x 1.4 cm). 13. Chatelaine perfume bottle sold at world fairs and major tourist outlets, England, c. 1890, size 2.4" x 1" (6.2 x 2.5 cm). 14. Chatelaine perfume bottle, ring, and chain for attachment to a belt, England, c. 1875, size 3" x 1.6" (7.7 x 4 cm). 15. Perfume bottle, Elizabeth Ames, USA, c. 1940–50, size 1.8" x 1.2" (4.5 x 3.1 cm). 16. Perfume atomizer, Primadonna, USA, c. 1950, size 2.1" x 1.4" (5.3 x 3.5 cm). 17. Perfume atomizer, France, c. 1920, size 3.1" x 1.6" (8 x 4 cm). 18. Perfume bottle, Hollywood, USA, c. 1950, size 2" x 0.6" (5 x 1.5 cm). 19. Perfume bottle for evening use, similar shape to opera glasses, France, c. 1890–1910, size 2.2" x 0.8" (5.7 x 2 cm). 20. Perfume bottle, Wiesner of Miami, USA, c. 1950, size 2.1" x 1" (5.3 x 2.5 cm). 21. Perfume bottle, Wiesner of Miami, USA, c. 1950, size 2.4" x 0.8" (6 x 2 cm). 22. Perfume bottle and funnel, probably Wiesner of Miami, USA, c. 1950, size 1.7" x 1.5" (4.4 x 3.8 cm).

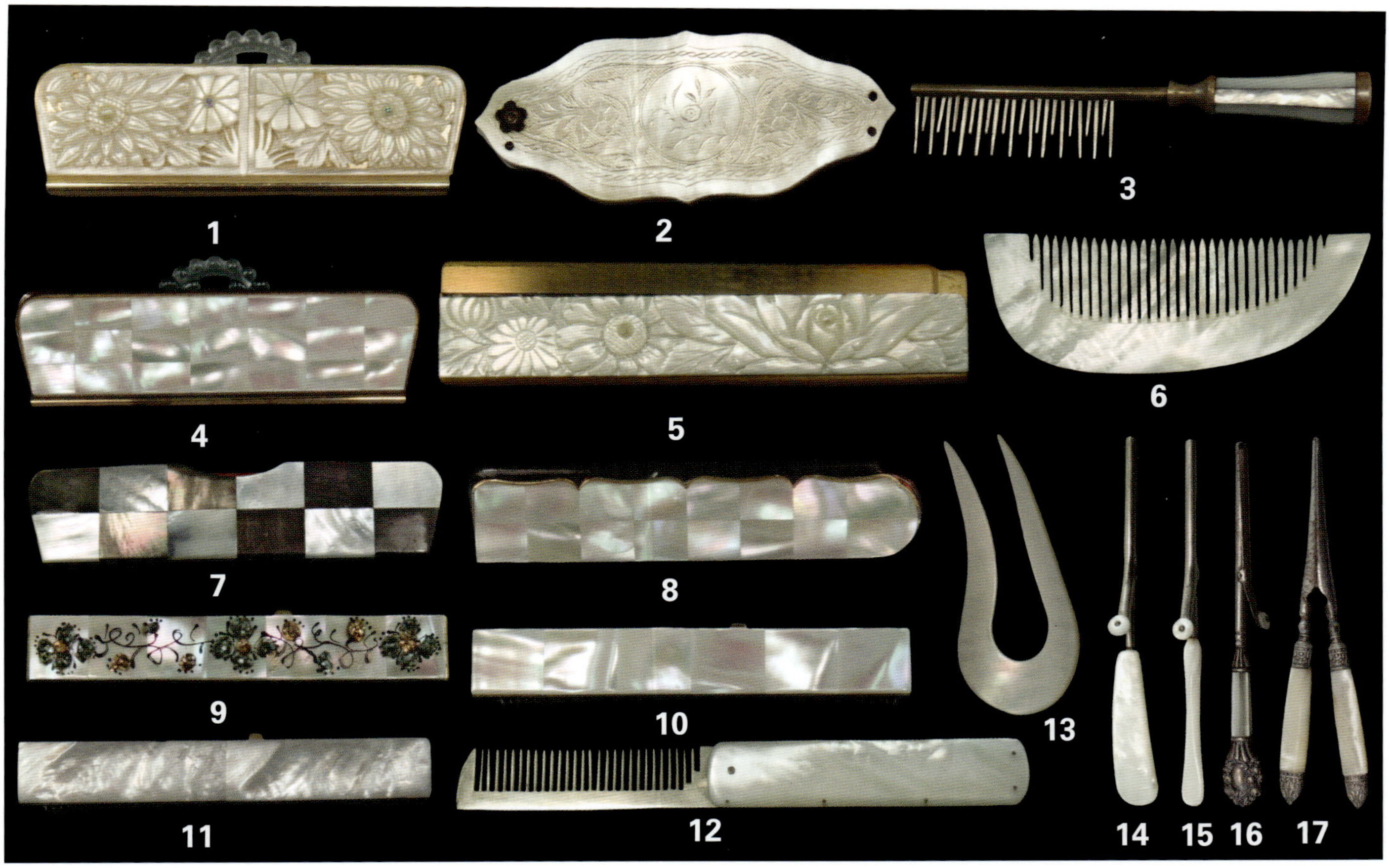

## PLATE 167 – COMBS AND CURLING IRONS

1. Comb in pearl case with carved flowers, with mirror, USA, c. 1950, size 4.3″ x 1.3″ (11 x 3.2 cm). 2. Folding comb, initials *L.N.*, China for the export market, c. 1850–60, size 2.6″ x 1.1″ (6.5 x 2.8 cm). 3. Comb, Germany, c. 1890–1910, size 5.5″ x 1″ (14 x 2.6 cm). 4. Comb in pearl case, USA, c. 1950, size 4.6″ x 1.2″ (11.7 x 3 cm). 5. Folding comb, carved rose and flowers, USA, c. 1950, size 4.1″ x 1″ (10.4 x 2.5 cm). 6. Comb made from solid pearl, Japan, c. 1868–1912, size 3.9″ x 1.4″ (10 x 3.6 cm). 7. Comb, pearl case, Fuller USA, c. 1940–50, size 4.3″ x 1″ (11 x 2.6 cm). 8. Folding comb, Stratton England, c. 1940–50, size 4.1″ x 0.8″ (10.3 x 2 cm). 9. Folding comb, USA, c. 1940, size 4.2″ x 0.7″ (10.6 x 1.8 cm). 10. Folding comb, Marhill, USA, c. 1940–50, size 4.3″ x 0.7″ (11 x 1.7 cm). 11. Folding comb, Bliss, USA, c. 1930–40, size 4.3″ x 0.6″ (11 x 1.6 cm). 12. Folding silver comb, hallmarked, USA, c. 1850–70, size 3.2″ x 0.8″ (8.2 x 2 cm). 13. Comb or hair decoration, England, c. 1920–40, size 3.1″ x 1.4″ (8 x 3.6 cm). 14. Curling iron, USA, c. 1930, size 6.3″ (16 cm). 15. Curling iron, USA, c. 1920, size 6.5″ (16.5 cm). 16. Curling iron, USA, c. 1910–20, size 7.1″ (18 cm). 17. Glove stretcher, France, c. 1885, size 8.3″ (21 cm).

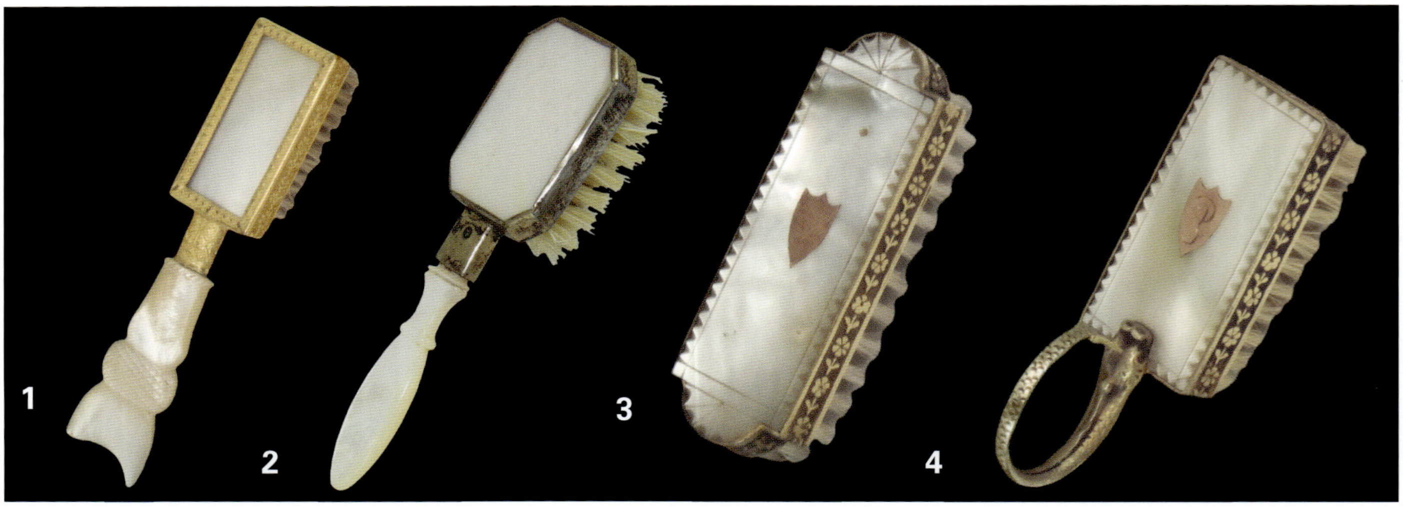

## PLATE 168 – MOUSTACHE BRUSHES

These moustache brushes were all made in France, c. 1810–20. Most were from boxed sets made for travelers. 1. Size 3.7″ x 1″ (9.5 x 2.3 cm). 2. Size 2.4″ x 0.9″ (6 x 2.2 cm). 3. Size 3″ (7.5 cm). 4. Size 2.4″ x 0.8″ (6 x 2 cm).

## PLATE 169 – MIRRORS

**1.** Exceptional decorative hand mirror, France, c. 1850–75, possibly part of a boxed set, size 4.3″ x 1.6″ (11 x 4 cm). **2.** Hand mirror, China, made for export market, c. 1830–60, size 10″ x 2.6″ (25.5 x 6.6 cm), etched roses. **3.** Small vanity mirror, USA, c. 1950, size 4.7″ x 2.4″ (12 x 6.2 cm). **4.** Small vanity mirror, USA, c. 1940, size 5.1″ x 2″ (13 x 5.2 cm). **5.** Small vanity mirror, USA, likely Marhill, c. 1950, size 3.5″ x 2″ (9 x 5 cm). **6.** Hand mirror, Esfahan, Iran, c. 1895, size 5.7″ x 2.4″ (14.6 x 6 cm), painted horsemen. **7.** Small vanity mirror, USA, c. 1950, size 4.7″ x 2.4″ (12 x 6.2 cm). **8.** Hand mirror, hallmarked Birmingham, England, 1905, size 5.3″ x 2.2″ (13.5 x 5.5 cm). **9.** Purse mirror or top of a patch box, Japan, c. 1890, size 2.4″ x 1.6″ (6 x 4 cm). **10.** Handbag souvenir mirror with pearl cover, USA, c. 1900, inscribed *Niagara Falls*, size 2.7″ x 2″ (6.8 x 5 cm). **11.** Mirror with carved fisherwomen cover, inscribed *Greuville*, France, c. 1890, size 2.4″ x 1.8″ (6 x 4.5 cm). **12.** Purse set: mirror, comb, vanity, inscribed *La Havre*, France, c. 1930–50, size 2.8″ x 1.8″ (7 x 4.5 cm).

## PLATE 170 – VANITY SETS AND BRUSHES

1. Hair grooming brush decorated with a carved urn and flowers with stiff natural boars' bristles for polishing the hair, France, c. 1880–1920, size 9.8″ (25 cm). 2a, 2b, 2c. Vanity set, France, c. 1900–1920, size mirror 10.1″ x 5.9″ (25.6 x 15 cm), hair brush 9.4″ x 2.4″ (24 x 6 cm), clothes brush 6.3″ x 5.5″ (16 x 14 cm). 3a, 3b, 3c. Vanity set, hallmarked sterling silver, Percy James Finch, Birmingham, England, 1922, mirror 10.2″ x 5.4″ (26 x 13.6 cm), hair brush 9.8″ x 3″ (24.8 x 7.5 cm), clothes brush 6.5″ x 1.8″ (16.7 x 4.5 cm). 4. Clothes brush, France, c. 1910, likely once part of a set, size 7.7″ x 2″ (19.5 x 5.2 cm), abalone shell and mother-of-pearl oyster. 5. Clothes brush, France, c. 1900–1910, likely once part of a set, size 7.6″ x 1.3″ (19.2 x 3.3 cm). 6. Hair brush, England, c. 1910–20, size 6.7″ x 1.7″ (17 x 4.3 cm). 7a, 7b. Vanity set, USA, c. 1940–50, mirror 12.9″ x 4.3″ (32.8 x 11 cm), hair brush 9.8″ x 3.1″ (25 x 7.8 cm). 8a, 8b. Vanity set, France, c. 1930–50, mirror 14.6″ x 4.3″ (37 x 11 cm), hair brush 9.1″ x 3″ (23 x 7.5 cm). 9a, 9b. Vanity set, USA, c. 1950, mirror 12.2″ x 4.7″ (31 x 12 cm), hair brush 10 x 3.3″ (25.6 x 8.5 cm).

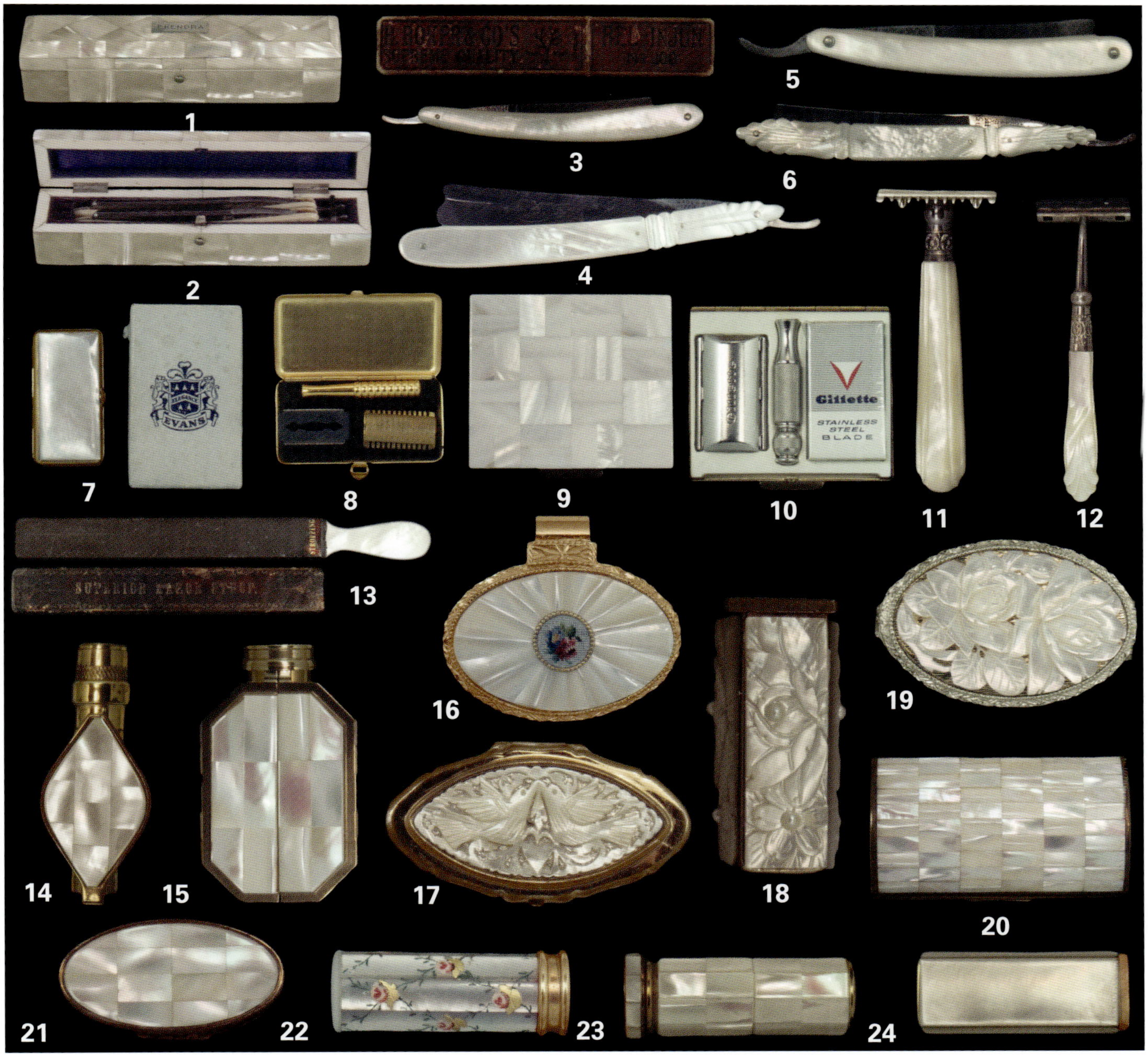

## PLATE 171 – SHAVING and LIPSTICK HOLDERS

**1–2.** Two straight razors in a pearl box, inscribed *F. Kendra*, Kropp, Sheffield, England, 1888, size 7.1″ x 1.6″ (18 x 4 cm). **3.** Straight razor, model Red Injun100, H. Boker, USA, c. 1900, size 6.2″ (15.7 cm). **4.** Straight razor, Wade & Butcher, Sheffield, England, c. 1895, size 6.1″ (15.5 cm). **5.** Corn razor, Vom Cleff, Germany, c. 1900, size 3.7″ (9.5 cm). **6.** Straight razor, J A Henckels, Germany, c. 1895, size 6.1″ (15.5cm). **7–8.** Ladies safety razor in a pearl box, Evans, USA, c. 1924, size 2″ x 1″ (5 x 2.5 cm). **9–10.** Safety razor in pearl box, razor by Gillette, box by Marhill, USA, c. 1960, size 2.4″ x 2.8″ (6 x 7 cm). **11.** Safety razor, Gillette type, England, c. 1910–20, size 4.1″ (10.5 cm). **12.** Safety razor, England, c. 1910, size 4.9″ (12.5 cm). **13.** Razor strop, England, c. 1880, size 12″ x 1.3″ (30.5 x 3.2 cm). **14.** Lipstick holder, Wiesner of Miami, USA, c. 1950 size 3.1″ x 1.2″ (8 x 3 cm). **15.** Lipstick holder, Wiesner of Miami, USA, c. 1950, size 2.6″ x 1.5″ (6.5 x 3.8 cm). **16.** Lipstick holder and mirror, Schildkraut, USA, c. 1950, size 2.8″ x 2.4″ (7 x 6 cm). **17.** Lipstick container with two love birds, Stratton, England, c. 1950, size 2.6″ x 1.4″ (6.5 x 3.5 cm). **18.** Lipstick holder and mirror, Schildkraut, USA, c. 1960, size 2.8″ x 1.9″ (7 x 4.7 cm). **19.** Lipstick holder, likely Schildkraut, USA, c. 1950–60, size 2″ x 0.8″ (5 x 2 cm). **20.** Lipstick holder, Ronson, USA, c. 1950, size 3″ x 1.7″ (7.5 x 4.3 cm). **21.** Lip stick holder, Max Factor, England, c. 1950, size 2.6″ x 1.1″ (6.7 x 2.8 cm). **22.** Lipstick holder, possible Marcel Franck, France, c. 1925, size 2″ x 0.8″ (5 x 2 cm). **23.** Lipstick holder, USA, c. 1950–60, size 2.16″ x 0.8″ (5.5 x 2 cm). **24.** Lipstick holder, Wiesner of Miami, USA, c. 1950, size 1.9″ x 0.8″ (4.8 x 2 cm).

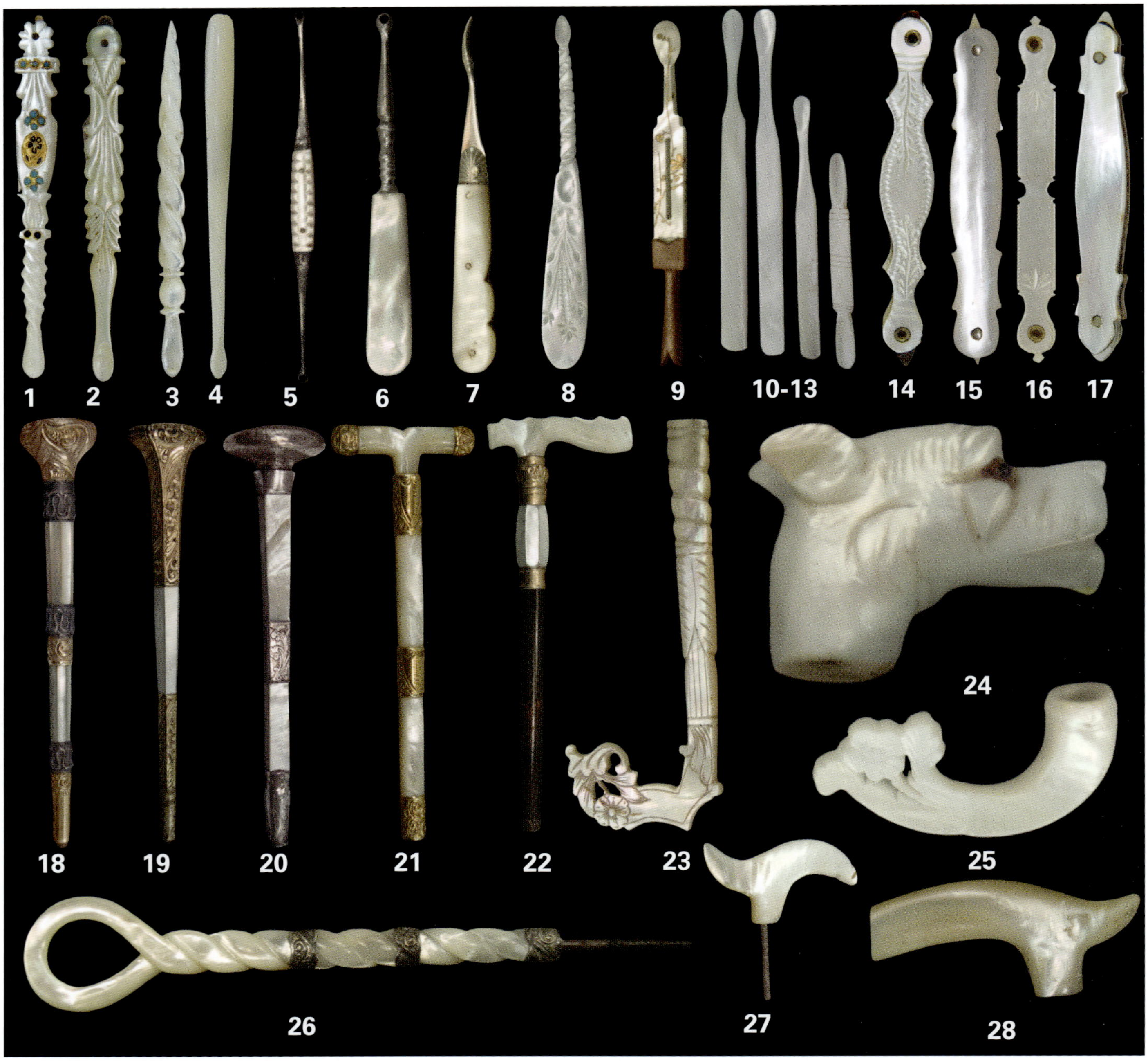

## PLATE 172 – EAR SCOOPS and HANDLES

**1, 2.** Ear scoop with the enameled pansy from Palais Royal, Paris, France, c. 1820, size 2.8" (7 cm). **3.** Ear scoop from a sewing set sold in the arcades of Palais Royal, Paris, France, c. 1820, size 2.4" (6 cm). **4.** Ear scoop, from a boxed set, France, 1830, size 2.8" (7 cm). **5.** Ear scoop, England, c. 1900, size 4.5" (11.5 cm). **6.** Ear scoop, Germany, for the export market, c. 1900, size 3" (7.5 cm). **7.** Folding ear scoop, hallmarked I.E.& S. Sheffield, England, 1910, size open 3.5" (9 cm), closed 2.2" (5.5 cm). **8.** Ear scoop, USA, c. 1910, size 3.7" (9.5 cm). **9.** Ear scoop, England, c. 1900, size 3.5" (9 cm). **10–13.** Ear scoop, USA, c. 1920–30, size 2.2" to 3.5" (5.5 to 9 cm). **14–17.** Folding ear scoop from a Palais Royal boxed set, France c. 1820, size #**14**: 2.2" (5.5 cm), #**15**: 2.4" (6 cm), #**16**: 2.6" (6.5 cm) , #**17**: 2.4" (6 cm). **18.** Walking stick handle inscribed *NGT*, England, 1908, size 10" (25.5 cm). **19.** Walking stick handle inscribed *LRL*, England, c. 1890, size 11 ¼" (28.5 cm). **20.** Walking stick handle inscribed with initial *C*, USA, c. 1900, sterling, size 8.9" (22.5 cm). **21.** Walking stick handle inscribed *M. Anderson, Hamilton Sept. 1899,* England, 1899, size 7.9" (20 cm). **22.** Walking stick handle, England, c. 1900, size 8.1" (20.5 cm). **23.** Parasol handle, England, c. 1850, size 4.3" (11 cm). **24.** Walking stick handle in the shape of a dog's head, France, c. 1890, size 1.18" (3 cm). **25.** Parasol handle, England, c. 1880, size 2.2" (5.5 cm). **26.** Parasol handle inscribed *Sterling*, USA, c. 1890, size 6.9" (17.5 cm). **27, 28.** Walking stick handles, France, c. 1880–1900, size 2.6" (6.5 cm).

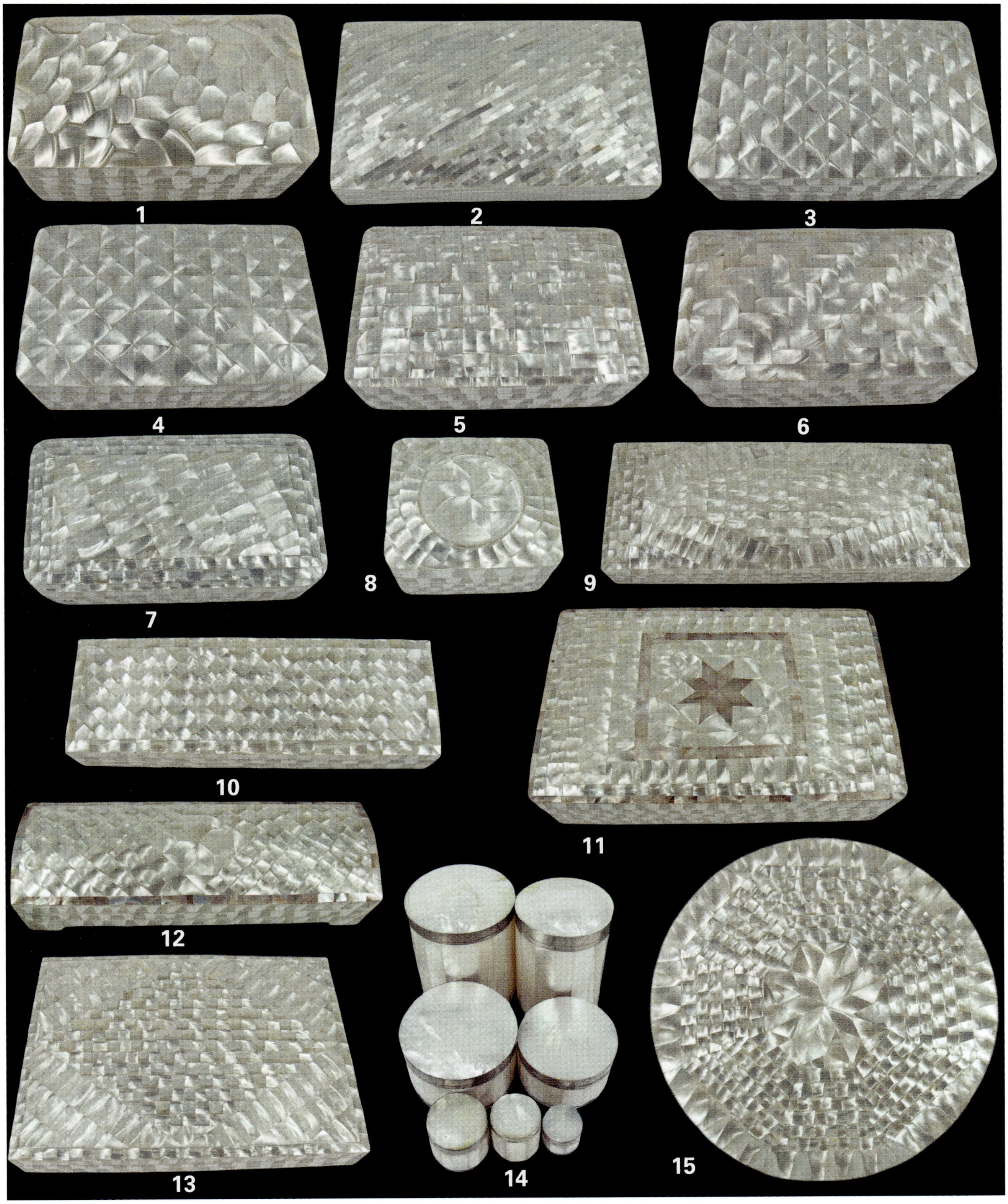


## PLATE 173 – JEWELRY and TRINKET BOXES FROM MYANMAR/BURMA

The wide range of variation in this selection of jewelry boxes from Myanmar/Burma shows what can be achieved by cutting the mother-of-pearl into different shapes and overlaying in different patterns. These designs are unique to this region. They are all c. 1995–2000. **1–2.** Size 7″ x 4″ x 3″ (17.8 x 10.3 x 7.5 cm). **3–5.** Size 8″ x 5.1″ x 2.6″ (20.5 x 13 x 6.5 cm). **6.** Size 7″ x 4″ x 3″ (17.8 x 10.3 x 7.5 cm). **7.** Size 7.1″ x 4″ x 1.5″ (18 x 10 x 3.8 cm). **8.** Size 4.6″ x 4″ x 2.6″ (11.8 x 10.4 x 6.7 cm). **9–10.** Size 8.9″ x 3″ x 1.4″ (22.6 x 7.5 x 3.5 cm). **11.** Size 11″ x 7.1″ x 2.6″ (28 x 18 x 6.5 cm). **12.** Size 12″ x 4″ x 2″ (30.5 x 10 x 5 cm). **13.** Size 10″ x 7″ x 1.5″ (25.2 x 17.8 x 3.7 cm). **14.** Trinket boxes in many different sizes, Myanmar, c. 1999, size from 1″ x 0.8″ diameter (2.5 cm x 2 cm) to 3″ x 3.5″ diameter (7.5 cm x 9 cm). **15.** Size 10.1″ (25.8 cm) diameter.

## PLATE 174 – JEWELRY BOXES FROM THE HOLY LAND

1. A magnificent jewelry box, Palestine, c. 1900, size 10.6″ x 7.9″ x 4.9″ (27 x 20 x 12.5 cm). 2. Box attributed to the collection of the Israeli Prime Minister Ehud Barak, who was reportedly given it in 1999 by the Palestine Authority, Palestine, 1999, size 12.6″ x 9.6″ x 3.3″ (32 x 24.5 x 8.5 cm). 3. Palestine, c. 1910, size 5.9″ x 5.9″ x 3.1″ (15 x 15 x 7.8 cm). 4. Box with Nativity scene in center, Palestine, c. 1950, size 9″ x 6.3″ x 3.1″ (23 x 16 x 8 cm). 5. Palestine, c. 1960, size 4.5″ x 3.5″ x 1.4″ (11.5 x 9 x 3.5 cm) the brass box was likely imported and pearl top added in Palestine. 6. Palestine, c. 1950–70, size 6.8″ x 4.9″ x 2″ (17.3 x 12.5 x 5 cm). 7. Palestine, c. 1950–70, size 2.4″ x 2.2″ x 1.7″ (6 x 5.5 x 4.3 cm). 8. Palestine, c. 1950–70, size 5.9″ x 5.9″ x 2″ (15 x 15 x 5 cm). 9. Box inscribed *With compliments of Jordan Armed Forces*, Jordan, c. 1986, size 7.1″ x 4.7″ x 0.7″ (18 x 12 x 1.7 cm). 10. Palestine, c. 1950–70, size 2.6″ x 2.6″ x 2″ (6.5 x 6.5 x 5 cm). 11. Palestine, c. 1950–70, size 6.1″ x 4.5″ x 1.6″ (15.5 x 11.5 x 4 cm). 12. Palestine, c. 1950–70, size 4.1″ x 3.5″ x 2″ (10.5 x 9 x 5 cm). 13. Palestine, c. 1950–70, size 11.8″ x 4.9″ x 2″ (30 x 12.5 x 5 cm). 14–15. Boxes made for tourism trade to be sold as souvenirs of a visit to a royal area, town, or castle, Palestine, c. 1960, size #8: 6.3″ x 4.7″ x 2″ (16 x 12 x 5 cm) size #9: 4″ x 4″ x 2″ (10 x 10 x 5.2 cm).

## PLATE 175 – JEWELRY, BOOK, and GLOVE BOXES

1. Jewelry box in the shape of a bathing machine, France, c. 1880–1910, size 3.2″ x 2.8″ x 4.4″ (8.2 x 7 x 11.3 cm), roof opens to show a padded interior. 2. Secret box made in the shape of a book, France, c. 1900–20, size 5.3″ x 4.3″ x 1.5″ (13.5 x 11 x 3.8 cm). 3. Jewelry box, France, c. 1890, size 6.5″ x 3.5″ x 2.4″ (16.5 x 9 x 6 cm). 4. Jewelry box, Myanmar, c. 1910, size 8.1″ x 4.3″ x 3.3″ (20.5 x 11 x 8.5 cm). 5. Secret box made in the shape of a photo album, England, c. 1867, size 5.9″ x 4.7″ x 1.9″ (15 x 12 x 4.8 cm). 6. Secret book box, England, c. 1870, size 9.8″ x 6.3″ x 2.2″ (25 x 16 x 5.5 cm) 7. Jewelry or vanity casket, France, c. 1870, size 4.1″ x 2.1″ x 3.1″ (10.5 x 5.3 x 8 cm). 8, 12. Jewelry box with pearl inlay, Egypt, c. 1950, size #8: 8.7″ x 7.5″ x 3.1″ (22 x 19 x 8 cm), #12: 6.3″ x 3.9″ x 2″ (16 x 9.8 x 5 cm). 9. Glove box, England, c. 1895, size 10.7″ x 3.6″ x 0.9″ (27.2 x 9.2 x 2.2 cm). 10. Glove box, England, c. 1895, size 10.9″ x 2.8″ x 1.2″ (27.8 x 7.2 x 3 cm). 11. Jewelry box, France, c. 1880, size 5.5″ x 3.9″ x 2.6″ (14 x 9.8 x 6.5 cm). 13. Jewelry box, France, c. 1880, size 11.8″ x 3.9″ x 3.5″ (30 x 10 x 9 cm). 14. Jewelry or playing cards box, Tahiti, c. 1940–50, size 7.9″ x 7.5″ x 1.8″ (20 x 19 x 4.5 cm).

## PLATE 176 – PILL and TRINKET BOXES

1. China, 1997, size 1.4" (3.5 cm). 2–4. Philippines, 1998, size 1.5" to 2.5" (3.9 to 6.4 cm). 5. India, c. 1960, size 1.3" diameter x 0.8" (3.2 cm x 2 cm). 6. Myanmar/Burma, c. 1999, size 1.4" diameter (3.5 cm). 7. Double pill box, China, c. 1950, size 2.4" x 1.2" x 0.5" (6.2 x 3 x 1.2 cm). 8. Stratton, England, c. 1940, size 1.4" x 1.4" x 0.5" (3.5 x 3.5 x 1.3 cm). 9. England, c. 1850, size 3" x 1" x 0.9" (7.5 x 2.7 x 2.2 cm). 10. India, c. 1980, brass inside, size 4.5" x 3.1" x 1.6" (11.4 x 8 x 4 cm). 11. With cameo, Italy, c. 1950, size 1.3" x 1" x 0.7" (3.4 x 2.5 x 1.8 cm). 12. Patch or pill box with the armorial crest of Baron Petre of Writtle, Essex, England, c. 1880, size 1.2" diameter x 0.4" (3.1 cm x 1.1 cm). 13. Salve pot, inscribed *RWC,* England, c. 1860, size 1.6" diameter x 0.4" (4 cm x 1.1 cm). 14. Patch box with a basket of flowers carved on the lid, France, c. 1750, size 2" diameter x 0.4" (5 x 1 cm). 15. Pomander box for pot pourri, France, c. 1800–20, size 2" diameter x 0.3" (0.5 cm x 0.8 cm), this box is similar to a whist marker box, but is much larger. 16. China, 1996, size 2.2" x 1.3" (5.5 x 3.5 cm). 17–18. Gentleman's pill box, pendant loop added later, France, c. 1800–1810, size 1.4" x 1" x 0.2" (3.6 x 2.6 x 0.6 cm). 19. Philippines, 1998, size 1.6" to 2" (4 to 5.2 cm). 20. Myanmar, c. 1999, size 3.3" diameter x 1.4" (8.5 cm x 3.5 cm). 21. Philippines, 1998, size 3.1" x 2" x 1.8" (7.8 x 5 x 4.5 cm). 22. France, c. 1860, size 2.5" x 1.6" x 0.2" (6.3 x 4 x 1.6 cm). 23. With initial *D,* China, c. 1820–40, size 1.6" x 1.6" x 1" (4 x 4 x 2.6 cm). 24. Initial *GAM*, China, c. 1820–40, size 1.6" x 1.6" x 1.2" (4 x 4 x 3 cm). 25. India, c. 1998, size 3" diameter x 3.3" (7.7 x 8.4 cm).

## PLATE 177 – JEWELRY and TRINKET BOXES

**1a, 1b.** Jewelry box with a carving of Pliny's doves, France, c. 1830–60, size 9.4″ x 6.5″ x 5.5″ (24 x 16.5 x 14 cm). **2.** Handkerchief box, China, c. 1850, with fine inlays showing three musicians, size 7.9″ x 7.7″ x 2.8″ (20 x 19.5 x 7 cm). **3.** Jewelry box, Philippines, c. 1996, size 11.2″ x 8.3″ x 4.5″ (28.5 x 21.2 x 11.5 cm). **4.** Presentation box, inscribed *Lund,* London, c. 1880, size 3.9″ x 2.4″ x 1.4″ (8.8 x 6 x 3.6 cm). **5.** Trinket box, England, c. 1880, size 3.9″ x 2.2″ x 1.8″ (9.8 x 5.6 x 4.5 cm). **6.** Jewelry box, India, c. 1950, size 5.9″ x 4″ x 3.7″ (15 x 10.2 x 9.5 cm). **7–8.** Multipurpose box, England, c. 1890, used for holding thimbles, a rosary, or day to day articles, size 2.7″ x 1.6″ (7 x 4 cm). **9.** Trinket with music box, India, c. 1970, size 4.8″ x 3.5″ x 2.8″ (12.2 x 9 x 7 cm). **10.** Trinket box, France, c. 1880, made from Chinese gaming counter that dates to c. 1800, size 2.5″ x 1″ x 0.6″ (6.4 x 2.5 x 1.4 cm).

## PLATE 178 – PURSES and VANITY ITEMS

1. Lady's purse or handbag, India, c. 1960–70, size 5.9" x 5.3" (15 x 13.5 cm). 2. Lady's purse or handbag, India, c. 1960–70, size 5.7" x 5.3" (14.5 x 13.5 cm). 3. Lady's purse or handbag, Thailand, c. 1900, size 5.1" x 3.1" (13 x 8 cm). 4. Vanity box, India, c. 1950, size 3.1" x 1.8" (8 x 4.5 cm). 5. Lady's purse or handbag in fish shape, marked *Elaine Shops,* China, c. 1950, size 9" x 5.3" (23 x 13.5 cm). 6. Vanity box, India, c. 1960, size 3.1" x 1.6" (8 x 4 cm). 7. Vanity bottle with Kohl applicator for applying dark eye/lid lines, India, c. 1970, size 2.8" x 3.1" (7 x 8 cm). 8. Flask type container, India, c. 1950, size 2" x 1.6" (5 x 4 cm). 9. Purse from a river shell, England, c. 1930, size 3.1" x 1.8" (7.8 x 4.5 cm). 10. Trinket box, India, c. 1998, sized 2.8" diameter x 2.4" (7 cm x 6 cm). 11. Escutcheon or box keyhole cover, England, c. 1920, size 1.8" x 1.2" (4.5 x 3 cm). 12. Kina, New Guinea, currency used as part payment for a wife, New Guinea, c. 1948, size 6.1" x 5.1" (15.5 x 13 cm). 13. Rouge or salve pot, France, c. 1850–75, size 2.3" diameter x 0.8" (6 cm x 2 cm). 14. Rouge or salve pot, France, c. 1850–75, size 2.4" diameter x 0.6" (6 cm x 1.5 cm). 15. Jewelry box, Thailand, 2007, size 3.1" x 3.1" x 1.3" (8 x 8 x 3.2 cm). 16. Trinket box (bamboo symbolizes longevity in Eastern philosophies), China, c. 1870, size 1.4" x 2" x 1.2" (3.5 x 5 x 3 cm).

## PLATE 179 – VANITY SETS, RING BOXES, ETC.

**1, 2.** Boxed vanity set, contains mirror, hair brush, clothes brush, compact, toothbrush bottle, and three vanity bottles, USA, c. 1925–35, size 9.5" x 6.2" x 3.9" (24.2 x 16 x 10 cm). **3, 4.** Rouge box, once thought to be a patch box, now believed for rouge and a brush, hallmarked Paris, France, 1744–1750, size 2.5" x 2" x 1.2" (6.3 x 5 x 3 cm). **5, 6.** Powder box, top of the box is for a puff and the bottom for powder, France, c. 1820–30, size 2.2" x 2.8" x 1.6" (5.5 x 7 x 4 cm). **7–9.** Ring boxes, England, c. 1890, size 1.3" x 0.8" x 1.2" (3.2 x 2 x 3 cm). **10.** Ring stand, hallmarked Birmingham, England, 1921, size 3.5" (9 cm). **11.** Ring stand, hallmarked Chester, England, 1912, size 3.9" (9.8 cm). **12.** Jewelry box with crystals, Thailand, c. 2007, size 2" (5 cm) square. **13.** Vinaigrette suitable for a housekeepers chatelaine, England, c. 1840–60, size 2.8" x 1" (7 x 2.5 cm). **14.** Rouge pot, France, c. 1906–1920, size 1.1" diameter x 0.4" (2.8 x 1 cm). **15.** Powder puff, made by PLI, France, c. 1920, size 2.2" x 0.7" (5.8 x 1.8 cm).

## PLATE 180 – LADIES' FANS 1

1. Exceptional fan with gilded figures, France, c. 1850, size 10.6″ x 20.5″ (27 x 52 cm). 2. Fan with excellent carving of the pearl sticks, France, c. 1850, size 10.6″ x 19.7″ (27 x 50 cm).

## PLATE 181 – LADIES' FANS 2

1. Fan, France, c. 1850–60, size 10.6" x 19.7" (27 x 50 cm). 2. Fan with ostrich feathers, France, c. 1920, size 6.3" x 9.4" (16 x 24 cm). 3. Fan, France, c. 1810–20, size 8.5" x 16.14" (21.5 x 41 cm). 4. Fan, France, c. 1850, size 10.6" x 20" (27 x 51 cm). 5. Fan with cloute work, France, c. 1880, size 7.9" x 14.6" (20 x 37 cm). 6. Fan, France or Belgium, c. 1870, size 9.4" x 17.7" (24 x 45 cm). 7. Fan, France, c. 1850–60, leaf might be later c. 1890–1900, size11.6" x 22.2" (29.5 x 56.5 cm).

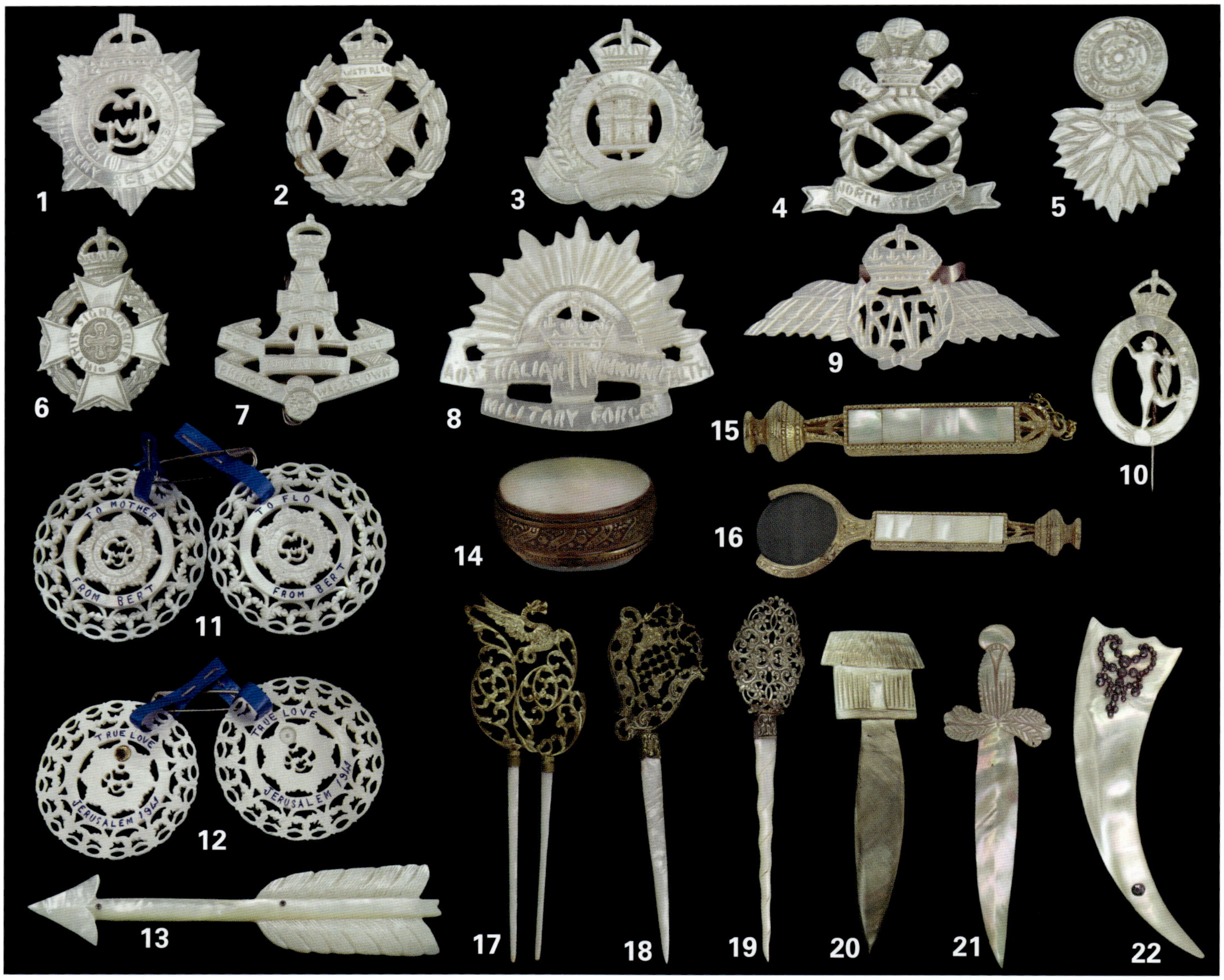

## PLATE 182 – REGIMENTAL BADGES, HAIR DECORATION

Regimental badges, also known as sweetheart brooches, were purchased during World War 2 by the troops who passed through Palestine. They were sent home to loved ones and worn with pride by wives and girlfriends. **1.** Royal Army Service Corps, Palestine, c. 1941–45, size 1.4″ x 1.4″ (3.5 x 3.5 cm). **2.** Rifle Brigade, Palestine, c. 1941–45, size 1.3″ x 1.2″ (3.2 x 3 cm). **3.** Suffolk Regiment, Palestine, c. 1941–45, size 1.5″ x 1.4″ (3.8 x 3.5 cm). **4.** North Stafford Regiment, Palestine, c. 1941–45, size 1.2″ x 1.2″ (3 x 3 cm). **5.** Honorable Artillery Co., Palestine, c. 1941–45, size 1.6″ x 1.2″ (4 x 3 cm). **6.** Royal Army Chaplins, Palestine, c. 1941–45, size 1.1″ x 1.4″ (2.8 x 3.6 cm). **7.** The Alexandra Princess Wales Own Yorkshire Regiment, Palestine, c. 1941–45, size 1.8″ x 1.6″ (4.6 x 4 cm). **8.** Australian Commonwealth Military Force, Palestine, c. 1941–45, size 1.5″ x 1.3″ (3.8 x 3.2 cm). **9.** Royal Air Force, Palestine, c. 1941–45, size 2″ x 1″ (5 x 2.5 cm). **10.** Royal Corps of Signals, Palestine, c. 1941–45, size 1.6″ x 0.6″ (4 x 1.5 cm). **11, 12.** Royal Army Service Corp, inscribed *Jerusalem 1941 To Mother from Bert* and *To Flo from Bert*. Did Bert make it through the war? We will never know. Size 1.7″ (4.3cm) diameter. **13.** Arrow, possible insignia from a fraternal group, uniform, or fashion, USA, c. 1950, size 4.9″ x 1.2″ (12.5 x 3 cm). **14.** Memorial box, other side glass for holding a memorial piece, England, c. 1870–80, size 1.8″ x 1.5″ (4.8 x 3.8 cm). **15.** Telephone dialer, possibly by Schildkraut, USA, c. 1960, size 3″ (7.6 cm). **16.** Telephone dialer with page magnifier, possibly by Schildkraut, USA, c. 1960, size 3.9″ (10 cm). **17.** Hair decoration with griffin, Europe, c. 1890–1910, size 5.1″ (13 cm). **18.** Hair decoration, Europe, c. 1890–1910, size 5.7″ (14.5 cm). **19.** Hair decoration, Europe, c. 1890–1910, size 5.8″ (14.7 cm). **20.** Hair decoration, Tahiti, c. 1980, size 4.1″ (10.5 cm). **21.** Hair decoration, USA, c. 1905, size 4.7″ (12 cm). **22.** Bag decoration, England, c. 1920, size 4.3″ x 1.2″ (11 x 3 cm).

**PLATE 183 – NECKLACES**

Thousands of different designs of mother-of-pearl necklaces have been made over the years. This is a small glimpse, mainly made in the Philippine Islands, c. 1960–1999.

## PLATE 184 – BROOCH – PINS

Many different designs have been made over the centuries. This is a small selection, mainly from China, the Philippines, and England, c. 1950–1999.

## PLATE 185 – PENDANTS

There is no end to the variety produced over the years. This is a small selection, mainly from China, the Philippines, and England, c. 1950–1999.

## PLATE 186 – BUCKLES

A small section from a very large collecting field. The dog and intricate carved buckles are from France, gold dragons buckle from Japan, the oval dragon buckle from China, and the rest from the USA and England, c. 1875–1975.

## PLATE 187 – BULGARIAN BUCKLES – PAFTI

Pafti, traditional woman's buckles from Bulgaria, often given as a wedding gift. Legend tells that the buckles protect the wearer from evil spells. The mother-of-pearl carving was done in Jerusalem and imported to Bulgaria, where Chiprovska goldsmiths made the metal buckle and assembled the item. The most popular design incorporates the eagle or falcon. Some buckles were also produced in Greece from the mother-of-pearl carvings imported from Palestine and used in northern Greece (mainly religious themes), and neighboring Bulgaria. 1. The falcon drinking, symbolizing hope, liberty, and victory, c. 1850–70, size 7.3" (18.5 cm). 2. The falcon, c. 1850–70, size 8.3" (21 cm). 3. Nativity scene, c. 1830–50, size 8.9" (22.5 cm). 4. One half of a buckle illustrating the Christian martyr Saint Demetrius, based on an early Orthodox icon, Palestine, c. 1830–50, size 4" x 2.8" (10.2 x 7.3 cm).

## PLATE 188 – HAIR BARRETTES

Hair clips, hair slides or hair barrettes from Philippine Islands and China, c. 1980–99. Many different designs have been made.

## PLATE 189 – KEY CHAINS

A wonderful series of key chains in the form of animals and marine life from Thailand, c. 1995. The Otter is from China, c. 1980. The square and ball is from the Philippines, c. 1995. Boxed—a musical keychain by Clover USA, c. 1950.

## PLATE 190 – PINS: HAT, STOCK, STICK

Top two hat pins, c. 1900. From left, stock pin, two stick pins from the Charles Darwin family line, c. 1830, rest stick pins: ones with metal covers are from China, the rest England and USA, c. 1960–80.

## PLATE 191 – CAMEOS

A selection of cameos made from mother-of-pearl from China, c. 1990.

## PLATE 192 – WATCH FOBS

A section from 1890–1920, mainly from England and the USA. They were attached to pocket watches and clipped on to the waistcoat to allow easy access to the watch.

## PLATE 193 – EARRINGS

Thousands of different designs have been made. This is a small section, mainly from China and the Philippine Islands, c. 1950–99.

# POWDER COMPACTS

During the Victorian era, the use of artificial beauty aids was frowned upon, and everyone was expected to rely on exercise and proper food to achieve rosy cheeks. It was only after Queen Victoria's death and the emancipation of women, that the use of cosmetics experienced a revival. With large numbers of women joining the work force, all of whom wanted to look fashionable, the portable powder compact developed. It was usually a round, flat container containing a mirror on the lid interior, pressed powder or loose powder on the bottom interior and a powder puff.

Some of the famous names for the manufacturers of mother-of-pearl topped compacts were Stratton, Melissa, Max Factor, Marhill, Schildkraut, Elgin, Kigu, Crown, W & W Light, and Evans. There were many smaller manufacturers. With the decline in popularity of the compact in the last quarter of the twentieth century, most manufacturers have long since disappeared.

It is interesting to note that although the more well-known manufacturers labeled compacts with their origins, this information was not completely correct. The mother-of-pearl tops were carved in large volumes and imported from China and a limited number from Palestine. These were attached by the manufacturers onto the standard metal compact that had been produced by the company. The Chinese top was usually a solid pearl piece that had been carved, whereas the Palestinian top was carved by piercing. The raw mother-of-pearl was not harvested in these regions, but imported from Australia, the Philippines, and Asia, so these pearl pieces had a long journey across the world before ending up as compact tops.

This collection is a mere fraction of the variety of mother-of-pearl compacts produced and there are enough compacts on the market to keep any collector going for decades. Most are inexpensive and this can be a very enjoyable collecting field.

**PLATE 194 – POWDER COMPACT**

In our opinion, the rarest mother-of-pearl topped compact is the Pygmalion grand piano with folding legs, England, c. 1940, size 2.8" x 2.4" (7 x 6 cm).

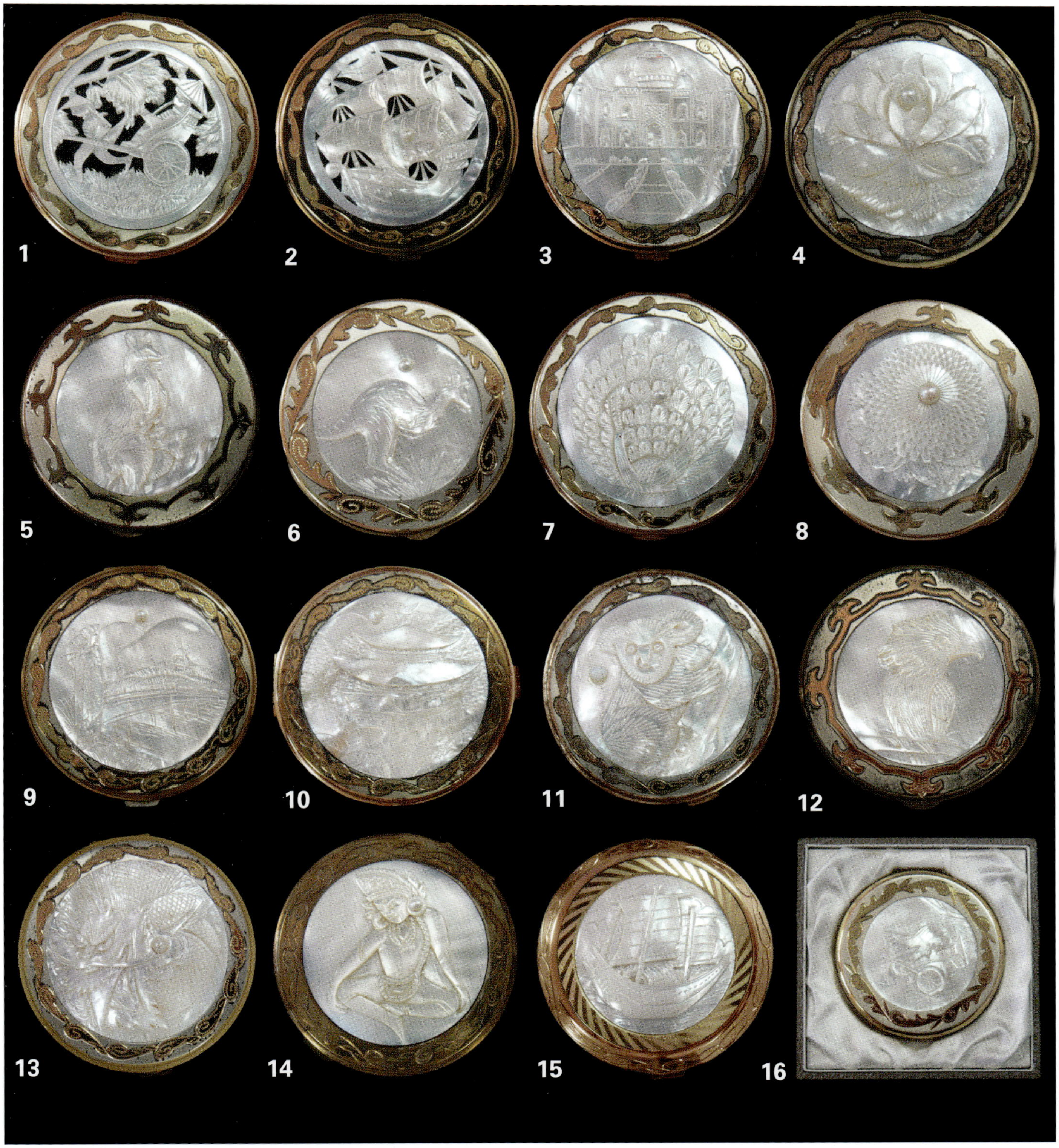


## PLATE 195 – POWDER COMPACTS

The compacts illustrated on this page are made by one manufacturer but are not marked. Inspection of over fifty examples has only produced one paper label giving the manufacturers name of W & W Light Japan. It is believed they are all made by this manufacturer. By subject matter, they were made with locally themed carvings for the tourist centers throughout the world. All sizes are the diameter of the compact. Japan, c. 1950. **1.** Rickshaw, size 3.1″ (8 cm). **2.** Galleon, size 3.1″ (8 cm). **3.** Taj Mahal, (India) size 3.1″ (8 cm). **4.** Rose, size 3.1″ (8 cm). **5.** Kangaroo, size 2.8″ (7 cm). **6.** Kangaroo, size 2.8″ (7 cm). **7.** Peacock, size 3.1″ (8 cm). **8.** Flower, size 2.8″ (7 cm). **9.** Japanese scene, size 3.1″ (8 cm). **10.** Pagoda, size 3.1″ (8 cm). **11.** Koala, size 3.1″ (8 cm). **12.** Bird, size 2.8″ (7 cm). **13.** Dragon, size 3.1″ (8 cm). **14.** Dancer, size 3.1″ (8 cm). **15.** Galleon, size 2.8″ (7 cm). **16.** Rickshaw, size 2.8″ (7 cm), in original box.

**PLATE 196 – POWDER COMPACTS**

1. Buddha, Japan, c. 1950, size 3.1″ (8 cm), in original box. 2. Dragon head, Japan, c. 1950, size 2.8″ (7 cm), in original box. 3. Mount Fuji, Japan, c. 1950, size 2.8″ (7 cm), in original box with a mother-of-pearl lipstick holder. 4. Fancy pattern, Japan, c. 1950, size 2.8″ (7 cm), in original box. 5. Star pattern, Stratton, England, c. 1950, size 3″ (7.5 cm). 6. Bird, Stratton, England, c. 1940, size 3.3″ (8.5 cm). 7. Jerusalem Cross, a Christian symbol, Stratton, England, c. 1950, size 3″ (7.5 cm). 8. Flower, Stratton, England, c. 1950, size 2.8″ (7 cm). 9. Star, Stratton, England, c. 1950, size 3″ (7.5 cm). 10. Flower, Stratton, England, c. 1940–50, size 3.3″ (8.5 cm). 11. Flower, Stratton, England, c. 1950, size 3″ (7.5 cm). 12. Shell shape, Stratton, England, c. 1950, size 2.6″ (6.5 cm). 13. Compact and lipstick holder set, Stratton, England, c. 1940, size 3.3″ (8.5 cm), in the original box. 14. Compact and inset lipstick holder, Stratton, England, c. 1950, size 3.1″ x 2.8″ (8 x 7 cm). 15. Pearl top, Stratton, England, c. 1950, size 2.6″ (6.5 cm). 16. Pearl top in gilt holder, Whiting and Davis, USA, c. 1930, size 2.4 x 2.8″ (6 x 7 cm).

## PLATE 197 – POWDER COMPACTS

Although items 9 to 13 are all star patterns, it is interesting to see the variety that can be achieved with hand carving by different craftsmen (all carved in Palestine for Melissa, England). **1.** Bird, Mascot, England, c. 1950, size 2.9" (7.3 cm). **2.** Flower, Mascot, England, c. 1950, size 2.8" (7 cm). **3.** Abalone and pearl star design, Mascot, England, c. 1950, size 3.1" (8 cm). **4.** Abalone and pearl flower design, Zenette, England, c. 1950, size 3.5" (9 cm). **5.** Flowers in a basket, Noailles, France, c. 1930, size 2.4" x 3.1" (6 x 8 cm). **6.** Flowers, Mirelle, France, c. 1930–40, size 2.8" square (7 cm). **7.** Star compact, Houbigant, France, c. 1930, size 2" x 1.6" (5 x 4 cm). **8.** Cameo Lady's Head, possibly Maxley, Germany, c. 1930, size 2.2" (5.5 cm). **9.** Star, Melissa, England, c. 1950–60, size 3" (7.5 cm). **10.** Star, Melissa, England, c. 1950–60, size 3" (7.5cm). **11.** Star, Melissa, England, c. 1950–60, size 3" (7.5 cm). **12.** Star, Melissa, England, c. 1950–60, size 3" (7.5 cm). **13.** Star, Melissa, England, c. 1950–60, size 3" (7.5 cm). **14.** Flower, Melissa, England, c. 1950–60, size 3" (7.5 cm). **15.** Dome of the Rock, Jerusalem, possibly Melissa, England, c. 1950–60, size 3" (7.5 cm). **16.** Carved Lady's head, possibly Melissa, England, c. 1950–60, size 3" (7.5 cm).

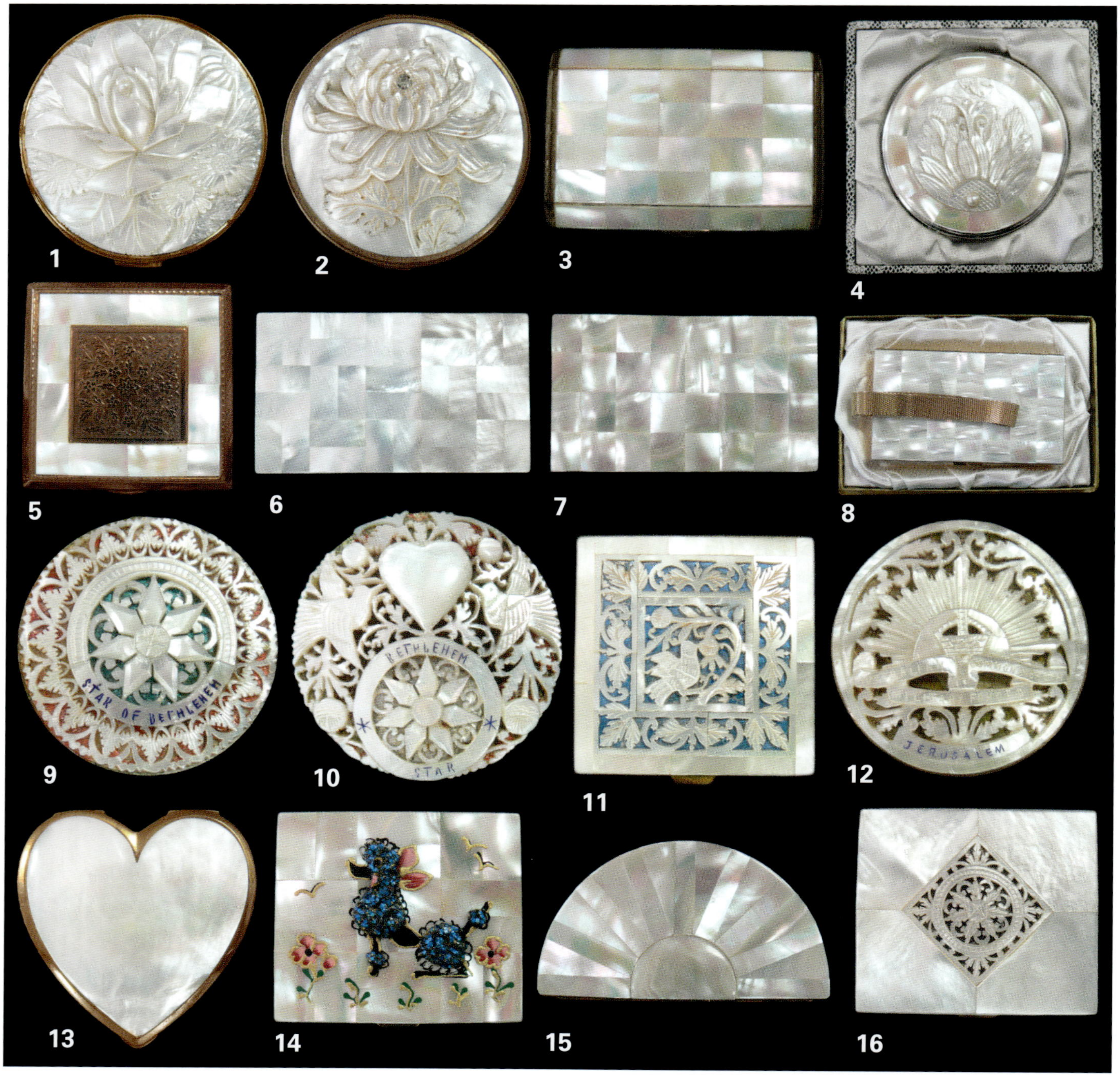


## PLATE 198 – POWDER COMPACTS

Evans used different types of mother-of-pearl to give their product a different look. If you look at items 6 to 8, which are similar carryalls, you will see the effect of using white mother-of-pearl oyster (item 6) green turban shell (item 7) and silver turban shell (item 8). **1.** Flower, Melissa, England, c. 1950–60, size 3″ (7.5 cm). **2.** Star, Melissa, England, c. 1950–60, size 3″ (7.5 cm) **3.** Rectangle, Melissa, England, c. 1950–60, size 3″ x 2″ (7.5 x 5 cm). **4.** Flowers, possibly Melissa, England, c. 1950–60, size 3″ (7.5 cm), in original box **5.** Square, Melissa, England, c. 1950–60, size 2.5″ square (6.3 cm). **6.** Carryall, rectangle, Evans, USA, c. 1950, size 5.3″ x 3.1″ (13.5 x 8 cm). **7.** Carryall, rectangle, Evans, USA, c. 1930, size 5.3″ x 3.1″ (13.5 x 8 cm). **8.** Carryall, rectangle, Evans, USA, c. 1950, size 5.3″ x 3.1″ (13.5 x 8 cm), in original box. **9.** Star of Bethlehem, pearl top carved in Palestine, c. 1940, size 2.4″ (6 cm). **10.** Heart, inscribed *Bethlehem,* pearl top carved in Palestine, c. 1940, size 2.4″ (6 cm). **11.** Bird, pearl top carved in Palestine, c. 1940–50, size 2″ x 2″ (5 x 5 cm). **12.** Inscribed *Australian Commonwealth Military Forces*, pearl top carved in Palestine and brought back by soldier returning from WW2, c. 1940–45, size 2″ (5 cm). **13.** Heart, Marhill, USA, c. 1940, size 3″ (7.5 cm). **14.** Poodle, Marhill, USA, c. 1940, size 2.8″ x 2.4″ (7 x 6 cm). **15.** Half round, Marhill, USA, c. 1940, size 4.1″ x 2.2″ (10.5 x 5.6 cm). **16.** Diamond pattern, Marhill, USA, c. 1940 size 2.7″ x 2.4″ (7 x 6 cm).

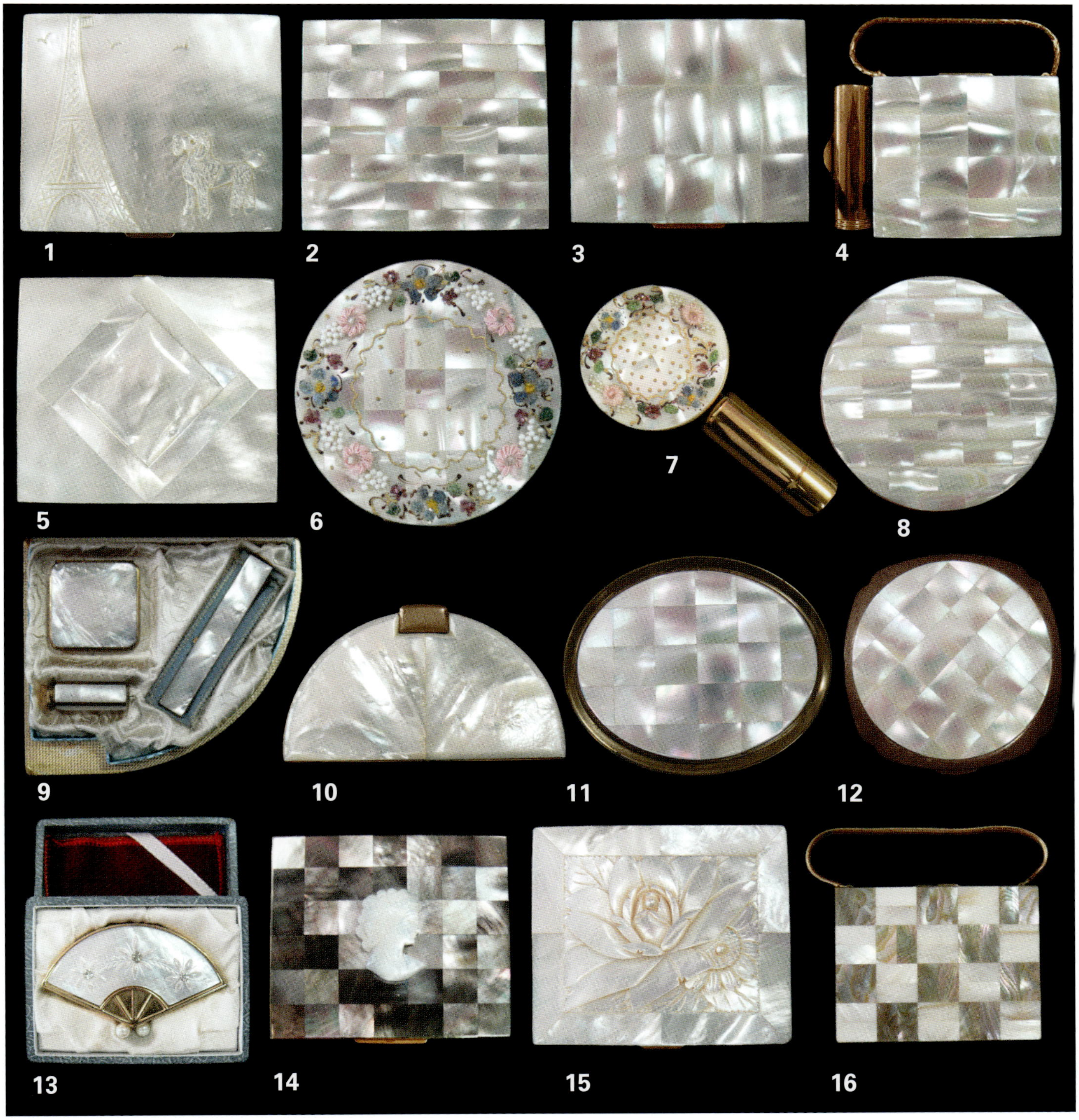


## PLATE 199 – POWDER COMPACTS

1. Eiffel Tower, Paris, with poodle, Marhill, USA, c. 1940, size 2.4" x 2" (6 x 5 cm). 2. Pearl rectangle veneer, Marhill, USA, c. 1940, size 2.8" x 2.4" (7 x 6 cm). 3. Pearl squares, Marhill, USA, c. 1940, size 2.8" x 2.4" (7 x 6 cm). 4. Carryall with handle, Marhill, USA, c. 1940–50, size 3.5" x 2.4" (9 x 6 cm). 5. Diamond shape, USA, c. 1940, size 2.8" x 2.4" (7 x 6 cm). 6–7. Compact and lipstick holder set, Marhill, USA, c. 1940, size 2.8" (7 cm) compact; 2'' (5 cm) lipstick holder. 8. Round, Regent of London, England, c. 1950, size 2.8" (7 cm). 9. Compact, comb and lipstick holder, Bliss, USA, c. 1930–40, size 2.3" x 2.3" (5.8 x 5.8 cm), in original box. 10. Half round, Bliss, USA, c. 1940, size 3.3" x 2" (8.5 x 5 cm). 11. Oval compact with music box, Kigu, Hungary, c. 1950, size 3.1" x 2.6" (8 x 6.5 cm). 12. Round, Kigu, England and Hungary, c. 1950, size 3" x 3" (7.5 x 7.5 cm). 13. Fan shape, Pink Lady, Japan, c. 1950, size 2.6" x 1.6" (6.5 x 4 cm). 14. Brownlip pearl with cameo, Ritz, USA, c. 1940, size 2.8" x 2.4" (7 x 6 cm). 15. Rose, possibly Anisco, USA, c. 1950, size 2.8" x 2.4" (7 x 6 cm). 16. Carryall with handle, possibly Kaycraft, USA c. 1960–70, size 3.9" x 3" (10 x 7.5 cm).

## PLATE 200 – POWDER COMPACTS

1. Bird and rose, Schildkraut, USA and Austria, c. 1950, size 2.8″ x 2.4″ (7 x 6 cm). 2. Flowers, Schildkraut, USA and Austria, c. 1950, size 2.4″ x 2″ (6.2 x 5.2 cm). 3. Flowers, likely Schildkraut, USA and Austria, c. 1950, size 2.4″ x 2″ (6.2 x 5.2 cm). 4. Bird and flowers, likely Schildkraut, USA and Austria, c. 1950, size 2.8″ (7 cm). 5. Oval, Schildkraut, USA and Austria, c. 1940, size 3.3″ X 2.1″ (8.5 x 5.4 cm). 6. Rectangle, Schildkraut, USA and Austria, c. 1940, size 2.8″ x 2.4′′ (7 x 6 cm). 7–9. Flower set, compact, lipstick holder, pill box, Schildkraut, USA and Austria, c. 1950, size 2.4″ x 2.1″ (6.2 x 5.3 cm) compact; 2.8″ x 2″ (7 x 5 cm) lipstick holder; 1.2″ x 1.2″ (3 x 3 cm) pill box. 10–12. Needlepoint set, Schildkraut, USA and Austria, c. 1940, size 3.9″ x 3″ (10 x 7.5 cm) cigarette case; 2.4″ x 2″ (6 x 5 cm) compact; 1.6″ x 1.4″ (4 x 3.5 cm) lighter. 13–15. Bird and flower set, Schick Mfg., USA, c. 1950, size 2.8″ x 2.4″ (7 x 6 cm) compact; 4″ x 1′′ (10.2 x 2.5 cm) comb; 2″ x 0.6 ″ (5 x 1.5 cm) lipstick holder. 16. Flower, Crown, Japan, c. 1950, size 3″ (7.5 cm), in original box. 17. Pearl with design, Crown, Japan, c. 1950, size 3″ (7.5 cm).18. Square, Volupte, USA, c. 1930–40, size 3″ x 3″ (7.6 x 7.6 cm). 19. Diamond pattern, Volupte, USA, c. 1940, size 2.8″ x 2.4″ (7 x 6 cm).

## PLATE 201 – POWDER COMPACTS

1. Round, black lip pearl, Elgin, USA, c. 1930, size 3″ (7.5 cm). 2. Square with diamond shape, Elgin, USA, c. 1930–40, size 2.8″ x 2.8″ (7 x 7 cm). 3. Abalone and pearl with removable key, Zell, USA, c. 1940–50, size 2.4″ (6 cm). 4. Abalone and pearl oyster, Zell, USA, c. 1940–50, size 2.8″ x 2.8″ (7 x 7 cm). 5. Rose, New Light, Japan, c. 1950, size 3.1″ (8 cm). 6. Rose, New Light, Japan, c. 1950, size 3.1″ x 2.4″ (8 x 6 cm). 7. Set compact, pill or rouge box, lipstick holder, Max Factor, USA, c. 1940, size 7.5″ x 4.3″ (19 x 11 cm). 8. Abalone and pearl oyster, USA, c. 1940, size 2.8″ (7 cm). 9. Abalone and pearl oyster, USA, c. 1950, size 2.8″ x 2.4″ (7 x 6 cm). 10. Squirrel, USA, c. 1950, size 2.8″ x 2.4″ (7 x 6 cm). 11. Lady's head powder box, England. c. 1890, size 1.8″ (4.5 cm). 12. Carryall with handle, USA, c. 1960–70, size 2.8″ x 2.6″ (7 x 6 cm). 13. Brown lip pearl oyster, USA, c. 1930, size 3.2″ (0.8 cm). 14a, 14b, 14c. Wrist compact with a strap to attach to the wrist, England, c. 1920, size 1.2″ (0.3 cm). 15. Wat Arum Temple, Bangkok, W & W Light Japan, c. 1950, size 3.1″ (8 cm).

## COIN PURSES

Mother-of-pearl coin (or change) purses were popular during the Victorian era. While much of the leather or fabric used in such purses disintegrated with time, the wonderful mother-of-pearl carved ornamentation on these purses withstood the effects of time. Purses with carvings of courting couples were in demand as gifts for a betrothed or wife. It was a meaningful gift from a loved one that was kept close and shown with pride to friends.

**PLATE 202 – FRENCH COIN PURSES 1**

All these purses were made and carved in France. 1. Lady sitting under a tree, c. 1835–55, size 2.9" x 2.4" (7.3 x 6 cm). 2. Lady with man playing a flute, c. 1835–55, size 2.8" x 2.4" (7.2 x 6 cm). 3. Hunting dog chasing a bird, c. 1835–55, size 3" x 2.4" (7.5 x 6 cm). 4. Dog watching man holding a stick, c. 1835–55, size 2.6" x 2" (6.6 x 5 cm). 5. Lady on a bench with child, c. 1835–55, size 2.5" x 1.9" (6.4 x 4.7 cm). 6. Flowers, c. 1850–80, size 2.6" x 2.1" (6.7 x 5.4 cm). 7. Man at the seaside with sailboat in background, c. 1835–55, size 2.6" x 2" (6.8 x 5.2 cm). 8. Fountain, c. 1850–80, size 2.8" x 2.3" (7.2 x 5.8 cm). 9. Hunter with rifle, c. 1835–55, size 3" x 2.4" (7.5 x 6 cm).

## PLATE 203 – FRENCH COIN PURSES 2

1. Flowers, France, c. 1870–90, size 2.4″ x 2″ (6 x 5 cm). 2. House or chateau, France, c. 1835–55, size 2.9″ x 2.3″ (7.4 x 5.8 cm). 3. Lady watching a swan, France, c. 1835–55, size 2.9″ x 2.4″ (7.3 x 6 cm). 4. Pierced design, France or Europe, c. 1835–55, size 3″ x 2.4″ (7.5 x 6 cm). 5. Lady with sheep, England, c. 1830–50, size 2.9″ x 2.8″ (7.4 x 7 cm). 6. Man on horseback with dog, France, c. 1835–55, size 2.9″ x 2.2″ (7 x 5.5 cm). 7. Bird on a branch, France, c. 1870–80, size 3″ x 2.4″ (7.5 x 6 cm). 8. Basket of flowers, France, c. 1870–80, size 2.7″ x 1.8″ (6.8 x 4.5 cm). 9. Horse, France, c. 1835–55, size 3″ x 2.4″ (7.5 x 6 cm). 10. Vase of flowers, France, c. 1835–55, size 2.9″ x 2.3″ (7.3 x 5.8 cm). 11. Gilt dog, marked *Monnaie* (currency), France, c. 1850–70, size 2.9″ x 2.4″ (7.4 x 6 cm). 12. Man reading a book, France, c. 1835–55, size 3″ x 2.4″ (7.5 x 6 cm).

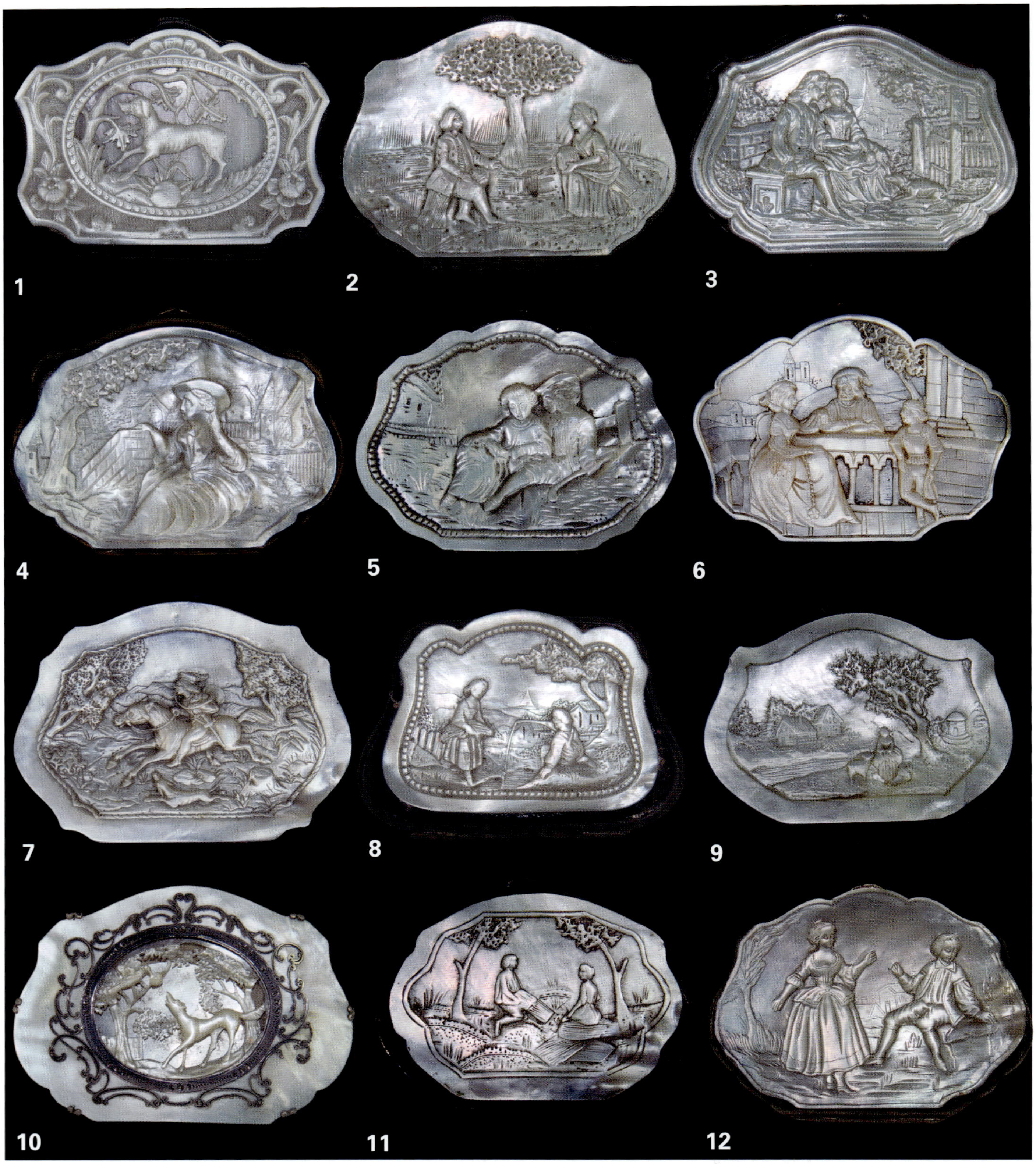


## PLATE 204 – FRENCH COIN PURSES 3

These coin purses were all made and carved in France: 1. Dog carved in relief, c. 1835–55, size 2.8″ x 3.1″ (7.2 x 8 cm). 2. Lady and man talking under tree, c. 1835–55, size 2.8″ x 2″ (7 x 5 cm). 3. Lady, man and dog, c. 1835–55, size 2.8″ x 2″ (7 x 5 cm). 4. Lady sitting near a river, c. 1835–55, size 2.9″ x 2″ (7.3 x 5.2 cm). 5. Man and lady on a riverbank, c. 1850–70, size 2.8″ x 2″ (7 x 5 cm). 6. Family at table, c. 1835–55, size 3.2″ x 2.2″ (8.2 x 5.7 cm). 7. Rider on a horseback with dog, c. 1835–55, size 3.1″ x 2.2″ (8 x 5.7 cm). 8. Man fishing with a lady watching, c. 1850–70, size 2.2″ x 1.6″ (5.5 x 4 cm). 9. Lady with lamb, c. 1850–70, size 2.8″ x 2″ (7 x 5 cm). 10. Dog, purse top converted to a brooch with silver backing, c. 1835–55, size 3.1″ x 2.2″ (8 x 5.5 cm). 11. Lady with man under trees, c. 1850–70, size 2.8″ x 1.9″ (7 x 4.7 cm). 12. Lady and man, c. 1835–55, size 2.8″ x 2″ (7 x 5 cm).

## PLATE 205 – FRENCH COIN PURSES 4

These coin purses were all made and carved in France: **1.** Carved in a diamond pattern, silver decoration, c. 1850–70, size 2.8" x 2" (7 x 5 cm). **2.** Diamond pattern, c. 1850–70, size 3.1" x 2.4" (8 x 6 cm). **3.** Rope pattern, c. 1850–70, size 2.4" x 1.8" (6 x 4.5 cm). **4.** Flowers, c. 1850–70, size 2.8" x 2" (7 x 5 cm). **5.** Flowers, c. 1850–70, size 3" x 2" (7 x 5 cm). **6.** Owner's monogram in center, c. 1850–70, size 2.8" x 2" (7 x 5 cm). **7.** Scallop shell shape, c. 1850–70, size 2.8" x 2" (7 x 5 cm). **8.** Fancy frilled decoration, c. 1850–70, size 2.8" x 2" (7 x 5 cm). **9.** Fancy carved overall repetitive decoration with central stylized bow motif, c. 1850–70, size 2.8" x 2" (7 x 5 cm). **10.** Silver stars in a fancy decoration, c. 1870–90, size 3.3" x 2.2" (8.5 x 5.5 cm). **11.–12.** Overall cross-hatched work with carved circles surrounding the escutcheon, decorated with silver, inscribed *Brevette SGDC*, c. 1870–90, size 3.3" x 2" (8.5 x 5 cm).

## PLATE 206 – FRENCH COIN PURSES 5

These coin purses were all made and carved in France. **1.** Ceres, Roman goddess of agriculture and motherly love, c. 1850–70, size 3.1″ x 2.8″ (8 x 7 cm). **2.** Lady and man, c. 1850–70, size 3.1″ x 2″ (8 x 5 cm). **3.** Lady holding a jug, c. 1850–70, size 3.1″ x 2″ (8 x 5 cm). **4.** Lady and man walking, c. 1850–70, size 2.8″ x 1.8″ (7 x 4.5 cm). **5.** Lady and man at a well, c. 1850–70, size 3.1″ x 2″ (8 x 5 cm). **6.** Dancing lady, c. 1850–70, size 3″ x 2″ (7.5 x 5 cm). **7.** Lady looking at a bird, c. 1850–70, size 3″ x 2″ (7.5 x 5 cm). **8.** Lady under a tree, house in background, c. 1850–70, size 2.8″ x 1.7″ (7 x 4.3 cm). **9.** Lady outside a house, c. 1850–70, size 3.1″ x 2″ (8 x 5 cm). **10.** Lady standing next to a fence looking out at the garden, c. 1850–70, size 3.1″ x 1.8″ (8 x 4.5 cm). **11.** Mary, Mother of Jesus Christ, c. 1875–90, size 2.4″ x 1.6″ (6 x 4 cm). **12.** Gentleman in eighteenth century garb at a fence, c. 1850–70, size 3.3″ x 2″ (8.3 x 5 cm).

## PLATE 207 – FRENCH COIN PURSES 6

These coin purses were all made and carved in France. **1.** Man and servant in a wine cellar, c. 1850–70, size 3.9" x 2.5" (10 x 6.3 cm). **2.** Lady and man talking, c. 1850–70, size 3.3" x 2" (8.5 x 5 cm). **3.** Man blowing a hunting horn, c. 1850–70, size 3.3" x 2" (8.4 x 5 cm). **4.** Lady talking to a seated man, c. 1850–70, size 3.1" x 1.9" (8 x 4.8 cm). **5.** Bird on a branch inscribed *San Sebastian* (Spain), c. 1865–80, size 3.1" x 2" (8 x 5 cm). **6.** Kissed by a cherub, c. 1850–70, size 3.3" x 2" (8.3 x 5.2 cm). **7.** Man reading a book, France, c. 1860–70, size 3.1" x 2" (8 x 5 cm). **8.** Vase of flowers, c. 1835–55, size 3.9" x 2.6" (9.8 x 6.5 cm). **9.** Cameo of lady's head, c. 1880–95, size 3.1" x 2" (8 x 4.5 cm). **10.** Flower arrangement, c. 1860–80, size 3.3" x 2" (8.3 x 5 cm). **11.** Fisherwoman with net, c. 1870–90, size 3.1" x 2" (8 x 5 cm). **12.** Notre Dame De Croas Batz, a sixteenth century church in Roscoff, France, c. 1880–90, size 2.5" x 1.4" (6.3 x 3.6 cm).

## PLATE 208 – FRENCH COIN PURSES 7

These coin purses were all made in France, except #10. 1. Silver Flowers in an urn, c. 1835–55, size 2.9" x 2.2" (7.4 x 5.6 cm). 2. Decoration in silver cutwork, c. 1850–70, size 3" x 2.4" (7.5 x 6 cm). 3. Extensive silver coverage, c. 1850–70, size 2.6" x 2" (6.5 x 5 cm). 4. Round, with the word *Paris* on the central medallion, c. 1890–1900, size 1.5" (3.8 cm) diameter. 5. Inscribed *Souvenir* on central banner, c. 1890–1900, size 3.7" x 2.7" (9.5 x 6.8 cm). 6. Inscribed *Souvenir* on central banner, c. 1890–1900, size 3.3" x 2.1" (8.5 x 5.4 cm). 7. Inscribed *Souvenir* on central banner, c. 1890–1900, size 4.1" x 2.6" (10.5 x 6.5 cm). 8. Simple silver decoration, c. 1890–1900, size 2" x 1.4" (5 x 3.5 cm). 9. Inscribed *Brevette SGDC,* c. 1890–1900, size 3.3" x 2" (8.5 x 5 cm). 10. Brown and white pearl, the framework was made in England and the pearl decoration done in Bethlehem, Palestine, c. 1900–15, size 3.1" x 2.4" (7.8 x 6 cm). 11. Flowers, c. 1870–90, size 2.4" x 1.8" (6 x 4.5 cm). 12. Sun ray pattern with a chain handle, c. 1870–90, size 3.4" x 2" (8.6 x 5.2 cm). 13. Carved leaf pattern with central silver decoration, c. 1880–95, size 3.1" x 2" (8 x 5 cm). 14. Shield with initials *BS,* c. 1860–80, size 3.1" x 1.8" (7.8 x 4.6 cm). 15. Cross, possibly a communion gift, c. 1880–90, size 2.4" x 1.6" (6 x 4 cm). 16. Man raking the garden, c. 1950, size 2.8" x 1.9" (7 x 4.8 cm). 17. Armorial, c. 1850, size 3" x 2.4" (7.5 x 6 cm).

## PLATE 209 – FRENCH COIN PURSES 8

These coin purses were all made and carved in France. The brown lip mother-of-pearl was sourced from the colonies of French Polynesia. **1.** Dog, c. 1850–60, size 2.8″ x 2″ (7 x 5 cm). **2.** A hunter on horseback holding a spear and advancing on a male lion, France, c. 1850–60, size 2.8″ x 2″ (7 x 5 cm). **3.** Flowers, c. 1870–90, size 2.8″ x 1.7″ (7 x 4.2 cm). **4.** Dog in a farmyard, c. 1880–1900, size 3.1″ x 2″ (8 x 5 cm). **5.** Man on horseback with dog, c. 1860–80, size 3.3″ x 2″ (8.3 x 5 cm). **6.** Fisherwoman with net, c. 1870–90, size 2.2″ x 1.5″ (5.5 x 3.7 cm). **7.** Fisherman with hand net, c. 1870–90, size 2.6″ x 2″ (6.5 x 5 cm). **8.** Fisherman with net, inscribed *Jersey* (off Normandy, France) c. 1870–90, size 2.8″ x 2″ (7 x 5 cm). **9.** Carved portrait of a woman with classical influence, c. 1870–80, size 2.8″ x 2″ (7.2 x 5.2 cm). **10.** Fisherwoman, inscribed *Soulae Gomer* on rear, c. 1870–90, size 2.6″ x 1.6″ (6.5 x 4 cm). **11.** Lady playing with a dog, c. 1860–80, size 2.4″ x 2.4″ (6.2 x 6 cm). **12.** Flowers, France, c. 1870–90, size 2.4″ x 1.7″ (6 x 4.2 cm). **13.** Ballerina, France, c. 1870–90, size 2.2″ x 1.6″ (5.6 x 4 cm).

## PLATE 210 – COIN PURSES

1. Inscribed *World's Columbia Exposition Chicago 1893*, USA, 1893, size 3.3" x 2.2" (8.5 x 5.5 cm). 2. Heart, China, c. 1920–30, size 2.8" x 2.3" (7 x 5.8 cm). 3. Fish, China, c. 1920–30, size 2.8" x 2" (7 x 5 cm). 4. Inscribed *Cherbourg*, c. 1900–10, size 1.8" x 2" (4.5 x 5 cm). 5. Painted bird and flowers, USA, c. 1870–90, size 1.6" x 2.1" (4 x 5.3 cm). 6. Pink and blue flowers, USA, c. 1870–90, size 2.1" x 1.7" (5.3 x 4.2 cm). 7. Awabi abalone shell, USA, c. 1870–90, size 2.6" x 1.6" (6.5 x 4 cm). 8. Flowers in center oval, c. 1890–1900, size 2.3" x 2" (5.8 x 5 cm). 9. Inscribed *Franco-British Exhibition 1903*, size 2.8" x 2" (7 x 5 cm). 10–11. Wallet type, England, c. 1860, size 3.5" x 2.4" (9 x 6 cm). 12. Souvenir of 1st Communion, France, c. 1880–90, size 2.1" x 1.7" (5.3 x 4.3 cm). 13. Made by Schiderkraut, Austria, for the USA market, 1886, size 4.7" x 2" (12 x 5 cm). 14. Inscribed *Boulogne Sur Le Mer*, France, c. 1880–1900, size 2.4" x 1.7" (6 x 4.4 cm). 15. Diamond pattern, France, c. 1880–1900, size 2.4" x 1.6" (6 x 4 cm). 16. Round, carved in a delicate floral motif, France, c. 1870–90, size 2" (5 cm) diameter. 17–18. Freshwater pearl shell, USA, c. 1900–10, size 3" x 1.3" (7.7 x 3.4 cm), #17 an internal view. 19. Simple shield, c. 1875–90, size 2.6" x 1.8" (6.5 x 4.5 cm). 20. Initial *D* carved in central escutcheon, c. 1875–90, size 2.4" x 1.8" (6 x 4.5 cm).

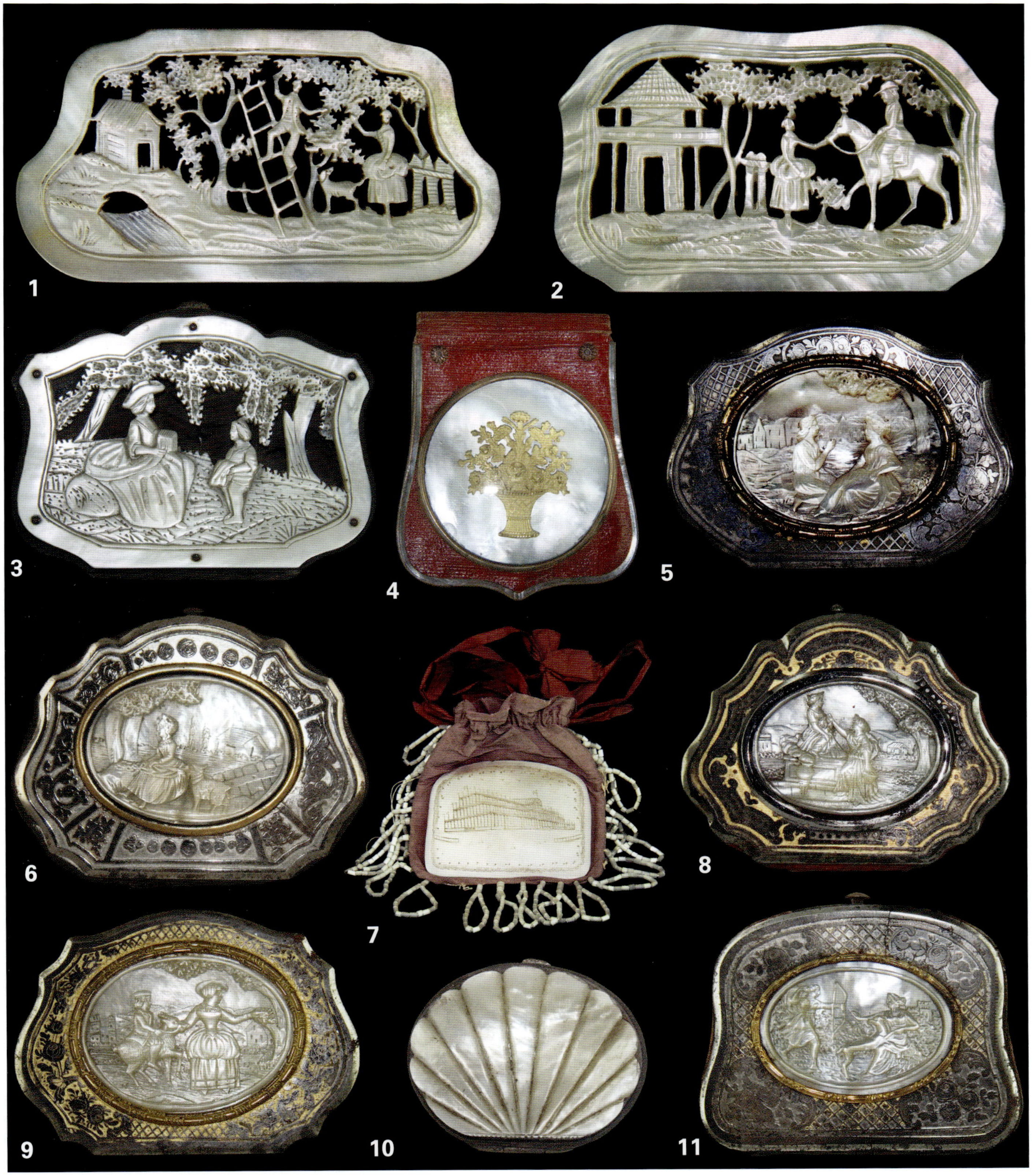

## PLATE 211 – COIN PURSES

1. Pierced carving: fruit pickers, France, c. 1850–80, size 3.5″ x 1.9″ (9 x 4.8 cm). 2. Pierced carving: man on horseback talking to a lady, France, c. 1850–80, size 3″ x 1.8″ (7.6 x 4.5 cm). 3. Pierced carving: lady and servant under trees, France, c. 1850–80, size 3″ x 2.2″ (7.5 x 5.7 cm). 4. Urn of flowers on mother-of-pearl with red leather, France, c. 1820, size 3.1″ x 2.8″ (8 x 7 cm). 5. Man talking to a lady, gilt metal edging, possibly Germany or France, c. 1850, size 3″ x 2″ (7.5 x 5 cm). 6. Lady and sheep, gilt metal edging, possibly Germany or France, c. 1850, size 2.8″ x 2″ (7 x 5.2 cm). 7. Draw string purse created from a coin purse top, Crystal Palace, England, c. 1850, size 4.3″ x 3.1″ (11 x 8 cm). 8. Lady with statue, gilt metal edging, possibly Germany or France, c. 1850, size 3″ x 2.2″ (7.5 x 5.7 cm). 9. Lady with child on a donkey, gilt metal edging, possibly Germany or France, c. 1850, size 3.1″ x 2.2″ (8 x 5.5 cm). 10. Scallop shape, France, c. 1870–90, size 2.3″ x 1.8″ (5.8 x 4.5 cm). 11. Lady, dog, and man with a bow and arrow gilt metal edging, possibly Germany or France, c. 1850, size 2.6″ x 2″ (6.5 x 5 cm).

CHAPTER 8

# Desk Accessories

Included in this chapter is a large variety of items used for writing, sealing, notebooks, dance cards, and visiting card cases, illustrating the popularity of mother-of-pearl during the nineteenth and early twentieth centuries.

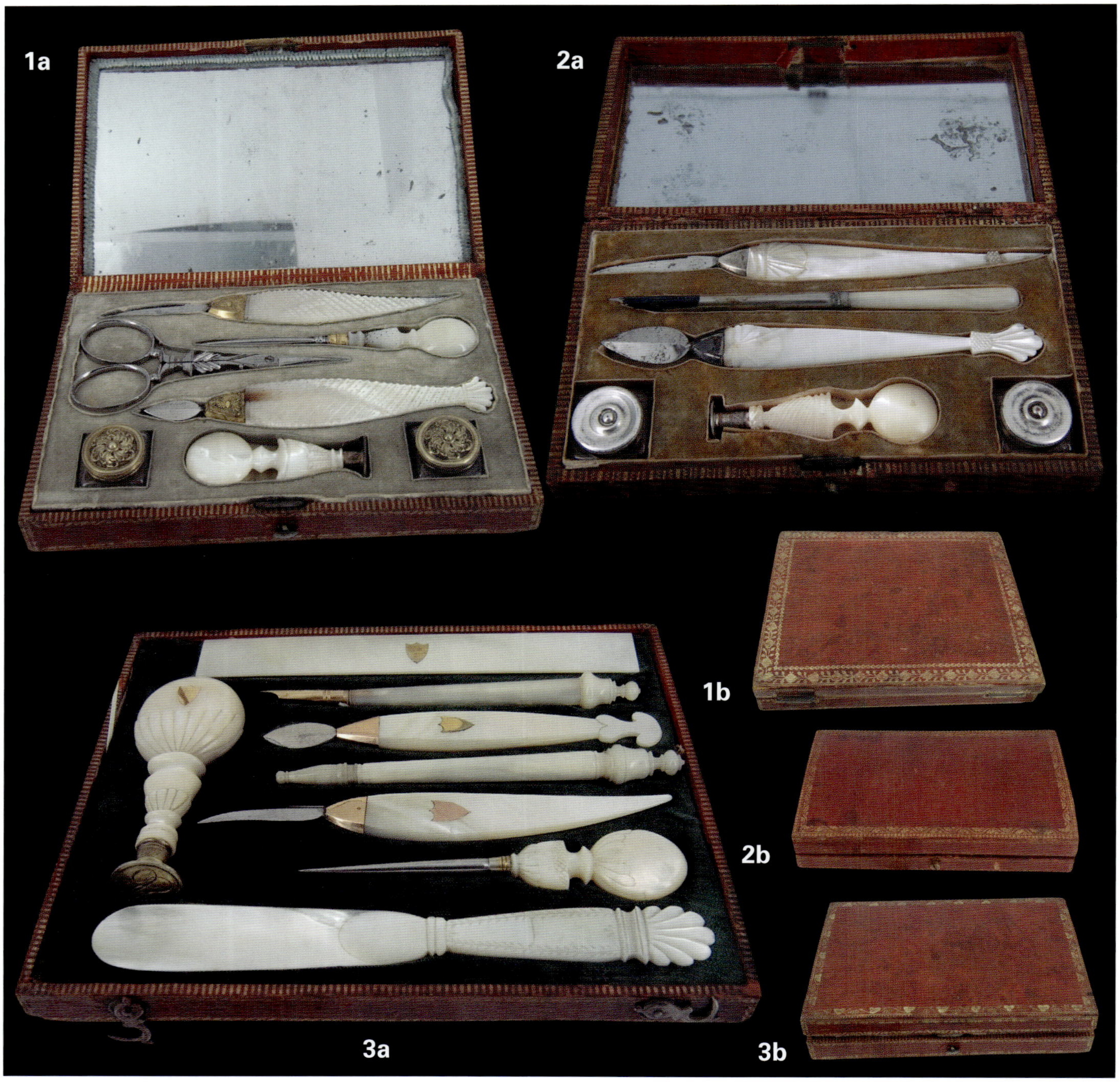


## PLATE 212 – PALAIS ROYAL WRITING SETS

These writing sets were sold in the arcades of Palais Royal in Paris, France, c. 1810–20, where only the best quality was offered. **1a, 1b.** Consists of a seal, ink scraper, quill knife, stiletto, scissors, and two ink bottles, size 5.9" x 3.7" (15 x 9.5 cm). **2a, 2b.** Consists of a dip pen, quill knife, ink scraper, wax seal, and two ink bottles, size 5.6" x 3.1" (14.2 x 8 cm). **3a, 3b.** Consists of a ruler, dip pen, ink scraper, pencil, quill knife, stiletto, letter opener, and wax seal, size 7.1" x 5.7" (18 x 14.5 cm).

## PLATE 213 – NOTEBOOKS 1

Notebooks or *aide memoires* were popular from the eighteenth century. These were used for essential notes but also during visiting. A caller would write his name on the pages (often ivory) and have the servant take the note to the person visited. It would be brought back with a written response. Fine mother-of-pearl covers were made, which gave the impression of wealth. There is an incredible variety of these notebooks and they were very popular. **1.** Man sitting under a tree, France, c. 1840–60, size 3.8″ x 2.8″ (9.6 x 7 cm). **2.** Lovers on a swing, based on the painting *Spring,* 1873, by Pierre Auguste Cot, France, c. 1875, size 4″ x 2.7″ (10.2 x 6.8 cm). **3.** Flowers, France, c. 1840–50, size 3.5″ x 2.6″ (9 x 6.5 cm). **4.** Lady, man, and chaperone, France, c. 1840–60, size 3.7″ x 2.4″ (9.5 x 6 cm). **5.** Lady sitting under a tree, France, c. 1840–60, size 3.8″ x 2.4″ (9.7 x 6.2 cm). **6.** Lady and a boy, France, c. 1840–60, size 3.8″ x 2.5″ (9.6 x 6.3 cm). **7.** Lady picking grapes, France, c. 1840–60, size 3.7″ x 2.6″ (9.5 x 6.5 cm). **8.** Shield, France, c. 1850, size 3.7″ x 2.4″ (9.4 x 6.2 cm). **9.** Diamond decoration, France, c. 1870–90, size 2.6″ x 3.7″ (6.5 x 9.5 cm). **10.** Tiled, France, c. 1870–90, size 3.9″ x 2.8″ (9.8 x 7 cm). **11.** Flowers, France, c. 1850, size 3.7″ x 2.4″ (9.4 x 6 cm). **12.** Silver decoration, France, c, 1880, size 2.4″ x 3.5″ (6 x 9 cm).

**PLATE 214 – NOTEBOOKS 2**

1. Lady and man, France, c. 1850–60, size 2.4" x 3.7" (6 x 9.5 cm). 2. Lady and a dog, France, c. 1850, size 3" x 1.8" (7.5 x 4.5 cm). 3. Putti, France, c. 1860, size 3.9" x 2.6" (9.8 x 6.6). 4. Dog, France, c. 1850–70, size 3.8" x 2.6" (9.6 x 6.5 cm). 5. France, c. 1860, size 3.7" x 2.6" (9.5 x 6.6 cm). 6. Silver decoration, France, c. 1860, size 3.7" x 2.6" (9.5 x 6.5 cm). 7. France, c. 1850, size 3.7" x 2.6" (9.5 x 6.5 cm). 8. France, c. 1850, size 3.7" x 2.6" (9.4 x 6.5 cm). 9. Rope decoration, France, c. 1850–60, size 3.7" x 2.6" (9.5 x 6.6 cm). 10. Etched garden scene, France, Germany or Italy, c. 1850–60, size 3.4" x 2.4" (8.6 x 6.2 cm). 11. Red leather and pearl, official enameled pansy of the Palais Royal, Paris, France, c. 1810, size 4.7" x 3.1" (12 x 8 cm). 12. Pierced design, France, c. 1840, size 3.5" x 2.2" (9 x 5.5 cm), inscribed *Given to Maria Charles in 1847.*

## PLATE 215 – NOTEBOOKS 3

1. Dog carved in white pearl set on black pearl background, France, c. 1850–70, size 3.7″ x 2.3″ (9.4 x 5.8 cm). 2. Painted scene, England, c. 1850, size 3.7″ x 2.4″ (9.5 x 6 cm). 3. Lady and man, France, c. 1850–60, size 3.5″ x 2.2″ (9 x 5.5 cm). 4. Ladies in a garden, France, c. 1825–50, size 3.9″ x 2.4″ (10 x 6 cm). 5. Fisherwomen, inscribed *Le Havre*, France, c. 1870–90, size 3.5″ x 2″ (8.6 x 5 cm). 6. Angels, France, c. 1840, size 2.4″ x 3.7″ (6.3 x 9.5 cm). 7. Walled city, Germany or Austria, c. 1850, size 3.7″ x 2.4″ (9.5 x 6 cm). 8. France, c. 1860, size 3″ x 1.9″ (7.7 x 4.8 cm). 9. Silver decoration, France, c. 1880, size 4.5″ x 2.6″ (11.5 x 6.5 cm). 10. Box type, France, c. 1865, size 3.1″ x 2.2″ (8 x 5.5 cm), for hand made visiting cards and notes. 11. With many of these early notebooks, the pad of pages is missing and all that survives is the cover, which has pockets on the inside.

## PLATE 216 – NOTEBOOKS 4

Most of the notebooks in this section have ivory pages on a swivel join. (See open example on Notebooks 5 page 223, #13.) **1.** Exceptional pierced carving of a lady and man under a tree, France, c. 1850, size 3.5″ x 2″ (9 x 5.2 cm). **2.** Flowers, England, c. 1860–80, size 3″ x 1.6″ (7.5 x 4 cm). **3.** Carisbrooke Castle, England, c. 1880, size 3.1″ x 1.8″ (8 x 4.6 cm). **4.** England, c. 1880, size 3.3″ x 1.6″ (8.4 x 4 cm). **5.** Thistle, Scotland/England, c. 1880, size 3″ x 1.6″ (7.5 x 4 cm). **6.** England, c. 1875–80, size 2.9″ x 1.8″ (7.3 x 4.5). **7.** Flowers, England, c. 1880, size 3″ x 1.4″ (7.6 x 3.6 cm). **8.** France, c. 1825, size 2.5″ x 1.6″ (6.3 x 4 cm). **9.** France, c. 1810, size 2.5″ x 1.6″ (6.3 x 4 cm), with official enamelled pansy of Palais Royal. **10.** France, c. 1810–20, size 2.1″ x 1.4″ (5.4 x 3.6 cm). **11.** Flowers, blue decoration, England, c. 1860–80, size 3″ x 1.6″ (7.5 x 4 cm). **12.** France, c. 1800, size 2.2″ x 1.8″ (5.5 x 4.5 cm), would have sold in Palais Royal shops. **13.** France, c. 1800, size 2.2″ x 1.6″ (5.6 x 4 cm), with official enamelled pansy of Palais Royal. **14.** Gothic Arches, would been have sold in Palais Royal shops, France, c, 1790–1810, size 2.6″ x 2.1″ (6.7 x 5.3 cm). **15.** Lady and man, France, c. 1850, size 3.1″ x 2″ (8 x 5 cm).

## PLATE 217 – NOTEBOOKS 5

1. Etched genre scene, China, c. 1850–60, size 3″ x 2″ (7.7 x 5 cm). 2. Etched genre scene, China, c. 1850–60, size 3.5″ x 1.6″ (9 x 4.1 cm). 3. Lady, France, c. 1840–50, size 3.7″ x 2.5″ (9.5 x 6.4 cm), in presentation box. 4. Lady watching a man with a flute, France, c. 1850–60, size 4.1″ x 2.5″ (10.4 x 6.4 cm). 5. Silver decoration, France, c. 1850–60, size 4.1″ x 2.8″ (10.5 x 7 cm). 6. Silver decoration, France, c. 1860, size 3.7″ x 2.8″ (9.5 x 7 cm). 7. Silver decoration, France, c. 1880–90, size 4.1″ x 2.8″ (10.5 x 7 cm). 8. Notebook holder, France, c. 1820, size 3.1″ x 2″ (8 x 5 cm). 9. Inscribed *Dydd Ian*, China, c. 1840–60, size 3.7″ x 2.9″ (9.5 x 7.3 cm). 10, 12. Brief case type, France, c. 1850–70, size 3.7″ x 2.8″ (9.3 x 7 cm). 11. France, c. 1840–60, size 3.5″ x 2.4″ (9 x 6 cm), has band with lock. 13. Swivel type notebook (see plate 222) showing the ivory pages.

## PLATE 218 – NOTEBOOKS 6 AND HOLDERS

1. Notebook holder, France, c. 1800–10, size 3.3″ x 2″ (8.4 x 5 cm). 2. Notebook holder, France, c. 1800, size 3″ x 2″ (7.8 x 5 cm). 3. Man and lady, France, c. 1840, rebound in a new notebook in Italy in 1949, size 3.7″ x 3.1″ (9.5 x 8 cm). 4. Putti, France, c. 1850, size 3.9″ x 2.8″ (10 x 7 cm). 5. York Minster, England, c. 1860, size 3.9″ x 2.8″ (10 x 7 cm). 6. Lincoln Cathedral, England, c. 1860, size 3.9″ x 2.8″ (10 x 7 cm). 7. England, c. 1880, size 3.9″ x 2.8″ (10 x 7 cm). 8. Bird, England, c. 1860, size 3″ x 1.9″ (7.5 x 4.7 cm). 9. Inscribed *San Remo*, Italy, c. 1860–90, size 2.7″ x 1.8″ (6.8 x 4.6 cm). 10. Two ladies and a goat, France, c. 1860–90, size 2.6″ x 1.7″ (6.5 x 4.4 cm). 11. Inscribed *Souvenir*, France, c. 1850–80, size 3.1″ x 2.1″ (8 x 5.3 cm). 12. Inscribed *Y Dr de Fournier,* France, c. 1880–1900, size 1.8″ x 2.6″ (4.6 cm x 6.5 cm). 13. Lady and man talking, France, c. 1850–70, size 3.7″ x 2.4″ (9.5 x 6 cm). 14. Gilt decoration, France, c. 1840, size 3.1″ x 2.1″ (8 x 5.4 cm). 15. Silver decoration, France, c. 1880, size 3.7″ x 2.4″ (9.5 x 6 cm). 16. Inscribed *St. Jean de Sur*, France, c. 1890, size 2.8″ x 2.1″ (7.2 x 5.3 cm). 17. Etched pearl, France, c. 1830–50, size 3.7″ x 2.4″ (9.3 x 6 cm). 18. Chatelaine notebook, England, c. 1875, size 1.2″ (3 cm) diameter.

## PLATE 219 – *CARNET DE BAL* 1

The *carnet de bal* is much smaller than a normal notebook and was used for recording partners for upcoming dances. They can be separated into men's (a very small book-shaped booklet) and ladies' (swivel type, many with a ring to fit on the finger.) It is possible that some of these originated in Austria. **1.** Men's, France, c. 1850–60, size 2" x 1.4" (5 x 3.6 cm). **2.** Men's, France, c. 1850–60, size 2" x 1.4" (5 x 3.6 cm). **3.** Men's, France, c. 1850–60, size 2.4" x 1.6" (6.3 x 4 cm). **4.** Men's, France, c. 1850–60, size 2" x 1.4" (5 x 3.5 cm). **5.** Men's, France, c. 1850–60, size 1.9" x 1.4" (4.7 x 3.5 cm). **6.** Men's, France, c. 1850–60, size 2" x 1.4" (5 x 3.5 cm). **7.** Men's, France, c. 1800, size 2.1" x 1.7" (5.3 x 4.3 cm). **8.** Men's, France, c. 1860–70, size 2" x 1.3" (5 x 3.4 cm). **9.** Inside of a better men's *carnet de bal* with space for listing names of partners. **10.** Ladies', France, c. 1850–60, size 2.2" x 1.4" (5.6 x 3.5 cm). **11.** Ladies', France, c. 1850–60, size 2" x 1.3" (5 x 3.3 cm). **12.** Ladies', France, c. 1860, size 1.9" x 1.2" (4.8 x 3 cm). **13.** Ladies', France, c. 1850, size 2.4" x 1.6" (6 x 4 cm). **14.** Ladies', France, c. 1860, size 2" x 1.3" (5 x 3.3 cm). **15.** Ladies', France, c. 1880, size 2" x 1.2" (5 x 3 cm). **16.** Ladies', France, c. 1860, size 2" x 1.3" (5 x 3.3 cm).

## PLATE 220 – *CARNET DE BAL* 2

These are all ladies' *carnet de bal*. It is possible that some of these originated in Austria. **1, 12.** Vase of flowers, France, c. 1860, size 3.7″ (9.3 cm), item 12 shows the same item opened, displaying the ivory pages, pencil, and finger ring. **2.** Lady picking fruit, France, c. 1800, size 3.1″ (8 cm), only the top carved pearl plate survives. **3.** Man fishing, France, c. 1800, size 3.1″ (8 cm), only the top carved pearl plate survives. **4.** Lady at a fence, France, c, 1850–60, size 2.3″ x 1.4″ (5.8 x 3.5 cm). **5.** Patterned, France, c. 1850–70, size 2.2″ x 1″ (5.6 x 2.6 cm). **6.** Silver decoration, France, c. 1860–70, size 2.3″ x 1.6″ (5.8 x 4 cm). **7.** Pattern, France, c. 1860–70, size 1.9″ x 1.2″ (4.8 x 3 cm). **8.** Flowers, France, c. 1880, size 3.1″ (8 cm). **9.** Flowers, France, c. 1880, size 3.1″ (8 cm). **10.** Flowers, France, c. 1880, size 3.4″ (8.6 cm). **11.** Silver decoration, France, c. 1870, size 3.9″ (10 cm). **13.** Etching, France, c. 1850–70, size 2.2″ x 1.4″ (5.6 x 3.5 cm).

## PLATE 221 – VISITING CARD CASES 1

Visiting cards have been exchanged since the eighteenth century, but it was not until the end of the 1700s that the visiting card gained in popularity and by the early 1800s was established in society. Nobility and the upper class used fine printed and engraved cards, whilst lower classes used white paper on which their names were written. A card case was a popular receptacle for holding these cards. The earliest case lids would pull off, but by 1835 hinge tops were used. The best cases had a carved front piece, but many interesting designs were made by varying the inlay of mother-of-pearl oyster with abalone shell. The height of popularity was 1840–50. A tray to hold the visiting cards presented to the servant who answered the door was usually kept on the hall table. The visiting card tray is only rarely made of mother-of-pearl. Various styles of visiting card cases include a hinged lid (item 12), side opening (item 11), and a combined notebook type (item 10).

**1, 2.** China, c. 1840, size 3.5″ x 1.8″ (9 x 4.5 cm), exceptionally well carved. **3.** Pierced carving, China, c. 1850, size 3.9″ x 2.3″ (10 x 6 cm). **4.** Pierced carving, China, c. 1850, size 3.7″ x 2.4″ (9.5 x 6.2 cm). **5.** Base with indoor genre vignette, lid with terrace genre vignette, France, c. 1850, size 4.3″ x 2.6″ (11 x 6.6 cm). **6.** England, c. 1870, size 4.1″ x 3.1″ (10.3 x 8 cm). **.** England, c. 1855, size 3.9″ x 3.1″ (10 x 8 cm). **8.** China, c. 1790, size 3.7″ x 2.1″ (9.5 x 5.4 cm) made during a time of shortage of mother-of-pearl and a lower grade capiz shell was used instead. **9.** Palais Royal, inscribed *Vister* (= visit), France, c. 1810–30, size 3.2″ x 1.9″ (8.2 x 4.9 cm). **10.** England, c. 1860, size 4.1″ x 3″ (10.5 x 7.6 cm), this card case has a notebook and pencil in addition to space for visiting cards. **11.** England, c. 1860, size 4.1″ x 3″ (10.5 x 7.6 cm), shows a typical side opening card case with a concertina effect holder for cards. **12.** England, c. 1870, size 4″ x 3″ (10 x 7.6 cm). **13.** England, c. 1865, size 3.1″ x 2.2″ (8 x 5.5 cm).

## PLATE 222 – VISITING CARD CASES 2

All these examples of visiting card cases are from England. **1.** c. 1860–70, size 3.9" x 2.8" (10 x 7 cm). **2.** c. 1860–70, size 3.7" x 2.5" (9.4 x 6.3 cm). **3.** c. 1860–70, size 3.5" x 2.5" (9 x 6.3 cm). **4.** c. 1850, size 3.5" x 2.6" (9 x 6.5 cm). **5.** c. 1860–70, size 3.9" x 2.6" (10 x 6.6 cm). **6.** c. 1860–70, size 3.7" x 2.8" (9.3 x 7 cm). **7.** c. 1860–70, size 3.7" x 2.6" (9.5 x 6.5 cm). **8.** c. 1850, size 3.6" x 2.6" (9.2 x 6.5 cm), with cameo center. **9.** c. 1860–70, size 3.9" x 2.8" (10 x 7 cm). **10.** c. 1850, size 3.5" x 2.2" (9 x 5.5 cm). **11.** c. 1850, size 4.1" x 3.1" (10.3 x 7.8 cm). **12.** c. 1870, size 3.9" x 3" (10 x 7.6 cm). **13.** c. 1845, size 4.3" x 3.1" (10.8 x 8 cm), with notebook. **14.** c. 1850, size 4.1" x 3" (10.5 x 7.5 cm). **15, 16.** c. 1850, size 4" x 3" (10.1 x 7.6 cm).

## PLATE 223 – VISITING CARD CASES 3

These examples of visiting card cases are all from England. **1.** Carved flowers, c. 1840, size 3.9″ x 3″ (10 x 7.5 cm). **2.** Carved flowers, c. 1845, size 3.9″ x 3.1″ (10 x 8 cm). **3.** c. 1850, size 4.1″ x 3″ (10.5 x 8 cm). **4.** Flowers, c. 1845, size 3.7″ x 2.7″ (9.4 x 6.8 cm). **5.** c. 1850, size 3.9″ x 3″ (10 x 7.5 cm). **6.** c. 1850, size 4.1″ x 3.1″ (10.5 x 8 cm). **7.** The three muses, Melete (meditation), Mneme (memory), and Aoede, (song) c. 1845, size 3.7″ x 2.8″ (9.5 x 7 cm). **8.** Flowers, c. 1845, size 3.7″ x 2.4″ (9.5 x 6 cm). **9.** Vase of flowers, c. 1845, size 3.4″ x 2.6″ (8.7 x 6.5 cm). **10.** c. 1860, size 4.2″ x 3″ (10.6 x 7.5 cm). **11.** c. 1860–70, size 3.9″ x 3″ (10 x 7.5 cm). **12.** c. 1860–70, size 3.5″ x 2.8″ (9 x 7 cm). **13.** Flowers, c. 1845, size 4.3″ x 3.1″ (10.8 x 8 cm). **14.** Boxed, c. 1845, size 4.3″ x 3.1″ (10.8 x 8 cm). **15.** c. 1860, size 4.1″ x 3″ (10.5 x 7.5 cm).

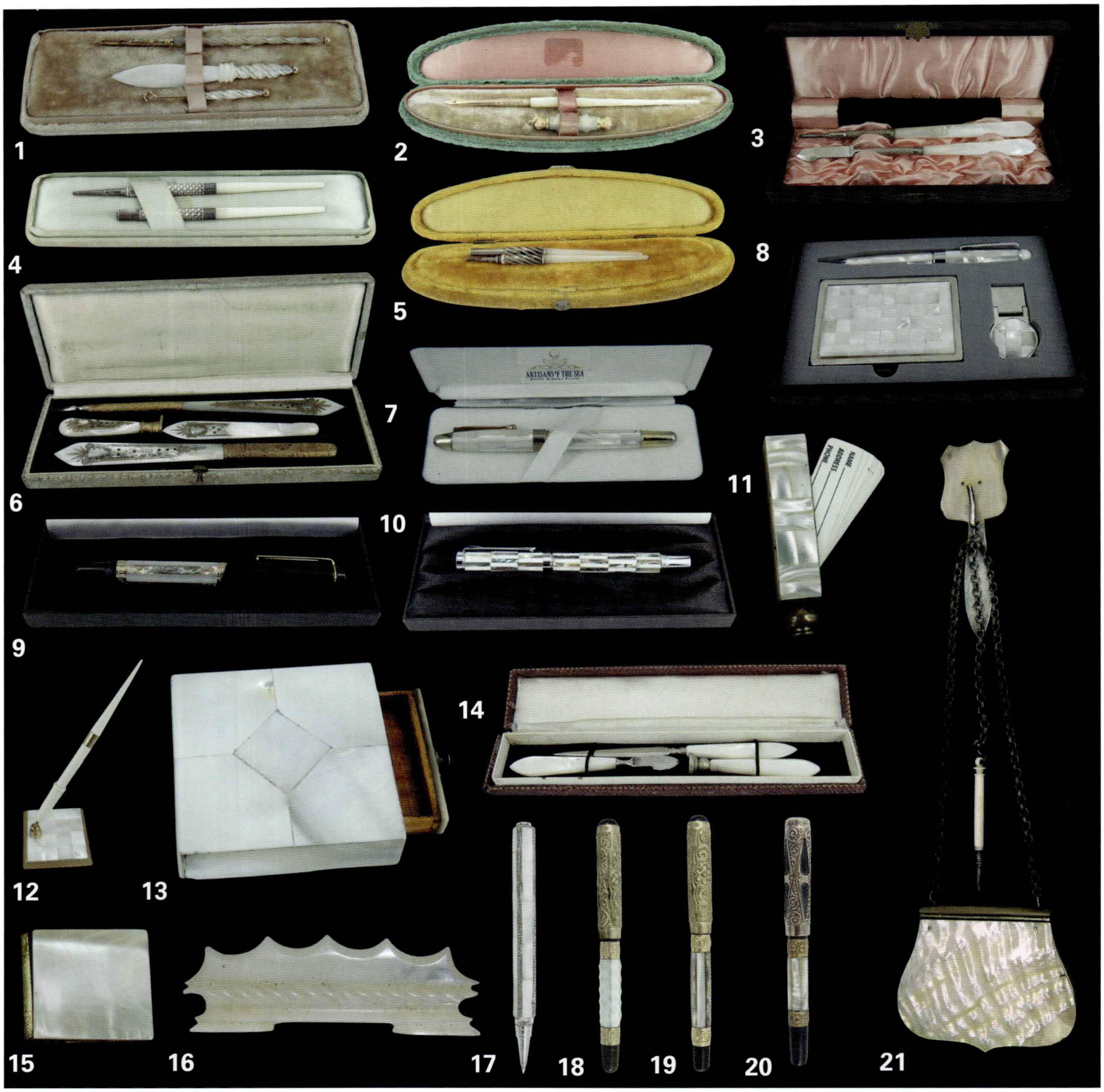


## PLATE 224 – PENS, WRITING SETS

1. Writing set, consisting of a dip pen, letter opener, and button hook, USA, c. 1885, size 2.8" to 5.7" (7 to 14.5 cm). 2. Pen and pencil set, USA ,c. 1880–1900, size 5.9" (15 cm). 3. Writing set consisting of a pencil and ink scraper, Europe, c. 1890, size 6 ¼" (15.5 cm). 4. Pen and pencil set, Mabie Todd, USA, c. 1890, size 6.1" (15 cm). 5. Pen and pencil set, missing a seal or letter opener, USA, c. 1850–80, size 4.1" (10.5 cm). 6. Writing set consisting of a dip pen, seal, letter opener, and bookmark, France, c. 1880, size 2.8" to 7" (7 to 17 cm). 7. Ball point pen, China, c. 1980, for Kailis Pearls Broome, size 5.9" (15 cm). 8. Men's gift set consisting of a pen, money clip, and card holder, China, c. 1999, size 4.7" x 6.7" (12 x 17 cm). 9. Fountain pen, Coles, USA, c. 1995, size 5.5" (14 cm). 10. Fountain pen, China, c. 1999, size 5.5" (14 cm). 11. Address book, USA, c. 1950, size 2.9" (7.4 cm). 12. Ball point pen in a pearl stand, USA, c. 1956, size 3.1" x 2.8" (8 x 7 cm). 13. Stamp or nib box, France, c. 1850, size 2.8" x 2.8" (7 x 7 cm). 14. Desk set consisting of a seal, ink eraser, and letter opener, USA, c. 1910, size 3.1" to 5.5" (8 to 14 cm). 15 . Stamp book, England, c. 1860, size 1.4" x 1.2" (3.5 x 3.1 cm). 16. Dip pen stand from a boxed set, France, c. 1820, size 1.8" (4.5 cm). 17. Ball point pen, India, c. 1990, size 5" (12.8 cm). 18. Eye dropper pen with squeeze bulb like a medicine dropper, USA, c. 1910, size 5.2" (13.2 cm). 19. Eye dropper pen, USA, c. 1910, size 5.5" (14 cm). 20. Eye dropper pen, USA, c. 1910, size 5.1" (13 cm). 21. Chatelaine notebook and pencil, USA, c. 1890, size 10.8" (27.5 cm).

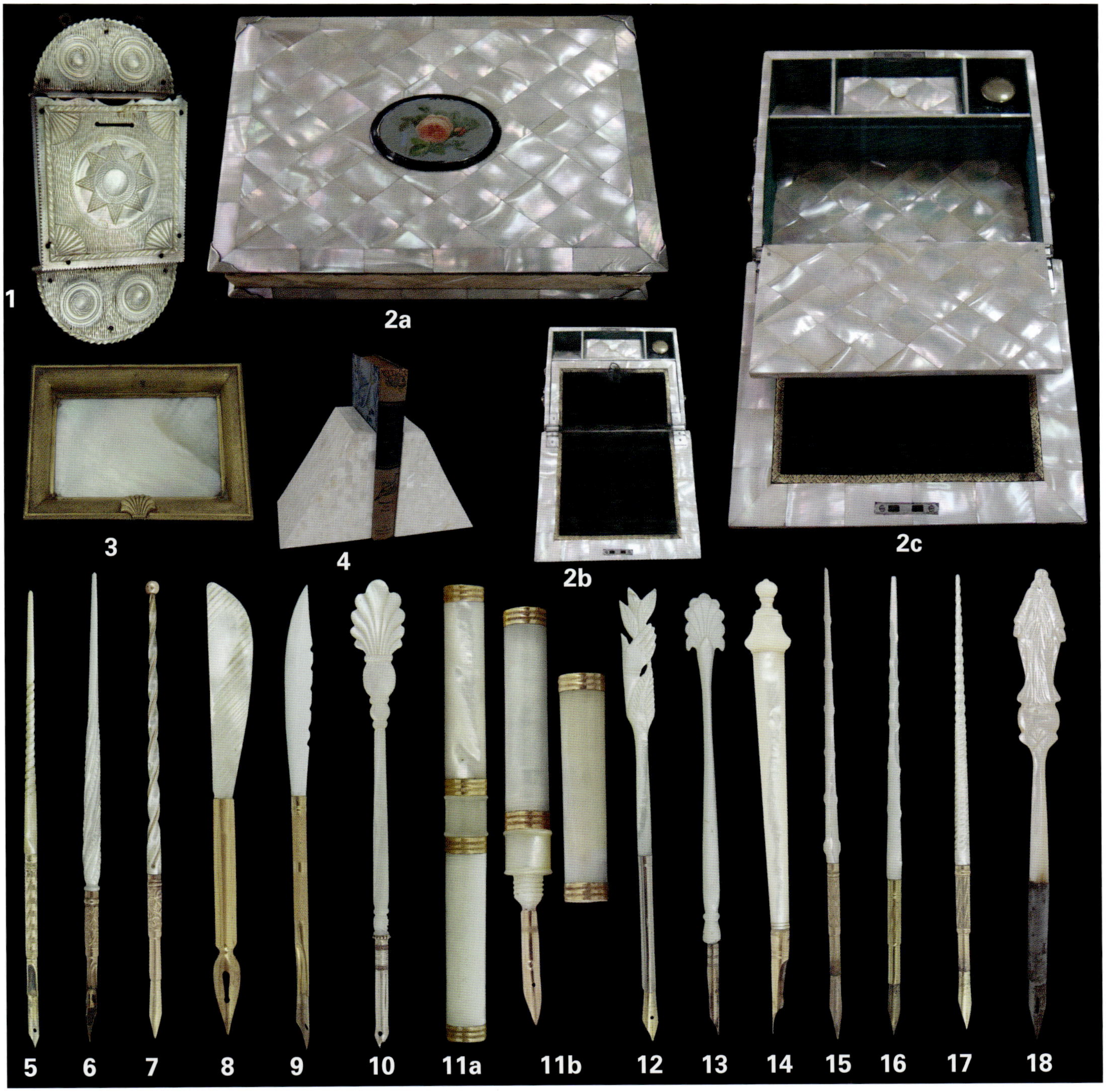


## PLATE 225 – DIP PENS and DESK ACCESSORIES

Dip pens have been around from 550 A.D., but mother-of-pearl was first used as a handle in 1790. Fountain pens took over from the dip pen around 1880. **1.** Wall visiting card holder. The butler would put visiting cards into this wall mounted holder near the front door, England, c. 1875, size 5.8″ x 2.6″ (14.8 x 6.7 cm). **2a–2c.** Ladies writing slope box with pearl veneered inside and outside, England, c. 1875, size 8.5″ x 6.7″ x 3.1″ (21.5 x 17 x 8 cm). **3.** Visiting card tray. A card tray on the hall table was a necessary receptacle for visiting cards, England, c. 1840–50, size 4.3″ x 2.8″ (11 x 7 cm). **4.** Bookends, Thailand, c. 1995, size 4.5″ x 5.5″ (11.4 x 14 cm). **5.** USA, c. 1885–1895, size 6.3″ (16 cm). **6.** USA, c. 1885–1895, size 6.3″ (16 cm). **7.** USA, c. 1875–1890, gold, size 6″ (15.3 cm). **8.** USA, c. 1890, size 5.1″ (13 cm). **9.** USA, c. 1900, size 6″ (15.2 cm). **10.** From a Palais Royal writing set, France, c. 1820, size 5.1″ (13 cm). **11a, 11b.** From a writing set, France, c. 1790–1810, size 3.1″ (8 cm). **12.** England, made for USA market, c. 1850–60, size 7.1″ (18 cm). **13.** From a Palais Royal writing set, France, c. 1820, size 4.9″ (12.5 cm). **14.** From a Palais Royal writing set, France, c. 1820, size 4.7″ (12 cm). **15.** USA, c. 1875–90, size 6.1″ (15.6 cm). **16.** USA, c. 1875–90, size 6.1″ (15.6 cm). **17.** USA, c. 1890, size 6.3″ (16 cm). **18.** Mary, mother of Jesus, France, c. 1850, size 6.1″ (15.5 cm).

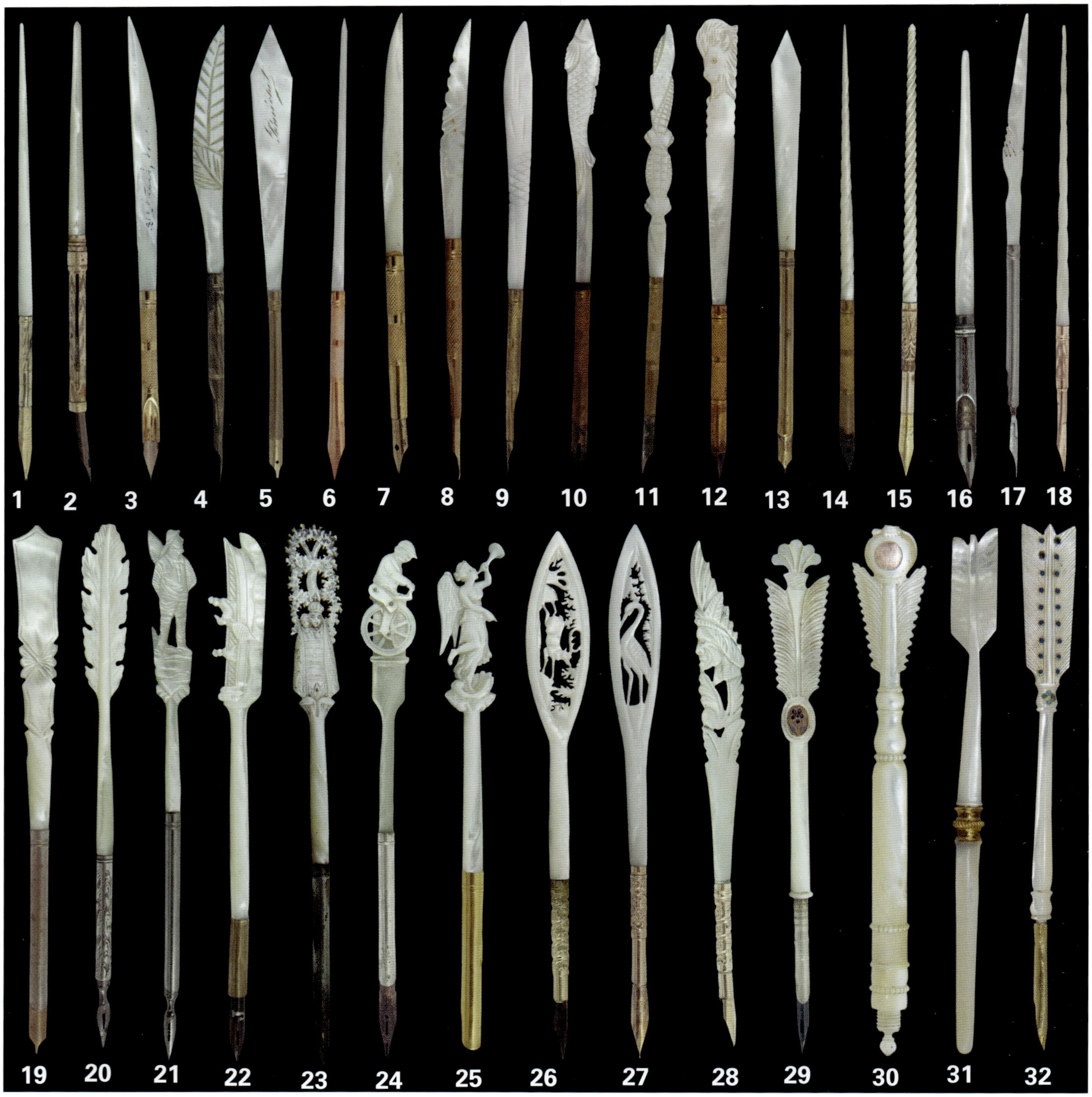


## PLATE 226 – DIP PENS

1. USA, c. 1900, size 6.9" (17.5 cm). 2. Retractable nib, USA, c. 1900, size 5.4" (13.7 cm). 3. USA, c. 1900, size 5.6" (14.1 cm). 4. USA, c. 1900, size 5.9" (15 cm). 5. France, c. 1880–1890, size 7.4" (18.7 cm). 6. USA, c. 1900, size 6.2" (15.8 cm). 7. USA, c. 1900, size 6.1" (15.5 cm). 8. USA, c. 1900, size 6" (15.2 cm). 9. USA, c. 1900, size 6.1" (15.5 cm). 10. Fish, USA, c. 1900, size 6.5" (16.5 cm). 11. Alligator, USA, c. 1900, size 6.7" (17 cm). 12. Buffalo head, USA, c. 1900, size 6.3" (16 cm). 13. France, c. 1890, size 6.2" (15.8 cm). 14. USA, c. 1890–1900, size 6" (15.2 cm). 15. USA, c. 1885, size 6.3" (16 cm). 16. Sterling, Birmingham, England, 1902 size 5" (12.7 cm). 17. Hand, USA, c. 1885, size 7.3" (18.5 cm). 18. USA, c. 1890, size 6.4" (16.2 cm). 19. France, c. 1875, size 7.4" (18.7 cm). 20. Feather plume, England, c. 1880 size 6.9" (17.5 cm). 21. Fisherman, France, c. 1875–90 size 7.5" (19 cm). 22. Boating, inscribed *Souvenir de Notre Dame de Sion,* France, c. 1875, size 6.9" (17.5 cm). 23. Mary and Infant Jesus, inscribed *Ste de Notre Dame de la Delivrande*, France, c. 1850, size 7.5" (19 cm). 24. Man on cycle, early automation dip pen, legs and wheel on the cycle move, France, c. 1850, size 7.3" (18.5 cm). 25. Angel blowing a trumpet, France, c. 1820, size 5.5" (14 cm), from a writing set. 26. Deer, England, c. 1890, size 6.25" (15.9 cm). 27. Crane, England, c. 1890, size 6.7" (17.1 cm). 28. Native American head, USA, c. 1885–95, size 6.3" (15.9 cm). 29–32. From boxed sets, France, c. 1820, size 4.1"- 5" (10.5 to 12.7 cm).

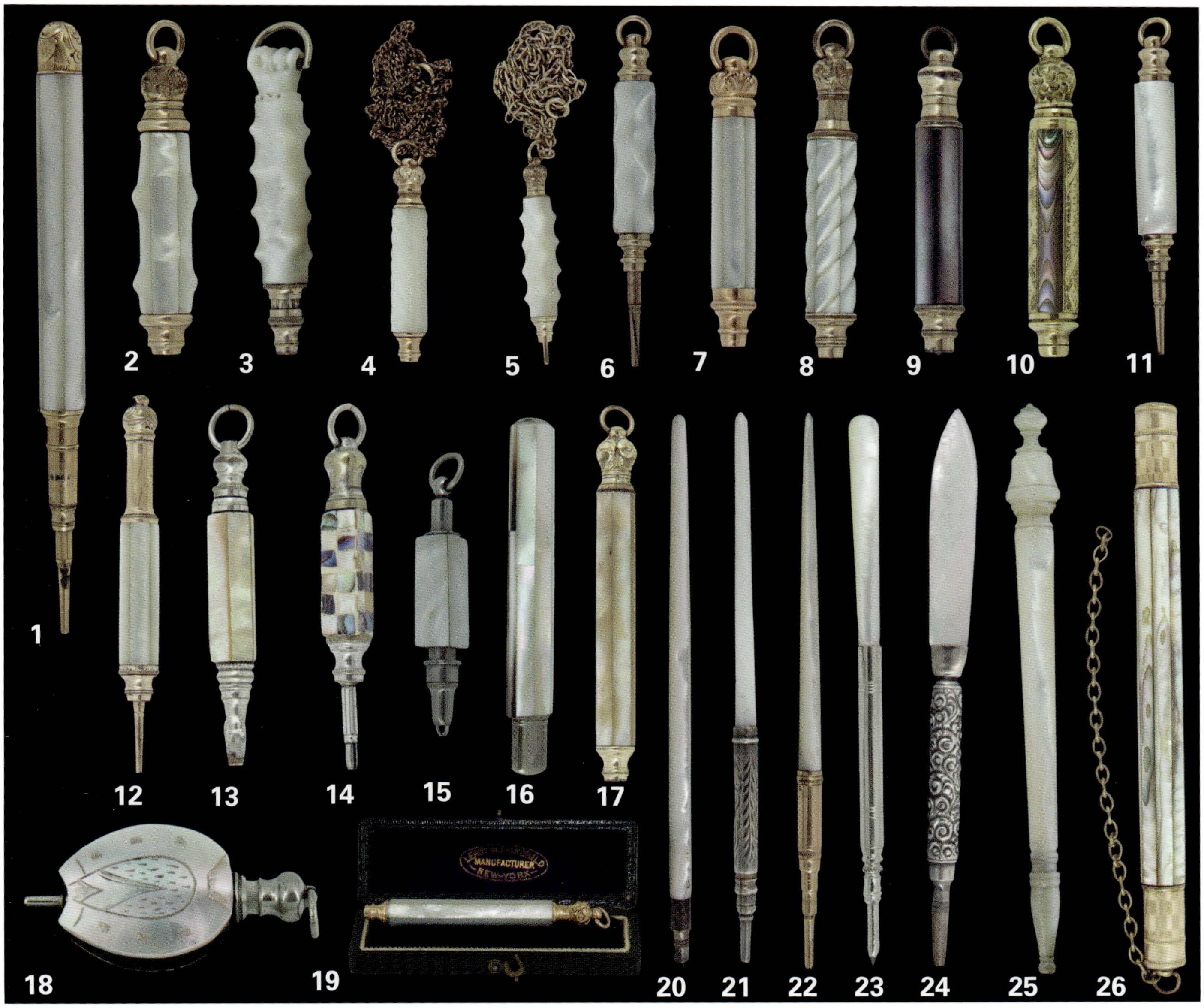

## PLATE 227 – PENCILS

Early mother-of-pearl pencils can be divided up into tablet form (solid), magic pencils (when you pull on the top, the front shoots out), screw pencils (a screw action is used to achieve the full size). **1.** Tablet pencil, USA, c. 1880–1890, size 4.7" (12 cm). **2.** Screw pencil, USA, c. 1873–89, size 2.4" (6 cm). **3.** Screw pencil with hand holding the ring, USA, c. 1873–89, size 2.3" (5.8 cm). **4.** Magic pencil, Aitken Lambert, USA, c. 1871–80, size 2" (5 cm). **5.** Magic pencil, USA, c. 1871–80, size 2.5" (6.3 cm). **6.** Magic pencil *Fairchild pat 5 Dec 71*, USA, c. 1871–80, size 2.5" (6.3 cm). **7.** Magic pencil *Pat Dec 71*, USA, c. 1871–80, size 2" (5 cm). **8.** Magic pencil, USA, c. 1871–80, size 2.2" (5.5 cm). **9.** Magic pencil, USA, c. 1871–80, size 1.9" (4.8 cm). **10.** Magic pencil, *Fairchild pat 5 Dec 71*, USA, c. 1871–80, size 1.8" (4.5 cm). **11.** Screw pencil, USA, c. 1873–80, size 2.4" (6.2 cm). **12.** Magic pencil, USA, c. 1871–80, size 3.1" (7.8 cm). **13.** Magic pencil, USA, c. 1871–80, size 2.2" (5.5 cm). **4.** Screw pencil, USA, c. 1873–80, size 2.2" (5.6 cm). **15.** Spring grip pencil, England, c. 1900, size 2" (5.1 cm). **16.** Tablet pencil, *Made in England*, England, c. 1890, size 3.3" (8.5 cm). **17.** Magic pencil, USA, c. 1871–80, size 2.8" (7cm). **18.** Magic pencil, *Gescesch*, Germany, c. 1880, size 1.8" (4.5 cm). **19.** Magic pencil, *Fairchild pat 5 Dec 71*, USA, c. 1871–80, size 2.5" (6.3 cm), in its original Fairchild box. **20.** Tablet pencil, USA, c. 1830–50, size 6" (15.2 cm). **21.** Tablet pencil, hallmarked Birmingham, England, 1898, size 4.7" (12 cm). **22.** Tablet pencil, H. Lambert, USA, c. 1880, size 5.5" (13.9 cm). **23.** Pencil from a writing set, France, c. 1820, size 3.5" (9 cm). **24.** Pencil, possible maker Hicks, USA, c. 1885, size 4.9" (12.5 cm). **25.** Pencil from a Palais Royal writing set, France, c. 1810, size 3.3" (8.5 cm). **26.** Container for pencil lead, USA, c. 1915, size 4.9" (12.5 cm).

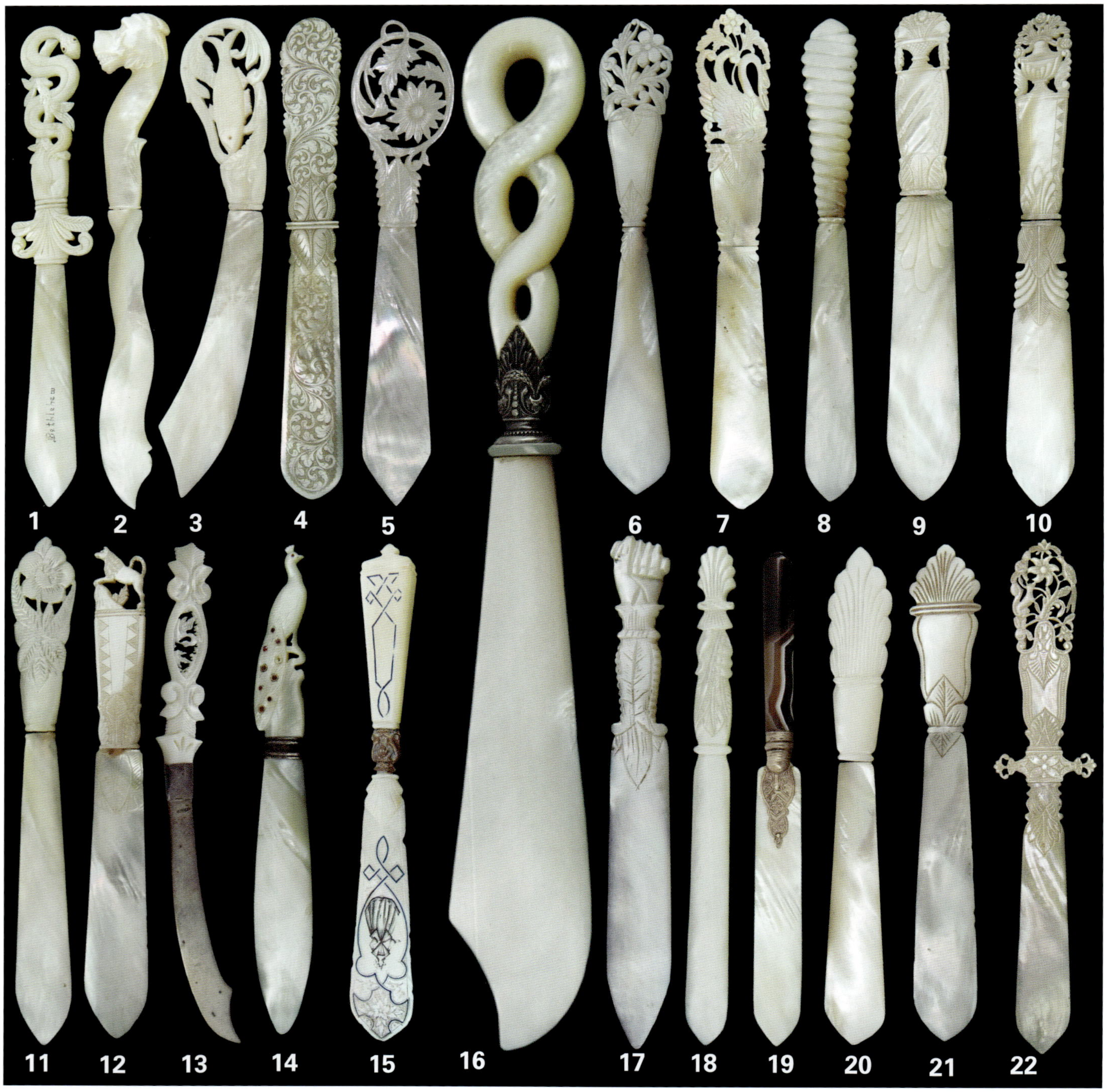


## PLATE 228 – LETTER OPENERS 1

Letter openers were first made around 1880, when gummed envelopes became common and the wax seal disappeared. They used to stay on desks, and were a show piece of wealth or importance. Large numbers were made in mother-of-pearl. 1. Snake, marked Bethlehem but thought to have originated in France, c. 1850, size 9.8" (25 cm), likely purchased for use in the tourist souvenir trade in Bethlehem. 2. Dragon's head, France, c. 1890, size 7.9" (20 cm). 3. Fish, England, c. 1890–1900, size 7.6" (19.3 cm). 4. Exquisite etching, England, c. 1870, size 8.7" (22 cm). 5. Flowers, England, c. 1880, size 8.7" (22 cm). 6. Flowers, England, c. 1850, size 9" (23 cm). 7. Swan, France, c. 1850, 9.4" (24 cm). 8. Cord carving, England, c. 1880–1900, size 7.5" (19 cm). 9. Flowers in urn, France, c. 1880, size 7.5" (19 cm). 10. Urn of flowers, France, c. 1840, size 8.5" (21.5 cm). 11. Single flower, England, c. 1875–85, size 6.5" (16.5 cm). 12. Poodle, France, c. 1850, size 7.3" (18.5 cm). 13. Swan, England, c. 1890, size 7.7" (19.5 cm). 14. Peacock, France, c. 1880–1900, size 7.5" (19 cm). 15. Etched lady, England or Netherlands, c. 1850, size 7.5" (19 cm). 16. Twisted handle ceremonial or presentation piece, France, c. 1850–65, size 13" (33 cm). 17. Hand holding a rod or baton, France, c. 1890, size 4.5" (11.5 cm). 18. Hand holding leaves, England, c. 1880, size 4.9" (12.5 cm). 19. Agate handle, Scotland, c. 1860, size 8.3" (21 cm). 20. Simple pattern, France, c. 1875–85, size 7.3" (18.5 cm). 21. France, c. 1875–85, size 6.9" (17.5 cm). 22. Dog, pierced carving, France, c. 1850, size 9.8" (25 cm).

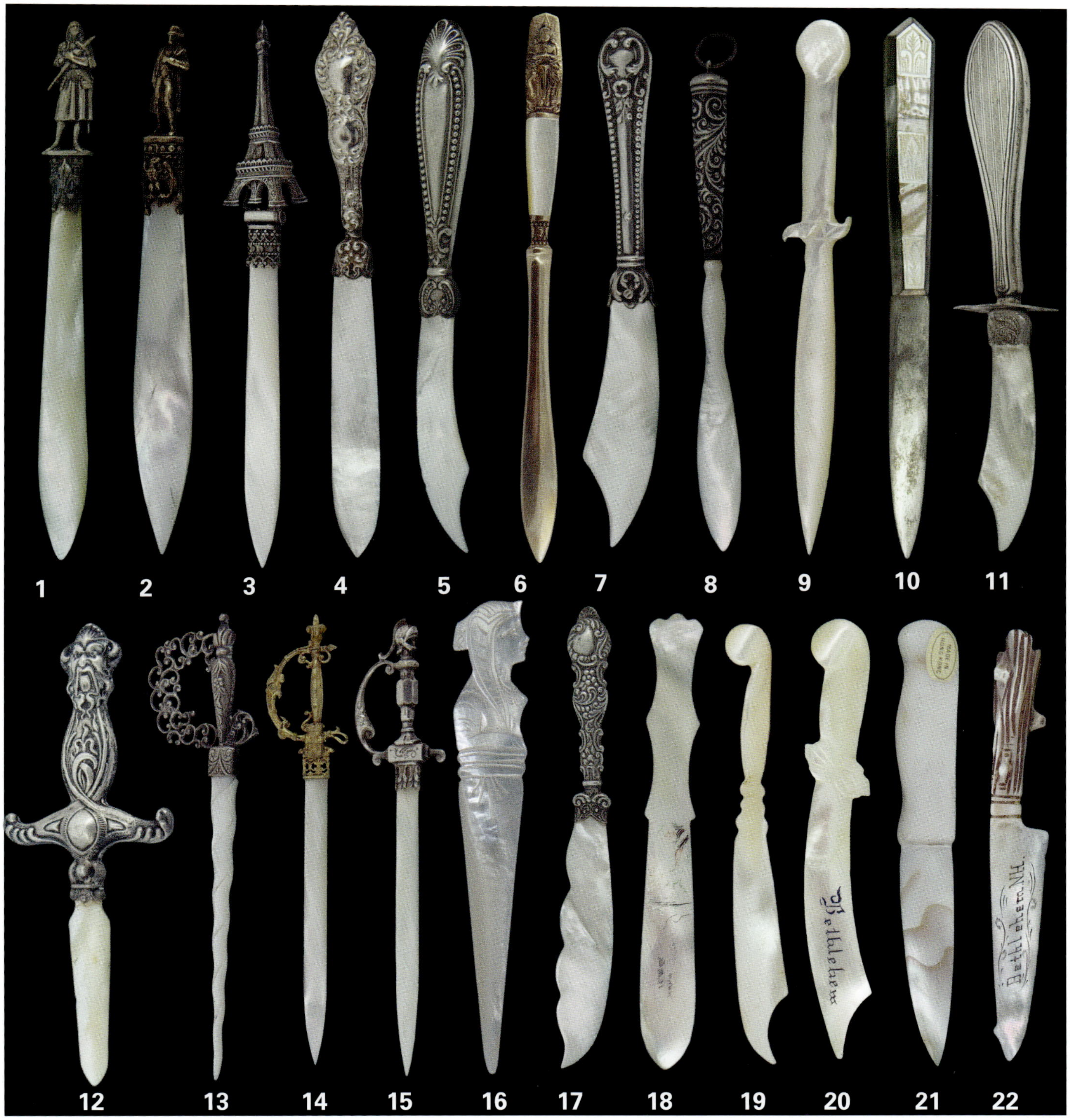


## PLATE 229 – LETTER OPENERS 2

**1.** Joan of Arc, France, c. 1898–1910, size 6.1″ (15.5 cm). **2.** Napoleon, France, c. 1898–1910, size 4.5″ (11.5 cm). **3.** Eiffel Tower, Paris, France, c. 1898–1910, size 5.5″ (14 cm). **4.** Sterling silver, USA, c. 1890, size 4.7″ (12 cm). **5.** Sterling silver, USA, c. 1890, size 6.4″ (16.2 cm). **6.** Elephant, Thailand, c. 2000, size 7.5″ (19 cm). **7.** Sterling silver, USA, c. 1890, size 6.4″ (16.2 cm). **8.** Sterling silver, USA, c. 1890, size 6.3″ (16 cm). **9.** Dirk-like handle, England, c. 1890, size 5.1″ (13 cm). **10.** Abalone and pearl handle, USA, c. 1925, size 9.4″ (24 cm). **11.** Sterling silver, USA, c. 1920, size 6.7″ (17 cm). **12.** Sterling silver, USA, c. 1890, size 4.9″ (12.5 cm). **13.** Sword shape, England, c. 1900–1925, size 5.6″ (14.2 cm). **14.** Sword shape, England, c. 1900–1925, size 5.4″ (13.8 cm). **15.** Sword shape, England, c. 1900–1925, size 6.1″ (15.5 cm). **16.** Cleopatra carved in the handle of a letter opener made during the height of Egyptian archeological discoveries, France, c. 1920, size 4.3″ (11 cm). **17.** Sterling silver, USA, c. 1900–1915, size 5.3″ (13.5 cm). **18.** Flat, China, c. 1920, size 5.9″ (15 cm). **19, 20.** Souvenir of *Bethlehem*, Palestine, c. 1900–25, size 4.3″ (11 cm). **21.** Souvenir of Muscatine, Iowa, made in Hong Kong, c. 1985, size 4.5″ (11.5 cm). **22.** *Bethlehem*, N.H., USA, c. 1900, size 4.5″ (11.5 cm).

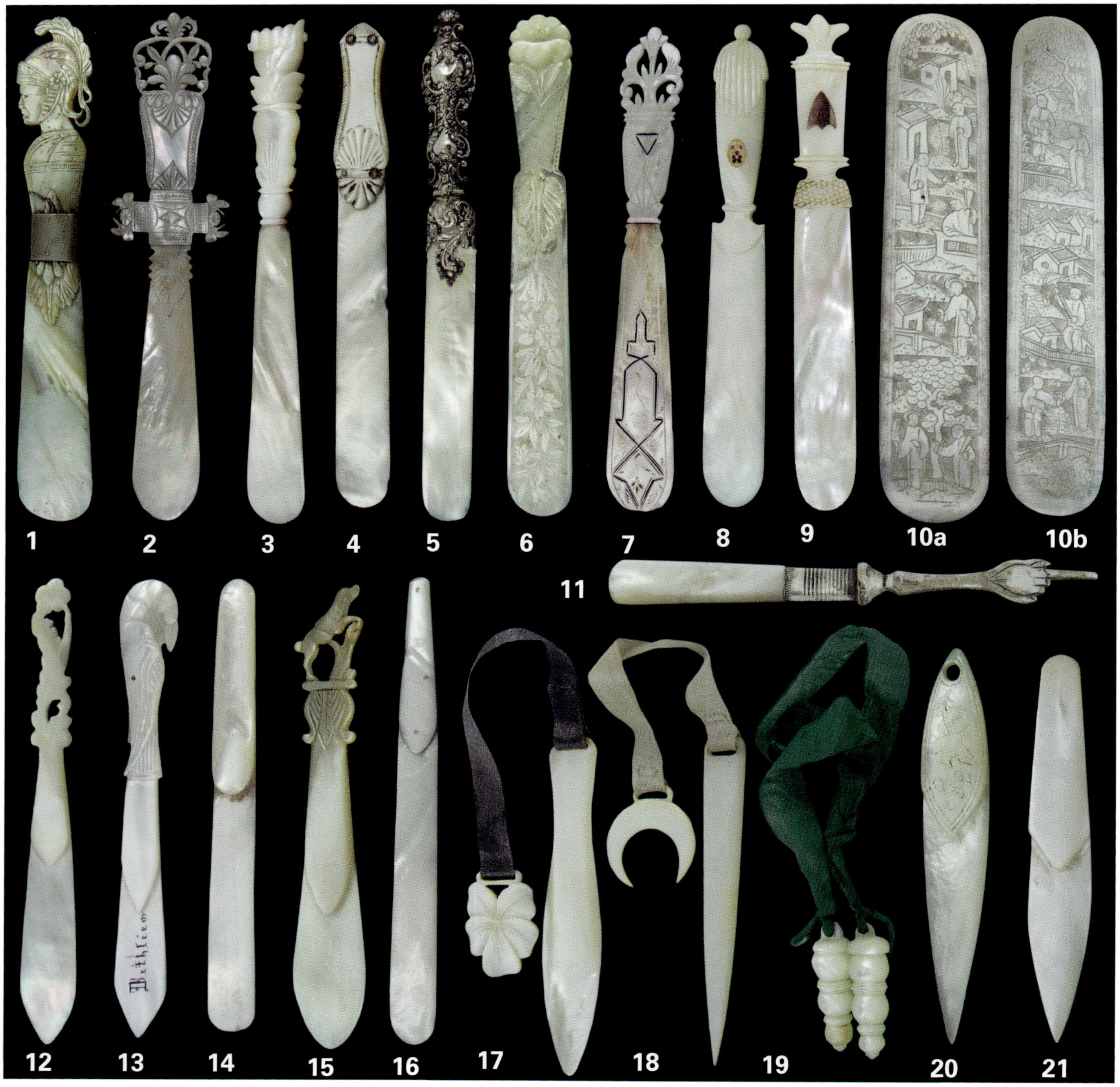


## PLATE 230 – PAGE TURNERS AND BOOKMARKS

Page turners can be separated from letter openers by the round end to the blade, and were needed, as many of the early texts were made of cloth or parchments. **1.** Roman soldier, old silver repair, France, c. 1875, size 7.7" (19.5 cm). **2.** Pierced pattern, France, c. 1850, size 9.3" (23.5 cm). **3.** Hand holding a rod or baton, France, c. 1830–50, size 7.5" (19 cm). **4.** With pen knife in the handle, England, c. 1875–1900, size 5.7" (14.5 cm). **5.** Sterling silver handle, USA, c. 1890, size 7.7" (19.5 cm). **6.** Flower, England, c. 1850, size 6.1" (15.5 cm). **7.** Decorated blade, France, c. 1880, size 7.1" (18 cm). **8.** With Palais Royal enameled pansy, France, c. 1820, size 5.1" (13 cm). **9.** From a boxed set, France, c. 1820, size 5.3" (13.5 cm). **10a, 10b.** Unusual page turner, China, c. 1830–40, size 4.3" (11 cm). **11.** Yad, Jewish ritual pointer to read the Torah without touching the sacred text, hallmarked Sheffield, England, 1909, size 5.5" (14 cm). **12.** Flowers, England, c. 1890, size 4.7" (12 cm). **13.** Shrimp inscribed *Bethlehem*, believed to have been purchased in France for the Holy Land tourist market, France, c. 1920, size 4.7" (12 cm). **14.** England, c. 1890, size 4.3" (10.8 cm). **15.** Poodle, France, c. 1880, size 4.9" (12.5 cm). **16.** With pen knife in handle, England, c. 1875–1900, size 7.1" (18 cm). **17.** Bookmark, flower with ribbon, England, c. 1900, size 3.3" (8.3 cm). **18.** Bookmark, sickle with ribbon, England, c. 1900, size 3.1" (8 cm). **19.** Bookmark, ribbon with pearl ends, England, c. 1880, size of ends 1.4" (3.5 cm). **20.** Bookmark, England, c. 1890, size 3" (7.5 cm). **21.** Bookmark, England, c. 1890, size 2.4" (6.2 cm).

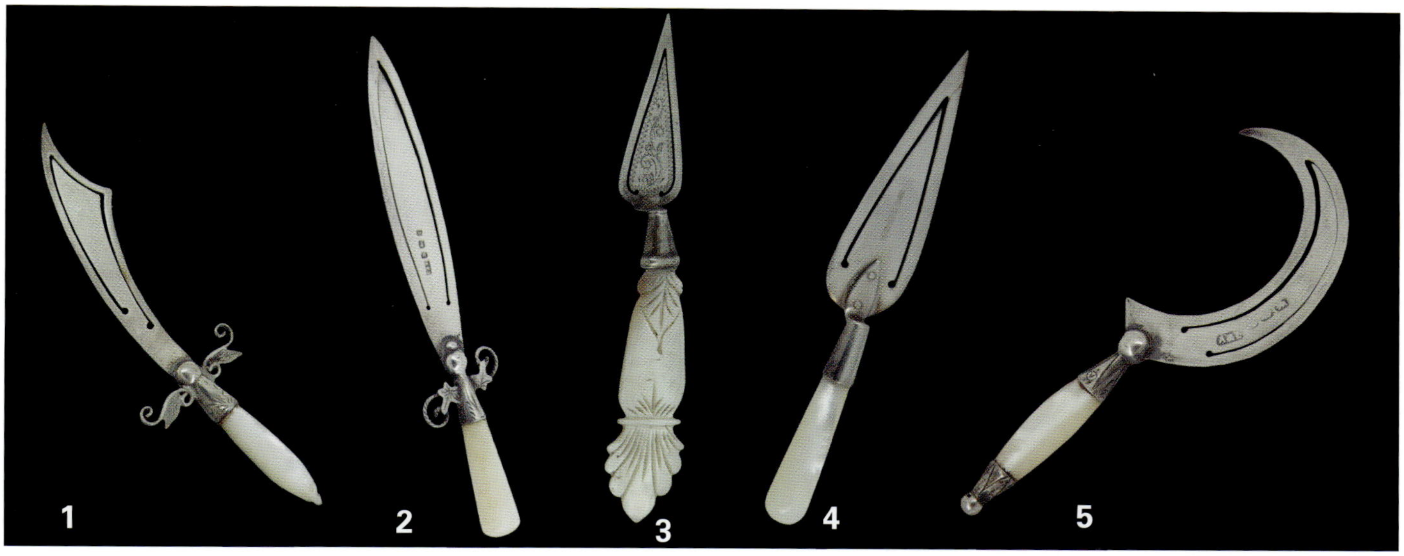

## PLATE 231 – SILVER BOOKMARKS

1. Hallmarked Birmingham, England, 1897, size 4.1″ (10.4 cm), maker's mark worn. 2. Hallmarked Birmingham, England, 1906, size 4.1″ (10.4 cm), maker Crisford & Norris. 3. No marks, England, c. 1890, size 4.6″ (11.6 cm). 4. Worn hallmarks, England, c. 1900, size 3″ (7.5 cm). 5. Sickle shape, hallmarked Birmingham, England, 1875, size 3″ (7.6 cm), makers mark worn.

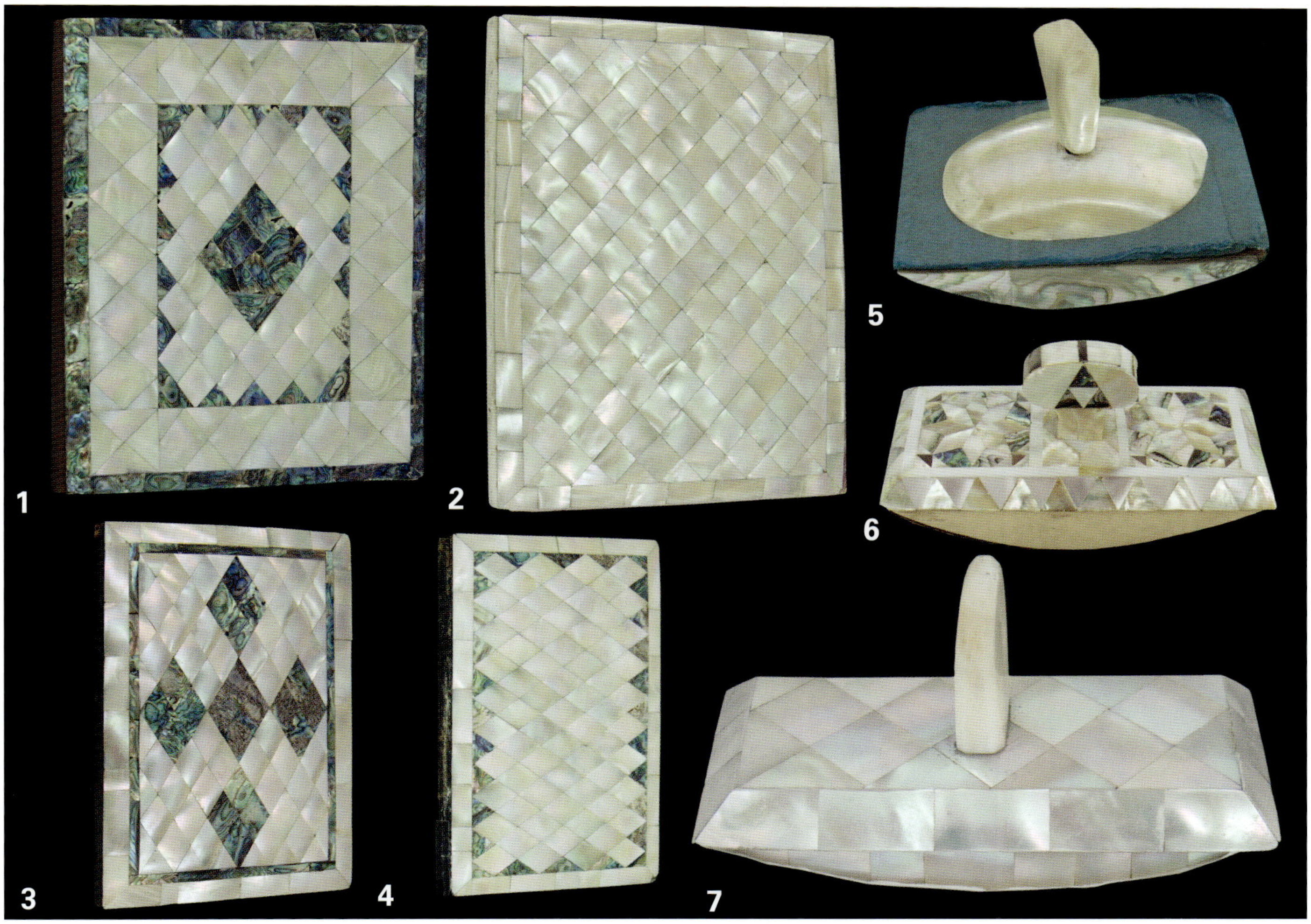

## PLATE 232 – BLOTTERS

A blotter (rocker type or book type) was essential to absorb the excess ink on freshly written items. 1. Folder blotter, England, c. 1875, size 12″ x 9.3″ (30.5 x 23.5 cm). 2. Folder blotter, England, c. 1875, size 12″ x 9.3″ (30.5 x 23.5 cm). 3. Folder blotter, England, c. 1875, size 9.1″ x 6.3″ (23 x 16 cm). 4. Folder blotter, England, c. 1875, size 9.1″ x 6.3″ (23 x 16 cm). 5. Hand held blotter, USA, c. 1925–30, size 4″ x 2.6″ (10.2 x 6.5 cm). 6. Hand held blotter, USA, c. 1920, size 5.9″ x 2.8″ (15 x 7 cm). 7. Hand held blotter, England, c. 1895–1900, size 4.3″ x 2.2″ (11 x 5.5 cm).

## WAX SEALS

The need for a wax seal on envelopes developed out of the need for secrecy of sensitive information or to ensure the letter was read only by the recipient. Early seals of mother-of-pearl were mainly produced in the first three quarters of the nineteenth century and predominantly in France. Of particular interest are the extra large French seals over 3.7" (9.5 cm), which are rarely seen and are thought to have been used by aristocrats.

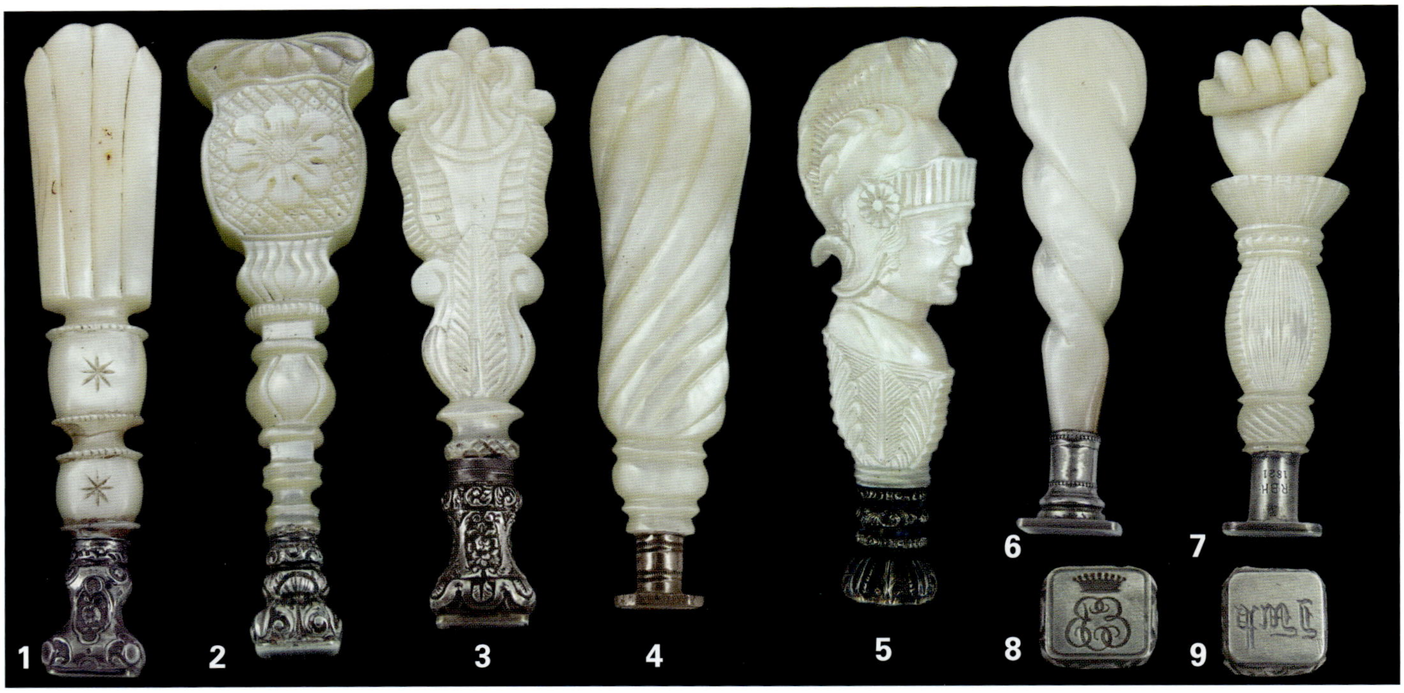

**PLATE 233 – SEALS 1**

1, 9. France, c. 1845, size 4.5" (11.5 cm). 2. France, c. 1830, size 4.3" (10.9 cm). 3, 8. France, Count's crown on the base, c. 1830, size 3.9" (10 cm). 4. Twisted, France, c. 1880, size 3.9" (10 cm). 5. Roman soldier, France, c. 1825, size 3.8" (9.7 cm). 6. France, c. 1830–50, size 3.9" (10 cm). 7. An outstanding example of the popular motif of a hand holding a rod or a baton, France, dated 1821, size 3.7" (9.5 cm).

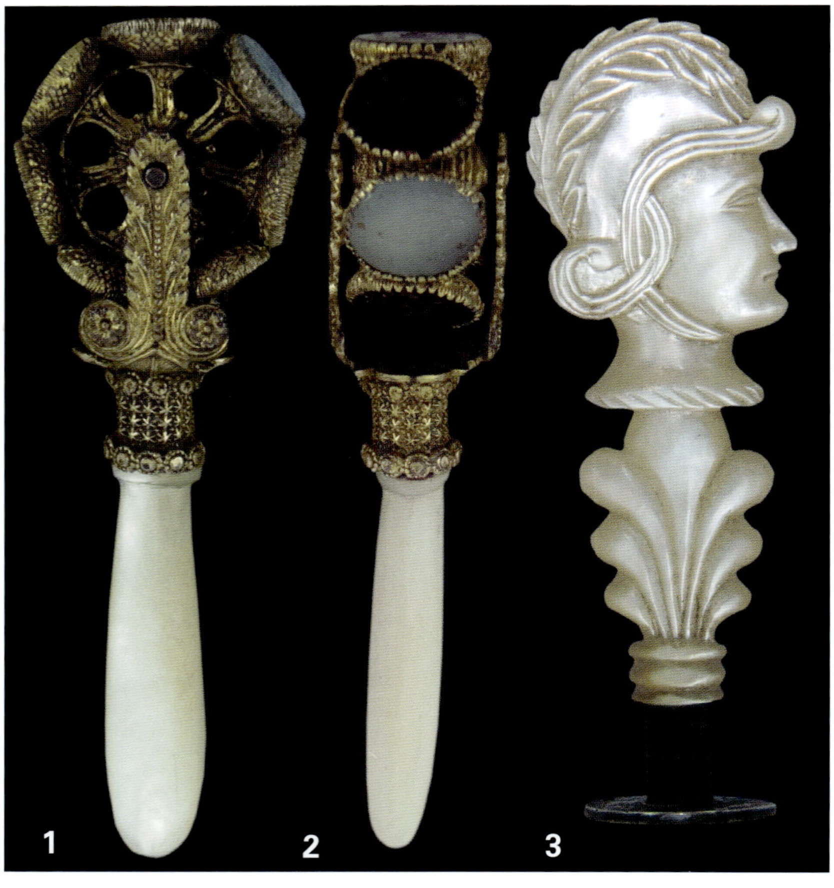

**PLATE 234 – SEALS 2**

1–2. Another item in the wax seal category is the seal wheel. This example contains seven seals each with a different dedication and image. Seals are: *A* (letter) softens the pain of absence; Forget me not; *Je meurs ou je m'attache* (I will hang on or die) with a tree; *Qui me neglige me perd* (He who neglects me loses me) with a caged bird taking flight; *Repondez vite* (Reply quickly) with a bird carrying a letter; *Je ne chance qu'en mourant* (I remain steadfast until death) with a veined leaf; *Telle est la vie* (Such is life) with a ship on rough seas. The seals are of various colored and foiled glass. France, c. 1790. size 3.7" (9.5 cm). 3. Carvers interpretation of an early Roman soldier, France, c. 1800–25, size 2.5" (6.2 cm).

## PLATE 235 – SEALS 3 – CHINESE AND ENGLISH

Seals 1 to 10 were made in China for export markets in England and Europe. **1–3.** Passion seals, intertwined passion fruit to symbolize the love of two people, China, c. 1820, size 2.4″ (6 cm) to 2.8″ (7 cm). **4–6.** Carved hollow seals, China, c. 1860–80, size 0.9″ (2.3 cm) to 2.4″ (6 cm). **7.** Fish, Canton, China, c. 1850, size 2.8″ (7 cm). **8, 9.** Shou Star, Deity of Longevity, China, c. 1875, size 2.6″ (6.7) to 2.8″ (7.1 cm). **10.** Dog's head chop seal, China, c. 1875, size 1.7″ (4.2 cm). **11.** Double intaglio dolphin, England, c. 1850, size 2.5″ (6.3 cm). **12.** Double ended seal, England, c. 1870, size 2.4″ (6 cm). **13, 14.** Fob seals, England, c. 1870–90, two designs, size 1.1″ (2.7 cm). **15, 16.** Clenched fist, England, c. 1850–75, size 2.4″ (6 cm) to 2.8″ (7.2 cm). **17.** Clenched fist, France, c. 1850–75 size 2″ (5 cm). **18–21.** Mixed designs, England, c. 1870, size 2″ (5 cm) to 2.3″ (5.8 cm).

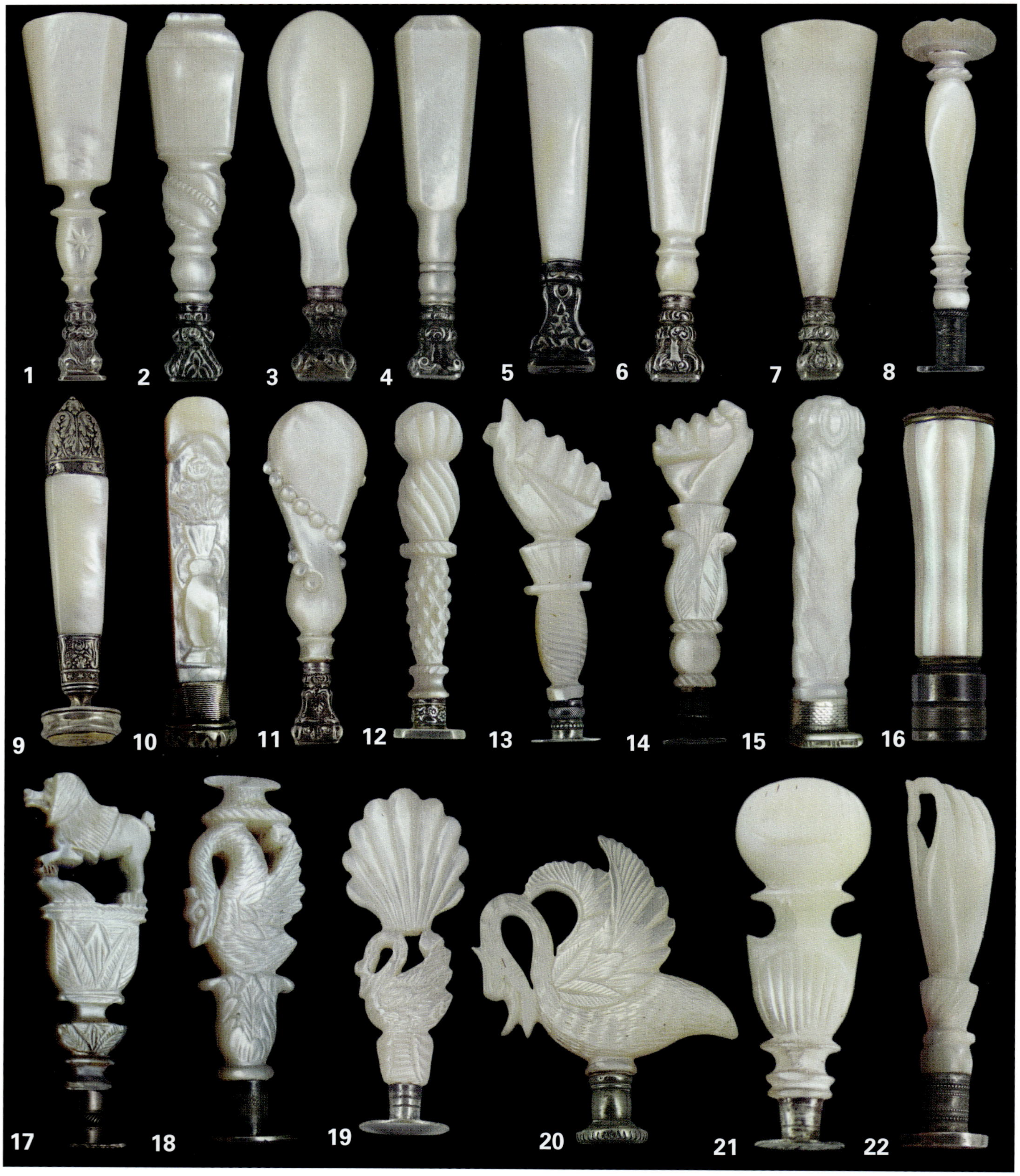


## PLATE 236 – SEALS 4 – FRANCE

**1–7.** Various designs, France, c. 1870–80, size 2.4″ to 3″ (6 cm to 7.7 cm). **8.** Unusual shape, France, c. 1850, size 2.6″ (6.5 cm). **9.** Silver marked *925*, France, c. 1860, size 3.1″ (8 cm). **10.** Carved flower urn, France, c. 1890, size 3.5″ (8.9 cm). **11, 12.** Various designs, France, c. 1850–70, size 2.6″ (6.7 cm) to 3.3″ (8.3 cm). **13, 14.** Hand holding rod or baton, France, c. 1850–70, size 2.5″ (6.3 cm) to 3″ (7.5 cm). **15.** Silver marked *925,* France, c. 1850, size 2.9″ (7.3 cm). **16.** Flower carved on top of the handle, France, c. 1897, size 2.9″ (7.3 cm). **17.** Carved poodle, France, c. 1850–70, size 2.9″ (7.2 cm). **18–20.** Swan seals various designs, France, c. 1850, size 2″ (5.3 cm). **21.** Classic design, France, c. 1875, size 2″ (5.1 cm). **22.** Open hand with a count's crown on the seal, France, c. 1860–70, size 2.4″ (6.2 cm).

## PLATE 237 – SEALS 5 – FRANCE

1-5, 8. Classic design, most from boxed sets sold at Palais Royal shops, France, c. 1800–1820, size #1 3.3″ (8.5 cm); #2–5. 2.6″ (6.5 cm) to 2.8″ (7 cm); #8. 1.6″ (4.1 cm). 6. Seal wax container, France, c. 1820, size 2.8″ x 1.2″ (7 x 3.2 cm). 7. Brass inlay decoration, France, c. 1850–70, size 3.3″ (8.5 cm). 9, 10. Seal wafer container with the enameled pansy, official symbol of higher quality sold at Palais Royal shops, France, c. 1800–1810, size 2.4″ (6 cm) and 2.8″ (7 cm). 11. Clenched fist, France, c. 1870, size 3″ (7.5 cm). 12. Cardinal Richelieu, France, c. 1820, size 3.2″ (8.2 cm). 13. Aristocrat's seal, France, c. 1850, size 4.3″ (10.8 cm). 14, 15. Hand holding a baluster form, two designs, France, c. 1850–60, size 3″ (7.5 cm) to 3.3″ (8.5 cm). 16, 17. Different patterns, France, c. 1860–70, size 3.1″ (8 cm) to 3.4″ (8.6 cm). 18. Snake intertwined on handle, France, c. 1880, size 3.1″ (8 cm).

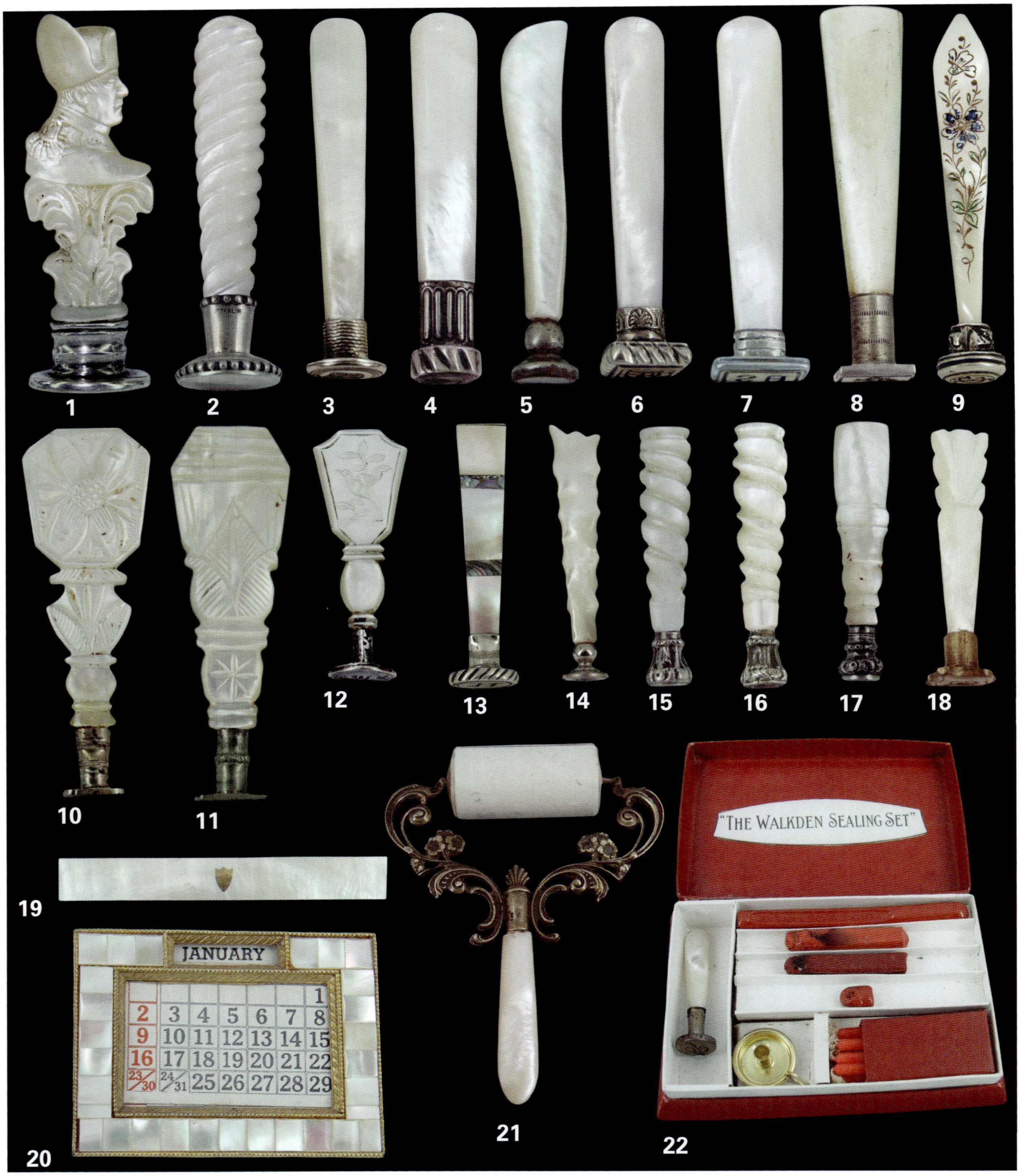


## PLATE 238 – SEALS 6 AND OTHER DESK ACCESSORIES

1. Napoleon, France, c. 1820, size 2.4″ (6 cm). 2. Carved design, USA, c. 1890, size 2.6″ (6.7 cm). 3–8. Assorted designs, USA, c. 1910–15, size 2.6″ (6.7 cm) to 3.3″ (8.4 cm). 9. Painted design, USA, c. 1870–90, size 4.1″ (10.4 cm). 10–12. Flat decorated seal, France, c. 1870–1880, size 2″ (5.3 cm) to 2.8″ (7 cm). 13. Abalone and pearl, USA, c. 1925, size 3.2″ (8.2 cm). 14. Carved, USA, c. 1890, size 2.8″ (7.2 cm). 15–17. Tiny seal with stone face, USA, c. 1900, size 1.6″ to 1.7″ (4 cm to 4.4 cm). 18. Small seal, France, c. 1880, size 1.8″ (4.5 cm). 19. Straight edge from a boxed writing set, France, c. 1810–20, size 5.7″ (14.5 cm). 20. Desk calendar, USA, 1956, size 3.1″ x 2.4″ (8 x 6 cm). 21. Ink stabilizer, Germany, c. 1900, size 5.5″ x 5.5″ (14 x 14 cm). 22. *The Walden Sealing Set*, (seal, sealing wax, candles, candle holder), USA, c. 1905–15, size 5.5 x 3.5″ (14 x 9 cm).

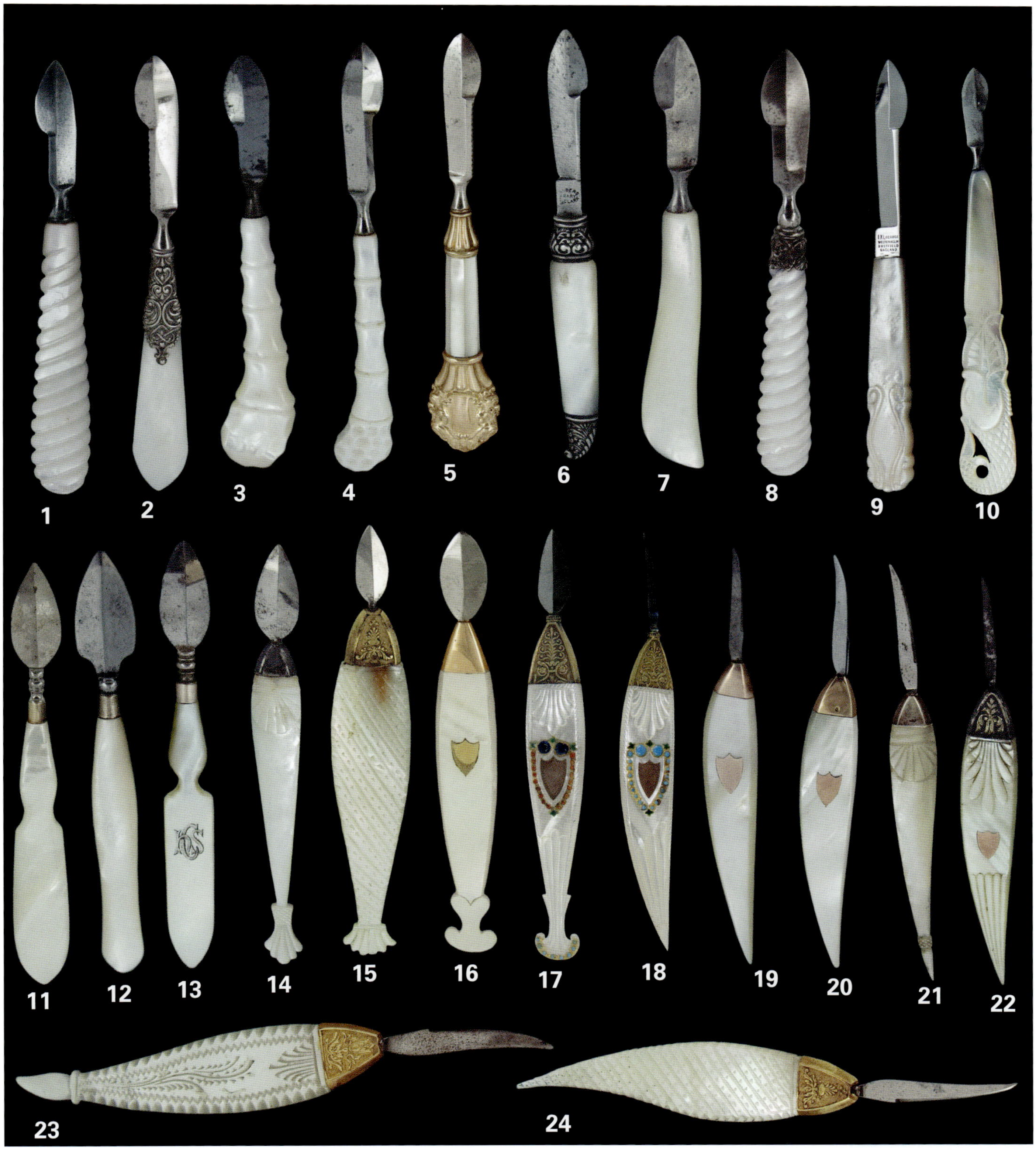


## PLATE 239 – INK ERASERS AND QUILL KNIVES

Ink erasers (numbers 1–17) were used to scrape off ink errors on a page, whilst the quill knife (numbers 18–24) was used to sharpen a quill for use as a dip pen. **1.** England, c. 1880, size 3.7″ (9.5 cm). **2.** USA, sterling, c. 1880, size 5.3″ (13.5 cm). **3, 4.** USA, c. 1890, size 3.9″ to 5.1″ (10-13 cm). **5.** USA, c. 1870, size 5.3″ (13.5 cm). **6.** USA, maker *Landers Frary & Clark*, c. 1880, size 6″ (15.2 cm). **7.** USA, c. 1895–1900, size 3.9″ (10 cm). **8.** England, c. 1880, size 4.1″ (10.5 cm). **9.** England, maker *George Wostenholm*, Sheffield, c. 1880, size 5.5″ (14 cm). **10.** USA, c. 1840–60, size 5.9″ (15 cm). Similar handles were made by US dental tool manufacturers. **11–13.** England, likely Sheffield, c. 1885, size 4.3″ (11 cm) to 4.8″ (12.3 cm). **14–17.** Originally from boxed sets sold at Palais Royal arcades, Paris, France, c. 1810–20, size 4.3″ to 4.8″ (11 to 12.2 cm). **18–24.** Quill knife originally from boxed sets sold at Palais Royal arcades, Paris, France, c. 1810–20, size 4.6″ to 5.6″ (11.8 to 14.3 cm).

## PLATE 240 – INKWELLS 1

Mother-of-pearl inkwells were a popular souvenir of trips to the seaside, and many had town names painted on them. Most of the pearl inkwells were made between 1850 and 1930. By 1920, the fountain pen gained tremendously in popularity and in ten years saw the demise of the inkwell. 1. England, c. 1880–1890, size 12.4″ x 9.1″ (31.5 x 23 cm). 2. England, c. 1890–1900, size 10.6″ x 8.1″ (27 x 20.5 cm). 3. Carved Native American, USA, c. 1900, size 3.1″ (8 cm). 4. England, c. 1890, size 8.3″ x 5.3″ (21 x 13.5 cm). 5. England, c. 1880–90, size 9.4″ x 6.7″ (24 x 17 cm). 6. India, c. 1950, size 2″ (5 cm) diameter. 7. England, c. 1880–90, size 8.9″ x 5.9″ (22.5 x 15 cm). 8. France, c. 1890–1900, seaside town souvenir, size 5.9″ x 3.5″ (15 x 9 cm). 9. France, inscribed *Cherbourg*, c. 1890–1900, size 3.9″ x 3″ (10 x 7.5 cm). 10. Desk caddy, France, c. 1890, size 6.9″ x 6.5″ (17.5 x 16.5 cm). 11. Desk caddy, France, c. 1890, size 5.5″ x 3.9″ (14 x 10 cm). 12. USA, c. 1900–1910, size 4.6″ (11.8 cm). 13. France, c. 1850, size 3.5″ x 2.4″ (9 x 6 cm).

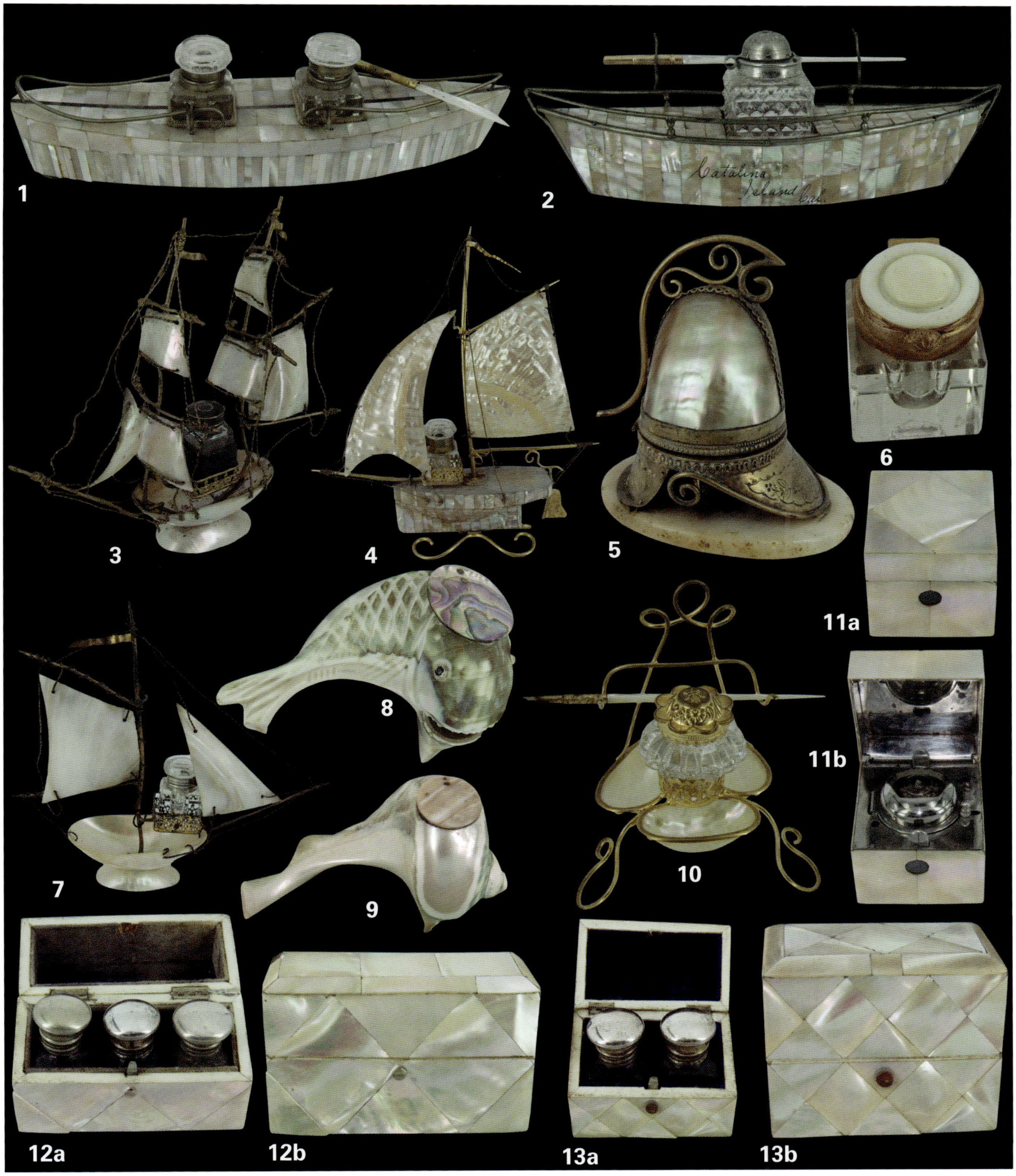


## PLATE 241 – INKWELLS 2

**1.** Boat, seaside souvenir, USA, c. 1890, size 11.2″ (28.5 cm). **2.** Boat, inscribed *Catalina Island*, USA, c. 1890, size 4.1″ (10.5 cm). **3.** Boat, France, seaside souvenir, c. 1880, size 7.5″ x 7.3″ (19 x 18.5 cm). **4.** Boat, France, c. 1870, size 8.3″ x 9.1″ (21 x 23 cm), seaside town name partly worn off. **5.** Helmet top opens to reveal an ink bottle, France, c. 1860, size 5.1″ x 4.1″ (13 x 10.5 cm). **6.** Ink bottle, England, c. 1900, size 1.4″ (3.5 cm) square. **7.** Boat, inscribed *Le Treport*, France, c. 1880, size 7.7″ x 6.9″ (19.5 x 17.5 cm). **8.** Fish, inkwell under the lid, USA, c. 1900, size 4.7″ (12 cm). **9.** Shell inkwell, USA, c. 1900, size 5.5″ (14 cm). **10.** France, c. 1880–1900, size 3.9″ x 3.2″ (10 x 8 cm). **11.** Traveller's ink bottle in a pearl box, England, c. 1870, size 2″ x 2″ (5 x 5 cm). **12a, 12b.** Three ink bottles in a pearl box, England, c. 1870, size 3.9″ x 1.6″ (10 x 4 cm). **13a, 13b.** Two ink bottles in a pearl box, England, c. 1870, size 2.8″ x 1.6″ (7 x 4 cm).

CHAPTER 9

# Time Pieces

Collecting clocks and watches has always been a popular hobby. Large numbers of time pieces have been manufactured, but the ones made of mother-of-pearl are truly rare.

In our opinion, the most visually arresting pearl timepieces are the early nineteenth century French clocks. The clock faces of pearl were set into cathedrals and churches. Please refer to our plate below. Manufacturing of mother-of-pearl timepieces continued through the nineteenth century into the first half of the twentieth century.

**PLATE 242 – CLOCKS**

1. Exceptional cathedral clock, France, c. 1810, size 8.1" x 3.7" (20.5 x 9.5 cm). 2. Wall clock maker *JBB,* likely Johann Baptist Beha, Germany, c. 1850, size 5.9" x 2.4" (15 x 6.2 cm). 3. Cathedral clock, maker *Le Roi Paris*, France, c. 1810, size 5.9" x 4.3" (15 x 11 cm).

## PLATE 243 – CLOCKS

**1.** Table clock, Imhoff, Switzerland, c. 1950–60, size 4.5" x 3.9" (11.5 x 10 cm). **2.** Table clock, Bucherer, Switzerland, c. 1950–60, size 5.7" x 3.9" (14.5 x 10 cm), Imhoff movements. **3.** Table clock, Lux, USA, c. 1928, size 4.7" x 6.3" (12 x 16 cm). **4.** Table clock, Dep, France, c. 1920–30, size 4.3" x 3.7" (11 x 9.5 cm). **5.** Table clock, Amarin, Thailand, for USA market, c. 1998, size 3.1" x 3.1" (7.8 x 7.8 cm), Japanese movements. **6.** Wall clock, Embassy, Switzerland, c. 1930–60, size 6.3" x 3.9" (16 x 10 cm), Imhoff movements,18 Jewels, backing carved by Valerie Meyer. **7.** Miniature travel clock, Japan, c. 1995, size 2.3" x 1.3" (5.8 x 3.4 cm). Case made in China, movements Japan. **8, 9.** Mantle clock, Lenzkirch, Germany, c. 1885, size 11" x 6.9" (28 x 17.5 cm), patent number 655321. **10.** Table clock, Hamburg American Clocks, England, c. 1940–50, size 3.5" x 2.6" (9 x 6.5 cm). **11.** Carriage clock, England, c. 1880, size 2.7" x 1.9" (6.8 x 4.7 cm), Swiss movements.

## PLATE 244 – CLOCKS AND WATCH HOLDERS

1. Travelling clock with protective brass doors, Imhoff, Switzerland, c. 1950, size 3.1″ x 3.5″ (8 x 9 cm). 2. Table clock, Brevette SGDC, France, c. 1915–25, size 5.4″ x 3.7″ (13.7 x 9.5 cm). 3. Table clock, Germany, c. 1920, size 2.8″ x 2.3″ (7 x 5.8 cm). 4. Traveling clock, Solomax Watch Co., Switzerland, c. 1910, size 2.5″ x 2.4″ (6.3 x 6 cm), in box for traveling. 5. Table clock, Fleur de Lys, Paris, France, c. 1920–30, size 2.4″ x 1.5″ (6 x 3.8 cm), movements by Lenox. 6. Wall clock, Australia, 2008, size 7.1″ (18 cm) diameter. 7. Pocket watch holder with hinged door, France, c. 1850–60, size 6.7″ x 4.5″ (17 x 11.4 cm). 8, 9. Helmet watch holder, France, c. 1860, size 5.3″ x 2.8″ (13.5 x 7.2 cm). 10. Chair watch stand, France, c. 1850, size 4.9″ x 2.4″ (12.5 x 6 cm). 11. Barrel clock, Medana, Switzerland, c. 1900, size 1.5″ x 1.3″ (3.8 x 3.3 cm). 12. Boat watch stand, France, c. 1870, size 5.8″ x 3.3″ (14.7 x 8.5 cm).

## PLATE 245 – CLOCKS AND WATCH HOLDERS

1. Pocket watch, Hob, Switzerland, c. 1910–20, size 1.6″ x 1.2″ (4 x 3 cm). 2. Pocket watch, Switzerland, c. 1910–20, size 1.8″ x 1.2″ (4.5 x 3 cm). 3. Pocket watch, Lady Grant, Switzerland, c. 1910–20, size 1.6″ x 1.2″ (4 x 3 cm). 4. Pocket watch, Agora, Switzerland, c. 1910–20, size 1.2″ (3 cm) diameter. 5. Wrist watch, Switzerland, c. 1910–20, size 1.1″ x 1.3″ (2.8 x 3.2 cm). 6. Wristwatch, Lady Tess, Switzerland, c. 1910–20, size 1″ (2.5 cm) diameter. 7. Clip on watch, Switzerland, c. 1920, size 1.2″ (3 cm) diameter. 8. Wrist watch, La Marne, Switzerland, c. 1910–20, size 1.1″ x 1.3″ (2.8 x 3.2 cm). 9. Pocket watch, England, c. 1880, size 2.7″ x 1.9″ (6.8 x 4.7 cm) Swiss movements. 10. Clock key, USA, c. 1890–1900, size 3.7″ x 2.4″ (9.5 x 6 cm), Native American head. 11. Box for pocketwatch, England, c. 1880, size 3.1″ x 2.4″ x 1.8″ (7.8 x 6 x 4.5 cm). 12, 13. Box for pocketwatch, England, c. 1870–80, size 3.1″ x 2.4″ x 2″ (7.8 x 6.2 x 5 cm). 14. Wristwatch, Gem Time, Japan, c. 1995, size 1.2″ (3 cm) diameter, assembled in Hong Kong. 15. Wristwatch, Miyoto, Japan, c. 1990, size 0.9″ x 1.4″ (2.3 x 3.5 cm). 16. Box for wristwatch, Myanmar, c. 1999, size 8.1″ x 2″ x 1.6″ (20.5 x 5.2 x 4 cm). 17. Clock hand, England, c. 1850, size 3.2″ (8.2 cm). 18. Clock key, China, c. 1890, for the English market, size 2.1″ x 1″ (5.3 x 2.6 cm).

CHAPTER 10

# Spectacles and Optical Aides

## SCISSOR SPECTACLES

Mother-of-pearl was first used for making the handles of scissor spectacles during the late eighteenth century. George Adams of Fleet Street, London, first patented scissor spectacles in 1780. Both George Washington and Napoleon Bonaparte used them, which helped to make them popular. Production came to an end early in the 1800s, when the lorgnette took over as the most popular vision aide.

## LORGNETTES

George Adams (Fleet Street, London), who first patented scissor spectacles, was also the first to design a device in 1785 that would permit the spectacles to slide into the mother-of-pearl case, which also acted as a handle, and so protected the glasses. The lorgnette was meant to be carried in the pocket. The photos will show the big variety of mother-of-pearl handled lorgnettes. They died out slowly during the twentieth century as the bifocal spectacles gained popularity.

## BIFOCALS

Mother-of-pearl was not sturdy or flexible enough to be used for the manufacture of twentieth century spectacles. On occasion, you do see nose guards on the frames of bifocals made of mother-of-pearl, but this is rare.

## SPY GLASSES

Early spectacles often did not fit well, or hadn't been ground well, causing poor vision. As a result, by 1680, small versions of the telescope called monoculars or spy glasses, were being produced. The invention of opera glasses in 1825 caused the decline in popularity of the spy glass.

## OPERA GLASSES

Opera glasses were invented by Lumiere of Paris in 1825. As the theater was an important part of the social life in early times, there was a high demand for these glasses. Variations in form and decoration were used to attract buyers. Early examples of opera glasses were covered in shagreen (rough skin of sharks and rays), but soon pearl oyster, abalone shell, and combinations of various mother-of-pearl types were used. By the end of the nineteenth century, new attachments were necessary to attract customers. The adjustable, extendable pearl handle was produced. At first, these handles were sold separately, but later they were sold connected to the opera glasses' frames.

## SPECTACLE CASE

In the mid-1800s, pearl was used as inserts for lacquer and papier-mache spectacle cases. Later, for evening wear, wood cases were covered with a thin veneer of mother-of-pearl, which made for a visually attractive case of high status. Production was mainly in England.

## MAGNIFYING GLASS

The earliest mention of the magnifying glass with a mother-of-pearl handle was in the second half of the eighteenth century. By the end of the nineteenth century, these were being produced in small numbers. A reproduction precaution should be mentioned here: there was a growing industry in England at the end of the twentieth century, which involved putting antique mother-of-pearl handles onto new magnifying glasses. These were then being sold to the tourist trade as antiques. The genuine antique, all original magnifying glass with a mother-of-pearl handle is hard to find.

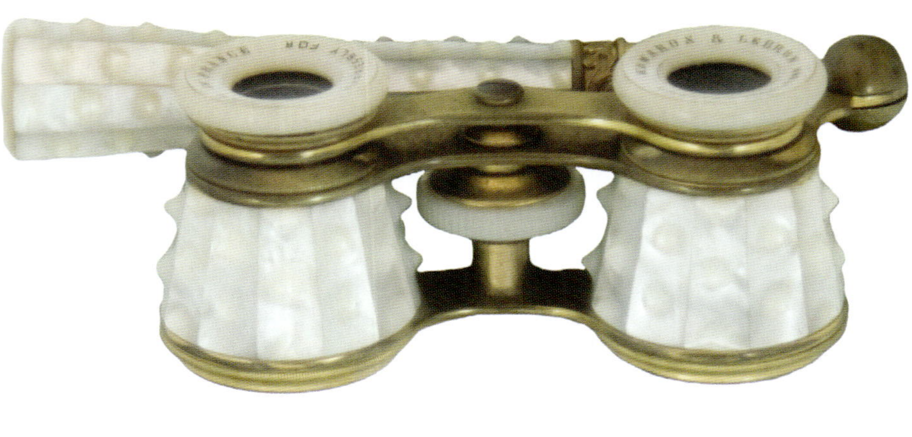

## PLATE 246 – OPERA GLASSES 1

1. Opera glasses, Zingraff, 184 Rue de Rivoli, Paris, France, c. 1870, size 3.3" x 1" (8.5 x 2.5 cm). 2. Opera glasses, made in France for Shreve, Crump & Low, Boston, April 1874, size 4.1" x 2" (10.5 x 5 cm). 3. Opera glasses, Colmont, Paris, France, c. 1890, size 3.1" x 1.4" (8 x 3.5 cm). 4. Opera glasses with original case, Le Maire, France, c. 1870, size 3.8 x 2.2" (9.6 x 5.5cm), rare solid pearl type. 5. Multi use, has different settings for theater, field, or marine use, *Le Maire 3349,* France, c. 1870–80, size 4.7" x 4.3" (12 x 11 cm). 6. Opera glasses 2.5X, Carton, Japan, c. 1960, size 3.5" x 1.8" (9 x 4.5 cm). 7. Opera glasses, Le Maire, Paris, France, c. 1880, size 4.1" x 3.1" (10.5 x 8 cm); it is unusual for pearl to be inlaid on the inner barrel. 8. Opera glasses, Le Maire, Paris, France, c. 1895, size 3.9" x 2.4" (10 x 6 cm). 9a+b. Opera glasses with case, Le Maire, Paris, France, c. 1870, size 4.3" x 3.3" (11 x 8.5 cm), rare solid pearl type. 10. Opera glasses, Le Maire, Paris, France, c. 1890, size 3.9" x 2.6" (10 x 6.5 cm), made from the Aribi pearl.

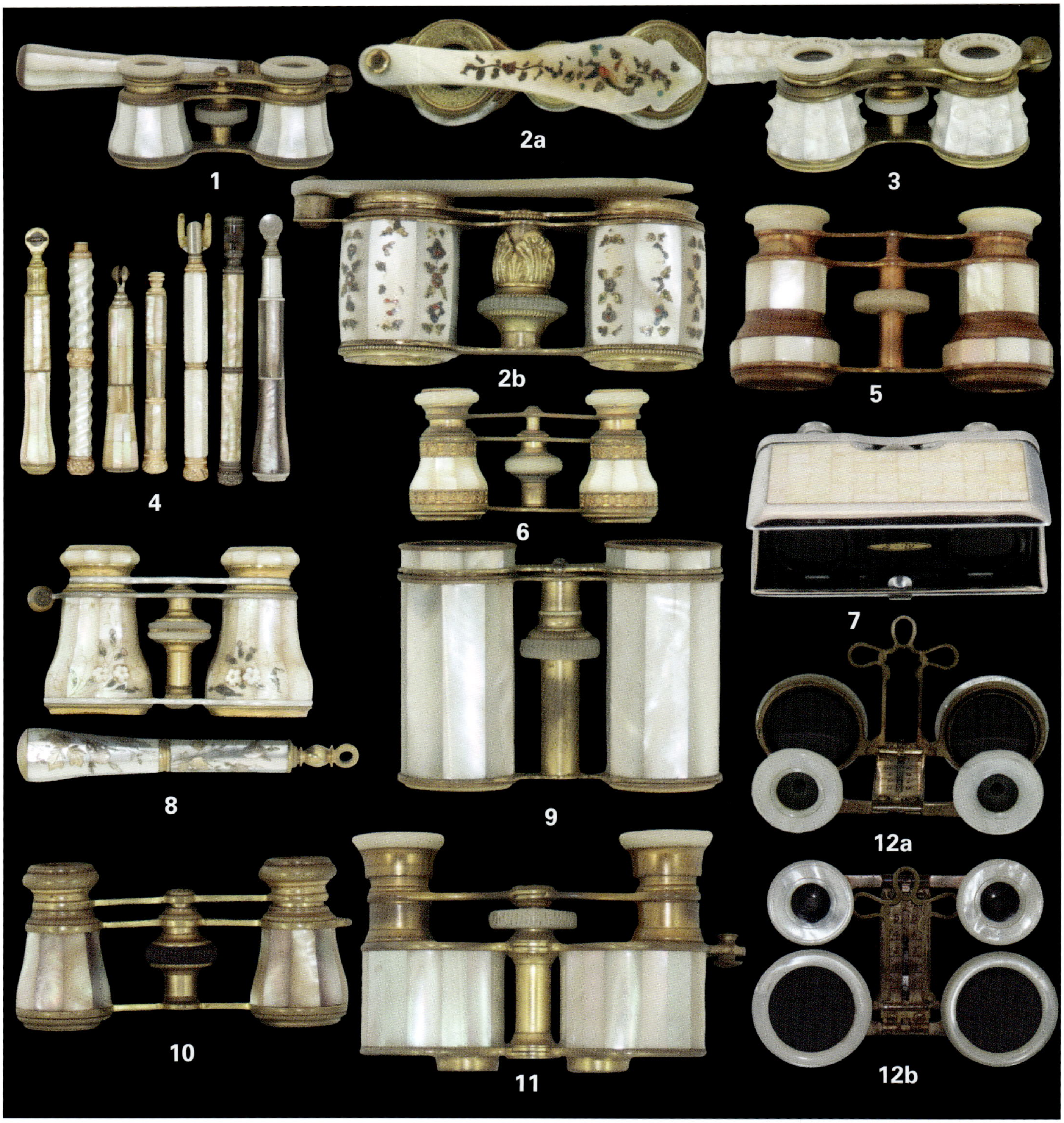


## PLATE 247 – OPERA GLASSES 2

**1.** Opera glasses with handle, France, c. 1890, size 3.9″ x 2″ (10 x 5 cm). **2a+b.** Opera glasses, Parinvention, France, c. 1870, size 3.7″ x 1.8″ (9.5 x 4.5 cm). **3.** Opera glasses, made in France for Edwards Lebron, Chattanooga, Tenn., USA, c. 1900, size 3.7″ x 1.8″ (9.5 x 4.5 cm). **4.** Opera glass handles showing great variety in design, France, c. 1890–1920, size 4.5″ to 5.9″ (11.5 to 15 cm). **5.** Opera glasses, France, c. 1880, size 3.7″ x 2″ (9.5 x 5 cm). **6.** Opera glasses, Colmont, Paris, France, c. 1880, size 3.5″ x 1.8″ (9 x 4.5 cm). **7.** Pocket folding glasses, *S-W,* Japan, c. 1925, size 4.3″ x 2.8″ (11 x 7 cm). **8.** Opera glasses, made in France for Tiffany & Co., c. 1890, size 3.9″ x 2.4″ (10 x 6 cm). **9.** Opera glasses, France, c. 1900, size 3.9″ x 3″ (10 x 7.5 cm). **10.** Opera glasses, La Tosca, Paris, France, c. 1900, size 3.5″ x 1.6″ (9 x 4 cm). **11.** Opera glasses, *G.E.Pryor, Opticien, 1 bis Rue Aubert, Paris,* France, c. 1870, size 3.5″ x 2.4″ (9 x 6 cm). **12a &12b.** Jumella Mars folding opera glasses, France, c. 1895, size 3.9″ x 2.8″ (10 x 7 cm).

## PLATE 248 – OPTICAL 1

1. Lorgnette, France, c. 1850, size 3″ (7.5 cm). 2. Lorgnette, France, c. 1850, size 3″ (7.5 cm). 3. Lorgnette, France, c. 1850, size 3″ (7.5 cm). 4. Lorgnette, France, c. 1850, size 3″ (7.5 cm). 5. Lorgnette, France, c. 1850, size 3″ (7.5 cm). 6. Lorgnette, England, c. 1800–1825, size 2.2″ (5.5 cm). 7. Lorgnette, England, c. 1800–1825, size 2.8″ (7 cm). 8. Lorgnette, England, c. 1840, size 2.4″ (6 cm). 9. Lorgnette, England, c. 1800–1820, size 4.3″ (11 cm). 10. Lorgnette, France, c. 1875, size 3.1″ (8 cm). 11. Scissor glasses, England, c. 1795–1800, closed 4.3″ (11 cm), open 7.3″ (18.5 cm).

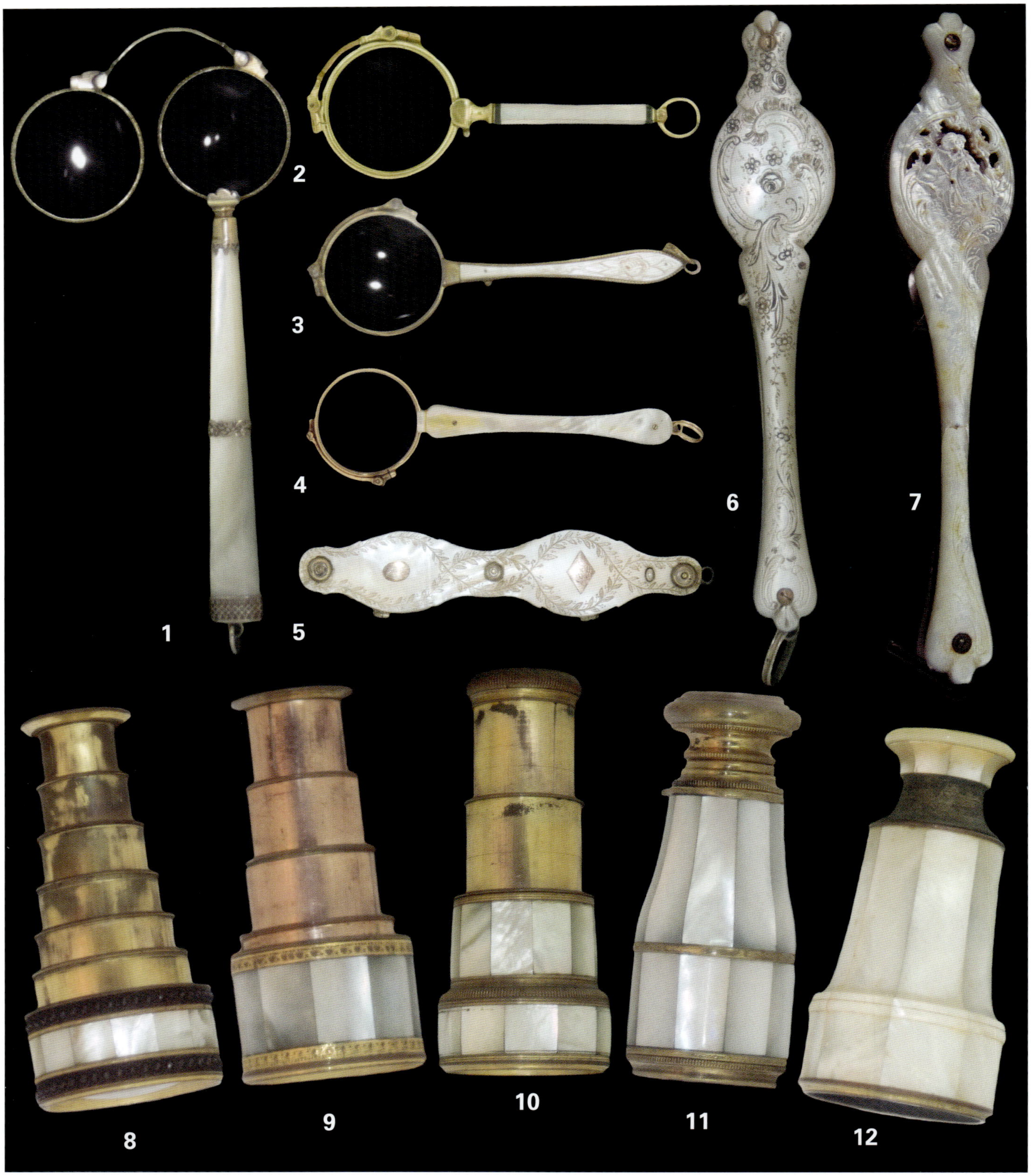


## PLATE 249 – OPTICAL 2

1. Lorgnette, England, c. 1880, size 6.1″ (15.5 cm). 2. Lorgnette, England, c. 1890–1920, size 3.5″ (9 cm). 3. Lorgnette, England, c. 1895, size 4.5″ (11.5 cm). 4. Lorgnette, England, c. 1890–1920, size 5.7″ (14.5 cm). 5. Lorgnette, inscribed *AB 1818*, England, size 4.3″ (11 cm). 6. Lorgnette, France, c. 1880, size 5.9″ (15 cm). 7. Lorgnette, France, c. 1880, size 5.5″ (14 cm). 8. Monocular or spy glass, six barrels (or draws), France, c. 1820, size 3.5″ (9 cm). 9. Monocular or spy glass, four barrels (or draws), France, c. 1840, size 2.8″ (7 cm). 10. Monocular or spy glass, two barrels (or draws), France, c. 1840, size 4.7″ (12 cm). 11. Monocular or spy glass, France, c. 1890, size 2.8″ (7 cm). 12. Monocular or spy glass, France, c. 1820, size 4.1″ (10.5 cm).

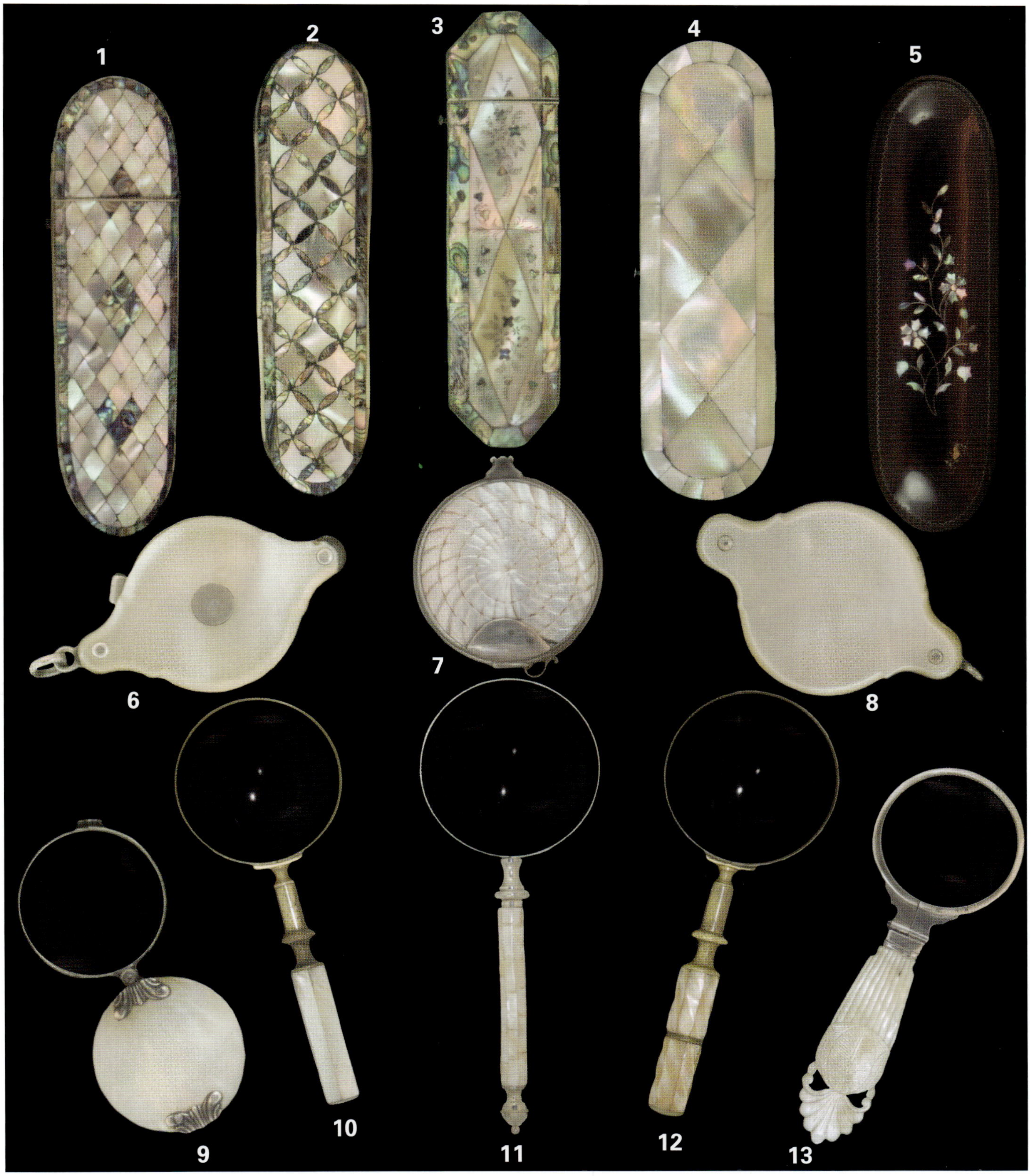


## PLATE 250 – OPTICAL 3

1. Glasses case, England, c. 1870–80, size 5.5" (14 cm). 2. Glasses case, England, c. 1870–80, size 5.7" (14.5 cm). 3. Glasses case, England, c. 1870–1880, size 5.5" (14 cm). 4. Glasses case, England, c. 1870–80, size 5.9" (15 cm). 5. Glasses case, papier-mache, England, c. 1870–80, size 5.1" (13 cm). 6. Magnifying glass, England, c. 1840, size 2.3" (5.8 cm). 7. Reducing lens, England, c. 1840, size 1.5" (3.8 cm). 8. Magnifying glass, England, c. 1840, size 2.3" (5.8c m). 9. Magnifying glass, England, c. 1800, size 1.6" (4 cm). 10. Magnifying glass, England, c. 1895, size 6.7" (17 cm). 11. Magnifying glass, India, c. 1975, size 10" (25.5 cm). 12. Magnifying glass, England, c. 1895, size 6.7" (17 cm). 13. Magnifying glass, France, c. 1880, size 5.5" (14 cm).

CHAPTER 11

# Dental And Medical

## DENTAL

Mother-of-pearl was used in handles for dental instruments as far back as the late eighteenth century. It was felt that using richly decorated tools was appropriate when seeing wealthy clients. Possibly, it even made the clients feel better about the pain they had to endure!

Elisabeth Bennion, in her book *Antique Dental Instruments* (Sotheby's Publications, London, 1986), illustrates magnificent dental sets from the first half of the nineteenth century. These wonderful sets are seldom seen out of museums today. Included in these sets are mother-of-pearl handled picks, pluggers, drills, tongue scrapers, mirrors, lancets, and others tools. Early 1800s dental hygiene sets, made in France, also used mother-of-pearl in the handles of the toothbrushes and toothpicks, and even for the covering of toothpick boxes.

By the mid-1800s, these mother-of-pearl instruments lost their popularity, no doubt caused by the advancement of dentistry and the need to sterilize tools, which damaged the mother-of-pearl.

## MEDICAL

Possibly because medical tools do not have visual prominence, as do dental tools, medical tools did not have much mother-of-pearl decoration on them. Also, as in the later dental tools, the need for sterilization necessitated that the tools be made of metals rather than decorative materials such as pearl. That being said, there are records of pearl having been used in scalpel handles, lancets, and lancet cases, and also for cases that held thermometers.

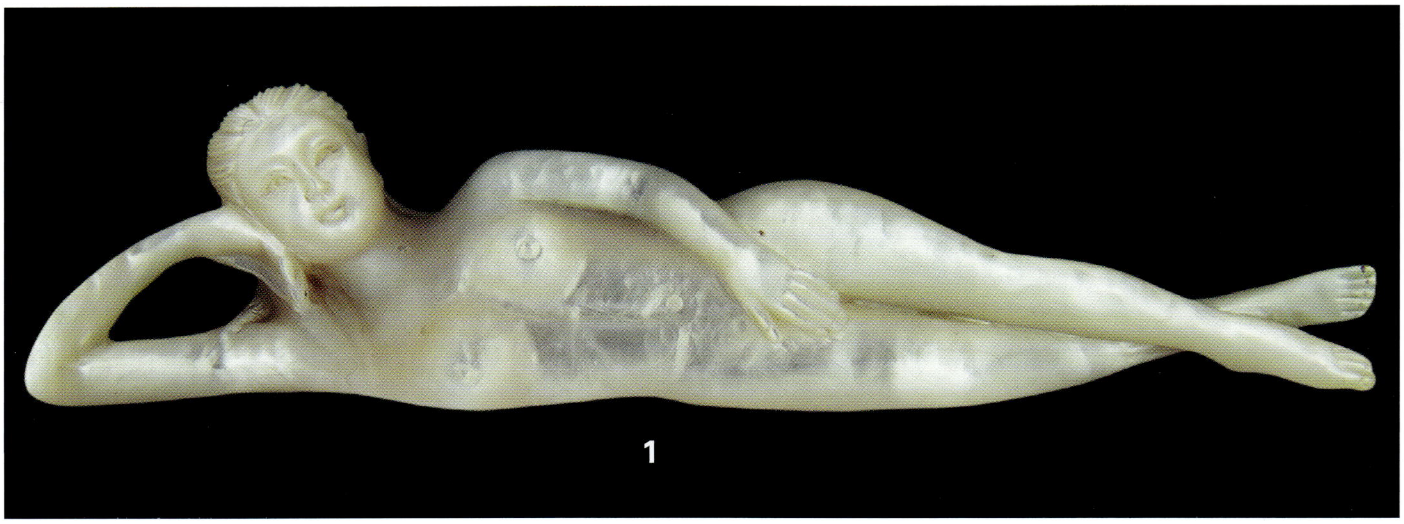


### PLATE 251 – MEDICAL DOLL

1. Chinese medical doll or "doctor's lady", China, c. 1850, size 5.1" (13 cm). Taken by a servant to the doctor to aid in diagnosing the illness of a mistress. Also used in consultations with a male doctor where the location of the problem could be indicated on the doll without pointing to the patient's body. Doctors would not examine female patients directly.

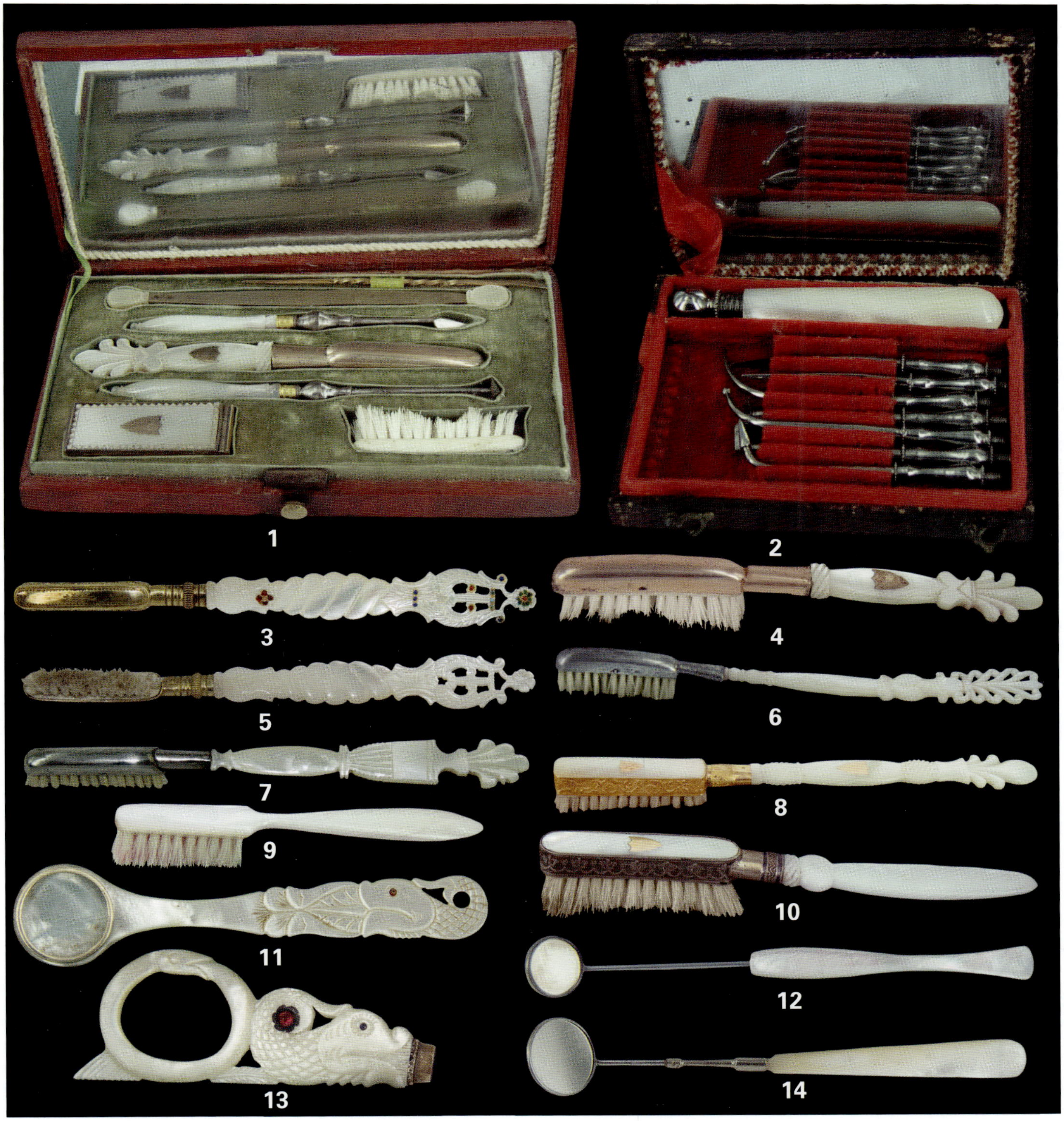


## PLATE 252 – DENTAL SETS, MIRRORS and TOOTHBRUSHES

1. Dental hygiene set for personal use, France, c. 1820, size 4.9″ x 2.8″ (12.5 x 7 cm), consists of a toothbrush, tongue scraper, two dental scalers, and a tooth powder box. It has the mark of goldsmith Pierre Leplain. 2. Seven dental scalers with single screw-in handle, France, c. 1820, size 3.5″ x 2.8″ (9 x 7 cm). 3, 5. Toothbrush with inset gem stones, France, c. 1810, size 5.3″ (13.5 cm), from a boxed set. 4. Toothbrush, France, c. 1820, size 3.9″ (10 cm), from a boxed set. 6. Toothbrush, France, c. 1800–20, size 6.1″ (15.4 cm), from a boxed set. 7. Toothbrush, France, c. 1800, size 5.2″ (13.2 cm). 8. Toothbrush with gold hallmark, France, 1809, size 4.6″ (11.7 cm). 9. Toothbrush, animal hair bristle, England, c. 1890, size 3.9″ (10 cm). 10. Toothbrush with silver, animal hair bristle, England c. 1870, size 3.9″ (10 cm). 11. Dental mirror with fish handle, USA, c. 1840, size 5.1″ (13 cm). 12. Dental mirror, USA, c. 1910, size 6.1″ (15.4 cm). 13. One handle from a pair a dental scissors, USA, c. 1840, size 3.5″ x 1.4″ (9 x 3.5 cm), similar carved fish are seen in the dental mirror #11. 14. Dental mirror, Boilo, USA, c. 1890–1900, size 6.7″ (17 cm).

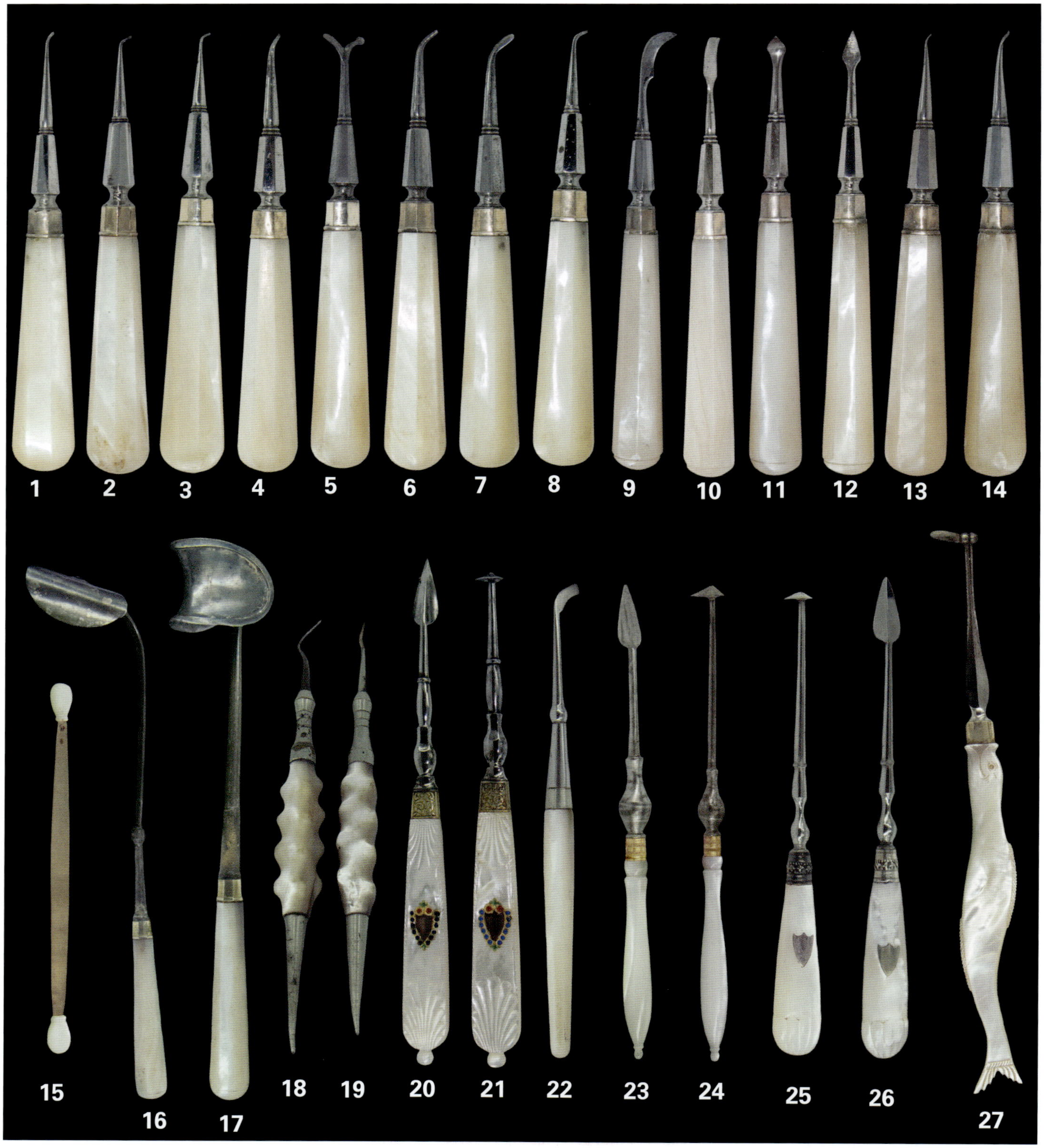


## PLATE 253 – DENTAL TOOLS

**1–14.** Set of fourteen dental pluggers or scalers with thick pearl handles, J. D. Chevalier, USA, c. 1860, size 5.5" (14 cm). **15.** Tongue scraper, France, c. 1800, size 3.9" (9.8 cm), from a boxed set. **16.** Dental tongue depressor, J. D. Chevalier, USA, c. 1860, size 9.1" (23 cm), would be held by the patient. **17.** Dental lip depressor, J. D. Chevalier, USA, c. 1860, size 9.1" (23 cm), would be held by the patient. **18, 19.** Dental pluggers, USA, c. 1870–80, size 6.3" (16 cm). **20, 21.** Dental pluggers or scalers from a boxed set, France, c. 1810, size 5.1" and 5.7" (13 and 14.5 cm). **22.** Dental plugger or scaler, USA, c. 1880, size 5.7" (14.5 cm). **23, 24.** Dental plugger or scaler, France, c. 1800, size 3.3" to 3.5" (8.5 to 9 cm), from a boxed set. **25, 26.** Dental plugger or scaler, France, c. 1820, size 3.4" to 3.8" (8.7 to 9.6 cm), from a boxed set. **27.** Dental lancet, likely J.D. Chevalier, USA, c. 1840, size 7.6" (19.2 cm), handle in the shape of a fish.

## PLATE 254 – MEDICAL and DENTAL TOOLS

**1, 3, 6.** Lancet case with two lancets, China for export to England, c. 1840, size 2.8" x 1.1" (7 x 2.8 cm), used for blood letting. **2, 7.** Lancet case for four lancets, China for export to England, c. 1840, size 2.2" x 1.2" (5.5 x 3 cm), used for blood letting. **4.** Lancet case with two lancets, England, c. 1850, size 2.6" x 1.2" (6.5 x 3 cm), used for blood letting. **5.** Lancet for blood letting, England, c. 1850, size 2.2" (5.5 cm). **8.** Replica of a Chinese medical doll or "doctor's lady," Thailand, 2000, size 5.7" (14.5 cm), aid in diagnosing the illness without pointing to the patient's body. (See the introduction to this chapter for another example.) **9.** Doctor's desk bell, hallmarked London, England, 1913, size 2.2" x 2.2" (5.5 x 5.5 cm). **10, 11.** Believed to be scalpels, USA, c. 1880, size 4.5" to 5.1" (11.5 to 13 cm), easily confused with later manicure tools. **12.** Thermometer in pearl case, NTCO, England, c. 1900, size 5.1" (13 cm). **13.** Thermometer case, USA, c. 1900, size 4.5" (11.5 cm). **14.** Tooth powder box, France, c. 1800, size 1.4" x 0.6" (3.5 x 1.5 cm), likely from a travel set. **15.** Baby thermometer in a pearl case, worn as a pendant by a nurse, England, c. 1880, size 0.9" (2.4 cm). **16.** Dental mirror with paste decoration, France, c. 1820, size 9.4" (24 cm), used by the patient to see progress. **17.** Dental mirror with paste decoration, France, c. 1820, size 9.1" (23 cm), used by the patient to see progress. **18.** Dental mirror, France, c. 1875–1900, size 9.4" (24 cm). **19–21.** Dental mirrors, France, c. 1830, size 4.1" x 1.3" (10.3 x 3.2 cm). **22.** Dental screw for removal of tooth stubs, France, c. 1825–50, size 2.8" (7 cm).

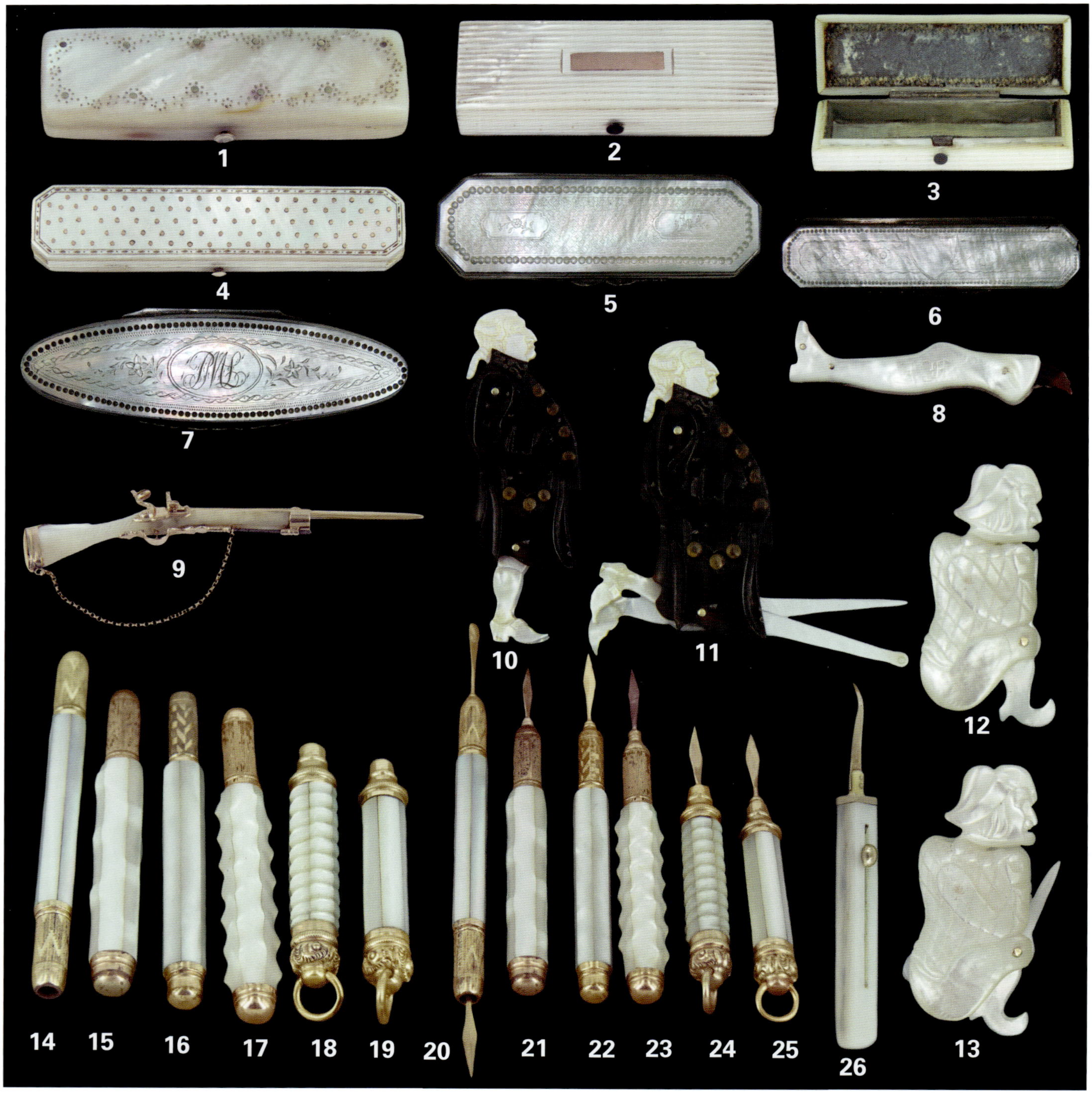

## PLATE 255 – TOOTHPICKS and TOOTHPICK BOXES

The toothpick boxes would likely have held a gold toothpick. **1.** Toothpick box, England, c. 1800, size 2.9″ x 0.6″ (7.4 x 1.6 cm). **2, 3.** Toothpick box with mirror, France, c. 1780, size 2.8″ x 0.8″ (7 x 2 cm). **4.** Toothpick box with mirror, France, c. 1780, size 3.1″ x 0.6″ (8 x 1.5 cm). **5.** Toothpick box, China, c. 1800, size 3.3″ x 1″ (8.5 x 2.5 cm). **6.** Toothpick box, China, c. 1800, size 2.8″ x 0.6″ ( 7 x 1.4 cm). **7.** Toothpick box with engraved owner's initials, China, c. 1800, size 3.1″ x 0.8″ ( 8 x 2 cm). **8.** Leg toothpick, England, c. 1880, size 2.8″ (7 cm). **9.** Toothpick in shape of a flintlock rifle, as was used during this era, the bayonet is the toothpick and slides in and out, there is a small compartment in the rifle butt, France c. 1800, size 2.2″ (5.7 cm). **10, 11.** Toothpick, King Louis XVI, the picks swivel out by moving the legs, the head also swivels (reminder of the King's execution by the guillotine), France, c. 1810, size 3.1″ (8 cm). **12–13.** Toothpick, Jester, the pick swivels by moving the legs, France, c. 1800, size 1.7″ (4.2 cm). **4–25.** Folding toothpicks, assorted designs, the toothpick extends by swiveling the metal winder, #20 is a toothpick on one end and ear scoop at the other, USA, c. 1871–1880, size 1.9″ to 2.6″ (4.7 to 6.7 cm). **26.** Sliding toothpick, 12k gold, England, c. 1890, size 2.2″ (5.5 cm).

CHAPTER 12

# Religion

Mother-of-pearl has been used to make religious items universally for many major religions. We have come across items representing Buddhism, Christianity, Hinduism, Islamism, Judaism, and Taoism. Each of these religions has its own section in this chapter, with symbolism, dogma, and beliefs explained, in so far as is relevant to the particular carved mother-of-pearl article.

## PLATE 256 – BUDDHISM 1

1–3. Guan Yin, commonly known as the goddess of mercy. In the Chinese art of pendant making, a blank insert in the shape of the form required is inserted into the living pearl oyster. This is done in the same way a nucleus is inserted in a cultured pearl. The shell covers this irritant with pearl. It is harvested in two years, cut out, and used in jewelry. China, c. 1990, size 5.1″ x 3.3″ (13 x 8.4 cm) to 6.3″ x 3.9″ (16 x 10 cm). 4. Buddha with a third eye, eye of wisdom or enlightenment. Made with a production process similar to that used in items #1–3. China, c. 1990, size 5.9″ x 3.9″ (15 x 10 cm). 5. Kuan Eim, riding a dragon, Chanthaburi, Thailand, 2006, size 4.1″ x 2.4″ (10.3 x 6.2 cm). 6. Four armed Buddha Avalokiteshvara, or Soo Li Yak Thep, an ancient compassionate Buddha, Chanthaburi, Thailand, 2006, size 5″ x 3.3″ (12.8 x 8.5 cm). 7. Sukhothai Buddha, as seen in a temple in Sukhothai, Thailand, 2006, size 4.9″ x 3.3″ (12.5 x 8.4 cm).

## PLATE 257 – BUDDHISM 2

This set has been carved by master carver Samai Sehua of Chanthaburi in Thailand in 2006. **1.** Portrayal of the Thai Buddha image for one of the days of the week, this one being the Saturday image. (Thai Buddha protected by seven Nagas, deities taking the form of snakes.) In this statue, Thai Buddha is protected by the Naga king, Paang Naga Prok. The Buddha sits on a coiled serpent, which rises to protect him from the raging storm. The Buddha sits in profound meditation, unaware of the tumult as he is lifted over the rising waves by the King of Nagas. Size 4.1″ x 2.8″ (10.5 x 7 cm). **2.** Phah Pathang Phon or Buddha Pathang Pong, size 4.7″ x 3.3″ (12 x 8.5 cm). **3.** Sukhothai Buddha in a temple. Sukhothai is a historical city and the first capital of Thailand, size 5.4″ x 3.4″ (13.8 x 8.6 cm). **4.** Thai four faces Buddha. This is the Thai representation of the Hindu god Brahma, who is worshipped by Thai Buddhists, size 6.7″ x 6.1″ (17 x 15.6 cm). **5.** Chatukam Ramathep, founder of a temple in southern Thailand. He is generally considered an incarnation of the Bodhisattva Avalokitesvara. Believed to provide protection and good fortune to the owner. Size 5.9″ x 4.7″ (15 x 12 cm). **6.** Kuan Eim, Thai goddess of mercy, riding a dragon. She is regarded by many as the protector of women and children and is also seen as a fertility goddess capable of granting children. She is the champion of the unfortunate, the sick, the disabled, and the poor, size 5.1″ x 3.7″ (13 x 9.5 cm).

## PLATE 258 – BUDDHISM 3

1, 2. Buddha, a magnificent statue, China, c. 1996, size 6.1" x 5.1" (15.5 x 13 cm). 3–5. Buddhist offering bowls, which can be filled with rice, salt, or other offerings to be placed on a home altar for the deities or at a Buddhist temple, Burma/Myanmar, 2003, size #3 & #5 9.8" diameter x 3.5" (25 cm x 9 cm), #4 11.8" diameter x 3.9" (30 cm x 10 cm). 6. Buddha and the Wheels of Life, the worldly wheel and the religious wheel existing alongside each other, China, c. 1920, size of frame 4.7" x 3.1" (12 x 8 cm). 7. Buddha, made for the tourist trade, China, c. 1960, size 2.2" x 1.6" (5.5 x 4 cm).

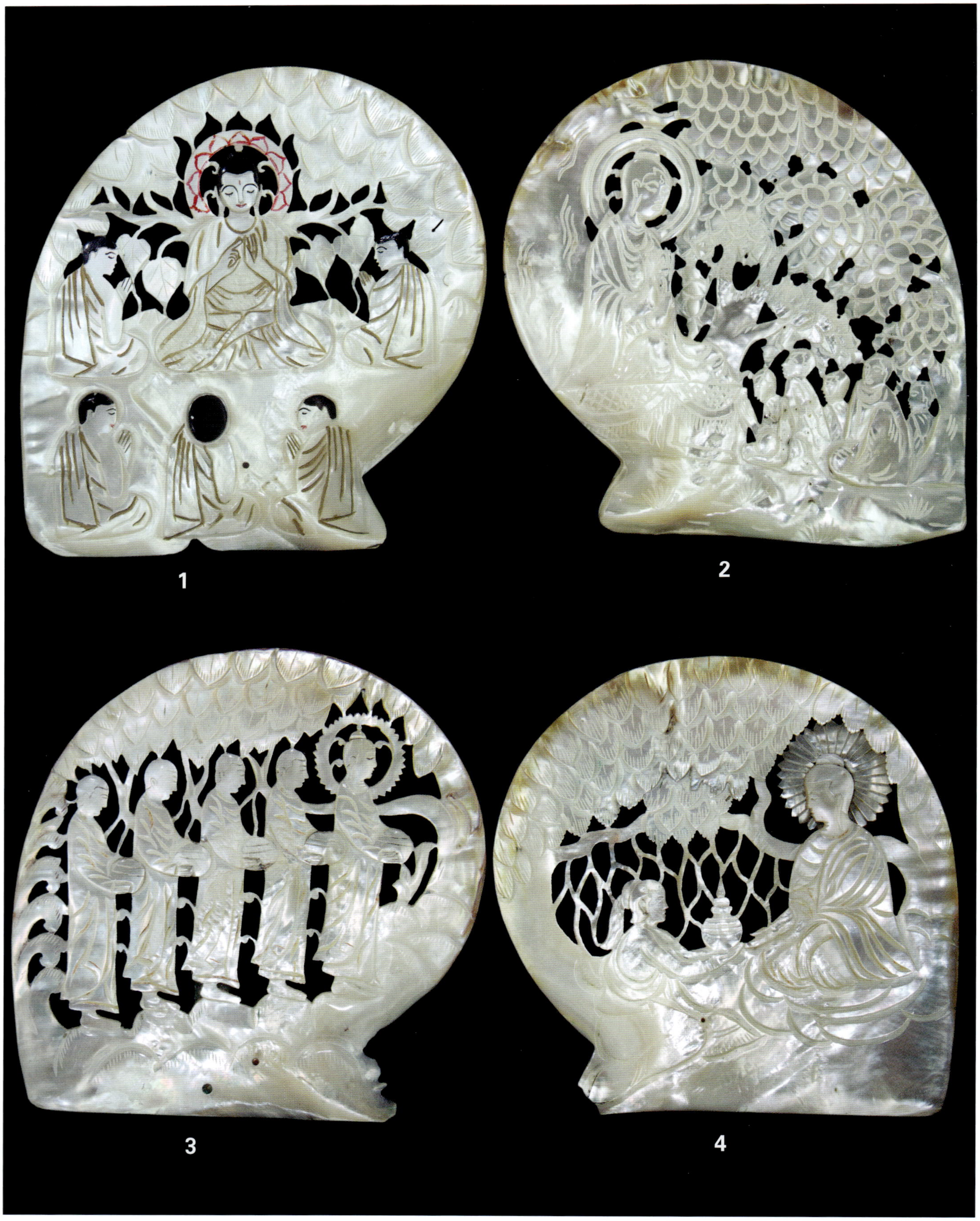


## PLATE 259 – BUDDHISM 4

These carvings are all from Burma/Myanmar. **1.** Buddha teaching five monks, c. 1950, size 8.9″ x 8.5″ (22.7 x 21.5 cm). **2.** Buddha teaching five monks under the trees, c. 1950, size 7.9″ x 7.5″ (20 x 19 cm). **3.** Buddha and four monks holding offering bowls, based on the statues in the Buddhist temple in Bhamo, Myanmar/Burma, c. 1950, size 7.7″ x 7.5″ (19.5 x 19 cm). **4.** A lay person offering food to Buddha, who is sitting under the Bodi trees where he attained enlightenment, Myanmar/Burma, c. 1950, size 6.9″ x 6.9″ (17.5 x 17.5 cm).

# CHRISTIANITY

Christianity has a long history of the use of mother-of-pearl in religious souvenirs and decorative items, especially from Europe and Palestine. The whiteness of the pearl shell represented purity and this was particularly suitable for these holy souvenirs. The history of early mother-of-pearl carving in the Holy Land is discussed in an earlier chapter.

There is no doubt that famous paintings of the past were the inspiration for many of the pearl carvings. In Palestine, it is believed that the churches must have had books of the famous paintings and they would have guided the carvers. The use of symbolism in some carvings would seem far too advanced for the normal carvers, indicating the guiding hand of the church.

The majority of the full shell carvings emanated from the Holy Land. A few were carved in Europe, but more examples are needed to establish the origin. In general, the European pearl carvings are far more intricate and detailed compared to the Palestinian carvings, but there are always exceptions, as Palestine was home to a number of master carvers. Most carvings were produced in Jerusalem, and the name on the shell (Bethlehem or Jerusalem) refers to where the scene took place and not where the shell was carved.

We acknowledge the significant contribution made by Dino Basilissi, of Florence, Italy, who has mentored us with an understanding of the subjects and the symbolism used on these religious carved shells. His knowledge is extensive, as is his collection. This is a vast field of research that cannot be covered in depth in the limited space available.

**PLATE 260 – CHRISTIANITY – CARVED PLATE**

This exceptional carving in black lip pearl oyster was made in France. Jesus, the Good Shepherd, with his flock of sheep (symbol for Christians), signed by the carver Taillefort, France, c. 1850, size 9.8″ x 8.7″ (25 x 22 cm).

## PLATE 261 – CHRISTIANITY – ICONS 1

1. St. Joseph with Infant Jesus, with symbolism of the triangle (symbolizes the Trinity, with God's eye that never closes), *IHS* (*Iesus Honinum Salvator* translated Jesus Savior of Men) surmounted by a cross, Cross of Jerusalem (four crosses in a large cross), pole, and two fish (first Christian symbol), Palestine, c. 1820–40, size 5.3" x 4.3" (13.5 x 10.8 cm). 2. Nativity scene, Mary and Joseph present Jesus to the visitors, the Magi bring gifts, an angel holds a palm branch to remember the fate of Jesus, a camel in the background from one of the Magi, Germany, c. 1750, size 3.8" (9.7 cm). 3. Reliquary with the Holy family, an ox, a donkey, the star of Bethlehem, angels, inscribed *Nativitas D.N.J.C.* (*Domini Nostri Jesu Christ*), *Ex crjpta bmv lactis in C* (Crypt of the Blessed Virgins Mary's milk in C—Christ?) and *Glor.in.Exc* (*Gloria in Excelsis Deo*; Latin for Glory to God in the Highest), signed and dated Solaiman Roc, Bethlehem, Palestine, 1884, size 9.6" x 7.3" (24.5 x 18.5 cm). 4. Nativity *Nativitas DNJC* (*Domini Nostri Jesu Christi*), likely the work of Solaiman Roc, Palestine, c. 1880–95, size 4.3" x 4.9" (11 x 12.5 cm).

## PLATE 262 – CHRISTIANITY – ICONS 2

On three of these icons, God the Father looks down on the scene. 1. Inscribed *Arcangelo Raffello*, Archangel Raphael and Tobias, based on the painting by Filippino Lippi c. 1475–1480, Palestine, c. 1800–50, size 5.7" x 6.7" (14.5 x 17 cm). 2. Nativity scene, Palestine, c. 1850–70, size 4.7" x 4" (12 x 10.2 cm). 3. The Last Supper inscribed *La Cena*, Palestine, c. 1830–60, size 6.9" x 5.9" (17.5 x 15 cm). 4. Saint Constantine standing next to the cross, Palestine, c. 1850–70, size 4.3" x 4.9" (11 x 12.5 cm).

## PLATE 263 – CHRISTIANITY – ICONS 3

1. St. Christina of Bolsena, who was tortured because of her faith. Two soldiers aim arrows, the instrument of her martyrdom, while two soldiers look on. Palestine, c. 1800, size 7.2" x 5.7" (18.4 x 14.5 cm). 2. St. James, generally identified with James the Less and James the Just, apostle to Jesus Christ, holding the fuller's club, which was the instrument of his martyrdom. Inscribed *S.Iacobus* (Latin for St. James) Palestine, c. 1850, size 4.7" x 6.5" (12 x 16.5 cm). 3. *Rosa Mystica*: Mary rises out of the center rose; seven stars around Her head represent the components of the material world. There are two relic chambers inscribed *D N S SEPUL* (*Domini Nostri Sepulchrum Jesu Christi*) and *S M CALVAR* (relic from Mount Calvary) Palestine, c. 1850, size 8.9" x 6.1" (22.5 x 15.6 cm). 4. Icon of Jesus, inscribed Jerusalem, Palestine, c. 1850–70, size 7.9" x 5.6" (20 x 14.3 cm).

## PLATE 264 – CHRISTIANITY – ICONS 3

1. Greek Orthodox icon, Mary with the Infant Jesus, with symbols *XCXC* (Mary), *MP* (Mother of God), three stars on the veil (symbolizing pure before, during, and after), a halo ("I am all"), and a globe (power of Christ to the world); Palestine, c. 1820–40, size 6.3" x 7.5" (16 x 19 cm). 2. Madonna Di Montenero, based of the original painting by Jacopo de Michele in 1354, now in a sanctuary near Livorno, Italy; inscribed *Vera Immagine di Maria SS di Montenero*, Palestine, c. 1820–40, size 9.8" x 7.1" (25 x 18 cm). 3. Orthodox Icon, St. Simeon and St. Eleuterio Vescovo E. Martire, Palestine, c. 1800–40, size 6.9" x 5.9" (17.5 x 15 cm). 4. Icon, Ecstasy of St. Francis, with symbolism of eye (ever watching eye of God), *IHS* (*Iesus Honinum Salvator* translated Jesus Savior of Men) , XX (Symbol of Mary), cross of Jerusalem (four crosses in a large cross), Palestine, c. 1840–70, size 7.6" x 6" (19.4 x 15.5 cm).

## PLATE 265 – CHRISTANITY – ICON 4 & CARTAGLORIA

1

1. Inscribed *S.Iosephus Labore Occupatus est cui Iesus* (translated, "St. Joseph employed in work together with Jesus"), St. Joseph and Jesus cut a wood table with a two-person saw while Mary, mother of Jesus, sits on the steps sewing. Archangel Raphael watches over the family. Palestine, c. 1800, size 7.9" x 7.9" (20 x 20 cm).

2

2. Reproduction of a Palestinian *cartagloria* from c. 1840; *cartaglorias* usually consisted of three frames placed on the altar of a church, which contained part of the Mass recited by the priest. Made in 2009 by E. Yidi, size 12.8" x 10.6" (32.5 x 27 cm).

## PLATE 266 – CHRISTIANITY – MODELS

1. Christ's Church, Jerusalem, consecrated 21st January 1849, Jerusalem, Palestine, c. 1870–90, size 4.7" x 4.3" (12 x 11 cm). 2, 3. A model of the Church of the Holy Sepulchre in Jerusalem, a site venerated by many Christians as Golgotha where Jesus was crucified, Palestine, c. 1840–60, size 10.2" x 9.8" (26 x 25 cm). 4, 5. Tabernacle, contains a picture of Mary and Infant Jesus, which is kept in the home to give blessing on the family, Palestine, c. 1930, size 5.8" x 3.4" (14.8 x 8.6 cm). 6. Tabernacle with a painting of Mary, mother of Jesus, France, c. 1880, size 3.3" x 2.1" (8.5 x 5.4 cm).

## PLATE 267 – CHRISTIAN PICTURES

1. *The Last Supper*, with a medallion of the nativity scene on the top, Jerusalem, Palestine, c. 1930–50, size 11.4″ x 13.2″ (29 x 33.5 cm). 2. Nativity scene inscribed *Hic de Virgine Maria Iesus Christus Natus est* (translated Here is Jesus Christ born to the Virgin Mary), Palestine, c. 1960, size 7.5″ x 7.5″ (19 x 19 cm). 3. Nativity in standing frame, once the top of a box frame creation, Palestine, c. 1950–60, size 7.5″ x 6.7″ (19 x 17 cm). 4. Ascension of Jesus Christ, Jerusalem, c. 1960–80, size 5.9″ x 8.5″ (15 x 21.5 cm). 5. Nativity, Palestine, c. 1980, size 6.1″ x 8.7″ (15.5 x 22 cm), shows the movement away from quality to bulk tourist production. 6. T*he Last Supper*, Palestine, c. 1940, size 8.3″ x 9.3″ (21 x 23.5 cm), brought to Australia by a returning soldier from WWII.

## PLATE 268 – CHRISTIANITY HOLY WATER FONTS

A holy water font is a vessel to hold holy water. There are three types: the one seen in churches, portable fonts, and private or household fonts. The fonts illustrated here were used at home by Catholics. They were usually hung inside the home at the entrance, or in the bedroom at the head of the bed. They contained holy water that had been blessed by the priest, and were used to make the sign of the cross in the morning and evening before going to bed. In 1905, with the separation of the church and state in France, and the reconciliation of the various Christian religions, blessing of holy water by the priests was suspended and the use of these home holy fonts was discontinued. This was a regional development, and it was different in every country, but France was the region where the pearl fonts were most used. Some fonts were converted into wall hangings for the home by removal of the holder for holy water. Mother-of-pearl examples are very rare and found mainly in France, Spain and their colonies. Many have a carving of God our Father looking down from the top of the font. 1. Central carving of St. John baptizing Jesus, Palestine, c. 1860–90, size 9.8″ (25 cm). 2. Central carving of St. John baptizing Jesus, Palestine, 1890, size 8.3″ (21 cm). This font has an old label attached to the rear with sealing wax. Label's message is blurred with age, but date of 10 August 1890 is still visible. 3. Jesus at the column, with stations of the cross, Palestine, c. 1860–90, size 7.3″ (18.5 cm). 4. Basilique du Sacre Coeur de Jesus (Basilica of the Sacred Heart of Jesus of Paris), Paris, France, c. 1890–1910, size 5.9″ (15 cm). 5. Sanctuary of Our Lady of Lourdes, Lourdes, France, c. 1890–1910, size 6.1″ (15.5 cm). 6. Jesus appears to St. Margaret Mary Alacoque, a nun in the Visitandine Monastery in the mid-1670s, France, c. 1890–1910, size 5.3″ (13.5 cm). 7. Jesus on the crucifix, France, c. 1870, size 4.1″ (10.5 cm).

## PLATE 269 – CHRISTIANITY HOLY WATER FONTS

1. Central carving of Jesus carrying the cross, Palestine, c. 1860–90, size 10″ (25.5 cm) adapted as a wall hanging with silver decoration where the holy water container was positioned. 2. Central carving of St. John baptizing Jesus, Palestine, c. 1860–90, size 9.8″ (25 cm), adapted as wall hanging with silver decoration where the holy water container was once positioned.

## PLATE 270 – CHRISTIANITY – COMMUNION GIFT SET and BAPTISM SCOOP

1. An angel appears to Mary, mother of Jesus, a communion gift set consisting of a missal, notebook and coin purse. The missal is entitled *Oficio Divino para Todos Los Dias de Fiesta Y De Precepto*, published by Laplace Sanchez Y Ca, Paris, France, 1869, size box 10.6″ x 6.5″ (27 x 16.5 cm). 2. Baptism scoop used at font for holy water, maker Susanna Baker and Edward Wiban, London, England, 1895, size 2.4″ (6 cm).

## PLATE 271 – CHRISTIANITY – ICONS and BIBLES

**1.** Carving, Joseph of Arimathea and Nicodermis remove the nails from Jesus, St. John and another disciple receiving the body, watched by Virgin Mary and Mary, wife of Cleopas, France, c. 1820, size 4.7" x 3" (12 x 7.7 cm). **2.** St. Francis of Assisi, founder of the order of Friars Minor, more commonly known as the Franciscans, Bethlehem, Palestine, c. 1875, size 4.7" x 3.9" (12 x 10 cm). **3–4.** The Holy Bible, Collins, London, England, 1957, inscribed *Jerusalem*, size 7.5" x 4.9" (19 x 12.5 cm). **5.** The Red Letter New Testament, Collins, London, England, 1935, size 4.5" x 3.3" (11.5 x 8.5 cm), stamped on the title page *Made in Palestine*.

## PLATE 272 – CHRISTIANITY – BIBLES AND PRAYER BOOKS 1

Although most of these Bibles were printed in England, the pearl work on the covers was done in Palestine and sold to visiting pilgrims to the Holy Land. The covers often have the star of Bethlehem on the one side and the cross of Jerusalem on the other side. **1, 2.** The Holy Bible, Collins, London, England, 1953, size 7.1″x 5.1″ (18 x 13 cm). **3.** The Red Letter New Testament, Collins, London, England, 1941, size 6.3″ x 4.3″ (16 x 11 cm). **4, 5.** The Red Letter New Testament, Wm. Collins Son & Co., London, England for The American Colony Stores, Jerusalem, Palestine, 1945, size 6.3″ x 3.9″ (16 x 10 cm). **6.** The Red Letter New Testament, Collins, London, England, 1950, carved on front cover *Jerusalem*, size 3.5″ x 4.5″ (9 x 11.5 cm).

## PLATE 273 – CHRISTIANITY – BIBLES AND PRAYER BOOKS

1, 2. The Book of Common Prayer, Oxford University Press, London, England, 1930, size 4.7″ x 3.1″ (12 x 8 cm). 3. The Imitation of Christ, Franciscan Press, Jerusalem, Palestine, 1941, size 2.2″ x 3.5″ (5.5 x 9 cm). 4, 5. The Red Letter New Testament, Collins, London, England, 1945, size 6.3″ x 4.1″ (16 x 10.5 cm). 6. Bible covers, allows the inside book to be changed from a Bible to a prayer book, England, c. 1870, size 4″ x 3 ¼″ (10 x 8 cm). 7. Diamond pattern, Little Path to Heaven, printed by The C. Wildermann Co., New York, USA, c. 1895, inscribed *bound in Belgium,* size 3.7″ x 2.8″ (9.5 x 7 cm). 8. Gold decoration on a pearl cover, Meu Thesourinho, published by Benziger Einsiedeln & Co., Switzerland, 1898, size 4.7″ x 3″ (12 x 7.5 cm). 9. Silver decoration on plain pearl cover, Tesoro De La Juventud Mejicana, published by F. Deslandes, Paris, France, c. 1901, size 4.7″ x 2.8″ (12 x 7 cm). 10. Pearl and abalone decorative pattern, *Mein Gott und mein Alles*, published by Berlag von Fr Stein, Gaarlouis, Germany, 1871, size 4.3″ x 3″ (11 x 7.5 cm). 11. Pearl cover with enamel oval of Mary, mother of Jesus, Nuevo Ramillete De Oro, published De La Autoridad Eclesiastica, Cuba, c. 1880, size 5″x 3″ (12.5 x 8 cm).

## PLATE 274 – CHRISTIANITY – MISSALS

1. Mary, mother of Jesus, Joya del Cristiano, publisher Morizot, Paris, France, c. 1870, size 3.7″ x 2.6″ (9.5 x 6.5 cm). 2. Mary, mother of Jesus, with Infant Jesus and St. Anna, based on the painting by Leonardo da Vinci, Imitation de Jesus Christ, published by Bellin Le Prieur, Paris, France, c. 1850, size 5.5″ x 3.7″ (14 x 9.5 cm). 3. Jesus praying in the Garden of Gethsemane, the cross symbolizing His destiny, Doble Ordinario De La Santa Misa, publisher Laplace, Sanchez Y Ca, Paris, France, c. 1870, size 4.1″ x 2.8″ (10.5 x 7 cm). 4. The marriage of the Virgin, based on the painting by Raphael, with Mary holding her hand to Joseph to slip on the ring, watched by the priest, Paroissien Romain, published by Antoine Maitre, Dijon, France, 1886, size 4.1″ x 2.8″ (10.5 x 7 cm). 5. Joseph, Mary, and baby Jesus in a manger with an ox and donkey watching, Oficio Divino Para Todos Los De Dias Fiesta Y De Precepto, publisher Laplace, Sanchez Y Ca, Paris, France,1879, size 4.7″ x 3.5″ (12 x 9 cm). 6. Mary, mother of Jesus, standing on a crescent moon, Oficio Divino para Todos Los Domingos Y Dias de Fiesta, published Libreria De Delarue, Paris, France, 1869, size 4.7″ x 3.5″ (12 x 9 cm).

## PLATE 275 – CHRISTIANITY – MISSALS

1. A faithful follower kneeling down in front of Jesus, who blesses with two fingers, La Mujer Catolica, published Llorens Hermanos, Barcelona, Spain, 1879, size 4.7" x 3.5" (12 x 9 cm). 2. St. John the Baptist, with cross and dressed in animal skins, together with Jesus, the Good Shepherd of souls, who has a flock of sheep (symbolizing Christians), marked with the cross and decorated with a ribbon, Doble Ordinario de La Santa Misa, publisher Hennelle, Bruxelles, Belgium, c. 1870, size 4.1" x 2.8" (10.5 x 7 cm). 3. The Holy Family escapes to Egypt, Diamante Del Paraiso, published Se Hallara, Madrid, Spain, 1856, size 4.3" x 2.8" (11 x 7 cm). 4. Jesus, praying in the garden of Gethsemane, Paroissien Romain, publisher Dalpayrat Et Depelley, Limoges, France, 1895, size 4.3" x 2.8" (11 x 7 cm). 5. Jesus wearing a crown of thorns, Doble Ordinario De La Santa Misa, publisher Libreria De A Mezin, Paris, France, c. 1880, size 3.9" x 2.8" (10 x 7 cm). 6. Jesus as the Good Shepherd, holding a lamp and a shepherd's staff, Paroissien Romain, published by Marc Barbou & Cie, Limoges, France, 1885, size 4.1" x 3.1" (10.5 x 7.8 cm).

## PLATE 276 – CHRISTIANITY – MISSALS

1. The Holy Family with John the Baptist kneeling before the Infant Jesus, Horas Divinas, published by Laplace, Sanchez Y Cia, Paris, France, 1872, size 4.7" x 3.5" (12 x 9 cm). 2. Mary, mother of Jesus, crowned Queen of the angels and saints, Missel De Jeanne d'Arc, Paroissien Romain, publisher Dalpayrat & Depelley, Limoges, France, 1898, size 4.7" x 3.1" (12 x 8 cm). 3. Jesus in the Garden of Gethsemane, deep in prayer, battles to accept the will of the Father whilst an angel comforts and strengthens Jesus who finally accepts His destiny, symbolized by the chalice of martyrdom. Oraciones Y Meditaciones, published by Laplace, Sanchez Y Cia, Paris, France, 1871, size 4.7" x 3" (12 x 7.5 cm). 4. Mary, mother of Jesus, standing on a snake in the universal symbol of good trumphing over evil, Oficio Divino Para Todos Los Dais de Fiesta Y De Precepto, publisher Laplace, Sanchez Et Cia, Paris, France, 1869, size 4.7" x 3.5" (12 x 9 cm). 5. Carving of an archangel (likely archangel Michael) holding a globe crucifix, Oficio Divino Para Todos Los Dias De Fiesta Y De Precepto, published by Laplace,Sanchez Et Cia, Paris, France, 1869, size 4.7" x 3.1" (12 x 8 cm). 6. Sacred Heart of Mary, with Jesus and John the Baptist, La Via Del Paradiso, published by Laplace, Sanchez Et Ca, Paris, France, c. 1880, size 4.7" x 3.5" (12 x 9 cm).

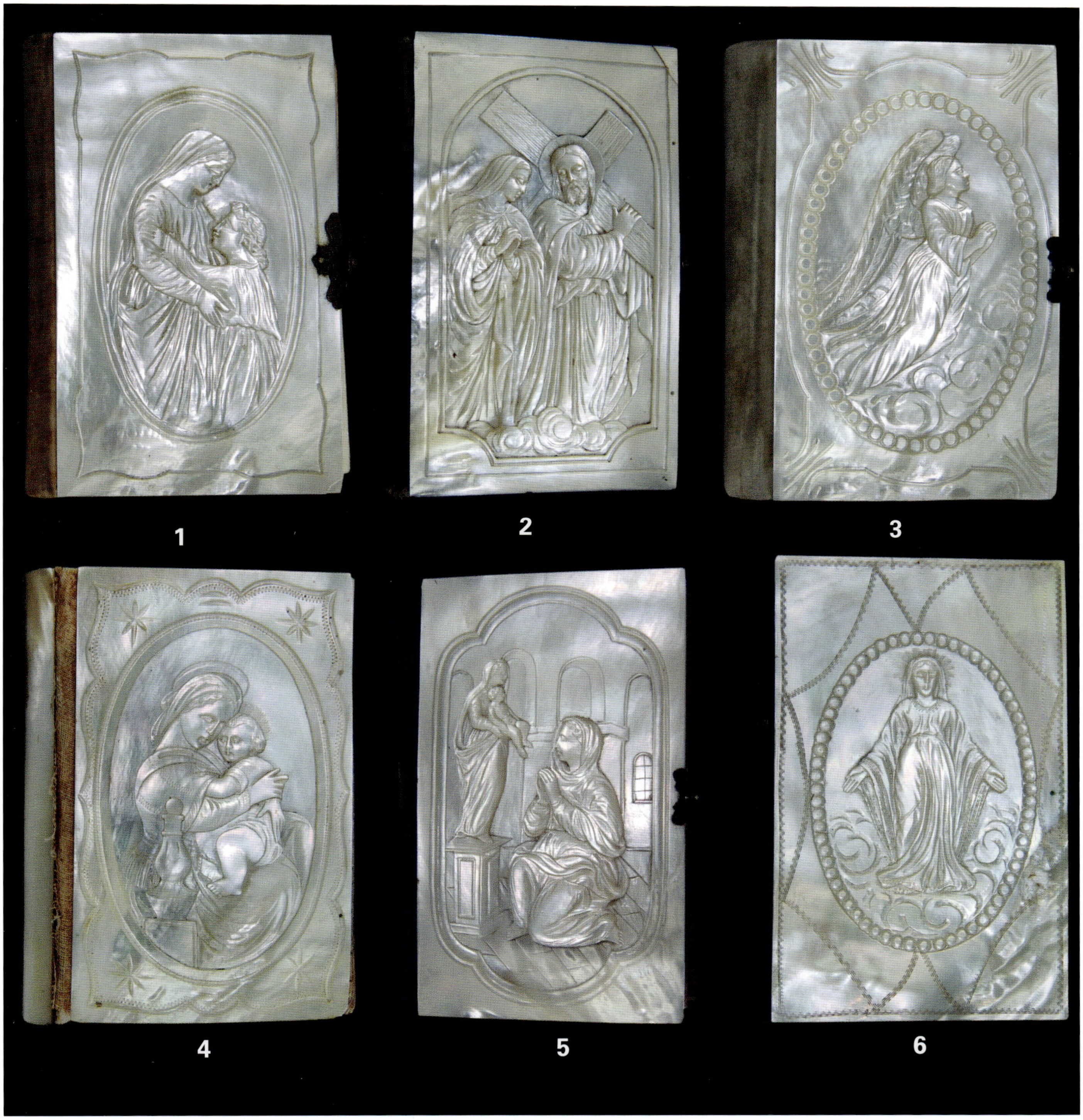


## PLATE 277 – CHRISTIANITY – MISSALS

1. Mary, mother of Jesus, with young Jesus, Paroissien Romain, Les Offices Des Dimanches, publisher G. Jeener, Paris, France, 1898, size 4.2" x 2.8" (10.7 x 7 cm). 2. Jesus, carrying the cross, meets his mother, Mary, the fourth station of the cross, Imitation of Jesus Christ, published Libraire Catholique De Perisse Freres, Paris, France, 1845, size 5.5" x 3.3" (14 x 8.5 cm). 3. An angel, Paroissien Romain, publisher Laplace, Sanchez Et Cie, Paris, France, c. 1869, size 4.1" x 3" (10.5 x 7.5 cm). 4. Mary, mother of Jesus, with young Jesus, based on the painting *Madonna of the Chair* by Raphael in 1513–4, Nuevas Horas Sagradas, published Libreria De Garnier Hermanos, Paris, France, 1862, size 4.8" x 3.3" (12.2 x 8.5 cm). 5. Young woman kneeling in prayer before the statue of Mary holding Infant Jesus, possibly a wedding gift signifying hopes for a family for the newlyweds, Oficio Divino Para Todos Los Dias Fiesta Y De Precepto, published by F De P. Mellado Y Co, Paris, France, 1869, size 4.7" x 3.1" (12 x 8 cm). 6. Mary, mother of Jesus, L'Imitation de Jesus Christ, published by Alfred Mame Et Fils, Tours, France, 1869, size 4.1" x 2.6" (10.4 x 6.5 cm).

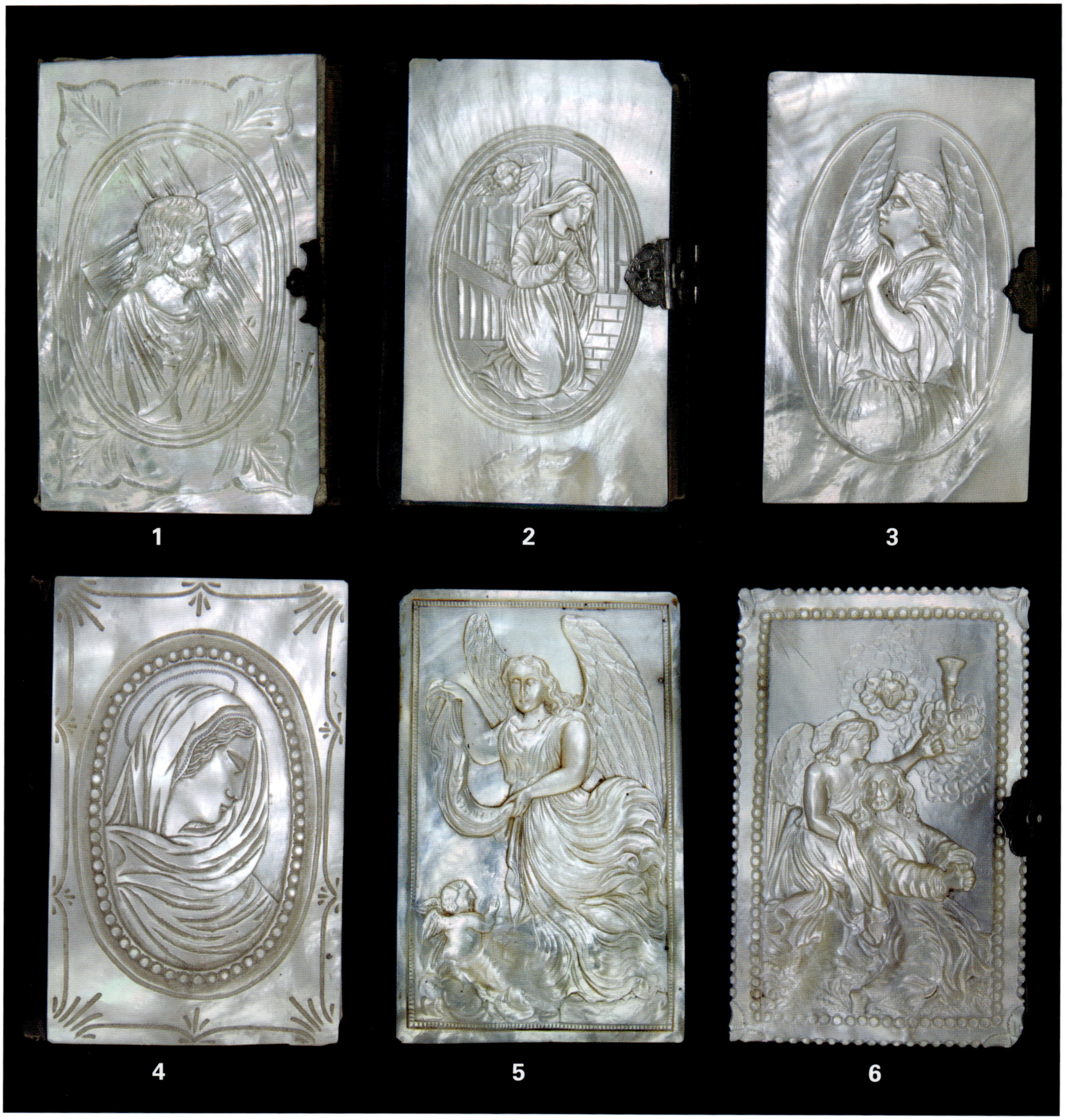


## PLATE 278 – CHRISTIANITY – MISSALS

Interestingly, covers for missals printed in Spain and Belgium where all carved in France. 1. Jesus carrying the cross, Oraciones Santo Sacrificio De La Misa, published Sociedad de S.Juan Evangelista Tornai, Belgium, 1890, size 4.3" x 3.1" (11 x 8 cm). 2. Carving of Mary, mother of Jesus, praying, watched by an angel, La Perla Del Cristiano Conteniendo El Oficio Divino, printed by Dejardin Editore, Paris, France, 1878, size 4.3" x 2.8" (11 X 7 cm). 3. An angel praying, Joya Del Cristiano, publisher Laplace, Sanchez Y Ca, Paris, France, 1845, size 3.7" x 2.6" (9.5 x 6.5 cm). 4. Mary, mother of Jesus, Oraciones Y Meditaciones, published by Laplace, Sanchez Y Cia, Paris, France, 1871, size 4.7" x 3" (12 x 7.5 cm). 5. An angel holding a banner and welcoming a baby that passed away, likely a custom-made gift to a grieving mother, La Mujer Catholica, published Liberia Espanola, Barcelona, Spain, 1853, size 4.8" x 3.1" (12.3 x 8 cm). 6. Jesus in prayer in the Garden of Gethsemane battles to accept the will of the Father, whilst an angel comforts and strengthens Him and reminds Him of His destiny as symbolized by the chalice of martyrdom. Oficio Divino printed by Libreria de Morizot, Paris, France, 1860, size 4.7" x 3.1" (12 x 8 cm).

## PLATE 279 – CHRISTIANITY – MISSALS

Often when missal books disintegrated from use, the carved covers were kept and reused on other missals. **1.** Mary, mother of Jesus, carving originally on a missal Key of Heaven published by Isaacs & Co, New Orleans, USA, c. 1925, printed in Czechoslovakia, but now attached to Paroissien Roman, published by Auzemery Freres Et Lagueny, Limoges, 1878, size 3.9" x 2.8" (10 x 7 cm). **2.** Mary, mother of Jesus, Key of Heaven, published Marks Isaacs & Co, New Orleans, USA, 1925, printed in Czechoslovakia, size 3.8" x 2.8" (9.7 x 7 cm). **3.** Celebrating communion, this was intended for a child of 10–12 years at first communion, and, out of respect, Christ is shown as a child instead of a bearded man, the carving originally on Key of Heaven, published Isaacs & Co., New Orleans, USA, c. 1925, printed in Czechoslovakia, but now attached to Paroissien Roman, published by A Maitre, Dijon, 1879, size 3.9" x 2.8" (10 x 7 cm). **4.** Jesus Christ, the carving originally on Key of Heaven, published Isaacs & Co., New Orleans, USA, c. 1925, printed in Czechoslovakia, but now attached to *Visites au Saint Sacrement*, Paris, published by F Curot, Paris, France, c 1900, size 3.9" x 2.8" (10 x 7 cm). **5.** Jesus, the Good Shepherd, with his sheep (symbolizing Christians) marked *JHS* (Christogram derived from the Greek name of Jesus), Key to Heaven, printed by Catholic Publications Press, printed in Czechoslovakia, 1925, in box size 3.7" x 2.8" (9.5 x 7 cm). **6.** Joseph, Mary, and Infant Jesus, printed by Sociedad de San Juan Evangelista, Tornai, Belgium, 1888, size 4.7" x 3.1" (12 x 8 cm).

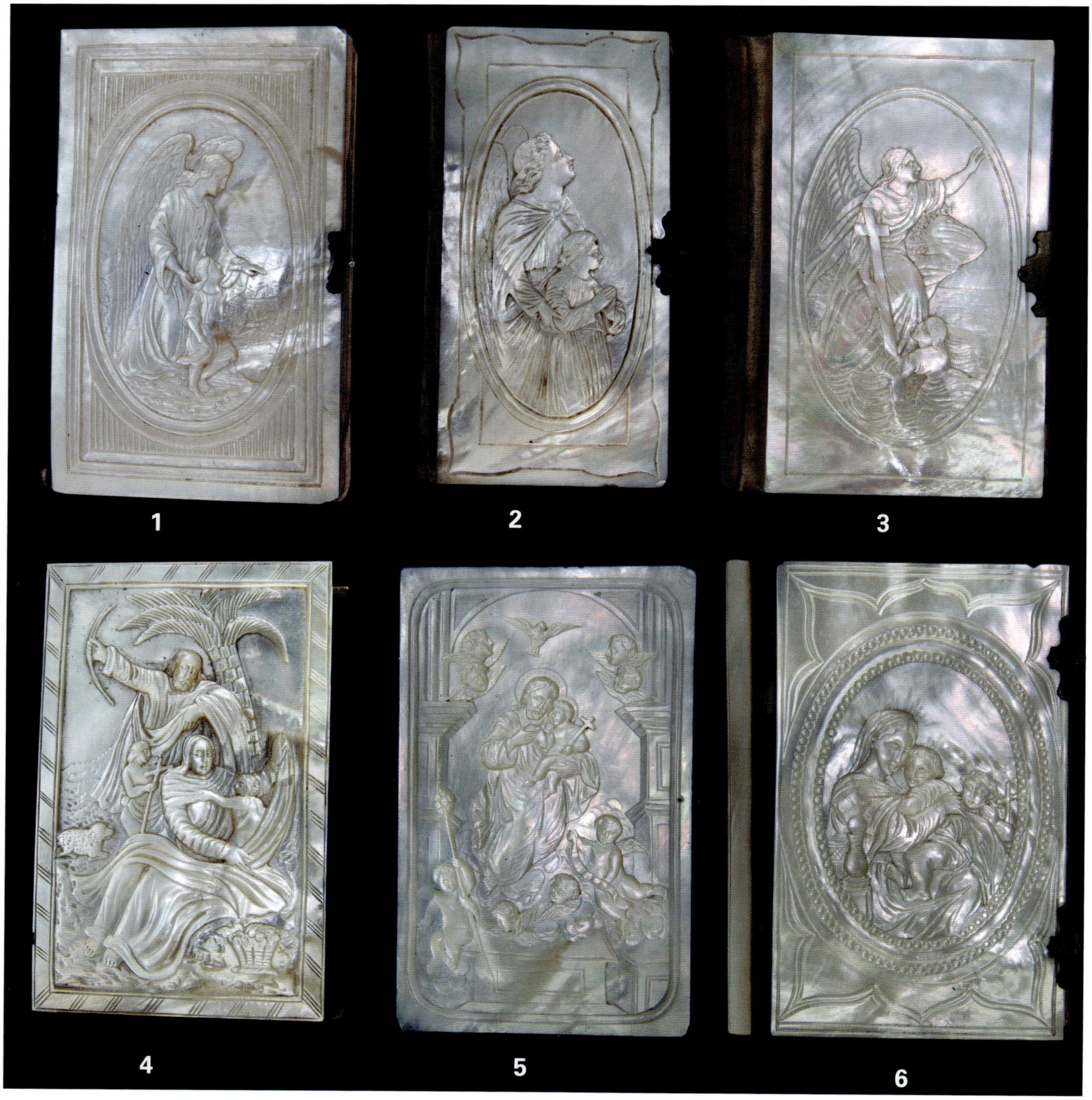


## PLATE – CHRISTIANITY – MISSALS

1. Angel with child, Oficio Divino, publisher Libereria De Morizet,Paris, France, 1843, size 4.7″ x 3.1″ (12 x 8 cm). 2. Angel with child, Pequeno Oficio Divino, publisher F Deslandes, Paris, France, c. 1875, size 4.7″ x 2.5″ (12 x 6.3 cm). 3. An angel holding a long cross to save a sinner drowning in a sinful humanity (symbolized by the sea) and shows the sinner the direction of heaven, Geiftliches Sentkornlein, publisher Benjiger Brothers, New York, 1855, size 4.3″ x 3″ (10.8 x 7.5 cm). 4. Joseph, with palm frond in hand to remember the passion of Christ, together with Mary, young Jesus, and John the Baptist, the sheep symbolizing the flock of mankind, Horas Divinas Coleccion De Ejercicios, publisher Libreria De Vincens, Tolosa, Spain, 1843, size 4.7″ x 4.3″ (12 x 8.5 cm). 5. Joseph with Jesus, holding a cross to show His destiny, surrounded with putti and angels, with one angel holding the lily, also called the club of St. Joseph. Geest Des Gebeds, published by Brepols en Turnhout, Belgium, 1870, size 4.7″ x 3.1″ (12 x 8 cm). 6. Mary, with a young Jesus and John the Baptist, based on the painting *Madonna of the Chair* by Raphael in 1513–4, Eucologio Romano, publisher Llorens Hermanos, Barcelona, Spain, 1866, size 4.7″ x 3.5″ (12 x 9 cm).

## PLATE 281 – CHRISTIANITY – STANDING CRUCIFIX 1

These crucifix are all from Jerusalem, Palestine. Most crucifixes have carvings of the four evangelists at the ends of the arms of the cross, Our Lady of Sorrows present at the base and a banner INRI (*Iesus Nazarenus Rex Iudaeorum*: Latin for Jesus the Nazarene, King of the Jews). The stations of the cross are usually at the rear of the crucifix. **1.** Crucifix with a carving of Jesus at the column, c. 1840–60, size 17.1″ (43.5 cm). **2.** Crucifix with a carving of Mary, mother of Jesus, in the base, c. 1840–60, size 15″ (38 cm). **3.** Crucifix with a carving in the base of Mary, with St. Francis and St. Anthony, c. 1840–60, size 15″ (38 cm). **4.** Crucifix, with nativity scene in the base and stations of the cross, c. 1870–90, size 11.4″ (29 cm). **5.** Pedestal from a crucifix (all that remains) with carvings of St. Simon the zealot, sacred heart of Jesus and St. Peter the apostle, with relics of the crib, c. 1850–80, size 3″ x 3.7″ (7.7 x 9.5 cm). **6.** Crucifix, minimal carving, c. 1960–80, size 5.2″ (13.2 cm). **7.** Crucifix with medallion of Jesus, c. 1920–50, size 14.6″ (37 cm). **8.** Crucifix, with nativity scene in the base, c. 1880–90, size 11″ (28 cm). **9.** Crucifix with nativity scene and in the middle, the skull of Adam, c. 1870–90, size 11.8″ (30 cm).

## PLATE 282 – CHRISTIANITY – CRUCIFIX 2

These crucifixes are all from Jerusalem, Palestine. 1, 2. Orthodox crucifix with pearl decoration on both sides, c. 1870–90, size 11.4" (29 cm). Side 1: God on the top, Jesus in the middle, on the left and right side Mary of Cleophas and Mary Magdalene holding handkerchiefs, the base St. Catherine of Alexandria, a Christian saint and martyr. Side 2: Four corners are the apostles John, Luke, Mark, and Matthew, in the center St. John baptizing Jesus, and on the base St. Basil the Great. 3. Crucifix, smaller than above and one-sided only, decorated with Mary, mother of Jesus on the base, c. 1890–1900, size 8.7" (22 cm). 4. Crucifix, smallest, decorated with Mary, mother of Jesus on the base, c. 1900–20, size 6.5" (16.5 cm). 5. Bishop's crucifix, 1923, size 11.6" (29.5 cm), this was a gift to a US bishop by the Commissariat of the Holy Land, Franciscan Monastery, and has papers for indulgences, including "enriched with indulgence of a happy death." 6. Crucifix with fine fret work, c. 1880–1900, size 9.8" (25 cm). 7. Crucifix with fine carved decoration, c. 1880–1900, size 14.2" (36 cm).

## PLATE 283 – CHRISTIANITY – CRUCIFIX 3

Of this selection of crucifixes, all except #3 are from Jerusalem, Palestine. 1. Crucifix with pierced decoration, c. 1880–1900, size 14.7″ (36 cm). This cross is enriched with the indulgence of a happy death and the stations. 2. Crucifix, pearl and abalone decoration, c. 1940–60, size 10″ (25.5 cm). 3. Wood cross with pearl inlay, Macau, China, c. 1880–1900, size 16.7″ (42.3 cm), likely made with imported labor from Vietnam and exported mainly to France. 4. Crucifix, c. 1940–60, size 5.7″ (14.5 cm). 5. Crucifix, c. 1880–95, size 6.7″ (17 cm). 6. Crucifix, c. 1924–60, size 5.7″ (14.5 cm). 7. Crucifix, c. 1920–40, size 6.7″ (17 cm). 8. Crucifix, c. 1950–60, size 8.8″ (22.3 cm). 9. Crucifix, c. 1895–1900, size 7.4″ (18.7 cm). 10. Crucifix, c. 1940–50, size 9.6″ (24.5 cm). 11. Crucifix, c. 1920–40, size 5.7″ (14.5 cm). 12. Crucifix, c. 1890–1900, size 5.3″ (13.5 cm).

## PLATE 284 – CHRISTIANITY – SMALL CRUCIFIX 4

1. France, c. 1890–1910, size 3″ (7.5 cm). 2. France, c. 1890–1910, size 3″ (7.5 cm). 3. France, c. 1890–1910, size 3.7″ (9.3 cm). 4. France, c. 1890–1910, size 2″ (5 cm). 5. France, c. 1890–1910, size 1.8″ (4.6 cm). 6. France, c. 1890–1910, size 2.6″ (6.5 cm). 7, 8. Cross with two sides Jesus and Mary, France, c. 1870–90, size 3.1″ (8 cm). 9. France, c. 1890–1910, size 2.1″ (5.4 cm). 10. France, c. 1780–1800, size 2.6″ (6.5 cm). 11. France, c. 1860–80, size 2.8″ (7 cm). 12 Jerusalem, Palestine, c. 1900–20, size 2.2″ (5.5 cm). 13. Jerusalem, Palestine, c. 1890–1900, size 2.4″ (6 cm). 14. Jerusalem, Palestine, c. 1910–20, size 4.3″ (11 cm).

## PLATE 285 – CHRISTIANITY – CROSS

**1.** Palestine, c. 1890–1910, size 2.5″ (6.3 cm). **2.** China, c. 1990, size 2.1″ (5.3 cm). **3.** China, c. 1990, size 2″ (5 cm). **4.** Palestine, c. 1920–40, size 1.7″ (4.3 cm). **5.** Palestine, c. 1970–90, size 1.3″ (3.2 cm). **6.** Philippine Islands, 1996, size 1.6″ (4 cm). **7.** Palestine, c. 1970–90, size 1.2″ (3 cm). **8.** Palestine, c. 1970–90, size 1.2″ (3 cm). **9.** Palestine, c. 1970–90, size 1.2″ (3 cm). **10.** Cross of Jerusalem, Palestine, c. 1840, size 1.2″ (3 cm). **11.** Palestine, c. 1900–1930, size 1.2″ (3 cm). **12.** Palestine, c. 1870–90, size 3.1″ (7.8 cm). **13.** France, c. 1860–80, size 2.4″ (6 cm). **14.** France, c. 1890, size 1.8″ (4.5 cm). **15.** Palestine, c. 1950, size 3.4″ (8.7 cm).

## PLATE 286 – CHRISTIANITY – CARVED SHELL 1

**Annunciation, an Angel Appears to Mary**

Archangel Gabriel appears to Mary in a city of Galilee named Nazareth, to give her the news that she would bear a son whom she must call Jesus, and that he will be called the Son of the Highest. **1.** Inscribed *Jn Anunsiasione* (Annunciation), Palestine, c. 1850–80, size 5.7″ x 6.1″ (14.5 x 15.5 cm). **2.** Inscribed *Souvenir de Bethleem* (Souvenir of Bethlehem), Palestine, c. 1870–90, size 5.7″ x 5.7″ (14.5 x 14.5 cm).

**The Star of Bethlehem**

**3.** The Star of Bethlehem revealed the birth of Jesus to the Magi and led them to Bethlehem, Palestine, c. 1920, size 5.3″ x 4.5″ (13.5 x 11.5 cm).

**The Nativity**

Mary places baby Jesus in a manger. She is accompanied by her husband, Joseph, and they are watched by local shepherds. **4.** This carving has an additional base decoration of the Last Supper, plus to the left, a carvings of the Baptism of Christ by John the Baptist and, to the right, annunciation, an angel appearing to Mary, Palestine, c. 1870–90, size 7.1″ x 6.7″ (18 x 17 cm).

## PLATE 287 – CHRISTIANITY – CARVED SHELL 2

**The Nativity**

Mary and Joseph with baby Jesus in a manger and watched by local shepherds. 1. Intricate carving incorporating extra medallions, Palestine, c. 1830–50, size 6.8″ x 6.9″ (17.2 x 17.4 cm). 2.The carved medallions show an angel on either side and in the center bottom small medallion, the Cup of Passion, Bethlehem, Palestine, c. 1880–1900, size 5.3″ x 5.7″ (13.5 x 14.5 cm). 3. An unusual pierced scene, Palestine, c. 1850–70, size 5.1″ x 5.5″ (13 x 14 cm). 4. An extra large sized presentation piece, Palestine, c 1933–50, size 9.4″ x 8.5″ (24 x 21.5 cm), comes in a presentation box (not shown).

## PLATE 288 – CHRISTIANITY – CARVED SHELL 3

**Adoration of the Magi**

Mary and Joseph present baby Jesus to the Magi. **1.** Very deep early carving. The base decoration is of the Last Supper, Palestine, c. 1800–30, size 8.5" x 9.3" (21.5 x 23.5 cm). **2.** The central carving includes the Three Wise Men bearing gifts of gold, myrrh, and frankincense, Palestine, c. 1880–90, size 6.1" x 6.3" (15.5 x 16 cm). **3.** Inscribed *Rei Magi*; *Rei* is a biblical term for those who retain allegiance to King David, whilst the Magi refer to the Three Wise Men who came bearing gifts of gold, myrrh, and frankincense, Palestine, c. 1820–50, size 6.1" x 6.1" (15.5 x 15.5 cm). **4.** Inscribed *Glornexcelsisdeo*. (abbreviation for *Gloria in Excelsis Deo*, translated Glory to God in the highest). In this carving, the scene is watched over by angels, Palestine, c. 1800–40, size 6.1" x 6.1" (15.5 x 15.5 cm).

## PLATE 289 – CHRISTIANITY – CARVED SHELL 4

**Escape to Egypt**
Joseph leads a donkey carrying Mary and the Infant Jesus in their escape to Egypt. Different artists show their own interpretations of this scene. 1. An early example, which has the addition of an angel guiding the way; note the unusual hat worn by Joseph, Palestine, c. 1840, size 5.1″ x 5.3″ (13 x 13.5 cm). 2. A pierced carving still on its original round board, Palestine, c. 1850–70, size 5.3″ x 5.3″ (13.5 x 13.5 cm). 3. The more recent carvings are applied on top of a shell, embellished by the use of abalone shell, Palestine, c. 1930–50, size 6.1″ x 5.5″ (15.5 x 14 cm). 4. The black spots in the eyes are often indications of early carving, Palestine, c. 1840, size 5.3″ x 5.1″ (13.5 x 13 cm).

## PLATE 290 – CHRISTIANITY – CARVED SHELL 5

**Young Jesus with Joseph and His Family**

St. Joseph, husband of Mary, holding Infant Jesus. St. Joseph has his staff with lily blossoms. 1. Inscribed *S. Giuseppe* (St. Joseph), signed by the carver *Bethlehem, Solaiman Roc*, Bethlehem, Palestine, c. 1880, size 5.5″ x 6.7″ (14 x 17 cm). 2. Inscribed *Sacra Familia*, (Sacred Family) Palestine, c. 1880–90, size 6.1″ x 5.6″ (15.5 x 14.3 cm). 3. Inscribed *S.Giusebe* (St. Joseph), Palestine, c. 1880–1900, size 4.7″ x 4.7″ (12 x 12 cm). 4. St. Joseph holding his staff, with a young Jesus Christ, inscribed San Josef (St. Joseph), Palestine, c. 1850–80, size 4.8″ x 4.3″ (12.3 x 11 cm).

## PLATE 291 – CHRISTIANITY – CARVED SHELL 6

**John the Baptist Baptizes Jesus**
John the Baptist in his traditional hide clothing holds a cross as he baptizes Jesus. 1. Two winged angels watch while the dove, representing the Holy Spirit, flies overhead, Palestine c. 1840–50, size 5.5" x 5.9" (14 x 15 cm). 2. An angel watches the baptism, Palestine, c. 1870–90, size 5.9" x 5.9" (15 x 15 cm). 3. Baptism, Palestine, c. 1870–90, size 5.9" x 5.9 (15 x 15 cm). The bottom medallion displaying Instruments of the Passion, possibly crown of thorns and the three nails from the crucifix. 4. Baptism, Palestine, c. 1850–80, size 6.6" x 6.2" (16.8 x 15.8 cm).

## PLATE 292 – CHRISTIANITY – CARVED SHELL 7

**The Mysteries of Faith**

Also known as the mysteries of the rosary, these carvings are often confused as unconnected scenes from the life of Jesus. 1. Nine mysteries of faith, Palestine, c. 1880–1900, size 5.9″ x 6.1″ (15 x 15.5 cm). 2. Four mysteries of faith, Palestine, c. 1870–90, size 6.7″ x 5.5″ (17 x 14 cm). 3. Four mysteries of faith in a pierced carving, Palestine, c. 1850–70, size 6.3″ x 6.2″ (16 x 15.8 cm).

**Stations of the Cross**

4. Six stations of the cross, Palestine, c. 1870–90, size 5.3″ x 5.5″ (13.5 x 14 cm). 5. The last supper, surrounded with fourteen stations of the cross, Palestine, c. 1870–90, size 8.1″ x 7.4″ (20.5 x 18.7 cm).

## PLATE 293 – CHRISTIANITY – CARVED SHELL 8

**Jesus, Palm Sunday, The Last Supper**

1. Palm Sunday, Jesus rides into Jerusalem on a donkey, welcomed with praise and palm branches, music and hymns, inscribed *Bethleem* (Bethlehem), Palestine, c. 1880, size 5.5″ x 6.3″ (14 x 16 cm). 2. Jesus, nail signs visible in his hand, basket of corn at his feet to symbolize the bread that he gave to his disciples saying "This is my body," and the cup of wine saying, "This is my blood," Eastern Europe or Palestine for the Orthodox Church, c. 1890, size 5.1″ x 4.7″ (13 x 12 cm). 3. The Last Supper, medallions around the edge from the mysteries of faith, Palestine, c. 1870–90, size 6.5″ x 6.7″ (16.5 x 17 cm). 4. The Last Supper, the base of this carving has a nativity scene, Palestine, c. 1870–90, size 8.3″ x 8.3″ (21 x 21 cm).

## PLATE 294 – CHRISTIANITY – CARVED SHELL 9

**The Last Supper**

Some of these carvings have been based on the painting by Leonardo Da Vinci *The Last Supper,* 1545–98. **1.** With medallions around the edge from the mysteries of faith, inscribed *Bethlemme* (Bethlehem), Palestine, c. 1850–70, size 6.7" x 7.2" (17 x 18.5 cm). **2.** This carving is dated on the back 1865, being one of a very few dated items found, Palestine, 1865, size 5.7" x 5.7" (14.5 x 14.5 cm). **3.** Inset on a carved wood backing, Palestine, c. 1880–1900, size 5.7" x 5.7" (14.5 x 14.5 cm). **4.** Palestine, c. 1870–90, size 7.1"x 7.1" (18 x 18 cm).

## PLATE 295 – CHRISTIANITY – CARVED SHELL 10

**<u>Praying, Stations of the Cross</u>**
1. Jesus prays in the Garden of Gethsemane on the night before He is arrested; the surrounding carvings show twelve disciples, Palestine, c. 1870–90, size 5.5″ x 5.9″ (14 x 15 cm). 2. The soldiers give Jesus the cross, the second station of the cross, Palestine, c. 1800–30, size 4.8″ x 4.6″ (12.3 x 11.7 cm). The number of the station has been reversed by the carver, likely during copying. 3. Jesus is forced to carry the cross to Golgotha outside Jerusalem's walls. In the fifth Station of the Cross Jesus is assisted by Simon of Cyrene, Palestine, c. 1800–30, size 5.9″ x 5.9″ (15 x 15 cm). 4. Jesus is nailed to the cross, the eleventh Station of the Cross, Palestine, c. 1800–30, size 5.5″ x 5.7″ (14 x 14.5 cm).

## PLATE 296 – CHRISTIANITY – CARVED SHELL 11

**The Crucifixion**

Jesus is crucified on the cross. According to the Gospel of St. John, witnessing the crucifixion was Mary, the mother of Jesus, Mary's sister, Mary the wife of Clopas, and Mary Magdalene. Some carvings show different numbers of women present. **1.** Palestine, c. 1820–50, size 6.5″ x 6.1″ (16.5 x 15.5 cm). **2.** Inscribed *Statio XII*, 12th Station of the cross, Palestine, c. 1820–50, size 4.9″ x 5.1″ (12.5 x 13 cm). **3.** Palestine, c. 1870–1900, size 6.3″ x 6.7″ (16 x 17 cm) **4.** Palestine, c. 1880–1900, size 5.7″ x 6.1″ (14.5 x 15.5 cm).

## PLATE 297 – CHRISTIANITY – CARVED SHELL 12

**Deposition: Jesus descends from the cross and is laid in a tomb**

1. Joseph of Arimathea and Nicodemus remove the nails, St. John and another disciple receiving the body and, to the left, Virgin Mary and Mary, wife of Cleopas, Palestine, c. 1780–1820, size 6.7" x 6.3" (17 x 16 cm). 2. Includes a bottom medallion of the Cross of Jerusalem, Palestine, c. 1850–90, size 6.1" x 5.9" (15.5 x 15 cm). 3. Palestine, c. 1850, size 6.3" x 6.7" (16 x 17 cm). 4. Jesus is laid in the tomb and covered in incense, the 14th Station of the Cross, Palestine, c. 1860–80, size 5.9" x 5.9" (15 x 15 cm).

## PLATE 298 – CHRISTIANITY – CARVED SHELL 13

**Resurrection**

On the third day, Jesus Christ rises from the tomb. 1. Soldiers drank and gambled at the foot of the cross, Mary Magdalene and Ruth carrying containers of balm and censor with incense; has the coat of arms of a high ranking Vatican official, Palestine, c. 1850, size 6.7" x 7.1" (17 x 18 cm). 2. Based on a painting by Bellini, Palestine, c. 1870–90, size 5.1" x 5.5" (13 x 14 cm). 3. Christ rises, Palestine, c. 1840–60, size 5.9" x 6.1" (15 x 15.5 cm). 4. Palestine, c. 1830–40, size 7.1" x 7.5" (18 x 19 cm).

## PLATE 299 – CHRISTIANITY – CARVED SHELL 14

**Ascension**

For forty days after The Resurrection, Jesus continued to teach his followers. At Bethany, while in the act of blessing them, Jesus was carried up to Heaven. **1.** Transfiguration of Jesus Christ, with Moses and Elijah at his side, his disciples Peter, James, and John watch in amazement, Palestine, c. 1870–1900, size 6.3″ x 6.3″ (16 x 16 cm). **2.** The Trinity: God, Jesus, and the Holy Spirit (dove) receiving Mary, mother of Jesus, into Heaven, Palestine, c. 1780, size 6.9″x 6.5″ (17.5 x 16.5 cm). **3.** Inscribed *Assunzione di Maria Virgine*, based on the painting by Rubens *Assumption of Mary*. Mary, mother of Jesus, ascends to Heaven, Palestine, c. 1820, size 7.2″ x 7.2″ (18.5 x 18.5 cm). **4.** Angels crown Mary, mother of Jesus, in Heaven based on the painting by Filippo Venuti, Palestine, c. 1840–50, size 4.9″ x 4.7″ (12.5 x 12 cm).

## PLATE 300 – CHRISTIANITY – CARVED SHELL 15

**The Saints**

1. Inscribed *S.Thadeeo S. Jonnes*, being St. Jude (Thaddeus) and St. John, both apostles of Jesus Christ, Palestine, c. 1850–80, size 6.1" x 6.1" (15.5 x 15.5 cm). 2. St. Melania, the younger and elder, Palestine, c. 1870–90, size 5.7" x 5.3" (14.5 x 13.5 cm). 3. Inscribed *S Chrle,* St. Charles Borromeo, a skull and a Bible sits on the lectern, Palestine, c. 1870–90, size 3.9" (10 cm). 4. St. Christina of Bolsena, feast day 24 July, Palestine, c. 1870–90, size 5.9" x 5.7" (15 x 14.5 cm). 5. St. Francis receives the Stigmata, Palestine, c. 1870–80, size 5.9" x 6.1" (15 x 15.5 cm).

## PLATE 301 – CHRISTIANITY – CARVED SHELL 16

**The Saints**
1. Inscribed *S.Antonio*, Saint Anthony of Padua, Franciscan Order, Palestine, c. 1800, size (4.7″ x 4.7″) 12 x 12 cm. 2. Inscribed *S. Marco Evangelista*, St. Mark the Apostle, Palestine, c. 1800 size 3.9″ x 3.9″ (10 x 10 cm). 3. St. George and the dragon is based on a painting by Rubens in 1620; this example includes the King of Silene's daughter, whose life St. George saved, Palestine, c. 1850–80, size 5.7″ x 5.5″ (14.5 x 14 cm). 4. St. George and the dragon, carved out of black pearl oyster, Palestine, c. 1950–90, size 6.3″ x 6.7″ (16 x 17 cm).

## PLATE 302 – CHRISTIANITY – CARVED SHELL 16

**The Saints**

1. St. Peter, apostle, and regarded as the first Pope of the Roman Catholic Church, holding the key to heaven, Palestine, c. 1880, size 4.3" x 3.1" (10.8 x 7.8 cm). 2. St. Anna and a young Jesus inscribed *Santa Ana;* St. Anna was the mother of Virgin Mary and grandmother of Jesus, Palestine, c. 1880, size 5.8" x 5.5" (14.8 x 14 cm). 3. St. Paschal Baylon, a Spanish Friar and saint in the Roman Catholic Church, Palestine, c. 1860–80, size 5.5" x 5.5" (14 x 14 cm). 4. Inscribed *S. Roce*; St Roch showing the plague on his leg, Palestine, c 1860–80, size 4.9 x 4.7" (12.5 x 12 cm).

## PLATE 303 – CHRISTIANITY – CARVED SHELL 17

**The Saints**
1. St. George killing the dragon, inscribed Vinnichenko, Palestine, c. 1972, size 7.1" x 5.9" (18 x 15 cm). 2. St. Barbara, a third century saint and martyr, Palestine, c. 1800, size 5.1" x 5" (13 x 12.7 cm). 3. Virgin Mary in Glory with Saints Jude and James the Less, Palestine, c. 1850, size 6.3" x 5.9" (16 x 15 cm). 4. Saints Leander, Fulfentius, Isidore and Florentina were brothers and sisters, a remarkable family who produced three bishops and an abbess. Inscribed *Itelapopulivestr* and *Filii Carthagines,* which translates "Go among your people and children of Cartagena" (in Spain). Palestine, c. 1850–80, size 4.8" x 4.3" (12.3 x 11 cm).

1

## PLATE 304 – CHRISTIANITY – CARVED SHELL 17

1. This incredible shell has more symbolism than any other shell we have seen, and includes:

The triangle represents the Holy Trinity: the dove represents the Holy Spirit, the rays of light represent Heavenly glory, Holy Spirit bringing down three crowns inserted on the arm of the cross, representing that Jesus completed His supreme sacrifice and only then does man gain control of the Underworld, the earth, and the sky. (This is the second time; the first time was when Adam and Eve were created, but this was lost to them when they ate the forbidden fruit.)
Symbolism continues with the large central heart full of love (*Mi Amor*), representing the Sacred Heart of Jesus surrounded by thorns and beams of light, and the sacred heart of Mary; the sword represents her heart pierced with pain; the stars around and at the foot of the moon according to the gospel of John; the snake represents evil and a reminder of the snake handing the forbidden fruit to Adam and Eve, this deed leading to the condemnation of man; a globe crucifix on the left, representing Jesus dying on the crucifix for the world, the inner wording translated to "Remain in Me and I in Him."
The two archangels portrayed are Michael with the sword and Gabriel. The edging translates to "Detection and conception of the climb to the cross in the Holy Spirit of the Sacred Heart of Jesus and Mary in the time of His Holy Animation."
This item is inscribed on the back that it was blessed in the most high Holy Sepulchre, Jerusalem, Palestine, c. 1820, size 3.7" x 3" (9.3 x 7.6 cm).

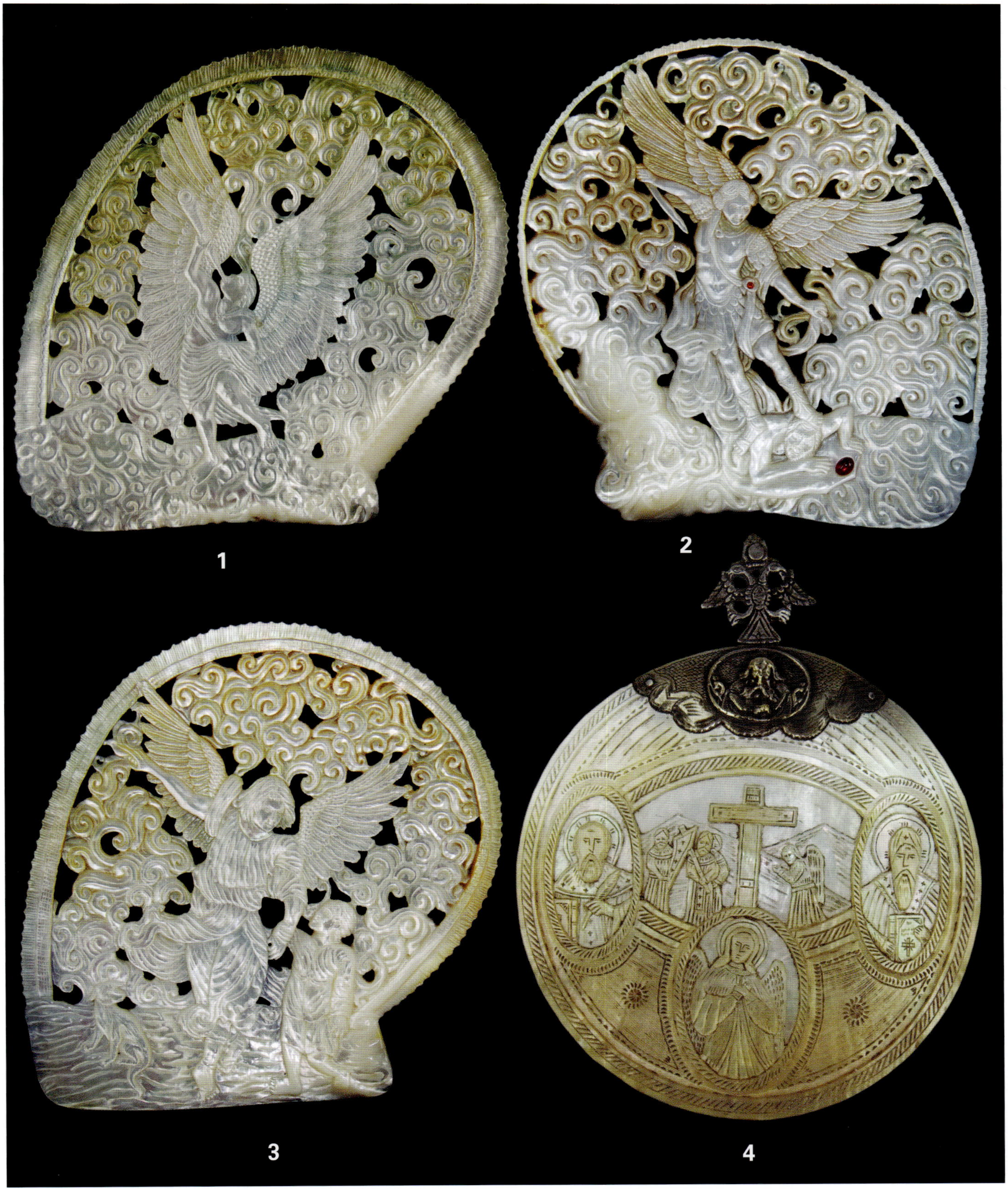

## PLATE 305 – CHRISTIANITY – ARCHANGELS and ANGELS

1. Archangel Gabriel, with his trumpet, which he will blow at the Last Judgment, Indonesia, 2011, size 6.5" x 6.7" (16.5 x 17 cm). 2. Powerful carving representing Archangel Michael crushing Satan, based on the painting by Guido Reni in 1635, inset rubies, Indonesia, 2011, size 6.7" x 7" (17 x 17.8 cm). 3. Archangel Raphael and Tobias, Indonesia, 2011, size 6.7" x 7.1" (17 x 18 cm). 4. Empty crucifix, Orthodox Church, the silver top depicting God with a beard blessing with three fingers, in the central scene an angel with Mary, mother of Jesus, and Mary Magdalena or Mary, wife of Clopas, whilst in the two side ovals are possibly John Chrysostom and St. Basil the Great, Palestine, c. 1875, size 5.1" x 5.1" (13 x 13 cm).

## PLATE 306 – CHRISTIANITY – CARVED SHELL 18

**Etched shells**

1. Jesus stumbles while carrying the cross, soldiers watch, Palestine, c. 1840–50, size 4.7″ x 4.3″ (12 x 11 cm). 2. Our Lady of Mount Carmel, the name given to the Blessed Virgin Mary in her role as patroness of the Carmelite order. Inscribed *Maria.Sma* (Blessed Mary) Palestine, c. 1840–50, size 5.5″ x 5.3″ (14 x 13.5 cm). 3. Mary, mother of Jesus, Palestine, c. 1840, size 3.9″ x 3.5″ (10 x 9 cm). 4. St. Basil the Great, inscribed *Brlci*, Palestine for the Orthodox Church, c. 1850, size 3.9″ x 4.1″ (10 x 10.5 cm). 5. Mary, mother of Jesus, inscribed *Regina Sanctorum Omnium* (Queen of all Saints), together with St. Peter, St. Lawrence, St. Agnes, St. Lucia, St. Blaise, St. Bonaventure who offer a crown to Queen Mary, Palestine, c. 1840–50, size 5.5″ x 5.5″ (14 x 14 cm).

## PLATE 307 – CHRISTIANITY – CARVED SHELL 2

1. Joseph, Mary, and Infant Jesus in a Nativity scene, Palestine, c. 1870, size 3″ x 2.2″ (7.6 x 5.6 cm). 2. The Holy Family in a Nativity scene, watched by two shepherds, Palestine, c. 1880, size 3.7″ x 2.3″ (9.5 x 5.8 cm). 3. The Annunciation: an angel appears to Mary, watched by a dove representing the Holy Spirit, carving from Palestine, c. 1890, size 3.8″ x 2.6″ (9.7 x 6.7 cm) set in silver in Russia, hallmarked Assayer Anatolii Apollinovich Artisbashev, Moscow, 84 zolothnik, silversmith Roman Ariotarkhov. 4. Inscribed *B.V. Addolorata*, Mary, mother of Jesus with a sword in her heart for the sorrow, based on the painting in *S. Ciriaco D'Ancona*, Palestine, c. 1860–70, size 4.1″ x 3.5″ (10.5 x 9 cm). 5. *S. Antonio* (St. Anthony) of Padova, Palestine c, 1890, size 3.5″ x 2.5″ (9 x 6.4 cm), with St. Francis of Assisi, he founded the order of Franciscan Friars. 6. *L'Agonie au Jardin* (The Agony in the Garden), Jesus praying in the garden of Gethsemane, Palestine, c. 1880, size 4.9″ x 3.1″ (12.4 x 8 cm). 7. The resurrection of Jesus Christ, Palestine, c. 1880, size 3.4″ x 2.3″ (8.7 x 5.8 cm). 8. The Sacred Heart of Mary, Palestine, c. 1880, size 3.5″ x 2.6″ (9 x 6.7 cm). 9. Nativity scene, Palestine, c. 1880, size 3.9″ x 2.5″ (10 x 6.3 cm). 10. Sacred Heart of Jesus, Palestine, 1860–80, size 2.8″ x 1.9″ (7 x 4.8 cm). 11. Our Lady of Sorrows; the swords represent the seven sorrows in the life of the Virgin Mary, Palestine, c. 1840, size 2.4″ (6 cm) diameter. 12. St. George and the dragon, Palestine, c. 1950 size 2.8″ x 2.2″ (7.2 x 5.5 cm).

## PLATE 308 – CHRISTIANITY – CARVED SHELL 1

Small medallions were often sewn on undergarments close to the skin to avoid annoyance when working and were not worn as necklaces as is the practice today. **1 & 2.** Double-sided carving: (**1**) The resurrection of Jesus Christ watched by an angel and a soldier holding a sword; (**2**) Mary, mother of Jesus with a sword in her heart for sorrow of the crucifixion, Palestine, c. 1700–1740, size 3.5″ x 2.8″ (9 x 7 cm). **3.** Inscribed *Adorasione di Pastore* (Adoration of the Shepherds) and *Gloria.e.x.celsis*, (*Gloria in Excelsis Deo*, Latin for "Glory to God in the highest"), Palestine, c. 1880, size 3.5″ x 2.8″ (9 x 7 cm). **4.** Presenting baby Jesus to the Magi, Palestine, c. 1860–80, size 3.5″ x 2.8″ (9 x 7 cm). **5–6.** Double sided carving (**5**) St. Joseph holding Infant Jesus, (**6**) Jesus Christ, the Shepherd of souls, Palestine, c. 1700–1740, size 3.5″ x 2.8″ (9 x 7 cm). **7.** Madonna and Infant Jesus, both wearing crowns to represent their aureole or circle of light showing their glory, Palestine, c. 1890, size 3.6″ x 2.6″ (9.2 x 6.5 cm). **8.** Ascension of Jesus Christ, watched by his disciples and three angels, Palestine, c. 1870, size 3.7″ x 2.8″ (9.4 x 7 cm). **9.** Jesus carries the cross, Palestine, c. 1890–1910, size 1.7″ x 1.2″ (4.3 x 3 cm). **10.** Mary and Infant Jesus, both wearing crowns to represent their aureole or circle of light showing their glory, Philippine Islands, 1996, size 2.6″ x 1.8″ (6.5 x 4.5 cm). **11.** Last Supper brooch, Palestine, c. 1910, size 2.4″ (6 cm) diameter. **12.** Medallion marked *S. Maria Maddalena* (St. Mary Magdalene) Palestine, c. 1890, size 1.8″ x 1.7″ (4.8 x 4.2). **13.** Resurrection of Jesus Christ, Palestine, c. 1900–20, size 2.5″ x 1.6″ (6.3 x 4 cm).

## PLATE 309 – CHRISTIANITY – CARVINGS

1. St. Patrick, Patron Saint of Ireland, Palestine, c. 1860–80, size 3.9″ x 2.7″ (10 x 6.8 cm). 2. Palm Sunday, Jesus rides into Jerusalem on a donkey, welcomed with praise and palm branches, music, and hymns, Palestine, c. 1860–80, size 3.9″ x 2.6″ (10 x 6.8 cm). 3. St. John Chrysostom, Orthodox Bishop, Palestine, c. 1880, size 2.6″ x 1.8″ (6.5 x 4.5 cm).
4. Joseph leading a donkey that is carrying Mary and Infant Jesus in their escape to Egypt, Palestine, c. 1860, size 3.7″ x 2.6″ (9.3 x 6.5 cm). 5. St. Joan of Arc, inscribed *Јерусалим* (Jerusalem), Palestine, c. 1920–40, size 2.6″ x 2″ (6.7 x 5 cm).
6. The Last Supper, inscribed *Cena D.N.J.C.* (Cena Domini Nostri Jesu Christi translated Last Supper of our Lord Jesus Christ), Palestine, c. 1880, size 2.9″ x 2.2″ (7.4 x 5.5 cm). 7 The Holy Family with the ox and donkey in the Nativity scene, Palestine, c. 1890, size 4.1″ x 3.3″ (10.5 x 8.4 cm). 8. Commemorative medallion of Pope Pius IX 1846–1878, Giovanni Maria Mastai-Ferretti, Italy, c. 1850–70, size 2″ x 1.7″ (5.2 x 4.4 cm). 9. King David playing his harp; David was the second king of Israel to reign during the period 1003–970 BC, Palestine, c. 1860, size 3.8″ x 2.5″ (9.6 x 6.4 cm).

## PLATE 310 – CHRISTIANITY – ICON, MONSTRANCE, and CARVINGS

**1.** Icon with a crucifix at the center. Jesus Christ is shown in the top medallion, surrounded by Seraphim (six-winged angels), the highest order of angels in the Christian world, ranked above cherubim and below God. Angels stand at each side of the scene, with eagles and snakes to symbolize the struggle of good (eagles) against evil (snakes). The theme of the base carving is St. Veronica, who gave Jesus her veil (some sources say handkerchief) to wipe His brow as He carried the cross to Golgotha, and when returned she miraculously found the imprinted face of Jesus on the veil. Palestine, c. 1780, size 21.3" x 13" (54 x 33 cm). **2.** Monstrance, used in Catholic, Anglican, and Lutheran Churches to display consecrated Eucharistic Host during specific rites. The host is made from dough, squeezed between two hot irons and placed in the center of the monstrance, protected by glass panels (absent in this example). Reproduction of an 1858 Palestinian example by E. Yidi, 2010, size 14.6" x 6.3" (37 x 16 cm). **3.** Statue of Mary, mother of Jesus, China, c. 1900, size 3.5" (9 cm). **4.** Jesus Christ, a relic from the Dominican Convent in Peru. It was custom amongst superstitious mountain folk to break of fingers off statues and to use them as relics. The Incas regarded items made from mother-of-pearl were worth more than gold. This carving must have traveled via Spain, possibly from France or Palestine, c. 1800, size 3.3" (8.5 cm). **5.** The three Magi before the massacre of the innocents when Archangel Michael warns the Magi not to return to Herod, Europe, c. 1820, size 4.3" x 2" (10.8 x 5 cm), likely the lid of a relic box. **6.** St. Joseph dying, with Jesus and Mary in attendance, Palestine or France, c. 1850, size 3.2" x 2.4" (8.2 x 6.2 cm), likely the cover of a missal or prayer book.

## PLATE 311 – CHRISTIANITY – RELIC OR ROSARY BOXES

There has been much confusion on the origins of these boxes, which are meant to house relics, rosaries, or any precious objects. Only box #6 was hallmarked for Erfurt City, Germany, but it is believed the pearl carving was made in Palestine. Generally, the more detailed carving is indicative of Europe (Germany or France), whilst the carving that lacks detail is indicative of Palestine. More examples are needed to clarify the origins. **1.** Inscribed *Anunziazione* (the Annunciation), an angel appears to Mary, Palestine, c. 1850, size 2.8″ x 2″ (7 x 5 cm). **2.** Inscribed *Iesu, Maria, S.Gusepe*, Mary sews, Joseph, holding a hammer works on wood, while Infant Jesus feeds the bird, Palestine, c. 1850, size 2.8″ x 2″ (7 x 5 cm). **3.** The Last Supper, Palestine, c. 1850, size 2.8″ x 2″ (7 x 5 cm). **4.** The resurrection of Jesus Christ, lid only, Palestine, c. 1850, size 2.8″ x 2″ (7 x 5 cm). **5.** The Nativity, only the lid of the box remains, Palestine, c. 1850, size 2.8″ x 1.8″ (7 x 4.6 cm). **6.** Jesus Christ is crucified, watched by his mother Mary, and Mary Magdalene. Silver frame hallmarked 13/16 Erfurt City, Germany, carving Palestine, c. 1850, size 2.7″ x 2″ (6.8 x 5 cm). **7.** Inscribed *Silete Dominus Dorm*, St. John the Baptist holds his finger on his lips to indicate silence and with the other hand he shows us Jesus is asleep, the cross lying next to him confirming His identity, Europe, c. 1840–50, size 2.8″ x 1.9″ (7 x 4.7 cm). **8.** An open box, to show the mother-of-pearl on all sides. **9.** The Last Supper, lid and base only, Palestine, c. 1850, size 3.1″ x 2.2″ (8 x 5.5 cm).

## PLATE 212 – CHRISTIANITY

**1.** Traveler's Tabernacle, taken with the owner and opened at night to give blessings, France, c. 1925–45, size 6″ x 3.1″ (15.4 x 7.8 cm). **2.** Rosary in a pearl container inscribed Souvenir de Lourdes, France, c. 1910, size 2.4″ x 1.5″ (6 x 3.8 cm). **3.** Rosary in a pearl container inscribed Ostende, France, for the Belgium market, c. 1900, size 2.2″ x 1.7″ (5.5 x 4.3 cm). **4.** Rosary, France or Italy, c. 1920, size of pearl crucifix 2″ (5.2 cm). **5.** Orthodox pectoral cross worn by a bishop as a sign of his office, Israel, c. 2005, size of central cross 5.9″ (15 cm). **6.** Panagia worn by an Orthodox bishop when not vested for service, Israel, c. 2002, size of central medallion, 5.5″ (14 cm). **7.** Necklace created from a c. 1880 Bethlehem carving and placed in a fashionable setting for 1970, US, size of pendant 2″ (5 cm). **8.** Tray with inlaid scene of Jerusalem, likely the work of Elias Yacamen, Palestine, c. 1960, size 9.8″ x 7.1″ (25 x 18 cm).

## PLATE 313 – HINDUISM

1. Hanuman, a Hindi deity, is considered the most powerful and intelligent amongst gods and is one of the most important personalities in the Hindu epic *The Ramayana*. He shows his devotion by carrying heavy rocks from the mountain to build a temple, Chanthaburi, Thailand, 2006, by master carver Samai Sehua, size 4.9" x 3.5" (12.5 x 9 cm). 2. Phra Phrom is the Thai representation of the Hindu god Brahma, Chanthaburi, Thailand, 2006, size 6.7" x 6.1" (17 x 15.5 cm). 3. Ganesh, one of the widely worshipped Hindu deities, Bali, Indonesia, 2000, size 6.7" x 6.3" (17 x 16 cm). 4. Lakshmi, Hindu god of peace, prosperity, and good luck, Thailand, c. 1935, size 4.7" x 2" (12 x 5 cm).

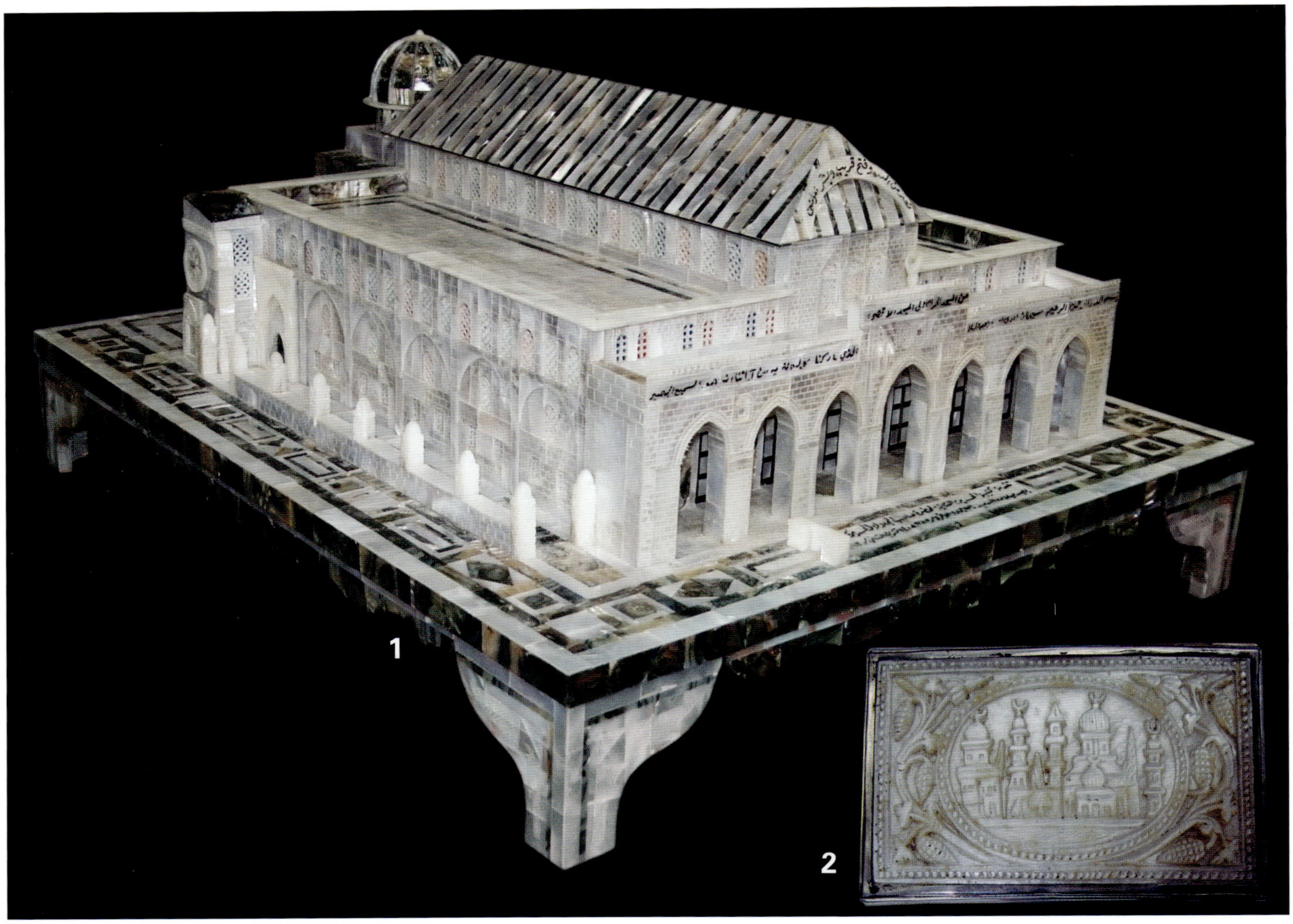

1

2

## PLATE 314 – ISLAMISM

1. Model of El Aqsa Mosque, an Islamic holy place in the old city of Jerusalem, Palestine, c. 1956, size 22.4″ x 19.3″ x 11″ (57 x 49 x 28 cm), comes in a presentation box with the inscription (translated from Arabic) *Gift from the Second Battalion to King Hussein of Jordan*, complete with the coat of arms of Jordan. 2. Carved Mosque box for holding Islamic prayer beads, Palestine, c. 1845–65, size 2.8″ x 1.7″ (7 x 4.3 cm).

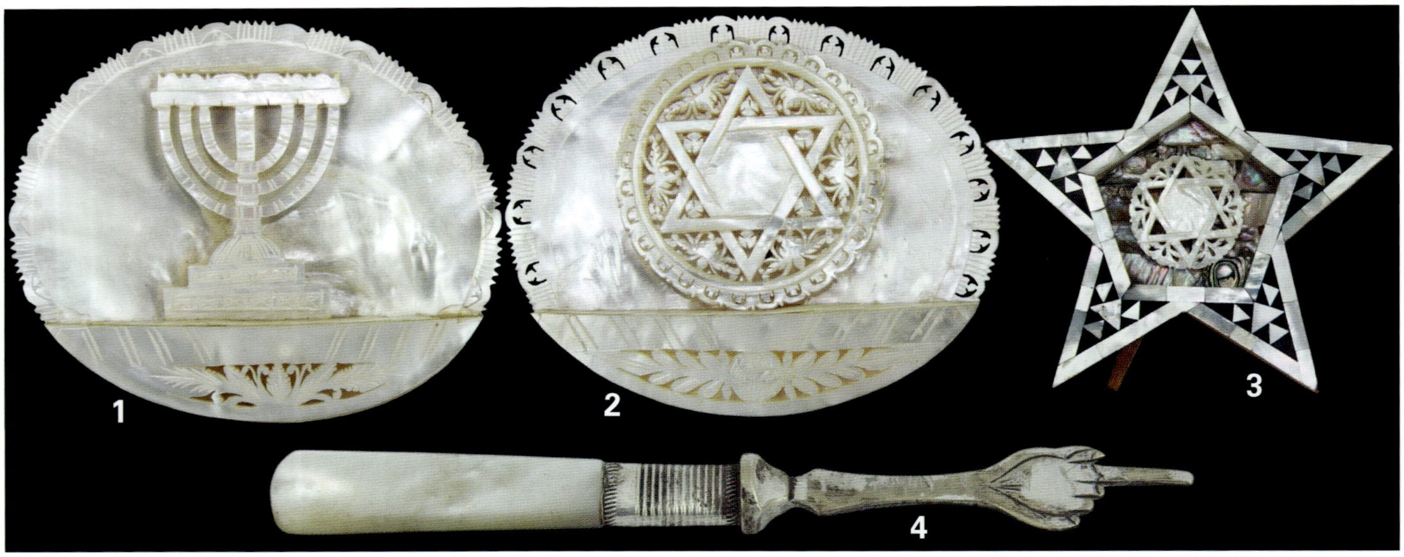

1 2 3 4

## PLATE 315 – JUDAISM

1. Menorah, celebrating the forming of the State of Israel, Israel, c. 1950, size 5.7″ x 4.9″ (14.5 x 12.5 cm). 2. Star of David, celebrating the forming of the State of Israel, Israel, c. 1950, size 6.1″ x 4.7″ (15.5 x 12 cm). 3. Star of David in a star frame, Israel, November 1973, size 7.7″ x 7.7″ (19.5 x 19.5 cm). 4. Yad, a Jewish ritual pointer to read the Torah without touching the sacred text, hallmarked Sheffield, England, 1909, size 5.5″ (14 cm).

## PLATE 316 – TAOISM 1

A magnificent set of Fu Lu Shou, a concept of good fortune, prosperity, and longevity believed to date back to the Ming Dynasty when Fu Star, Lu Star, and Shou Star were considered personified deities of these attributes.
**1, 2**. Fu—Deity of happiness and fortune
**3, 4**. Lu—Deity of prosperity, affluence
**5, 6**. Shou—Deity of Longevity
China, 2010, size 6.3" (16 cm).

1

2a

2b

## PLATE 317 – TAOISM 2

1. The Eight Immortals are legendary deities and considered to be signs of prosperity and longevity. They are popular themes in art. Included are He Xiangu, Cao Guojiu, Li Tieguai, Lan Caihe, Lu Dongbin, Han Xiang Zi, Zhang Guo Lao and Zhongli Quan, Vietnam, 1996, size 62.1" x 31.5" (158 cm x 80 cm). 2a, 2b. Shou Star, the deity of longevity, who is said to control the life span of mortals. This example has been carved out of a mother-of-pearl freshwater shell and comes in a silk-lined box, China, c. 1920, size 5.9" x 3.1" (15 x 8 cm).

CHAPTER 13

# Tobacciana

Tobacciana covers a very wide range of articles connected to smoking. Mother-of-pearl was used in the manufacture of cigarette holders, cigarette cases, and etuis, cheroot cases, snuff boxes, and bottles, lighters, and holders, match safes, tampers, and cigar cutters.

We think the most beautiful of all the carved examples in the category of Tobacciana are the snuff boxes and cheroot boxes. Mother-of-pearl snuff boxes were produced by European manufacturers in the eighteenth century. They produced beautifully carved examples in mother-of-pearl, the likes of which have not been seen again. China also manufactured delicately engraved snuff boxes especially for the export market to England and Europe. Only a small percentage of snuff boxes produced were made in mother-of-pearl, so it was always a product for the high end of the market.

Early nineteenth century cheroot cases were also wonderfully carved from mother-of-pearl. To compare the nineteenth century examples to the twentieth century examples shows the movement away from works of art to mass production with the resultant poor quality. The carved examples in both snuff boxes and cheroot cases are in high demand and difficult to obtain.

Most of the production of pearl tobacciana was discontinued by middle to the end of the twentieth century, as concerns for health reduced smoking and the demand for these top end lighters and cases.

**PLATE 318 CIGAR ETUI**

**1a, 1b**. An amazingly large cigar etui, France, c. 1870, size 12.6" x 6.3" (32 x 16 cm), the central rod can be turned, which swivels the pearl cigar holders to the open position, when not in use it is swiveled close.

## PLATE 319 – SNUFF BOXES 1

1. Snuff box, dock, or ship scene, Europe, c. 1780–1800, said to have belonged to the Duchess of Wellington, size 2.8″ x 2.2″ x 0.8″ (7 x 5.5 x 2.1 cm). 2a, 2b. Snuff box, scene of party with wine, Europe, c. 1775–1800, base made from tiger cowry, size 3.1″ x 2.4″ x 1.7″ (7.8 x 6 x 4.3 cm). 3. Snuff box, initials *C.K.* on gold, England, c. 1830–50, size 2.2″ x 0.6″ x 0.2″ (5.5 x 1.5 x 0.6 cm). 4. Snuff box, lady in a garden, France, c. 1830–50, size 2.8″ x 2″ x 1.4″ (7 x 5 x 3.5 cm). 5. Snuff box, oxen and a farming scene, China, c. 1800–1810, carved at a time when white pearl was in short supply and black pearl oyster was used as a substitute, size 2.4″ x 1.6″ x 0.7″ (6 x 4 x 1.8 cm). 6. Snuff mull, carved bird, England, c. 1850, size 2″ x 1.3″ x 0.7″ (5 x 3.4 x 1.8 cm). 7. Snuff box, pierced carving after the French style, Argentina, c. 1950–90, size 1.8″ x 0.8″ (4.5 x 2 cm). 8. Snuff box, pierced carving, after the French style, Argentina, c. 1950–90, size 1.8″ x 0.8″ (4.6 x 2 cm). 9. Snuff box, man fishing, England, c. 1750–60, size 1.4″ x 0.4″ (3.5 x 1.1 cm). 10. Snuff box, oval, France, c. 1775–1810, size 3.3″ x 2.5″ x 0.4″ (8.5 x 6.4 x 1 cm). 11. Snuff box, hinged lid, England, c. 1860, size 2.4″ x 0.7″ x 0.3″ (6.2 x 1.9 x 0.8 cm). 12. Snuff box, two birds in a tree, France, c. 1850–70, size 2.5″ x 1.8″ x 0.6″ (6.3 x 4.5 x 1.5 cm). 13. Snuff box with a top carving of a French interpretation of two Japanese maidens, France, c. 1800, size 3.3″ x 2.6″ (8.5 x 6.5 cm). 14. Snuff box illustrating three musicians, France or Austria, c. 1800, size 4.1″ x 3.1″ (10.5 x 8 cm).

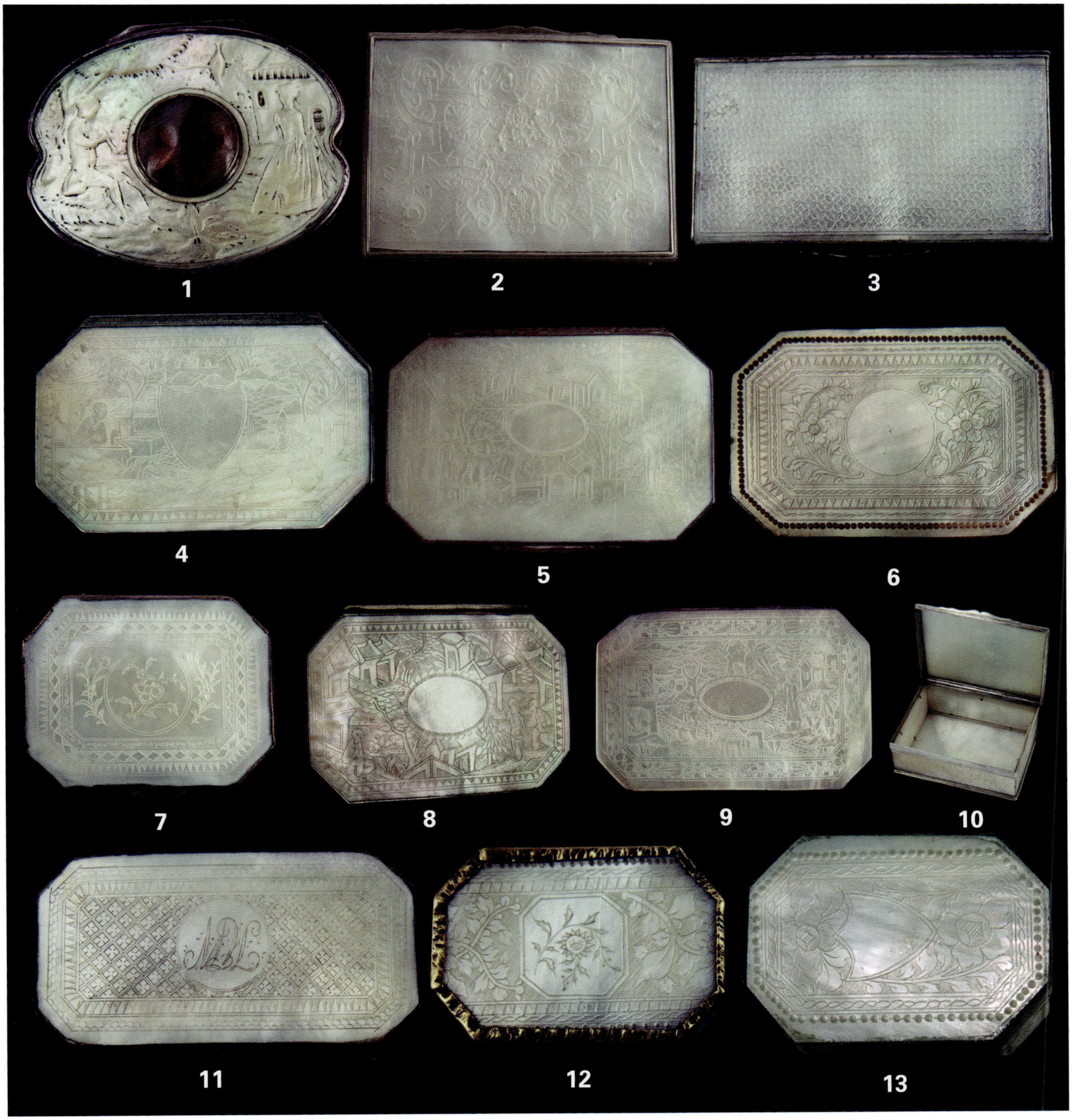


## PLATE 320 – SNUFF BOXES 2

1. Snuff box, man and lady, agate center, Europe, c. 1750–1780, size 2.7″ x 2.1″ x 0.4″ (6.8 x 5.4 x 1 cm). 2. Snuff box, scroll design, France, c. 1800–50, size 2.8″ x 2″ x 1.1″ (7 x 5.2 x 2.8 cm). 3. Snuff box, fine repeating pattern, France, c. 1860, size 3″ x 1.6″ x 1.5″ (7.5 x 4 x 3.8 cm). 4. Snuff box, village scene, China, c. 1840–60, size 2.2″ x 1.5″ x 0.6″ (5.7 x 3.8 x 1.5 cm). 5. Snuff box, village scene, China, c. 1840–60, size 2.6″ x 1.8″ x 0.7″ (6.5 x 4.5 x 1.7 cm). 6. Snuff box, flowers, China, c. 1840–60, size 2.4″ x 1.6″ x 0.8″ (6 x 4 x 2 cm). 7. Snuff box, flowers, the slender size suggests that this box is most likely a lady's snuff box, China, c. 1840–60, size 2.2″ x 1.7″ x 0.2″ (5.5 x 4.2 x 0.5 cm). 8. Snuff box, the slender size suggests that this box is most likely a lady's snuff box, China, c. 1840–60, size 2.5″ x 1.7″ x 0.2″ (6.3 x 4.3 x 0.5 cm). 9. Snuff box, village scene, China, c. 1840–60, size 2.6″ x 1.8″ (6.5 x 4.6 cm). 10. Inside of a typical snuff box showing pearl on all sides. 11. Snuff box, initials *MH,* China, c. 1840–60, size 2.8″ x 1.4″ x 1.1″ (7 x 3.5 x 2.8 cm). 12. Snuff box, floral pattern, China, c. 1840–60, size 1.7″ x 1.2″ x 1.1″ (4.3 x 3 x 2.8 cm). 13. Snuff box, village scene, China, c. 1840–60, size 1.7″ x 1.2″ x 1.1″ (4.3 x 3 x 2.8 cm).

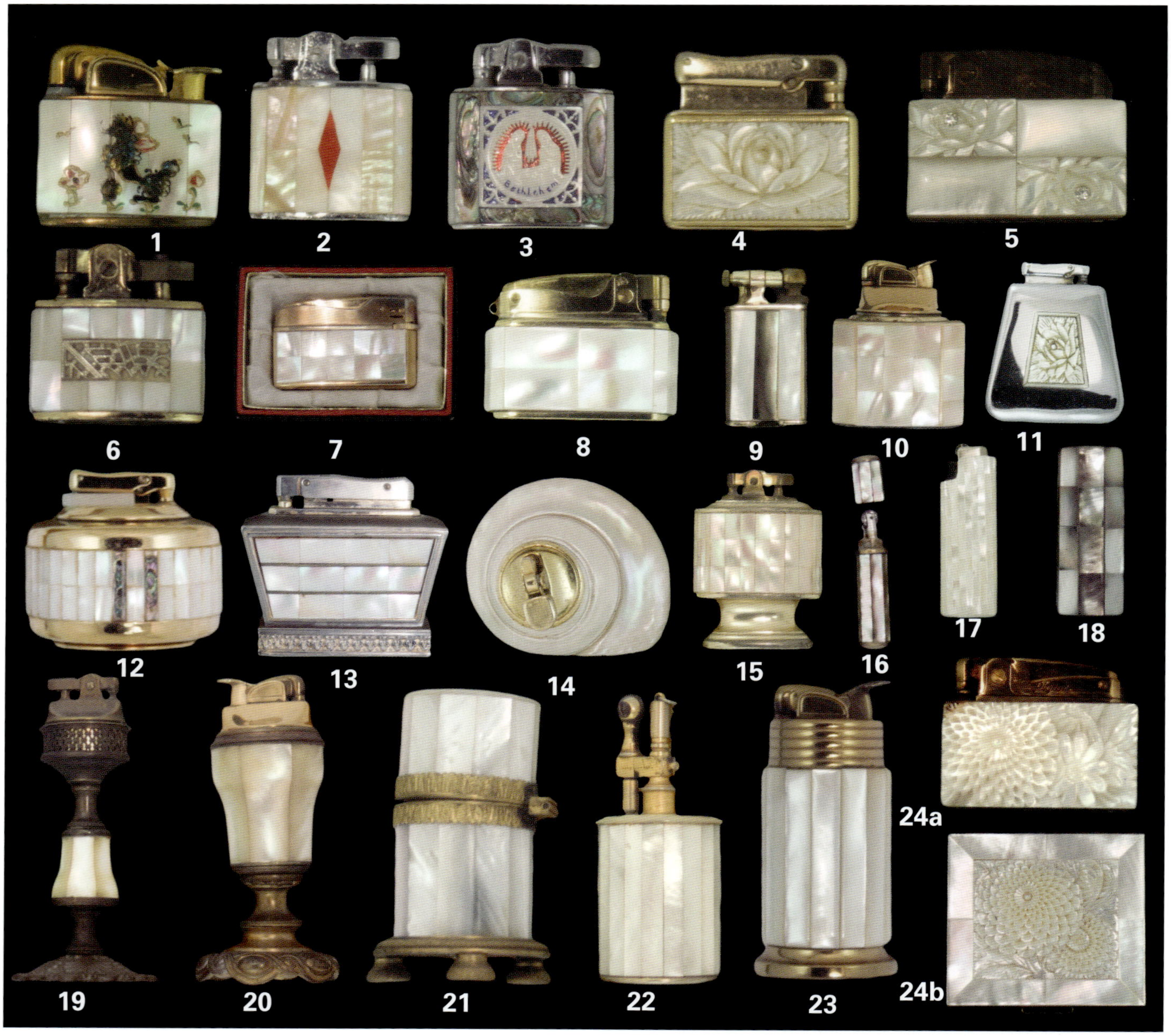

## PLATE 321 – LIGHTERS

1. Poodle lighter, Evans, USA, c. 1950, size 1.5″ x 1.5″ (3.8 x 3.8 cm). 2. Red diamond lighter, Elight, Japan, c. 1948, size 2″ x 1.8″ (5 x 4.2 cm). 3. Nativity lighter, Mosda, England, c. 1949, size 1.8″ x 2″ (4.5 x 5 cm), pearl carving done in Palestine. 4. Rose lighter, Colibri, Germany, c. 1960, size 1.6″ x 1.4″ (4 x 3.6 cm). 5. Lighter, two roses, Pidgeon, Japan, c. 1960, size 1.7″ x 1.4″ (4.3 x 3.5 cm). 6. Trickette lighter, Wiesner, Japan, c. 1950, size 1.6″ x 1.6″ (4 x 4 cm). 7. Boxed lighter, Sarome, Japan, c. 1954, size 2.4″ x 1.6″ (6 x 4 cm). 8. Pearl lighter, Arrow, Japan, c. 1950, size 1.7″ x 1.3″ (4.2 x 3.2 cm). 9. Two tone lighter, Golden Wheel, USA, c. 1920, size 1.6″ x 0.8″ (4 x 2 cm). 10. Table lighter, Evans, USA, c. 1950, size 2.8″ x 2.2″ (7 x 5.7 cm). 11. Rose table lighter, Colibri, Germany, c. 1950, size 3.3″ x 2.8″ (8.5 x 7 cm). 12. Table monogas lighter, Colibri, Germany, c. 1959, size 2.4″ x 2.6″ (6 x 6.5 cm). 13. Table lighter, Crest, Canada, c. 1938, size 2.8″ x 2.4″ (7 x 6 cm). 14. Trocha shell table lighter, Penguin, Japan, c. 1960, size 4.5″ x 3.1″ (11.5 x 8 cm). 15. Table lighter, Marhill, Japan, c. 1950, size 3.5″ x 2.4″ (8.8 x 6.2 cm). 16. Cylindrical lighter, inscribed *Ministere des Finances,* France, c. 1915, size 2.8″ x 0.6″ (7 x 1.5 cm). 17. Holder for disposable lighter, Thailand, 1996, size 3.1″ x 1.2″ (8 x 3 cm). 18. Holder for disposable lighter, Philippines, 1998, size 2.8″ x 1.2″ (7.2 x 3 cm). 19. Table lighter, Evans, USA, c. 1930, size 5.7″ x 2.8″ (14.5 x 7 cm), looks like pearl opera glasses shape. 20. Table lighter, Evans, USA, c. 1930, size 5.1″ x 2.4″ (13 x 6 cm), looks like pearl opera glasses shape. 21. Table lighter, Evans, USA, c. 1940, size 3.7″ x 1.8″ (9.5 x 4.5 cm). 22. Lift Arm table lighter, France, c. 1936, size 3.9″ x 1.6″ (9.8 x 4 cm). 23. Table lighter, Evans, USA, c. 1950, size 3.7″ x 1.9″ (9.5 x 4.8 cm). 24a, 24b. Lighter and cigarette case set, Pidgeon, Japan, c. 1960, size lighter 1.3″ x 1.7″ (3.4 x 4.4 cm), case 3″ x 3.3″ (7.5 x 8.5 cm).

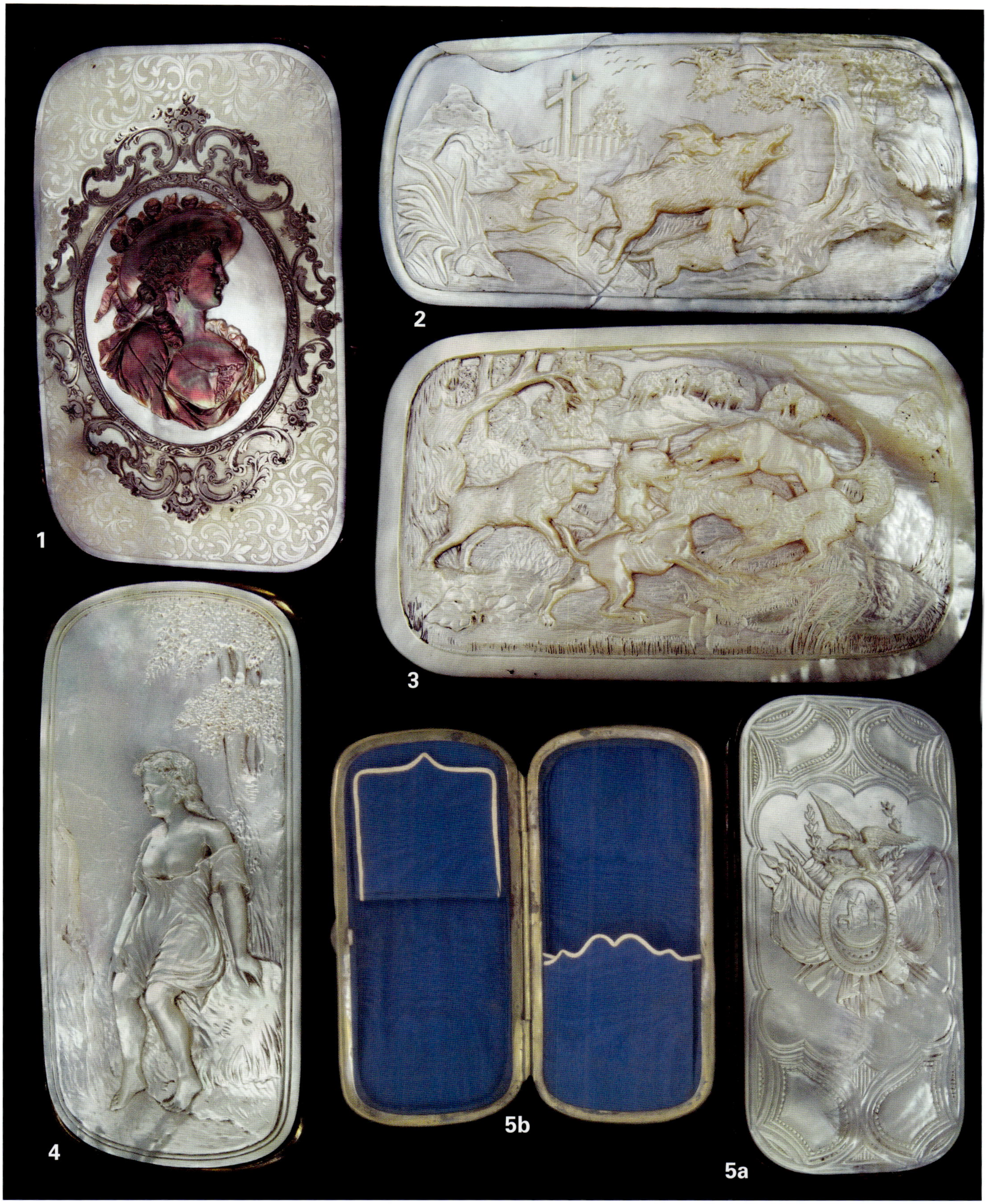


## PLATE 322 – CHEROOT CASES

1. Cheroot case, cameo of a lady of Marie Antoinette period carved from black lip pearl shell, France, c. 1850, size 5.5″ x 2.8″ (14 x 7 cm). 2. Cheroot case, dogs attacking a wild boar, France, c. 1840, size 5.7″ x 2.8″ (14.5 x 7 cm). 3. Cheroot case, pack of dogs hunting, France, c. 1840, size 5.5″ x 3.5″ (14 x 8.8 cm). 4. Cheroot case, carved lady, France, c. 1850, size 5.5″ x 2.8″ (14 x 7 cm). 5a, 5b. Cheroot case, coat of arms of the Republic of Bolivia, possibly carved in Palestine, c. 1880, size 5.3″ x 2.8″ (13.5 x 7 cm).

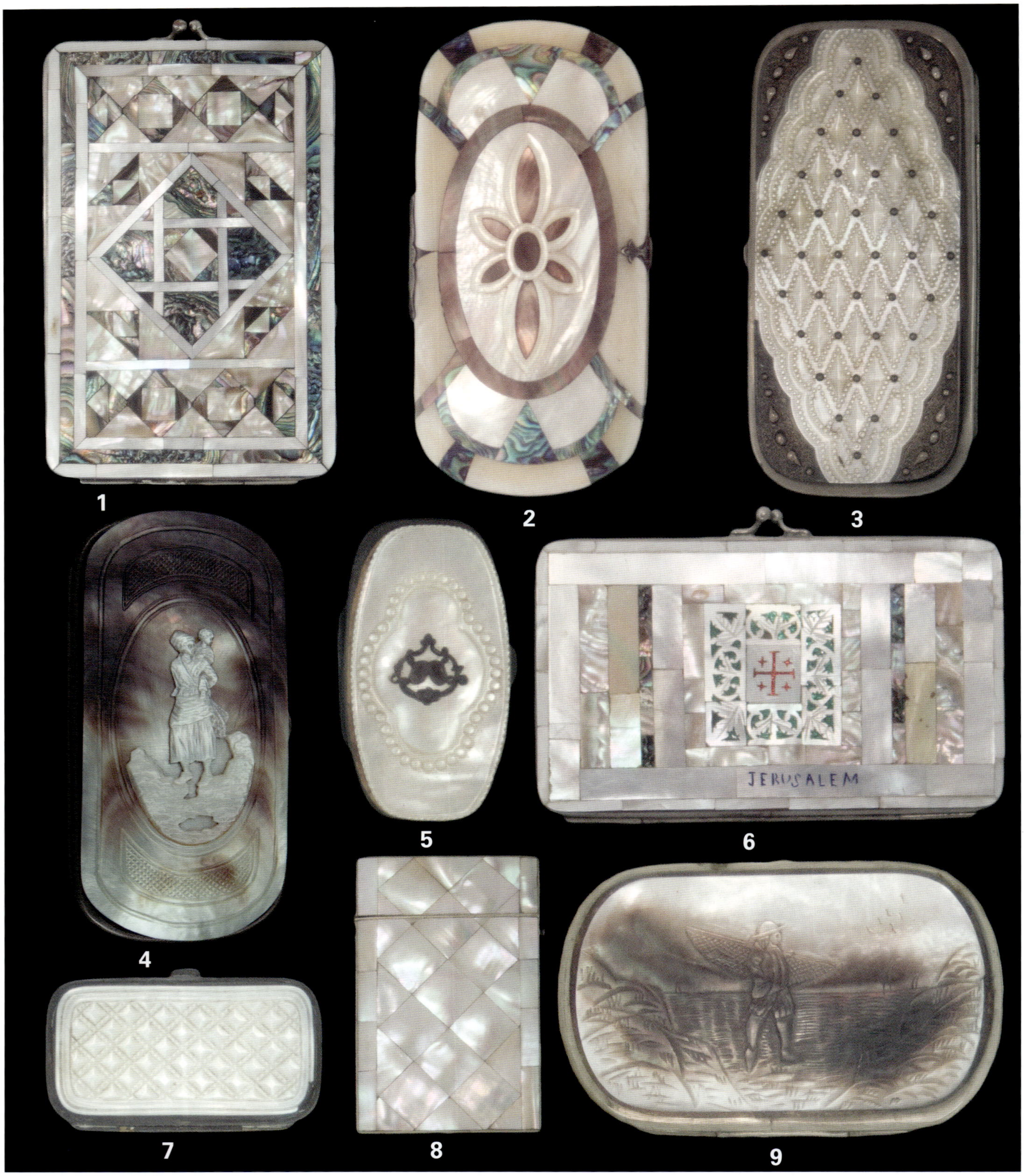


## PLATE 323 – CHEROOT CASES

1. Cheroot case, abalone shell and pearl oyster inlays, England, c. 1900, size 5.5″ x 3.5″ (14 x 9 cm). 2. Cheroot case made with three different types of mother-of-pearl, France, c. 1870, size 5.4″ x 2.8″ (13.7 x 7 cm). 3. Cheroot case, diamond pattern, England, c. 1855, size 5.5″ x 2.8″ (14 x 7 cm). 4. Cheroot case, lady and child, France, c. 1870, size 4.7″ x 2.4″ (12 x 6 cm). 5. Cheroot case, silver decoration, France, c. 1870, size 2.6″ x 1.4″ (6.5 x 3.5 cm). 6. Cheroot case, inscribed *Jerusalem,* souvenir item, framework of the case likely from England, Palestine, c. 1950, size 5.1″ x 3.1″ (13 x 8 cm). 7. Cheroot case, France, c. 1870, size 2.8″ x 1.4″ (7 x 3.5 cm). 8. Cheroot case, card case style, England, c. 1800, size 4.5″ x 3″ (11.5 x 7.5 cm). 9. Cheroot case, inscribed *Souvenir Chalard*, France, c. 1880, size 3.3″ x 2″ (8.5 x 5 cm).

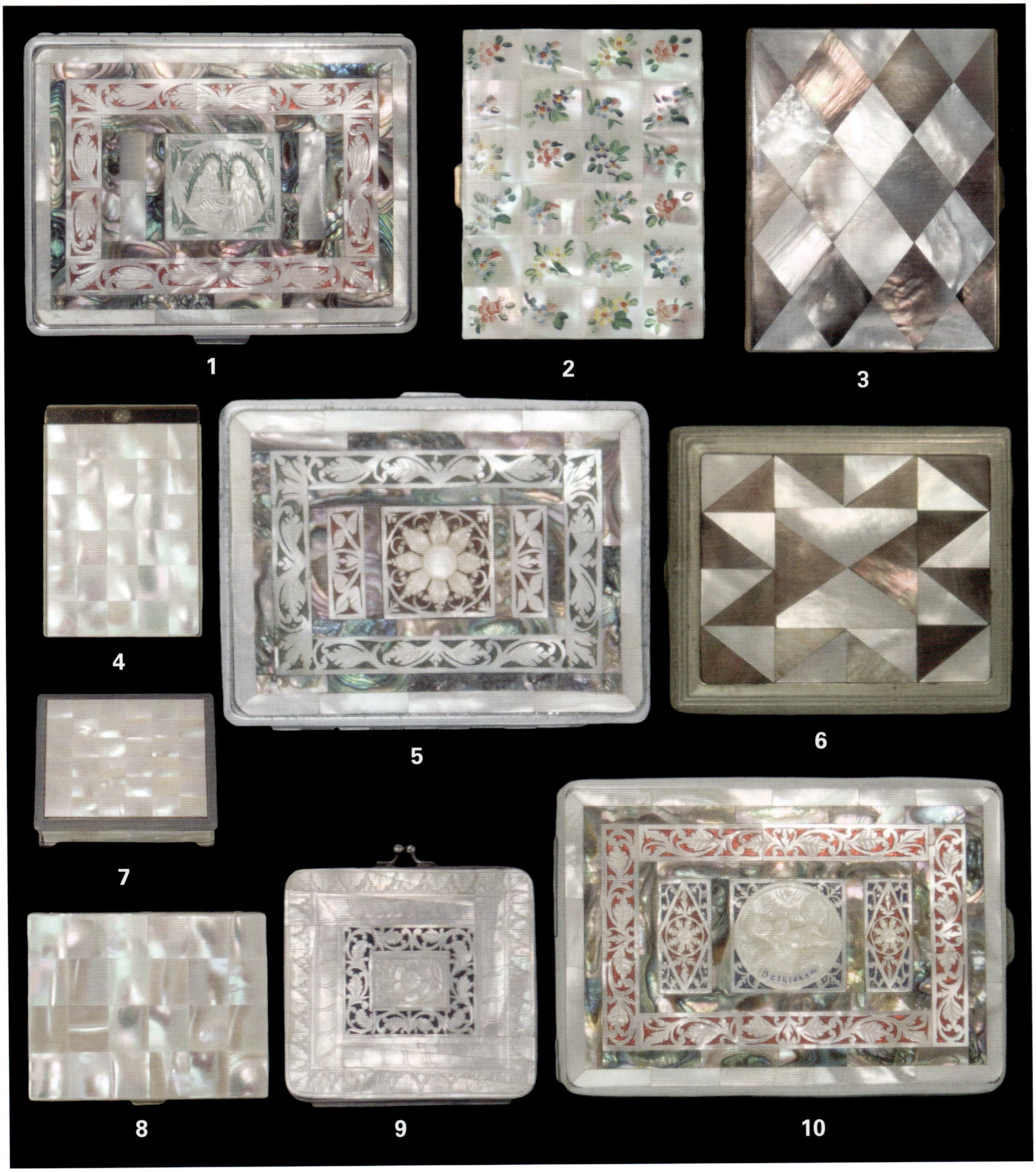



## PLATE 324 – CHEROOT AND CIGARETTE CASES

1. Cigarette case, nativity, pearl work done in Palestine, Emu Brand, England, c. 1950, size 4.3" x 3.1" (11 x 8 cm). 2. Cigarette case, flower, Schildkraut, Austria, for the US market, c. 1940, size 3.9" x 3.1" (10 x 7.8 cm). 3. Cigarette case, Schildkraut, Austria, for the US market, c. 1940, size 3.9" x 3" (10 x 7.7 cm). 4. Cigarette case, Evans, US, c. 1938, size 3.5" x 2.4" (9 x 6 cm). 5. Cigarette case, flower, pearl work done in Palestine, Emu Brand, England, c. 1950, size 4.3" x 3.1" (11 x 8 cm). 6. Cigarette case, Presto, US, c. 1940, size 3.5" x 3" (9 x 7.5 cm). 7. Desk cigarette case, Marhill, US, c. 1950, size 4.2" x 3.5" (10.6 x 9 cm). 8. Cigarette case, Marhill, US, c. 1940–50, size 3.9" x 3" (10 x 7.7 cm). 9. Cheroot case, pearl work done in Palestine, Mayell, England, c. 1950–60, size 3.3" x 3.1" (8.5 x 8 cm). 10. Cigarette case, *Bethlehem,* case made in Austria, pearl work done in Palestine, c. 1950, size 4.5" x 3.1" (11.5 x 8 cm).

## PLATE 325 – CIGAR CUTTERS AND MATCH SAFES

1. Cigar cutter, Herder, Germany, c. 1905, size 2.3" x 1.7" (5.8 x 4.4 cm). 2. Cigar cutter, Singers, Germany, 1904, size 2.3" x 1.8" (5.8 x 4.5 cm). 3. Cigar cutter, Germany, c. 1910, size 2.3" x 1.8" (6 x 4.5 cm). 4. Cigar cutter, Henkels, Germany, c. 1915, size 4.3" x 0.5" (11 x 1.2 cm). 5. Cigar cutter, Germany, c. 1920, size 2.7" x 0.9" (6.9 x 2.2 cm). 6. Cigar cutter, US, c. 1920, size 2.4" x 0.8" (6 x 2 cm). 7. Cigar cutter, US, c. 1925, size 1.4" x 0.6" (3.6 x 1.5 cm). 8. Cigar cutter, Germany, c. 1920, size 1.3" x 0.6" (3.3 x 1.4 cm). 9. Match safe, card case style, Europe, c. 1885, size 2.2" x 1.3" (5.8 x 3.2 cm). 10. Match safe, card case style, Europe, c. 1885, size 2.3" x 1.3" (5.8 x 3.2 cm). 11. Match safe, Germany, made for USA market, c. 1900, size 2.4" x 1.6" (6 x 4 cm). 12. Match safe, inscribed *Daytona*, Germany, made for USA market, c. 1900, size 2.6" x 1.4" (6.5 x 3.6 cm). 13. Match safe in the shape of a book, Europe, c. 1900, size 1.8" x 1.4" (4.6 x 3.5 cm). 14. Match safe, inscribed *Atlantic City,* Germany, made for the USA market, c. 1900, size 2.6" x 1" (6.5 x 2.5 cm).

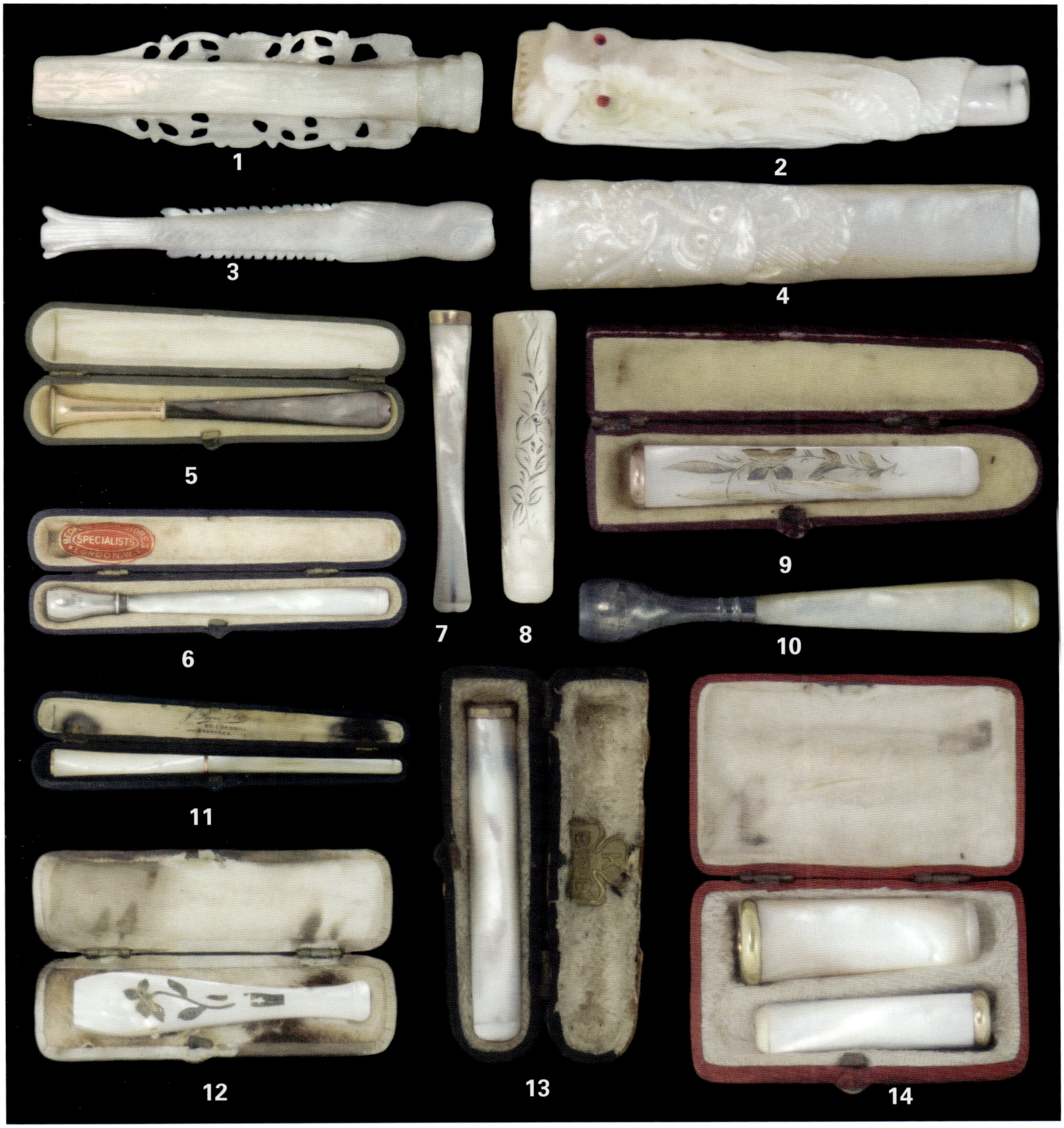


## PLATE 326 – CIGARETTE HOLDERS

**1.** Cigarette holder with fancy carving, England, c. 1915, size 2.6" (6.5 cm). **2.** Cigarette holder, carved dragon, China, c. 1910–20, size 2.8" (7 cm). **3.** Cigarette holder, fish shape, England, c. 1915–25, size 3.2" (8.2 cm). **4.** Cigarette holder, carved dragon, China, c. 1910–20, size 3" (7.5 cm). **5.** Cigarette holder, gold mark, unusual use of black lip pearl shell for the handle, boxed, France, c. 1925, size 3.9" (10 cm). **6.** Cigarette holder, box inscribed *Bedford Cigar Store,* William Shaw, London, England, 1920, size 4.5" (11.5 cm). **7.** Cigarette holder, England, c. 1920, size 3.3" (8.5 cm). **8.** Cigarette holder with engraving, France, c. 1910, size 2.2" (5.5 cm). **9.** Cigarette holder with gold leaf decoration, France, c. 1910–20, size 2.8" (7 cm). **10.** Cigarette holder, sterling silver, USA, c. 1920, size 3.1" (8 cm). **11.** Cigarette holder, box inscribed *J. Leom & Co, 60 Cornhill*, England, c. 1920, size 5.9" (15 cm). **12.** Cigarette holder with gold leaf decoration, France, c. 1910, size 2.8" (7.2 cm). **13.** Cigarette holder, box inscribed *KB+B*, England, c. 1910–20, size 2.8" (7 cm). **14.** Cigarette and cheroot holders in box, England, c. 1910–20, size 1.8" (4.5 cm).

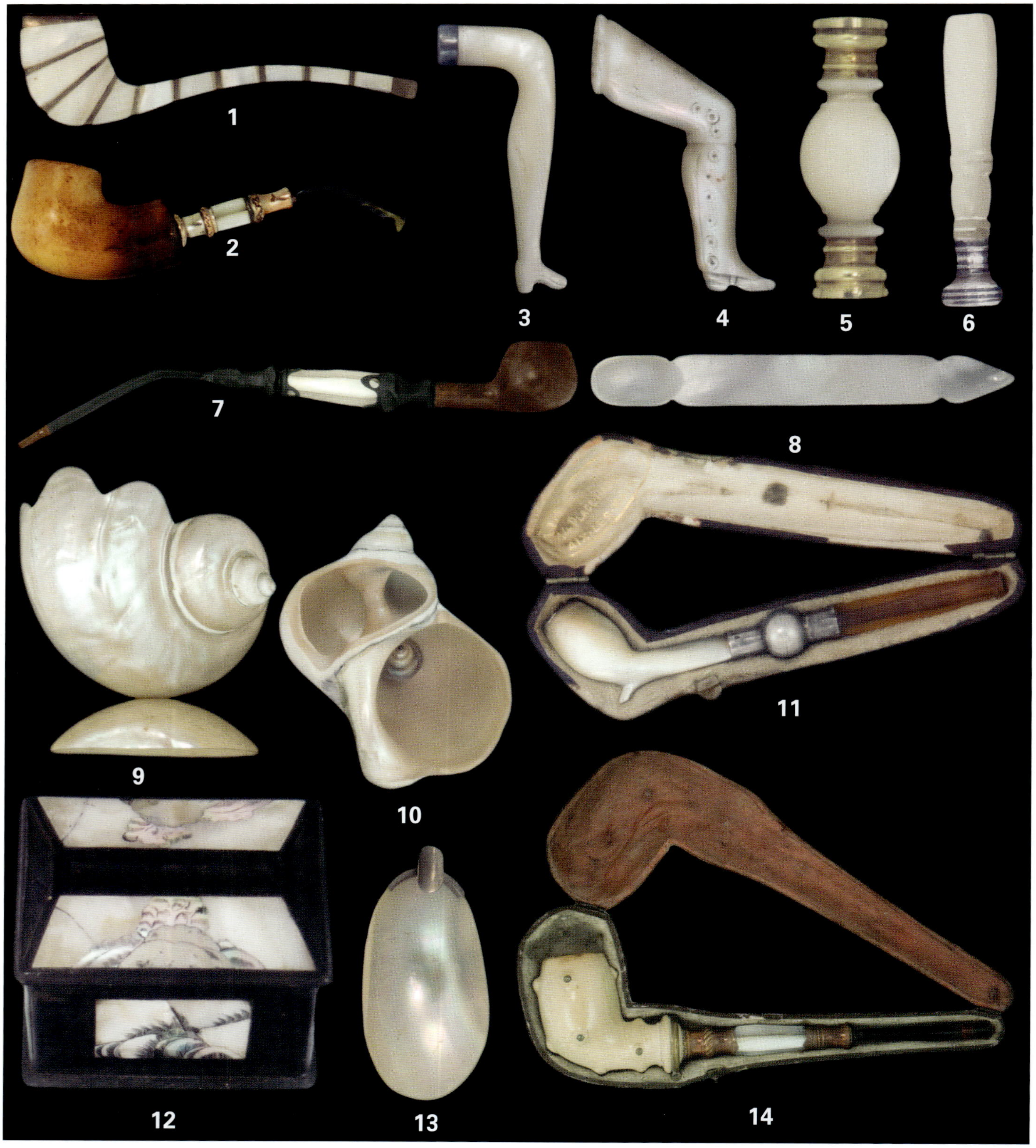


## PLATE 327 – PIPES, TAMPERS, AND ASHTRAYS

1. Pipe for herbs or tobacco, brass, India, c. 1950, size 3.9″ (10 cm). 2. Pipe, England, c. 1920, size 6.1″ (15.5 cm). 3. Pipe tamper based on Lady Ilchester's leg, England, c. 1760, size 2.8″ x 1.2″ (7 x 3 cm). 4. Pipe tamper, calvary trousers, likely a military tamper, England, c. 1850, size 2 x 0.8″ (5 x 2 cm). 5. Pipe tamper, England, c. 1875, size 1.6″ x 0.6″ (4 x 1.5 cm). 6. Pipe tamper, England, c. 1850, size 1.4″ x 0.3″ (3.5 x 0.7 cm). 7. Pipe, London, England, c. 1910, size 11″ (28 cm). 8. Pipe and snuff tool likely adapted from a manicure tool, England, c. 1900, size 2.8″ x 0.4″ (7 x 1 cm). 9–10. Cigarette and match holders, Philippines, for US market, c. 1940, size #9 3.8″ x 3″ (9.75 x 7.5 cm), #10 3.1″ x 2.4″ (8 x 6 cm). 11. Lady's pipe, inscribed *Aix Les Bains,* France, c. 1900–20, size 4.1″ (10.5 cm). 12. Cigarette dispenser, China, c. 1900, size 4.3″ x 3.1″ x 2.8″ (11 x 8 x 7 cm). 13. Ashtray, England, c. 1930–40, size 3.7″ x 2.4″ (9.5 x 6 cm). 14. Pipe, boxed, England, c. 1900, size 7.2″ (18.5 cm).

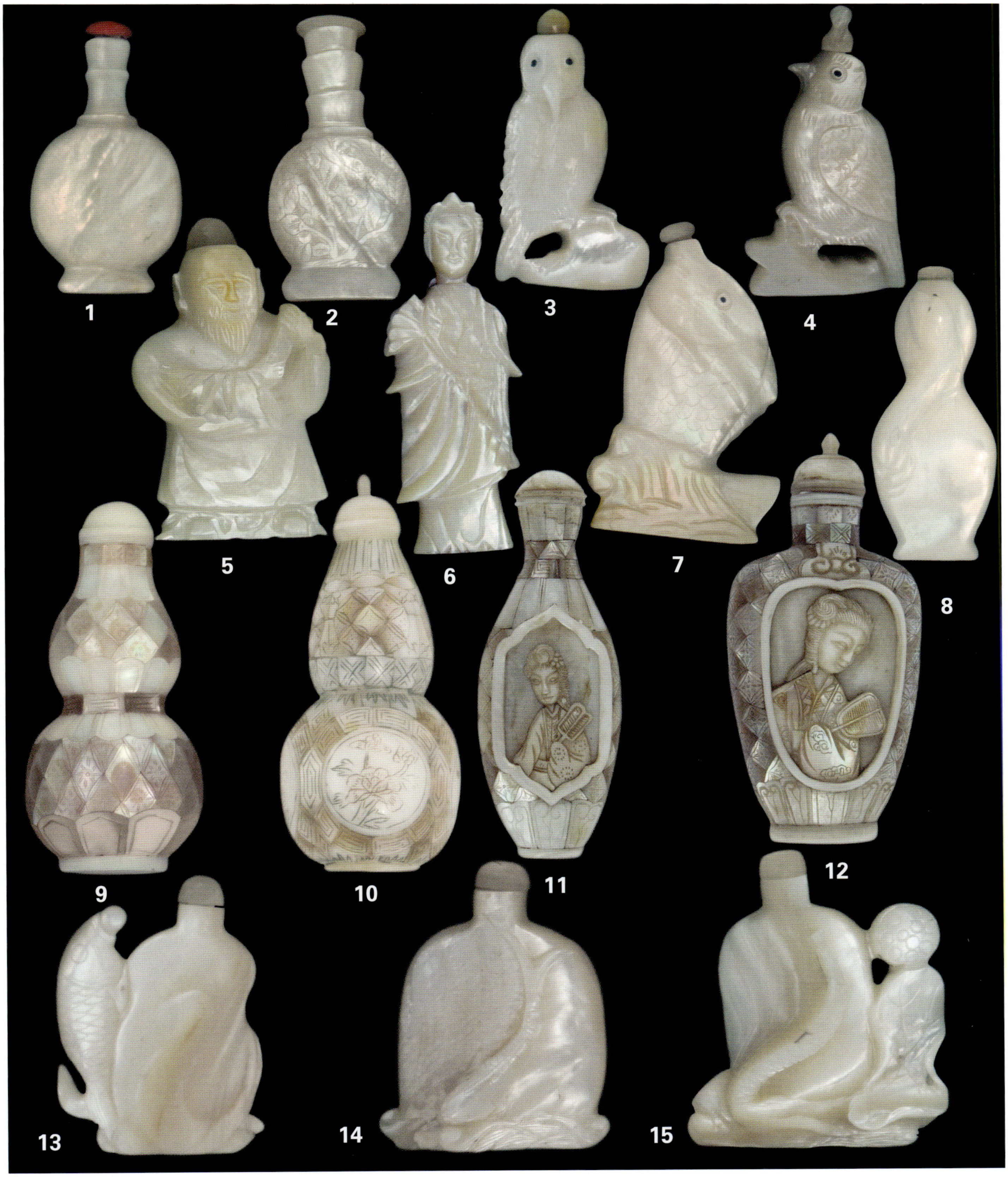


## PLATE 328 – CHINESE SNUFF BOTTLES 1

All these snuff bottles are from China: **1.** c. 1890–1910, size 2.8″ x 1.6″ (7 x 4 cm). **2.** c. 1890–1910, size 2.8″ x 1.4″ (7 x 3.5 cm). **3.** Owl, c. 1950, size 3.1″ x 1.8″ (8 x 4.5 cm). **4.** Owl, c. 1950, size 3.3″ x 1.8″ (8.5 x 4.5 cm). **5.** Man, c. 1890–1900, size 2.4″ x 1.3″ (6 x 3.4 cm). **6.** Lady, c. 1875–1900, size 3.7″ x 1.3″ (9.5 x 3.2 cm). **7.** Fish, c. 1830, size 3.5″ x 1.9″ (9 x 4.8 cm). **8.** Fish design, c. 1900, size 3.3 x 1.4″ (8.3 x 3.5 cm). **9.** c. 1845–50, size 2.8″ x 1.3″ (7 x 3.2 cm). **10.** c. 1850, size 2.8″ x 1.3″ (7 x 3.2 cm). **11.** Lady's head, c. 1845–50, size 3″ x 1.4″ (7.5 x 3.5 cm). **12.** Lady's head, c. 1845–50, size 3″ x 1.1″ (7.5 x 2.8 cm). **13.** Fish design, c. 2005, size 2.8″ x 2″ (7 x 5.3 cm). **14.** Fish design, c. 2005, size 2.6″ x 2″ (6.5 x 5 cm). **15.** Fish design, c. 2005, size 2.8 x 2.1″ (7 x 5.4 cm).

## PLATE 329 – CHINESE SNUFF BOTTLES 2

All these snuff bottles are from China, with exception item 8, which is from Thailand. **1.** Dragon, c. 1950, size 2.8″ x 1.8″ (7 x 4.5 cm). **2.** Green & red ink, c. 1950–80, size 2″ x 1″ (5 x 2.6 cm). **3.** Green & red ink, c. 1950–80, size 2 x 1.4″ (5.2 x 3.5 cm). **4.** Green & red ink, c. 1950–80, size 2″ x 1.4″ (5 x 3.5 cm). **5.** Green & red ink, c. 1950–80, size 2.2″ x 1.2″ (5.5 x 3 cm). **6.** Flowers, c. 1920–35, size 2.4″ x 1.5″ (6 x 3.8 cm). **7.** c. 1940–50, size 2.5″ x 1.4″ (6.4 x 3.5 cm). **8.** Made from the turban shell, Thailand, c. 1910, size 1.9″ x 1.3″ (4.8 x 3.2 cm). **9.** Table snuff bottle, fisherman, c. 1890–1910, size 3.6″ x 1.9″ (9.2 x 4.8 cm). **10.** Table snuff bottle, c. 1890–1910, size 3.5″ x 1.8″ (9 x 4.5 cm). **11.** c. 1940–50, size 2.5″ x 1.4″ (6.4 x 3.5 cm). **12.** c. 1940–50, size 2.5″ x 1.4″ (6.4 x 3.5 cm). **13.** Table snuff bottle, bird, c. 1890–1910, size 3.1″ x 1.8″ (8 x 4.5 cm). **14.** c. 1940–50, size 2.5″ x 1.4″ (6.4 x 3.5 cm). **15.** c. 1940–50, size 2.5″ x 1.4″ (6.4 x 3.5 cm). **16.** China, c. 1940–50, size 1.6″ x 1.2″ (4 x 3 cm). **17.** c. 1940–50, size 1.6″ x 1.2″ (4 x 3 cm). **18.** c. 1940–50, size 1.6″ x 1.2″ (4 x 3 cm).

CHAPTER 14

# Leisure Times

Mother-of-pearl was first recorded as being used in games in the early eighteenth century. Card games such as Ombre, Quadrille, and Pope Joan were very popular in England and Europe at that time. These games needed gaming counters for scoring.

The Chinese were quick to capitalize on this need and started producing counters cut from mother-of-pearl, which were etched or scratch carved. Over the years, the quality of these counters developed into the most intricate designs ever seen.

This trade was made possible by captains and supercargo aboard ships visiting Canton in China, who, to supplement their salary, would purchase sets of these counters from the Hongs (factories) in Canton, which they resold when they got home. The sets became very popular, and soon the wealthy made special orders to have their coats of arms etched on gaming counters (armorial counters). As ships were not in port long enough to have these special sets made, it is believed that captains of subsequent vessels would bring the filled orders back to England.

These counters were popular until 1820–1840, when changing trends saw new games emerging that did not need the high quantity of gaming counters. The Chinese manufacturers tried improving the quality with a very deep carved variety of counter, but they could not stop the drop off in demand.

The popularity of mother-of-pearl saw this shell being used in sets of dominoes, chess sets, whist markers, card boxes, and many other leisure time activities, as the following plates will show.

1a 1b 2a 2b 3a 3b 4

**PLATE 330 – LEISURE TIMES – DOMINOES**

**1a, 1b.** Dominoes, 28 tiles in a pearl box, France, c. 1880–1900, size 7″ x 2.4″ x 2.2″ (17.9 x 6 x 5.5 cm); tiles 1.8″ x 0.8″ (4.5 x 2 cm). **2a, 2b.** Dominoes, 28 tiles in wood box, France, c. 1860–1890, box size 7.1″ x 2.8″ x 2.8″ (18 x 7 x 7 cm); tiles size 1.8″ x 0.9″ (4.5 x 2.3 cm). **3a, 3b.** Dominoes, 45 tiles in a leather box, France, c. 1890–1920, size 9.4″ x 2.4″ x 2.8″ (24 x 6 x 7 cm); tiles 2″ x 1″ (5 x 2.5 cm). **4.** Dominoes, 24 miniature tiles in a pearl box, France, c. 1920, tile size 0.2″ x 0.1″ (0.6 x 0.3 cm); box size 1.7″ x 1.4″ (4.2 x 3.5 cm).

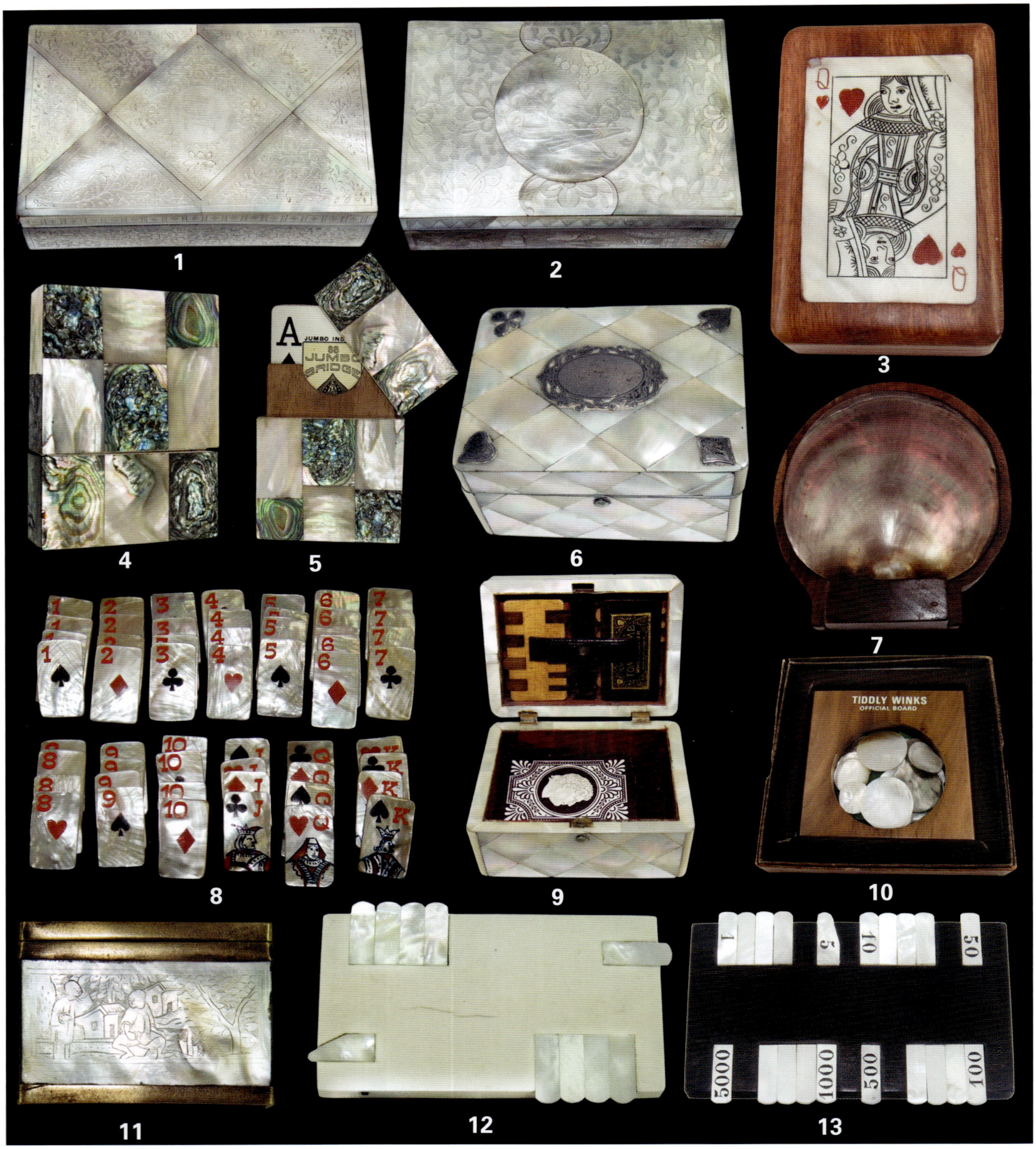


## PLATE 331 – LEISURE TIMES – CARDS

1. Playing card box, initials *JHB,* China, c. 1820–40, size 4.5″ x 2.8″ (11.5 x 7 cm). 2. Playing card box, Valentine's pattern of two billing birds, China, c. 1745, size 4.5″ x 3″ x 1.5″ (11.5 x 7.6 x 3.7 cm). 3. Playing card box, Vietnam, c. 1998, size 4.3″ x 3″ x 1.6″ (11 x 7.5 x 4 cm); similar boxes were made with other card suites. 4, 5. Playing card box with Russell & Morgan cards, US, c. 1930, size 4″ x 3″ x 1″ (10 x 7.5 x 2.5 cm). 6, 9. Games box, contents cards, and two game markers, England, c. 1840, size 3.9″ x 2.9″ x 2.2″ (10 x 7.3 x 5.6 cm). 7. Playing card box, Tahiti, c. 1940, size 7.1″ x 6.7″ (18 x 17 cm). 8. Pearl playing cards, full set by Peter Meyer, Australia, 2005, size per card 1.9″ x 1.1″ (4.7 x 2.7 cm). 10. Tiddly Winks, 2 colors of pearl, US, c. 1950, size 4.3″ x 4.3″ (11 x 11 cm). 11. Playing card box for miniature cards, China, c. 1840–50, size 1.6″ x 1.2″ (4 x 3 cm). 12. Piquet game counter or marker for the popular card game, France, c. 1880, size 3.1″ x 1.8″ (8 x 4.5 cm). 13. Bezique game counter or marker, France, c. 1890, size 3.5″ x 2.4″ (9 x 6 cm).

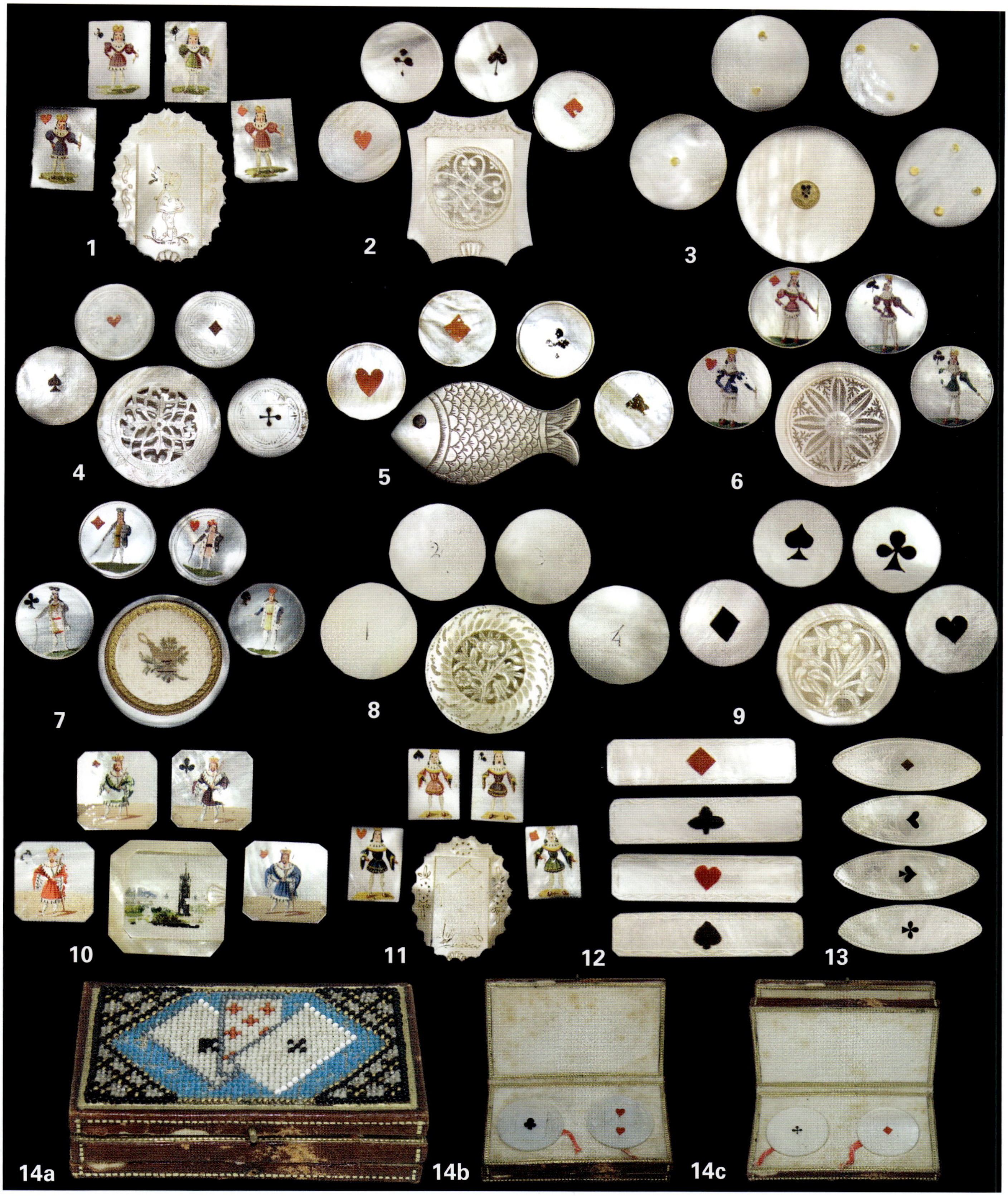


## PLATE 332 – LEISURE TIMES – WHIST MARKERS

Whist was a classic English card game that was played widely in the eighteenth and nineteenth centuries by everyone, including such famous leaders as Queen Victoria, Napoleon, and Benjamin Franklin. **1–11.** Whist markers in a pearl box, France, c. 1800–20. There are always four markers in a box. Some of these are marked with a card suite and a painting of kings, others are numbered 1 to 4, while others just have I to 4 dots. The boxes measure from 0.8" to 2" (2.1 to 5.2 cm) diameter. **12–13.** Make-Do whist markers, converted from gaming counters by addition (or cutting out) of the four card suites, the original gaming counters from China c. 1760–1800, converted in France or Europe, c. 1820, size 2.2" (5.7 cm). **14.** Whist markers in a bead covered box; box has two compartments, each holding 2 markers, France, c. 1800, size 2.8" x 1.6" (7 x 4 cm).

## PLATE 333 – LEISURE TIMES – GAMING COUNTER BOXES 1

**1a, 1b, 1c.** Gaming box for counters, China, c. 1830, box size 6.5″ x 4.9″ x 1.4″ (16.5 x 12.5 x 3.6 cm), contents 4 pearl boxes, each pearl box has an engraved card suite on the lid and should contain 140 counters in the 4 boxes, size 2.1″ x 2.8″ x 1″ (5.3 x 7.2 x 2.6 cm). **2a, 2b.** Gaming box, France, c. 1850–80, blank chips in 3 shapes with 2 game counters or markers, size 11.6″ x 9″ x 2″ (29.5 x 23 x 5 cm). **3a, 3b.** Gaming tray for counters, China, c. 1750–80, tray size 12.2″ x 10.2″ x 2″ (31 x 26 x 5 cm), contents 4 wood boxes, each 4.3″ x 3.4″ x 1.6″ (11 x 8.6 x 4 cm); should contain 140 counters.

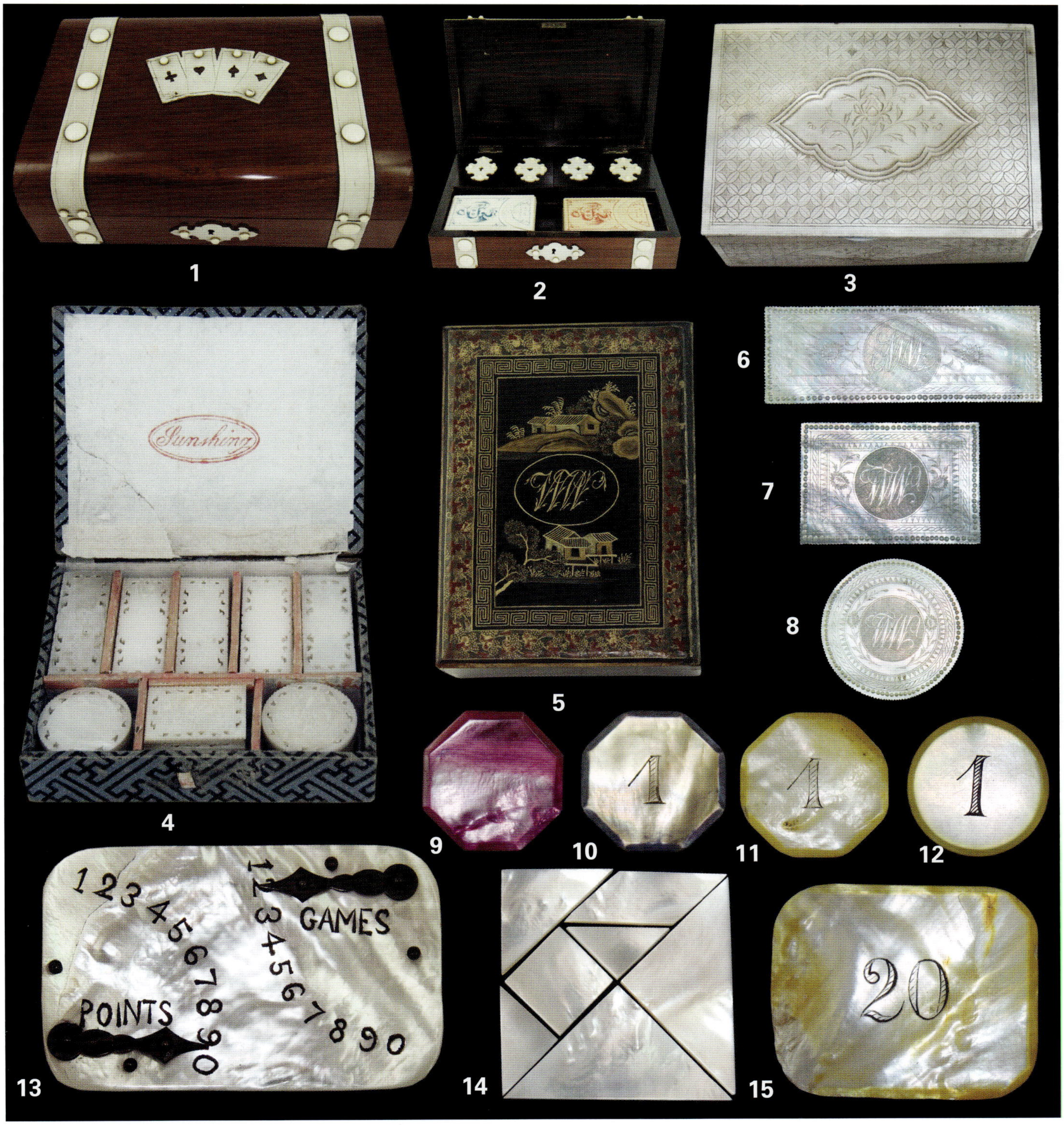


## PLATE 334 – LEISURE TIMES – GAMING COUNTER BOXES 2

1, 2. Gaming box, Europe and China, c. 1820, the box and cards came from Europe, while the counters came from China, size 10.2″ x 6.9″ x 1.2″ (26 x 17.5 x 7.5 cm); contents: 4 boxes which originally contained 140 pearl counters. 3. Gaming counter box, China, c. 1819–30, size 2.4″ x 1.7″ x 0.9″ (6.2 x 4.2 x 2.2) would have been a part of a set of 4 boxes, which contained gaming counters. 4. Gaming counter set, maker Sunshing (Hong Merchant in Canton), the set consists of 80 long oblong, 40 round, and 20 short oblong; total 140 counters, China, c. 1820, size of box 3.7″ x 3.1″ (9.5 x 8 cm). 5–8. Wealthy clients would order their monograms to be etched on the counters and the box. This box (would have been one of four boxes) measures 4.5″ x 3.3″ (11.5 x 8.5) and shows the monogram on the different shapes of counters, China, c. 1760–90, size 1.3″ to 2″ (3.4 to 5 cm). 9–12, 15. Gaming counters, dyed for different values, South America, first half of the twentieth century. 13. Game marker, helps keep game scores, England, c. 1880, size 2.4″ x 1.6″ (6 x 4 cm). 14. Tangram Geometric Silhouetting, a Chinese puzzle from c. 1850, where the pieces can be arranged in an infinite number of pictorial silhouettes, reproduction, size 2″ x 2″ (5 x 5 cm).

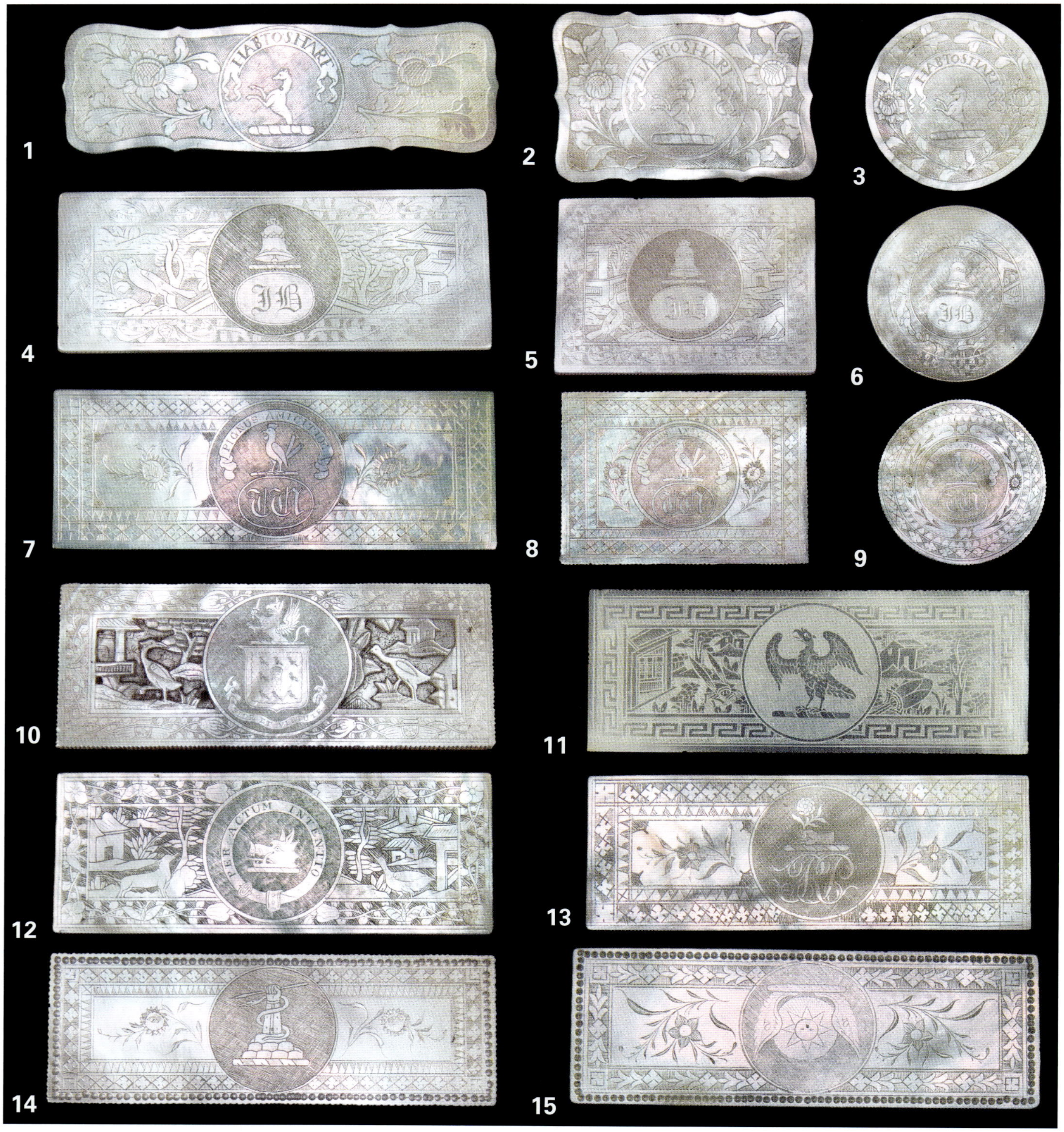


## PLATE 335 – LEISURE TIMES – GAMING COUNTERS 1

These are examples of armorial gaming counters, which where made in Canton. Some crests have not yet been identified with a family name. Cowan (see bibliography) estimates that between 1500–2000 armorial sets where made. **1–3.** Habtosharf family, China, c. 1810, long oblong 2.5″ x 0.8″ (6.3 x 2 cm), short oblong 1.5″ x 1″ (3.9 x 2.5 cm), round 1.3″ (3.2 cm) diameter. **4–6.** Bell, initials *JB*, China, c. 1800–30, size long oblong 2.5″ x 1″ (6.4 x 2.5 cm), short oblong 1.8″ x 1.2″ (4.5 x 3 cm), round 1.5″ (3.8 cm) diameter. **7–9.** Moore family, China, c. 1810, size long oblong 2.3″ x 0.8″ (5.9 x 2.1 cm), short oblong 1.5″ x 1.1″ (3.9 x 2.8 cm), round 1.3″ (3.4 cm) diameter. **10.** Dragon with sword crest, China, c. 1840, size 2.8″ x 1″ (7 x 2.6 cm). **11.** Eagle crest, China, c. 1810, size 2.6″ x 1″ (6.5 x 2.5 cm). **12.** Urquhart family, China, c. 1800, size 2,5″ x 0.9″ (6.4 x 2.3 cm). **13.** Hand holding a rose crest, China, c. 1810, size 2.3″ x 0.8″ (5.8 x 2.1 cm). **14.** Arm holding a spear, snake coiled around arm, China, c. 1810, size 2.4″ x 0.8″ (6.1 x 2.1 cm). **15.** Sun crest between wings, China, c. 1810, size 2.4″ x 0.8″ (6.1 x 2.1 cm).

1 2 3 4 5 6 7 8 9 10 11 12

## PLATE 336 – LEISURE TIMES – GAMING COUNTERS 2

The deep carved gaming counters from China are the most stunning of all counters. Each counter had a different scene and must have taken a considerable time to carve. **1–3.** Large sized range: long oblong 2.9" x 2.8" (7.4 x 7.1 cm) , short oblong 1.6" x 1.2" (4.2 x 3 cm), round 1.8" (4.5 cm) diameter, China, c. 1840. **4–6.** Medium sized range: long oblong 2.5" x 1" (6.4 x 2.5 cm), short oblong 1.7" x 1.2" (4.2 x 3 cm), round 1.4" (3.6 cm) diameter, China, c. 1840. **7–9.** Smaller sized range: long oblong 2.3" x 1" (5.8 x 2.5 cm), short oblong 1.3" x 1" (3.4 x 2.5 cm), round 1.4" (3.5 cm) diameter, China, c. 1840. **10–12.** Large fretted border: long oblong 2.6" x 1" (6.5 x 2.5 cm), short oblong 1.2" x 1.7" (3 x 4.3 cm), round 1.6" (4 cm), China, c. 1840.

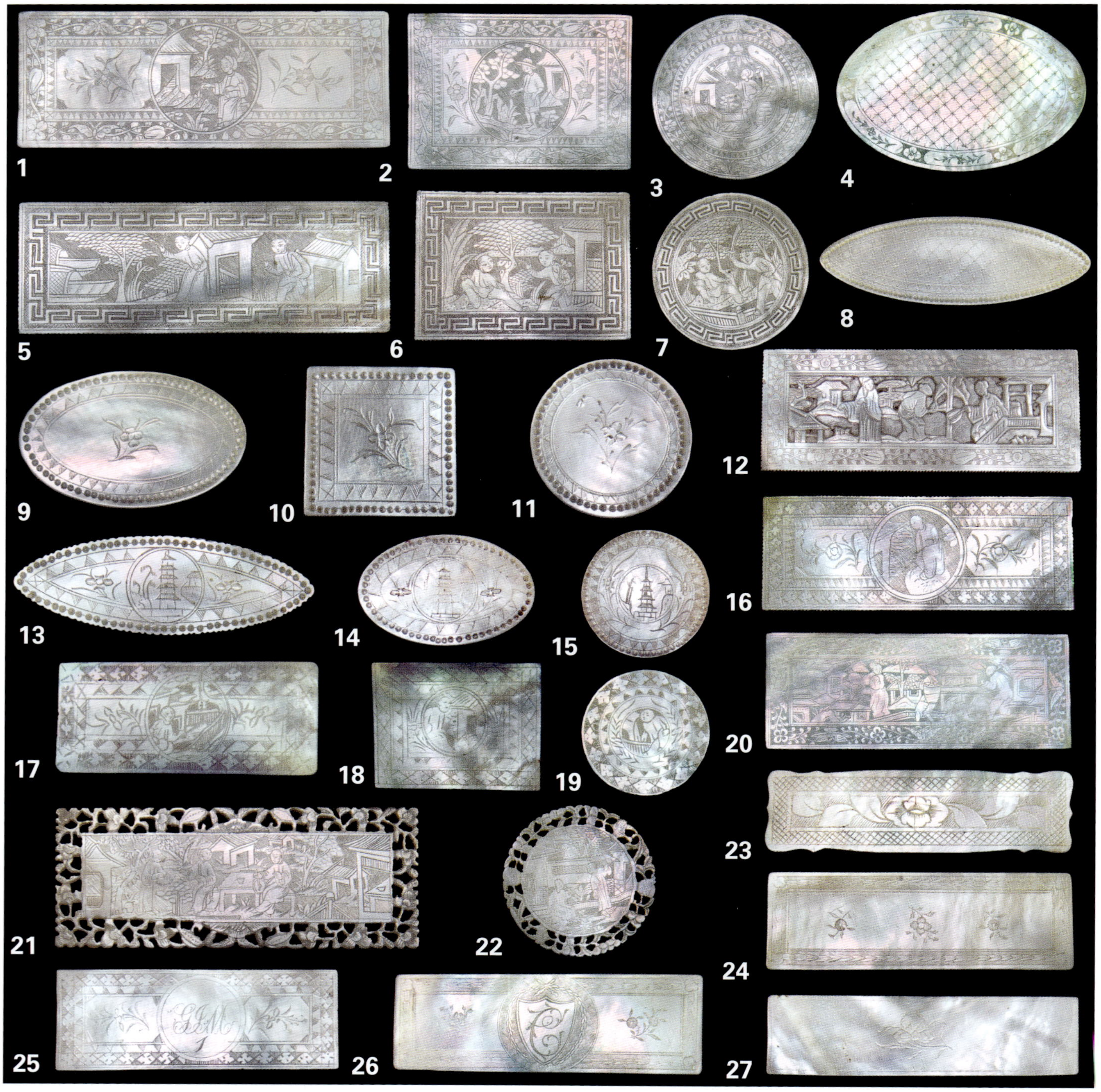

## PLATE 337 – LEISURE TIMES GAMING COUNTERS 3

1–3. Genre scenes, China, c. 1800, size long oblong 2.8" x 1.1" (7 x 2.7 cm), short oblong 1.9" x 1.4" (4.9 x 3.5 cm), round 1.5" (3.9 cm) diameter. 4. Oval, China, c. 1790, size 2.5" x 1.6" (6.3 x 4 cm). 5–7. Greek key border, China, c. 1785, size long oblong 2.3" x 0.9" (5.9 x 2.2 cm), short oblong 1.6" x 1.5" (4 x 3.7 cm), round 1.4" (3.5 cm) diameter. 8. Drilled border, China, c. 1760–1825, size 2.4" x 0.8" (6.1 x 2.1 cm). 9–11. Simple floral motif, China, c. 1810, size oval 1.2" x 0.8" (3.1 x 2 cm), square 0.7" x 0.7" (1.7 x 1.7 cm), round 0.8" (2 cm) diameter. 12. Deep carved, China, c. 1840, size 2.8" x 1" (7 x 2.6 cm). 13–15. Pagoda decoration, China, c. 1760–1825, size long oval 1.9" x 0.6" (4.7 x 1.6 cm), oval 1.4" x 0.9" (3.6 x 2.2 cm), round 1.1" (2.7 cm) diameter. 16. Detailed border, China, c. 1760–90, size 2.3" x 0.8" (5.9 x 2.1 cm). 17–19. Genre scenic, China, c. 1820, size long oblong 1.6" x 0.6" (4 x 1.6 cm), short oblong 1.1" x 0.8" (2.8 x 2 cm), round 1" (2.6 cm) diameter. 20. Genre scenes, China, c. 1810–20, size 2.5" x 0.9" (6.4 x 2.4 cm). 21–22. Large fretted border, China, c. 1840, size long oblong 2.7" x 1.1" (6.9 x 2.7 cm), round 1.7" (4.3 cm) diameter. 23. Wavy edge, China, c. 1750–70, size 2" x 0.6" (5.2 x 1.5 cm). 24. Long oblong, China, c. 1750–70, size 2.5" x 0.8" (6.4 x 2.1 cm). 25. Monogram *GJM,* China, c. 1770–80, size 2.2" x 0.8" (5.5 x 2 cm). 26. Initial *C*, China, c. 1750–70, size 2.5" x 0.8" (6.4 x 2.1 cm). 27. Simple floral motif, China, c. 1730–40, size 2" x 0.6" (5.2 x 1.5 cm).

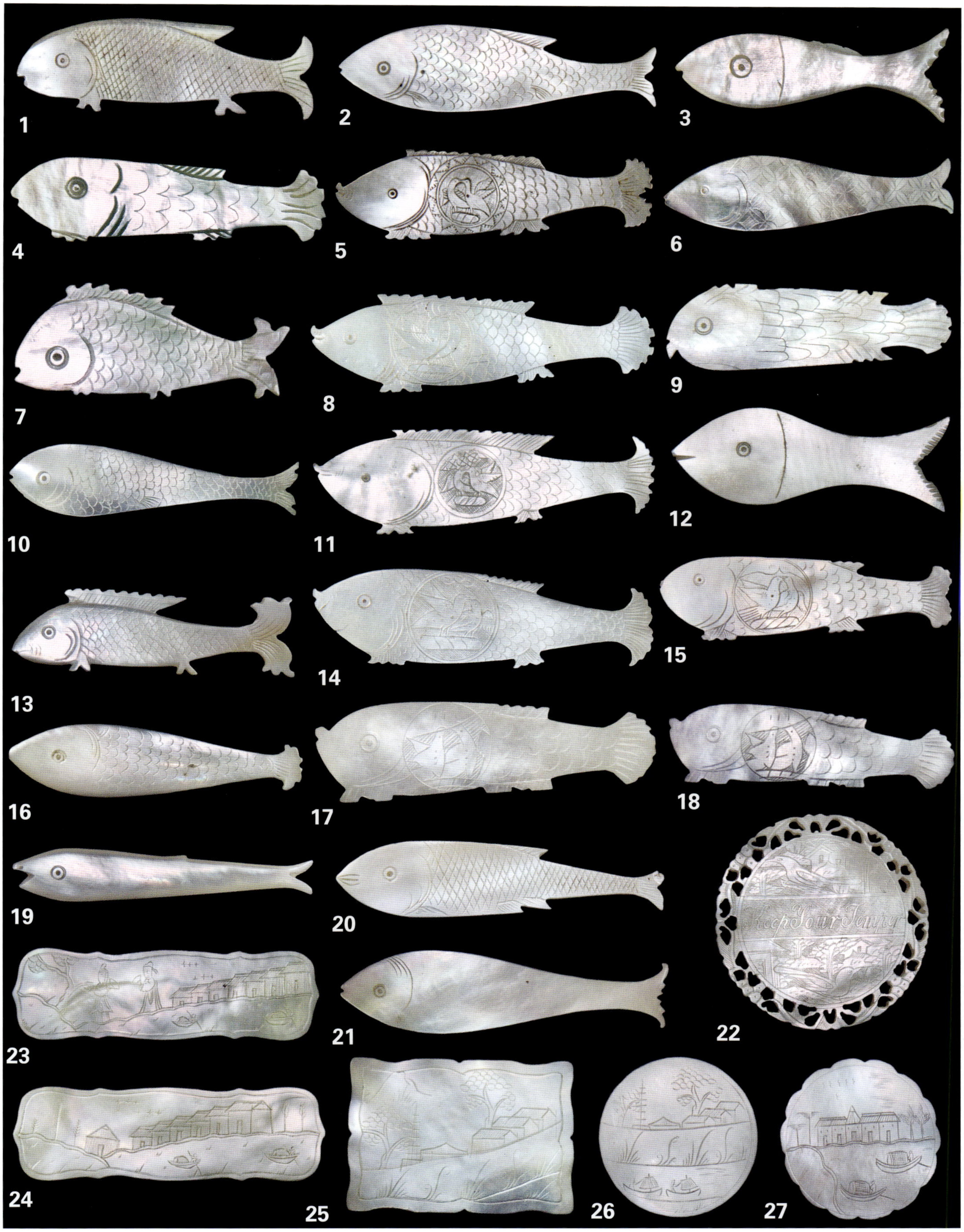


## PLATE 338 – LEISURE TIMES GAMING COUNTERS 4

**1–21.** Fish, China, c. 1740–1800, size 1.6″ to 2.7″ (4 cm to 6.9 cm), the large variety in designs is incredible. **22.** *Keep your temper*, China, c. 1820, size 1.5″ (3.7 cm) diameter. **23–27.** Hongs at Canton; Hongs are trading factories or merchant's premises in China under the Qing Government, China, c. 1745, size from 1.4″ to 1.5″ (3.5 cm to 3.9 cm).

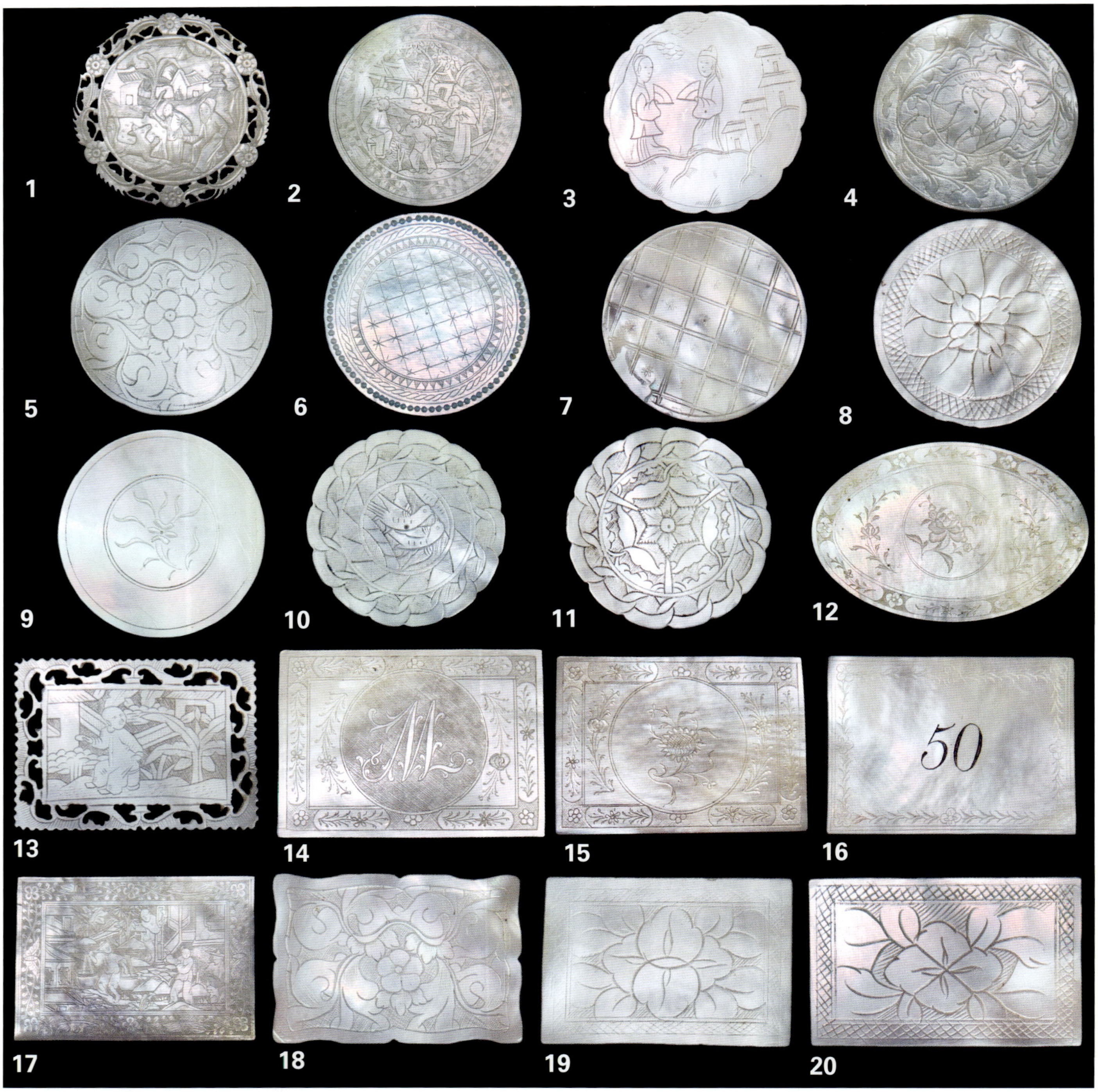


## PLATE 339 – LEISURE TIMES GAMING COUNTERS 5

The variety in these gaming counters is very large and many collectors specialize in collecting the different patterns. **1.** Fretted border, China, c. 1820, size 1.7″ (4.3 cm) diameter. **2.** Genre scene, China, c. 1800, size 1.5″ (3.9 cm diameter). **3.** Two people at the Hongs of Canton, China, c. 1745, size 1.2″ (3 cm). **4.** Two billing birds, China, c. 1760–90, size 1.3″ (3.3 cm) diameter. **5.** Flower, China, c. 1745, size 1.2″ (3 cm) diameter. **6.** Large diamond pattern, China, c. 1760–90, size 1.4″ (3.5 cm) diameter. **7.** Large diamond pattern, China, c. 1760–90, size 1.3″ (3.3 cm) diameter. **8.** Flower with crosshatched border, China, c. 1760–1825, size 1.1″ (2.7 cm) diameter. **9.** Flower, China, c. 1730–40, size 1″ (2.6 cm diameter). **10.** Bird, China, c. 1760–90, size 1.3″ (3.3 cm) diameter. **11.** Flower, China, c. 1750–70, size 1.3″ (3.3 cm) diameter. **12.** Oval, China, c. 1790, size 2.5″ x 1.6″ (6.3 x 4 cm). **13.** Small fretted scene, China, c. 1800–20, size 1.2″ x 0.9″ (3.1 x 2.2 cm). **14.** Monogram *M* or *W*, China, c. 1800, size 1.5″ x 1.1″ (3.9 x 2.8 cm). **15.** Simple floral decoration, China, c. 1800, size 1.5″ x 1.1″ (3.9 x 2.8 cm). **16.** Inscribed *50*, China, c. 1780, size 1.8″ x 1.3″ (4.6 x 3.4 cm). **17.** Genre scene, China, c. 1800, size 1.9″ x 1.4″ (4.9 x 3.5 cm). **18.** Wavy edge, China, c. 1745, size 1.5″ x 1.1″ (3.9 x 2.8 cm). **19.** Simple flower, China, c. 1730–40, size 1.2″ x 0.8″ (3 x 2 cm). **20.** Simple flower with crosshatched border, China, c. 1730–40, size 1.2″ x 0.8″ (3 x 2 cm).

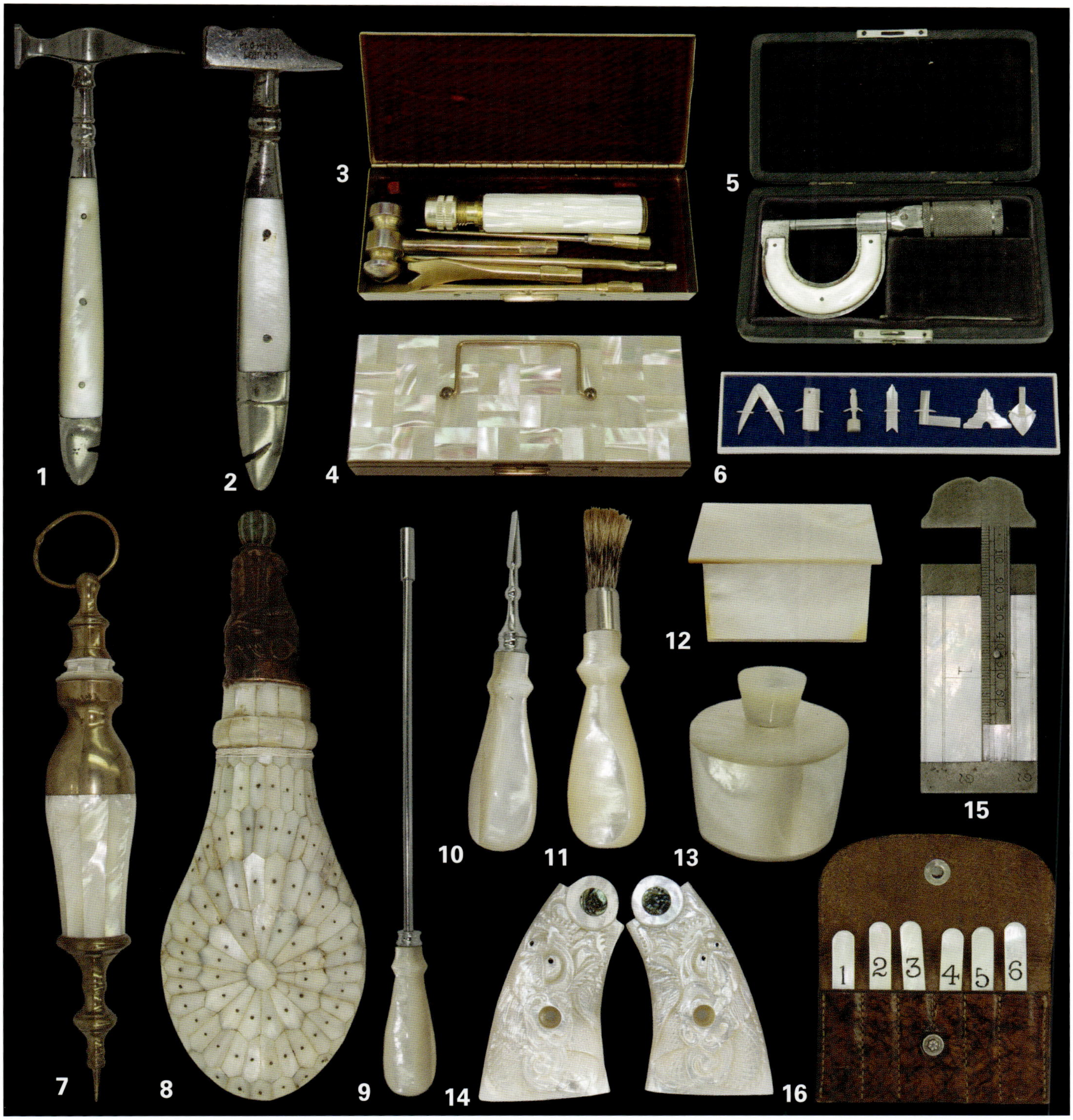


## PLATE 340 – LEISURE TIMES – TOOLS & GUN ACCESSORIES

1. Pearl handled hammer used for opening cigar boxes, maker Zwilling, Germany, c. 1879, size 6.5" (16.5 cm). 2. Pearl handled hammer, used for opening cigar boxes, maker Arnohubold, Leipzig, Germany, c. 1890–1900, size 4.5" (11.5 cm). 3 & 4. Lady's tool set, pearl covered box, pearl handle multi-tool, China, c. 1950, size 5.1" x 2.2" (13 x 5.5 cm). 5. Micrometer with pearl, England, c. 1880, size 4" x 1.8" (10.3 x 4.5 cm). 6. Masonic symbolic tools of the stone mason, USA, c. 1960, size 8.6" x 1.9" (22 x 4.8 cm). 7. Plumb bob, US, c. 1960, size 11.8" (30 cm). 8. Powder flask for gunpowder, India, c. 1930, size 9.7" x 3.3" (24.6 x 8.5 cm). 9–13. Colt handgun cleaning set made by Eagle, US, c. 1970, size rod 10.8" (27.5 cm), driver 5.1" (13 cm), brush 5.1" (13 cm), boxes for cleaning materials 1.7" to 3.2" (4.2 to 8.1 cm) 14. Colt hand gun grips, China, c. 1960, size 3" x 1.8" (7.5 x 4.5 cm), a retirement present given to a Chicago police officer. 15. Button measure: ligne measure of a button maker, likely from Birmingham, England, c. 1889, size 2.4" x 1" (6.2 x 2.6 cm). 16. Shooting peg markers numbered 1–6, England, c. 1900, size of each peg 1.8" x 0.3" (4.5 x 0.7 cm).

## PLATE 341 – LEISURE TIMES – CHESS AND COLLECTABLES

1. Chess board, Myanmar/Burma, c. 1990, open box, size 8″ x 8.1″ x 1″ (20.3 x 20.6 x 2.5 cm), folds in half. 2. Chess set, Japan, c. 1920, open size 11.8″ x 15″ x 1″ (30 x 38 x 2.5 cm), folds in half. 3. Cribbage board, England, c. 1890, size 10″ x 2.4″ x 0.4″ (25.5 x 6 x 1 cm). 4, 7. Cribbage board, England, c. 1880, open size 6.1″ x 3.3″ x 1.1″ (15.6 x 8.3 x 2.8 cm), folds in half. 5, 6. Pocket chess set, Vietnam, c. 1980, open box size 6.7″ x 6.5″ x 0.7″ (17 x 16.6 x 1.7 cm). 8. Save the whales coin series, with a mother-of-pearl carving, Tokelau, 2002, size 1.6″ (4 cm) diameter; there are 4 different coins in the series. 9, 10. Pearl box with 1965 proof set of coins from Jordan, box inscribed *Central Bank of Jordan,* 1965, size 4.5″ x 3.3″ (11.5 x 8.5 cm). 11. Fishing spoon or lure used to fish salmon in NW USA, c. 1950–60, size 1.6″ to 5.5″ (4 to 14 cm). 12. Fishing spoon or lure made from twine, horn, and pearl, South Pacific, c. 1890, size 3″ (7.8 cm). 13. Postal scale, likely a retirement gift to a postal worker, England, c. 1880–90, size 7.5″ x 5.1″ (19 x 13 cm). 14. Nuclei implanter: tool used for implanting nuclei in pearl oyster farming, China, c. 1980, size 4.8″ (12.3 cm).

CHAPTER 15

# Photographic

Mother-of-pearl plays a part in photographic collectibles when it comes to the decoration of the early photo cases and photo albums.

## DAGUERREOTYPE AND OTHER EARLY PROCESSES

With the discovery of Louis Daguerre's process of photography in 1839, there was huge interest in this subject, but the daguerreotype was easy to damage. The solution was to house these images in cases and soon the miniature case manufacturers were producing large numbers of these cases for this purpose. Mother-of-pearl (as well as other materials) was used as decoration in both inlay and veneer processes for boxes. The very best examples had a mother-of-pearl carving on the front.

## PHOTO ALBUMS

As photographic knowledge evolved, and it was possible to print photographs on paper, it was not long until photo albums were used to store pictures, along with comments to remind the owner of cherished memories.

Mother-of-pearl was used in covering the finest quality albums. It was found that different types of mother-of-pearl shells and different cuts produced different effects to appeal to buyers at that time. The albums came in different sizes, often with a fancy clasp to secure the covers and hold the contents safely.

For a brief period in the early twentieth century, small pocket albums fitted into metal cases were popular. Many of these albums had mother-of-pearl covers.

**Plate 342 – Photographic**

1. Photo album, England, c. 1885, size 11.8" x 9.3" (30 x 23.5 cm). Albums such as the one pictured here took considerable time and talent to inlay the many tiny pieces of mother-of-pearl.

## PLATE 343 – PHOTOGRAPHIC

**1a, 1b.** Photo album, England, c. 1870–95, size 11.8″ x 9.3″ (30 x 23.5 cm). **2.** Photo album, England, c. 1870–95, size 4.7″ x 5.7″ (12 x 14.5 cm). **3.** Photo album, England, c. 1870–95, size 8.3″ x 5.7″ (21 x 14.5 cm). **4.** Photo album, England, c. 1870–95, size 4.7″ x 5.9″ (12 x 15 cm). **5.** Photo holder, US, c. 1950, size 2.6″x 1.8″ (6.5 x 4.5 cm), holds 12 photos. **6.** Photo holder, US, c. 1950, size 2.4″x 2.8″ (6 x 7 cm); holds 2 photos. **7a, 7b.** Photo case, 6th plate daguerreotype, US, c. 1850, size 3.1″ x 3.7″ (8 x 9.5 cm). **8.** Daguerreotype, 16th plate, US, c. 1850, size 2″ x 1.7″ (5 x 4.3 cm). **9.** Photo case, 6th plate daguerreotype, US, c. 1850, size 3.3″ x 3.7″ (8.5 x 9.5 cm). **10a, 10b.** Photo case, 9th plate tin type, US, c. 1860, size 3.1″ x 2.6″ (8 x 6.5 cm). **11.** Photo case, 6th plate, US, c. 1860, size 4.3″ x 3.5″ (11 x 9 cm). **12.** Photo case, France, c. 1850, size 3.4″ x 3″ (8.7 x 7.5 cm).

CHAPTER 16

# Housewares

Shell was first used in society in a strictly functional way. Shells were used in exchange for goods or services. They were used as an early form of money. Shells also were used as utensils and as containers for food. The shell has always held a significant place within man's day-to-day life. As society developed, so did humanity's penchant for the creation of beauty, the human appreciation of art. Craftspeople showed their talents with the carving and etching of natural materials. Mother-of-pearl was valued wherever it was available, and tradesmen found ways early on to import/export pearl along the trade routes. The Victorian era saw a serious growth in the popularity of pearl pieces. It was only natural that it came to be fashioned into functional household pieces, with elaborate artistry on pieces made for the wealthy classes.

It was often difficult to acquire a large enough single piece of flat pearl for the purpose of making an entire fork, knife, spoon, or other utensil. Therefore, pearl was often used as handles only and then set with a metal or silver tine stem, knife blade, spoon bed, or other piece that was more long lasting. A large industry developed in Sheffield and Birmingham, UK, which supplied pearl handled flatware worldwide. France also manufactured pearl flatware, to a lesser degree.

Plates of carved mother-of-pearl were popular in Europe for serving caviar. Pearl was one of the few natural materials that didn't react to caviar.

So popular was carved mother-of-pearl, its use spread to the manufacture of all sorts of functional household pieces. During the nineteenth and twentieth centuries, candlestick holders, candle shades, individual salts, master salts and pepper pots, and also salt and pepper sets, household bells, along with a myriad of other things, were manufactured widely and sold well. Mother-of-pearl retained its popularity well into the twentieth century for housewares, especially pieces designed for the tourist trade. Many are the pearl gifts brought home from travels abroad, to be used within the home.

Sadly, the end of the twentieth century brought a shortage of raw mother-of-pearl. Thailand and the Philippines, both having easy access to raw mother-of-pearl, were the main producers still supplying souvenir housewares.

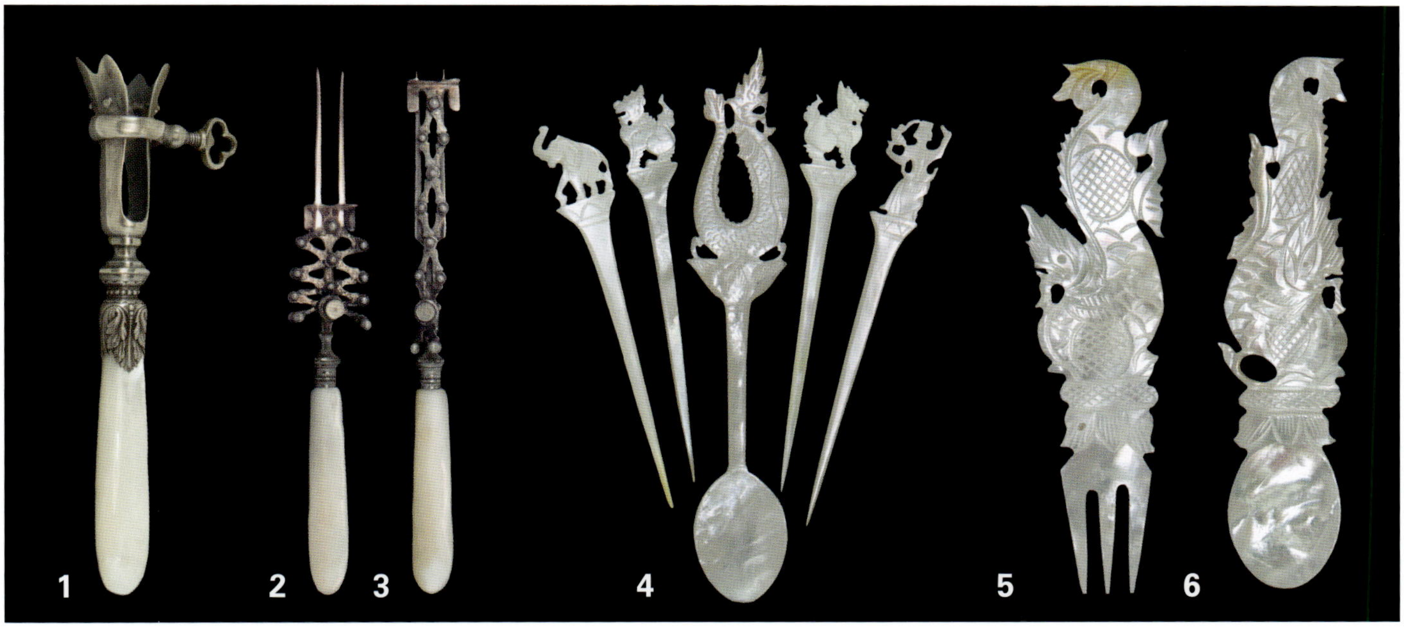


**PLATE 344 – HOUSEWARES**

1. Drum stick holder, France, c. 1890–1905, size 8.3" (21 cm). 2–3. Meat fork, England, c. 1870, size 7.7" (19.5 cm), handle pushes meat off the fork when required. 4. Dragon spoon and *Hors d'Oeuvre* picks, Myanmar/Burma, c. 1920, size spoon 6.3" (16 cm), picks 3.7" (9.5 cm). 5–6. Dragon fork and spoon, Thailand, c. 1996, size 4.1" (10.5 cm).

## PLATE 345 – TEA CADDIES AND TEA SETS, HOUSEWARES

Tea was an expensive commodity in the early days and the supply was locked up in a special box called a tea caddy. Many designs of these caddies have been made with mother-of-pearl, but they are hard to find and very costly. **1.** A marvelous tea set, Thailand, c. 1996, made entirely from the brown lip mother-of-pearl shell; the set consists of a tray size 8.7" (22 cm) diameter, a teapot, size 7.5" x 7.5" x 2.2" (19 x 19 x 5.5 cm), and 5 cups size 2.2" x 2.1" (5.5 x 5.4 cm). **2a, 2b.** Tea caddy with two lead lined compartments, pagoda shape, England, c. 1820, size 5.1" x 5.1" x 3.1" (13 x 13 x 8 cm). **3a, 3b.** Tea caddy, single compartment, Philippines, 2004, reproduction of an early nineteenth century example, size 7.5" x 6.7" x 5.1" (19 x 17 x 13 cm). **4.** Miniature tea pot, India, c. 1970, size 3.9" x 3.9" (10 x 10 cm). **5.** Tea caddy made with brown lip mother-of-pearl, apple shape, France, c. 1950, reproduction of an eighteenth century example, which would have been made out of wood, extra large size 11" x 9.4" x 9.4" (28 x 24 x 24 cm). **6.** Tea Caddy in white mother-of-pearl, apple shape, France, c. 1950, reproduction of an eighteenth century example, which would have been made out of wood, size 6.7" x 5.1" x 5.1" (17 x 13.5 x 13.5 cm).

## PLATE 346 – PICNIC and TEA SETS, HOUSEWARES

1. Picnic set, consisting of 6 cups and saucers, 6 tea spoons, and a shell holder to hold the spoons or napkins, all packed in a picnic box, Italy, c. 1950, size 17.3″ x 12.2″ (44 x 31 cm). 2. Tea set, Italy, c. 1960, consisting of 6 cups, size 1.7″ diameter x 2.8″ (4.4 x 7 cm), 6 saucers, size 4.1″ diameter (10.5 cm), 6 spoons size 3.9″ (10 cm), and a shell holder for spoons and napkins, size 4.7″ x 4.9″ x 3.4″ (12 x 12.5 x 8.7 cm). 3–4. Picture frames, Philippines, c. 1997, size 9″ x 7.1″ (23 x 18 cm). 5. Goblet set, made from the trocha shell, Italy, c. 1980, size 3.9″ (10 cm) high. 6–7. Vases, Thailand, c. 1996, size 7.3″ x 3.5″ (18.5 x 9 cm). 8. Vase, Indonesia, c. 2000, size 8.1″ diameter x 5.1″ (20.5 x 13 cm). 9. Vase, India, c. 1980, size 10.6″ diameter x 4.7″ (27 x 12 cm). 10. Vase, US, c. 1950, size 4.9″ x 3.7″ x 3.9″ (12.5 x 9.5 x 10 cm).

## PLATE 347 – RADIO, LAMP, and TRINKET BOWLS

**1.** General Electric tube radio model 512F with mother-of-pearl veneer, US, c. 1951, size 10.6″ x 6.5″ x 5.5″ (27 x 16.5 x 14 cm), only 6 mother-of-pearl examples are known that were made for awards to the six top G.E. salesmen. **2.** Lamp, England, c. 1900, size 11.4″ (29 cm), with a light in the turban shell. **3.** Decorative bowl, has many uses in the home for vanity, sewing, etc., France, c. 1898–1905, size 10″ x 6.7″ x 3.1″ (25.5 x 17 x 8 cm). **4.** Trinket bowl, France, c. 1880–90, size 5.5″ x 3.3″ x 4.9″ (14 x 8.5 x 12.5 cm). **5.** Decorative plate or tray, England, c. 1900, size 6.3″ x 6.1″ (16 x 15.5 cm). **6.** Decorative bowl or dish, England, c. 1860–80, size 9.8″ (25 cm).

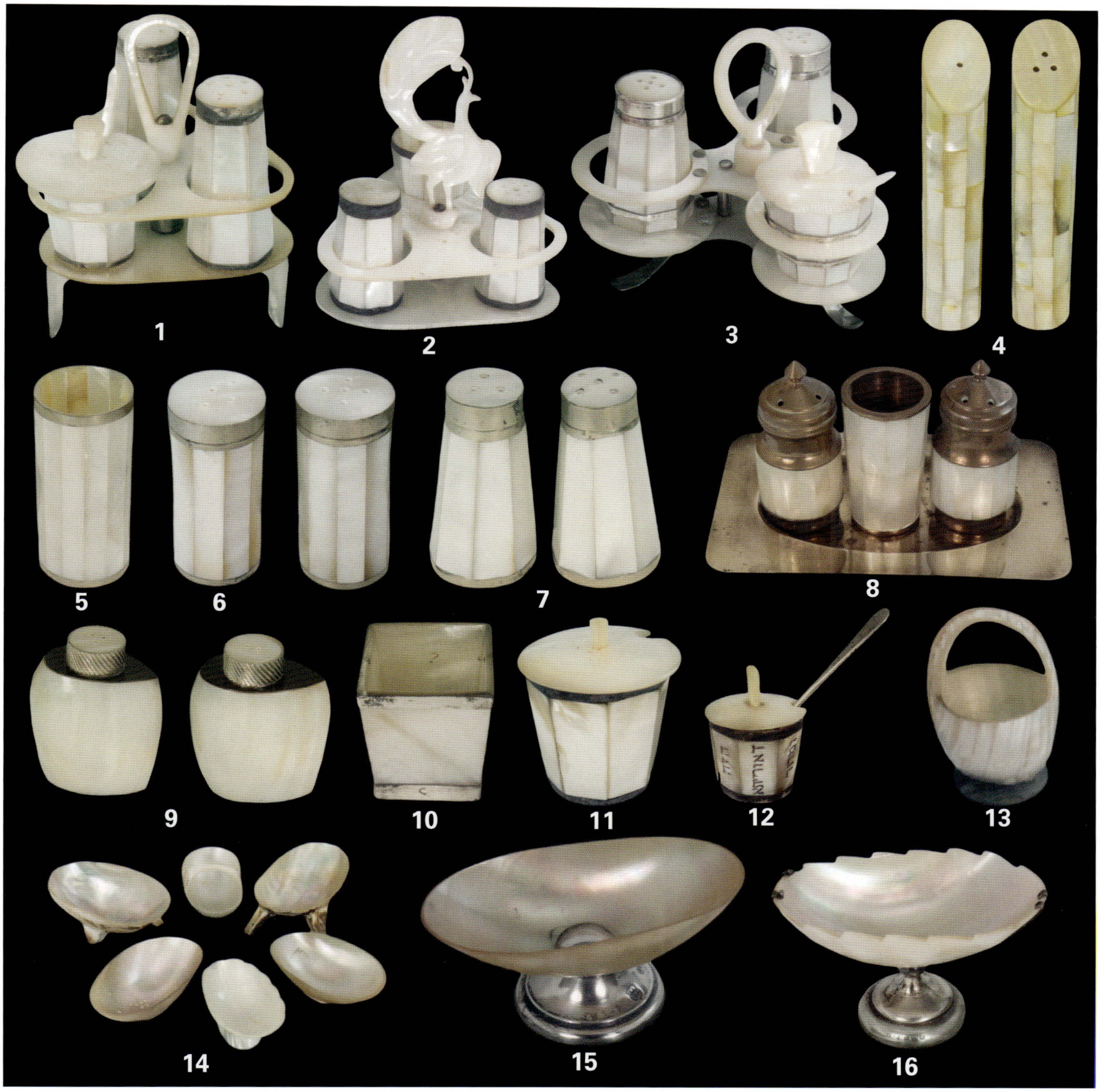


## PLATE 348 – SALT, PEPPER, AND CONDIMENT SETS

1. Condiment set, includes salt, pepper, mustard, Thailand, c. 1950–60, size 4.3″ x 2.4″ (11 x 6 cm). 2. Condiment set with peacock center, includes salt, pepper, mustard, Thailand, c. 1950–60, size 5.1″ x 3.5″ (13 x 9 cm). 3. Condiment set, consisting of salt, pepper, mustard, Thailand, c. 1950–60, size 4.3″ x 3.9″ (11 x 10 cm). 4. Salt and pepper, Thailand, c. 2005, size 4.7″ x 1″ (12 x 2.5 cm). 5. Toothpick holder, Thailand, c. 2003, size 2.4″ x 1.2″ (6 x 3 cm). 6. Salt and pepper, Thailand, c. 1996, size 2″ x 1″ (5.2 x 2.5 cm). 7. Salt and pepper, Thailand, c. 1995, size 2.4″ x 0.8″ (6 x 2 cm). 8. Condiment set, consisting of salt, pepper, toothpick holder, India, c. 1980, size 4.5″ x 2.8″ (11.5 x 7.2 cm). 9. Salt and pepper, India, c. 2000, size 2″ x 2.4″ (5 x 6 cm). 10. Master salt pot with silver banding, England, c. 1900, size 1.6″ x 1.8″ (4 x 4.5 cm). 11. Mustard pot with silver banding, England, c. 1920, size 2″ diameter x 2.2″ (5 x 5.5 cm). 12. Marrow container with old style Jewish script, Jerusalem, c. 1900, size 2″ diameter x 1.6″ (5 x 4 cm), the lid has a gap for the marrow spoon. 13. Open salt, England, c. 1920, size 2″ x 1.2″ (5 x 3 cm). 14. Open salts, England, c. 1920, size 1.8″ to 3.1″ (4.5 to 8 cm). 15. Master salt, sterling silver hallmarked Birmingham, England, 1907, size 2.8″ x 1.6″ (7 x 4 cm). 16. Master salt with sterling silver base hallmarked Birmingham, England, 1906, size 3.9″ x 2.4″ (10 x 6 cm).

## PLATE 349 – CAVIAR PLATES

Mother-of-pearl plates and utensils are the number one choice for serving caviar, as the pearl does not react with the caviar. Both sterling silver and stainless steel affect the caviar's fragile flavor. The caviar plates were supplied in sets of matching patterns, but few of these complete sets survived. We must be content with the single plates that are seen from time to time. Sizes for round plates are the diameter. 1. An unusual pierced design, Europe, c. 1890, size 5.7″ (14.5 cm). 2. Beautifully engraved with a central scene of a fisherman and a sail boat, Europe, c. 1875, size 7.2″ (18.5 cm). 3. Europe, c. 1880, size 6.7″ (17 cm). 4. Pierced edging, Europe, c. 1890, size 7.1″ x 5.5″ (18 x 14 cm). 5. Europe, c. 1890, size 7.1″ x 5.9″ (18 x 15 cm). 6. Europe, c. 1890, size 4.9″ (12.5 cm). 7. Europe, c. 1890, size 8.1″ x 5.5″ (20.5 x 14 cm). 8. Europe, c. 1890, size 6.3″ (16 cm). 9. Europe, c. 1890, size 5.1″ x 3.9″ (13 x 10 cm). 10. Europe, c. 1870, size 6.3″ (16 cm). 11. Europe, c. 1880, size 6.7″ (17 cm). 12. Europe, c. 1880, size 6.7″ (17 cm). 13. Europe, c. 1890, size 4.9″ (12.5 cm).

## PLATE 350 – TRINKET BOWLS AND DISHES

1. Washstand dish for soaps, vanity, US, c. 1950, size 5.1″ x 3.9″ x 2.8″ (13 x 10 x 7 cm). 2. Nut dish, US, c. 1950, size 4.3″ x 6.3″ x 3″ (11 x 16 x 7.5 cm). 3. Master salt, England, c. 1880, size 6.3″ x 3.5″ x 2.4″ (16 x 8.8 x 6 cm). 4. Trinket dish, inscribed Newport, Rhode Island, USA, c. 1950–60, size 5.5″ x 4.3″ x 4.1″ (14 x 11 x 10.5 cm). 5. Trinket dish, inscribed *Block Island*, Rhode Island, US, c. 1950, size 4.5″ x 2.4″ x 2″ (11.5 x 6 x 5 cm). 6. Trinket dish, US, c. 1950–60, size 3.3″ x 2″ x 0.9″ (8.5 x 5.1 x 2.2 cm). 7. Trinket dish with bird carving, US, c. 1950–60, size 4.1″ x 3.1″ x 2.6″ (10.5 x 8 x 6.5 cm). 8. Trinket dish, US, c. 1950–60, size 5.3″ x 2.4″ x 4.7″ (13.5 x 6 x 12 cm). 9. Trinket basket cut from a turban shell, England, c. 1900, size 6.9″ x 3.7″ x 3.3″ (17.5 x 9.5 x 8.5 cm). 10. Trinket dish made from a turban shell, England, c. 1920, size 4.3″ x 2.6″ x 1.4″ (11 x 6.5 x 3.5 cm). 11. Trinket dish in shape of a leaf, US, c. 1950–60, size 3.9″ x 2.4″ x 1.2″ (10 x 6 x 3 cm). 12. Trinket dish with dog and space needle from Seattle World's Fair, US, c. 1962, size 2.8″ x 2.4″ (7 x 6 cm). 13. Decorative plate, Myanmar/Burma, c. 1996, size 4.1″ x 6.7″ (10.5 x 17 cm). 14. Decorative plate, Myanmar/Burma, c. 1996, size 6.9″ x 5.7″ (17.5 x 14.5 cm). 15. Fish plates, illustrating 1 of a set of 6, made by Rex, Japan, c. 1970, size 5.5 x 3.5″ (14 x 9 cm). 16. Footed plate, mimicking a Victorian visiting card holder, England, c. 1950, size 4.7″ (12 cm) diameter. 17. Snack plate, Myanmar/Burma, c. 1996, size 5.7″ (14.5 cm) diameter. 18. Snack plate, Myanmar/Burma, c. 1996, size 5.9″ (15 cm) diameter. 19. Snack plate, Myanmar/Burma, c. 1996, size 5.9″ (15 cm) diameter. 20. Snack plate, Myanmar/Burma, c. 1996, size 5.5″ (14 cm) diameter. 21. Caviar plate, Europe, c. 1880, size 4.9″ (12.5 cm) diameter.

## PLATE 351 – HOUSEWARES

1a, 1b. An exceptional ornamental plate: The stand was likely made in China, while the carving was created in Austria, France, or Germany, c. 1880, size 9.4″ x 8.5″ (24 x 21.5 cm). 2a, 2b. Bonbonniere for holding treasures such as sugar candy, France, c. 1810, size 3.4″ x 2″ (8.7 x 5.2 cm). 3. Decorative plate with kneeling French Guard, France, c. 1900, size 6.2″ x 5.5″ (15.8 x 14 cm). 4. Book or Bible stand, Thailand, c. 1990, size 10.2″ x 5.9″ x 5.5″ (26 x 15 x 14 cm). 5. Occasional table, Thailand, c. 2000, size 12.2″ x 11.2″ x 11.2″ (31 x 28.5 x 28.5 cm).

## PLATE 352 – TRAYS and PLATES

This plate illustrates the wide range of effects that can be achieved by overlaying the mother-of-pearl pieces in different patterns. These trays were produced only in small numbers, often to a specific order. They are graphic testament to the artistic ability of the craftsman. Items 1–5 are all from Myanmar/Burma. 1. c. 1996, size 17.7″ x 11.1″ (45 x 28.3 cm). 2. c. 1996, size 17.7″ x 11.1″ (45 x 28.3 cm). 3. c. 1996, size 17.7″ x 11.1″ (45 x 28.3 cm). 4. c. 1998, size 13.7″ x 11″ (35 x 28 cm). 5. c. 1996, size 17.7″ x 11.1″ (45 x 28.3 cm). 6. Tray with overlay of the awabi abalone, France, c. 1900–20, size 9.4″ x 7.4″ (24 x 18.8 cm). 7. Cebu, Philippine Islands, c. 2003, size 17.3″ x 16.1″ (44 x 41 cm). 8. Decorative plate, Myanmar/Burma, c. 1996, size 9.6″ (24.5 cm) diameter. 9. Cebu, Philippine Islands, c. 2003, size 12.2″ x 12.2″ (31 x 31 cm). 10. Decorative plate, Myanmar/Burma, c. 1996, size 9.6″ (24.5 cm) diameter. 11. Decorative plate, Myanmar/Burma, c. 1996, size 9.6″ (24.5 cm) diameter. 12. Decorative plate, Myanmar/Burma, c. 1996, size 7″ (17.8 cm) diameter. 13. Kitchen hanger, *Souvenir of Le Creport,* France, c. 1900–20, size 7″ x 11.4″ (17.8 x 29 cm).

## PLATE 353 – CANDLEHOLDERS and SNUFFERS

Nowadays we forget how important candles were to our ancestors who did not have electricity. There were huge volumes of candleholders made, but only a few have been found made in mother-of-pearl. In certain countries they are called a chamber stick or candle stick. **1.** An exceptional candleholder, France, c. 1860, it has an intricate pierced border, etched plate and a handle in the shape of a swan, size 6.3" x 4.7" (16 x 12 cm). **2.** Candleholder, Thailand, c. 1996, size 10" x 2.4" (25.5 x 6 cm). **3.** Mini candleholder, France, c. 1870–90, size 3" x 2" (7.5 x 5 cm). **4.** Candleholder, inscribed *Souvenir Aracachon*, made from black lip pearl oyster, France, c. 1890–1900, size 4.3" x 4.3" (11 x 11 cm). **5.** Candleholder, made from the turban shell, France, c. 1880–1890, size 5.9" x 3.1" (15 x 8 cm). **6.** Candleholder, England, c. 1850–75, size 6.5" x 8.3" (16.5 x 21 cm). **7.** Candleholder in the shape of a flower, France, c. 1890, size 3.9" x 2.4" (10 x 6 cm). **8.** Candlesticks, Thailand, c. 1996, size 10" x 2.8" x 2.8" (25.5 x 7 x 7 cm). **9.** Candle snuffer, India, c. 1990, size 12.2" (31 cm). **10.** Candle snuffer, England, c. 1910, size 9.4" (24 cm).

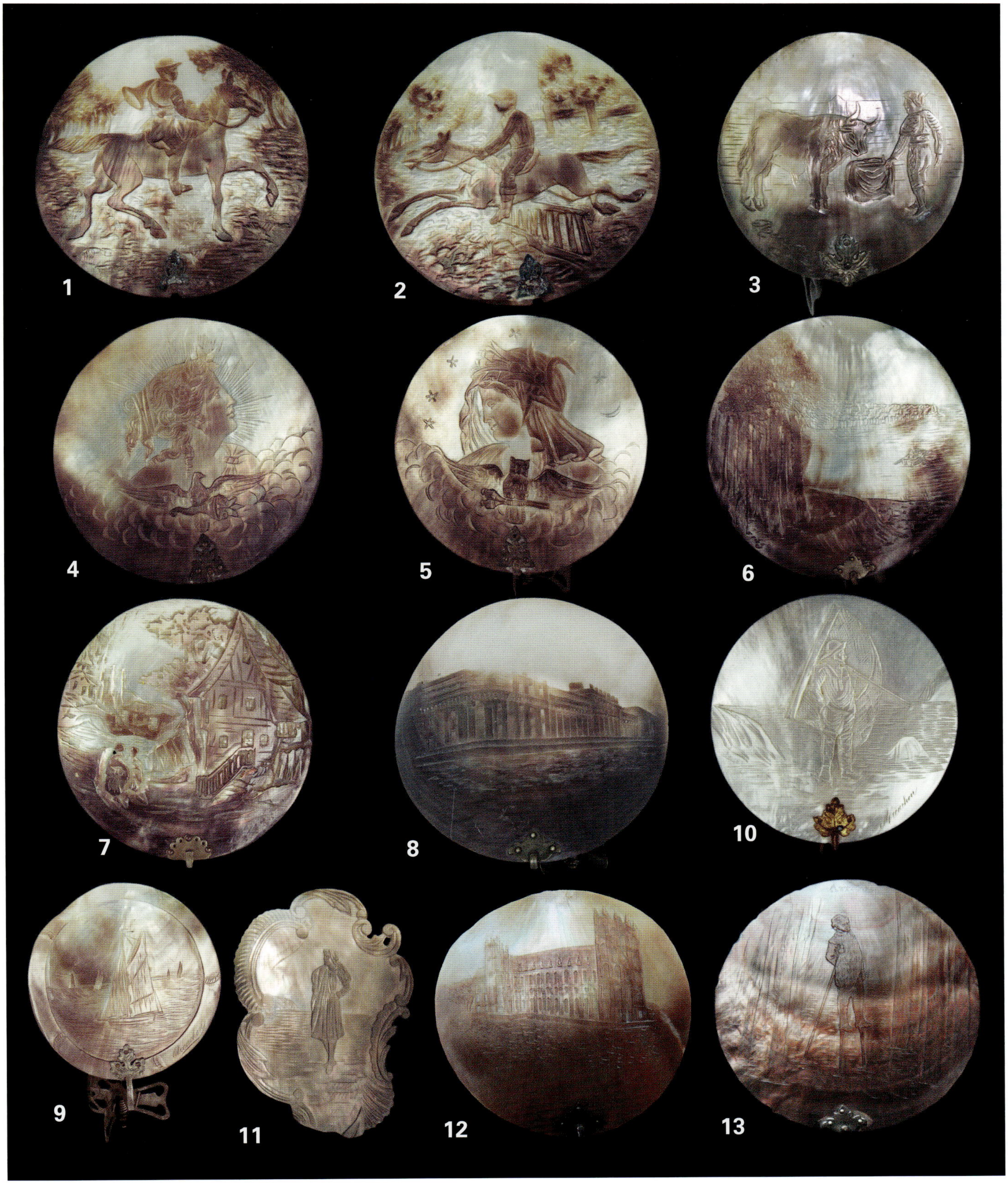

## PLATE 354 – CANDLE SHADES

1. Huntsman on horse, France, c. 1880, size 4.3" (11 cm) diameter. 2. Huntsman on horse, France, c. 1880, size 4.3" (11 cm) diameter. 3. Bull fighting, France, c. 1890, size 3.3" (8.5 cm). 4. Lady's head, France, c. 1880, size 3.7" (9.5 cm) diameter. 5. Lady's head, France, c. 1880, size 3.7" (9.5 cm) diameter. 6. Forest scene, inscribed *Aracachon*, France, c. 1900, size 4.5" (11.5 cm). 7. House scene, France, c. 1890, size 3.5" (9 cm). 8. Building in France, c. 1890, size 4.1" (10.5 cm). 9. Sailboat, inscribed *Aracachon*, France, c. 1900, size 3.1" (8 cm). 10. Fisherman, inscribed *Aracachon,* France, c. 1890–1900, size 3.5" (9 cm). 11. Fisherwoman, inscribed *Scheveningen*, Netherlands, c. 1890, size 3.9" x 3.1" (10 x 8 cm). 12. A carving of an unidentified French building, France, c. 1880, size 4.2" x 3.9" (10.7 x 10 cm). 13. Inscribed *Arcachon*, with a carving of a French shepherd on stilts, helping them tend their sheep in a boggy countryside, France, c. 1880, size 4.5" x 4.5" (11.5 x 11.5 cm).

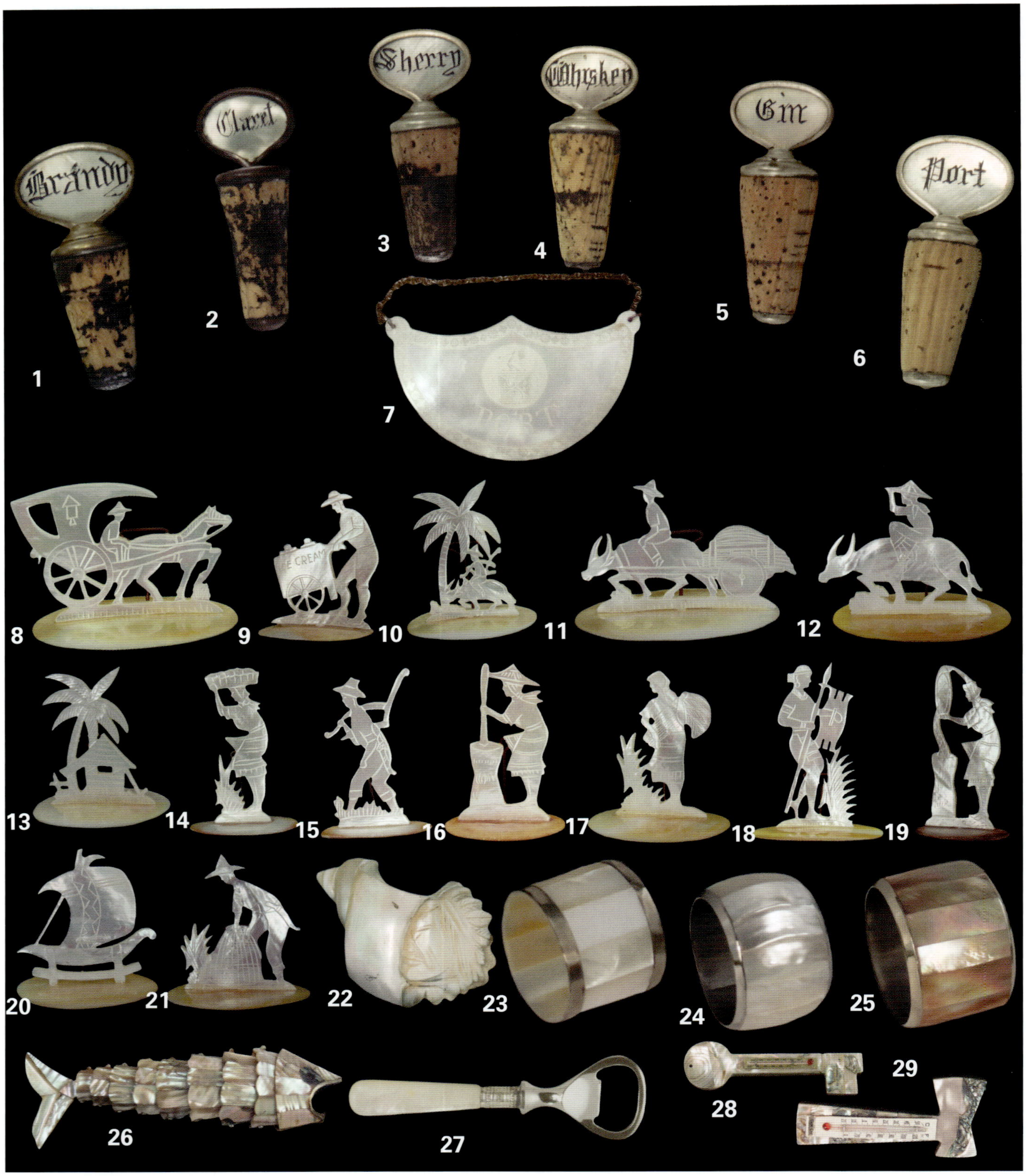


## PLATE 355 – BOTTLE STOPPERS, LABELS, and NAPKIN HOLDERS

1–6. Six bottle stoppers, England, c. 1910–20, size 3.1″ (8 cm). 7. Port bottle label, France, c. 1810, made for the English market, size 2.8″ (7 cm). 8–21. Napkin holders, Philippines, c. 1950, various designs and sizes from 2.4″ x 1.6″ x 3.1″ (6 x 4 x 8 cm). There is a metal stand behind the carving to hold the napkin. 22. Napkin holder, Native American head, US, c. 1900, size 3.5″ x 2.2″ (9 x 5.5 cm). 23. Napkin holder (part of set of 6), Thailand, c. 1970, size 1.5″ (3.7 cm). 24. Napkin holder (part of set of 6), Cebu, Philippine Islands, c. 1996, size 1.8″ (4.5 cm). 25. Napkin holder (part of set of 6), Cebu, Philippine Islands, c. 1997, size 1.7″ (4.3 cm). 26. Articulated fish bottle opener, US, c. 1950, size 5.9″ (15 cm). 27. Bottle opener, US, c. 1960, showing how easy it is to be fooled: this is a new top on an old tableware handle, size 4.7″ (12 cm). 28. Thermometer, *Souvenir of San Diego*, USA, c. 1910–20, size 5.1″ x 1.2″ (13 x 3 cm). 29. Thermometer, *Souvenir of Cape Cod,* US, c. 1910–20, size 3.7″ x 1.8″ (9.5 x 4.5 cm).

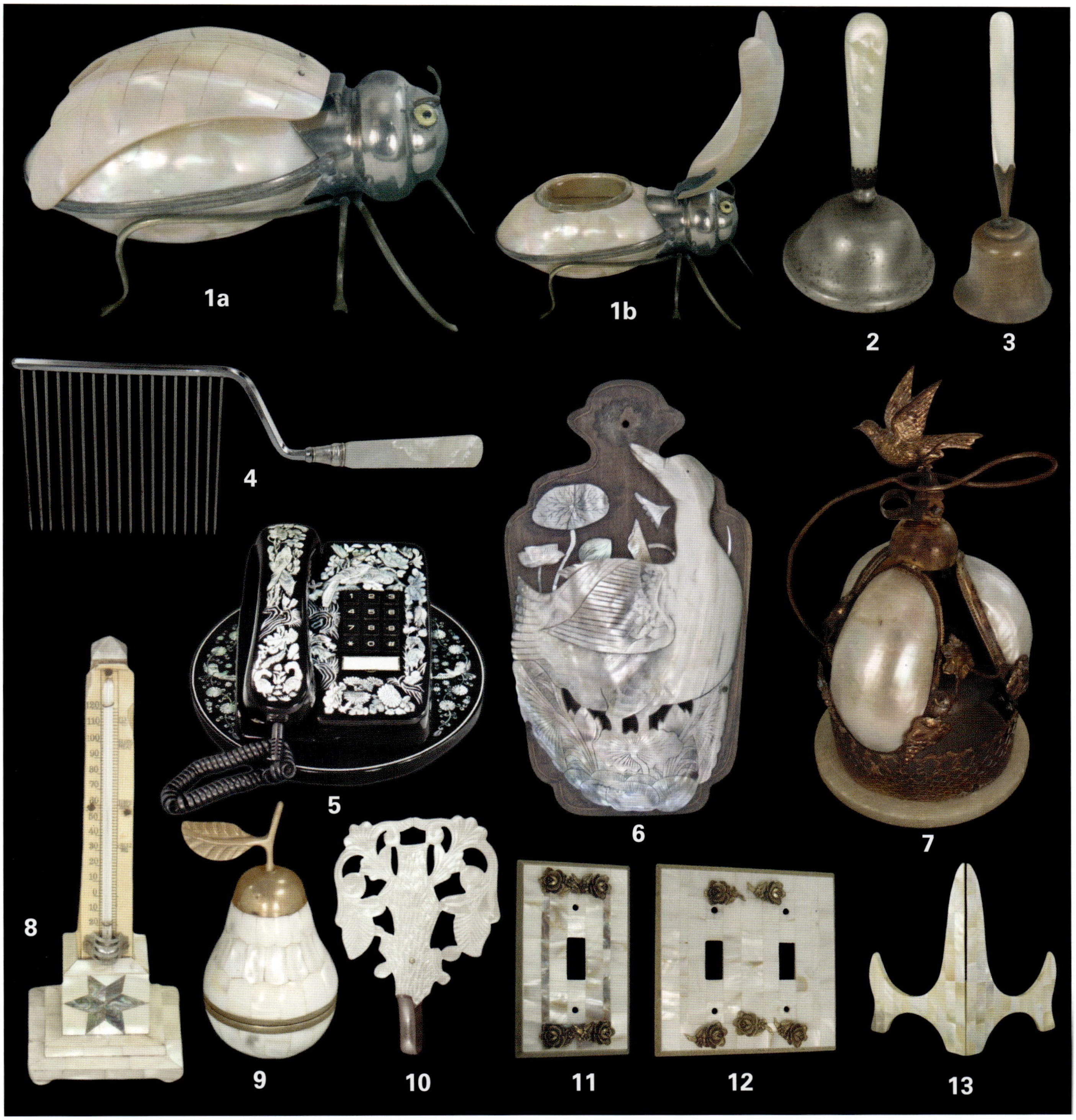


## PLATE 356 – BELLS, NAPKIN HOLDERS, SERVERS

**1a & 1b.** An unusual master salt in the shape of a bee, the wings lift up to reveal the hidden salt pot, maker Mustershultz, Germany, c. 1879, size 5.1" x 2.6" (13 x 6.6 cm). **2.** Table bell, US, c. 1900, size 3.3" (8.5 cm). **3.** Table bell, US, c. 1900, size 4.7" (12 cm). **4.** Cake breaker, sterling, John Hasselbring, Brooklyn, US, c. 1950, size 10.4" x 3.8" (26.5 x 9.8 cm). **5.** Telephone with pearl inlay of birds and flowers, Vietnam, c. 1950, size 9.8" x 9.8"x 6.2" (25 x 25 x 16 cm). **6.** Duck letter or note holder, Vietnam, c. 1940, size 5.1" x 9" (13 x 23 cm). **7.** Hotel bell from a reception desk, France, c. 1850–70, size 6.3" x 3.1" diameter (16 x 8 cm). **8.** Thermometer on an Obelisk, made during the height of popularity of Egyptian artifacts after the discovery of Tutankhamen's tomb, England, c. 1920, size 8.6" x 3" x 3" (22 x 7.5 x 7.5 cm). **9.** Pear trinket container, India, c. 1960, size 5.9" x 2.8" x 2.8" (15 x 7 x 7 cm). **10.** Picture hanger, used with a decorative ribbon, England, c. 1890, size 3.3" x 2.3" (8.5 x 6 cm). **11.** Light switch cover, single switch, India, c. 1990, size 4.5" x 2.8" (11.5 x 7 cm). **12.** Light switch cover, double switch, India, c. 1990, size 4.5" x 4.5" (11.5 x 11.5 cm). **13.** Plate holder, Thailand, c. 1980, size 5.9" (15 cm).

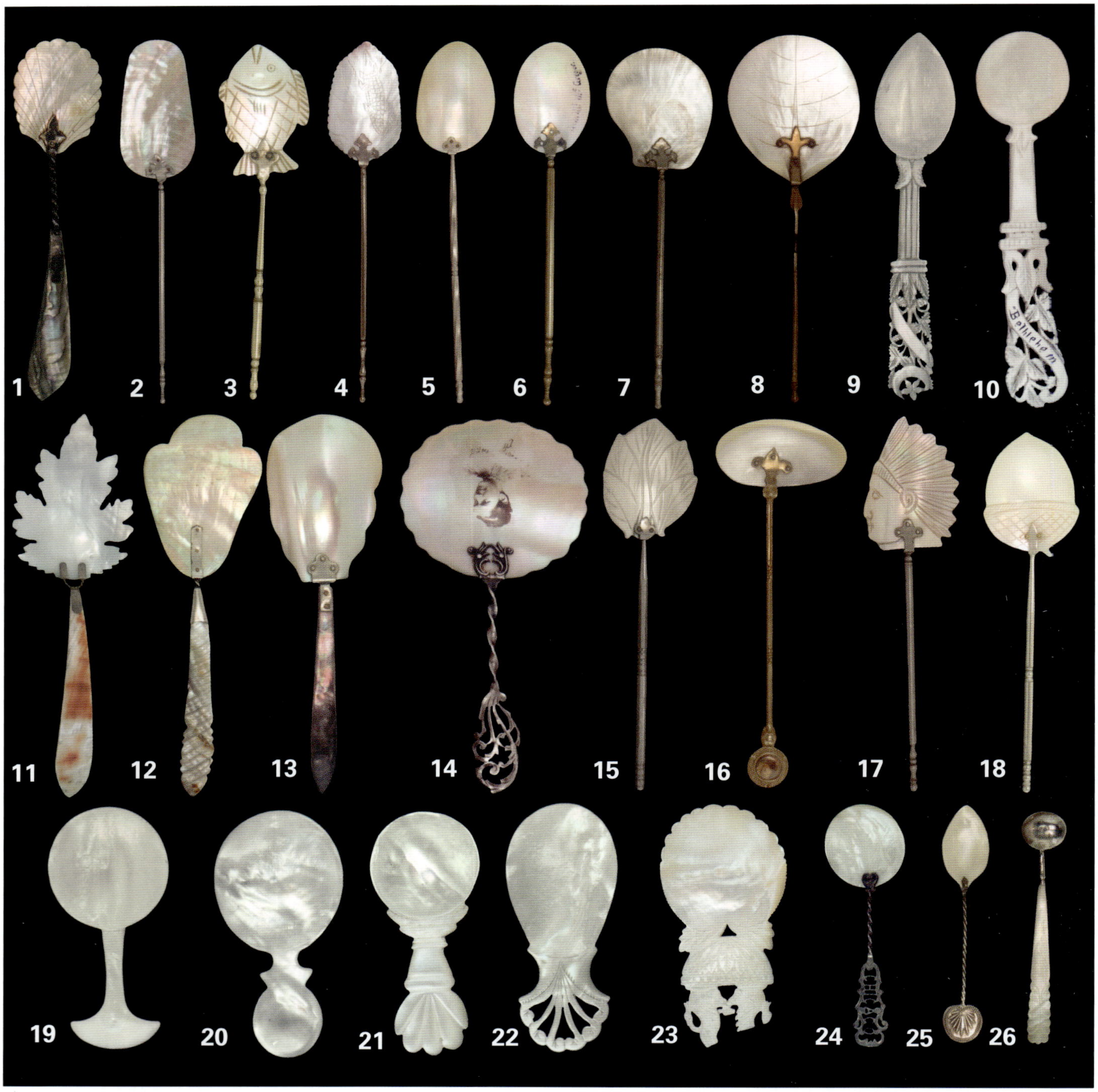


## PLATE 357 – TABLEWARE

1. Server, US, c. 1900–25, size 9.8″ (25 cm). 2. Server, USA, c. 1900–25, size 11″ (28 cm). 3. Fish spoon, US, c. 1916–25, mimic of Chinese pieces, size 4.3″ (11 cm). 4. Alligator server, US, c. 1900–15, size 9.4″ (24 cm). 5. Souvenir spoon, US, c. 1900–15, size 9″ (23 cm). 6. Souvenir spoon, USA, c. 1900–15, size 9″ (23 cm), inscribed *Mt Mc Gregor*. 7. Souvenir spoon, US, c. 1900–15, size 9.8″ (25 cm). 8. Server, France, c. 1895, size 9.8″ (25 cm). 9. Souvenir spoon, Bethlehem, Palestine, c. 1890–1900, size 4.5″ (11.5 cm). 10. Souvenir spoon, *Bethlehem*, Palestine, c. 1890–1900, size 3.5″ (9 cm). 11. Server, Canada, c. 1900, size 9.4″ (24 cm). 12. Server, USA, c. 1900–25, size 7.9″ (20 cm). 13. Server, USA, c. 1900–25, size 8.9″ (22.5 cm). 14. Sterling silver handle, photo transfer of a lady on mother-of-pearl, US, c. 1870–90, size 5.3″ (13.5 cm). 15. Souvenir spoon, US, c. 1900–15, size 7.5″ (19 cm). 16. Portrait spoon, US, c. 1900, photo of a French lady, size 7.5″ (19 cm). 17. Native American head server, US, c. 1890, size 9″ (23 cm), Atlantic coast souvenir. 18. Acorn spoon, US, c. 1885–1915, size 6.7″ (17 cm). 19. Tea caddy spoon, England, c. 1915, size 2.8″ (7.2 cm). 20. Tea caddy spoon, England, c. 1890, size 2.8″ (7.2 cm). 21. Tea caddy spoon, England, c. 1890, size 3.1″ (7.8 cm). 22. Tea caddy spoon, England, c. 1890, size 3″ (7.5 cm). 23. Tea caddy spoon, swan, France, c. 1820, size 3.3″ (8.5 cm). 24. Tea caddy spoon, US, c. 1890, inscribed *Chicago*, sterling, size 4.4″ (11.2 cm). 25. Preserve or fruit spoon, US, 1892, engraved *Gladys Dec 25 1892*, size 4.3″ (11 cm). 26. Master salt spoon, Birmingham, maker Francis Clark, England, c. 1831, size 4.5″ (11.5 cm).

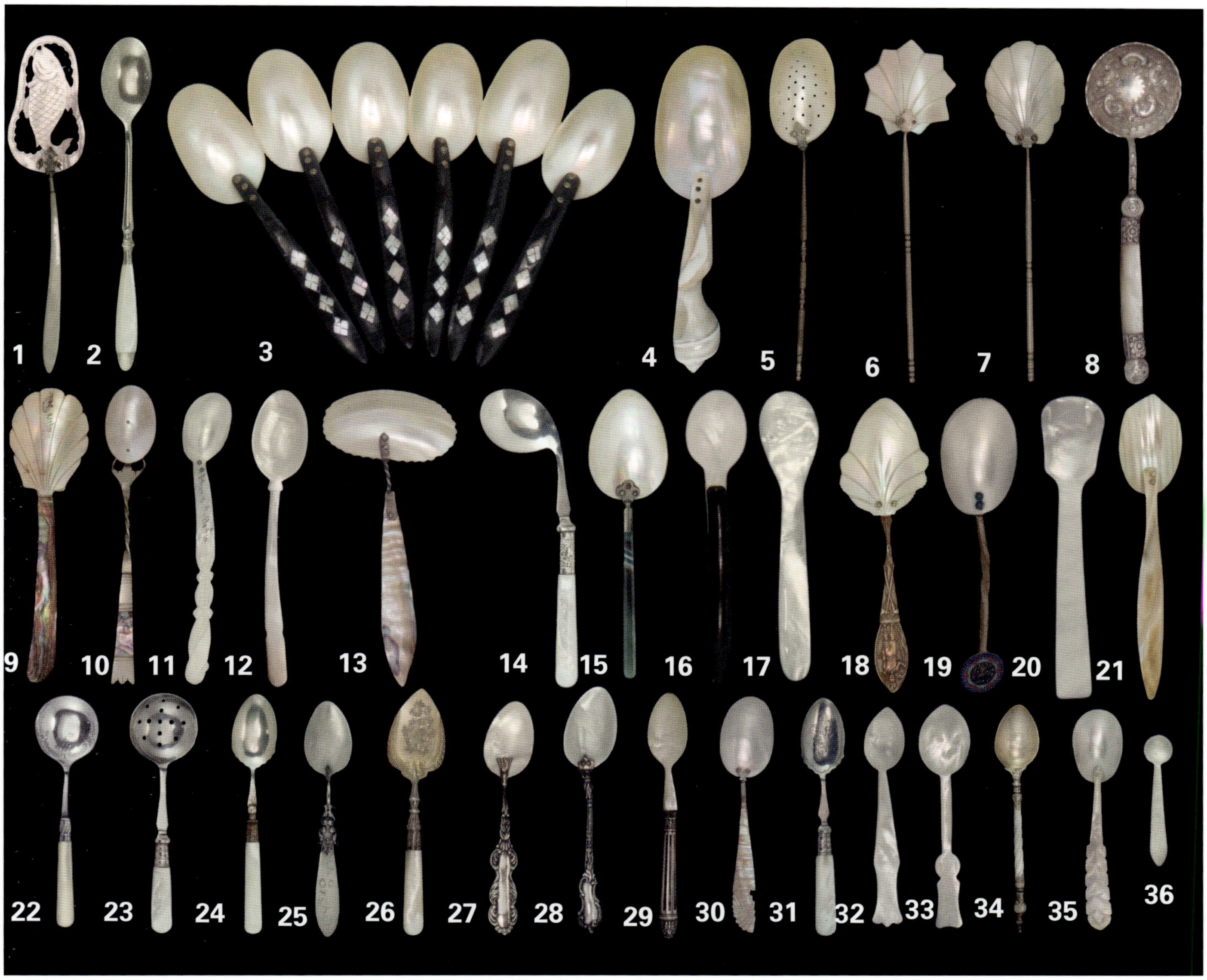


## PLATE 358 – TABLEWARE

**1.** Fish server, US, c. 1880, size 11″ (28 cm). **2.** Serving spoon, Thailand, c. 1993, size 7.5″ (19 cm). **3.** Salad servers, set of 6, Thailand, c. 1950, size 5.7″ (14.5 cm). **4.** Server, Thailand, c. 1920, size 7.7″ (19.5 cm). **5.** Powdered sugar spoon, US, c. 1910, size 6.7″ (17 cm). **6.** Souvenir spoon, US, c. 1910–20, size 5.3″ (13.5 cm). **7.** Souvenir spoon, US, c. 1895–1915, size 4.7″ (12 cm). **8.** Berry spoon, Charles James Allen and Sidney Darwin, Sheffield, England, 1880, hallmark, size 5.5″ (14 cm). **9.** Scallop spoon, US, c. 1895–1915, size 5.9″ (15 cm), *Niagara Falls*. **10.** Souvenir spoon, Mexico, c. 1930, size 6.9″ (17.5 cm). **11.** Alligator spoon, US, c. 1910, size 6.3″ (16 cm), *Passe Gallie,* Fla. **12.** Pearl spoon, Philippine Islands, c. 1950, size 6.9″ (17.5 cm). **13.** Ladle, US, c. 1900–25, size 4.1″ (10.5 cm). **14.** Invalid spoon, England, c. 1900, size 6.5″ (16.5 cm), inscribed *Argyle*. **15.** Display spoon, agate handle, England, c. 1850, size 5.7″ (14.5 cm). **16.** Souvenir spoon, Bahamas, c. 1930–40, black coral handle, size 5.2″ (13.3 cm). **17.** Souvenir spoon, Thailand, c. 1950, size 4.5″ (11.5 cm). **18.** Acorn and Native American souvenir spoon, US, c. 1895–1915, size 4.5″ (11.5 cm). **19.** Souvenir spoon, Mideast, c. 1920, size 4″ (10.2 cm). **20.** Souvenir spoon, Thailand, c. 1960, size 4.9″ (12.5 cm). **21.** Souvenir spoon, US, c. 1955, size 5.5″ (14 cm). **22.** Desert spoon, England, c. 1920, inscribed *Bros S*, size 4.5″ (11.5 cm). **23.** Powdered sugar spoon, England, c. 1895, size 5.7″ (14.5 cm). **24.** Jam or conserve spoon, England, c. 1900, size 6.3″ (16 cm). **25.** Souvenir spoon, US, c. 1900, size 4.3″ (10.8 cm), *Old Orchard* (Maine). **26.** Cake server, hallmarked Birmingham, England, 1938, size 6.7″ (17 cm). **27.** Sterling spoon, US, c. 1890, size 5.3″ (13.5 cm). **28.** Sterling spoon, US, c. 1890, size 3.9″ (10 cm). **29.** Sterling spoon, US, c. 1890, size 6.3″ (16 cm). **30.** Native American head spoon, US, c. 1890, size 6.1″ (15.5 cm). **31.** Jam or conserve spoon, England, c. 1920, size 6.2″ (15.7 cm). **32.** Souvenir spoon, China, c. 1950, size 4.1″ (10.5 cm). **33.** Souvenir spoon, China, c. 1950, size 4.5″ (11.5 cm). **34.** Souvenir spoon, US, c. 1880–95, New York, size 4.7″ (12 cm). **35.** Souvenir spoon, US, c. 1910, size 5.3″ (13.5 cm). **36.** Salt spoon, China, c. 1890, etched, size 2″ (5 cm).

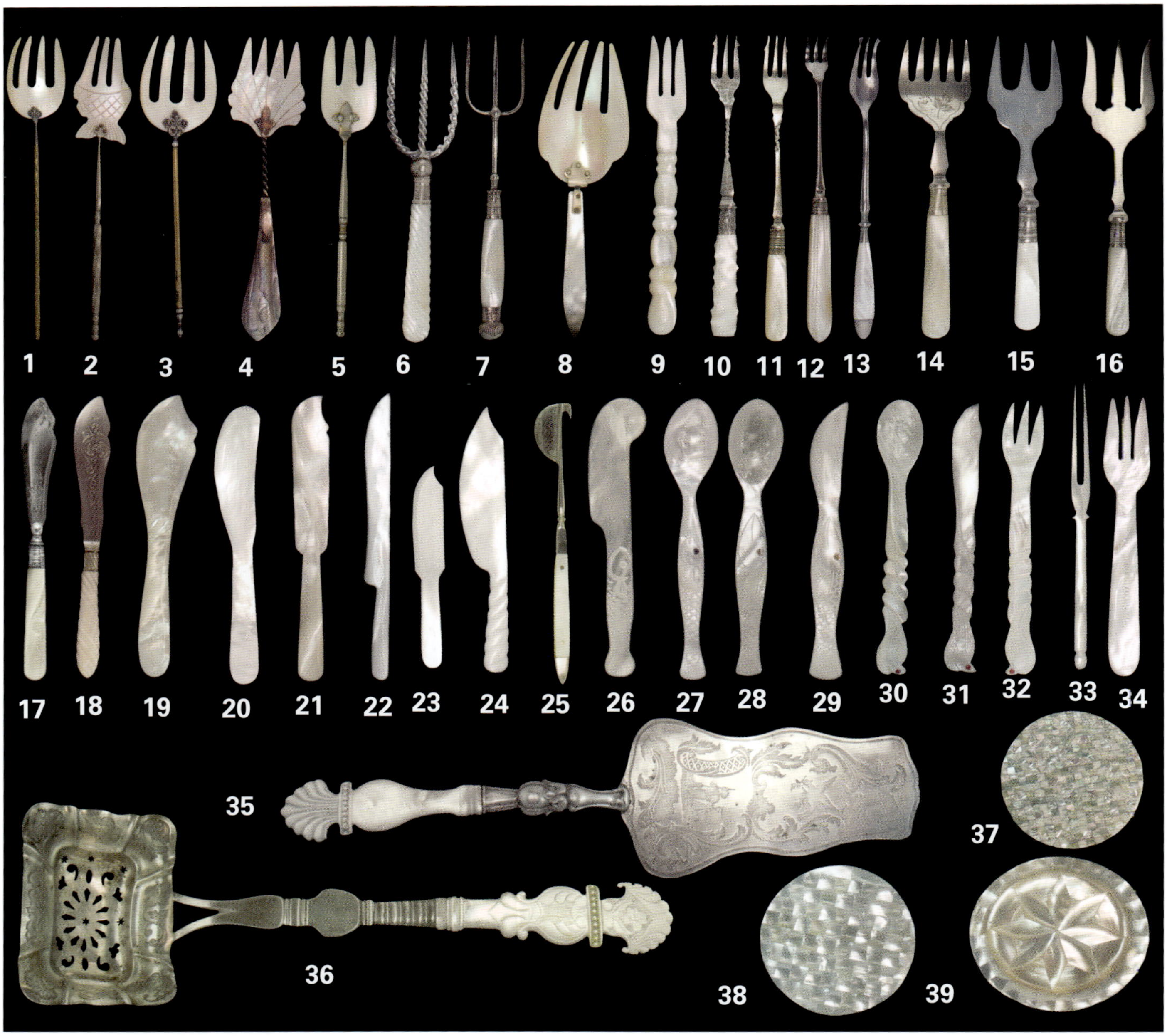

## PLATE 359 – TABLEWARE

1. Serving fork, US, c. 1895–1905, size 9.4″ (24 cm). 2. Fish server, US, c. 1890, size 7.1″ (18 cm). 3. Serving fork, US, c. 1895–1905, size 9.4″ (24 cm). 4. Serving fork, US, c. 1895–1905, size 9.8″ (25 cm). 5. Serving fork, US, c. 1890, size 4.5″ (11.5 cm), for fruit or side server. 6. Bread fork, England, c. 1880, size 6.5″ (16.5 cm). 7. Bread fork, England, c. 1880, size 9.4″ (24 cm), inscribed *Wingfield*. 8. Serving fork, US, c. 1930, size 7.1″ (18 cm). 9. Fancy fork, Thailand, c. 1995, size 5.5″ (14 cm). 10. Pickle fork, England, c. 1890, size 7.3″ (18.5 cm) inscribed *H.F.*S.* 11. Pickle fork, England, c. 1900, size 7.1″ (18 cm), *EPNS*. 12. Cheese or fondue fork, England, c. 1900, size 6.5″ (16.5 cm). 13. Pickle fork, Thailand, c. 1995, size 7.7″ (19.5 cm). 14. Sardine fork, England, c. 1880, size 5.9″ (15 cm), *EPNS*. 18. Bread fork, England, c. 1910, size 5.9″ (15 cm). 15. Bread fork, England, c. 1910, size 5.7″ (14.5 cm). 16. Bread fork, England, c. 1910, size 6.3″ (16 cm). 17–18. Butter spreader, England, c. 1920–50, size #1 6.1″ (15.5 cm) #2 7.7″ (19.5 cm). 19. Butter spreader, China, c. 1920, size 4.9″ (12.5 cm). 20. Butter spreader, Thailand, c. 1950, size 4.9″ (12.5 cm). 21. Butter spreader, China, c. 1920, size 4.9″ (12.5 cm). 22. *Hors d'Oeuvre* knife, China, c. 1950, size 4.5″ (11.5 cm). 23. Butter spreader, US, c. 1900–20, size 2.2″ (5.5 cm). 24. Butter spreader, US, c. 1900–20, size 2.8″ (7 cm). 25. Orange peeler, Germany, c. 1920, size 5.3″ (13.5 cm). 26–29. Souvenir set, fish handle, Thailand, c. 1996, size 4.9″ (12.5 cm). 30–32. Souvenir set, snake handle, Thailand, c. 2006, size 5.7″ (14.5 cm). 33. *Hors d'Oeuvre* pick, Thailand, c. 1955, size 3.5″ (9 cm). 34. Souvenir fork, Philippine Islands, c. 1993, size 5.1″ (13 cm). 35. Server, France, etched *J.D. 15 Sept 1877*, size 10.4″ (26.5 cm). 36. Ladle, France, etched *J.D. 15 Sept 1877*, size 9.1″ (23 cm). 37. Coaster, Philippine Islands, c. 1994, size 3.3″ (8.5 cm). 38. Coaster, Myanmar, c. 2003, size 3.1″ (8 cm). 39. Coaster, Myanmar, c. 2003, size 3.1″ (8 cm).

## PLATE 360 – TABLEWARE

1. Cutlery set, England, c. 1900, size 11.4″ x 8.7″ (29 x 22 cm), EPNS. 2–3. Two tray cutlery set, England, c. 1900, size 9.8″ x 7.1″ (25 x 18 cm), inscribed *F & C. Osler*. 4. Butter or caviar knife set, Hong Kong, c. 1980, box size 5.5″ x 4.6″ (14 x 11.8 cm). 5. Tea set, six spoons, six forks, six knives, Thailand, c. 1996, size 4.5″ (11.5 cm). 6. Bread fork, hallmarked Sheffield, England, 1896, box size 9.1″ x 2.8″ (23 x 7 cm). 7. *Hors d'Oeuvre* pick set of 7, Thailand, c. 1950–60, size 4.3″ (11 cm). 8. Knife sharpener, US, c. 1925, size 12.2″ (31 cm). 9. Skewer, hallmarked Sheffield, England, c. 1904, size 14″ (35.5 cm). 10. Pen knife, ladies leg shape, England, c. 1880, size 1.7″ (4.2 cm). 11–13. Serving set, Thailand, c. 1996, size 10.2″ to 11″ (26 to 28 cm). 14–15. Salad serving set, India, c. 2003, size 6.3″ (16 cm). 16–17. Salad serving set, Thailand, c. 2004, size 6.7″ (17 cm). 18. Pen knife, Germany, c. 1900, size 2.4″ (6 cm), inscribed *Argyle*. 19. Pen knife, Thailand, c. 1995, size 3.1″ (8 cm). 20. Pen knife, England, c. 1910, inscribed *Rodgers*, size 3.1″ (8 cm). 21. Pen knife, hallmarked Birmingham, England, 1900, size 2.8″ (7 cm). 22. Pen knife, hallmarked Chester, England, 1887, size 2.8″ (7 cm). 23. Pen knife, hallmarked Sheffield, England, 1897, size 2.6″ (6.5 cm). 24. Pen knife, hallmarked Sheffield, England, 1908, size 2.8″ (7 cm). 25. Pen knife, hallmarked Sheffield, England, 1905, size 3.1″ (8 cm). 26–28. Salt or mustard spoon, England, c. 1890, size 3″ to 3.7″ (7.5 to 9.5 cm). 29–30. Salt spade and shovel, US, c. 1900, size 3″ (7.5 cm). 31. Crumb scoop with etching, England, c. 1890, size 11″ (28 cm). 32. Butter pick, used to spear fancy butter balls, England, c. 1880, size 6.4″ (16.2 cm).

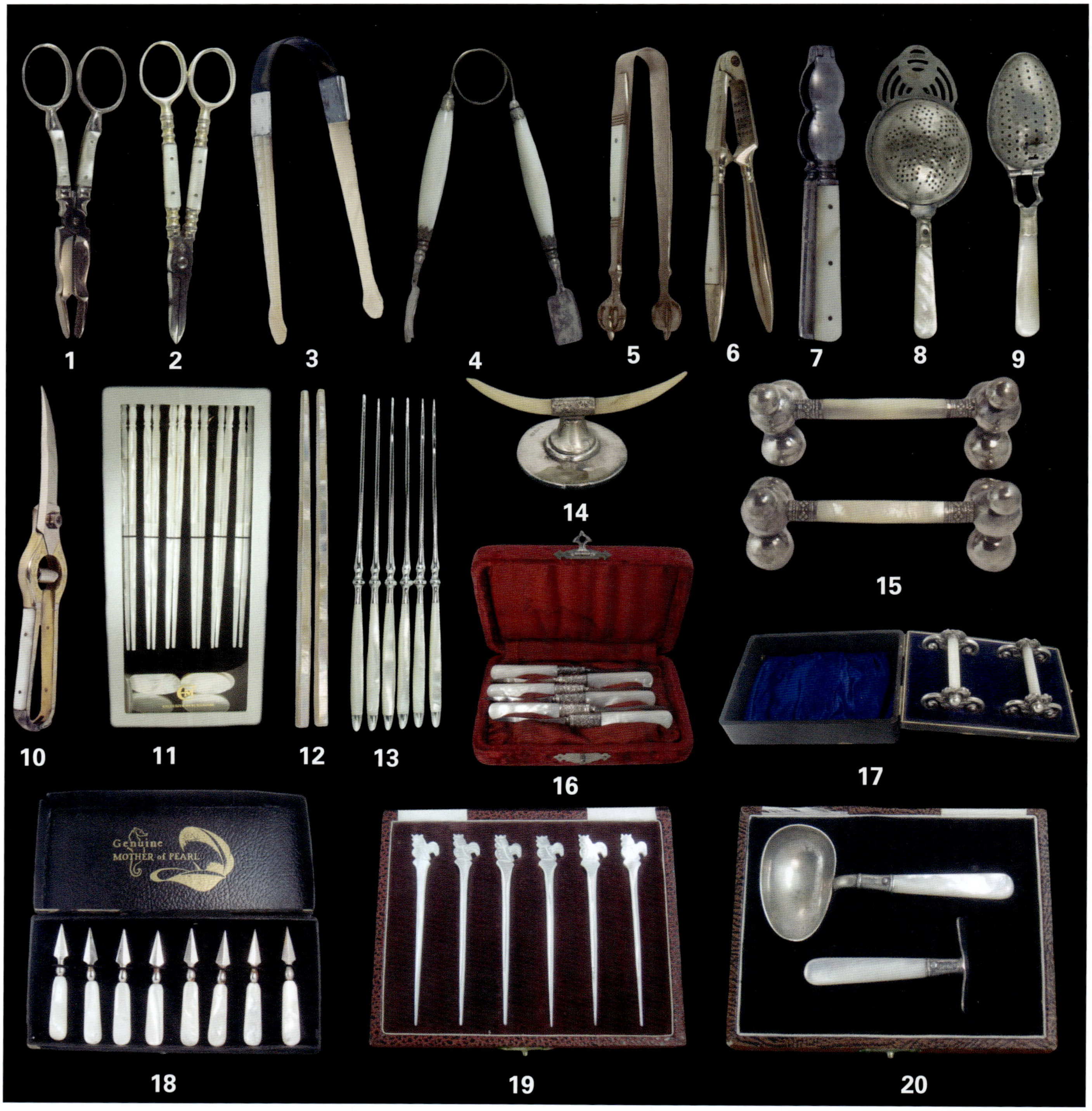


## PLATE 361 – HOUSEWARES

1. Sugar nips, Germany, c. 1910, size 5.1″ (13 cm). 2. Grape scissors, Von Cleef, Germany, c. 1890–1900, size 5.5″ (14 cm). 3. Tongs hallmarked Exeter, England, 1864, size 4.7″ (12 cm). 4. Pastry tongs, US, c. 1920, size 4.3″ (11 cm). 5. Pastry tongs, US, c. 1920, size 4.3″ (11 cm). 6. Nut cracker, Von Cleef, Germany, c. 1900, size 5.9″ (15 cm). 7. Nut cracker, US, c. 1920–30, size 5.7″ (14.5 cm). 8. Tea spoon strainer, England, c. 1930, size 5.9″ (15 cm). 9. Tea strainer, England, c. 1920, size 5.1″ (13 cm). 10. Kitchen shears, Natenberg Strauss Co., Germany, c. 1925, size 10.2″ (26 cm). 11. Six set chopsticks with stands, Thailand, c. 2007, box size 12.2″ x 5.9″ (31 x 15 cm). 12. Pearl chopsticks, Thailand, c. 1980, size 6.9″ (17.5 cm). 13. Three pairs chopsticks, Thailand, c. 1996, size 7.9″ (20 cm). 14. Knife stand, England, 1890, size 3.1″ (8 cm). 15. Knife stand, England, 1920, size 3.9″ (10 cm). 16. Set of six nut picks, US, c. 1910, box size 6.3″ x 3.9″ (16 x 10 cm). 17. Knife stand, hallmarked Birmingham, England, 1898, size 3.1″ (8 cm). 18. Oyster picks, set of 8, US, c. 1930, size 7.9 x 3.7″ (20 x 9.5 cm). 19. *Hors d' oeuvre* picks, six cockerel, England, c. 1910, box 5.3″ x 4.3″ (13.5 x 11 cm). 20. Gift set for a baby, including a pap spoon and food pusher, England, c. 1915–25, box size 3.9″ x 4.7″ (10 x 12 cm).

# Bibliography


## GENERAL

Beeck, Eric Van Ees. *L'Art & La Matiere*. France: Editions Communes des Sablons, 2005.

Bonnet, Laurence. *La Nacre La Tabletterie, Le Bouton, L'eventail*. France: Edition District Des Sablons, 1998.

Cinamon, Diana Sanders. *All about Antique Silver*. San Bernardino: AAA Publishing, 2005.

Clarke, Antigone & Joseph O'Kelly. *Antique Boxes, Tea Caddies & Society 1700–1880*. Atglen, PA: Schiffer Publishing, 2003.

Cossignani, Tiziana. *Conchiglie, perle e Madreperla*. Piceno: L'informatore, 2003.

Cummins, Genevieve. *Antique Boxes Inside and Out*. Woodbridge: Antique Collectors Club, 2006.

Joyce, Kristin, & Shellei Addison. *Pearls Ornament and Obsession*. London: Thames and Hudson, 1992.

Leidy, Denise Patry. *Mother-of-Pearl A tradition in Asian Lacquer*. New York: The Metropolitan Museum of Art, 2006.

Musee Oceanographique. *Art de la Nacre Coquilllages Sacres*. Monaco: Musee Oceanographique, 1993.

Orilla, Enrico. *La Madreperla*. Milan: Ulrico Hoepli, 1908.

Perfect, Sue. *The Birmingham Pearlies – An account of The Pearl Shell Industry in Birmingham*. UK: George Hook & Co., 2001.

Pickford, Ian–Editor. *Jackson's Hallmarks English, Scottish, Irish silver and gold marks*. UK: Antique Collectors Club, 2005.

Saul, Mary. *Shells An illustrated guide to a timeless and fascinating world*. London: Country life, 1974.

Shirai, Shohei. *Pearls and Pearl Oysters of the World*. Japan: Marine Planning, 1994.

Springsteen, F.J. & F.M. Leobrera. *Shells of The Philippines.* Manila: Carfel Seashell Museum, 1986.

Wenk, Klaus. *The Art of Mother-of-Pearl in Thailand*. Zurich: Verslag Inigio Von Oppersdorff, 1980.

*Wikipedia online.* http://en.wikipedia.org/wiki/Main_Page

Yidi Daccarett, Enrique & K D Daccarett & M L Angarita. *El Arte Palestino De Taller El Nacar*. Barranquilla: Private Printing, 2005.

## CARVINGS

Carson, Ritchie. *Shell Carving History and Techniques*. New Jersey: A.S. Barnes, 1974.

Carson, Ritchie. *Carving Shells and Cameos*. London: Arthur Baker Limited, 1970.

Musee de la Ville de Noumea. *Ile d'exil, terre d'asile.* Noumea: Published by the Museum, 2004.

## SEWING TOOLS and ACCESSORIES

Andere, Mary. *Old Needlework Boxes and Tools*. Devon: David & Charles, Newton Abbot, 1971.

Burn, Diane Pelham. *Thread Winders: A Collectors Guide*. UK: Private Printing, no date.

Colby, Averil. *Pincushions*. London: B. T. Batsford, 1975.

Collett, Sylvie. *Palais Royal Needlework Tools*. Wimborne: Minster Press, 2009.

Crestin-Billet, Federique. *Catalogue Ouvrages de Dames. Mercerie, Broderie*. Paris: Tana, 2005.

Crestin-Bellet, Frederique. *La Folie des Cieaux*. Paris: Flammarion, 2003.

Crestin-Bellet, Federique. *La Folie des A Coudre*. Paris: Flammarion, 2003.

Cummins, Genevieve, & Nerylla Taunton. *Chatelaines Utility to Glorious Extravagance*. UK: Antique Collectors Club, 1996.

Epstein, Diana, and Millicent Safro. *Buttons.* New York: Harry Abrams, 2001.

Groves, Sylvia. *The History of Needlework Tools and Accessories*. Feltham: Country Life Books, 1968.

Houart, Victor. *Sewing Accessories: An Illustrated History*. London: Souvenir Press, 1984.

Hughes, Elizabeth & Marion Lester. *The Big Book of Buttons*. Sedgwick: New Leaf Publishers, 1993.

Luscomb, Sally. *The Collector's Encyclopedia of Buttons*. West Chester: Schiffer Publishing, 1992.

Mathis, Averil. *Antique and Collectable Thimbles and Accessories*. Kentucky: Collector Books, 1986.

McConnel, Bridget. *The Story of Antique Needlework Tools*. Atglen, PA: Schiffer Publishing, 1999.

Meacham, Carolyn. *Elegant Arts Antiques Points of Interest Newsletters 2006-7.* Electronic Newsletters.

Palmer, Pat. *Tattling Shuttles—Related Tools and Accessories*. England: Rugby, 2003.

Proctor, Molly. *Needlework Tools and Accessories: A Collectors Guide*. London: B.T Batsford, 1990.

Roberts, Joan. *Stilettos.* Dorset: Thimble Society, 2007.

Rogers, Gay Ann. *An Illustrated History of Needlework Tools*. London: John Murray, 1983.

Sullivan, Kay. *Needlework Tools and Accessories*. Woodbridge: Antique Collectors Club, 2004.

Taunton, Nerylla. *Antique Needlework Tools and Embroideries*. England: Antique Collectors Club, 1997.

Thompson, Helen Lester. *Sewing Tools and Trinkets*. Volume 1 and 2. Kentucky: Collectors Books, 1997 & 2005.

Whiting, Gertrude. *Old Time Tools and Toys of Needlework*. New York: Dover Publications, 1971.

Zalkin, Estelle. *Thimbles & Sewing Implements*. USA: Warman Publishing, 1988.

## RATTLES

Bailly Pommery & Voutier. *Collection D'un Amateur Hochets*. Paris: (Auction catalogue) 2005.

Hersey, Marcia. *Collecting Baby Rattles and Teethers*. Iola: Krause Publications, 1998.

## DRESSING ACCESSORIES

Brandon, Sue, *Button Hooks and Shoe horns*, UK: Shire Album number 122, 2000.

Clements, Monica & Patricia, *Cameos – Classical to Costume*, Atglen, PA: Schiffer Publishing, 1998.

Compton, Cynthia, *Button hooks, Collecting and Price guide*, Private Printing, 1983.

Gostelow, Mary, *The Fan,* Dublin: Gill and Macmillan, 1976.

Mayor, Susan, *The Letts Guide to collecting Fans*, London: Charles Letts, 1991.

Miller, Anna, *Cameos old and new*, New York: Van Nostrand Reinhold, 1991.

Musee Cognacq-Jay, *Porte bouquets*, Paris: Paris Musees, 2005.

Ritchie, Roy & Ron Stewart, *Standard guide to Razors*, Kentucky: Collector Books, 2007.

Tcherviakov, Alexander, *Fans,* Bournemouth: Parkstone Press, 1998.

## DRESSING ACCESSORIES - COMPACTS

Clayton, Larry. *The Evans Book*. Atglen, PA: Schiffer Publishing Ltd, 1998.

Ettinger, Roseann. *Compacts and Smoking Accessories*. Atglen, PA: Schiffer Publishing Ltd, 1999.

Gerson, Roselyn. *Vintage and Vogue Ladies Compacts*. Kentucky: Collector Books, 2001.

Mueller, Laura. *Collectors Encyclopedia of Compacts, Volume 1.* Kentucky: Collector Books, 1996.

Mueller, Laura. *Collectors Encyclopedia of Compacts, Volume 2.* Kentucky: Collector Books, 1997.

## DESK ACCESSORIES

Badders, Veldon. *Collectors Guide to Inkwells Volume 1 and 2.* Kentucky: Collector Books, 1995 & 1998.

Banfield, Edwin. *Visiting Cards and Cases*. Trowbridge: Baros Books, 1989.

Crosby, Deborah. *Victorian Pencils, Tools to Jewels*. Atglen, PA: Schiffer Publishing, 1998.

Grist, Everett. *Collector's Guide to Letter Openers*. Kentucky: Collector Books, 1998.

Hunting, Jean & Franklin. *The Collectors World of Inkwells*. Atglen, PA: Schiffer Publishing, 2000.

Jaegers, Ray and Bevy. *The Write Stuff—Collectors Guide*. Iola: Krause Publications, 2000.

Joannis-Deberne, Henri. *Carnets de bal,* Memoire de l'ephemere. France: Musee de Carouge, 2004.

Riley, Noel. *Visiting Card Cases*. Guildford: Lutterworth Press, 1983.

## SPECTACLES, OPTICAL AIDES AND PHOTOGRAPHIC

Crestin-Bellet, Frederique. *La Folie des Lunettes*. Paris: Flammarion, 2003.

Fleishman, David. Antique Spectacles. http://www.antiquespectacles.com/slide_shows/mop/mop.htm#

Rosenthal, J. William. *Spectacles and Other Vision Aids*. San Francisco: Norman Publishing, 1996.

Berg, Paul K. *Nineteenth Century Photographic Cases and Wall Frames*. Private Printing, 2003.

## DENTAL AND MEDICAL

Bennion, Elisabeth. *Antique Dental Instruments*. London: Sotheby's Publications, 1986.

Bennion, Elisabeth. *Antique Medical Instruments*. London: Sotheby Parke Bernet, 1979.

## RELIGION

Bagatti, Bellarime. *Mother-of-Pearl Industry of Bethlehem 1342–1942*. Bethlehem: Custody of the Holyland, Lund Humphries.

*Pilgrim Treasures from the Hermitage–Byzantium Jerusalem*. Amsterdam: Hermitage, c. 1990.

Orthodox Society. *The Industry of Mother-of-Pearl in Bethlehem.* Bethlehem: Orthodox National Charitable Soc., 1986.

## TOBACCIANA

Clayton, Larry. *The Evans Book—Lighters Compacts Perfumes Handbags.* Atglen, PA: Schiffer Publishing, 1998.

Flanagan, James. *The Big Book of Cigarette Lighters*. Kentucky: Collector Books, 2005.

## LEISURE TIMES

Cowan, Derek. *Mother-of-Pearl Game Counters*. Palo Alto: Past Pleasures, 1998.

Neal, Bill. *Chinese Mother-of-Pearl Gaming Counters*. UK: Published by the author, 2007, www.chezbill.com

Neal, Bill. *Armorial Chinese Gaming Counters.* UK: Published by the author, 2008, www.chezbill.com

Seymour, Dale. *Antique Gaming Chips*. Palo Alto: Past Pleasures, 1985.

# Appendix

1

2

## PLATE 362 – FAKE/FAUX MOTHER-OF-PEARL

Many materials are sold as mother-of-pearl but are not genuine shell. Often the seller is not doing this intentionally, but does not know the difference. The most common misidentification is lucite, which is Polymethyl methacrylate (plastic) #1 first marketed in 1933. It is easy to spot the difference when you hold examples of both in your hands.
1) Mother-of-pearl shell #2 is cool to the touch while plastic #1 is warm.
2) Mother-of-pearl shell #2 has a high luster of many colors, while plastic #1 is milky and shows whitish layers with no depth or color.
3) Mother-of-pearl shell #2 is heavy while plastic #1 is extremely light.